Special Effects Artists

Special Effects Artists

*A Worldwide Biographical
Dictionary of the Pre-Digital Era
with a Filmography*

Rolf Giesen

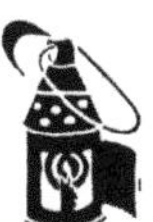

McFarland & Company, Inc., Publishers
Jefferson, North Carolina

The present work is a reprint of the library bound edition of Special Effects Artists: A Worldwide Biographical Dictionary of the Pre-Digital Era with a Filmography, *first published in 2008 by McFarland.*

LIBRARY OF CONGRESS CATALOGUING-IN-PUBLICATION DATA

Giesen, Rolf.
Special effects artists : a worldwide biographical dictionary
of the pre-digital era with a filmography / Rolf Giesen.
p.   cm.
Includes bibliographical references and index.

ISBN 978-0-7864-9551-1 (softcover : acid free paper) ∞
ISBN 978-1-4766-0819-8 (ebook)

1. Cinematographers — Biography — Dictionaries.
2. Cinematography — Special effects — Dictionaries.
3. Motion pictures — Catalogs.   I. Title.
TR849.A1G54   2014   778.5'30922 — dc22   2008023209

BRITISH LIBRARY CATALOGUING DATA ARE AVAILABLE

On the cover: Behind the scenes of an effects shot from the 1994 film *The High Crusade* (Karl-Heinz Christmann and Deutsche Kinemathek Berlin); (inset) the Medusa model from the 1981 film *Clash of the Titans* (MGM/Photofest)

Manufactured in the United States of America

*McFarland & Company, Inc., Publishers
Box 611, Jefferson, North Carolina 28640
www.mcfarlandpub.com*

To the memory of my late friend, Albert Whitlock,
matte artist and visual effects artist extraordinaire

Acknowledgments

L.B. Abbott, Linwood G. Dunn, Gerhard Huttula, Jan W. Jacobsen, Nathan Hertz Juran, Danny Lee, Fritz Maurischat, Derek Meddings, Theodor Nischwitz, Lester Novros, Karl Ludwig Ruppel, H.O. Schulze, Curt Siodmak, Harry Thomas, George E. Turner and Albert Whitlock, who have since passed away.

Over the years I met, talked to and in some cases worked with Henri Alékan, Henry Alvarez, Colin Arthur, Bob Baker, Rick Baker, Craig Barron, Peter Bartoschek, Sacha Bertram, Piet De Rycker, Syd Dutton, Richard Edlund, Roland Emmerich, Chris Endicott, Volker Engel, Scott Farrar, Uwe Fleischer, Warren Franklin, Steve Gawley, Stuart Gordon, Ned Gorman, Erich Günther, Helmut Herbst, Werner Hierl, Antonín Horák, Gregory Jein, Werner Keppler, Vit Komrzy, Mme. Madeleine Malthète-Méliès, Kurt Marks, Phil Meador, Claudia Meglin, Theo Mezger, Jimmy Murakami, Dennis Muren, John Nelson, Richard Patterson, Thilo Graf Rothkirch, Ron Seawright, Robert Short, Paul Swendsen, Bill Taylor, Richard Taylor, Philipp Timme, Phil Tippett, Douglas Trumbull, Paul Verhoeven, Howie Weed, Götz Weidner and Paul Wilson.

Grateful thanks to the masters of stop-motion, Jim Danforth and Ray Harryhausen. Danforth as well as Ernest D. Farino took some time to read the manuscript and suggest valuable corrections.

I have to mention also my fellow writers and historians Forry (Forrest J) Ackerman, Norbert Bolewski, Bob Burns, Tony Dalton, Hellmuth Dimko, Herbert Gehr, Mike Hankin, Josef Hilger, Paul Mandell, Hans Helmut Prinzler, Don Shay (editor, *Cinefex* magazine), Mark Cotta Vaz, Wang Lei and Prof. Dr. Bernd Willim†. For help with the stills I have to acknowledge the kind assistance of my colleagues at Deutsche Kinemathek Berlin, Peter Latta and Gerrit Thies. I would also like to thank Pancho Kohner for allowing me to quote a letter to his father Paul written by producer George Pal in 1936.

Contents

Preface

The volume you hold in your hands covers almost 100 years of visual effects which have enriched moviemaking throughout the world. Some reviewers might call it rather arbitrary to terminate a book about effects-laden pictures with the release of Steven Spielberg's *Jurassic Park*, because the genre of *sfx* blockbusters would reach its peak in the years to follow.

The success of artists, technicians and craftsmen in the pre-digital era was extremely limited when compared to the apparently boundless possibilities of CGI (computer-generated images) today supported by unreasonably high, inflated budgets. Very often in the past there was not much money at hand and only primitive techniques to accomplish the impossible: to travel 20,000 leagues under the sea, dare a trip to the moon, visit the gods of Mt. Olympus and fight the monsters and behemoths of mythology.

The filmmakers of the past tried hard. They often failed, with their work ridiculed (*Plan 9 from Outer Space*, *The Beast with a Million Eyes*, *Reptilicus*), but sometimes they created unforgettable images that for a lifetime stuck in the minds of viewers (the original *King Kong*, *The Thief of Bagdad*, *The 7th Voyage of Sinbad*, *The Time Machine*). In the 21st-century war of the blockbusters, scores of sfx technicians are listed in the on-screen credits but in the old days they had to work anonymously. Only the department heads were credited and sometimes not even them. Quite often their work was regarded as top secret.

This selection of biographies is a tribute to some very innovative people who contributed to our imagination. But in most cases their names remained obscure: cinematographers, designers, matte artists, model makers and prop men as well as animators, mainly in mainstream filmmaking. There are the pioneers, the guys who enhanced early slapstick comedy via ingenious in-camera effects. There is the fellowship of American, British, German and Japanese special effects departments which had its heyday from the mid–1920s until the late 1950s, when film studios began to lose audiences to television and many departments folded due to lack of funding and resources. Among them are men who received more than one Academy Award: Americans Gordon Jennings, John P. Fulton, and L.B. "Bill" Abbott. There are Karel Zeman of Czechoslovakia, Mario Bava of Italy, Emilio Ruiz Del Rio of Spain, Henri Alékan of France, Eiji Tsuburaya of Japan, Ernst Kunstmann of Germany, Alexander Ptushko of Russia, George Pal of Hungary (who crowned his career as a producer in America), Albert Whitlock who went from Britain to the United States, and Ray Harryhausen who did the opposite.

There is Stanley Kubrick's landmark movie *2001: A Space Odyssey*, created with the help of established supervisors (Wally Veevers and Tom Howard) and young talent (Con Pederson, Douglas Trumbull). For many years it remained the last outstanding sfx movie. Then came George Lucas, who changed it all with *Star Wars* and Industrial Light & Magic.

A filmography of selected special effects films is provided after the biographies. This adds credits for feature films that often come to mind when speaking about the bygone days of mechanical, analog effects — such films as *The Student of Prague*, *Metropolis*, *Things to Come*, *The Wizard of Oz*, *Gone with the Wind*, *Citizen Kane*, *Destination Moon*, *Gojira*, *The Incredible Shrinking Man*, *Earth vs. the Flying Saucers*, *Darby*

O'Gill and the Little People, The Birds, Jason and the Argonauts and *Planet of the Apes.*

This filmography is personal and therefore subjective. Basically, productions were selected which either can be described as genuine special effects films or contain at least a substantial number of special effects scenes and memorable sequences. It not only covers most of the key work done in the period the book deals with, including entries recognized by the Academy of Motion Picture Arts and Sciences, it also includes some dismal failures that are part of this writer's early cinema exposure. Many of the artists and technicians were not properly credited in those days. I tried to give credit where credit is due.

In some cases, production and release year of a picture differ. For instance, the bulk of the original *King Kong* was shot in 1932 while the movie itself was released in spring 1933. Thus I would indicate 1932–33. *The 7th Voyage of Sinbad* was filmed in 1957, with postproduction and release in 1958: 1957–58. Some exceptional films were years in production. Cecil B. DeMille's VistaVision version of *The Ten Commandments* was started in 1953, finished and released in 1956: 1953–56.

Ernest Farino found the method of indicating a span of years for a given film confusing: "The confusion is especially compounded by the inconsistency of having many other titles with only one date."

Nevertheless I decided to stick with it, and will have to take the blame for it.

Of course a book like this, a data nightmare, is far from complete. Books, magazines and (who would deny it?) the Internet proved invaluable in compiling all material. Sometimes I had to count on nothing else than my memory. The sources from which I took interviews are cited. If not, the statements are drawn from interviews I personally conducted with the respective artist or technician, as in the case of the late German cinematographer H.O. Schulze.

With the completion of this book, I will have finished my work on sfx exhibitions and on building a vast collection of effects-related objects and documents for the Deutsche Kinemathek in Berlin, which I started in 1984. Therefore I decided to only use stills and photographs from this collection, which mostly cover the achievements of a selected few celebrities in the field.

Introduction

When Peter Jackson unveiled his 2005 remake of that innocent special effects hybrid *King Kong* (1933), it became clear to everybody that, despite the miniatures he used, the age of mechanical film effects was gone forever. Technically, Jackson's *King Kong* had more to do with the few minutes of computer-generated dinosaurs in Steven Spielberg's *Jurassic Park* than with Willis O'Brien's crude but inventively designed and machined stop-motion effects. Jackson's remake certainly was a triumph of digital techniques but it was what one might call a Pyrrhic victory: A movie which will overwhelm you when you see it but once you have seen it you have no real desire to watch it again and you will forget it in months, weeks, days. The computer apparently has no limits in creating and rendering images with a seemingly photo-realistic touch, even those that are physically impossible. (Umberto Eco once said that the Americans' striving for naturalism is primitive in the context of the history of art, and Jim Danforth lamented a tendency towards hard-edged hyper-realism.) According to the rules of virtual democracy, the software they used in Jackson's native New Zealand to re-invent the giant ape of the days of the Great Depression is basically available to amateurs, too. There will be a new generation of dilettantes not only using adequate software in order to invent their individual 3D images but to evoke a new horizon of interactive parallel worlds of digital picturemaking as well. We know that what we see today is nothing compared to the interactive opportunities of tomorrow, which don't need cameras any more. Everything can be manipulated through bytes and pixels. That process took decades but the ambi-tion to create those virtual parallel worlds were there right in the beginning. There were challenges and innovative multimedia ideas even in the early days of moviemaking.

The Time Traveler

When film pioneer Robert William Paul joined H.G. Wells for a time at the turn of the last century, they tried to create what Wells had envisioned on paper: a film event, something we would call a "ride" today, inspired by Wells' novel *The Time Machine*. Their proposed multimedia vehicle would allow one to travel through space and time without even moving. Real Rube Goldberg stuff. From the British patent application, No. 19984, drawn up by Robert William Paul under the date of October 24, 1895:

> My invention consists of a novel form of exhibition whereby the spectators have presented to their view scenes which are supposed to occur in the future or past, while they are given the sensation of voyaging upon a machine through time, and means for presenting these scenes simultaneously and in conjunction with the production of the sensation by the mechanism described below, or its equivalent.
>
> The mechanism I employ consists of a platform, or platforms, each of which contains a suitable number of spectators and which may be enclosed at the sides after the spectators have taken their places, leaving a convenient opening towards which the latter face, and which is directed towards a screen upon which the views are presented.
>
> In order to create the impression of traveling, each platform may be suspended from cranks in shafts above the platform, which may be driven by an engine or other convenient source of power. These cranks may be so placed as to impart to the

platform a gentle rocking motion, and may also be employed to cause the platform to travel bodily forward through a short space, when desired, or I may substitute for this portion of the mechanism similar shafts below the platforms, provided with cranks or cams, or worms keyed eccentrically on the shaft, or wheels gearing in racks attached to the underside of the platform or otherwise.

Simultaneously with the forward propulsion of the platform, I may arrange a current of air to be blown over it, either by fans attached to the sides of the platform, and intended to represent to the spectators the means of propulsion, or by a separate blower driven from the engine and arranged to throw a regulated blast over each of the platforms.

The screened picture elements would have been projected by several (magic) lanterns or film machines composed of:

1. A hypothetical landscape, containing also the representation of the inanimate objects in the scene.
2. A slide, or slides, which may be traversed horizontally or vertically and contain representations of objects such as a navigable balloon etc., which is required to traverse the scene.
3. Slides of film, representing in successive instantaneous photographs, after the manner of the kinetoscope, the living persons or creatures in their natural motions. The films or slides are prepared with the aid of the kinetograph or special camera, from made up characters performing on a stage, with or without a suitable background blending with the main landscape.
4. Changeable colored, darkened, or perforated slides may be used to produce the effect on the scene of sunlight, darkness, moonlight, rain, etc.

In order to enable the scenes to be gradually enlarged to a definite amount, I may mount these lanterns on suitable carriages or trolleys, upon rails provided with stops or marks, so as to approach to or recede from the screen a definite distance, and to enable a dissolving effect to be obtained, the lantern may be fitted with the usual mechanism. In order to increase the realistic effect I may arrange that after a certain number of scenes from a hypothetical future have been presented to the spectators, they may be allowed to step from the platforms, and be conducted through grounds or buildings arranged to represent exactly one of the epochs through which the spectator is supposed to be traveling.

After the last scene is presented I prefer to arrange that the spectators should be given the sensation of voyaging backwards from the last epoch to the present, or the present epoch may be supposed to have been accidentally passed, and a past scene represented on the machine coming to a standstill, after which the impression of traveling forward again to the present epoch may be given, and the rearrival notified by the representation on the screen of the place at which the exhibition is held, or of some well-known building which by the movement forward of the lantern can be made to increase gradually in size as if approaching the spectator.

Optical Lyric

Paul and Georges Méliès, one of the founding fathers of special effects, to whom Paul sold one of his first camera projectors, were not only imaginative mechanics and engineers, they also were great showmen who luckily could count on a still rather superstitious audience that would believe it all too readily. They had learned their lesson from conjurors and magic lantern wizards. One of those had been Robertson (Étienne Gaspar Robert), who had presented his *Fantasmagories* in Paris in 1794. Those were specially projected ghost shows. "It principally worked by a movable projecting lantern and awesome figures painted on glass slides projected on to a screen, also on to clouds of smoke emerging from braziers. This entertainment was given at the Pavillon de l'Exchequer. It was a great success, and later moved to a disused chapel. This was approached by corridors of tombs and other monuments, which helped produce the weird atmosphere necessary. The interior of the chapel was draped in black, and the only light came from a single lamp burning with a pale flame."[1]

Resurrection of the Dead

Paul Wegener, an actor and major force in the German silent film whose fascination with the fantastic helped shape the creative destiny of his nation's fledgling movie industry, was one of the earliest advocates of synthetic cinema — a cinema utilizing all possible effects of the camera. In a lecture held on Easter Monday 1916 in Berlin, Wegener spoke prophetically of his dream to engender an absolutely artificial movie:

You have all seen films in which suddenly a line appears, curves and changes its form. Out of it grows faces and the line disappears. To me the impression seems highly remarkable. But such things are always shown as an intermezzo and nobody has ever thought of the colossal possibilities of this technique. I think the film as art should be based — as in the case of music — on tones, on rhythm. In these changeable planes, events unreel which are partly identified with natural pattern, yet partly beyond real lines and forms. Imagine one of Böcklin's sea paintings with all the fabulous tritons and nereids. And imagine an artist duplicating this work in hundreds of copies but with each copy having small displacements so that all copies revealed in succession would result in continuous movement. Suddenly we would see before our very eyes a world of pure fantasy come to life. Such effects can also be achieved with specially constructed little models animated like marionettes — in this field there are great achievements nowadays. One also can change the pace of different movements by shooting too slow or too fast, developing a fantastic vision which will produce entirely new associations of ideas. We are entering a new pictorial fantasy world as we would enter a magic forest. We are setting foot in the field of pure kinetics — or optical lyric, as I call it. This field will perhaps be of major importance and will open new beautiful sights. This eventually is the final objective of each art, and so cinema would gain an autonomous aesthetic domain for itself. A movie could be created which would become an experience of art — an optical vision, a great symphonic fantasy! That it will happen one day, I am sure — and beyond that, I am certain, later generations will look upon our early efforts as upon childish stuttering.

That lecture was held at the time of World War I. Walt Disney tried similar things with his *Fantasia* made at the start of World War II. Alas, these two big wars of the 20th century made positive imagery almost impossible. Not beautiful paintings but monsters from the subconscious mind would dominate our minds and the screen.

The Legacy of King Kong

When I was a child, not much information was available on what is called special effects or visual effects. I saw *The 7th Voyage of Sinbad* in 1958, the militaristic Japanese *The Mysterians* in 1960 and *Godzilla Raids Again*, *Gorgo* and *Konga* in 1961; men in monster suits and robots destroying whole cities and miniature landscapes fueled the powerless, puerile mind of a seven-year-old

kid. I became highly interested in effects and animation such as Walt Disney stuff, having seen *Sleeping Beauty* in 1959 and being an avid reader of Disney's comic strips, especially those drawn by Carl Barks. But I found only two volumes that helped to bring some light into darkness: *Die neue Trickfilm-Schule*, an amateur filmer's account of all kinds of tricks, and a German translation of *Walt Disney: The Art of Animation* (*Die Kunst des Zeichenfilms*) by Bob Thomas.

There was no *Cinefex*, there were no "Making Of"s, no Internet Movie Data Base to consult then.

My father told me that he saw and enjoyed *King Kong* so much when it was mass-released in Germany in November 1933 that he never forgot the cinematic experience but I myself had to wait a few years until I managed to catch a screening on TV. That was in 1971. By then I was too old to really enjoy the naive story that I saw as we had started to seriously discuss the efforts of New German Cinema. With filmmakers like Rainer Werner Fassbinder and Volker Schlöndorff, there was no place for special effects and imaginary Skull Island or Sinbad's Colossa or Peter Pan's Neverland. There was no magic password such as "From the land beyond beyond...." In my spare time, however, I kept in touch with the magic of my childhood and in 1972 read Ray Harryhausen's *Film Fantasy Scrapbook*, which unfortunately revealed not too much because the magician (and that he certainly was to us) preferred to keep some secrets for himself. Then I attended sociology courses at Free University in Berlin and wrote a thesis about fantasy films in which I went on to painfully scrutinize the genre that I had loved so much. When I met Wim Wenders in 1985, he still claimed, "I myself consider special effects special *defects*." (Later he "apologized" and used matte shots and other effects in his movies.) By then, although still despised by the scholars of *cinéma vérité*, special effects movies, due to inflation and higher admissions, were more successful than ever.

Destination Moon and Beyond

Stanley Kubrick's *2001: A Space Odyssey* (although entirely produced in analog technique) became the first confusing but mind-boggling

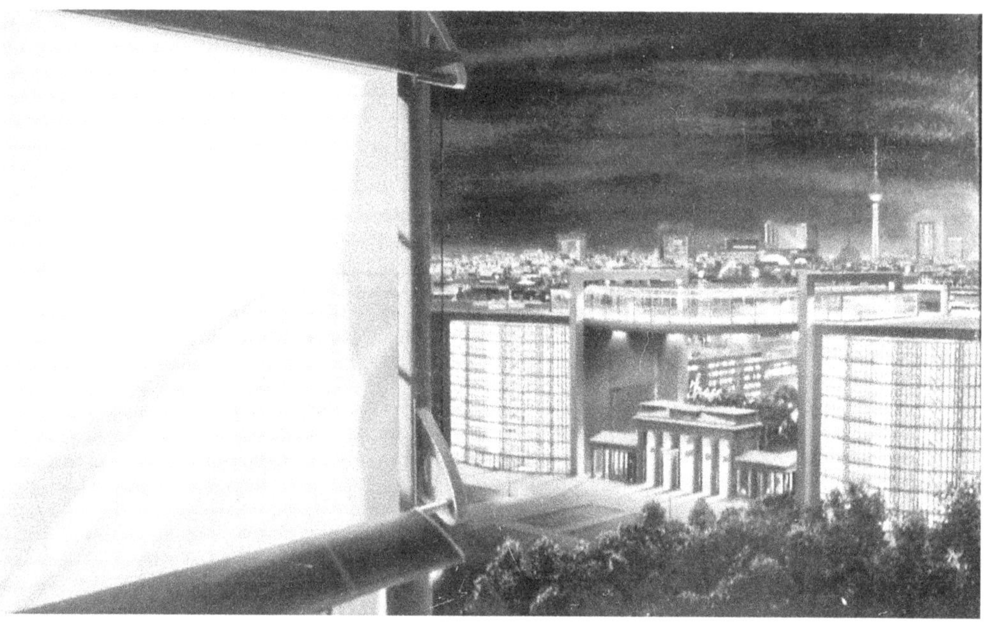

Matte painting for the Wim Wenders production *Bis ans Ende der Welt* (*Until the End of the World*) (courtesy Deutsche Kinemathek Berlin).

sfx experience in the changing world of 1968. The moon landing in 1969 (I have no doubt that they made it) turned its vision into reality and some years later George Lucas mixed Walt Disney and Wernher von Braun, a former SS *Vergeltungswaffen* official, who both had made *Man in Space* for American TV in 1955–56 (directed by innovative animator Ward Kimball). These were the sources from which emerged 1977's *Star Wars*, which eventually revived the NASA spirit. When I left the Berlin cinema which ran *Star Wars* I immediately knew that nothing would be the same again. The innocence of the old mechanics was gone. The days of Japanese rubber suit monsters and spaceships on clearly visible wires were *passé*. Thanks to Boeing and NASA, electronics would reshape moving images and destroy the fairy-tale nickelodeon.

So the change came not from within the cinema industry but from TV as well as aerial and space technology. As movies were adapting and absorbing techniques from photography in the early stages, such as double exposure to create ghostly images, static background projection or glass paintings, now movies themselves were absorbed by the digital age. Not only *Star Wars* or earlier science-fiction pics such as George Pal's *The War of the Worlds* (1953) made me aware that

war more than peace was affecting the imagery of movie special effects. The peaceful airmen, "Wings Over the World," who had fought for a never-ending progress in H.G. Wells' 1936 film adaptation, *Things to Come*, transformed into the pilots who bombed Guernica, Warsaw, London, Coventry. During World War II the film industries of various countries had built effects departments capable of reconstructing aerial attacks and spectacular sea battles, and some effects personnel even went out to film atomic blasts (as did Lloyd Knechtel). A. Arnold Gillespie, a longtime employee of MGM, won an Academy Award for *Thirty Seconds Over Tokyo*. At Toho in Japan, Eiji Tsuburaya miniaturized *The War at Sea from Hawaii to Malaya* in grand style; this became the forerunner of his *Godzilla* series. In Nazi Germany, Ufa and Tobis created *Stukas* and *Front in the Sky* respectively and added considerably to the propaganda for Hermann Göring's *Luftwaffe*. Even Cinerama began as sort of a gunnery trainer for B-17 flying fortress crews, and early TV was used by the Germans not only to entertain the home front but also as camera surveillance for V1 and V2 ballistics. (The pilots who man today's aircraft were in a way raised by *Star Wars*.)

Artificial Worlds

At the end of World War II, David Rawnsley, who had a background in architecture and engineering, and director Michael Powell (*The Red Shoes, The Tales of Hoffmann*) suggested to J. Arthur Rank a streamlined and therefore more effective process of filmmaking which they called "New Design for Films." Out of Rank's Research Department hatched Independent Frame. What could have been the breeding ground for a new kind of artificial filmmaking didn't turn out well at that time, however, as it relied heavily on background projection, models and miniatures instead of real locations which was what they would call for in post-war filmmaking. Nevertheless, it was an early step towards the process of digital and therefore entirely synthetic filmmak-

ing. (Some of the process work at MGM, such as that on *Green Dolphin Street,* resembles the Independent Frame concept — panning from studio sets to large rear-screen set-ups.) Years later Douglas Trumbull suggested shooting movies in virtual studios, with actors in front of green or blue screens (and put this idea into practice with his Magicam process). So post-war British filmmakers were pretty innovative and seemed to have set new standards. Even Ray Harryhausen and producer Charles H. Schneer eventually located their operation in London as Hollywood had invested too much into rear projection while in London they offered blue screen and other goodies at the same time.

When I became associated with Ray Harryhausen, he had recently finished *Clash of the Titans*, his stop-motion swansong. We did several

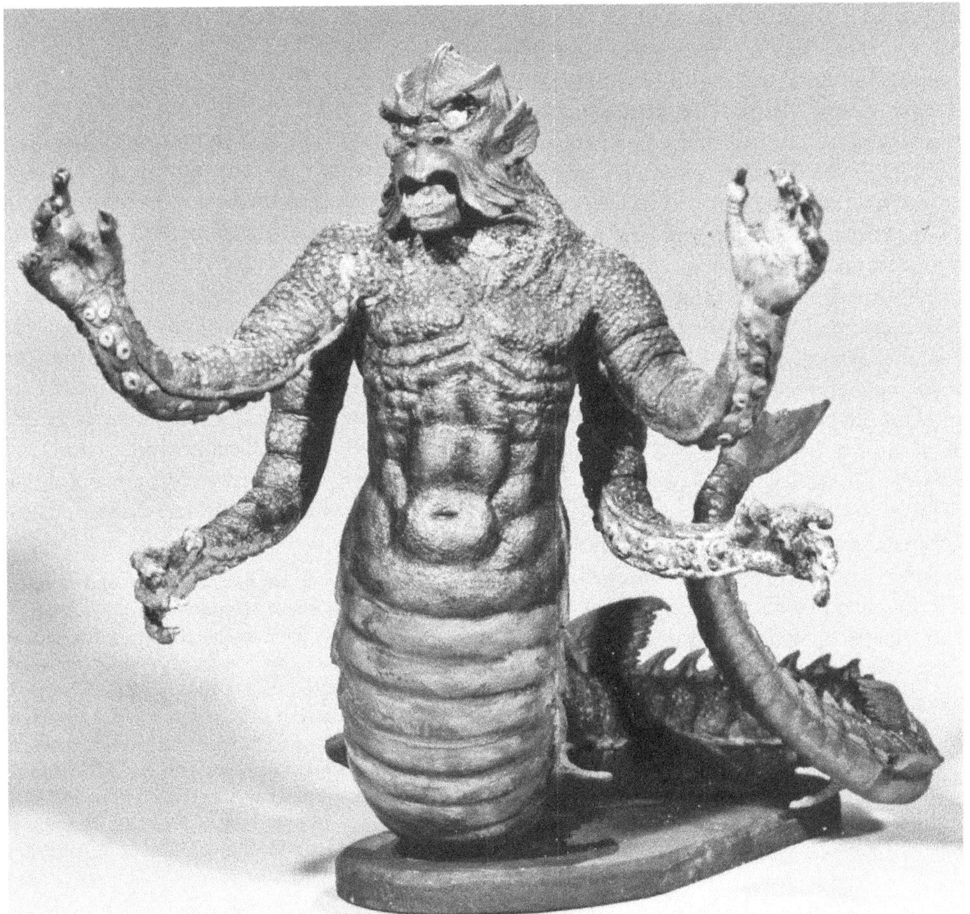

Kraken, the four-armed sea monster, from *Clash of the Titans* (courtesy Ray and Diana Harryhausen Collection as displayed by Deutsche Kinemathek Berlin).

exhibitions together, the first at the 1985 Berlin Film Fest, and for more than 15 years I curated and displayed most of his collection for the Deutsche Kinemathek, finally shown at Filmmuseum Berlin, right in the center of the German capital. You bet it was a nostalgic experience. The images Ray helped to create are cemented in my still youthful mind. As is the work of Jim Danforth, who did most of the dragon's animation in *The Wonderful World of the Brothers Grimm*, and of Willis O'Brien, the late lamented technical creator of *Kong* (who had had some other wild ideas never to reach the screen).

In Hollywood I saw some of the original *King Kong* models deteriorating at Forry Ackerman's vast Ackermansion. "I like to see them rot like myself," Forry told me whimsically (and years later had to sit down and witness his major collection being destroyed by ignorance). In 1984 I met L.B. Abbott, Lin Dunn and Danny Lee, who re-created his *Mary Poppins* flying rig in miniature for use at the Berlin Kinemathek; at the same time I visited Digital Productions, where they just finished computer-generated spaceships for *The Last Starfighter*. I realized then that a whole era, the age of mechanics, had passed. At that time, *Tron* and *The Last Starfighter* were not highly successful but a few years later, with morphing-technique commercials, the Nonterrestrial Water Pseudopod seen in *The Abyss*, the Cyborg, Liquid Metal Prototype, of *Terminator 2* and the dinosaurs of *Jurassic Park*, digital images became industry standard. Some technicians made the transition to the computer; others didn't and, alas, faded away.

This book is a tribute to those who made the mechanical age of cinema so entertaining. But computer-wise I have to disappoint my readers. I am not going to offer much digitally. A second volume has to be written by someone else.

But where to finish what I had in mind? Where would I set the turning point? For Filmmuseum's exhibition "Artificial Worlds," as a tribute to Ray Harryhausen, Phil Tippett gave me some items on loan. One was an armature that looked like a two-legged dinosaur. In fact, it was the mechanical D.I.D. (Direct Input Device) used to create believable digital movements for *Jurassic Park* (and the blueprint of motion capture). When they started to reconstruct prehistoric life in the computer, they realized that

the creatures walked with a limp. So they referred to ordinary stop-motion as a guideline and animated an armature that was equipped with encoders connected to a computer. Thus the frame-by-frame (keyframe only) information was fed into the computer which was used to construct an internal pictorial wire-frame figure, render and animate it properly.

I often call this device the missing link between the mechanical and the digital age of picture making. At that turning point a hundred years of mechanical filmmaking end, and a new chapter is begun which I will not cover. *Tempora mutantur, et nos mutamur in illis,* as the Latin phrase goes: Times are changing and we are changing with them ... but sometimes it's good to look back, not in anger but in awe to acknowledge what an inventive generation accomplished with much simpler means.

Pandora's Box

The era of digital filmmaking is just beginning. It is only one part within the concert of expanding digital media power, mostly interactive, while the film medium still is (and always will be) analog, at least in storytelling. The magic word is convergency. Transmitting artificial people from one medium to another, from mobile phones to computer games, from computer games to TV and vice versa. And the software is or will be easily available (to every dilettante, so to speak). Dennis Muren (ILM), who when he was a teenager was inspired and influenced by the work of Ray Harryhausen, recently stated:

> Almost anyone can do effects now; and so we have people out there happily turning out images, whether they have any talent or not. Effects are so commonplace that if I were growing up today, I don't know that the spark would be there to attract me. But lots of young people *are* attracted — some of whom consider us old-timers practically obsolete. We have people now at ILM who look at the work we did on *Star Wars* like people of my generation used to look at silent movies. Some of them are pretty scornful about it. "What did you guys think you were doing? We're *really* doing it now." I know that's just youth talking — and youth is important for change to happen — but it's oddly disturbing to have your life's work dismissed and thrown out. But it will happen to them, too.

Someday their work will also be thrown out — and it will be up to historians to look back on it and recognize it for what it was.[2]

Muren might be right, for what will lie beyond the computer which is basically a TV set with a typewriter placed in front? His boss, George Lucas, is thinking already about new frontiers (in fact it was Lucas who termed the availability of digital media to everybody a "democracy") and has no reservations to enter and conquer the delicate dream sphere of the human mind and subconscious:

I see true environments being created and combined with a lot of the biotech things going on, in terms of manipulating people's senses through drugs.... This combination will have the most powerful effect on the kind of storytelling we're doing today. It's too far off for me to worry about, and I'm not interested in virtual reality at its current level because it's just too crude. But the interface will improve dramatically, and if you can program virtual reality or simulator rides with biotech, you will have every interesting non-world. The first step would be to take the simulator ride part of an environment with the biotech part so that you believe the room is shaking or moving, that you are in a situation. At some point they may do away with the mechanical part of it, but that's serious biotech where you can just implant the story in a pill and live it. That's not outside the realm of possibility. You take the pill and go to sleep. It'd be like a dream and you have an actual real, physical experience of something completely imaginary. What that'll mean for society I have no idea....[3]

Something frightening seems to have evolved since the "innocent" mechanical days of R.W. Paul. Dreamsmiths like Lucas actually consider the human brain the true interface and may want to create images and fictitious parallel worlds right in the human brain, *à la* William Gibson's *Cyberspace* visions. Media might absorb new developments in medicine and neurology to make the blind see. We know that interactive scenarios are already more popular with young people than conventional cinema or TV. One day, those avatars will command artificial intelligence and create their own synthetic environment and life. No chance to do things like that on the ordinary silver screen of yesteryear.

"Is there still a chance for the true-and-honest cinema?" a film student recently asked. Yes, I answered, the experience of the audience, the very human event of being one of them in front of the giant silver screen. Of course, there is a schism between the *personal* experience provided by the digital age and the *communal* experience of audience viewing. Jim Danforth, while reading this, said that he, personally, thinks there is an atavistic power that extends from the days when mankind huddled around fires and told stories, and that we will sacrifice this power if viewing becomes entirely an isolated experience; "But then, I tend to be conservative."

Notes

1. David Devant, *My Magic Life*, London: Hutchinson, 1931.
2. *Cinefex*, Number 65, March 1996, p. 111.
3. As quoted by Gundolf S. Freyermuth: "The future of the cinema: Synthetic realities," in: *Filmmuseum Berlin*: Nicolai, 2000.

Glossary

Animation Stand   Movable table to place animated artwork and metal scaffold that supports the camera.

Bipack   Two strips of film are run simultaneously through camera or projector.

Blue Screen   Actors or objects are filmed in front of a blue backing. In the laboratory the color blue is separated, matte and counter-matte are produced and the image composited with a different background. In 1939 Larry Butler used the process in Britain for the Technicolor *The Thief of Bagdad* (with 50 Blue-Backing set-ups for a total of 99 cuts). After the war, with the advent of more color films, it became industry standard in films like *The Gift Horse* (1952), made at Shepperton Studios. In the early years of the process, the biggest disadvantage was a tendency to get "edging" (clearly noticeable matte lines through shrinking of film stock).

Chroma Key   Blue box, similar to blue screen. In the 1950s, TV applied electronic technology which used a monochrome background with even lighting. Through electronic processing, the background color was replaced by another image and a composite was created. It was used, for instance, at Clokey Films for the 1959 Easter episode of *The Dinah Shore Chevy Show*.

Composite   A film frame combined out of separately filmed elements.

Double Exposure   Cameraman rewinds film to expose it twice or several times in order to achieve superimpositions.

Effects Animation   2D-animated elements are optically added to live-action and through rotoscoping.

Floor Effects *see* **Mechanical Effects**

Front Projection   Needs less soundstage space than rear projection while the projected image is much sharper. A two-way mirror is placed between camera lens and a screen made of highly reflective material originally developed by the 3M company for use in road signs. The mirror, which acts as a beam splitter, is set at a 45-degree angle to the axis of a projector lens and used to project a plate onto the large reflex surface screen which reflects the light rays back towards the projector lens. In the direct line of the reflected beam, behind the two-way mirror, a camera is positioned. Actors in front of the screen are self-matting. Several people experimented with it. In France, Alékan and Gerard got a patent which was confirmed in Britain in 1957. The prologue sequence in *2001: A Space Odyssey* (1968) is done with front projection; also *Superman*'s flying scenes. The first person in the United States to use front projection with motion picture backgrounds might have been Dennis Muren on the 16mm amateur effort *Equinox*, filmed in early 1966.

Glass Shots *see* **Matte Paintings and Glass Shots**

Hanging Miniatures   Lining (or hanging) up a foreground or, as set designer Vincent Korda called it, front miniature which represents the upper part portions of a structure such as towers and roofs with a full-size set. By measuring the distance between the camera and the set and the shots required, one can plan the scale of the miniature top. The miniature then is placed on location between camera and main set at an appropriate distance and in an appropriate position. If a miniature is built one-third life-size, for instance, it has to be placed one-third as far from the camera as the full-size set. While the model is placed in front of the set, it often serves to fill the background. Camera can be panned or tilted during shooting. Method has been used to great advantage in F. W. Murnau's *Der letzte Mann* (U.S.: *The Last Laugh*, 1924); the silent 1924 and sound 1939 *Thief of Bagdad*; *Don Q, Son of Zorro* (1925); the silent *Ben-Hur* (1925; the stadium includes miniature people, designed by A. Arnold Gillespie); *The Scarlet Pimpernel* (1935); and *Things to Come* (1936). Key exponents of this technique in America and Britain were Ned Mann, Ross Jacklin and Wally Veevers. In Germany and France, Russian émigré Nicholas Wilcke created some stunning images by hanging miniatures. In Spain there were the flawless achievements of Emilio Ruiz del Rio. Nowadays the technique has been replaced by digital set extension.

High-Speed Filming   By filming movement of people or action with more than 24 frames per second, often 96 frames a second or more, the action is slowed down. Miniatures appear larger.

In-Camera Effects   In-camera effects include double exposures, dissolves and superimpositions, stationary mattes, prisms and all kind of filters, high-speed filming, stop-frame photography, etc.

Matte/Counter Matte   Opaque mask that blocks a portion of a scene.

Matte Paintings and Glass Shots   Part of a scene is painted on a pane of glass (or Masonite), on location (and then a sheet of glass is mounted in front of the camera like a hanging miniature) or in postproduction (then the images are filmed separately as mattes or with the live action projected into the painting). The matte artist ad-

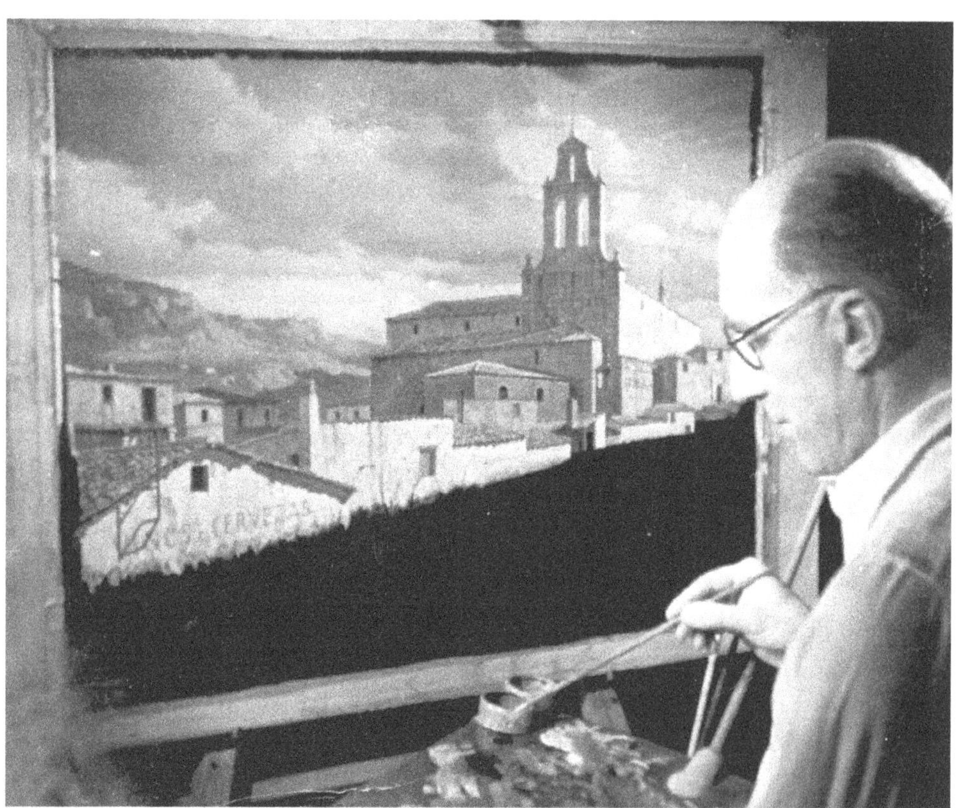

Above and opposite page: These unidentified examples of matte paintings (and preparing live action plates for matte art) are from Spain and were found in the files of the Paul Kohner Archives at Deutsche Kinemathek Berlin.

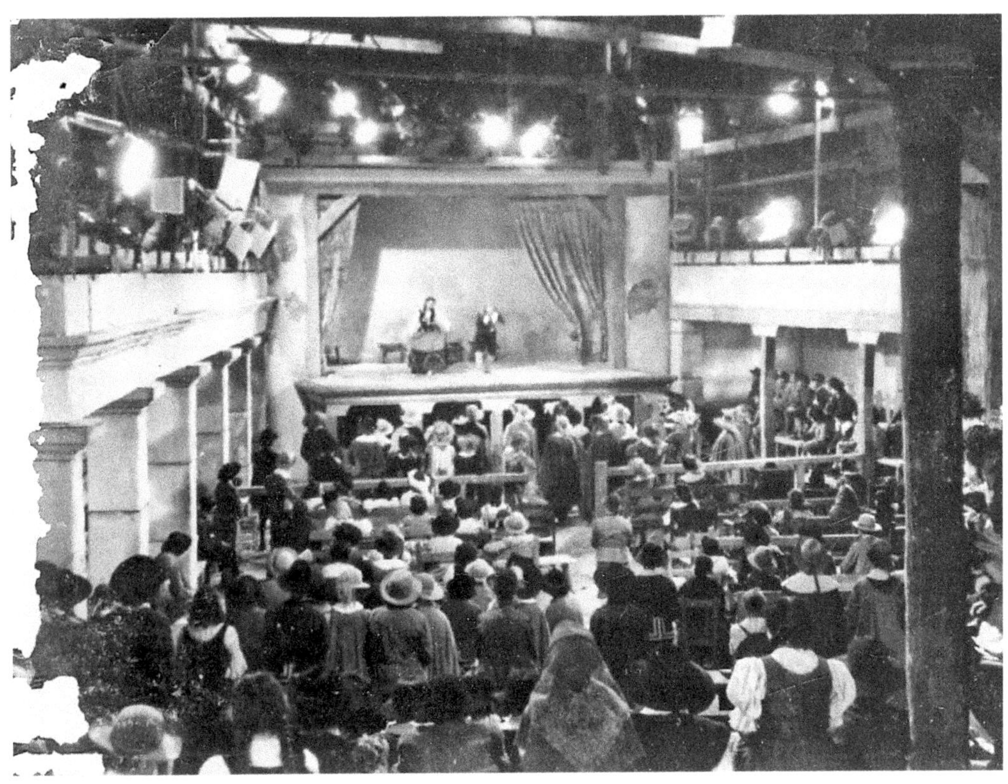

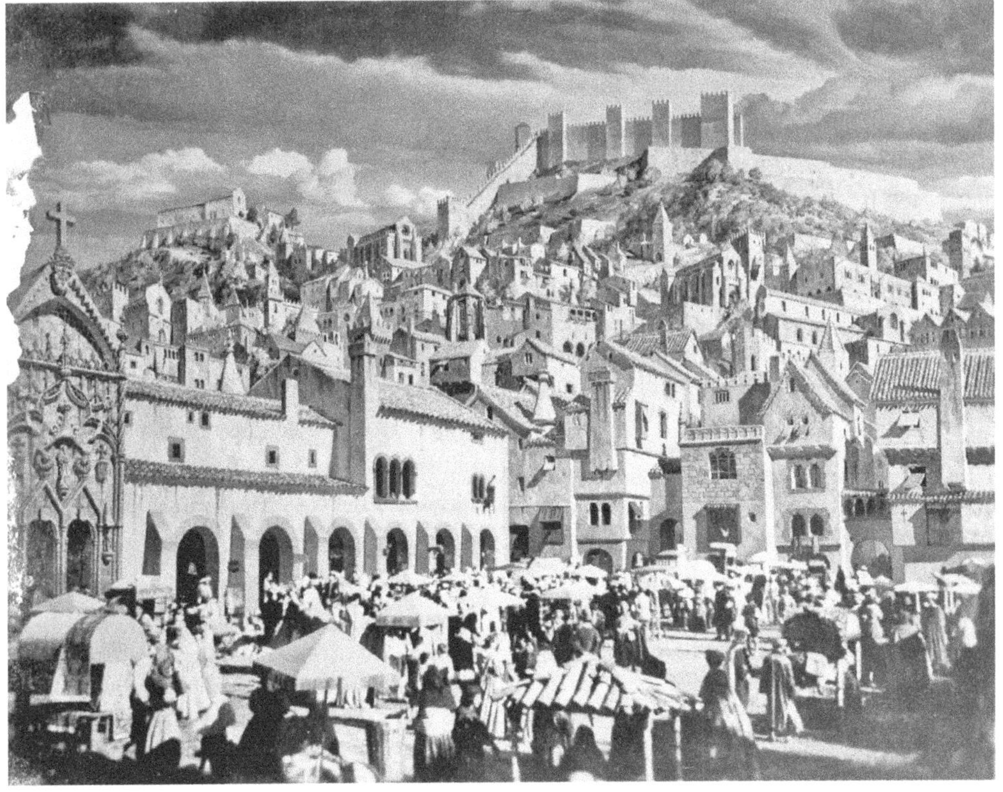

justs the colors according to the lighting of the original location or set. The first artists to use the technique were Norman Dawn, Ferdinand Pinney Earle, Paul Detlefsen, Paul Grimm, Mario Larrinaga and, in France and Britain, Percy Day. Before it became digital matte painting, the art of painted mattes was greatly refined by Albert Whitlock, a British artist who emigrated to America and enjoyed a career at Disney and Universal.

Mechanical Effects   Practical effects that take place right on the set in front of the camera. Involves hydraulics, pneumatics, electronics, engineering, construction, ballistics and pyrotechnics, utilizes motors, cables and pulleys, gimbals and, of course, explosives. In Britain they are called Physical or Floor Effects.

Miniature Projection   Patented by Willis O'Brien to combine glass paintings with background projection. When *King Kong* producer Merian C. Cooper became involved, this process was adapted to the idea of using small projections with miniature sets and stop-motion animation.

Miniatures   Individual models, but also miniature sets and studio tanks to film maritime action.

Motion Control   Computer-control performs exact, repeatable camera movements and functions exposure by exposure to coordinate the movement of separately filmed elements. The motion control basically comes from sound engineering and employing audio channels. In 1949 a member of MGM's sound department, O.L. Dupy, constructed a pioneering system, called a "repeater head," which allowed for pans and tilts over matte painting composites. Also in 1949, Paramount used a punch-tape repeater system to make repeater moves for *Samson and Delilah.* At Industrial Light & Magic they named it originally "Dykstraflex" after John C. Dykstra.

Multifilm Systems   Use cameras with two identical movements so that a traveling matte can be shot at the same time as the ordinary negative. Multifilm systems involve the Infra-red process, the Ultraviolet process and, for some time at Rank in Britain and Disney in the U.S., the Sodium vapor process.

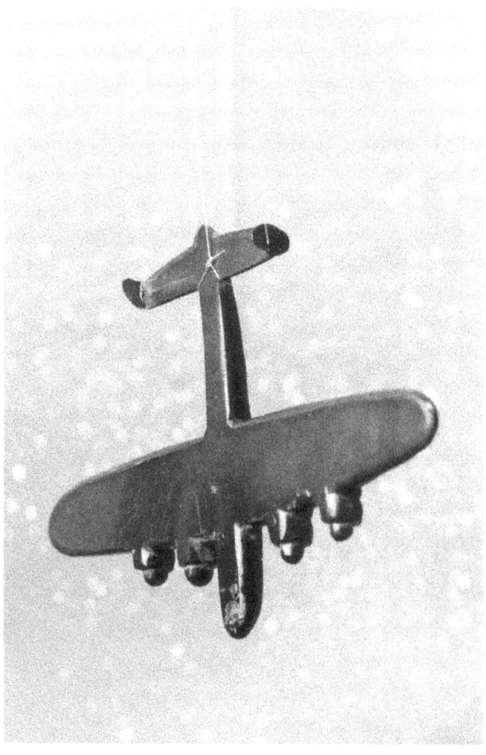

Tiny model of Flying Fortress for the German movie *Aimee & Jaguar* (courtesy Hans Joachim Thunack and Deutsche Kinemathek Berlin).

Optical Effects   Mainly done in optical printing: dissolves, split-screens, superimpositions, freeze-frame shots, optical "flops" (left to right or vice versa), repeating action, changing the rate of speed per second and so on.

Optical Printing   A postproduction technique. Previously photographed images are changed in an optical printer by re-photographing them. Optical printers have been equipped with one or more projectors and lamphouses that project the elements into the lens of a taking camera.

Physical Effects *see* **Mechanical Effects**

Pyrotechnics   These include fire, smoke, bullets and all kinds of explosives.

Rear Projection   A projector throws a previously filmed background image (or "plate") onto a screen. In front of the translucent screen, the actors play a scene. Camera and projector are synchronized or interlocked. Slide projection was already known in photography. Background projection for moving scenes was first seen in Fox and Warner productions. Among the pioneers are George J. Teague and Ralph Hammeras at Fox, and Hans Koenekamp at Warner-First National. A plastic screen recommended by Sidney Saunders was used for the first time in the production of RKO's *King Kong* (1933). The biggest process department, however, was at Paramount Studios, operated by Farciot Edouart. To receive a brighter image, Edouart used a triple-projector that was developed in a joint venture effort so that three prints of the same scene could be projected by three projectors simultaneously, with the images precisely overlapped (Warner Bros.–First National had a similar device in Burbank).

From an unpublished research paper written by German trickfilm pioneer Guido Seeber, who passed away in 1940:

> When a photographer named Sonntag proposed in 1912 to add to portrait photographs any background by projecting it from behind onto a background screen, he couldn't imagine that one day his idea, then smiled at, would become important — not so much in photography, but rather in cinematography. Today, background projection is indispensable in film production. And there are possibilities in process cinematography waiting for further development. For example, it was criticized that the projected background images were not large enough to materialize the director's ideas. To overcome this problem, two background projectors were installed side by side projecting adjoining images, with the junction of the two scenes made unrecognizable by suitable set pieces such as a tree or a pillar. Nevertheless, there were problems with this system too. It is nearly impossible to have two projector lamphouses with equal illuminating power. One had to look for other ways. A stimulation came from touring exhibitors who had used not only a double apparatus but a triple-headed projector called an Agioscope for projecting slides. After a series of experiments, first with slides, an apparatus has been developed for projecting three identical *moving* plates exactly one upon another. The construction consists of three projectors — the two outer ones projecting inward by means of surface mirrors, and the center one projecting directly onto the process screen.

There was also *Interlaced Projection*, in which three segments were extracted from a 65mm image and re-projected side by side using three separated 35mm projectors. By overlapping the images with soft blends, a continuous image was formed; this had the advantage of three light sources (three *hot spots*) evenly distributed across the wide screen, which was then re-photographed in anamorphic 35mm, or in Cinerama. Jim Danforth used a two-image version of this to get super-clear miniature projection backgrounds for John Carpenter's *They Live* (1988). The plate recording area for this system is larger than VistaVision. Occasionally back projection (with digital projectors) is still used today.

Reverse Action   By running the film backwards during shooting, an action can be reversed; for instance, a person might jump out of the water.

Rostrum Camera *see* Animation Stand

Rotoscoping   Isolating a filmed object or person by tracing around its edges frame-by-frame allows for creating a silhouette. Live-action is thus combined with effects animation. It is not exactly known who came up with this technique. It's usually credited to Max Fleischer (1915–16) but Jim Danforth thinks that Fleischer used cutouts for his early films and didn't use projected rotoscope animation until around the time of his feature-length *Gulliver's Travels* (1939) and *Mr. Bug Goes to Town* (1941). Phil Kellison once told Danforth that it was Leonard Pickley who really invented rotoscoping and had sued Disney for using the process without paying royalties. Disney knew Pickley was right, but extended the legal process until Pickley ran out of money. (Pickley had worked on the "A Night on Bald Mountain" sequence of 1940's *Fantasia*, and passed away in 1958.)

Schüfftan Process [Mirror Trick]   This was developed by Eugen Schüfftan and associates in the early 1920s. Patent was used throughout Europe. The technique entailed the employment of a mirror positioned in front of the camera lens at an angle of 45 degrees. (Later, however, they used the advantage of a semi-transparent mirror.) The camera is opposite to a life-sized set, while the ancillary set (usually a model or miniature) is placed on the right hand side of the camera. Actual set, mirror and model form a right angle. By selectively scraping away the silvering, part of the mirror would be rendered transparent. Thus the camera can shoot the actual set through the open part of the mirror, while capturing the model in the mirror's reflection at the same time. This way, the image of the miniature is superimposed on the life-size set. During shooting, the distance between miniature and camera has to be adjusted so that the scale of he model will be consistent with that of the actual set. The shorter the distance between model and camera, the larger its reflection in the mirror and the larger it appears in the final scene. Since the camera is shooting the reflection of the model in a mirror, the image is side-inverted. That means that the model has to be built on how it would look in the mirror. Can only be applied to studio lighting. Requires a 25–40mm camera lens so that life-size set and miniature will be equally distinct and merge seamlessly. Sometimes a positive diopter lens was used on the reflected image so that focus could be exact for both distances.

Sodium Light Process   A Traveling Matte Color Process (Multifilm System) which involved a beam-splitting camera to photograph actors in front of a yellow-lit background. The matte is simpler to make than with blue screen; foreground colors are virtually unlimited in this process. Developed by the Rank Laboratories, and first used in 1956 in *Plain Sailing*. In America it was exclusively adopted by Disney in the early 1960s for use in *Mary Poppins* (1964).

Split-Screen   By masking an image in two-halves, it is possible to create *Doppelgänger* shots and other effects.

Stop-Motion Animation   Creates lifelike movement out of lifeless 3D objects such as models and jointed puppets by means of stop-frame photography. Willis O'Brien, Ray Harryhausen, Jim Danforth, David Allen and Phil Tippett were the chief effects people using the process.

Studio Tank   Some of the bigger studios, such as MGM, Fox and Warners, were equipped with large outdoor and indoor pools to film model ships at sea. Wind machines and special paddles were used to create waves which, due to the smaller scale of the model, moved too quickly; as water cannot be reduced in size or "miniaturized," these scenes have to be filmed high-speed. The center of the tank is usually

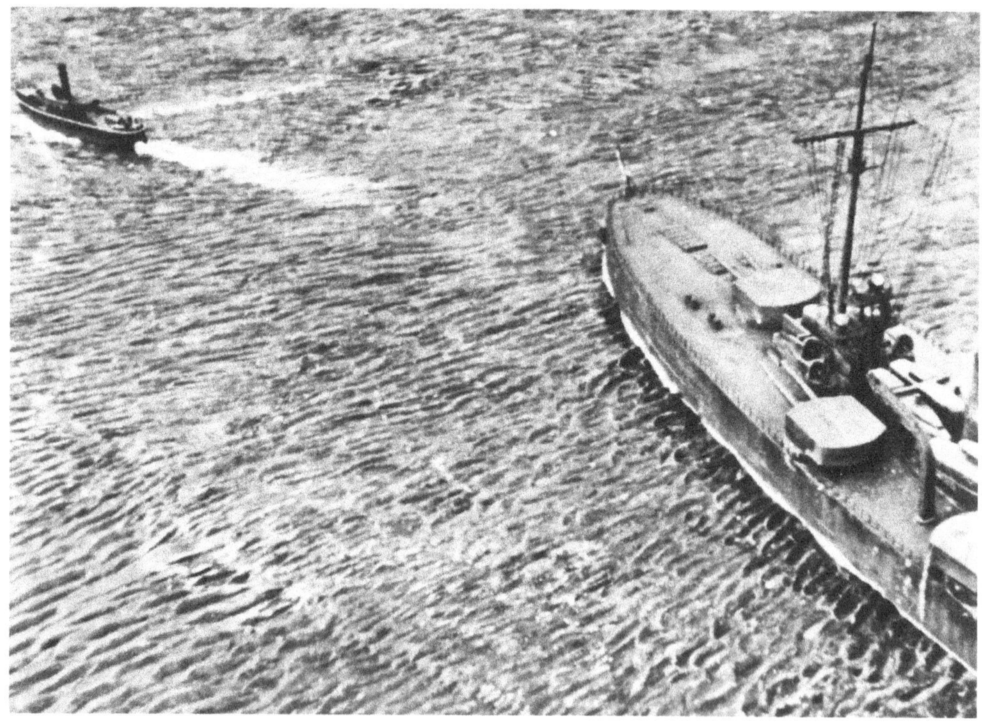

Ernst Kunstmann: Model ships for DEFA (1950s) (courtesy Deutsche Kinemathek Berlin).

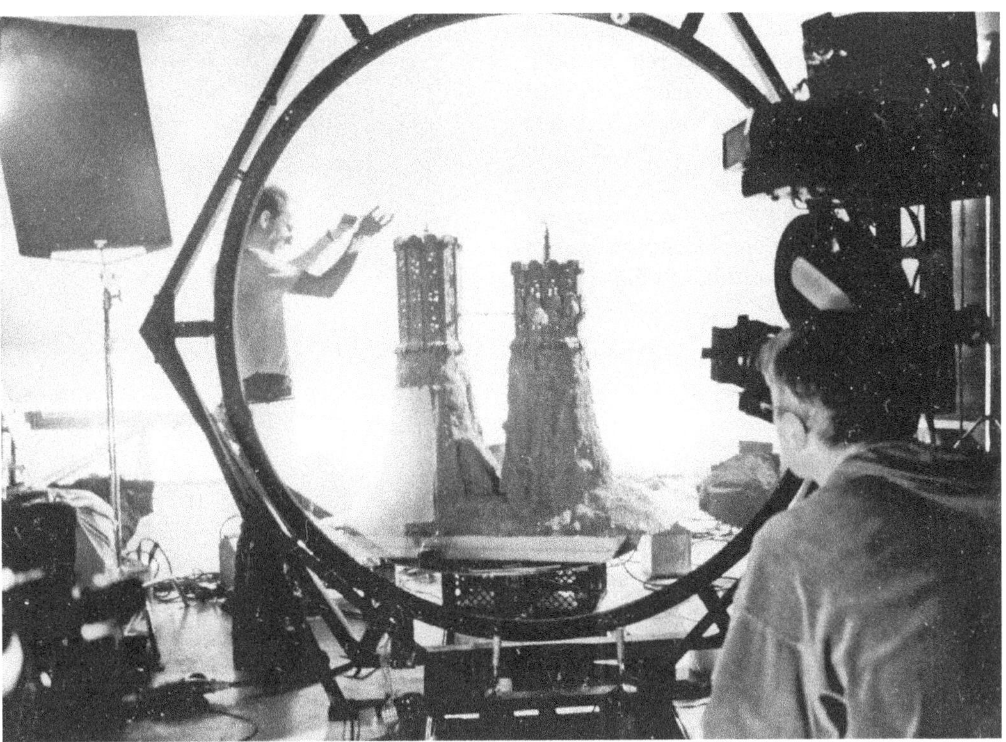

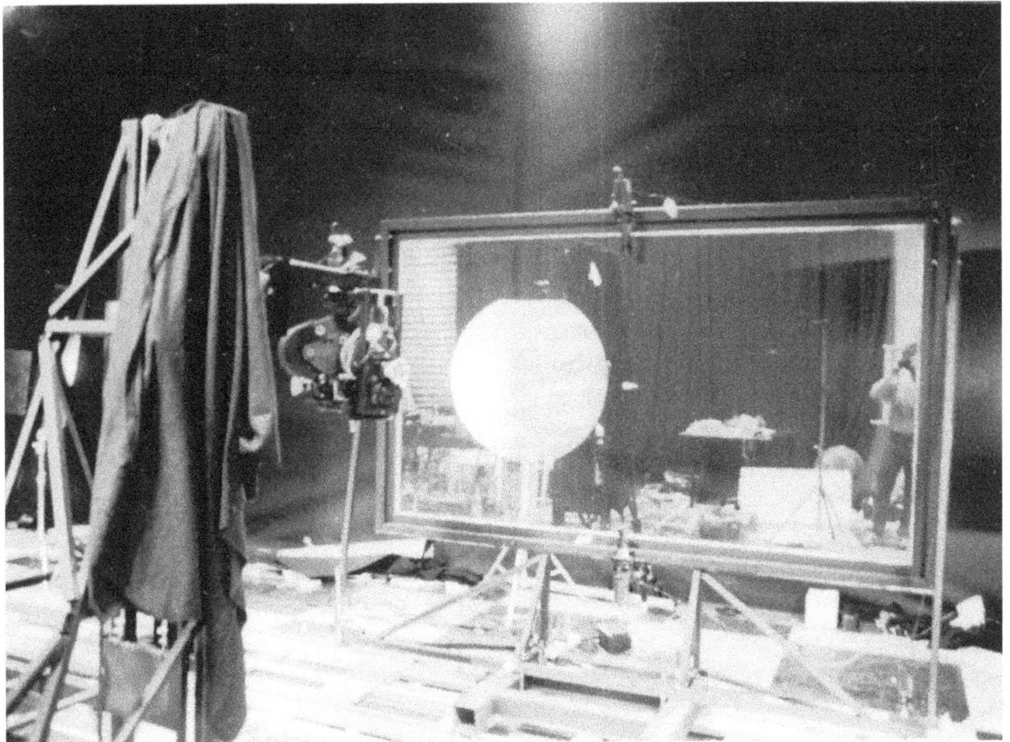

The model stage of *The High Crusade* (1994), produced by Roland Emmerich (courtesy Karl-Heinz Christmann and Deutsche Kinemathek Berlin).

deeper, also in order to sink model ships pulled by off-screen tractors and other vehicles along underwater rails through the respective artificial lake in front of a huge painted horizon. A. Arnold Gillespie, with credits such as *Mrs. Miniver* (1942), *Thirty Seconds Over Tokyo* (1944) and *They Were Expendable* (1945), was a leading expert in this type of picture; he once claimed to have spent half his life in MGM's big outdoor tank in Culver City.

Superimposition   Used from time to time for transitionary, montage, and ghost effects. *See also*: double-exposure.

Suspending *see* **Wirework**

Traveling Mattes   In order to combine people walking with a different background, no static mattes can be used. Instead, silhouettes exactly duplicate the actors' movements but therefore the actors have to be filmed in front of a neutral (black or blue) background to combine them frame by frame with a new, separately filmed background. Thus, a matte film traveled along with the background and foreground film.

Trick Perspective   Similar to hanging or foreground miniatures, but often used with actors to increase or reduce the apparent size of the characters. One of the best examples for trick perspective are the scenes involving leprechauns in Disney's *Darby O'Gill and the Little People* (1959) or some shots in Harryhausen's *The 3 Worlds of Gulliver* (1960).

Wirework   Actors and props are flown through the air by different types of wires and flying rigs. Examples: *The Absent Minded Professor* (1961), *Mary Poppins* (1964).

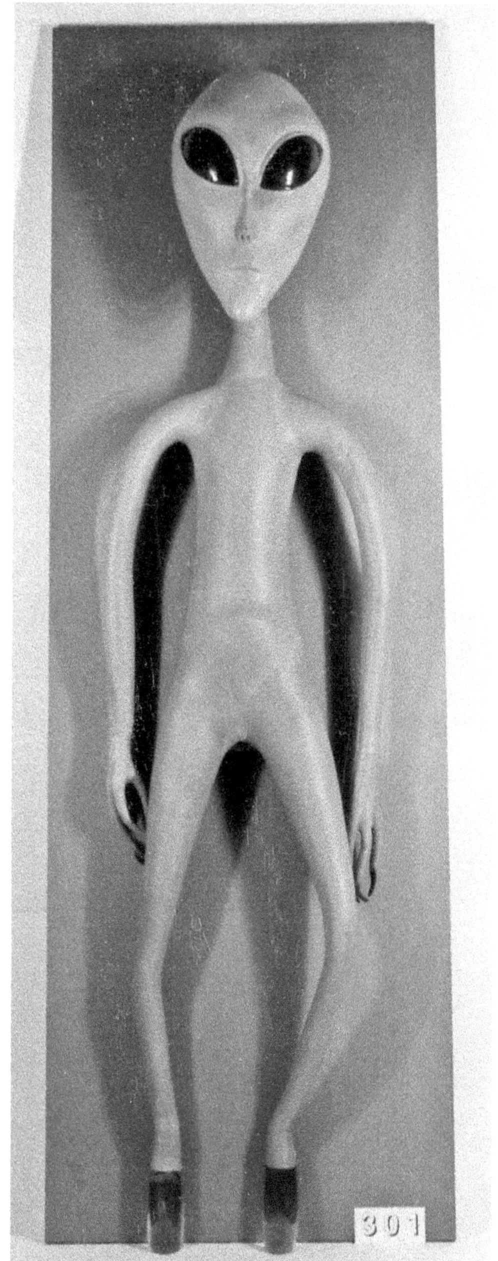

Alien marionette (*Communion*) (courtesy Deutsche Kinemathek Berlin).

The Biographies

L.B. [Bill] Abbott (1908–1985)

American Special Effects Cinematographer

L.B. (Lenwood Ballard) Abbott's father started his career as cameraman in the silent era, as did his son, who entered Fox Studios in 1926 when he was 18. L.B. assisted on Raoul Walsh's *What Price Glory?* (1926), F.W. Murnau's highly acclaimed *Sunrise* (1927) and *Just Imagine* (1930). In 1936 he became a camera operator. He photographed some effects footage for *In Old Chicago* and *Suez* (both in 1938) and helped with *Swamp Water* (1941).

When Fred Sersen, head of the 20th Century–Fox photographic effects division, needed another regular cameraman, Abbott volunteered and eventually was promoted to director of photography, special effects department in 1943: *The Song of Bernadette* (1943), *Sweet Rosie O'Grady* (1943), *Crash Dive* (1943), *Heaven Can Wait* (1943), *Moon Over Miami* (1943), *The Gang's All Here* (1943), *The Meanest Man in the World* (1943), *Buffalo Bill* (1944), *Pin-Up Girl* (1944), *Wilson* (1944), *A Wing and a Prayer* (1944), *A Tree Grows in Brooklyn* (1945), *Captain Eddie* (1945), *State Fair* (1945), *Where Do We Go from Here?* (1945), *Anna and the King of Siam* (1946), *The Razor's Edge* (1946), *The Ghost and Mrs. Muir* (1947), *Forever Amber* (1947), *Miracle on 34th Street* (1947), *Captain from Castile* (1947), *Deep Waters* (1948), *The Snake Pit* (1948), *Call Northside 777* (1948), *Unfaithfully Yours* (1948), *Down to the Sea in Ships* (1949), *A Letter to Three Wives* (1949), *Slattery's Hurricane* (1949), *Twelve O'Clock High* (1949), *For Heaven's Sake* (1950), *All About Eve* (1950), *Two Flags West* (1950), *The Big Lift* (1950), *David and Bathsheba* (1951), *The Desert Fox* (1951), *The Day the Earth Stood Still* (1951), *Follow the Sun* (1951), *Fourteen Hours* (1951), *Bird of Paradise* (1951), *The Snows of Kilimanjaro* (1952), *The Desert Rats* (1953), *Niagara* (1953), *The Robe* (1953; the first Cinema-Scope picture), *Titanic* (1953), *Inferno* (1953, 3D), *Desiree* (1954), *The Egyptian* (1954), *Garden of Evil* (1954), *Hell and High Water* (1954), *Prince Valiant* (1954), *River of No Return* (1954), *Three Coins in the Fountain* (1954), *Demetrios and the Gladiators* (1954), *The Girl in the Red Velvet Swing* (1955), *The Left Hand of God* (1955), *Love Is a Many Splendored Thing* (1955), *The Racers* (1955), *The Rains of Ranchipur* (1955), *The Seven Year Itch* (1955), *Untamed* (1955), *The Girl Can't Help It* (1956), *The King and I* (1956), *The Bottom of the Bottle* (1956), *Bus Stop* (1956), *D-Day, the Sixth of June* (1956), *The Man in the Grey Flannel Suit* (1956), *The Revolt of Mamie Stover* (1956), *The True Story of Jesse James* (1957).

When Sersen's successor, Ray Kellogg, left Fox, Abbott took over the department and was in charge from 1957 to 1970: *The Wayward Bus* (1957), *The Enemy Below* (1957), *Will Success Spoil Rock Hunter* (1957), *Bernardine* (1957), *The Sun Also Rises* (1957), *Desk Set* (1957), *The Three Faces of Eve* (1957), *Peyton Place* (1957), *The Fly* (1958), *The Hunters* (1958), *Rally Round the Flag, Boys* (1958), *South Pacific* (1958), *The Young Lions* (1958), *The Roots of Heaven* (1958), *The Diary of Anne Frank* (1959), *Journey to the Center of the Earth* (1959), *The Blue Angel* (1959), *Holiday for Lovers* (1959), *High Time* (1960), *The Lost World* (1960, which began a cycle of movie and TV work with producer Irwin Allen), *North to Alaska* (1960), *Sink the Bismarck!* (1960, filmed

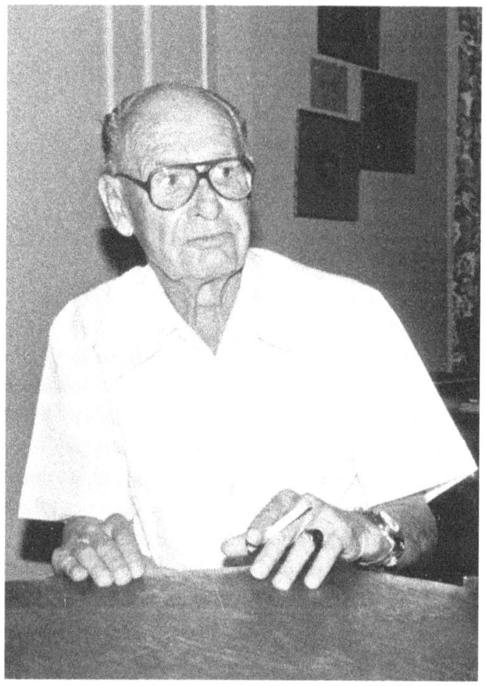

L.B. (Bill) Abbott, who for many decades worked at 20th Century–Fox, a year before his death. Photograph by Hans Helmut Prinzler (courtesy Deutsche Kinemathek Berlin).

in Britain; consultant), *Wake Me When It's Over* (1960), *Francis of Assisi* (1961), *Snow White and the Three Stooges* (1961), *Voyage to the Bottom of the Sea* (1961), *Return to Peyton Place* (1961), *Five Weeks in a Balloon* (1962), *The Longest Day* (1962, a Darryl F. Zanuck production filmed in Europe; consultant), *Mr. Hobbs Takes a Vacation* (1962), *Cleopatra* (1963), *Move Over, Darling* (1963), *The Birds* (1963, additional effects in school sequence), *Fate Is the Hunter* (1964), *Goodbye, Charlie* (1964), *Hush ... Hush, Sweet Charlotte* (1964), *What a Way to Go* (1964), *Flight of the Phoenix* (1965), *The Agony and the Ecstasy* (1965), *Morituri* (1965), *The Sound of Music* (1965), *Those Magnificent Men in Their Flying Machines* (1965, filmed in Britain; consultant), *Von Ryan's Express* (1965), *Fantastic Voyage* (1965–66), *Batman* (1966), *Our Man Flint* (1966), *The Sand Pebbles* (1966), *Stagecoach* (1966), *Way Way Out* (1966), *The Flim Flam Man* (1967), *In Like Flint* (1967), *The St. Valentine's Day Massacre* (1967), *Valley of the Dolls* (1967), *The Boston Strangler* (1968), *Planet of the Apes* (1968), *Star!* (1968), *Butch Cassidy and the Sundance Kid* (1969), *Che!*

(1969), *Hello, Dolly!* (1969), *Justine* (1969), *Beneath the Planet of the Apes* (1969–70), *M*A*S*H** (1970), *Myra Breckinridge* (1970), *The Only Game in Town* (1970), *Patton* (1970), *Beyond the Valley of the Dolls* (1970). TV series and specials include *Voyage to the Bottom of the Sea* (1964–68), *Lost in Space* (1965–68), *The Time Tunnel* (1966–67), *Batman* (1966–69), *Land of the Giants* (1967–69), *City Beneath the Sea* (1970), *M*A*S*H* (1972–82), *Flood* (1976), *Fire* (1976), *The Return of Captain Nemo/The Amazing Captain Nemo* (1976), *The Night the Bridge Fell Down* (1977), *Code Red* (1980). Academy Awards for *Dr. Dolittle* (1967), *Tora! Tora! Tora!* (1969), *The Poseidon Adventure* (1972) and *Logan's Run* (1976), the latter made at MGM. As freelance effects director, he was involved in the shooting of *Jonathan Livingston Seagull* (1973), *The Towering Inferno* (1974), *Evel Knieval* (1976), *The Swarm* (1977–78), *1941* (1980), *When Time Ran Out* (1980), *Wrong Is Right* (1981). In 1984, ASC Press published his book *Special Effects: Wire, Tape and Rubber Band Style.*

Richard F. Albain

American Mechanical Effects Supervisor

Richard F. (Dick) Albain was apparently with Columbia Studios for some time. Credits include: *Valley of the Dragons* (1961), *The Underwater City* (1962), *The Man from the Diner's Club* (1963), *The Three Stooges Go Around the World in a Daze* (1963), *Strait-Jacket* (1964), *The Outlaws Is Coming* (1965). Television series: *Bewitched* (1964), *I Dream of Jeannie* (1965).

Henri Alékan (1909–)

French Cinematographer

Paris-born assistant to Eugene Schüfftan while the latter worked in France. As lighting cinematographer, he was in high demand with films like *La Belle et la bête* for Jean Cocteau in 1946, *Austerlitz* for Abel Gance in 1959 (using the simplifilm process) and *Der Himmel über Berlin* for Wim Wenders in 1987.

Alékan was one of the originators of front projection, which was then called the Alékan-Gerard process.

Nick Allder

British Mechanical Effects Supervisor

Often worked with Brian Johnson: *Alien* (1978–79), *The Empire Strikes Back* (1979–80), *Dragonslayer* (1980–81). For *Conan the Barbarian* (1982) he built a mechanical snake. Special effects work for: *Legend* (1985), *Leviathan* (1989), *The Fifth Element* (1997), *Braveheart* (1995), *Muppet Treasure Island* (1996), *Lost in Space* (1998).

David Allen (1944–1999)

American Stop Motion Animator

Stop-motion aficionado who was friends with Jim Danforth and Dennis Muren. Together they did the 16mm amateur film *Equinox* which was later blown up to 35mm and released theatrically by Jack H. Harris (in 1971). Danforth took Allen to Britain where he did 80 percent of the Chasmasaurus sequence for *When Dinosaurs Ruled the Earth* (1968–70) and helped out with *Willy Wonka and the Chocolate Factory* (1971). Allen tried to persuade Hammer Films to produce his *Raiders of the Stone Ring* (revised and reduced to *Zeppelin vs. Pterodactyls*), but Hammer did not green-light the film and Allen's lifelong pet project, later retitled *The Primevals*, was never finished. Did stop-motion animation for the low-budget projects *Flesh Gordon* (1973–74), *The Crater Lake Monster* (1977), *Laserblast* (1978), *The Day Time Ended* (1979), *Witches' Brew* (1980), *Caveman* (1980–81, with Jim Danforth again), *The Howling* (1981), *Q/The Winged Serpent* (1982), *The Hunger* (1983), *Twilight Zone: The Movie* (1983), *The Dungeonmaster* (1985), *The Stuff* (1985), *Ghoulies II* (1987), *The Puppetoon Movie* (1987, additional animation). Occasionally did some puppet work at ILM: *Young Sherlock Holmes* (1985), **batteries not included* (1987), *Willow* (1988). Also involved in: *Honey, I Shrunk the Kids* (1989). Over the years he joined forces with producer Charles Band and also took on directorial assingments: *Dolls* (1987), *Puppetmaster* (1989), *Robot Jox* (1989), *Bride of Re-Animator* (1990), *Crash and Burn* (1990), *Oscar* (1991), *Puppetmaster II* (1991), *Puppetmaster III* (1991), *Subspecies* (1991), *Demonic Toys* (1992), *Doctor Mordrid* (1992), *Bloodstone: Subspecies II* (1993), *Bloodstone: Subspecies III* (1993), *Dollman vs. Demonic Toys* (1993), *Prehysteria* (1993), *Dragonworld* (1994), *Freaked* (1994), *Oblivion* (1994), *Prehysteria 2* (1994), *Robot Wars* (1994), *Galgameth, the Arrival* (1996), *Puppetmaster IV* (1996), *Puppetmaster V* (1996).

Howard A. Anderson (1890–1979)

American Photographic Effects Supervisor

Did effects work for Cecil B. DeMille's silent epic *The King of Kings* (1927) and founded his own effects company in 1928: *White Zombie* (1932) starring Bela "Dracula" Lugosi, *Thunder Over Mexico* (1933), *The Duke of West Point* (1938), *The Flying Deuces* (1939, Laurel & Hardy), *Beyond Tomorrow* (1940), *The Corsican Brothers* (1941), *Angel on My Shoulder* (1946). He also was hired to do effects work for Chaplin Studios and producer Sol Lesser's perennially popular *Tarzan* series. After World War II he reorganized his company with sons Howard, Jr. and Darrell. Articles: "Dual photography matter of timing," *International Projectionist*, January 1942, and "Dual roles in pictures," *International Photographer*, March 1942. Died in Northridge, California.

Howard A. Anderson, Jr.

American Photographic Effects Supervisor

Saw his father produce lightning effects for DeMille's *The King of Kings* in 1927. Joined the company after World War II with brother Darrell and took assignments mostly from independent producers and TV: *Unknown Island* (1948), *The Flying Saucer* (1950), *Phantom from Space* (1953), *King Dinosaur* (1955, for Bert I. Gordon), *Nightmare* (1956), *Godzilla, King of the Monsters!* (additional work for U.S. release of Japanese monster movie *Gojira* in 1956), *The Black Scorpion* (1956–57), *Invasion of the Saucer Men* (1957), *The Time Machine* (1959–60, optical effects for Project Unlimited and producer George Pal), *The Angry Red Planet* (1959–60), *12 to the Moon* (1960), *Beyond the Time Barrier* (1960), *X-15* (1960), *Jack the Giant Killer* (1961–62, in cooperation with Project Unlimited), *The Underwater City* (1962), *Varan the Unbelievable* (1962, additional work for U.S. release of Japanese monster movie *Daikaiju Baran*). Bigger pictures included *Taras Bulba* (1962), *Tobruk* (1967), *Point Blank*

(1967), *The Party* (1968), *The Mephisto Waltz* (1971), George Pal's *Doc Savage: The Man of Bronze* (1973), *Gray Lady Down* (1978), *Superman* (1977–78), *Avalanche Express* (1979). TV: *The Untouchables, Star Trek, The Invaders, Mission: Impossible, The FBI, The Lucy Show, Cannon, Barnaby Jones, A Man Called Sloane, Mod Squad, Charlie's Angels, Happy Days*. Anderson's company was relocated onto the Desilu (former RKO) lot (that's the reason he did many of Desilu's TV shows) and, after merger with Paramount, in the former Paramount visual effects facilities where they also took over the old Vista-Vision Printer designed for *The Ten Commandments*. When it was sold to Industrial Light & Magic, it was known there as The Anderson Printer.

Apogee Productions, Inc.

American Visual Effects Company

When John Dykstra and some of his collaborators left George Lucas after *Star Wars,* they founded Apogee: *Star Trek: The Motion Picture* (1979–80), *Firefox* (1982), *Never Say Never Again* (1983). The company also did some preliminary work on *Dune* (1983–84). Went bankrupt in 1993.

Hidesaburo [Shuzaburo] Araki
(1913–1961)

Japanese Effects Cinematographer

Eiji Tsuburaya's brother-in-law. During World War II was combat cameraman in China. (...) In 1955 he photographed *Ginrin*. Photographed effects sequences for Eiji Tsuburaya's early color and/or Tohoscope releases and helped with blue screen and optical effects: *Chikyu boei-gun* (*The Mysterians*, 1957), *Bijo to ekitainingen* (*The H-Man*, 1958), *Sensukai I-57 kofuku sega* (*Submarine I-57 Will Not Surrender*, 1959), *Nippon tanjo* (*The Three Treasures*, 1959), *Son Go Ku* (*The Adventures of Sun Wu Kong*, 1959), *Daikaiju Baran* (*Varan the Unbelievable*, 1959), *Denso nin-gen* (1959), *Uchu daisenso* (*Battle in Outer Space*, 1959–60), *Hawai Middouei daikaikusen: Taiheyo no arashi* (*I Bombed Pearl Harbor*, 1960). At the time of his sudden death (cerebral hemorrhage), he was only 48 years old.

Roy Arbogast

American Mechanical Effects Supervisor

Worked on *Fantastic Voyage* (1966), *Bonnie and Clyde* (1967), *Jaws* (1972–73), *Close Encounters of the Third Kind* (1976–77), *Jaws 2* (1978), *Dracula* (1978–79), *Caveman* (1980–81), *The Incredible Shrinking Woman* (1981), *Escape from New York* (1981), *The Thing* (1982), *Return of the Jedi* (1982–83), *Jaws 3-D* (1983). TV series: *Night Gallery*.

Steven Archer (1957–)

British Stop-Motion Animator

In 1975 he became assistant to Cliff Culley in the matte department of Pinewood Studios: *The Pink Panther Strikes Again* (1976), *Candleshoe* (1976), *Escape from the Dark* (1976). In 1980 Ray Harryhausen selected him to assist on the animation for *Clash of the Titans*. Archer especially turned his attention to Bubo the mechanical owl. Harryhausen recommended him to Derek Meddings for the crystal spider animation for the Widow of the Web sequence in *Krull* (1982–83). Did some stop-motion on *Die unendliche Geschichte* (*The Neverending Story*, 1983–84; Falkor the Luck Dragon squirming in the sky), *The Adventures of Baron Munchausen* (1988–89) and *The Gate II* (1989, directed by Randy Cook). TV series: *Mr. Majeika* (1988), *Spitting Image* (1988), *Winjin' Pom* (1990).

He wrote the book *Willis O'Brien: Special Effects Genius* (published by McFarland in 1993). Unsuccessfully tried to resurrect some of Willis O'Brien's aborted projects left to him by O'Brien's widow Darlyne.

Teisho [Sadamasa] Arikawa
(1925–2005)

Japanese Effects Cinematographer

At the end of World War II, the Tokyo-born Arikawa was trained as a pilot for the Japanese Navy but survived Kamikaze. In 1945 he joined Toho Studios as sound recordist. Impressed by the effects work for *Battle of Hawaii,* he visited and talked to Eiji Tsuburaya. They hit it off immediately, and in 1948 Arikawa became part of Tsuburaya's independent Special Effects Technique Laboratory. Cameraman since 1953 when Tsuburaya was allowed to return to Toho. Went on to photograph all of Tsuburaya's war pictures as well as *Gojira* (*Godzilla, King of the Monsters!*, 1954) and related science fiction films: *Taiheyo no washi* (*Eagle of the Pacific*, 1953), *Gojira no gyakushu* (*Gigantis, the Fire Monster*, 1955), *Sora no daikaiju Radon* (*Rodan*, 1956), *Chikyu boeigun* (*The Mysterians*, 1957), *Nippon tanjo* (*The Three Treasures*, 1959), *Uchu daisenso* (*Battle in Outer Space*, 1959–60), *Mosura* (*Mothra*, 1961), *Yosei Gorasu* (*Gorath*, 1962), *Kingukongu tai Gojira* (*King Kong vs. Godzilla*, 1962–63), *Daitozoku* (*The Lost World of Sinbad*, 1963), *Kaitei gunkan* (*Atragon*, 1963), *Uchu daikaiju Dogora* (*Dagora, the Space Monster*, 1964), *San daikaiju: Chikyu saidai no kessen* (*Ghidrah, the Three-Headed Monster*, 1964), *Furankenshutain tai chitei kaiju Baragon* (*Frankenstein Conquers the World*, 1965), *Kaiju daisenso* (*Invasion of the Astro-Zombies*, 1965), *Furankenshutain no kaiju: Sanda tai Gaira* (*The War of the Gargantuas*, 1966), *Kingukongu*

no gyakushu (*King Kong Escapes*, 1967), *Ido Zero daisakusen* (*Latitude Zero*, 1969). In the mid–60s when the series got cheaper, he took over more and more directorial chores from Tsuburaya, who in the meantime was able to focus on his own TV activities: *Gojira, Ebira, Mosura: Nankai no daiketto* (*Ebirah, Horror of the Deep*, 1966), *Kaijuro no kessen: Gojira no musuko* (*Son of Godzilla*, 1967, in which he had numerous composite shots to show the size of the monsters and had 20 wire technicians operate a giant spider model which came in in six different sizes), *Kaiju soshingeki* (*Destroy All Monsters*, 1968). In between, Arikawa helped Tsuburaya direct his *Urutoraman* (*Ultraman*) and *Yasuyoshi ito Yasuji Morita* (*Mighty Jack*) series.

He left Toho shortly after Tsuburaya's demise and a last feature, *Gezora, Ganime, Kameba: Kessen! Nankai no daikaju* (*Yog: The Space Amoeba*, 1970–71). His last film was the 1977 *King Kong* rip-off *Xing xing wang* (*Colossus of Congo*). Died in his 80th year from lung cancer.

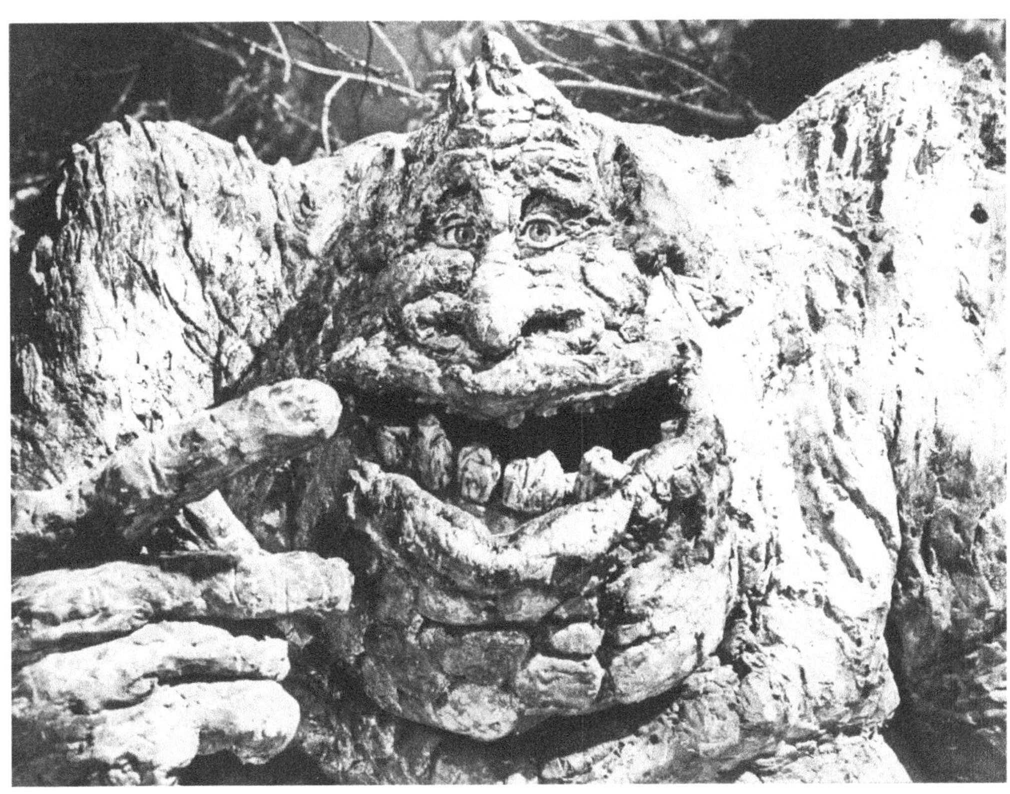

Colin Arthur's Rock Biter: *The Neverending Story* (1983–84) (courtesy Deutsche Kinemathek Berlin).

Colin Arthur

British Makeup Expert

An expert with latex foam. Staff member of Madame Tussaud's wax cabinet. Assisted Stuart Freeborn on *2001: A Space Odyssey* (1965–68). Did *Battle of Britain* (1968–69), *Ryan's Daughter* (1970), *The Devils* (1971), *Diamonds Are Forever* (1971), *The Abominable Dr. Phibes* (1971), *Conan the Barbarian* (1982), *Steiner—Das Eiserne Kreuz* (1977, with director Sam Peckinpah), *Christiane F.—Wir Kinder Vom Bahnhof Zoo* (1981, blood effects), *Die unendliche Geschichte* (*The Neverending Story*) *I* (1983–84) and *II* (1989–90). TV special: *Il Monsignore Quixote/Monsignor Quixote* (1988). With Ray Harryhausen on *The Golden Voyage of Sinbad* (1971–72; mask of the Vesir), *Sinbad and the Eye of the Tiger* (1976–77) and *Clash of the Titans* (1979–80).

Jerome H. [Jerry] Ash

(1893–1953)

American Cinematographer

As photographer, Jerome H. (Jerry) Ash did very early trick shots. He was in the movies first as an extra and actor in 1915, then lifelong cinematographer at Universal Studios where he inherited most of the trick and in-the-camera shots. Miniature photography for *The Cat and the Canary* (1927) and *King of Jazz* (1930). Did the three *Flash Gordon* serials (1936, 1938 and 1940) and *Buck Rogers* (1939) with Larry "Buster" Crabbe plus *The Phantom Creeps* (1939) with Bela Lugosi. Later joined the special photography department: *The Crimson Canary* (1945), *The Time of Their Lives* (1946), *The Scarlet Horseman, Abbott and Costello Meet Frankenstein* (1948; Lon Chaney's Wolf Man transformation), *Abbott and Costello Meet the Invisible Man* (1951).

Roy Ashton (1909–1995)

Australian-British Special Effects Makeup Man

Started as an architectural student but changed his mind and became an illustrator in a commercial firm of block-makers and designers in Australia. Came to England and went to an art school for about a year. On the art school's notice board, he saw an advertisement that Gaumont British Film Corporation was interested in training makeup artists. He applied, was chosen and assisted a former Ufa make-up man named Rosenthal. He encountered Boris Karloff while working on *The Man Who Changed His Mind* (1936). Two decades later did most of Hammer Films' monster gallery: *The Curse of Frankenstein* (1956–57, assistant to Phil Leakey), *Dracula* (1957, U.S.: *Horror of Dracula*, assistant to Phil Leakey), *The Man Who Could Cheat Death* (1959), *The Mummy* (1959), *The Brides of Dracula* (1960), *The Curse of the Werewolf* (1960), *The Evil of Frankenstein* (1963), *The Kiss of the Vampire* (1963–65), *The Gorgon* (1964), *The Curse of the Mummy's Tomb* (1964), *The Plague of the Zombies* (1966), *The Reptile* (1966). For Amicus did *Tales from the Crypt* (1971). Other productions include *Mr. Arkadin* (*Confidential Agent*, 1955) with Orson Welles, *Captain Nemo and the Underwater City* (1970), *The Private Life of Sherlock Holmes* (1970), *The Creeping Flesh* (1973).

James R. [Jim] Aupperle

American Stop-Motion/Miniature Expert

Credits include *Flesh Gordon* (1974), *Planet of Dinosaurs* (1978), *Caveman* (1980–81), *The Thing* (1982), *Dreamscape* (1984), *Ghostbusters* (1984), *Troll* (1985), *Evil Dead II* (1987), *The Gate* (1987), *Nightmare on Elm Street 3* (1987), *Beetlejuice* (1988), *After Midnight* (1989), *Nightmare on Elm Street 5* (1990), *Robocop 2* (1990), *The Addams Family* (1992), *The Nightmare Before Christmas* (1993), *Tremors II—Aftershocks* (1996).

Tim Baar (1902–1977)

American Miniaturist

Apparently he was at MGM for some time (he once mentioned to Jim Danforth that he contributed to that studio's 1939 *The Wizard of Oz*. Later joined Charles Baker at Universal Studio's Miniature Department: *The Mummy's Tomb* (1942), *Flesh and Fantasy* (1943), *Phantom of the Opera* (1943), *It Came from Outer Space* (1953), *Creature from the Black Lagoon* (1953–54), *Tarantula* (1955). Also did some work for Paramount's *When Worlds Collide* in 1951. While working at Universal he joined forces with Gene Warren and Wah Chang and co-founded Project Unlimited. Shared Academy Award for *The Time Machine* (1959–60). Credited on *Dinosaurus!* (1960), *Master of the World* (1960–61), *Jack the*

Giant Killer (1961–62), *The Wonderful World of the Brothers Grimm* (1962–63). Involved in other Projects stuff like *Spartacus* (1960), *7 Faces of Dr. Lao* (1963–64) and *Around the World Under the Sea* (1965). After Projects was disbanded he did *The Horse in the Gray Flannel Suit* (1968) and *Son of Blob* (*Beware! The Blob*, 1972).

Bob Baker

American Puppeteer

One of George Pal's original *Puppetoons* animators. In the late 1940s he opened a marionette

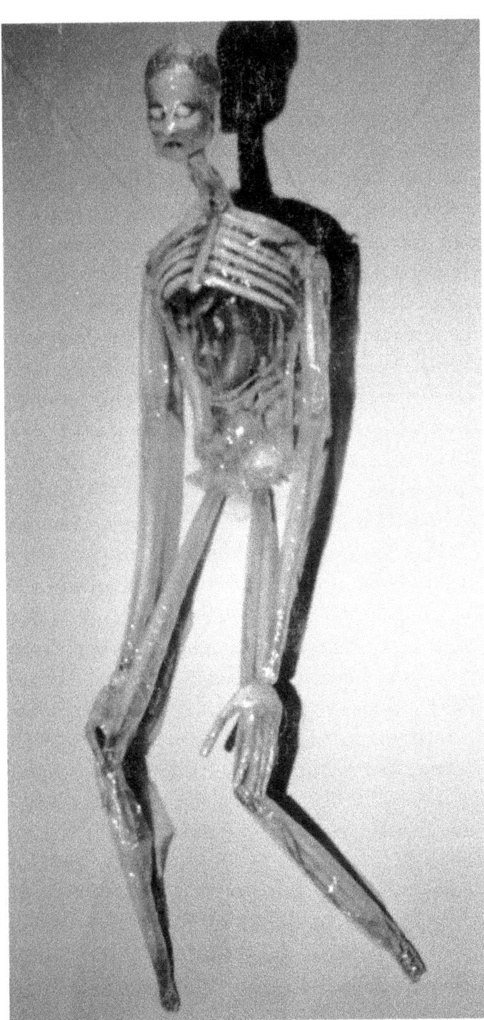

Alien marionette from *Close Encounters of the Third Kind* which in 1985 became one of the first displays of Deutsche Kinemathek (courtesy Deutsche Kinemathek Berlin).

theatre in Los Angeles. Took occasional puppeteering and wire works jobs for the film industry: *Monster from the Ocean Floor* (1954; a low-budget octopus for novice producer Roger Corman), *tom thumb* (1958), *The Angry Red Planet* (1959, puppeteering a bizarre Martian rat-bat-spider-crab), *Bedknobs and Broomsticks* (1971), *Escape to Witch Mountain* (1975), *Close Encounters of the Third Kind* (1976–77). TV series: *Star Trek*, *Voyage to the Bottom of the Sea*. Fabricated merchandising puppets for sale at Disneyland.

Charles Baker

American Miniaturist

Charles Cleon Baker joined the miniature crews of *The Lost World* (1924–25) and *Don Q, Son of Zorro* (1925) before entering Universal Studios for lifelong services in 1930: *Waterloo Bridge* (1930), *East of Java* (1930), *Frankenstein* (1931, miniature tower and windmill), *Air Mail* (1932), *The Invisible Man* (1933), *Bride of Frankenstein* (1935), *The Invisible Ray* (1935–36), *The Invisible Man Returns* (1939–40), *The Boys from Syracuse* (1940), *The Wolf Man* (1941), *The Invisible Woman* (1941), *The Ghost of Frankenstein* (1942), *Invisible Agent* (1942), *Frankenstein Meets the Wolf Man* (1942), *The Mummy's Tomb* (1942), *Flesh and Fantasy* (1943), *Phantom of the Opera* (1943), *You Gotta Stay Happy* (1948), *It Came from Outer Space* (1953), *Abbott and Costello Go to Mars* (1953), *Creature from the Black Lagoon* (1953–54), *This Island Earth* (1954), *Tarantula* (1955), *The Deadly Mantis* (1956), *Around the World in 80 Days* (1956, for producer Michael Todd), *The Incredible Shrinking Man* (1956–57), *The Monolith Monsters* (1957), *Run Silent, Run Deep* (1958), *Father Goose* (1964), *Earthquake* (1973), *Airport '77* (1977), *Airport '80: The Concorde* (1979).

Friend F. Baker

American Cinematographer

In 1915 he began as assistant cameraman at Universal. In 1916 he worked on the silent *20,000 Leagues Under the Sea*. Did photographic effects for Lon Chaney's *The Hunchback of Notre Dame* (1922–23) and staged the earthquake for the 1927 *Old San Francisco*. Later joined the effects department of Columbia Pictures. Then turned to 3D stereoscopic filmmaking and constructed a dual camera 16mm unit. Invented 3D-Natural Vision for Milton L. Gunzburg: "Baker, supported by O. S. 'Buddy' Bryhn and working with cameramen Joseph Biroc and Lothrop Worth, worked out the Natural Vision 3-Dimension process, as it was called, over a period of nearly six months beginning in mid (or late) summer 1951" (R. M. Hayes, *3-D Movies*, p. 21). As 3-dimension engineer he was involved in *Bwana Devil* (1952), the promotional short *Time for Beanie* (1952), *House of Wax* (1953) and *The Charge at Feather River* (1954), then completely disappeared from the scene. In *International Photographer*, October 1932, a piece written by Baker was published under the title "Inventor describes his process" (referring to a new composite process).

Rick Baker (1950–)
American Special Makeup Creator

Richard A. (Rick) Baker was born in Binghamton, New York. Two years after his birth, his parents moved to California, settling in Covina. He read about fx makeup in the pages of *Famous Monsters of Filmland* magazine and met part-time gorilla actor Bob Burns, a protégé of Paul Blaisdell, at Don Post's shop. In 1965 he devoured Dick Smith's magazine *Monster Makeup Handbook* and eventually met the great makeup artist in person. Professionally started taking jobs at Clokey Studios and Cascade of California and worked on TV commercials including the Jolly Green Giant and an "Un-hamburger" for 7-Up. His first feature assignment was a tentacled $500 monster suit for *Octaman* (1971) with associate Douglas Beswick. First project with John Landis, who became a frequent customer, was the apeman-like Schlockthropus, the Missing Link star of *Schlock* (1971), followed by *The Incredible 2-Headed Transplant/The Thing with Two Heads* (1971–72, a two-headed gorilla suit), *Black Caesar* (1973), *Cop Killers* (1973), *It's Alive!* (1974, monster baby), *The Chameleons* (1974), *Death Race 2000* (1975, death mask design for David Carradine), *Track of the Moon Beast* (1976), *Squirm* (1976), *Zebra Force* (1976), *The Kentucky Fried Movie* (1977,

John Landis), *The Incredible Melting Man* (1977–78), *It Lives Again* (1978). In between low-budget jobs he assisted his idol Dick Smith on *The Exorcist* (1972–73) and *The Fury* (1977) and got recommended by Dick to prepare an inflated fx head of actor Yaphet Kotto for the James Bond picture *Live and Let Die* (1973). Did some special model work on *Flesh Gordon* (1971–74, sculpting and casting the beetleman model to be animated by Jim Danforth and making a bronzed spider statue) and Bert I. Gordon's *The Food of the Gods* (1975–76). Became Dino De-Laurentiis' *King Kong* (1976) and was seriously injured by model helicopters in his apeman costume atop a Twin Towers miniature: "The first time that we actually started shooting with the helicopters, they're flying around, and the next thing I know, something goes and *Bam!*, it hits on me.... [I]t missed my head, but it hit my arm, and I thought my arm was just broken in half. It was really painful" (interviewed by Craig Reardon for *Closeup #3*). Cantina Sequence for George Lucas' *Star Wars* (1976–77). Did *Tanya's Island* (1980), *The Howling* (1981), *The Incredible Shrinking Woman* (1981), *The Funhouse* (1981), *Videodrome* (1983), Michael Jackson's *Thriller* video (1983, directed by John Landis), *Greystoke: The Legend of Tarzan, Lord of the Apes* (1983–84), *Starman* (1984, with Dick Smith), *Cocoon* (1985), *My Science Project* (1985), *Harry and the Hendersons* (1987), *Coming to America* (1988), *Gorillas in the Mist: The Story of Dian Fossey* (1988), *Missing Link* (1988), *Gremlins 2: The New Batch* (1990), *The Rocketeer* (1991), *Wolf* (1994), *Ed Wood* (1994, designed Lugosi makeup for actor Martin Landau), *Batman Forever* (1995), *The Nutty Professor* (1996), *Escape from L.A.* (1996), *Ghosts* (1997), *Men in Black* (1997), *Batman and Robin* (1997), *Psycho* (1998), *Mighty Joe Young* (1998), *How the Grinch Stole Christmas* (2001), *Planet of the Apes* (2001), *Men in Black II* (2002), *The Ring* (2002), *Hellboy* (2004), *The Ring Two* (2005), *Cursed* (2005), *X-Men: The Last Stand* (2006), *Click* (2006). Won his first Academy Award for Landis' *An American Werewolf in London* (1981). Animatronics makeup creator: *Captain Eo* (1986). TV series: *Beauty and the Beast* (1987). There are well-founded rumors that the basic design for E.T. was partly the work of Baker.

Ron Ballanger

British Mechanical Effects Supervisor

Credits include: *The Heroes of Telemark* (1965), *Those Magnificent Men in Their Flying Machines* (1965), *2001: A Space Odyssey* (1965–68), *Oh! What a Lovely War* (1969).

Peter Ballbusch (1902–1966)

Swiss-American Montage Effects Artist

Born in Switzerland. Created montage sequences for MGM: *The Good Earth* (1937), *Gone with the Wind* (1939), *Sergeant Madden* (1939), *Dr. Jekyll and Mr. Hyde* (1940–41, Spencer Tracy version), *Annie Get Your Gun* (1950), *Show Boat* (1951), *Scaramouche* (1952), *The Merry Widow* (1952).

Bent Barfod

Danish Illustrator, Animator and SFX Consultant

Barfod started as a stage designer and comic-strip artist. In 1949 he debuted with the animated short *They Guide You Across*, then founded his own studio to produce experimental, animation and documentary films. American producer Sid Pink hired him to do effects work for his Danish sci-fi movies *Reptilicus* (1962) and *Journey to the Seventh Planet* (1962). In 1983 Barfod did *Otto er et naesehorn*.

Harry Barndollar (1885–1963)

American Special Effects Supervisor

Started in the art department designing title paintings: *The Tiger Man* (1918), *The Toll Gate* (1920), *The Cradle of Courage* (1920), *So Long Letty* (1920), *O'Malley of the Mounted* (1921), *The Whistle* (1921), *White Oak* (1921), *Travelin' On* (1922). Eventually became a special effects director at Warner Bros.: *Danger Signal* (1945), *Two Guys from Milwaukee* (1946), *Shadow of a Woman* (1946), *Cloak and Dagger* (1946), *The Man I Love* (1947), *Nora Prentiss* (1947), *Love and Learn* (1947), *The Unsuspected* (1947), *Escape Me Never* (1947), *My Wild Irish Rose* (1947), *The Voice of the Turtle* (1947), *My Girl Tisa* (1948), *Winter Meeting* (1948), *The Decision of*

Christopher Blake (1948), *Night Unto Night* (1949), *Colt .45* (1950). Presumably on the strength of his aircraft models for Humphrey Bogart's *Chain Lightning* (1950), he was assigned to direct the flight of the space ark in George Pal's Paramount production *When Worlds Collide* (1951). Final credits for *Captain Horatio Hornblower, R.N.* (1951, in Britain) and *Submarine Command* (1951).

Craig Barron (1961–)

American Matte Cinematographer and Supervisor

Started as matte cameraman at Industrial Light & Magic: *The Empire Strikes Back* (1979–80), *Raiders of the Lost Ark* (1981), *Dragonslayer* (1981), *E.T. the Extra-Terrestrial* (1981–82), *Star Trek: The Wrath of Khan* (1982), *Poltergeist* (1982), *The Dark Crystal* (1982), *Return of the Jedi* (1982–83), *Die unendliche Geschichte* (*The Neverending Story*, 1983–84), *Indiana Jones and the Temple of Doom* (1983–84), *Star Trek III: The Search for Spock* (1984), *Starman* (1984), *The Goonies* (1985), *Cocoon* (1985), *Explorers* (1985), *Young Sherlock Holmes* (1985), *Enemy Mine* (1985), *Labyrinth* (1986), *Star Trek IV: The Voyage Home* (1986), *The Golden Child* (1986), *The Witches of Eastwick* (1987), *Empire of the Sun* (1987), **batteries not included* (1987), *Willow* (1988). In 1988 with fellow artists Michael Pangrazio, Chris Evans and Sean Joyce from ILM, he founded his own company, Matte World: *Steal the Sky* (HBO, 1988), *By Dawn's Early Light* (1990, TV), *RoboCop 2* (1990), *Flight of the Intruder* (1991), *Star Trek VI: The Undiscovered Country* (1992), *Batman Returns* (1992), *Bram Stoker's Dracula* (1992), *The Shadow* (1994), *The Jungle Book* (1994), *Casino* (1995), *Independence Day* (1995–96), *Titanic* (1997), *The Truman Show* (1998), *Mighty Joe Young* (1998), *X-Men* (2000), *The Mummy Returns* (2001), *The Ring* (2002), *Catwoman* (2004), *Invincible* (2006). Wrote the book *The Invisible Art* with co-author Mark Vaz.

Hans J. Bartholowsky

German-American Matte Artist

Did matte paintings for Columbia Studios and Warner Bros. In October 1940 published the research paper "Plastic Matte Shots" (*International Photographer*). Byron Haskin (interviewed by Joe Adamson) described him as someone "who could grab a brush and in ten minutes paint you a hillside full of weeds, which is an art, believe me!"

Dennis C. Bartlett

British Blue Screen Consultant

Assisted Victor Margutti at Pinewood Studios. His expertise as bluescreen expert went into many pictures: *Superman* (1977–78), *Clash of the Titans* (1979–80), *Saturn 3* (1980), *Dragonslayer* (1981), *Supergirl* (1984), *Santa Clause* (1984–85), *Enemy Mine* (1985, filmed at Bavaria Studios Munich), *The Adventures of Baron Munchausen* (1988), *Memphis Belle* (1990), *A Brief History of Time* (1999). TV: *The Muppet Show* (1976). Article: "Lighting and photographing traveling matte scenes," *American Cinematographer*, June 1981.

James Basevi (1890–1962)

British-American Art Director and Special Effects Supervisor

Born Plymouth, Devon, England. Came after World War I to Canada and the United States. As draughtsman and art director working at Metro-Goldwyn-Mayer, Basevi was appointed by Cedric Gibbons head of the special effects division, which was part of the art department of the studio complex in Culver City. In that capacity he worked on *The Mysterious Island* (1928–29), *Tarzan the Ape Man* (1932), *The Mask of Fu Manchu* (1932), *Tarzan and His Mate* (1934), *San Francisco* (1936) and after leaving MGM for Goldwyn and United Artists: *Dead End* (1937), Walter Wanger's *History Is Made at Night* (1937, shipwreck sequence), *The Adventures of Marco Polo* (1938), *Blockade* (1938) and *Wuthering Heights* (1939). For Goldwyn's *The Hurricane* (1937) he spent $400,000 to create a disaster sequence. In 1939 Basevi returned to art direction; in 1943 he won an Academy Award for *The Song of Bernadette*. Also worked on the effects-laden *A Yank in the R.A.F.* (1941), *Lifeboat* (1944) and *Spellbound* (1945), both for director Alfred Hitchcock, and *Mighty Joe Young* (1948–49).

Saul Bass (1920–1996)

American Title Expert and Artist

Did main titles for Otto Preminger, Alfred Hitchcock and others: *North by Northwest* (1959), *Spartacus* (1959–60), *Psycho* (1959–60), *Seconds* (1966). Directed the ant thriller *Phase IV* (1974).

Karl Baumgartner

German Explosives Expert

Nicknamed Charly Bum-Bum. Was resident effects expert at Bavaria Studios in Munich: *Die Brücke* (1959), *Captain Sindbad* (1962–63), *Die Niklashauser Fahrt* (1970), *Das Boot* (1981–82), *Enemy Mine* (1985). Was also hired for *The Longest Day* (1962).

Mario Bava (1914–1980)

Italian Cinematographer, Effects Expert and Director

Born in San Remo, Italy. His father, Eugenio, worked as a sculptor for the silents. The son became a director of photography (having worked his way through the ranks of second assistant and camera operator) who frequently did all sort of effects: *Le fatiche di Ercole* (*Hercules*, 1957) and *Ercole e la regina di Lidia* (*Hercules Unchained*, 1959) with Steve Reeves. For Jacques Tourneur's *La battaglia di Maratona* (*The Giant of Marathon*, 1959) he multiplied extras for battle scenes. Photographed and co-directed Riccardo Freda's monster movie *Caltiki, il mostro immortale* (1959) and used camera tricks to enhance his own *Ercole al centro della terra* (*Hercules in the Haunted World/Hercules at the Center of the Earth*, 1961), *Terrore nello spazio* (*Planet of the Vampires*, 1965, which heavily influenced *Alien*), and *Diabolik* (*Danger: Diabolik*, 1967). Second unit director: *Le meraviglia di Aladino* (*The Wonders of Aladdin*, 1961). Was invited to direct sequence with one-eyed cyclops Polyphem (Samson Burke) for TV mini-series *Les Aventures d'ulyssey/L'Odissea/L'Odyssée* (1968, *regia della seconda unità ed effete speciali nel quarto episodio*). Special effects consultant: *La morte viene dallo spazio* (1958), *Mosé* (*Moses—The Lawgiver*, 1974–75) with Burt Lancaster, *Bordella* (1975) and *Inferno* (1980) for son Lamberto Bava and director

Dario Argento. Turned down an offer from producer Dino DeLaurentiis to accompany him to America.

Ivor Beddoes
British Matte Artist and Illustrator

Besides taking jobs in the art department, Beddoes occasionally did matte and special paintings: *Black Narcissus* (1947, scenic artist), *The Red Shoes* (1948), *Attila* (1954, in Italy), *The Long Ships* (1963), *Superman 2* (1980). Storyboards for *The Empire Strikes Back* (1979–80).

Sass Bedig (1913–2000)
American Explosives Expert

Pyrotechnics for western, gangster, action and war films: *4 for Texas* (1963), *The Lively Set* (1964), *Cast a Giant Shadow* (1966), *The Fortune Cookie* (1966), *Hour of the Gun* (1967), John Wayne's Vietnam drama *The Green Berets* (1968), *Bullitt* (1968), *The Bridge at Remagen* (1969), *Gaily, Gaily* (1969), *The Hawaiians* (1970), *Le Mans* (1971), *The French Connection* (1971), *The Organization* (1971), Francis Ford Coppola's *The Godfather* (1972), *Walking Tall* (1973), *Magnum Force* (1973), *Thunderbolt and Lightfoot* (1974), *Freebie and the Bean* (1974), *Rollerball* (1975), *Doc Savage: The Man of Bronze* (1975, for producer George Pal), *Bound for Glory* (1976). With Sam Peckinpah on *The Killer Elite* (1975), *Convoy* (1976) and (in Germany) *Steiner—Das Eiserne Kreuz* (1977). Also did *Steiner—Das Eiserne Kreuz 2. Teil* (1979).

Jon Berg
American Stop-Motion and Model Expert

Started with David Allen and Cascade. Worked on the ill-fated *Primevals*, *The Crater Lake Monster* (1977), *Star Wars* (1976–77, chess game sequence), *Piranha* (1978), *Laserblast* (1979), *The Empire Strikes Back* (1979–80), *Dragonslayer* (1980–81), *Return of the Jedi* (1982–83), *Twilight Zone: The Movie* (1983), *The Ewok Adventure: Caravan of Courage* (1984), *Ghostbusters* (1984), *Ewoks: The Battle for Endor* (1985), *The Fly* (1986), *House II* (1986), *RoboCop 2* (1990), Tim Burton's *The Nightmare Before Christmas* (1993).

Doug Beswick
American Stop-Motion Animator

Under Wah Chang's supervision, he animated the educational short *Dinosaurs, the Terrible Lizards* (1968). With Rick Baker he co-created the monster suit for *Octaman* in 1971. Involved in *Beware! The Blob* (*Son of Blob*, 1972), *Timegate* (1977–78, Jim Danforth's unfinished feature film project), *Planet of Dinosaurs* (1978), *The Empire Strikes Back* (1979–80), *Ghostbusters* (1984), *The Terminator* (1984), *Evil Dead II* (1987), *Nightmare on Elm Street 3* (1987), *Beetlejuice* (1988), *After Midnight* (1989), *Drop Dead Fred* (1990), *Gremlins 2: The New Batch* (1990), *Nightmare on Elm Street 5* (1990), *The Addams Family* (1992), *Doctor Mordrid* (1992), *Cabin Boy* (1993), *Ticks* (1993).

Walter Beyer
American Blue Screen Expert

For several years he was the resident TM supervisor at Universal City Studios where he refined color difference techniques. Published research paper "Travelling matte photography and the blue screen system" (*American Cinematographer* 1963 and *Journal SMPTE* March 1965).

Maurice Binder (1925–1991)
American-British Title Expert

Born New York. Created the impressive main titles for the James Bond series. Also *Charade* (1963), *The Final Countdown* (1980) and *The Last Emperor* (1987). Died in London.

Raymond O. [Ray] Binger
(1888–1970)
American Process Cinematographer

Did background photography mainly for Samuel Goldwyn and other independent producers like Walter Wanger: *Kid Millions* (1934), *The Call of the Wild* (1935), *Barbary Coast* (1935), *The Dark Angel* (1935), *Splendor* (1935), *Strike Me Pink* (1936), *Dodsworth* (1936), *Come and Get It* (1936), *The Hurricane* (1937, directed by John Ford), *The Cowboy and the Lady* (1938),

Trade Winds (1938), *Stagecoach* (1939, John Ford), *The Long Voyage Home* (1940, Ford again), *House Across the Bay* (1940), Alfred Hitchcock's *Foreign Correspondent* (1940), *Sundown* (1941), *The Pride of the Yankees* (1942), *The North Star* (1943), *The Princess and the Pirate* (1944), *Up in Arms* (1944), *The Chase* (1946), *Northwest Stampede* (1948). At Universal: *The Land Unknown* (1957) with fellow cinematographer Clifford R. Stine.

James Stuart Blackton
(1875–1941)
American Film and Trick Pioneer

He began his career as a caricaturist. Founded Vitagraph Company with Albert E. Smith. Experimented with miniature tank (*The Battle of Santiago Bay*, 1898: photographs of the ships mounted on wooden bases and pulled with strings through a small water basin), stop-frame (*The Enchanted Drawing*), and composite photography (*The Life of Moses*, 1910).

George E. Blackwell
British Model Maker

Built models and miniatures for productions like *This Was Paris* (1942) and *Flying Fortress* (1942), then became a stalwart of Rank's staff of effects people: *The Chronicle History of King Henry the Fift with His Battell Fought at Agincourt in France* (*Henry V*, 1944), *Caesar and Cleopatra* (1945), *A Matter of Life and Death* (1946), *Uncle Silas* (U.S.: *The Inheritance*, 1947). Did miniatures and mechanical effects for *Captain Horatio Hornblower R.N.* (1952, Warner Bros. British production), *Angels One Five* (1952), *Rob Roy, the Highland Rogue* (1954, Disney British production), *The Dam Busters* (1954–55), *Moby Dick* (1954–56), *1984* (1956), *Yangtse Incident: The Story of H.M.S. Amethyst* (1957), *Tarzan and the Lost Safari* (1957), *Curse of the Demon/Night of the Demon* (1957–58, prepared devilish demon for appearance in Jacques Tourneur movie), *Ice Cold in Alex* (1958), *Bottoms Up* (1960), *Summer Holiday* (1963), *The Masque of the Red Death* (1964), *The Secret Invasion* (1964), *She* (1964–65), *One Million Years B.C.* (1965–66, volcano sequence for Ray Harryhausen movie), *Slave Girls* (1966–67/68), *The Abominable Dr. Phibes* (1971).

Paul Blaisdell (1929–1983)
American Monster Suit Expert

Sci-fi's Forrest J Ackerman suggested his client Blaisdell (who had illustrated some science-fiction stuff) for a job designing and building strictly low-budget monster suits and additional props for American-International, Roger Corman, Bert I. Gordon and cheap drive-in fare: *The Beast with a Million Eyes* (1955), *Day the World Ended* (1956), *It Conquered the World* (1956), *The She-Creature* (1956), *Voodoo Woman* (1956–57), *Cat Girl* (1957), *Invasion of the Saucer Men* (1957), *The Amazing Colossal Man* (1957), *It! The Terror from Beyond Space* (1958), *Attack of the Puppet People* (1958), *Earth vs the Spider* (1958), *How to Make a Monster* (1958), *Ghost of Dragstrip Hollow* (1959), *Invisible Invaders* (1959), *The Angry Red Planet* (1959). Blaisdell sometimes also played the monsters in these movies, wearing his own creations. Often was assisted by his wife, Jackie. In the early 1960s he edited the short-lived magazine *Fantastic Monsters of the Film* with friend Bob Burns.

Robert [Bob] Blalack (1948–)
American Optical Cinematographer

Born Canal Zone, Panama. Did optical work for the original *Star Wars* (1976–77) and founded his own company Praxis Film Works: *Airplane!* (1980), *Altered States* (1980), *Wolfen* (1981), *Cat People* (1982), *Jaws 3-D* (1983), *To Be or Not to Be* (1983), *The Day After* (1983), *The Last Dragon* (1985), *RoboCop* (1987). Article: "Composite optical and photographic effects for *Star Wars*," *American Cinematographer*, June 1981.

Irving A. Block (1913–1986)
American Matte Artist

Worked for major studios (20th Century–Fox, MGM, some time in Mexico and Europe) as well as on matte shots for Lou Bunin's puppet version of *Alice in Wonderland* (1951). Became partner of Jack Rabin, whom he had met in the mid–1940s while working at Fox. Together they collaborated on cheap sci-fi and fantasy projects: *Rocketship X-M* (1950), *Unknown World* (1951), *Flight to Mars* (1951, subcontracted by Jack Cosgrove), *Captive Women* (1952), *Invaders from Mars* (1953), *Cat-Women of the Moon* (1953, painted moonscape and extended left-over sets from a Marco Polo picture), *World Without End* (1956), *The Invisible Boy* (1957), *The Saga of the Viking Women and Their Voyage to the Waters of the Great Sea Serpent* (1957, basically it was Block's optically blown-up and rear-projected arm that served as the monster's neck), *Macabre* (1958), *War of the Satellites* (1958), *The Giant Behemoth* (1958–59), *The Thirty-Foot Bride of Candy Rock*, (1959), *The Atomic Submarine* (1959, the "Cyclops" creature again was built around Block's arm with the elbow encircled by a row of rubber tentacles). For the 1957 *Kronos* he provided the screen story and also the designs of a giant robotic machine. "I wanted it to be anthropomorphic, to look like a robot, but at the same time I wanted it to look like a piece of machinery. I spent a lot of time on it, it didn't come just like that! It was a long process of thinking. At one point it looked more like a construction by Picasso, but I reduced it down by a whole series of steps until it ultimately became just a black box" (interview in *Fantascene* Vol. 1 No. 2). TV: *The Pied Piper of Hamelin* (1957), *Men into Space* (1959). With Allen Adler (and a nod to Shakespeare and *The Tempest*) he wrote the original screen story for *Forbidden Planet* (1956) and sold it to MGM producer Nicholas Nayfack. Withdrew from Hollywood and became a full professor of art at California State College in Northridge where he taught courses ranging from anatomy to video-tape expression. Died in Los Angeles.

Chesley Bonestell (1888–1986)
American Matte Artist and Illustrator

San Francisco-born, Bonestell studied architecture. From 1932 through 1937 he was assistant to Joseph Strauss, chief engineer of the Golden Gate Bridge. In 1939 he became a matte artist at RKO Studios: *The Hunchback of Notre Dame* (1939), *Swiss Family Robinson* (1940), *Citizen Kane* (1941), *The Magnificent Ambersons* (1941–42). At Columbia he did *Only Angels Have Wings*

(1939); at Fox, *Charley's Aunt* (1941) and *How Green Was My Valley* (1941); at Warners, *The Adventures of Mark Twain* (1944), *The Horn Blows at Midnight* (1945), *Rhapsody in Blue* (1945), *The Fountainhead* (1949). In 1949 he illustrated the book *Conquest of Space* written by rocket pioneer Willy Ley and started to focus on astronomical art for several of George Pal's productions: *Destination Moon* (1949–50, painting lunar backdrops), *When Worlds Collide* (1951), *The War of the Worlds* (1952–53, prologue sequence), *Conquest of Space* (1955). Also did the lunar landscape for low-budget *Cat-Women of the Moon* (1953) and TV work for the series *Men into Space* (1959). Died in Carmel, California.

Frank J. Booth
American Effects Cinematographer

At Universal he did trick shots for the early sound films *Broadway* (1929), *All Quiet on the Western Front* (1930) and *Dracula* (1930).

Walter R. Booth
British Director

Conjuror-photographer. Did inventive magic films along the lines of Georges Méliès for pioneer producers Robert William Paul (*The ? Motorist*, 1906) and Charles Urban, Urban Trading Company (*Possibilities of War in the Air*, 1906). Created first British 2D-animation: *The Hand of the Artist* (1906). In 1912 he did the first color films for Urban's Natural Colour Kinematograph Company and a year later early sound films for U. K. Kineplastikon Films.

Boss Film Studios

Located in Marina Del Rey, Los Angeles. Evolved from Douglas Trumbull's Entertainment Effects Group. Here, assisted by 90 collaborators, Richard Edlund created top-notch, expensive effects for *Ghostbusters* (1983–84), *2010* (1983–84), *Poltergeist II* (1986), *Big Trouble in Little China* (1986), *Die Hard* (1988), *Air Force One* (1996–97), *Batman Returns* (1992), *Cliffhanger* (1993). In 1998, Edlund was forced to close his sfx operation as other companies were able to offer less expensive digital work.

Rob Bottin (1959–)

American Special Make-Up Expert

Bottin assisted Rick Baker, with whom he worked on the cantina sequence for *Star Wars* (1976–77), on *King Kong* (1976) and *The Incredible Melting Man* (1978). Worked on his own on *Piranha* (1978), *Rock'n'Roll High School* (1979), *Humanoids from the Deep* (1980), *The Howling* (1981); John Carpenter's *The Fog* (1980), *The Thing* (1982) and *Big Trouble in Little China* (1986); Paul Schrader's remake *Cat People* (1982) and Ridley Scott's *Legend* (1985). Academy Award for *Total Recall* (1990).

Les Bowie (1913–1979)

British-Canadian Special Effects Supervisor

Born in Vancouver. While he was a prisoner in World War II, he developed some rather artistic skills: "As well as helping out on stage shows by painting background scenery and adding some simple effects such as snow and rain, his versatility was put to use for more pressing matters when he was called upon to forge passports for escape attempts, manufacturing German rubber stamps from potatoes, and making German uniforms from blankets (dyeing them with vegetable and fruit dyes), as well as engineering air pumps for tunnel digging and building decoys to keep the captors occupied during escape attempts" (*Hammer Films: The Bray Studios Years*, pp. 24–25). After working as a scenic painter on *School for Secrets* (1946), *Great Expectations* (1946) and *The Red Shoes* (1948), he focused on matte paintings and landed a job with Walter Percy Day at Shepperton Studios. Realizing that matte shots could be done less expensively and much faster, he applied for a job at Rank's Pinewood Studios. His small unit included Albert Whitlock. Together they worked on *So Long at the Fair* (1949), *Give Us This Day* (working title: *Christ in Concrete*, 1949), *Trio* (1953), *Romeo and Juliet* (1953–54). Became independent by founding Bowie-Margutti Ltd. (or, Bowie, Margutti & Co.) with Victor Margutti and later Bowie Films Ltd.: *The Dam Busters* (1955). Known for his overall cheap effects for Hammer Films, perhaps most notably *The Quatermass Xperiment* (U.S.: *The Creeping Unknown*, 1954, for which he created an octopus-like space monster at different scales for the Westminster Abbey climax. He told *Kine Weekly*: "We went to the slaughterhouse, got some tripe, and cut it up. We made a wooden frame with lots of joints. After photographing it in miniature, we married it up with paintings on foreground glass — and eventually made it look like the monster in Westminster Abbey.") Other Hammer assignments: *Spaceways* (1952–53), *X the Unknown* (1956, photographing tiny worms you use for fishing and feeding to tropical fish and magnifying them into monstrous life), *Quatermass 2* (U.S.: *Enemy from Space*, 1956), *The Curse of Frankenstein* (1956–57), *Dracula* (U.S.: *Horror of Dracula*, 1957–58, mattes only), *The Mummy* (1959), *The Brides of Dracula* (1960), *The Terror of the Tongs* (1960), *The Curse of the Werewolf* (1960), *Taste of Fear* (1960–61), *The Shadow of the Cat* (1960–61), *The Damned* (U.S.: *These Are the Damned*, 1961/63), *The Pirates of Blood River* (1961–62), *Captain Clegg* (1961–62), *The Phantom of the Opera* (1961–62), *The Old Dark House* (1962), *Paranoiac* (1962), *The Kiss of the Vampire* (1962/64), *Nightmare* (1962–63), *The Scarlet Blade* (1963), *The Devil-Ship Pirates* (1963–64), *The Evil of Frankenstein* (1963–64), *She* (1964–65), *The Plague of the Zombies* (1965), *The Reptile* (1965–66), *One Million Years B.C.* (1965–66, prologue and glass matte only), *Frankenstein Created Woman* (1966–67), *The Mummy's Shroud* (1966–67), *Quatermass and the Pit* (U.S.: *Five Million Years to Earth*, 1967), *Moon Zero Two* (1969), *When Dinosaurs Ruled the Earth* (1970–71, only the final painting as others failed to please fx supervisor Jim Danforth), *Vampire Circus* (1971), *Dracula A.D. 1972* (1972), *Frankenstein and the Monster from Hell* (1972), *The Satanic Rites of Dracula* (1972), *Legend of the Seven Golden Vampires* (1974), *To the Devil ... a Daughter* (1974). For Hammer's *Dracula, Prince of Darkness* (1965) he revived Christopher Lee as the Count: "We created a whole sequence of stages, photographs, and married them together. They weren't animation at all. They were done for real with the actor we used. We dissolved one thing to another many many times, with them very carefully lined up. And they were real, they weren't models at all. We ended up with real people underneath bits and pieces. First of all, it was full-size. Full-sized skeleton, full-sized ashes, full-size smoke — everything was full-size. Models in a sense, but full scale" (*Little Shoppe of Horrors Number 4*). Bowie once remarked that one could call him the true Dr. Frankenstein. His former assistant Derek Meddings reminds us that there would be no real Hammer horror films before Les Bowie came aboard. Other Bowie films include: *The Trollenberg Terror* (U.S.: *The Crawling Eye*, 1957), *Grip of the Strangler* (1958), Disney's *Swiss Family Robinson* (1959), *The Day the Earth Caught Fire* (1961), *Deadlier Than the Male* (1966), *The Terrornauts* (1967), *Some Girls Do* (1968). As consultant he was involved in Roman Polanski's *Cul-De-Sac* (1966), François Truffaut's *Fahrenheit 451* (1966), Stanley Kubrick's *Dr. Strangelove* (1963) and *2001: A Space Odyssey* (1968, recommending his assistant Brian Johnson for the job), *The Assassination Bureau* (1968), Boris Sagal's *Mosquito Squadron* (1969), *The Adventures of Barry Mckenzie* (1972), and George Lucas' *Star Wars* (1976–77). Charles Schneer and Ray Harryhausen called for his services repeatedly (*Jason and the Argonauts*, 1962–63; *Sinbad and the Eye of the Tiger*, 1975–76) and even rented his studio operation in Slough as base for model work on *First Men in the Moon* (1964–65). Posthumous Academy Award for his matte shots for *Superman* (1977–78). Many British effects personnel were trained at some time at Bowie's: Roy Field, Ian Scoones, Ray Caple, Brian Johncock (Johnson), Colin Chilvers and Kit West.

William [Bill] Brace

American Illustrator, Art Director and Matte Artist

Was working for an LA paper when he was contacted by Project Unlimited to do art effects and mattes for *The Time Machine* (1959–60). Became in-house art director of Projects: art titles for *Atlantis, the Lost Continent* (1960–61) and *Jack the Giant Killer* (1961–62). Painted dragon and did covers for Grimm books for *The Wonderful World of the Brothers Grimm* (1962–63). Also *7 Faces of Dr. Lao* (1963–64). His wife Barbara did puppet costumes for *Atlantis*. Later retired to Hawaii.

William Bradford (1905–1959)

American Effects Cinematographer and Director of Photography

Born Vermont. Took over from Bud Thackery the job of photographing the miniatures created by the Lydecker Bros. for Republic serials. Other credits include *Women in War* (1940). Died in Los Angeles.

Eric Brevig (c. 1957–)

American Visual Effects Supervisor

Started in the 1980s: *The Man Who Wasn't There* (1983), *D.A.R.Y.L.* (1985), *The Seventh Sign* (1988), *Big Business* (1988), *Earth Girls Are Easy* (1988), *Scrooged* (1988), *The Abyss* (1989, at Dream Quest Images), *Total Recall* (1990), *Hook* (1991), *Wolf* (1994), *Honey, I Shrunk the Audience* (1994), *Disclosure* (1994), *The Indian in the Cupboard* (1995), *Men in Black* (1997), *Snake Eyes* (1998), *Wild Wild West* (1999), *Pearl Harbor* (2001), *K-19: The Widowmaker* (2002, at ILM), *Signs* (2002), *The Hunted* (2003), *Peter Pan* (2003), *Twisted* (2004), *The Day After Tomorrow* (2004), *The Village* (2004, at ILM), *The Island* (2005). 3D specials: *Magic Journeys* (1982) and *The Man Who Wasn't There* (1983). As Director: *Xena: Warrior Princess* (1995, TV series), *Journey 3-D* (2008).

Robert [Bob] Broughton (1917–)

American Optical Effects Technician

Born in Berkeley, Broughton attended University of California in Los Angeles studying chemistry, physics, math, and optics. He held a lifelong position at Disney Studios since 1937, starting with photography of animated features (*Snow White and the Seven Dwarfs*, tests). In 1940 he joined the newly founded special photographic effects and process department (the "A Night on Bald Mountain" segment of *Fantasia*). During World War II he served as cameraman in the field photographic branch of O.S.S. (*Battle of Midway* by director John Ford). Returning to Disney, he became a close collaborator of Ub Iwerks and others on live-action features including traveling matte work and sodium vapor process: *20000 Leagues Under the Sea* (1953–54), *The Absent Minded Professor* (1960–61), *The Birds* (1962–63, for director Alfred Hitchcock), *Mary Poppins* (1964), *Bedknobs and Broomsticks* (1971),

The Black Hole (1979). Broughton retired in 1982.

Gail Brown

American Model Expert

Head of 20th Century–Fox Model Shop during the shooting of *Fantastic Voyage* (1965–66), *Doctor Dolittle* (1967, created mechanical whale), and *Tora! Tora! Tora!* (1969–70, with Ivan Martin supervising the building of 10 American and 19 Japanese model ships).

Allan Bryce

British Mechanical Effects Technician

Was part of Brian Johnson's operation: *When Dinosaurs Ruled the Earth* (1970–71), *Alien* (1978–79), *The Empire Strikes Back* (1979–80).

Ivyl Burks

American Model Maker

In charge of miniatures at Paramount Studios: *Road to Utopia* (1946), *Samson and Delilah* (1949), *The War of the Worlds* (1952–53), *The Bridges at Toko-Ri* (1955), *Conquest of Space* (1954–55), *The Ten Commandments* (1953–56).

Robert Burks (1909–1968)

American Cinematographer and Special Effects Cinematographer

Born in Chino, California, he started at Warner Bros. doing second unit, effects and insert photography for Byron Haskin and occasionally Don Siegel: *A Dispatch from Reuter's* (1940), *Arsenic and Old Lace* (1941, released in 1944), *The Horn Blows at Midnight* (1945), *The Woman in White* (1948), *The Miracle of Our Lady of Fatima* (1952). One of three cinematographers on Warner's *House of Wax* (1953) and one of two on John Wayne's *Hondo* (1953), both in Eastmancolor and Natural Vision or Warner Vision 3D technology. Thanks to his technical skills he became Alfred Hitchcock's favorite cinematographer: *North by Northwest* (1959), *The Birds* (1963). He died with his wife in a tragic house fire after smoking in bed.

Ellis Burman

American Special Prop Maker

In his own shop he made props and mask appliances for Universal Studios: *The Wolf Man* (1941, Lon Chaney Jr.'s wolf-head silver stick), *The Ghost of Frankenstein* (1941–42, the rubber Monster head pieces for Chaney), *Frankenstein Meets the Wolf Man* (1942–43, with Bela Lugosi), *House of Frankenstein* (1944, with Glenn Strange) and *House of Dracula* (1945, with Strange as the Monster again). Also created a talking mule figure for *Francis* (1949), and dinosaurs and mammals for *Unknown Island* (1948), *Prehistoric Women* (1950), *Jungle Manhunt* (1951), and *Teenage Cave Man* (1958).

Lawrence W. [Larry] Butler
(1908–1988)

American Special Effects Director

Born in Akron, Ohio. His father, William Butler, worked on optical effects for Warner Bros. Larry joined him when he was only 15 and was chosen to accompany Ned Mann as an assistant to London. For Alexander Korda they did *The Ghost Goes West* (1935), *Things to Come* (1935–36), *The Elephant Boy* (1936, first picture of his friend Sabu), *Fire Over England* (1936), *The Man Who Could Work Miracles* (1936). When Mann returned to America, Butler resumed his position and started work on Technicolor epics: *The Drum* (1938) and *The Thief of Bagdad* (1939–40) for which he received an Academy Award and created the Blue Screen process for Color Photography which he himself called "Tri-Matte Process." For finishing touches on *Thief*, he returned with Korda to Hollywood: *That Hamilton Woman* (1941), *The Jungle Book* (1942), *To Be or Not to Be* (1942), then back to Warner Bros.: *Casablanca* (1942), *Edge of Darkness* (1943), *Destination Tokyo* (1943), *The Adventures of Mark Twain* (1944), *Janie* (1944), *Crime by Night* (1944), *Saratoga Trunk* (1944–45), *The Horn Blows at Midnight* (1944–45), *Tonight and Every Night* (1944–45). In 1944 he was appointed head of the effects department (and of his own optical printers) at Columbia Studios Corporation and the job included directing second units: *A Thousand and*

One Nights (1945), *Gilda* (1946), *The Lady from Shanghai* (1947–48, mirror maze sequence for Orson Welles), *To the Ends of the Earth* (1948), *We Were Strangers* (1949), *All the King's Men* (1949), *Lorna Doone* (1951), *Gun Fury* (1953, 3D), *The Caine Mutiny* (1953–54), *Earth vs. the Flying Saucers* (1955–56, second unit director), *The Giant Claw* (1956–57), *20 Million Miles to Earth* (1956–57, as second unit director accompanied Ray Harryhausen to Italy), *The 7th Voyage of Sinbad* (1957–58, fx department head). After Columbia closed its effects operation, Butler and former collaborator Donald C. Glouner founded Butler-Glouner, Inc.: *13 Ghosts* (1960, Illusion-O sequences in Ectoplasmic Color), *The Devil at Four O'Clock* (1961), *Taras Bulba* (1963), *Robinson Crusoe on Mars* (1964), *In Harm's Way* (1964–65), *Marooned* (1969). Butler helped his old friend, director Don Siegel, designing a special aerial rig for flight scenes with actor Walter Matthau in *Charley Varrick*; the 1972 film was photographed by one of his three sons, Michael Butler. In his autobiography Siegel mentioned Butler several times and called him "brilliant in optics." In April 1973 Butler-Glouner was sold and the partners retired. Award: Scientific or Technical Award Class III in 1975 (shared with Roger Banks): for the concept of applying low inertia and stepping electric motors to film transport systems and optical printers for motion picture production.

Butler-Glouner, Inc.

Independent effects house founded by Larry Butler and Donald C. Glouner: *13 Ghosts* (1960, Illusion-O sequences in Ectoplasmic Color), *House of Usher* (1960), *The Devil at Four O'Clock* (1961, volcano eruption filmed at Larry Butler ranch), *Pit and the Pendulum* (1960–61), *Master of the World* (1960–61), *The Guns of Navarone* (1961), *Taras Bulba* (1962), *X—The Man with the X-Ray Eyes* (1963), *Robinson Crusoe on Mars* (1964), *In Harm's Way* (1964–65, miniature ships), *Guess Who's Coming to Dinner* (1967), *Mackenna's Gold* (1968), *Marooned* (1969), *The Dunwich Horror* (1970), *Fools' Parade* (1971), *The Life and Times of Judge Roy Bean* (1972), *Lost Horizon* (1972–73). TV: *The Outer Limits.* In April 1973 the partners sold the Butler-Glouner Company and retired.

James Cameron (1954–)
American Director

Cameron has not only directed movies with spectacular effects sequences (*The Terminator, Aliens, The Abyss, Terminator 2: Judgment Day, True Lies, Titanic*) but, at the beginning of his career, did sfx himself. Inspired by *Star Wars*, he created a ten-minute film which featured all kinds of models and mattes; it got him a job with Roger Corman and New World Pictures: *Battle Beyond the Stars* (1980) and John Carpenter's *Escape from New York* (1981). Co-founded the CGI company Digital Domain.

Ray Caple (19??–1986?)
British Matte Artist

Ray Caple, a gifted artist and model maker, was trained by Les Bowie and started with Bowie-Margutti in the early days of Hammer Films. Ian Scoones: "He was an untrained artist that just listened to the way Les taught him. Always the quick gimmicks, such as holding two or three brushes at once, one with yellow, one with green, one with lighter green, and just twisting the wrists and doing a whole tree in seconds" (*Hammer Films: The Bray Studios Years*, p. 279). *The Quatermass Xperiment* (1955), *X the Unknown* (1956), *Captain Clegg* (1961–62), *The Kiss of the Vampire* (1962/64), *Nightmare* (1962–63), *The Evil of Frankenstein* (1963–64), *The Gorgon* (1963–64), *First Men in the Moon* (1963–64), *The Masque of the Red Death* (1964), *She* (1965), *City Under the Sea* (1965), *One Million Years B.C.* (1965–66), *Frankenstein Created Woman* (1965–66). Freelancing on *Mackenna's Gold* (1968), *The Battle of Britain* (1969), *When Dinosaurs Ruled the Earth* (1970), *The Slipper and the Rose* (1976), *Satyam Shivam Sundaram: Love Sublime* (1978), *Superman* (1977–78, assistant to Bowie), *The Thief of Bagdad* (1978), *Circle of Iron* (1978), *Alien* (1979), *Chariots of Fire* (1981), *Time Bandits* (1981), *Nineteen Eighty-Four* (1984), *Brazil* (1985), *Spies Like Us* (1985), *Batman* (1989). TV: *The Martian Chronicles* (1980, miniseries), *Prisoners of the Lost Universe* (1983).

Cascade Pictures

Founded in the 1960s by Roy Seawright and Barney Carr. Phil Kellison joined to handle stop-motion and effects-laden commercials. Among the talents who worked at Cascade on *Pillsbury Doughboy* ads and others were Jim Danforth, Dennis Muren, David Allen, Jon Berg, Peter Kleinow and Rick Baker. Kellison remembers that when Cascade went broke, stockholders got a dime on the dollar. The company's remnants formed CPC and later Coast Special Effects.

John Chambers (1924–2001)
American Special Makeup Artist

Chambers worked in Army hospitals as a dental technician and on prosthetic devices such as artificial noses and ears for wounded soldiers before landing a job at NBC-TV in 1953. In the 1960s he worked at Universal: *The Ugly American* (1962), *The List of Adrian Messenger* (1963), *Bedtime Story* (1964). Virtually created *Planet of the Apes*, both cinema and TV, and received an Academy Award for working on the first one (which was released in 1968). Other credits: *The Human Duplicators* (1964), *The Chase* (1966), *True Grit* (1969), *Phantom of the Paradise* (1974), *Beauty and the Beast* (1976, TV series), *The Island of Dr. Moreau* (1977, Burt Lancaster version), *Halloween II* (1981). Modeled Leonard Nimoy's Mr. Spock's Vulcan ears for *Star Trek* (although the prototype had been done by Charles Schram) and the head of a man killed by the shark in *Jaws* (1974–75). In charge of John Chambers Studio.

Wah Ming Chang (1917–2003)
American-Chinese Sculptor, Prop Maker,
Costume Designer, Miniaturist and
Puppeteer

Born in Honolulu, Hawaii. In 1919 his family moved to San Francisco and opened the Ho Ho Tea Room. His mother, Fai Hue Chang, was a talented artist, having graduated from the California School of Art and Crafts. She died when Wah was 11. While his father left for Europe, an artist friend, Blanding Sloane, and his wife took the young and talented boy under their wings. Blanding became Wah's mentor. Together they worked on the Technicolor *Lost Island* (1934), an unfinished *Kong* marionette spoof, with Wah playing a dinosaur battling Charles Gemora in a

gorilla suit. Wah attended the Peninsula School for Creative Education in Menlo Park. In 1939 he became the youngest member of Walt Disney's model department, creating three-dimensional maquettes for the animators to study during production of *Pinocchio* (1939), *Fantasia* (1940) and *Bambi* (1942). During this time he was afflicted with polio. Eventually he became head of George Pal's *Puppetoons* replacement model shop. He also worked with Pal competitor John Sutherland on a series of stop-motion shorts known as *Daffy Ditties*. In 1947 he produced *The Way of Peace*. In the 1950s did lots of freelance work for commercials and occasional feature films. Built big spider models for *Cat-Women of the Moon* (1953–54) and *Tarantula* (1955) as well as the infamous mechanical scorpion head for *The Black Scorpion* (1956–57; the head was seen in close-ups in between the stop-motion sequences). Made fanciful masks and costumes for 20th Century–Fox's *The King and I* (1956) and *Can-Can* (1960). In 1956, with his animator friend Gene Warren and former Universal Studios miniaturist Tim Baar, he founded Project Unlimited, Inc., and in the beginning did all kind of low-budget work such as *Kronos* (1956–57) and *Monster from Green Hell* (1957). They contributed to virtually all of George Pal's MGM features beginning with *tom thumb* (1958) and received an Academy Award for *The Time Machine* (1959–60), which was followed by *Atlantis, the Lost Continent* (1960–61), *The Wonderful World of the Brothers Grimm* (1962–63, in Cinerama), *7 Faces of Dr. Lao* (1963–64) and, after the dissolve of their company, *The Power* (1968). Project Unlimited did a forced perspective shot for *Spartacus* (1960) and stop-motion animation for *Dinosaurus!* (1960), *Goliath and the Dragon* (1960–61) and *Jack the Giant Killer* (1961–62), and miniatures for *Master of the World* (1960–61), *Flight of the Lost Balloon* (1961) and *Around the World Under the Sea* (1966). Wah made the beautiful headdress for Elizabeth Taylor's grand entrance in *Cleopatra* (1962–63). With partner Gene Warren he supervised the creation of monsters for *The Outer Limits* TV series, designed the original communicator and tricorder as well as imaginative aliens and "Tribbles" for *Star Trek* and helped to create simian masks for *Planet of the Apes* (1968). He also contributed to the low-budget *Voyage to the Planet of Prehistoric Women* (1968) directed by young Peter Bogdanovich. Wah produced the educational short *Dinosaurs, the Terrible Lizards* (1968), which was animated by Doug Beswick, and *Magic Pony* (1985). In his later years, he had considerable success as a fine-art sculptor of charming bronzes. His subjects tended to be children and animals. Died in Carmel, California.

Colin Chilvers

British Mechanical Effects Supervisor

Became part of Bowie Films, then on his own: *Superman* (1978), *Clash of the Titans* (1979–80), *Saturn 3* (1980), *X-Men* (2000).

The Chiodo Brothers: Charles, Stephen and Edward

American Stop-Motion Experts

Did stop-frame sequences for *Pee-wee's Big Adventure* (1985), *Killer Klowns from Outer Space* (1987, directed by Stephen, clowns designed by Charlie), *The Puppetoon Movie* (1987), *RoboCop* (1987), *Darkman* (1990), *Freaked* (1994), *Naked Gun 33 1/3* (1994), *Tales from the Hood* (1995), *Screamers* (1996), *The Stupids* (1996).

Charles [Chris] Christadoro

American Puppeteer and Model Maker

Christadoro made the Fay Wray puppet for *King Kong* (1932–33), a hand-carved wooden figure that had 32 pressure joints in it and could be animated. This led to work on the Technicolor Kong spoof *The Lost Island* (1934, never finished). With Wah Chang he made puppet characters as guidelines for Disney animators. Bob Baker, who joined him in George Pal's studio on the *Puppetoons*: "Chris was the third most famous ivory carver in the world, he'd done a lot of things for Disney sculpting figures of Pinocchio, etc., that the animators would work from…. Some of the things he did actually inspired Disney to do the Audio-Animatronics thing. He made this little tap-dancing figure — it moved its mouth and winked its eyes, and it was all done with cams and gears, and Disney kept saying 'Make it move, make it move! Make it do this and make it do that,' and Chris said 'Goddamit! You only can make these things do so much!' Chris was a brilliant artist" (*Closeup* Number 3).

Edward Cohen (later: Edward Coleman and Colman)

(1905–1994)

American Special Effects Cinematographer and Director of Photography

After assisting on *Hell's Angels* (1930), he became Ned Mann's miniature photographer and accompanied him to Korda in Britain: *Things to Come* (1934–36). Returned to America and photographed spider sequence for *The Thief of Bagdad* (1940). Joined Walt Disney Studios (*20000 Leagues Under the Sea*, 1953–54) and was promoted to director of photography: *The Absent Minded Professor* (1961), *Mary Poppins* (1964), *The Love Bug* (1969). Died in Newport Beach, California.

Randall William (Randy) Cook

American Stop-Motion Animator and Visual Effects Supervisor

Did animation for David Allen and others. He was part of the ill-fated *Primevals* project and *The Crater Lake Monster* (1977), *The Day Time Ended* (1979), *Laserblast* (1979), *The Howling* (1980), *Caveman* (1981), *Q* (1982). Was called in for stop-motion scenes of *The Thing* (1982), *Ghostbusters* (1984, terror dogs), *2010* (1984), *The Gate* (1987), *Hardcover* (1988), *Gate II* (1990), *Highway to Hell* (1991), *Oscar* (1991), *Puppetmaster II* (1991), *Subspecies* (1991), *Doctor Mordrid* (1992), *Dragonworld* (1994), *Puppetmaster IV* (1994). Left stop-motion and joined Peter Jackson in New Zealand on the *Lord of the Rings* CGI trilogy and *King Kong* (2004–2005).

Willis R. Cook

American Miniature and Special Effects Expert

Cook worked on miniatures such as the rollercoaster for *The Beast from 20,000 Fathoms*

(1952–53). Also credited for *The Blue Gardenia* (1953, director: Fritz Lang), *Cat-Women of the Moon* (1953–54), *New York Confidential* (1955), *The Pride and the Passion* (1957), *The Devil at Four O'Clock* (1961), *The Professionals* (1966), *Hurry Sundown* (1967), *Daring Game* (1968), *Mackenna's Gold* (1969), *The Molly Maguires* (1970).

Wilkie Cooper (1911–2001)
British Director of Photography

Camera operator at Alexander Korda's London Films: *Fire Over England* (1935). Assigned to do first blue screen tests in the car park at Denham Studios with American special effects director Larry Butler for *The Thief of Bagdad* (1939–40). Later photographed several of Ray Harryhausen's films: *The 7th Voyage of Sinbad* (1957–58), *The 3 Worlds of Gulliver* (1959–60), *Mysterious Island* (1960–61), *Jason and the Argonauts* (1961–63), *First Men in the Moon* (1964), *One Million Years B.C.* (1965–66). TV: *The Avengers*.

Ray Cory (1894–1968)
American Process Cinematographer and Director of Photography

At Columbia Pictures: *The Secret Command* (1944), *A Thousand and One Nights* (1945), *Counter-Attack* (1945), *Perilous Holiday* (1946). Second unit: *The Caine Mutiny* (1954). First camera: The Three Stooges' *Have Rocket, Will Travel* (1959).

John R. Cosgrove (1902–1965)
American Matte Artist

John R. (Jack) Cosgrove worked in a society-portrait studio in Kansas City for four years. A brilliant artist who had won the national photographic contest conducted by *Screenland* magazine, he came to Hollywood in the early 1930s, got in touch with Cecil B. DeMille and worked as a matte artist in close partnership with Russell E. Lawson at Universal Studios: *The Black Cat* (1934), *Bride of Frankenstein* (1935), *The Invisible Ray* (1935–36). He also worked for Chesterfield-Invincible (*Death from a Distance,*

1936). After a stint at Columbia Studios he was hired to build the matte department at Selznick International where he supervised over 100 Technicolor matte shots for *Gone with the Wind* (1938–39). Other pictures as executive for special filming effects at Selznick or on loan-out agreements include: *Little Lord Fauntleroy* (1936), *The Garden of Allah* (1936), *A Star Is Born* (1937), *The Prisoner of Zenda* (1937), *Nothing Sacred* (1937), *The Adventures of Tom Sawyer* (1938), *The Young in Heart* (1938), *Made for Each Other* (1939), *Intermezzo* (1939), *Beyond Tomorrow* (1940), *Kit Carson* (1940), *Rebecca* (1940), Charles Chaplin's *The Great Dictator* (1940), *So Ends Our Night* (1941), *Since You Went Away* (1944), *Spellbound* (1945), *Duel in the Sun* (1947). When Selznick pictures became few and far between, he took work at Warner Bros.: *Meet John Doe* (1941), *Action in the North Atlantic* (1943), *Passage to Marseille* (1944). Other work: *Our Town* (1940), *Joan of Arc* (1948), *She Wore a Yellow Ribbon* (1949, lightning effects, credited only in European versions), *Drums in the Deep South* (1951), *September Storm* (1960, in 3D). In the 1950s he spent some time with Louis Lichtenfield back at Warner Bros. Matte consultant on some notorious low-budget sci-fi pictures: *Flight to Mars* (1951), *Invaders from Mars* (1953), *Monster from Green Hell* (1957) and *Queen of Outer Space* (1958). Although a heavy drinker, he was always reliable. According to Larry Butler, Cosgrove was one of the few who really understood the meaning and importance of painted mattes. Died in Hermosa Beach, California.

Jack Cox (1896–1960)
British Cinematographer

Born in London and educated at New College, Worthing, John Jaffray (Jack) Cox entered the trade in 1912 as assistant to L. Fitzhamon. Worked as a cameraman with Gaumont; in the early 1920s, chief cameraman for Maurice Elvey. One of Alfred Hitchcock's early cameramen, selected for his vast knowledge of photographic effects — an expert in "blurred images, overlays, dissolves and double exposures" (Duncan Petrie, *The British Cinematographer*): *The Ring* (1927), *Blackmail* (1929, incorporating Shuftan shots to combine live-action with nine transparencies of the British Museum), *Juno and the Paycock*

(1930), *Rich and Strange* (1931). Became chief cameraman of British International Pictures, Elstree. Returned to Hitchcock in 1938 for *The Lady Vanishes*, a picture rich in miniatures. Died in Surrey.

John T. Coyle (1890–1970)
American Effects Supervisor and Producer

Originally an art director. In the early 1930s he supervised the effects department at Nat Levine's Mascot Pictures and did the effects for the serials *The Phantom Empire* (1935) and *The Fighting Marines* (1935). Coyle subsequently worked at Republic Pictures: special effects for *The Hit Parade* (1937), then as supervisor, *Wild Horse Rodeo* (1937), *The Purple Vigilantes* (1938); co-director, *Call of the Yukon* (1938). Finally became a producer at Republic and PRC.

Byron L. Crabbe
American Illustrator and Glass Artist

Willis O'Brien hired Crabbe to illustrate key scenes and do glass mattes for *Creation* (1930–31, defunct), *King Kong* (1932–33), *The Son of Kong* (1933) and *The Last Days of Pompeii* (1934–35). He painted Count Zaroff's chateau for *The Most Dangerous Game* (1932) and worked on *Kentucky Kernels* (1934). Apparently he did some matte art in the early stages of *Gone with the Wind* shortly before his death.

Arthur (Art) Cruickshank (1918–1983)
American Effects Cinematographer

The 1933 release of *King Kong* left the then 14-year-old boy spellbound. In February 1939 he joined Disney as animation cameraman. When Disney moved from Hyperion Avenue to its new Burbank plant at the end of '39, Cruickshank worked as a technician laying out shots at the Multiplane Camera: *Pinocchio* (1939–40), *Fantasia* (1940), *Bambi* (1942), then close collaboration with Ub Iwerks in the Special Process Laboratory. On *Melody* (1953, 3D), *20000 Leagues Under the Sea* (1953–54), *Darby O'Gill and the Little People* (1958–59) and *The Absent Minded Professor* (1960–61) Cruickshank operated an optical printer; on *Mary Poppins* (1963) he did yellow screen shots. When Iwerks had to turn down L.B. Abbott's offer to support him as cinematographer in the sfx unit at 20th Century–Fox he sent over Cruickshank in 1964. Cruickshank received an Academy Award for *Fantastic Voyage* (1965–66) and worked on *Dr. Dolittle* (1967), *The Flim-Flam Man* (1967), *A Guide for the Married Man* (1967), *In Like Flint* (1967), *The St. Valentine's Day Massacre* (1967), *Valley of the Dolls* (1967), *Planet of the Apes* (1967–68), *The Boston Strangler* (1968), *The Detective* (1968), *Lady in Cement* (1968), *The Secret Life of an American Wife* (1968), *Star!* (1968), *The Sweet Ride* (1968), *Butch Cassidy and the Sundance Kid* (1969), *Che!* (1969), *Hard Contract* (1969), *Hello, Dolly!* (1969), *John and Mary* (1969), *Justine* (1969), *100 Rifles* (1969), *The Undefeated* (1969), *Beneath the Planet of the Apes* (1970), *Cover Me Babe* (1970), *The Great White Hope* (1970), *M*A*S*H* (1970), *Move* (1970), *Myra Breckinridge* (1970), *The Only Game in Town* (1970), *Patton* (1970), *Tora! Tora! Tora!* (1970) as well as Irwin Allen's TV series *Land of the Giants*. In 1971 he returned to Disney to supervise effects work on *The Island at the Top of the World* (1974), *Pete's Dragon* (1977), *The Cat from Outer Space* (1978), *Return from Witch Mountain* (1978), *The Black Hole* (1979), *Tron* (1982, as lab supervisor) and *Something Wicked This Way Comes* (1983). Also did film work for Epcot and Disneyworld such as *Magic Journeys* (1982). Article: "In the Land of Magical Effects," *IATSE Official Bulletin*, Spring 1969. Died in Los Angeles County.

Bob Cuff
British Matte Artist

After four years at the Camberwell School of Art, in 1952 he was hired as trainee matte artist by production designer Vincent Korda. Started in the matte department at Shepperton Studios under Wally Veevers: *Hobson's Choice* (1953), *Devil Girl from Mars* (1954), *Richard III* (1955), *Three Men in a Boat* (1956), *A Killer in Korea* (1956), *The Smallest Show on Earth* (1957), *The Admiral Crichton* (1957), *A King in New York* (1957), *Silent Enemy* (1958), *I Was Monty's Double* (1958), *Carlton Brown of the F.O.* (1958), *Room at the Top* (1958), *I'm All Right Jack* (1959),

Expresso Bongo (1959), *Too Hot to Handle* (1960), *The Guns of Navarone* (1961), *The War Lover* (1962), *The Longest Day* (1962), *The Day of the Triffids* (1962), *Summer Holiday* (1962), *The Victors* (1963), *Heavens Above* (1963), *Dr. Strangelove or: How I Learned to Stop Worrying and Love the Bomb* (1963). In 1963 he left Shepperton and joined Bowie Films where he did mattes, closely working with Ray Caple and photographer John Mackey: *First Men in the Moon* (1963–64), *The Masque of the Red Death* (1964), *She* (1965), *City Under the Sea* (1965), *One Million Years B.C.* (1966). With Mackey he freelanced on *2001: A Space Odyssey* (1965–68, moon shots with compressed models) and *Mackenna's Gold* (1969). Together, with Bowie acting in the background, they founded Abacus Productions and produced commercials. After retiring from Abacus: *Young Winston* (1972), *Monty Python's Life of Brian* (1979), *The Princess Bride* (1987), *The Adventures of Baron Munchausen* (1988), *Erik the Viking* (1989).

Cliff Culley

British Matte Artist and Miniature Expert

Worked on *The Early Bird* (1965), *Khartoum* (1966), *Hands of the Ripper* (1971), *The Pink Panther Strikes Again* (1976), *Candleshoe* (1976), *Escape from the Dark* (1976), *Warlords of the Deep* (*Warlords of Atlantis*, 1978), *The Spaceman and King Arthur* (1979), *An Arabian Adventure* (1979), *Clash of the Titans* (1980–81), *Witness for the Prosecution* (1982 TV movie), *Hellbound: Hellraiser II* (1988), *A Kid in King Arthur's Court* (1995), *Knightskater* (1995), *A Midsummer Night's Dream* (1996). For many years he was the resident matte artist at Pinewood Studios and was involved in the early Bond films: *Dr. No* (1962), *From Russia with Love* (1963), *Goldfinger* (1964), and *Thunderball* (1965).

Russell A. Cully (1900–1990)

American Process and Effects
 Cinematographer

Born in San Pedro to Irish-American parents. His father was killed in a hunting accident when Russell was four. When Russell was 18 he found a job as laborer and night watchman in a motion picture studio. In 1921 he became lab technician at Famous Players–Lasky–Paramount West Coast Studio in Hollywood. In November 1923 he became a member of the Paramount Experimental Department which was later called the Technical Effects Department and eventually the Special Effects Department. Worked with Rolla Flora and Gordon Jennings. First cameraman since 1927. Did projection printing, high speed camera work, double printing and special trick effects, laying out as well as photographing full and top miniatures, glass shots, photo image, color transparencies and Vorkapich montage effects. He attended story conferences as a camera consultant, directed chase and action sequences, and cut effects scenes to match music tempo. After ten years at Paramount, he went to MGM in March 1933; his credits there include *San Francisco* (1936) and *The Good Earth* (1936–37; an eight-month stint in China to photograph process plates). Went as effects cinematographer to Great Britain. In 1936 joined RKO's camera effects department in Hollywood under Vernon L. Walker: *Make Way for a Lady* (1936), *The Man Who Found Himself* (1937), *The Woman I Love* (1937), *Annapolis Salute* (1937), *Super-Sleuth* (1937), *Gunga Din* (1939), *Citizen Kane* (1940–41, Cully's favorite project), *The Magnificent Ambersons* (1942), *It's a Wonderful Life* (1946). After Walker's demise in 1948, Cully was in charge of the department for several years. Other RKO credits include *Crack-Up* (1946), *Nocturne* (1946), *Child of Divorce* (1946), *Criminal Court* (1946), *Step by Step* (1946), *Dick Tracy Versus Cueball* (1946), *The Falcon's Adventure* (1946), *Vacation in Reno* (1946), *Without Reservations* (1946), *The Bachelor and the Bobby Soxer* (1947), *Crossfire* (1947), *Under the Tonto Rim* (1947), *Banjo* (1947), *Born to Kill* (1947), *Desperate* (1947), *Dick Tracy's Dilemma* (1947), *Honeymoon* (1947), *A Likely Story* (1947), *The Farmer's Daughter* (1947), *The Locket* (1947), *Thunder Mountain* (1947), *The Long Night* (1947), *They Won't Believe Me* (1947), *Trail Street* (1947), *The Woman on the Beach* (1947), *Dick Tracy Meets Gruesome* (1947), *Night Song* (1947), *Out of the Past* (1947), *Berlin Express* (1948), *Design for Death* (1948), *Fighting Father Dunne* (1948), *Guns of Hate* (1948), *If You Knew Susie* (1948), *I Remember Mama* (1948), *Mr. Blanding Builds His Dream House* (1948), *Return of the Bad*

Men (1948), *Mystery in Mexico* (1948), *Race Street* (1948), *The Twisted Road* (1948), *Western Heritage* (1948), *Good Sam* (1948), *The Velvet Touch* (1948), *Blood on the Moon* (1948), *Station West* (1948), *Every Girl Should Be Married* (1948), *Variety Time* (1948), *Bodyguard* (1948), *Rachel and the Stranger* (1948), *A Woman's Secret* (1949), *The Miracle of the Bells* (1948), *They Live by Night* (1949), *The Judge Steps Out* (1949), *Adventure in Baltimore* (1949), *Roughshod* (1949), *Walk Softly, Stranger* (1950), *The Whip Hand* (1951), *Androcles and the Lion* (1952). Died at his home in Rancho Palos Verdes, California.

H. G. (Harry) Cunningham

American Camera and Machine Constructor

At RKO Studios he built miniature projectors, process technique and armatures for the original *King Kong* (1932–33), *The Son of Kong* (1933), *Citizen Kane* (1941), and *Mighty Joe Young* (1947–49). Created a World War II aerial combat camera which was named after him. Became famous by finding a way to make Bell & Howell movements quiet enough for their cameras to be used for early sound films, thereby preventing the ubiquitous B&H cameras from becoming obsolete immediately. After his death, George Randle took over his operation.

Jim Danforth (1940–)

American Stop-Motion Animator, Matte Artist and Visual Effects Director

James (Jim) Danforth was born in Ohio and primarily grew up in Illinois, near Chicago. His father was a teacher of geology and biology. Young Danforth was mainly inspired by two movies: *King Kong* (1933) and *The Thief of Bagdad* (1940). When he was 12, the family moved to California. Soon the young film buff made home movies laden with effects and visited Disney's Effects Department where he met Peter Ellenshaw and Albert Whitlock. He encountered Ray Harryhausen while Ray was working on *The 7th Voyage of Sinbad* (1958), and Project Unlimited when they did a sequence for George Pal's *tom thumb* (1958). After some more amateur films, an attempt to launch his own *The Princess of Mars* (1958) and doing animation shorts for Art Clokey of Clokey Films (*Davey and Goliath*), he was continuously hired by Projects: *The Time Machine* (1959–60), *Goliath and the Dragon* (1960–61), *Master of the World* (1960–61), *Jack the Giant Killer* (1961–62, doing 50 percent of the animation), *Flight of the Lost Balloon* (1961), *Journey to the Seventh Planet* (1962), *The Wonderful World of the Brothers Grimm* (1962–63), *7 Faces of Dr. Lao* (1963–64, his first Academy

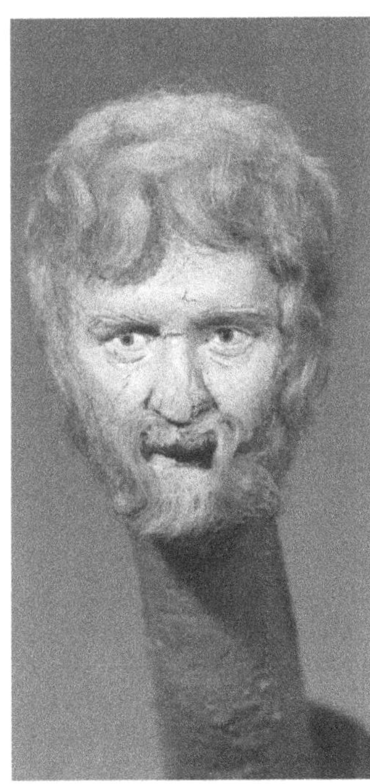
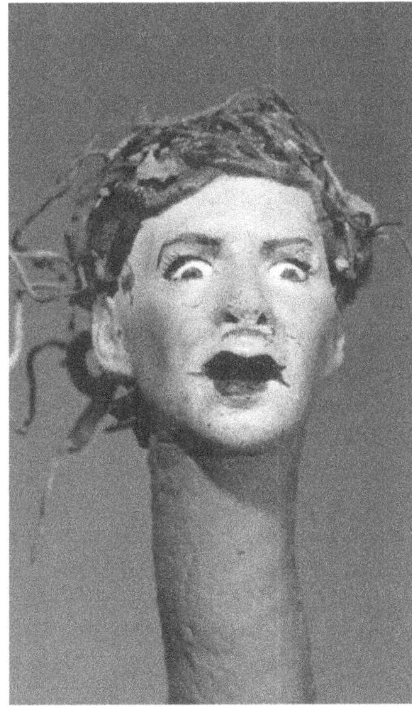

Above and following page: The stop-motion heads of the Loch Ness monster sculpted by Martha Armstrong and animated by Harryhausen aficionado Jim Danforth for the George Pal production *7 Faces of Dr. Lao.*

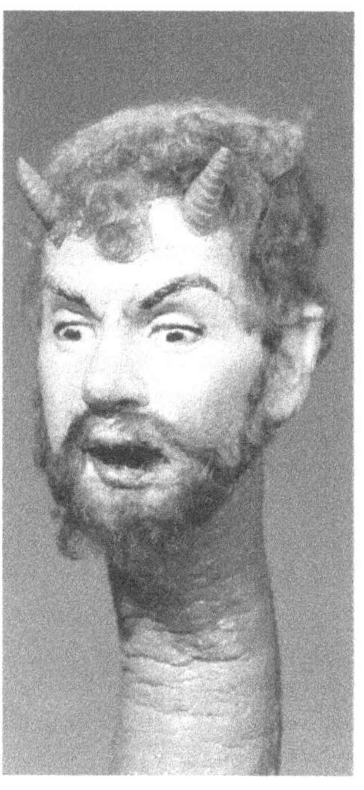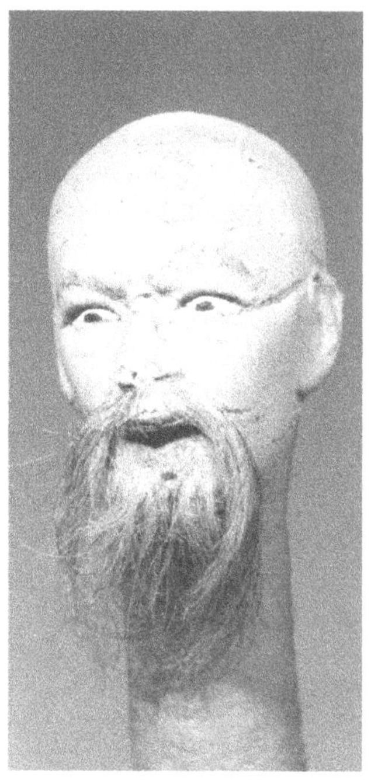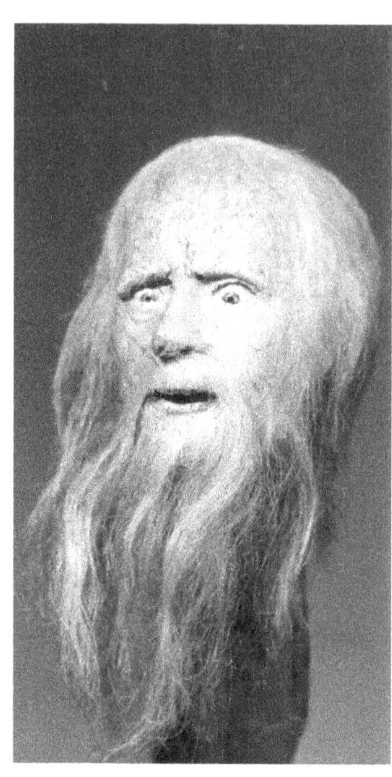

Award nomination), and *Around the World Under the Sea* (1965–66). TV series done at Projects include *The Twilight Zone* and the *Outer Limits* episodes "Don't Open Till Doomsday," "The Invisible Enemy" and "Counterweight." For some time he was at Universal Studios where he apprenticed briefly to matte artist Albert Whitlock and landed in the miniature department under Charles Baker. Did a stop-motion shot for *I'd Rather Be Rich* (1964) under Whitlock's supervision. When working on Pillsbury Doughboy commercials for Cascade Studios, he received an offer from Hammer Films (via Rudi Fehr at Warners) to do the visual effects for *When Dinosaurs Ruled the Earth* (1968–71, second Academy Award nomination). Also worked on *Willy Wonka and the Chocolate Factory* (1970, models and animation), *Diamonds Are Forever* (1971, submarine shot for Whitlock) and *Flesh Gordon* (1971–74, beetleman animation and glass mattes), and was special consultant for Universal's *The Legend of King Kong* (1976, to be directed from a Bo Goldman script by Joseph Sargent) which closed after four months of preproduction. Organized his own company Effects Associates and did animation jobs such as *Caveman* (1980–81) and mainly matte shots. Was matte artist on the 16mm amateur film *Equinox* by Dennis Muren (started in 1966 and released

commercially in 1971), *Portnoy's Complaint* (1972), *Dark Star* (1974), *Planet of the Dinosaurs* (1978), *The Day Time Ended* (1980), *The Scarlett O'Hara War* (1980, TV), *The Thing* (1982), *Conan the Barbarian* (1982, matte not used in final U.S. version but perhaps appeared in European prints), *Creepshow* (1982), *Megaforce* (1982), *Twilight Zone: The Movie* (1983), *Sahara* (1983), *Die Unendliche Geschichte* (*The Neverending Story*, 1983–84; Danforth's company Effects Associates, Inc. was subcontracted by ILM to do a matte painting job), *Ninja III: The Domination* (1984), *The Blue and the Grey* (1984, TV), *The Ewok Adventure: Caravan of Courage* (1984, subcontracted by ILM), *Runaway Train* (1985), *The Stuff* (1985), *Commando* (1985), *Bring 'em Back Alive* (1985, TV), *Day of the Dead* (1985), *Prince of Darkness* (1987), *They Live* (1988), *Deep Star Six* (1989), *Bugsy* (1991), *Body Bags* (1991, TV), *Memoirs of an Invisible Man* (1991–92), *Body Snatchers* (1994). Main titles: *Attack of the Fifty Foot Woman* (the 1993 remake). Optical effects: *The Wizard of Speed and Time* (1988, in which he also shared a short scene with his wife Karen). Danforth was offered supervision of *Star Wars* (1975–77) by George Lucas but had to turn him down as everything was laid out before production began. Animated titles for the *Hallmark Hall of Fame* series. Commercials include Ford

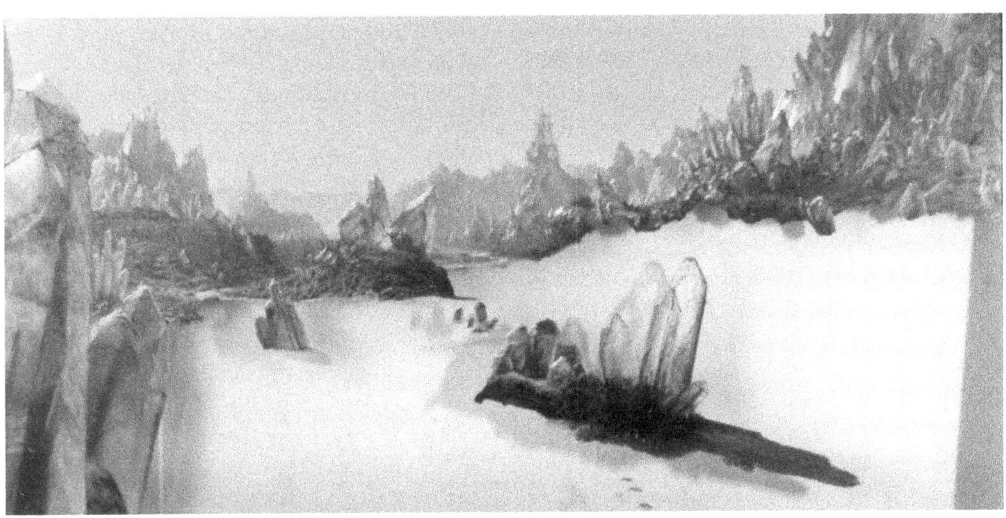

Matte painting by Jim Danforth (Effects Associates) for *The NeverEnding Story*, reused in *The NeverEnding Story II* (courtesy Deutsche Kinemathek Berlin).

Pinto and Recipe Brand Dog Food. Projects that fell through in various stages include *Thongor in the Valley of the Demons* (1976) and *Timegate* (1979), both of which were to have been directed by Danforth. Directed the skiing sequence in *Memoirs of an Invisible Man*. In 1991 he prepared a trailer for a Sherlock Holmes feature, *West of Kashmir*. Author of the *American Cinematographer* article "Improved Color for Process Projection Dupes." He has also written about the visual effects in producer Alexander Korda's *The Thief of Bagdad*.

Roy Davidge

American Process Pioneer

In the early 1920s, the Roy Davidge Lab was one of the few places in Hollywood where optical and process photography was made available to the industry. It became a good learning ground for future effects people such as Robert R. Hoag. Davidge rarely received screen credit.

E. Roy Davidson (1896–1962)

American Effects and Process Cinematographer

Was involved in shooting miniatures for Howard Hughes' *Hell's Angels* (1930). Hired to supervise photographic effects department of Columbia Pictures: *The Black Room* (1935, with Boris Karloff playing identical twins), Frank Capra's *Mr. Deeds Goes to Town* (1936) and *Lost Horizon* (1937), Hawks' *Only Angels Have Wings* (1939). Then as sfx director to Warner Bros.: *Passage to Marseille* (1944), *God Is My Co-Pilot* (1945), *A Stolen Life* (1946), *The Big Sleep* (1946), *Humoresque* (1946), *Fighter Squadron* (1948), *White Heat* (1949), *Task Force* (1949), *The Lady Takes a Sailor* (1949). Died in Los Angeles.

Mark H. Davis (1907–1995)

American Matte Cinematographer

Made approximately 3,000 matte shots. Worked on at least 470 feature films as well as numerous TV shows and commercials. Born in Troy, Idaho, he came to Los Angeles in 1928. Two years later he landed a job in MGM's photographic effects department as an assistant to process and matte cinematographer Thomas E. Tutwiler. Helped to create the famous Metro lion logo. Besides doing process, matte and miniature photography (*Tarzan and His Mate, Tugboat Annie, Queen Christina, Dancing Lady, Hollywood Party, Bombshell, The Cat and the Fiddle*), he also became an expert matte painter. Worked as matte photographer for Warren A. Newcombe, head of Metro's matte department. *Marie Antointette* (1938), *The Wizard of Oz* (1939), *Boom Town* (1940), *Dr. Jekyll and Mr.*

Hyde (1941), *Smilin' Through*, *Blossoms in the Dust* (1941), *Mrs. Miniver* (1942), *Tortilla Flat* (1942), *Random Harvest* (1942). Promoted to director of photography in 1942 (by John Arnold, head of MGM camera department) while he was working on *Lassie Come Home* (1942–43, first matte shots in Eastman monopack) and *Keeper of the Flame* (1942–43); also *Cry "Havoc"* (1943), *The Heavenly Body* (1943), *The White Cliffs of Dover* (1944), *Thirty Seconds Over Tokyo* (1944), *Kismet* (1944), *Keep Your Powder Dry* (1945), *The Cockeyed Miracle* (1946), *Green Dolphin Street* (1947), *The Three Musketeers* (1948), *Easter Parade* (1948, motion control shot with technique supplied by MGM sound man O.L. Dupy), *Annie Get Your Gun* (1950), *An American in Paris* (1951), *Show Boat* (1951), *Singin' in the Rain* (1952). Also did a lot of aerial photography (during World War II he was loaned out to the Navy) and was one of the designers of MGM's projection process system. Invented title-making equipment used at Metro and a special movie camera eventually acquired by the president of Technicolor. Remained at MGM until 1956, then took on freelance jobs for film (*Around the World in 80 Days* in 1956, *The Alamo* in 1960) and TV (*Alcoa Theatre, Cheyenne, Maverick, Sugarfoot, 77 Sunset Strip, Hawaiian Eye, Bourbon Street Beat, The Roaring Twenties, Lawman* and *Bronco*). Retired in 1973.

Norman O. Dawn (1886–1975)

American Effects Pioneer and Producer

Began as a still photographer at a photoengraving shop, the Thorpe Engraving Company, in Los Angeles. Met Georges Méliès and the Lumières in 1906 on his second trip to Paris. Did documentaries around the world as newsreel cameraman. Transferred the technique of glass shots, which he had used in still photography as early as 1905 (at the suggestion of fellow photoengraver Max Handschiegl, inventor of the Handschiegl process), to moving pictures in 1907 when he filmed the colonial Spanish-style Mission la Soledad in Monterey, California, that needed a roof which he painted on a sheet of glass in front of the camera lens: *Missions of California*, sold to Arthur Lee, the New York office manager of the French Gaumont company, for

$150. Further assignments from Lee took Dawn to the Panama Canal, Colombia, Hawaii, China, Australia, New Zealand, Sumatra, Java and New Guinea. In 1911 Lee released Dawn's first feature, *Story of the Andes*, for which the filmmaker used mattes and counter-mattes to combine paintings and live-action. The same year Dawn moved to Hollywood. In 1913 he did static rear projections for a western called *The Drifter*. In 1916–17 he was called in with his newly acquired Bell & Howell camera to enhance a Mack Sennett Keystone comedy for Triangle release called *Oriental Love* (directed by Walter Wright) with painted mattes; he applied for a patent on June 18, 1917 (granted 51 weeks later, on June 11, 1918, as Patent #1,269,061; described as a process to combine "real and artificially made subjects"). He did five years of trick work and painted mattes for Universal Studios before leaving in 1921. In 1922 he was with Robertson-Cole Pictures Corporation: *Five Days to Live* and *The Vermilion Pencil*, both starring Japanese actor Sessue Hayakawa. Eventually he was reunited with Irving Thalberg, the former studio manager of Universal, who had joined Louis B. Mayer at Selig Studio. For Thalberg, Dawn went to Canada for *Master of Woman*. In 1924, Dawn's *Valley of 10,000 Smokes*, a documentary made in Alaska, was released. Thalberg later talked him out of the matte patent for $10,000. Dawn continued to work as a director on exotic documentaries and features for Australasian Films Ltd. and directed *For the Term of His Natural Life* in Tasmania and a burlesque, *Show Girl's Luck*, Australia's first talkie. In 1930, when the Depression left him broke, Dawn had to return to Hollywood. He did the effects for *Mr. Robinson Crusoe* (1932) for Douglas Fairbanks, then gradually was reduced to the lowest of Poverty Row (for example, the serial *The Lost City* in 1935). For Edgar Rice Burroughs he made *Tundra* in 1936; it was re-released in 1949 as *Arctic Fury*. During World War II he worked for some time at Boeing, where gun cameras were integrated into the B-29 Flying Fortress to record aerial combat, and was involved in training and industrial films. The end of his career was lamentably marked by potboilers such as *Two Lost Worlds* (1950) and *Wild Women* (1951). His detailed notebooks, which include data on 861 effects shots, was left to the University of Texas at Austin.

Thomas Sydney (Tom) Day
(1912–1985)

British Matte Cinematographer

Son of matte artist Walter Percy Day. Joined his father as cameraman: *Things to Come* (1936), *The Man Who Could Work Miracles* (1936), *The Drum* (1938), *The Thief of Bagdad* (1939–40).

Walter Percy Day   (1878–1965)

British Matte Artist

Born in Luton, the son of Eli Day and his wife Lucy (born Crawley). A figure and landscape painter, he came from the classic school of painting. Introduced painted glass mattes, known as the Day process, to Europe. Served a three-year apprenticeship with photographer W. J. Roberts, then trained at Heatherley's Art School and the Royal Academy of Art in London (1901–1906). In 1908 he went to Tunisia and for four years painted Oriental scenes. Returned to Britain during World War I. His film effects career started right after the war in 1919 at Elstree Studios in Borehamwood with a company called Ideal Films. Three years later he went to Paris and did glass paintings for the French productions *Les Opprimés* (1923), *L'arriviste* (1924), *La Terre promise* (1925), *La Flamme* (1925), *Le Bossu* (1925), *L'homme à l'hispano* (1926), *Nana* (1926), *Michel Strogoff* (1926), *Le Mystère de la tour Eiffel* (1927), *Croquette* (1927), *Le Joueur d'échecs* (*The Chess Player*, 1927, spectacular glass shot of the Czar's Winter Palace with a military parade on the snowy ground in front), *The Ring* (1927), *Le Martyre de Sainte-Maxence* (1928), *Le Tourbillon de Paris* (1928), *Cagliostro* (1929), *La Vie miraculeuse de Thérèse Martin* (1929), *Verdun, visions d'histoire* (1929), *La Divine croisière* (1929), *Maman Colibri* (1929), *La merveilleuse vie de Jeanne d'arc* (1929), *Le Roi des aulnes* (1930), introducing matte paintings to Julien Duvivier's *Au Bonheur des dames* (1930), *La Bodega* (1930), *La Fin du Monde* (1930–31), *Les trois Mousquetaires* (1932). Day not only handled painting task but even played the small part of Admiral Hood in Abel Gance's *Napoléon* epic (1927). When he started to do matte shots, Day was highly disappointed with the steadiness of French Debrie cameras and in 1932 returned to Britain. There he acquired new camera equipment which would guarantee steadiness and opened a shop. In 1933 he teamed up with Alexander Korda and London Films and eventually set up a department at Denham Studios in 1936. Other credits include *The Private Life of Henry VIII* (1933), *The Scarlet Pimpernel* (1934), *Sanders of the River* (1935), *Scrooge* (1935), *The Ghost Goes West* (1935), *Things to Come* (1935–36), *Rembrandt* (1936), *The Man Who Could Work Miracles* (1936), *Fire Over England* (1937), *Storm in a Teacup* (1937), *Elephant Boy* (1937), *Knight Without Armour* (1937), *Victoria the Great* (1937), *The Drum* (1938), *Sixty Glorious Years* (1938), *Wuthering Heights* (1939, for Sam Goldwyn in Hollywood), *The Hunchback of Notre Dame* (1939, for RKO in Hollywood), *The Four Feathers* (1939), *Jamaica Inn* (1939), *The Thief of Bagdad* (1939–40), Also was involved in: *Major Barbara* (1940–41), *How Green Was My Valley* (1941, for 20th Century–Fox in Hollywood), *The First of the Few* (1942), *In Which We Serve* (1942, directed by David Lean), *Secret Mission* (1942), *The Life and Death of Colonel Blimp* (1943), *The Demi-Paradise* (1943), *A Canterbury Tale* (1944), *This Happy Breed* (1944), *The Chronicle History of King Henry the Fift with His Battell Fought at Agincourt in France* (*Henry V*, 1944–45, directed by Laurence Olivier), *Perfect Strangers* (1945), *I Know Where I'm Going!* (1945), *Caesar and Cleopatra* (1945), *Men of Two Worlds* (1946), *A Matter of Life and Death* (U.S.: *Stairway to Heaven*, 1946), *Black Narcissus* (1947), *Panique* (1947), *An Ideal Husband* (1947), *Mine Own Executioner* (1947). Rejoined Korda as director of special effects at London Films' Shepperton Studios: *Anna Karenina* (1948), *The Winslow Boy* (1948), *The Fallen Idol* (1948), *The Red Shoes* (1948), *Bonnie Prince Charlie* (1948), *The Last Days of Dolwyn* (1949), *The Third Man* (1949), *The Elusive Pimpernel* (1950), *The Black Rose* (1950), *Gone to Earth* (1950), *The Mudlark* (1950), *Pandora and the Flying Dutchman* (1951), *Outcast of the Islands* (1952), *The Wild Heart* (1952). For his services to British cinema, in 1948 he was decorated with the Order of the British Empire. Day, who preferred the term process shots to matte shots, worked with his sons Thomas Sydney (as cameraman) and Arthur George and later with Wally Veevers as his matte cinematographer. He retired from the film business in 1952. He married Adeline Ellenshaw, mother of Peter Ellenshaw, and thus became stepfather to his assistant. Other artists who worked with Day were Albert Julian, George Samuels, Joseph Natanson and for a short time Les Bowie and Albert Whitlock (on *Mine Own Executioner*). Day wrote the article "The origin and development of the matte shot process" for *British Kinematography*, September 1948. Died in Los Angeles. Nicknames: "Pop," "Poppa."

Segundo De Chomón (1871–1929)
Spanish Trickfilm Pioneer

De Chomón trained as an engineer in France and made trick shorts along the lines of Georges Méliès. Contributed imaginative effects and technical ideas for the feature films *Cabiria* (1913), *Maciste all'inferno* (1925) and Abel Gance's *Napoleon* (1927–28).

Marcel Delgado (1898–1977)
Mexican-American Sculptor and Miniaturist

Born La Parrita, state of Coahila, Mexico. The Delgado family moved to California in 1909. In 1911 Marcel's father died. Marcel loved to sculpt from an early age. While working at the Otis Art Institute in Los Angeles, Marcel was discovered by Willis O'Brien (O'Brien attended a "Still Life" class at Otis and invited Marcel to join him at First National Studios). "I had a job at the grocery that paid $18 a week and I wasn't about to give it up. Then Obie insisted that I should work for him. I must have turned him down fifteen or twenty times. When I saw the studio, I immediately changed my mind! Obie didn't know me from Adam. He was just taking a chance" (interview with Don Shay, 1965). Delgado would sculpt 49 rubber stop-motion dinosaurs for O'Brien for *The Lost World* (1924–25). Then he worked as model maker at

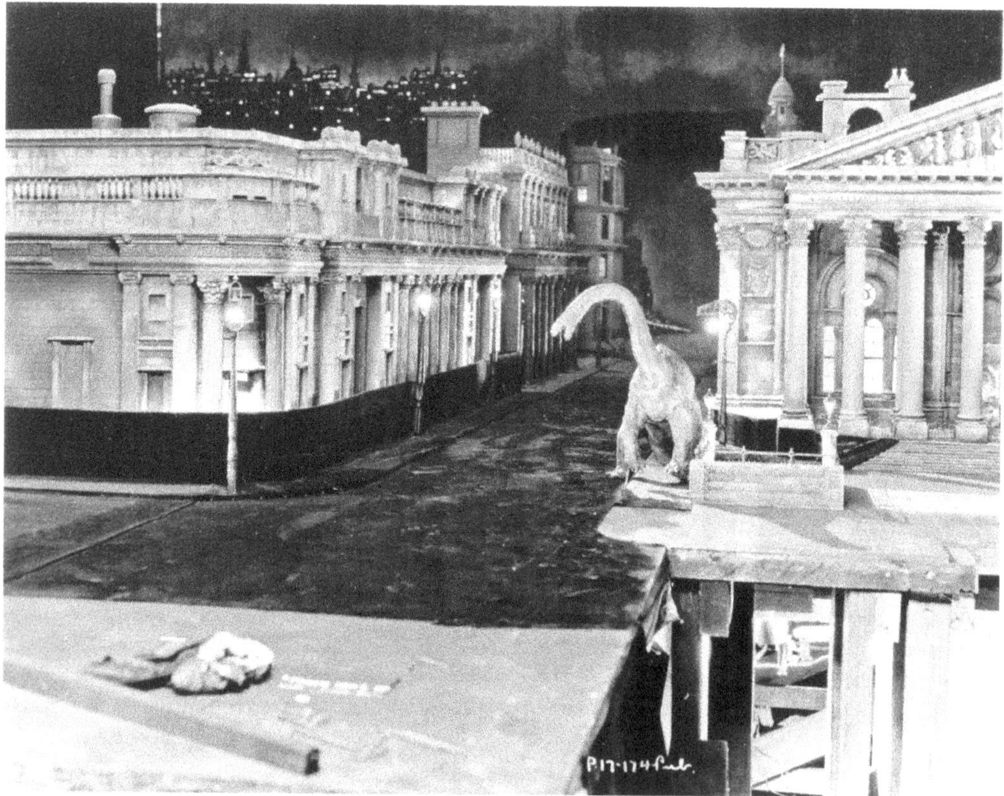

Brontosaurus model by Marcel Delgado for *The Lost World* (courtesy Deutsche Kinemathek Berlin).

First National for about two years before he was laid off. Got a job at William Fox Western Studios where (being able to read blueprints) he was involved in creating the city of the future for *Just Imagine* (1929–30). At that time he joined the union and worked at various studios. In 1930 a call from O'Brien brought him to RKO. There a dinosaur epic titled *Creation* (1930–31) was shelved in favor of *King Kong* (1932–33). Delgado covered the King Kong armature with rubber which was then overlaid with rabbit fur. "I made the two full body models used in *King Kong*. Both models were eighteen inches high, which is three-quarter inch to the foot…. The prehistoric animals were all three-quarters of an inch to the foot scale, and the miniature people were made one inch to the foot scale…. Occasionally I dropped in on the sets during the shooting or while Mr. O'Brien was animating the models. I was always busy trying to keep the models repaired as they would deteriorate or break. Many times I worked all night or on holidays in order to have them ready for use when needed. Many times I had to tear them down and build them over again because the rubber and muscles deteriorated from the heat of the lights and the constant movement of the animation" (*The Girl in the Hairy Paw*, p. 180). Delgado was part of most of O'Brien's unfinished, half-finished and finished projects: *The Son of Kong* (1933), *The Last Days of Pompeii* (1934–35; he made a swordfish for a sequence in a flooded arena which remained unfilmed), *War Eagles* (1939–40, unfinished at MGM: "I made a spearman riding a giant eagle and throwing a spear at a Tyrannosaurus"), *Gwangi* (1942, unfinished at RKO), *Mighty Joe Young* (1948–49). Of the latter he said, "I think Joe Young was my best ape. He was 15 or 16 inches high and the skin was unborn calf skin which I asked for so it wouldn't bristle like the rabbit fur on Kong [when touched by its animators]." Delgado was even more proud of the four-inch version of Joe that worked, he said, like a watch) and *It's a Mad Mad Mad Mad World* (1962–63, at Film Effects of Hollywood, for which he also did some animation which eventually was rejected by Lin Dunn and redone by Jim Danforth). In between he made miniatures, models and lots of tiny manikins for various model shops. RKO Studios: *Bird of Paradise* (1932), *The Most Danger-*

ous Game (1932), *The Monkey's Paw* (1932–33), *Flying Down to Rio* (1933), *She* (1935), *Days of Glory* (1944), *The Bells of St. Mary's* (1945), *Sister Kenny* (1946), *The Farmer's Daughter* (1947), *The Miracle of the Bells* (1948). Metro-Goldwyn-Mayer: *The Wizard of Oz* (1939), *Thirty Seconds Over Tokyo* (1944), *Annie Get Your Gun* (1950). Warner Bros.: *Saratoga Trunk* (1945). Paramount Studios: *The War of the Worlds* (1952–53). Walt Disney Studios: *20000 Leagues Under the Sea* (1953–54, as giant squid technician), *The Shaggy Dog* (1959, dog suit), *Mary Poppins* (1964); he also manufactured animals for Disneyland (Adventureland). Universal: *The Birds* (1963, some mechanical birds for use by Alfred Hitchcock). Project Unlimited: *Goliath and the Dragon* (1960–61, life-size head of fire–breathing dragon made out of leather in two weeks time), *Dinosaurus!* (1960, stop-motion and mechanical dinosaurs), *Master of the World* (1960–61, two balloons and assistance with the *Albatross*), *Jack the Giant Killer* (1961–62, started to sculpt two-headed giant), *The Outer Limits* (TV series), *The Twilight Zone* (TV). Butler-Glouner, Inc.: *Robinson Crusoe on Mars* (1964). 20th Century-Fox: *Fantastic Voyage* (1965–66, puppets). Retired in 1966. In the 1970s he fell off a ladder in his house and broke his back, never recovering from that severe accident. Died in Los Angeles.

Victor Delgado (191?–??)
Mexican-American Model Maker

Started by assisting his brother Marcel on *King Kong* (1932–33). For *The Son of Kong* (1933) he animated the model climbing a rock during the climax flood sequence. Assisted Marcel in manufacturing the body of a saber-tooth tiger for *She* (1935) and worked on other RKO features. Both Marcel and Victor, not very successfully, tried some stop-motion on *Mighty Joe Young* (1948–49). Later joined Centaur Productions and Project Unlimited as model shop foreman: *Goliath and the Dragon* (1960–61, stop-motion animation alternating with Jim Danforth), *Dinosaurus!* (1960), *Master of the World* (1960–61), *Jack the Giant Killer* (1961–62) and the TV series *The Outer Limits*. For a short time he worked at Universal. Lost parts of his fingers while operating a band saw. Although handicapped after the accident, he taught at Manual Arts High School in Los Angeles. Retired with his wife in Colorado.

Paul Detlefsen (1899 or 1900–1986)
American Matte Artist

The Detlefsen family came from Copenhagen, Denmark. Paul, the Chicago-born son of a medical doctor, studied at the Chicago Art Institute and the Academy of Fine Arts. His goal was to work in animated films but since he couldn't find a job he became a scenic painter. Because of his artistry in doing glass paintings, he was sought out by Cecil B. DeMille and Douglas Fairbanks. In 1923 he assisted Ferdinand Pinney Earle and painted mattes for *Dancer of the Nile* and *The Rubaiyat of Omar Khayyam*. In 1929 he teamed up with Lloyd W. Knechtel at RKO Studios; he painted on glass the foreground clouds for the original RKO radio tower trademark and worked on *Ringside*, one of that studio's earliest productions. After a while he went to Warner Bros. and stayed there for twenty years: *Cabin in the Cotton* (1932), *The Adventures of Mark Twain* (1944), *The Horn Blows at Midnight* (1945), *Escape in the Desert* (1945), *The Big Sleep* (1946), *Shadow of a Woman* (1946). Returned to RKO for *Androcles and the Lion* (1952). At age 50 he became a calendar artist focusing on nostalgic motifs. Detlefsen was a personal friend of Walt Disney.

Louis DeWitt
American Rostrum Cameraman and Title Artist

Did titles and inserts at 20th Century–Fox, then joined independent partners Jack Rabin and Irving Block at Studio Film Service: *The Big Combo* (1955), *Kronos* (1956–57), *The Invisible Boy* (1957), *Macabre* (1958), *War of the Satellites* (1958), *The Giant Behemoth* (1958–59). His involvement sometimes happened to be more financial than creative. On his own he did *The Phantom Planet* (1961).

Roger Dicken (1939–)
British Model Maker

A fan of Ray Harryhausen, he made models for Gerry Anderson's *Thunderbirds* series and lunar landscape for *2001: A Space Odyssey* (1965–68). Props for *Witchfinder General* (*Conqueror Worm*, 1968), *The Scars of Dracula* (1970), and *Trog* (1970). Did some dinosaur sculpting (plesiosaur) for *When Dinosaurs Ruled the Earth* (1968–70). For *The Land That Time Forgot* (1975) and *Warlords of the Deep* (*Warlords of Atlantis*, 1978) he sculpted mechanical creatures and dinosaurs. The chestburster from Ridley Scott's *Alien* (1978–79) is another Dicken creations. Later came to America: Wolves for *The Howling* (1980), a dinosaur for *Caveman* (1980–81) and a stop-motion monkey for *The Hunger* (1983); also worked on *Q/The Winged Serpent* (1982). Then he returned to England and had success manufacturing dolls from his own designs.

Patrick A. (Pat) Dinga
American Mechanical Effects Expert

Did effects for several low-budget legends such as Ed Wood and Roger Corman: *Return to Treasure Island* (1954), *Bride of the Monster* (1954), *Master of the World* (1960–61), *Pit and the Pendulum* (1961), *Tales of Terror* (1962), *The Raven* (1963), *The Comedy of Terrors* (1963), *Muscle Beach Party* (1964).

Jan Domela (1894–1973)
Holland-American Matte Artist

Born in Amsterdam, Holland, as Johan Domela Nieuwenhuis, Jan Marinus Domela came to San Francisco in 1915. He attended California School of Fine Arts and the Los Angeles School of Illustration. In 1925 he returned to Europe, studied at Rijks Academy in Holland and Académie Julian in Paris. A few years later he went back to the States and entered the film business. For many years he was resident matte artist at Paramount Studios (he even painted the Paramount logo): *Her Jungle Love* (1938), *Spawn of the North* (1938), *Union Pacific* (1939), *Dr. Cyclops* (1939–40), *Typhoon* (1940), *Aloma of the South Seas* (1941), *I Wanted Wings* (1941), *Reap the Wild Wind* (1941–42), *For Whom the Bell Tolls* (1943), *Unconquered* (1947), *A Connecticut Yankee in King Arthur's Court* (1949), *Samson and Delilah* (1949), *When Worlds Collide* (1951), *The War of the Worlds* (1952–53), *The Ten*

Commandments (1953–56). Maintained a studio in Santa Monica until his demise.

Dream Quest Images, Inc.
American Visual Effects Studio

Co-founded by Hoyt H. Yeatman, Scott Squires, Rocco Gioffre, Frederick Iguchi and Thomas and Robert Hollister. The plan evolved while they were jointly working on *Star Trek* (1979–80). They rented some space in Culver City and did some video graphics and visual displays for *Blade Runner* (1981–82). Involved in *E.T. the Extra-Terrestrial* (1981–82, additional visual effects), *Blue Thunder* (1983), *Captain Eo* (1986), *The Abyss* (1989), *Crimson Tide* (1995), *Armageddon* (1998), *Mighty Joe Young* (1998), *Mission to Mars* (2000).

Edwin B. Du Par (1890–1961)
American Special Effects Cinematographer

Du Par toured in a vaudeville act billed as "The Dancing Du Pars, the boys with the educated feet." He became prop man for director Eddie Cline at Mack Sennett's place. Eventually he was invited by Fred W. Jackman, Sennett's chief cinematographer, to join his staff:

> Of course, I jumped at the chance. One of the first jobs I had with him was down at the Palisades in Santa Monica. At that time the streetcar tracks crossed the mouth of the canyon on a bridge with telephone piling. Fred had figured out a shot with a couple of autos chasing each other as they went in and out of those pilings. In order to cover the shot we had to go up on top of the Palisades and come down a little ridge to a point where we could set up the camera. Well, we got the camera down and set up — and Fred said he would go down and direct the chase while I was to photograph it. He instructed me on the speed of the crank, and departed. In the meantime, a good stiff breeze came in from the ocean, hit the cliffs, and almost blew the camera and me off the cliff for a drop of about 100 feet. Despite this, we made the shot, and I did my best to crank at the speed and still keep it steady — but it was at speed of 6, while at the time the dramatic speed was 16 and the cranking for comedy 12. Fred told me I had better practice speeds, as I would be doing a lot of cranking, so I got a stopwatch and camera and practiced on the different speeds to get them set in my mind and make it more automatic in judging. I almost wore

out the camera practicing, but got so proficient that I could go from stop motion to 16 and back again in a scene [*American Cinematographer*, December, 1946].

After three years at Sennett, Du Par moved over to Fox, then, in 1920, to Warner Brothers, making about a dozen comedies with Monty Banks. In 1925 Jack L. Warner sent Du Par to New York for initial experimentation with sound films. He spent his time there making Vitagraph sound shorts. One of the last things Fred Jackman did while in charge of the special effects activities at Stage 5 on the Warner-First National Burbank lot was to re-hire Du Par, who then photographed miniatures, process and second units for *South of Suez, The Dawn Patrol* (1938), *The Roaring Twenties* (1939), *Desperate Journey* (1942), *Action in the North Atlantic* (1943), *Passage to Marseille* (1944), *God Is My Co-Pilot* (1945), *Pride of the Marines* (1945), *Objective, Burma!* (1945), *Three Strangers* (1946), *Johnny Belinda* (1948), *Embraceable You* (1948), *The Decision of Christopher Blake* (1948), *Always Together* (1948), *The Fountainhead* (1949), *Beyond the Forest* (1949), *Task Force* (1949), *The Inspector General* (1949), *Flaxy Martin* (1949), *Chain Lightning* (1950), *The West Point Story* (1950), *Three Secrets* (1950) and *Giant* (1956). He was director of photography on *The Bounty Hunter* (1954) in WarnerVision (3D but released only in flat format) and for his former Warner boss Byron Haskin on the Jules Verne picture *From the Earth to the Moon* (1958).

Linwood Dunn (1904–1999)
American Effects Cinematographer and Optical Effects Supervisor

Linwood Gale Dunn was born in Brooklyn and raised in Flatbush. During his high school years he was a self-trained dance band musician. In 1923 he started as a projectionist for the American Motion Picture Corporation in New York and carried a portable projector from schools to churches. In 1925 he assisted on the Pathé serial *The Green Archer* (directed by his uncle, Spencer Gordon Bennet). A year later when Pathé moved its serial unit to Fine Arts Studio, Dunn came to Hollywood as a camera assistant and operator: *Snowed In* (1926), *Hawk of the Hills* (1927), *Queen of the Northwoods* (1929; with this, his fourteenth serial job, he became a first cameraman), *Flight* (1929, Frank Capra's first sound film at Columbia Pictures). In 1929 he joined the camera effects department at RKO Radio Studios working with Lloyd W. Knechtel, model shop supervisor Don Jahraus and glass artists Paul Detlefsen: *Ringside* (1929), *Cimarron* (1931), *The Case of Sergeant Grischa* (1930), *Danger Lights* (1930, 63.5mm widefilm in George K. Spoor's Natural Vision Process, not to be confused with stereoscopic Natural Vision), *The Most Dangerous Game* (1932). Started to operate an optical printer for Knechtel and his successor, Vernon L. Walker. The crude printer consisted of a Mitchell camera and a projector in a lathe bed. Went to Willis O'Brien and convinced him to do composite shots on *King Kong* (1932–33) in the printer instead of bipacking right in the camera. Claimed to have had a hand in the famous scene of Kong climbing the Empire State Building. Jim Danforth, however, doubts that statement: "Lin told me this story twice. Once it was about *Mighty Joe Young*, once it was about *King Kong*. *Mighty Joe Young* shows evidence of this (and the shots are not of good quality in terms of sharpness), but there is little internal evidence of this in *Kong*. Of course the Williams mattes were done optically, but by Williams in his own, independent facility." Dunn's other credits include *Lucky Devils* (1932–33), *The Phantom of Crestwood* (1932–33), *Before Dawn* (1932–33), *The Son of Kong* (1933), a variety of optical wipes for the short *So This Is Harris!* (1933), *Melody Cruise* (1933), *Flying Down to Rio* (1933), *Hips, Hips, Hooray!* (1933–34), *Ace of Aces* (1933), *Down to Their Last Yacht* (1934), *Anne of Green Gables* (1934), *The Last Days of Pompeii* (1935), *Top Hat* (1935), *Bringing Up Baby* (1938), *Gunga Din* (1939), *The Hunchback of Notre Dame* (1939), *Swiss Family Robinson* (1940), *Citizen Kane* (1940–41; editor Robert Wise introduced director Orson Welles to the optical printer), *Cat People* (1942, produced by Val Lewton and magnificently directed by Jacques Tourneur), *The Navy Comes Through* (1942), *Bombardier* (1943), *Days of Glory* (1944), *Experiment Perilous* (1944), *It's a Wonderful Life* (1946), *Sinbad the Sailor* (1947), *The Thing from Another World* (1950–51, electrocuting the extraterrestrial invader), *The Whip Hand* (1951), *Androcles and the Lion* (1952), *The Narrow Margin* (1953), *The French Line* (1954), *Dangerous Mission* (1954, 3D), *The Sea Around Us* (1955), *The Conqueror* (1956) and *Jet Pilot* (made in 1950 and released in 1957). In the final years of RKO, Dunn directed the department. In February 1957, RKO Radio Pictures film production ceased and departmental operations were eventually terminated. Dunn decided to lease the photographic effects department facilities from RKO and merged this operation with his own independent company, Film Effects of Hollywood, founded in 1946 with Cecil D. Love and Don W. Weed. With his newly expanded scope, the facility could now offer to the increasing number of independent film producers highly sophisticated photographic effects services and optical printing techniques: *On the Beach* (1959), *Anatomy of a Murder* (1959), *West Side Story* (1961, end titles), *55 Days at Peking* (1962, commissioned by director Nicholas Ray to do multiple image effects which ultimately didn't materialize), *Circus World* (1962), *It's a Mad Mad Mad Mad World* (1962–63), *The Birds* (1963), *My Fair Lady* (1964), *Kiss Me, Stupid* (1964), *The Satan Bug* (1965), *The Hallelujah Trail* (1965), *Ship of Fools* (1965), *The Great Race* (1965), *The Bible* (1965–66), *Hawaii* (1966, storm sequence: an 80-foot ship was mounted to rock in front of a 100-foot special blue screen, then backgrounds were optically matted in), *Murderers' Row* (1966), *What Did You Do in the War, Daddy?* (1966), *Thoroughly Modern Millie* (1967), *The Russians Are Coming! The Russians Are Coming!* (1966), *Tobruk* (1967), *Gaily, Gaily* (1969), *Darling Lili* (1970), *Airport* (1970), *Song of Norway* (1970), *Catch-22* (1970), *The Neptune Factor* (1973), *The Devil's Rain* (1975), *The Reincarnation of Peter Proud* (1975), *Taxi Driver* (1976), *New York, New York* (1977), *Damnation Alley* (1977), *Sgt. Pepper's Lonely Hearts Club Band* (1978), *The Shape of Things to Come* (1979). TV: *Star Trek, Kung Fu, Wonder Woman*. Called in as consultant on both *2001: A Space Odyssey* (1968, process plates) and *Star Wars* (1976–77, judging effects set-up at ILM). Involved in special features: *Journey to the Stars* (1961, Cinerama-Boeing 70mm Spacearium film) and *A Place to Stand* (1967, 70mm Expo film, 1968 Academy Award Winner for Best Live Action Short Subject: very sophisticated multi-panel optical printing technique, as many as 15 panels on the screen at once). Also: *The Searching Eye* (Kodak Show, New York World's Fair), *The Billy Graham Story* (New York World's Fair), *Wonderful World of Chemistry* (Dupont, New York World's Fair), *The Earth Is Man's Home* (*Expo 67*, Montreal, Canada), *Flight Simulation* (Singer Simulation Systems), *Fisher Price Toys* (Mattel Toy Company), *Jacques Cousteau's Museum of the Sea* (Queen Mary), *Labyrinth* (Canadian Film Board for Ontario Place), *General Motors* (Hanna-Barbera), *Capture the Sun* (Reuben Fleet Space Center, San Diego), *John Deere Corporation Film* (Chicago Museum of Science and Industry), *In the Beginning* (International Harvester, Chicago), *Eclipse 75* (IMAX presentation at Ontario Place, Canada), *USAF Aircraft Tower Control Simulation* (AAI Corporation). For Eastman Kodak and U.S. Armed Forces in association with Cecil Love, he designed the Acme-Dunn Special Effects Printer:

In 1942 Bill Barry of Eastman Kodak approached me regarding the need for special effects optical printers by the United States Armed Forces Photographic Units. Kodak was handling much of the technical needs of such Governmental motion picture installations, and found that they were unable to find a source of supply of such optical printers, as they had never been manufactured as a commercial "shelf item" product. In all of the major studios, and in the few independent optical effects companies, such printers were always a hand-made "Rube Goldberg," such as the equipment I developed and operated over my early years at RKO Radio Pictures. I was then commissioned by the Government and Kodak to design and have manufactured a standardized machine that could be readily obtained as required for all optical printing needs of these motion picture units in various locations. The order I received had no specifications and no price, all of which was left to me to come up with. My RKO associate over many years, Cecil Love, and I worked out the design of the printer, based on our many years of being deeply involved in optical effects, working together at RKO. We welcomed this opportunity because we knew that the motion picture industry sorely needed a standardized optical printer, as such "home made" machines left so much to be desired. The cost of each one being individually custom designed, and in most cases with the studio machine shop handling the project, there appeared to be a lack of design that originated from the operator's standpoint, a most important factor. In this case I would be in full charge of the project, and with the valued as-

sistance of my colleague, Cecil Love, would provide optical printers that combined the many important operational features that we had found were needed to meet the fast-growing creative requirements in this very important field of motion picture production. With an order in hand for three Government printers I was in a position to select a quality manufacturer who would be interested in taking on such a new proprietary item, and would fill the Government orders on a high-priority basis. After a discussion with Edward Furer, an owner of the Acme Tool and Manufacturing Company, I felt I had found the interest, enthusiasm, talent and financial responsibility I needed to take on this most important project. It just so happened that Cecil Love had recently joined the United States Navy Photo Science Laboratory in Anacostia which, coincidentally, was to be the first installation of this new optical printer. This was surely a good break, because Cecil could keep me informed about any changes needed for future machines, based on his daily experience with this prototype printer, thus making us feel that our design could well become the industry standard. The Acme-Dunn Special Effects Optical Printer was not made available to our industry until World War II ended, at which time this equipment soon became the industry standard, and thus served as a nucleus for new independent special effects organizations, many appearing due to the closing down of the major studio departments.... This machine became the basic design for several optical printers to follow, such as the Oxberry, Photo Research, Producers Service, and others of more recent vintage, all now utilizing recent technological advances; but with the same concept as the Acme-Dunn machine, which was a radical departure from the earlier equipment used in our industry" [Linwood G. Dunn, *Historic Facts About the Acme-Dunn Optical Printer*].

For that printer, Dunn received a special Academy Award, Class III, in technological achievement (1944). He also received a Medal of Commendation in 1978 (in appreciation of outstanding service and dedication in upholding the high standards of the Academy of Motion Picture Arts and Sciences), an Award of Merit in 1980 and a Gordon A. Sawyer Award in 1984 for outstanding contributions toward advancement of the science or technology of motion pictures. Was twice president and long-time treasurer of ASC. With his protégé George E. Turner, he co-edited the 1983 book *The ASC Treasury of Visual Effects*. Dunn was a founding member of the Visual Effects Society.

C. Dodge Dunning and Carroll H. Dunning

American Camera Technicians and Inventors

In the mid–1920s, C. Dodge Dunning invented the instant double-printing bi-pack process which was presented to the film industry in 1927 by his father Carroll H. Dunning, who owned the Prizma Color Process Company. Until the breakthrough of background projection, it was used for scenes in movies like *Silver King Comes Through* (1927), *Just Imagine* (1930), *The Big Trail* (1930), *Anna Christie* (1930), *Trader Horn* (1931), *Dirigible* (1931), *Subway Express* (1931), *Africa Speaks* (1932), *Tarzan the Ape Man* (1932), *Mr. Robinson Crusoe* (1932), *Bird of Paradise* (1932), *King Kong* (1932–33), *The Son of Kong* (1933), *Deluge* (1933), *Tarzan and His Mate* (1934). Articles by Carroll Dunning appeared in *Journal SMPTE*, May 1929 ("Typical problems in process photography") and in *American Cinematographer*, April 1929 ("Patents vs. patents vs. practice") and June 1929 ("Some problems related to composite photography").

Syd Dutton

American Matte Artist

Dutton studied fine arts at the University of California at Berkeley. Attending a presentation by Linwood G. Dunn at the San Francisco Museum of Modern Art attracted him to film effects. In 1973 he moved with his family to Hollywood. Eventually he became an apprentice in Albert Whitlock's matte department: *Family Plot* (1976), *Buck Rogers in the 25th Century* (1979), *History of the World, Part I* (1981), *Ghost Story* (1981), *Masada, A.D.* (1985, TV miniseries). After Universal closed the department,

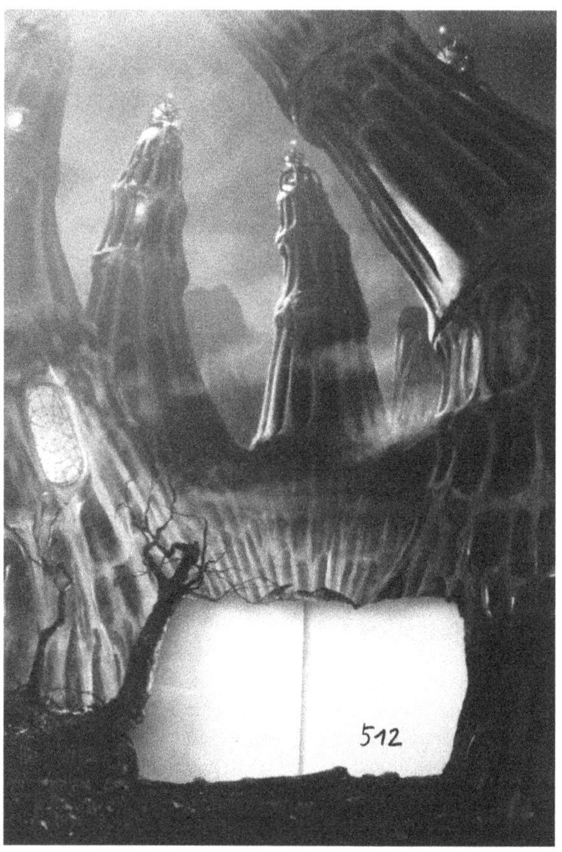

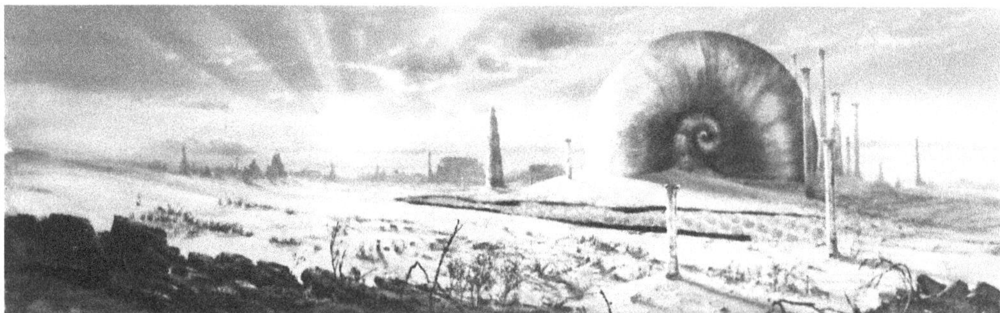

Various glass and matte paintings for **Die Unendliche Geschichte II** (***The NeverEnding Story II***), supervised by Albert Whitlock. The plates were shot at Bavaria Studios in Munich, painted by Syd Dutton and photographed by Bill Taylor at Illusion Arts in Van Nuys (courtesy Deutsche Kinemathek Berlin).

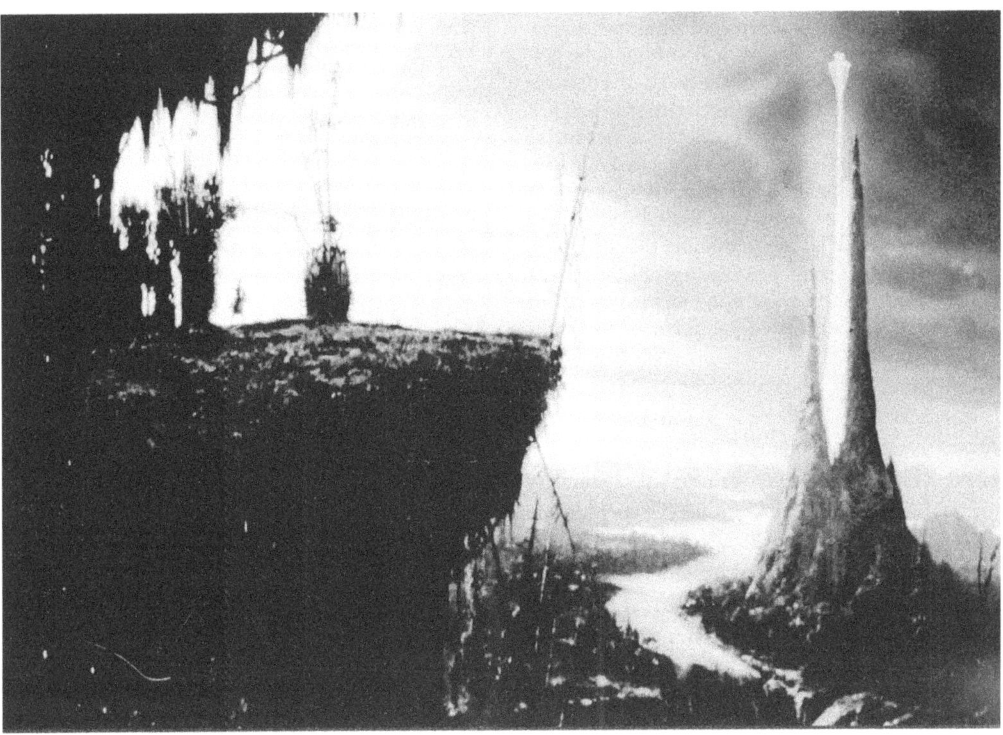

Anamorphic matte shot (optically "squeezed") for *The NeverEnding Story II* (1989–90), supervised by Albert Whitlock, painted by Syd Dutton and photographed by Bill Taylor at Illusion Arts (courtesy Deutsche Kinemathek).

Dutton and Bill Taylor, who was Whitlock's cameraman, founded Illusion Arts, Inc., in Van Nuys: *Red Sonja* (1985), *Die Unendliche Geschichte II* (*The NeverEnding Story II*, 1989–90) and many more. Last traditional matte painting for Martin Scorsese's *The Age of Innocence* (1993) and *Batman & Robin* (1997, jungle lab scene). Then right into the digital age: *Anna and the King* (1999).

Elmer G. Dyer (1892–1970)
American Aerial Cinematographer

With his own movie camera the Lawrence, Kansas-born Dyer started to contribute to newsreels, then in the early 1920s photographed westerns. Acknowledged for his second unit and aerial footage: *Hell's Angels* (1930), *The Dawn Patrol* (1930), *Dirigible* (1931), *Airmail* (1932), *Murder in the Clouds* (1934), *China Clipper* (1936), *Only Angels Have Wings* (1939), *The Flying Deuces* (1939, Laurel & Hardy), *Flight Command* (1940, second unit director), *I Wanted Wings* (1941),

Dive Bomber (1941), *Keep 'Em Flying* (1941), *Captains of the Clouds* (1942), *Wake Island* (1942), *Air Force* (1943), *Murder Is My Beat* (1955, special photography), *The Hot Angel* (1958). During World War II he contributed to training films for the U.S. Air Force.

John C. Dykstra (1947–)
American Visual Effects Supervisor

Born in Long Beach, Dykstra attended California State College and studied Industrial Design at Long Beach State. He worked for Lester Novros and Graphic Films (IMAX entry: *Voyage to the Outer Planets*) and on commercials, and joined Douglas Trumbull on *The Andromeda Strain* (1971) and *Silent Running* (1971). Trumbull recommended him to George Lucas for *Star Wars* (1975–77) for which Dykstra, with electronics designer Alvah J. Miller, developed a motion control unit called Dykstraflex:

I had the idea for years. This is just one permutation of the concept. It's not a *new* concept.

It's very old, like blue screen or front projection. It's been around for years, just waiting to be perfected or improved to suit the needs of a particular situation. Al Miller is an electronics designer. We sat down with two bottles of wine during the old Future General days and figured out what the machine ought to do, what it ought to look like, and how to program it. Basically, it is just a combination of all the techniques that have been used for years, combined into a sophisticated device capable of manufacturing techniques [*Cinefantastique* Double Issue Vol. 6 No. 4/Vol 7. No. 1, p. 11].

For *Star Wars* Dykstra received an Academy Award as well as a Scientific or Technical Award Class II for the development of a facility uniquely oriented toward visual effects photography. After the first *Star Wars*, Dykstra, who had a disagreement with Lucas, left Industrial Light & Magic, co-produced *Battlestar Galactica* (1977) with Glen A. Larson and founded with some partners his own optical house, Apogee Productions, Inc.: *Star Trek: The Motion Picture* (1979), *Firefox* (1981), *Starflight One* (1982), *Space Vampires* (1984). After Apogee folded, Dykstra continued to freelance right into the computer age: *Batman Forever* (1995), *Batman and Robin* (1997), *Stuart Little* (1998–99), *Spider-Man* (2002), *Spider-Man 2* (2004), *The Dreamless* (2006).

Paul E. Eagler (1890–1961)

American Special Effects Cinematographer

Born in Newman, Illinois. It was a gift he got from his father in 1900 that inspired young Eagler: a magic lantern which provided an avenue for his inventiveness. Soon after, a traveling show came to the small town of Newman. There were not only vaudeville acts but, during intermission, two-minute moving pictures. The projector resembled his magic lantern, with some sort of hand-cranked clockwork. Eagler became insistent and finally volunteered as projectionist. When the family moved to California, Eagler was supposed to study at U.S.C., but he was so taken with movies that his father bought a movie house in Sawtelle where Paul would hand-crank the projection machine. That was when he decided that he also should *make* movies. Armed

with an Eberhardt-Schneider catalogue and the innards of an old Méliès projector, he painstakingly built his own camera and immediately used it to shoot documentaries. In 1915 Eagler got a job in Hollywood at Inceville and landed in the title department and then in the trick department. Working with artist Irving Martin, he made his first matte shot for a picture entitled *Peggy*. He remained with Thomas Ince for nearly ten years as an effects photographer and production cameraman, then moved to the Pathé lot in Culver City. He did photographic effects for Douglas Fairbanks' *Robin Hood* (1922) and *Tess of the Storm Country* (1922). According to *American Cinematographer* he did his first background projection for a 1923 movie. The screen consisted of a six-foot-by-eight-foot piece of white silk. In those days there were no high-intensity arcs, no fast film, no fast lenses and no synchronous motors, so actors had to try to make like love while straddling an 80-foot drive shaft that connected the camera to the projector. When the Goldwyn people moved into Ince Studios, Eagler was sent to do second-unit camerawork on *Ben-Hur* (1925) in Rome, Italy. By the time he returned to Culver City, the Goldwyn Studios had merged with Metro and Louis B. Mayer to become Metro-Goldwyn-Mayer. Eagler stayed at MGM where he supervised process shots until 1933, then did process plates and second unit work for various independent producers such as Samuel Goldwyn and Walter Wanger at United Artists Studios on North Formosa Avenue in Hollywood: *Strike Me Pink* (1936), *Dead End* (1937), *The Hurricane* (1937), *The Cowboy and the Lady* (1938), *The Real Glory* (1939), *The Westerner* (1940) and Alfred Hitchcock's *Foreign Correspondent* (1940). In the 1940s he assisted Vernon L. Walker at RKO Studios, including process work for *Li'l Abner* (1940), *The Navy Comes Through* (1942), *Bombardier* (1943), *Days of Glory* (1944) and *Notorious* (1946), another Hitchcock vehicle that relied heavily on process (South America footage). He also went to Palm Beach, Florida, to photograph second unit and plates for *Unexpected Uncle* (1941). At Selznick he was involved in effects and process production for *Portrait of Jennie* (1948). In the 1950s, Eagler organized process service for B-pictures: *The Beast from 20,000 Fathoms* (1952–53), *The Monster That Challenged the World* (1957).

Ferdinand Pinney Earle
(1878–1951)

American Matte Artist

Son of a noted brigadier general and the eldest of four brothers. After early schooling near Trenton, New Jersey, he studied painting in Paris. His teachers were Bourguereau and Whistler. Traveled all over Europe. Also studied poetry (at Oxford) and dramatic literature (at Columbia) when he returned to the United States, then left again for Europe. In 1915 he started to paint backdrops and titles for the movies. Artistic effects (double exposing actors and painting): *Within the Law* (1917), *Womanhood, The Glory of the Nation* (1917, for film pioneer James Stuart Blackton). Art titles: *Social Hypocrites* (1918), *To Hell with the Kaiser!* (1918), *The Embarrassment of Riches* (1918), *Pals First* (1918), *Once to Every Man* (1918), *The Birth of a Race* (1918), *Daddy-Long-Legs* (1919), *Bill Apperson's Boy* (1919), *The Better Wife* (1919), *The Miracle Man* (1919), *Out of the Dust* (1920), *The Money Changers* (1920), *Domestic Relations* (1922). With *The Rubaiyat of Omar Khayyum* (1923), produced with his own money, he became one of the originators of the matte process (he fought over the patents with Norman Dawn). In an article published in the October 1921 issue of *American Cinematographer,* effects cinematographer Philip H. Whitman remarked that Earle "has solved the greatest economic problem of motion picture production. He is filming scenes in which a score of noted actors and actresses appear, but ... there is not one player on the payroll! The setting is the most beautiful of the production, but there are no actors before the camera. They're inside the camera. When the action was photographed by George Benoit, the setting was invisible to the eye. Now the setting is photographed and the actors in *proportia persona* are not needed. In Earle's production of *The Rubaiyat of Omar Khayyam* hundreds of scenes are photographed at separate times of action." Earle also worked on *Dancer of the Nile* (1923), *Souls in Bondage* (1923), *Ben-Hur* (1925, credited for "art effects") and *Liliom* (1934, directed by Fritz Lang in France for Fox Films; Earle received screen credit as *décorateur*). He is seen painting in a Marion Davies movie, *Show People* (1928).

Richard Edlund (1940–)
American Visual Effects Cinematographer and Supervisor

As a teenager, this native of Fargo, North Dakota, took high school sports pictures, some of them published in the *Los Angeles Examiner.* He learned photography in the U.S. Navy. Attended Film Classes at USC (University of Southern California) School of Cinema in 1961–62, then went to work at The Westheimer Company, a Hollywood optical house where he assisted founder Joseph Westheimer ("Joe was willing to teach me what he knew") and cinematographer William Reinhold on shots for the *Star Trek* TV series. He did title cards, built and repaired equipment, and photographed inserts for four years (*The Outer Limits, The Wild Wild West*). In 1968 he took a break from commercial filmmaking and shot still pictures of rock bands (including album covers). After doing some experimental film stuff and a stint at Robert Abel's, he met John Dykstra in a small effects company. Dykstra hired Edlund to work with him on the

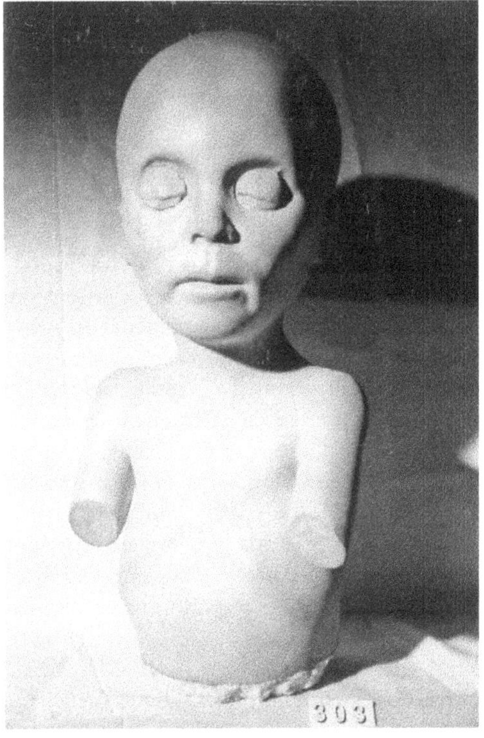

Star Child (torso of fetus) from *2010* (courtesy Deutsche Kinemathek Berlin).

Dykstraflex motion control scenes for *Star Wars* (1975–77). Edlund stayed with Dykstra to work on *Battlestar Galactica* (1978–79), then left for San Rafael and Industrial Light & Magic: *The Empire Strikes Back* (1979–80), *Raiders of the Lost Ark* (1981), *Poltergeist* (1982), and *Return of the Jedi* (1982–83). Returned from San Francisco to Los Angeles to take over what was known as Effects Entertainment Group (EEG) in Marina del Rey from Douglas Trumbull and transformed the facilities into Boss Films: *Ghostbusters* (1984), *2010* (1984), *Masters of the Universe* (1987), *Die Hard* (1988), *Vibes* (1988), *Ghost* (1990), *Alien³* (1992), *Species* (1995), *Starship Troopers* (1997), *Air Force One* (1997), *The Parent Trap* (1998). In 1998 Boss Film went out of business. Edlund continued in the industry by supervising *Bedazzled* (2000), *The Stepford Wives* (2004, collaborating with Tippett Studios), *Anamorph* (2007). Scientific and Engineering Awards in 1981 for the concept and engineering of a beam-splitter optical composite motion picture printer as well as for the engineering of the Empire Motion Picture Camera System.

Farciot Edouart (1894–1980)

American Rear-Projection Supervisor

Alexander Farciot Edouart was born in California. Both his grandfather and father had been portrait photographers. In 1915, Edouart started as assistant cameraman at Realart Studios, a forerunner of Paramount Pictures in Hollywood. After two years his activities were interrupted by service in World War I (as a member of the Army Photography Section he was sent overseas and promoted to sergeant). In 1918 he received his discharge and was given a lieutenant's commission in the Red Cross as special cinematographer in the Armistice Commission in Germany. For a short time he went back to Hollywood, then asked to return to Paris in complete charge of the Red Cross' motion picture operation. He returned to Los Angeles in 1921 to begin his own photographic business but got in touch with Lasky and Paramount where he stayed until the late 1960s. First he did glass shots, then went into traveling mattes. In 1928 he was credited as photographer on *Interference*. Eventually he found a niche for himself in the transparency department where background projection became his authoritarian domain: *A Farewell to Arms* (1932), *One Sunday Afternoon* (1933), *Alice in Wonderland* (1933), *Gambling Ship* (1933), *This Day and Age* (1933), *Thirteen Hours by Air* (1936), *The Plainsman* (1936), *Desire* (1936), *Waikiki Wedding* (1937), *I Met Him in Paris* (1937), *Easy Living* (1937), *Angel* (1937), *The Buccaneer* (1938), *Ride a Crooked Mile* (1938), *Men with Wings* (1938), *Spawn of the North* (1938, Academy Award), *Midnight* (1939), *Never Say Die* (1939), *Union Pacific* (1939), *Geronimo* (1939), *Honeymoon in Bali* (1939), *Dr. Cyclops* (1939–40, certainly his most interesting, most demanding work), *Road to Singapore* (1940), *North West Mounted Police* (1940), *Reaching for the Sun* (1941), *I Wanted Wings* (1941, Academy Award), *Virginia* (1941), *Sullivan's Travels* (1941), *Aloma of the South Seas* (1941), *Reap the Wild Wind* (1941–42, Academy Award), *Road to Morocco* (1942), *China* (1943), *So Proudly We Hail!* (1943), *For Whom the Bell Tolls* (1943), *The Uninvited* (1944), *The Story of Dr. Wassell* (1944), *Double Indemnity* (1944), *The Lost Weekend* (1945), *Road to Utopia* (1946), *Two Years Before the Mast* (1946), *O.S.S.* (1946), *The Searching Wind* (1946), *Unconquered* (1947), *The Paleface* (1948), *The Big Clock* (1948), *A Foreign Affair* (1948), *The Great Gatsby* (1949), *Rope of Sand* (1949), *My Friend Irma* (1949), *Samson and Delilah* (1949), *A Connecticut Yankee in King Arthur's Court* (1949), *Sunset Blvd.* (1950), *Carrie* (1950–52), *Submarine Command* (1951), *A Place in the Sun* (1951), *Detective Story* (1951), *Jumping Jacks* (1952), *Son of Paleface* (1952), *Shane* (1953), *Pony Express* (1953), *Flight to Tangier* (1953, 3-D), *Sangaree* (1953, 3D), *Those Redheads from Seattle* (1953, 3D), *Jivaro* (1953–54, 3D), *The Ten Commandments* (1953–56), *Money from Home* (1953, 3D), *Elephant Walk* (1954), *Alaska Seas* (1954), *The Naked Jungle* (1954), *Sabrina* (1954), *The Desperate Hours* (1954–55), *The Bridges at Toko-Ri* (1954–55), *Conquest of Space* (1954–55), *To Catch a Thief* (1955), *The Man Who Knew Too Much* (1956), *Hollywood or Bust* (1956), *Wild Is the Wind* (1957), *The Sad Sack* (1957), *The Space Children* (1958), *The Colossus of New York* (1958), *Vertigo* (1958), *The Buccaneer* (1958 remake), *Last Train from Gun Hill* (1959), *Visit to a Small Planet* (1960), *G.I. Blues* (1960), *Cinderfella* (1960), *One-Eyed Jacks*

(1961), *Breakfast at Tiffany's* (1961), *Pocketful of Miracles* (1961), *The Man Who Shot Liberty Valance* (1962), *Escape from Zahrain* (1962), *The Pigeon That Took Rome* (1962), *Girls! Girls! Girls!* (1962), *Hud* (1963), *Donovan's Reef* (1963), *Fun in Acapulco* (1963), *It's A Mad Mad Mad Mad World* (1963), *Robinson Crusoe on Mars* (1964, slide projection), *The Patsy* (1964), *The Disorderly Orderly* (1964), *Red Line 7000* (1965), *Ship of Fools* (1965), *In Harm's Way* (1965), *The Family Jewels* (1965), *Village of the Giants* (1965, for Bert I. Gordon), *Assault on a Queen* (1966), *El Dorado* (1966), *The Last of the Secret Agents?* (1966), *The Oscar* (1966), *Barefoot in the Park* (1967), *The Caper of the Golden Bulls* (1967), *Blue* (1968), *Rosemary's Baby* (1968). TV series: *Bonanza*. Scientific or Technical Awards, Class II, in 1937: For the development of the Paramount dual screen transparency camera setup, with two adjoining process screens divided by a prop element such as a tree; Class III in 1939 (shared with Joseph E. Robbins and William Rudolph) for the design and construction of a quiet portable treadmill; Class II in 1943 (shared with Earle Morgan and Barton Thompson) for the development and practical application to motion picture production of a method of duplicating and enlarging natural color photographs, transferring the image emulsions to glass plates and projecting these slides by especially designed stereopticon equipment; Class III in 1947 (shared with C. R. Daily, Hal Corl and H. G. Cartwright) for the first application of a special anti-solarizing glass to high intensity background and spot arc projectors; Class II in 1955 (shared with Hal Corl) for the engineering and development of a double-frame triple-head background projector; Class III the same year (again with Corl) for an improved dual stereopticon background projector. Co-created Paramount's short-lived 3D technology Paravision (with Loren L. Ryder, Dr. Charles R. Dailey and Ferdinand Eich).

Peter Ellenshaw (1913–2007)

British–American Matte Artist

The London-born Ellenshaw assisted his later stepfather W. Percy Day in the early days of Korda's London Film Productions: *The Ghost Goes West* (1936), *Things to Come* (1936), *Rembrandt* (1936), *The Man Who Could Work Miracles* (1936), *Elephant Boy* (1937), *Fire Over England* (1937), *Storm in a Teacup* (1937), *Victoria the Great* (1937), *The Drum* (1938), *Sixty Glorious Years* (1938), *The Four Feathers* (1939), *The Thief of Bagdad* (1939–40), *Major Barbara* (1940). After World War II, still a member of Day's team, he didn't feel like an assistant anymore so he began to compete with the master himself on several joint productions such as *A Matter of Life and Death* (U.S.: *Stairway to Heaven*, 1946), *Black Narcissus* (1947) and *The Red Shoes* (1948), then left Day to work on his own. Did mattes for *Quo Vadis* (1951) and *Captain Horatio Hornblower, R.N.* (1951). Eventually got some assignments on Disney's British quota pictures *Treasure Island* (1950), *Robin Hood* (1952) and *The Sword and the Rose* (1953), which led him to go overseas and work for Disney Studios in Burbank, California: *20000 Leagues Under the Sea* (1953–54), *Davy Crockett, King of the Wild Frontier* (1955), *Davy Crockett and the River Pirates* (1956), *The Great Locomotive Chase* (1956), *Westward Ho the Wagons* (1956), *Old Yeller* (1957), *The Light in the Forest* (1958), *Tonka* (1958), *Darby O'Gill and the Little People* (1958–59), *Third Man on the Mountain* (1959), *Toby Tyler* (1960), *Kidnapped* (1960), *Pollyana* (1960), *Ten Who Dared* (1960), *Swiss Family Robinson* (1960), *The Sign of Zorro* (1960), *The Absent Minded Professor* (1960–61), *Greyfriars Bobby* (1961), *In Search of the Castaways* (1961), *Summer Magic* (1963), *Lt. Robin Crusoe, U.S.N.* (1966), *The Fighting Prince of Donegal* (1966), *Monkeys, Go Home!* (1967), *The Adventures of Bullwhip Griffin* (1967), *The Gnome-Mobile* (1967), *The Happiest Millionaire* (1967), *Blackbeard's Ghost* (1968), *The Love Bug* (1968–69). Academy Award for *Mary Poppins* (1964). Designed Disney's *Johnny Tremain* (1957) and did a matte painting of ancient Rome on a loanout to Universal for *Spartacus* (1960). Returned to Disney to design *Bedknobs and Broomsticks* (1970–71), *The Island at the Top of the World* (1974), and *The Black Hole* (1979). Contributed paintings for his son Harrison (Peter, Jr.) for *Dick Tracy* (1990). Died in Santa Barbara, California.

Peter S. (Harrison) Ellenshaw, Jr. (1944–)

American Matte Artist

The son of artist Peter Ellenshaw was born in Harrisburg, Pennsylvania. To avoid being confused with his father, he renamed himself Harrison (after his birthplace). Majored in psychology at Whittier College, then three years service in the U.S. Navy (including three trips to Vietnam). Assisted Alan Maley in Disney's matte department in 1970: *Bedknobs and Broomsticks* (1970–71). When Maley left, Harrison, at age 29, became head of the department: *The Apple Dumpling* (1975), *The Man Who Fell to Earth* (1976, for actor David Bowie), *Pete's Dragon* (1977). Also became matte supervisor on Lucasfilm's first ventures *Star Wars* (1976–77) and *The Empire Strikes Back* (1978–79). Continued as Disney matte and sfx supervisor (later renamed Buena Vista Visual Effects) on *The Black Hole* (1979), which was designed by his father, *Tron* (1982), *Dick Tracy* (1990) as well as *Captain Eo* (1986).

John Ellis

American Optical Cinematographer

In 1978–79 he was camera assistant on *Star Trek: The Motion Picture*. Joining Lucasfilm, he operated optical printers on *Dragonslayer* (1982), *E.T. the Extraterrestrial* (1982) and *Star Trek II: The Wrath of Khan* (1982). In the mid–1980s, with *Goonies* (1985), he became supervisor of ILM optical department. For ILM he created an optical printer that was named after him.

Volker Engel (1965–)

German Visual Effects and Miniature Supervisor

In contrast to what he later claimed, there was a breeding ground for special effects in Germany which clearly helped Bremerhaven-born Engel to get an assignment in Sindelfingen to work as a model maker, then as sfx supervisor on Roland Emmerich's *Moon 44* (1988–89). After some model work for Emmerich's first U.S. feature *Universal Soldier* (1992) and lecturing at Filmakademie Baden-Württemberg in Ludwigsburg (where he contributed to TV's *Der letzte*

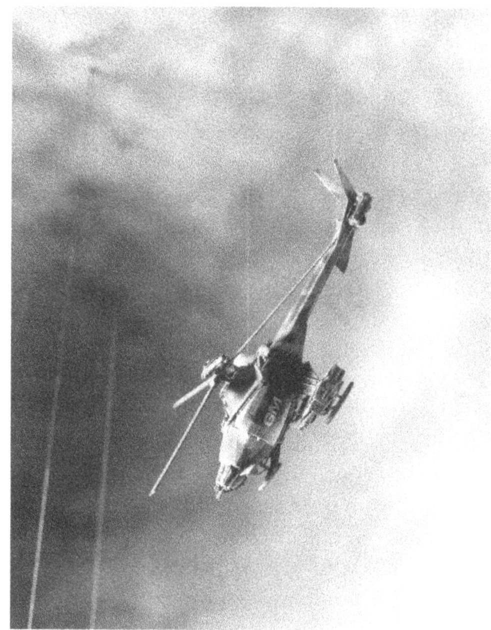

A helicopter model by Volker Engel made for the early Roland Emmerich picture *Moon 44* (courtesy Volker Engel and Deutsche Kinemathek Berlin).

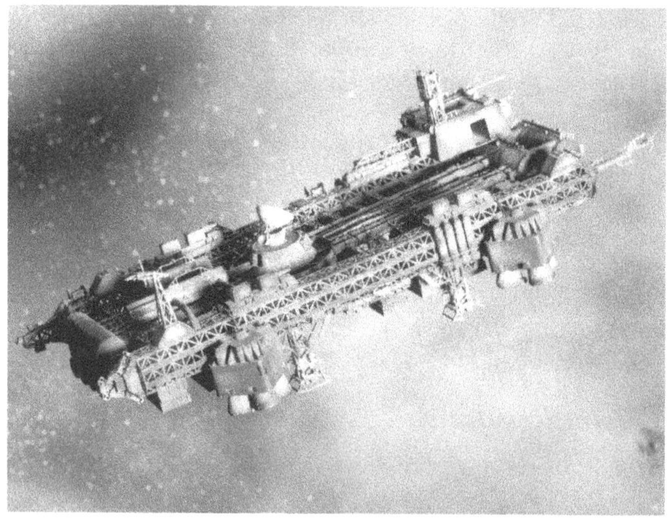

Volker Engel spaceship for Roland Emmerich's *Moon 44* (courtesy Volker Engel and Deutsche Kinemathek Berlin).

Kosmonaut in 1994 and to *Schlafes Bruder* in 1994–95), Engel renewed his contact with Emmerich and Centropolis. He won an Academy Award for his work on *Independence Day* (1995–96) and supervised *Godzilla* (1997–98). Later with partner Marc Weigand he opened his own production facilities, Uncharted Territories, near Los Angeles Airport. In 2003 they produced *Coronado*, an effects-filled adventure yarn, and did a CGI dragon for the TV mini-series *Ring of the Nibelungs* (2004). In 2006 Engel received an Emmy Award for the first part of the mini-series *The Triangle* (2005).

Jonathan Erland (1939–)
British-American Blue Screen Expert

London-born Erland attended London International Film School in 1956. In 1976 he got a job with John Dykstra on *Star Wars*. With Dykstra he co-founded Apogee Productions, Inc., where he became director of research. Scientific and Engineering Award 1983 (shared with Roger Dorney): For the engineering and development of a reverse blue screen traveling matte process for special effects photography, and in 1984 (with Donald Trumbull, Stephen Fog and Paul Burk) for design and development of the "Blue Max" high power blue-flux projector for traveling matte composite photography and (with Robert Bealmear) for an innovative design for front projection screens and an improved method for their construction. Article: "Reverse or negative blue-screen traveling matte process," *Journal SMPTE*, March, 1983.

Orien Ernest
American Mechanical Effects Expert

With Fred Knoth he was in charge of the Technical Department at Universal City Studios: *Abbott and Costello Meet Frankenstein* (1948). Shared Scientific or Technical Award Class in 1954: for the development of a hand-portable, electric dry oil-fog machine.

Christopher (Chris) Evans
American Matte Artist

In 1980 he graduated with a Master of Fine Arts degree from UCLA. When he saw *The Em-*pire Strikes Back* with its painted clouds he applied for a job at Industrial Light & Magic's matte painting department where he was tutored by Alan Maley: *Dragonslayer* (1981), *E.T. the Extra-Terrestrial* (1982), *Star Trek: The Wrath of Khan* (1982), *The Dark Crystal* (1982), *Return of the Jedi* (1982–83), *Die Unendliche Geschichte* (*The NeverEnding Story*, 1983–84), *Indiana Jones and the Temple of Doom* (1984), *Star Trek III: The Search for Spock* (1984), *Starman* (1984), *The Goonies* (1985), *Cocoon* (1985), *Enemy Mine* (1985), *Star Trek IV: The Voyage Home* (1986), *The Golden Child* (1986), **batteries not included* (1987), and the TV series *Young Indiana Jones*. After *Willow* (1988) he started to freelance. With matte cinematographer Craig Barron, he co-founded Matte World: *Flight of the Intruder* (1990), *Batman Returns* (1992), *Jurassic Park* (1993), *City Slickers 2* (1994), *Star Trek: First Contact* (1996), *Titanic* (1997), *The Mummy Returns* (2001), *The Alamo* (2004), *Invincible* (2006).

Maximilian Fabian (1891–1969)
Austrian-American Miniature and Special Effects Cinematographer

As director of photography at MGM, the Austrian-born Fabian was assigned to the special effects unit and for many years worked as A. Arnold Gillespie's cameraman: *Tarzan Escapes* (1934), *San Francisco* (1936), *The Wizard of Oz* (1939), *Tarzan Finds a Son!* (1939), *Mrs. Miniver* (1940), *Thirty Seconds Over Tokyo* (1944), *Quo Vadis* (1950–51), *Forbidden Planet* (1956). Died in Los Angeles.

Ernest D. Farino (1952–)
American Visual Effects Supervisor

Born in Massachusetts, this amateur-turned-pro's projects include *The Alien Factor* (1979), *The Howling* (1980), *The Strangeness* (1980), *Caveman* (1981, handling the rotoscope garbage mattes for the frontlite/backlite Pterodactyl sequence and machining the stop-motion armatures), *Galaxy of Terror* (1981), *Saturday the 14th* (1981), *Slapstick of Another Kind* (1982), *The Thing* (1982), *Dreamscape* (1984), *The Terminator* (1984), *The Dungeonmaster* (*Ragewar*, 1985, roto effects, opticals), *The Puppetoon Movie* (1987), *The Abyss* (1989), *Cyborg* (1990), *Snow White—A Tale of Terror* (1997). Visual effects supervisor: *From the Earth to the Moon* (1998, TV mini-series, Emmy nomination), *Frank Herbert's Dune* (2001, mini-series, Emmy winner). Directed *Josh Kirby—Time Warrior: Chapter 2* and *Chapter 4* (1995) but had nothing to do with the effects work. Co-published *FXRH* (1971–74) with Sam Calvin, a four-issue fanzine devoted to Ray Harryhausen. Animated the Pillsbury Doughboy for Coast Productions (1979).

Doug Ferris

British Matte Artist

Assisted on mattes for *When Dinosaurs Ruled the Earth* (1968–70). Painted mattes for *Alice's Adventures in Wonderland* (1972), Jack Gold's *The Medusa Touch* (1978), *Superman* (1977–78, assistant to Les Bowie), *Superman II* (1980).

Roy Field (1932–2002)

British Optical Cinematographer

Started at Bray Studios as a clapper-loader. He subsequently worked with Bowie-Margutti: *The Quatermass Xperiment* (U.S.: *The Creeping Unknown*, 1954), *X the Unknown* (1956). Accompanied Victor Margutti to Pinewood Studios and focused on optical printing processes: *Dr. No* (1962), *From Russia with Love* (1963), *Goldfinger* (1964), *Those Magnificent Men in Their Flying Machines* (1965), *Superman* (1977–78), *Clash of the Titans* (1979–80), *Saturn 3* (1980), *Superman II* (1980), *Dragonslayer* (1980–81), *Outland* (1981), *Superman III* (1983), *The Dark Crystal* (1983), *Supergirl* (1984), *A Christmas Carol* (1984), *Santa Claus* (1984–85), *King David* (1985), *White Hunter Black Heart* (1990), *Cleopatra* (1999, TV).

Film Effects of Hollywood, Inc.

American Optical Effects Company

An independent effects house founded in 1946 by partners Linwood G. Dunn, Cecil D. Love and Don W. Weed: *On the Beach* (1959), *Anatomy of a Murder* (1959), *West Side Story* (1960), *The Birds* (1962–63, one sequence only), *It's a Mad Mad Mad Mad World* (1962–63), *The Great Race* (1965), *The Bible* (1965), *Hawaii* (1966), *Airport* (1970), *Damnation Alley* (1977). TV: *Star Trek*. Later became Film Effects International.

Oskar Fischinger (1900–1967)

German Animation and Effects Artist

Born in Gelnhausen. In addition to his experimental (*Studie 1–14*) and animation work (*Komposition in Blau*, 1934–35) and stop-frame animated commercials (*Muratti greift ein*, 1934, animated cigarettes in Gasparcolor), he created photographic effects for the feature films *Der Weltkrieg* (1926–27), *Der Unüberwindliche* (1928), Fritz Lang's *Frau im Mond* (*Woman in the Moon/By Rocket to the Moon*, 1928–29), *Die Försterchristel* (1930), *Das Blaue vom Himmel* (1932), *Annette im Paradies* (1933–34). In 1936 he went to America: *Allegretto* (1936, Gasparcolor animation, originally envisioned as part of Paramount's *The Big Broadcast of 1937*), *Fantasia* (1939–40, preproduction concepts), *Jane Eyre* (1944, titles), Fritz Lang's *Secret Beyond the Door* (1947, dream sequence). Died in Hollywood.

Howard Fisher

American Matte Artist

One of the original Newcombe men at Metro-Goldwyn-Mayer's matte department where he worked on many productions from *Meet the Baron* (1933) up to *Forbidden Planet* (1956). Later did matte paintings at Film Effects of Hollywood for *It's a Mad Mad Mad Mad World* (1962–63).

Max Fleischer (1889–1972)

American Cartoon Producer

Viennese-born Max Fleischer pioneered American cartoons. In 1916 he invented and patented basics of the rotoscope process which was refined by Leonard Pickley.

Rolla Flora

American Effects Cinematographer

Pioneer technician with Paramount Studios in Hollywood. Later involved in entries like *The*

All-Star Bond Rally (1945), a short film starring Bob Hope, and the western *The Red Stallion* (1947).

A.D. Flowers

American Explosives Expert

At MGM he started by dressing trees for *The Wizard of Oz* (1939), then became their explosives expert: *Thirty Seconds Over Tokyo* (1944), *Battleground* (1949), *Quo Vadis* (1950–51), *The Red Badge of Courage* (1951), *Forbidden Planet* (1956), *Ben-Hur* (1959). Shared Academy Awards with L.B. Abbott for the 20th Century–Fox features *Tora! Tora! Tora!* (1969–70) and *The Poseidon Adventure* (1972). Other credits include: *Bloody Mama* (1970), *Rio Lobo* (1970), *The Godfather* (1972), *Sleeper* (1973), *The Fury* (1977), *Apocalypse Now* (1979), *1941* (1979). Technical Achievement Award in 1979 (shared with Logan R. Frazee) for the development of a device to control flight patterns of miniature airplanes during motion picture photography.

Anna F. Foerster

German Effects Cinematographer

Studied at Filmakademie Baden-Württemberg and joined Volker Engel on *Schlafes Bruder*

(1994–95) and later worked on *Independence Day* (1995–96). Visual effects photography for *Magicians* (2000), *Pitch Black* (2000) and *Stuart Little 2* (2002). Second unit director: *The Day After Tomorrow* (2004).

Stuart Freeborn (1914–)

British Makeup Artist

London-born Freeborn started in the industry working on such notable productions as *Rembrandt* (1936, Korda production starring Charles Laughton), *The Thief of Bagdad* (1939–40), *Oliver Twist* (1948, directed by David Lean, as "Stuart Freebourne"; made-up Alec Guinness as Fagin), *The Bridge on the River Kwai* (1957, directed by Lean), *Those Magnificent Men in Their Flying Machines* (1965). Did the apemen (*australopitecus*) for the prologue of Stanley Kubrick's *2001: A Space Odyssey* (1965–68). George Lucas hired him to create Yoda, Chewbacca, Tauntauns and similar creatures for early films in the *Star Wars* series.

Fitch Fulton

Swedish-American Scenic Painter and Matte Artist

After scenic painter Fitch Fulton retired from the theatrical stage and from vaudeville, his son,

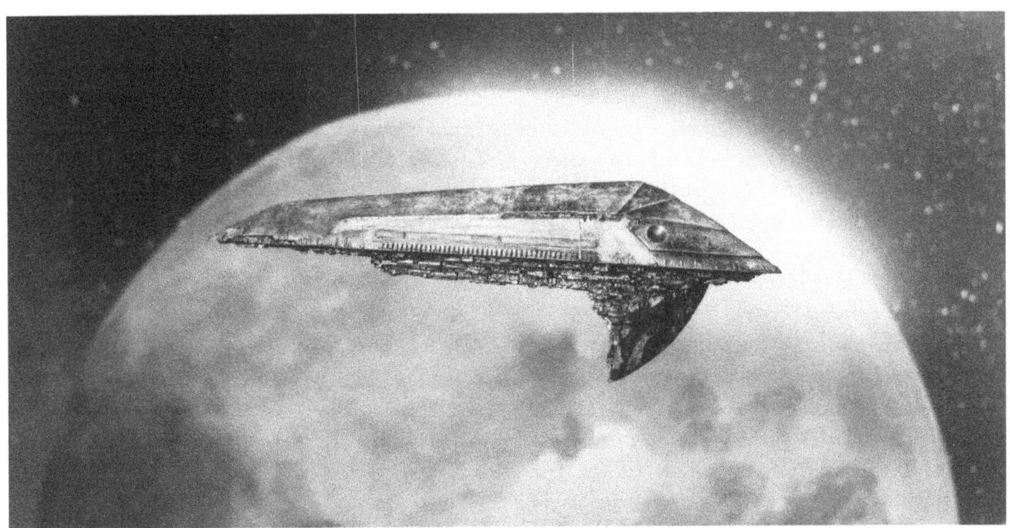

Spacecraft for the Roland Emmerich picture *Independence Day*, on display at Deutsche Kinemathek Berlin courtesy of 20th Century–Fox (photograph of display courtesy Deutsche Kinemathek Berlin).

special effects ace John P. Fulton, persuaded him to try his hand at matte paintings. Jack Cosgrove used him on *Gone with the Wind* (1939; Fitch and Al Simpson sketched the mattes on 30x40" masonite boards), and Larry Butler employed him on *The Jungle Book* (1942). Fulton worked as a matte artist for Fox (*How Green Was My Valley*, 1941) and RKO (*Citizen Kane*, 1940–41, and *The Whip Hand*, 1951). He was screen-credited for his *Mighty Joe Young* (1946–49) glass shots. Also was a talented landscape artist, focusing on Southern California and the Sierra Nevada.

John P. Fulton (1902–1966)

American Special Effects Cinematographer and Supervisor

A Swedish-American born in Nebraska, John Phipps Fulton was the son of scenic artist Fitch Fulton. The family moved to California in 1914. Fitch insisted that John study electrical engineering and would have no part in the entertainment industry. As a young man, then a surveyor for the Southern California Edison Company, John watched D.W. Griffith direct and decided to enter the movie industry after all. Camera assistant on Lloyd Hamilton and Larry Semon slapstick comedies. Eventually became director of photography at Universal Studios but switched to a technically more challenging filmmaking arena, trying his hand at trick shots. In 1931 he became head of Universal's new special effects department, creating the photographic effects for many horror and fantastic films (and supervising the construction of a new stage reserved for process and miniatures in 1932): *Frankenstein* (1931), *Murders in the Rue Morgue* (1931–32), *The Mummy* (1932), The *Invisible Man* series originated by director James Whale in 1933, *The Black Cat* (1934), *Bride of Frankenstein* (1935), *Werewolf of London* (1935), *The Raven* (1935), *The Invisible Ray* (1935–36), *Dracula's Daughter* (1936), *Son of Frankenstein* (1938–39), *The Invisible Man Returns* (1939–40, starring Vincent Price), *Black Friday* (1939–40), *The Invisible Woman* (1940), *Man Made Monster* (1941), *The Wolf Man* (1941), *The Ghost of Frankenstein* (1942), *Invisible Agent* (1942), *The Mummy's Tomb* (1942), *Frankenstein Meets the Wolf Man* (1942–43), *Son of Dracula* (1943), *Calling Dr.*

Death (1943), *Weird Woman* (1944), *Cobra Woman* (1944), *The Scarlet Claw* (1944, with Basil Rathbone as Sherlock Holmes and Nigel Bruce as Dr. Watson), *Ghost Catchers* (1944), *The Invisible Man's Revenge* (1944), *House of Frankenstein* (1944), *The Mummy's Curse* (1944), *House of Dracula* (1945). Other Universal work included: *Waterloo Bridge* (1931), *Heaven on Earth* (1931), *A House Divided* (1931, featuring a storm at sea), *Impatient Maiden* (1932), *Scandal for Sale* (1932), *Radio Patrol* (1932), *The Texas Bad Man* (1932), *Airmail* (1932, a production for which he learned to fly in order to do aerial photography; flying became his lifelong hobby), *Destination Unknown* (1933), *Her First Mate* (1933), *Cross Country Cruise* (1934), *Affairs of a Gentleman* (1934), *Let's Talk It Over* (1934), *The Love Captive* (1934), *One More River* (1934), *Romance in the Rain* (1934), *Wake Up and Dream* (1934), *Great Expectations* (1934), *Imitation of Life* (1934), *The Man Who Reclaimed His Head* (1934), *The Good Fairy* (1935), *Mystery of Edwin Drood* (1935), *Night Life of the Gods* (1935), *Princess O'Hara* (1935), *Stormy* (1935), *Remember Last Night?* (1935), *The Great Impersonation* (1935), *Magnificent Obsession* (1935), *Dangerous Waters* (1936), *Show Boat* (1936, directed by James Whale), *Postal Inspector* (1936), *My Man Godfrey* (1936), *The Girl on the Front Page* (1936), *My Little Chickadee* (1940), *Zanzibar* (1940), *This Woman Is Mine* (1941), *In the Navy* (1941), *Keep 'Em Flying* (1941), *Hellzapoppin* (1941), *Eagle Squadron* (1941–42, incorporating World War II footage filmed in Britain by Ernest B. Schoedsack for Walter Wanger production), *Saboteur* (1942, collaboration with Alfred Hitchcock), *The Spoilers* (1942), *Pittsburgh* (1942), *We've Never Been Licked* (1943), *Arizona Trail* (1943), *Corvette K-225* (1943), *Crazy House* (1943), *His Butler's Sister* (1943), *Gung Ho!* (1943), *Sing a Jingle* (1944), *Ali Baba and the Forty Thieves* (1944), *Ladies Courageous* (1944), *The Impostor* (1944), *Weekend Pass* (1944), *Hat Check Honey* (1944), *Follow the Boys* (1944), *This Is the Life* (1944), *Slightly Terrific* (1944), *Christmas Holiday* (1944), *Gypsy Wildcat* (1944), *In Society* (1944), *The Merry Monahans* (1944), *Babes on Swing Street* (1944), *San Diego I Love You* (1944), *Murder in the Blue Room* (1944), *My Gal Loves Music* (1944), *Here Come the Co-eds* (1945), *See My Lawyer* (1945), *Sudan* (1945), *That's the Spirit* (1945), *The Strange Affair of Uncle Harry*

(1945), *Lady on a Train* (1945), *That Night with You* (1945), *Frontier Gal* (1945), *Scarlet Street* (1945), *Night in Paradise* (1945–46). He also worked with John Ford's photographic unit in World War II. With the (unfulfilled) promise to make him a director, producer Samuel Goldwyn lured him away from Universal to invent effects for Danny Kaye comedies. First Academy Award for Kaye's Technicolor *Wonder Man* (1945). More Goldwyn productions Fulton worked on: *The Best Years of Our Life* (1946) and *The Secret Life of Walter Mitty* (1947). However, only one assignment as second unit director evolved from his stint at Goldwyn's: *The Bishop's Wife* (1947). Finally Fulton left Goldwyn, doing independent work for producer Walter Wanger on *Joan of Arc* (1948) and *Tulsa* (1949, burning oil field) and joining Louis Lichtenfield and the Warner Bros. matte department. After the untimely death of Gordon Jennings (and on recommendation by Lichtenfield and an old colleague, Universal's David Stanley Horsley) Fulton was made head of Paramount's Special Effects Department in 1953. Academy Awards for *The Bridges at Toko-Ri* (1954–55) and for parting the Red Sea in Cecil B. DeMille's VistaVision epic *The Ten Commandments* (1953–56). Received screen credit on virtually every Paramount production of that period including *Sangaree* (1953, 3D), *The Caddy* (1953), *Those Redheads from Seattle* (1953, 3D), *Flight to Tangier* (1953, 3D), *Money from Home* (1953–54, 3D), George Pal's *The Naked Jungle* (1953–54), *Jivaro* (1953–54, 3D), *Red Garters* (1954), *Casanova's Big Night* (1954), *Knock on Wood* (1954), *Elephant Walk* (1954), *About Mrs. Leslie* (1954), *Living It Up* (1954), *Sabrina* (1954), *White Christmas* (1954, introducing the VistaVision process), *The Country Girl* (1954), *3 Ring Circus* (1954), *Strategic Air Command* (1954), George Pal's *Conquest of Space* (1955), *Run for Cover* (1955), *Hell's Island* (1955), *The Far Horizons* (1955), *The Seven Little Foys* (1955), *We're No Angels* (1955), *You're Never Too Young* (1955), *The Desperate Hours* (1955), *Lucy Gallant* (1955), *Artists and Models* (1955), *The Rose Tattoo* (1955), *Bing Presents Oreste* (1956), *The Court Jester* (1956), *The Scarlet Hour* (1956), *Anything Goes* (1956), *The Leather Saint* (1956), *The Proud and Profane* (1956), *Pardners* (1956), *The Vagabond King* (1956), *The Search for Bridey Murphy* (1956), *The Mountain* (1956), *Hollywood or Bust* (1956), *The Rainmaker* (1956), *Three Violent People* (1957), *Funny Face* (1957), *Williamsburg: The Story of a Patriot* (1957), *The Delicate Delinquent* (1957), *Beau James* (1957), *Loving You* (1957), *The Lonely Man* (1957), *Omar Khayyam* (1957), *The Joker Is Wild* (1957), *Short Cut to Hell* (1957), *The Devil's Hairpin* (1957), *Hear Me Good* (1957), *Zero Hour!* (1957), *The Sad Sack* (1957), *Wild Is the Wind* (1957), *Spanish Affair* (1958), *Desire Under the Elms* (1958), *St. Louis Blues* (1958), *The Space Children* (1958), *The Colossus of New York* (1958), *King Creole* (1958), *Rock-A-Bye Baby* (1958), *The Matchmaker* (1958), *Hot Spell* (1958), *The Black Orchid* (1958), *I Married a Monster from Outer Space* (1958), *Houseboat* (1958), *Maracaibo* (1958), *The Buccaneer* (1958), *The Trap* (1959), *Alias Jesse James* (1959), *The Five Pennies* (1959), *Last Train from Gun Hill* (1959), *But Not for Me* (1959), *Career* (1959), *The Jayhawkers!* (1959), *Li'l Abner* (1959), *Heller in Pink Tights* (1960), *Visit to a Small Planet* (1960), *The Bellboy* (1960), *G.I. Blues* (1960), *All in a Night's Work* (1960), *One-Eyed Jack* (1960), *Cinderfella* (1960), *On the Double* (1961), *The Pleasure of His Company* (1961), *The Ladies Man* (1961), *Love in a Goldfish Bowl* (1961), *Breakfast at Tiffany's* (1961), *Too Late Blues* (1961), *Summer and Smoke* (1961), *Blue Hawaii* (1961), *Escape from Zahrain* (1962), *Hatari!* (1962), *The Pigeon That Took Rome* (1962), *It's Only Money* (1962), *My Six Loves* (1963), *The Patsy* (1964). Alfred Hitchcock and Fulton were reunited on *Rear Window* (1954), *To Catch a Thief* (1955), *The Trouble with Harry* (1955), *The Man Who Knew Too Much* (1956) and *Vertigo* (1958). TV series: *The Rebel* (1959). After leaving Paramount Pictures, Fulton and Rip Van Ronkel co-wrote typical Cold War B picture *The Bamboo Saucer* (released post-mortem in 1968). Went to Britain to supervise *The Heroes of Telemark* (1965) and to Spain for *Surcouf, L'eroe dei sette mari* (U.S.: *The Sea Pirate*, 1966). Fulton died during the preparation of *Battle of Britain* in a hospital in London.

William E. Garity

American Engineer

From 1929 until 1942 he worked at Walt Disney Studios and designed the Multiplane Camera System (as well as Fantasound for *Fantasia*).

Steve Gawley (1952–)
American Model Maker

In 1975, after graduating from California State University at Long Beach, Gawley was recommended for a job making models for Industrial Light & Magic by Joe Johnston. He is one of the few who worked on all episodes of the *Star Wars* saga. Also: *Raiders of the Lost Ark* (1981), *Star Trek II: The Wrath of Khan* (1982), *Star Trek III: The Search for Spock* (1984), *Back to the Future* (1985). Gradually taking over from Lorne Peterson, Gawley became head of ILM's model shop until it was closed.

Charles Gemora (190?–1961)
Philippine-American Sculptor, Special Makeup Creator and Gorilla Actor

Sculpted statues for the cathedral for the Lon Chaney version of *The Hunchback of Notre Dame* (1922–23). Head of the crew that built Universal's Phantom Stage and even helped Chaney with his special makeup for *The Phantom of the Opera* (1925). Also was with Chaney in *Where East Is East* (1929). At Paramount Studios he headed the makeup laboratory (Paramount's supervising makeup artist was Wally Westmore): *The War of the Worlds* (1952–53, created and played the briefly seen Martian), *The Colossus of New York* (1955), *I Married a Monster from Outer Space* (1958), *Curse of the Faceless Man* (1958), and was loaned out to Warners for James Dean's makeup in *Giant* (1956). Since the late 1920s Gemora's specialty were gorilla suits (creating a total of six at least, making them all from scratch). He was short in stature enough to play those gorillas in front of the camera himself: *The Unholy Three* (1930, sound remake starring Lon Chaney), *The Gorilla* (1930), *Ingagi* (1931), *Murders in the Rue Morgue* (1931–32, with Bela Lugosi as Dr. Mirakle and Joe Bonomo doubling Gemora on the Paris rooftops), *Blonde Venus* (1932, with Marlene Dietrich), Laurel & Hardy's *The Chimp* (1932 short) and *Swiss Miss* (1938; Gemora's name misspelled in the credits as Gamore), *The Monster and the Girl* (1941, obviously his best suit, which also ended up in *Africa Screams*, 1949), *Phantom of the Rue Morgue* (1953, in 3D, with Nick Cravat, Burt Lancaster's friend

from acrobat days, doubling in physically strenuous scenes as Gemora had recently suffered a heart attack) and *Gorilla at Large* (1954, in 3D). He never played *King Kong* and constantly denied the rumor that he had; he did play a Kong-like gorilla in the unfinished Technicolor short *Lost Island* (1934). In the 1950s, Bob Burns, a young fan eager to play gorillas himself (he eventually would), visited Gemora at his Paramount lab and was told how to build a gorilla suit:

> He had no secrets at all, he told me *everything*. He said, "You're going to need a cast of your face if you want it to fit well. That's one of the main things you gotta worry about. If you have daylight through those eyeholes, you're in trouble." That *was* one thing that put Charlie's gorilla suits above *all* the others. His eyes fit right up against the eyeholes. You could shoot an extreme close-up on his face and his eyes blended right in with the gorilla face, and it didn't look like a mask. All the other gorilla guys, if the camera got too close, you could tell there were eyeholes. But even in the early days, you could get real close on Charlie's face and it would look great…. To make his gorilla bulkier and more imposing, Charlie padded himself with kapok, the silky stuffing they used to use in sleeping bags. It's fine, it's good padding, but you *sweat* to death because *insulation* is what it is!…. Charlie was the first guy to ever come up with what he called "a water bag." He put it in the stomach of his later gorillas so there would be totally realistic movement — it moved the way a chubby person's stomach would if he was bouncing around…. Charlie also did extension arms, because gorillas' arms are a lot longer than human arms…. According to Charlie, what "makes" the performance is 90 percent body English and eye movement. He told me to do a lot of head movements and things like that; open and close your eyes; and if you want to make the gorilla look *really* mean, when you open the mouth, throw your head back so that people are now looking up *inside* the mouth. It gives the illusion that the mouth is open a lot wider than it actually is. Just tilt your head back, open your mouth as wide as you can get it, and it looks like you're really growling [Bob Burns and Tom Weaver, *Monster Kid Memories*, pp. 83–85].

Gemora's last films were *Jack the Giant Killer* (1960–61, making the gnomes and witches), *Flight of the Lost Balloon* (1961) and Marlon Brando's *One-Eyed Jack* (1961).

Wally Gentleman (1926–2001)

British-Canadian Visual Effects Designer and Cameraman

Born Yiewsley, England. Was an effects photographer on the classic *The Red Shoes* (1948). In association with Colin Low and Roman Kroner at National Film Board of Canada, he did the effects for the groundbreaking space documentary *Universe* (1959–60) and more Canadian films. Stanley Kubrick brought him to London to prepare *2001: A Space Odyssey* (1965–68): "From commencement I tried to impress upon Kubrick the necessity of having our special effects equipment set up in a sterile environment. The optical and process work on the animation stand *had* to be in a sterile environment — otherwise, every speck of dirt would become an unwanted star" (*Cinefex* number 85, p. 81). Many shots of the *Discovery*, the *Aries* and the moon bus, he revealed, were actually animated still photographs. Gentleman had to leave the production in the early spring of 1967:

> We were about nine to ten weeks into the floor production of the film when attention to an intestinal malignancy demanded exploratory surgery in the hospital. This meant that I would be at least eight months convalescent after the operation, so at that point it was agreed as a necessity to leave the production. By this time we had shot all the interiors on the *Aries* spacecraft, the *Orion* spacecraft and shooting on the space station wheel and the centrifuge was well into production. I didn't return to England after surgery in Canada [Interview in the Canadian magazine *Take One*, Vol. 1 #11, 1969].

The general impression, Ernest D. Farino writes in a mail to this author, is that Gentleman left the production because of some conflict with Kubrick or other dissatisfaction, but this is obviously not the case: He had been involved in early decisions about effects procedures, and was originally going to be the overall director of visual effects. In 1979 Gentleman did *H.G. Wells' the Shape of Things to Come*, in 1987 *Iron Warrior*. FX consultant: *One from the Heart* (1982). TV: *Wonder Woman* (1976). Ironically he died in 2001.

Buzz Gibson (1897–1985)

American Studio Technician, Key Grip and Stop-Motion Animator

Willis O'Brien assigned grip Elgen Brooks [Buzz] Gibson to work on *King Kong* (1932–33) and *The Son of Kong* (1933) and join him in three-dimensional animation. Gibson's best work was the Tyrannosaurus of *King Kong* and the agile Styracosaurus of *Son*. Supported by his brother, he tried some animation on *Mighty Joe Young* (1948–49) but was unable to turn out sufficient stop-motion and claimed that the puppets were too small.

Credited as chief technician on the low-budget films *Attack of the Puppet People* (1958, directed by Bert I. Gordon), *Invisible Invaders* (1959) and *The Four Skulls of Jonathan Drake* (1959).

According to his widow, he never liked to look back and never was interviewed about his involvement in *King Kong*. Died in Oceanside, California.

A. Arnold Gillespie (1899–1978)

American Special Effects and Miniature Unit Supervisor and Art Director

Born El Paso, Texas and educated at Columbia University, Art Students League, New York. In 1922 "Buddy" Gillespie landed a job at Paramount; the next year he went to Goldwyn Studios in Culver City. Over 200 credits as art director at Goldwyn and MGM (1925–1936), including *London After Midnight* (1927) with Lon Chaney.

He also worked in special effects (an integral part of MGM's art department, Gillespie often had to work on miniatures and hanging miniatures): *Ben-Hur* (1925), *Night Flight* (1933), *Mutiny on the Bounty* (1935), *San Francisco* (1936).

After James Basevi's departure in 1936, department head Cedric Gibbons appointed Gillespie head of the MGM special effects department which included studio tank and models as well as mechanical effects and background projection: *Tarzan Escapes* (1936), *Test Pilot* (1938), *Too Hot to Handle* (1938), *Tarzan Finds a Son!* (1939), *The Wizard of Oz* (1939), *Boom Town*

(1940), *Comrade X* (1940), *Flight Command* (1940), *Dr. Jekyll and Mr. Hyde* (1940–41), *The Bugle Sounds* (1941), *Tarzan's New York Adventure* (1942), *I Married an Angel* (1942), *Stand By for Action* (1943), *Assignment in Brittany* (1943), *Bataan* (1943), *Pilot #5* (1943), *The Man from Down Under* (1943), *A Guy Named Joe* (1943), *Song of Russia* (1943), *The Heavenly Body* (1944), *The White Cliffs of Dover* (1944), *Dragon Seed* (1944), *Kismet* (1944), *An American Romance* (1944), *Mrs. Parkington* (1944), *This Man's Navy* (1945), *Without Love* (1945), *The Clock* (1945), *Son of Lassie* (1945), *The Valley of Decision* (1945), *Our Vines Have Tender Grapes* (1945), *Yolanda and the Thief* (1945), *What Next, Corporal Hargrove?* (1945), *Up Goes Maisie* (1946), *The Green Years* (1946), *Lady in the Lake* (1947), *The Beginning or the End* (1947, mushroom atomic blast), *The Sea of Grass* (1947), *High Barbaree* (1947), *The Hacksters* (1947), *This Time for Keeps* (1947), *Desire Me* (1947), *Cass Timberlane* (1947), *High Wall* (1947), *Homecoming* (1948), *State of the Union* (1948), *On an Island with You* (1948), *Luxury Liner* (1948), *The Kissing Bandit* (1948), *Command Decision* (1948), *The Bribe* (1949), *The Secret Garden* (1949), *The Stratton Story* (1949), *Scene of the Crime* (1949), *Adam's Rib* (1949), *East Side, West Side* (1949), *Malaya* (1949), *The Magnificent Yankee* (1950), *Key to the City* (1950), *The Outriders* (1950), *Nancy Goes to Rio* (1950), *Side Street* (1950), *The Yellow Cab Man* (1950), *The Reformer and the Redhead* (1950), *Annie Get Your Gun* (1950), *Crisis* (1950), *A Lady Without Passport* (1950), *The Toast of New Orleans* (1950), *Devil's Doorway* (1950), *To Please a Lady* (1950), *Dial 1119* (1950), *Kim* (1950), *Watch the Birdie* (1950), *Pagan Love Song* (1950), *Quo Vadis* (1950–51, vast miniature of Rome burning), *Three Guys Named Mike* (1951), *Inside Straight* (1951), *Soldiers Three* (1951), *Go for Broke!* (1951), *No Questions Asked* (1951), *The Tall Target* (1951), *The Strip* (1951), *The People Against* O'Hara (1951), *Texas Carnival* (1951), *Angels in the Outfield* (1951), *Callaway Went Thataway* (1951), *The Unknown Man* (1951), *It's A Big Country* (1951), *An American in Paris* (1951), *Desperate Search* (1952), *The Light Touch* (1952), *Invitation* (1952), *Lone Star* (1952), *Just This Once* (1952), *Talk About a Stranger* (1952), *Young Man with Ideas* (1952), *Scaramouche* (1952), *Lovely to Look at* (1952), *The Sellout* (1952), *The Girl in White* (1952), *Carbine Williams* (1952), *Glory Alley* (1952), *Washington Story* (1952), *Fearless Fagan* (1952), *The Merry Widow* (1952), *Apache War Smoke* (1952), *Above and Beyond* (1952), *Million Dollar Mermaid* (1952), *The Bad and the Beautiful* (1952), *The Prisoner of Zenda* (1952), *Battle Circus* (1953), *I Love Melvin* (1953), *Jeopardy* (1953), *Bright Road* (1953), *Code Two* (1953), *Cry of the Hunted* (1953), *Scandal at Scourie* (1953), *Young Bess* (1953), *A Slight Case of Larceny* (1953), *Dream Wife* (1953), *Arena* (1953), *Ride, Vaquero!* (1953), *Latin Lovers* (1953), *All the Brothers Were Valiant* (1953, whaling scenes), *The Long, Long Trailer* (1954), *Rhapsody* (1954), *Rose Marie* (1954), *Prisoner of War* (1954), *Executive Suite* (1954), *Men of the Fighting Lady* (1954), *Valley of the Kings* (1954), *Seven Brides for Seven Brothers* (1954, avalanche), *Her Twelve Men* (1954), *Rogue Cop* (1954), *The Last Time I Saw Paris* (1954), *Green Fire* (1954), *The Prodigal* (1955), *Forbidden Planet* (1955–56, basically designed Robby the Robot and supervised spaceship miniature), *Gaby* (1956), *High Society* (1956), *The Power and the Prize* (1956), *The Opposite Sex* (1956), *The Great American Pastime* (1956), *The Wings of Eagles* (1957), *Gun Glory* (1957), *Tip on a Dead Jockey* (1957), *Until They Sail* (1957), *Jailhouse Rock* (1957), *Don't Go Near the Water* (1957), *Run Silent, Run Deep* (1958, World War II submarine epic, on loan-out for United Artists release), *Torpedo Run* (1958, submarines again), *Green Mansions* (1959), *North by Northwest* (1959), *The Wreck of Mary Deare* (1959, shipwreck), *The Adventures of Huckleberry Finn* (1960), *Bells Are Ringing* (1960), *Cimarron* (1960), *Atlantis, the Lost Continent* (1960–61), *Billy Rose's Jumbo* (1962), *The Prize* (1963). Retired after his eighth Oscar, for MGM's second *Mutiny on the Bounty* (1962–63), but came back for *The Greatest Story Ever Told* (1965, filmed on the MGM lot for United Artists release). Academy Awards for *Mrs. Miniver* (1942), *Stand by for Action* (1943), *Thirty Seconds Over Tokyo* (1944), *They Were Expendable* (1945), *Green Dolphin Street* (1947), *Plymouth Adventure* (1952) and the (however unfortunate) sea battle of numerous miniature galleys and pirate vessels of *Ben-Hur* (1959). Died in Los Angeles. An account of his work was supposed to be published after his death but was canceled.

Terry Gilliam (1940–)
American Director

In New York he worked for Harvey Kurtz-man's *Help* magazine. When he came to Britain and joined Monty Python, he not only acted and directed but did imaginative collage (cut-out) animation. For his own feature films he founded his own London effects house: *The Time Bandits* (1981), *Brazil* (1985), *The Adventures of Baron Munchausen* (1988–89, at Cinecittà Studios in Rome).

Rocco Gioffre
American Matte Artist

As a high school student in Lorain, Ohio, he did his own mattes and stop-motion puppets and got in touch with Matthew Yuricich asking for some advice: "Rocco had written me letters and I got him some things he needed, like front-projection screens. I was impressed by the fact that he was doing matte paintings right there at home. They weren't red-hot, but he was doing *all* of it. He had a damn good knowledge of this stuff. So when I got busy on *Close Encounters*, I talked to Doug Trumbull about this kid I wanted to train as a matte artist and he said sure" (*Cinefex* number 12, April 1983, p. 51). Gioffre started as Yuricich's assistant: *Close Encounters of the Third Kind* (1976–77), *Damnation Alley* (1977), *The Deer Hunter* (1978), *Star Trek: The Motion Picture* (1978–79), *Blade Runner* (1981–82). On his own he did matte paintings for *Caveman* (1980–81), *Blue Thunder* (1983), *National Lampoon's Vacation* (1983, painting of fictional theme park WalleyWorld), *D.A.R.Y.L.* (1985), *RoboCop* (1987), *RoboCop 2* (1989), *Predator 2* (1990), *Hook* (1991), *Gate II* (1992), *Cliffhanger* (1993), *Rob Roy* (1995), *What Dreams May Come* (1998), *Mystery Man* (2004). Co-founder of Dream Quest Images.

Jack R. Glass
American Photographic Effects Expert

Did visual effects for numerous low-budget shows for film and TV, some of them sci-fi: *Bad Men of Tombstone* (1949), *Massacre River* (1949), *Deputy Marshal* (1949), *Two Lost Worlds* (1950), *Tales of Robin Hood* (1951), *The Man from Planet X* (1951), *Jack and the Beanstalk* (1952), *Project Moon Base* (1953), *Captain Scarface* (1953), *The Magnetic Monster* (1953), *Riders to the Stars* (1954), *Superman's Peril* (1954), *Superman in Scotland Yard* (1954), *Superman Flies Again* (1954), *Superman and the Jungle Devil* (1954), *Born in Freedom: The Story of Colonel Drake* (1955), *The Naked Dawn* (1955), *The Lost Missile* (1958), *Go, Johnny, Go!* (1959). TV series and specials: *Racket Squad* (1950), *The Abbott and Costello Show* (1952), *Adventures of Superman* (1952), *Letter to Loretta* (1953), *The Public Defender* (1954), *Rocky Jones, Space Ranger* (1954), *Duel in Space* (1954), *Crash of Moons* (1954), *Renegade Satellite* (1956), *Forbidden Moon* (1956), *The Cold Sun* (1956), *Blast Off* (1956), *Beyond the Moon* (1956), *The Robot of Regalio* (1956), *Menace from Outer Space* (1956), *Jack the Ripper* (1958), *The Veil* (1958), *Destination Nightmare* (1958).

Dennis Glouner
American Matte Cinematographer

Son of Donald C. Glouner. Served as matte photographer on several of Albert Whitlock's projects: *Airport '77* (1977), *MacArthur* (1977), *The Wiz* (1978), *The Prisoner of Zenda* (1979), *History of the World, Part I* (1981), *Heartbeeps* (1981), *Cat People* (1982), *Dune* (1984), *Red Sonja* (1985).

Donald C. Glouner (1913–1994)
American Visual Effects Cinematographer

Born in Ronks, Pennsylvania. Brother of cinematographer Martin Glouner, whose career was terminated by blindness in 1933. Associated with Lawrence Butler in May 1944 and photographed matte paintings and other tricks for the effects department of Columbia Pictures: *Tonight and Every Night* (1945), *My Name Is Julia Ross* (1945), *A Thousand and One Nights* (1945), *Gilda* (1946), *The Walls Came Tumbling Down* (1947), *The Jolson Story* (1946), *The Swordsman* (1948), *The Loves of Carmen* (1948), *To the Ends of the Earth* (1948; for that production he traveled abroad to shoot process plates in several foreign countries), *The Wreck of the Hesperus* (1948), *The Sign of the*

Ram (1948), *Song of India* (1949), *Rogues of Sherwood Forest* (1950), *Father Is a Bachelor* (1950), *Lorna Doone* (1951), *The Petty Girl* (1951), *The Son of Dr. Jekyll* (1951, transforming Louis Hayward from Jekyll to Hyde), *The 7th Voyage of Sinbad* (1957–58, genie coming out of the lamp). With Butler, head of the department, he founded Butler-Glouner, Inc.: *13 Ghosts* (1960, Illusion-O sequences in Ectoplasmic Color), *Master of the World* (1960–61), Edgar Allan Poe features for American International Pictures, *The Guns of Navarone* (1961, additional effects), *Marooned* (1969), *Fools' Parade* (1971), *The Dunwich Horror* (1970), *The Life and Times of Judge Roy Bean* (1972), *Lost Horizon* (1972–73). In April 1973 the partners sold Butler-Glouner and retired. Donald was the uncle of cinematographer Richard Glouner and father of effects cameraman Dennis Glouner.

Bert I. Gordon (1922–)

American Director

Born in Kenosha, Wisconsin, Bert Ira Gordon was eight or nine years old when he got a film camera and achieved some ghostly effects with it, such as stop tricks to make people appear and disappear. Attended University of Wisconsin. Started in commercials, industrial films and television, including some animation. Came to Hollywood and made a name in low-budget horror and special effects films for American International Pictures, Allied Artists, United Artists, Embassy Pictures and other companies: *Serpent Island* (1954, made in 16mm for $18,000), *King Dinosaur* (1955), *Beginning of the End* (1957), *The Cyclops* (1957), *The Amazing Colossal Man* (1957), *War of the Colossal Beast* (1958), *Earth vs the Spider* (1958), *Attack of the Puppet People* (1958), *The Boy and the Pirates* (1960, the last film made with ship miniatures at Fox's Lake Sersen) and *The Magic Sword* (1962), this, too, filmed on the 20th Century–Fox lot. (Gordon interviewed by Marty McKee: "I built a big dragon. On the screen, he was like 25 feet tall, but in actuality, it was about 11 feet tall. I couldn't make it any smaller, because otherwise the fire wouldn't look real. I wanted to use real fire. So I had Fox built that, their effects department. And then we shot real fire out.")

Other credits: *Village of the Giants* (1965), *The Food of the Gods* (1976), *Empire of the Ants* (1977).

James B. Gordon

American Visual Effects Cinematographer

Supervised camera effects at 20th Century–Fox for Fred Sersen, Ray Kellogg and L.B. Abbott: *A Yank in the R.A.F.* (1941), *The Day the Earth Stood Still* (1951), *The Robe* (1953, first CinemaScope picture), *Hell and High Water* (1954), *The Rains of Ranchipur* (1955), *The Fly* (1958), *Journey to the Center of the Earth* (1959), *The Blue Angel* (1959), *From the Terrace* (1960) and many more. When work at 20th became scarce, he accepted independent work as 3D consultant for *The Mask* (1961), a Canadian picture. Producer Julian Roffman: "I took over the optical effects department at 20th Century–Fox for two months because they weren't busy and they were happy to have some sucker come in and pay them just to keep the doors open" (*Filmfax* no. 25). Then Gordon joined Film Effects of Hollywood as director of photography: *It's a Mad Mad Mad Mad World* (1962–63), *The Great Race* (1965), *Hawaii* (1965), *What Did You Do in the War, Daddy?* (1966), *Airport* (1970).

Graphic Films

American Animation Studio

Founded by Disney veteran Lester Novros, this Hollywood company did many documentaries for NASA, *To the Moon and Beyond* in Cinerama and preproduction work for Stanley Kubrick's *2001: A Space Odyssey* (1965–68). Also early IMAX films. Alumni of Graphic Films include: Douglas Trumbull, Con Pederson, John Dykstra, Robert Abel, Colin J. Cantwell.

Robert Greenberg and Richard Greenberg

American Optical Effects Consultants

In 1977 they founded R/Greenberg Associates and specialized in commercials. Also did title sequences for *Superman* (1977–78) and *Alien* (1978–79), optical effects for *Xanadu* (1980) and

Woody Allen's *Zelig* (1983). Turned to computer graphics as early as 1981.

Loyal C. Griggs (1906–1978)
American Director of Photography, Second Unit and Visual Effects Cinematographer

Born in Michigan, he entered the movie industry in the mid–1920s. At Paramount he photographed *The Bridges at Toko-Ri* (1954–55) and Cecil B. DeMille's *The Ten Commandments* (1953–56). Assisted on special effects as well as process and transparency photography mainly for Paramount Pictures, but also for 20th Century-Fox and MGM: *A Farewell to Arms* (1932), *Madame Butterfly* (1932), *The Eagle and the Hawk* (1933), *International House* (1933), *Gambling Ship* (1933), *College Humor* (1933), *Florida Special* (1936), *San Francisco* (1936), *Waikiki Wedding* (1937), *Men with Wings* (1938), *Spawn of the North* (1938), *Salty O'Rourke* (1945), *Love Letters* (1945), *Kitty* (1945), *Hold That Blonde* (1945), *The Lost Weekend* (1945), *Masquerade in Mexico* (1945), *Road to Utopia* (1946), *To Each His Own* (1946), *The Bride Wore Boots* (1946), *O.S.S.* (1946), *Our Hearts Were Growing Up* (1946), *The Searching Wind* (1946), *Monsieur Beaucaire* (1946), *Ladies' Man* (1947), *The Perfect Marriage* (1947), *Easy Come, Easy Go* (1947), *Golden Earrings* (1947), *Woman on the Run* (1950), *A Place in the Sun* (1951), *Detective Story* (1951), *My Son John* (1952), *The Robe* (1953, first CinemaScope picture), *Hot Spell* (1958). Second unit: *The Naked Jungle* (1954), *Vertigo* (1958), *Airport* (1970).

Paul A. Grimm (1891–1974)
German-American Matte Artist

Born in King Williams Town, South Africa, the son of German parents, Grimm came to the U.S. at age seven. He won scholarship in Rochester, New York, for a study at the Royal Academy in Düsseldorf. Went to Hollywood in 1919 to paint backdrops. Glass paintings for early pictures at Warner Bros. (Rin Tin Tin films such as *Where the North Begins* in 1923, photographed by Vernon Walker) and First National (*Noah's Ark*, 1929). Retired from the film business in 1932 and focused entirely on portraits and landscapes. Died in Palm Springs.

Joachim Grüninger (1962–)
German Miniature Supervisor

Born in Stuttgart, he started with Roland Emmerich on *Joey* (U.S.: *Making Contact*, 1984–86) and *Hollywood Monster* (1987), then founded his own company Magicom/Magicmove in Munich: *The High Crusade* (1993–94), *The Patriot* (1996–97), *An American Werewolf in Paris* (1997), *Anatomie* (2000), *Otto—Der Katastrofenfilm* (2000), *Die Wolke* (2005–2006).

George Gunn
British Optical Technician

Worked at Technicolor London. Developed Gunnshot traveling matte process. For *The Red Shoes* (1948) he matted a shot of Moira Shearer suspended on wires into a flat glass water tank colored by chemicals to show the actress dancing through space.

Erich Günther (1923–)
German Stop-Motion and Effects Cinematographer

Born in Gittersee near Dresden, where he photographed numerous puppet films for the Trickfilmstudio as well as director Kurt Weiler. Was involved in some animation for DEFA's sci-fi epic *Der schweigende Stern* (*First Spaceship on Venus*, 1959) and *Hans Röckle und der Teufel* (1974) but actually entered East-German (G.D.R.) Babelsberg Studios in 1977 for a children's film, *Konzert für Bratpfanne und Orchester*, that involved a stop-motion sequence, and even more ambitious composite shots of live-action and stop-motion for *Ein Schneemann für Afrika*, made the same year. He continued there with two young colleagues, animator Heiko Ebert and assistant cameraman Tony Loeser: *Der Prinz hinter den sieben Meeren* (1982), *Moritz in der Litfasssäule* (1982–83), *Die Geschichte vom goldenen Taler* (1984–85, TV), *Das Schulgespenst* (1985–86), *Der Froschkönig* (1988, stop-motion frog), *Der Drache Daniel* (1988–89). For composite shots he invented a special matte system

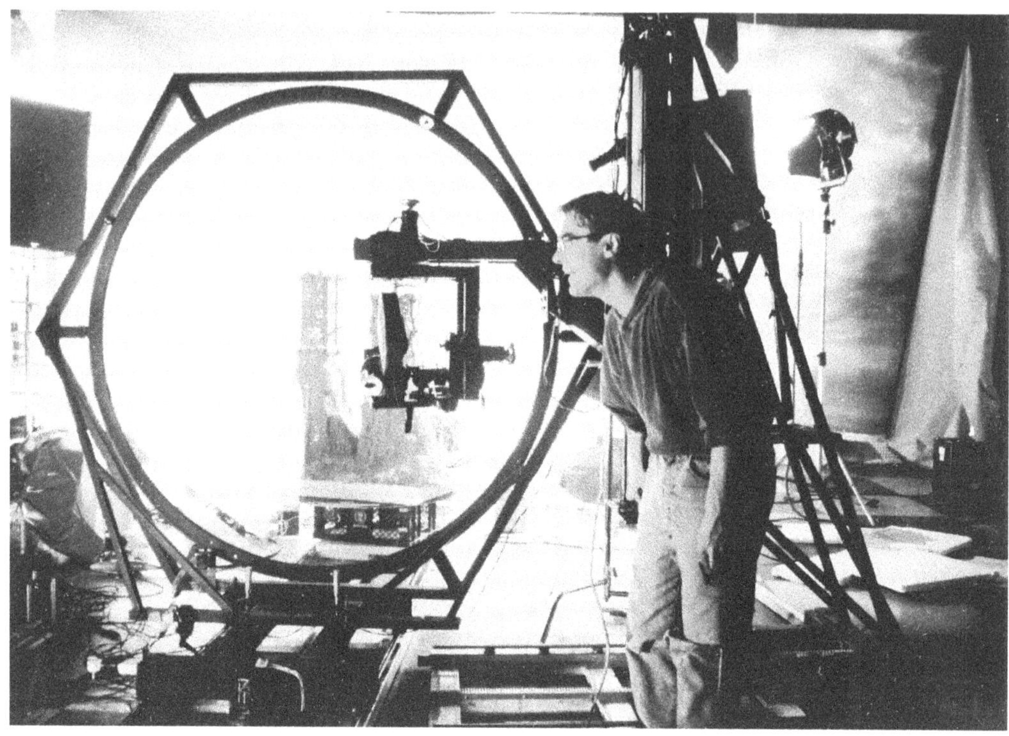

Behind the camera of *The High Crusade* (1994): motion control cinematographer Karl-Heinz Christmann (courtesy Karl-Heinz Christmann and Deutsche Kinemathek Berlin).

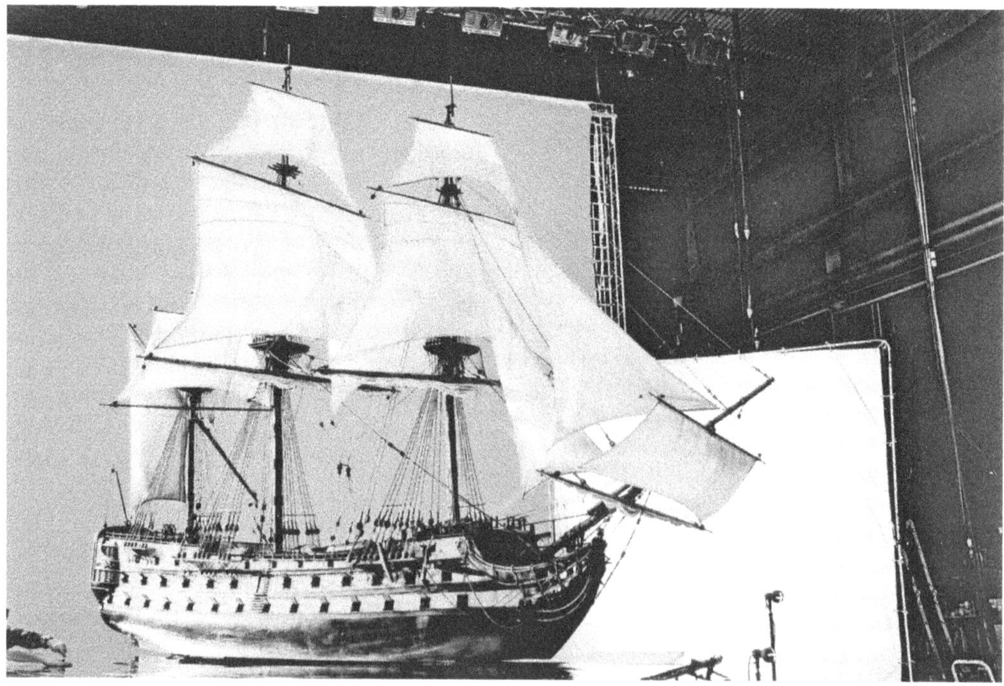

Above and following page: Joachim Grüninger model ships in front of a green screen for the Roland Emmerich production *The Patriot* (2000) (courtesy Joachim Grüninger and Deutsche Kinemathek Berlin).

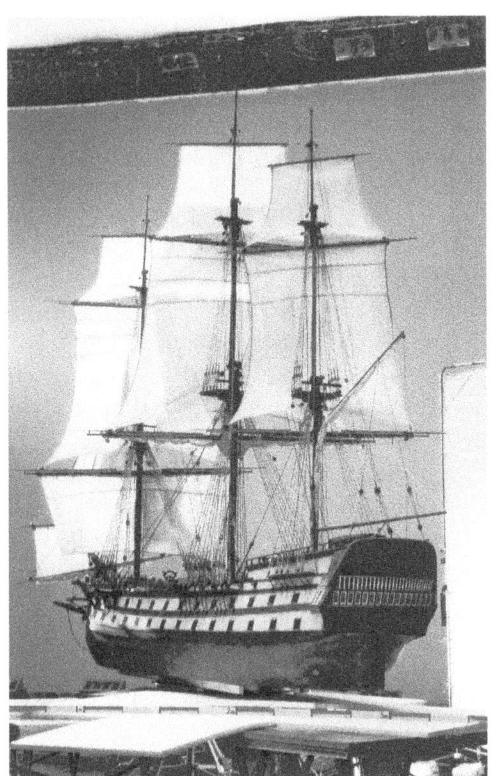

with a mirror and a setup of two cameras. After German reunification, his services were still called for: *Zirri—Das Wolkenschaf* (1992–93), *Novalis—Die blaue Blume* (1993), *Kondom des Grauens* (1996), and the Planet B series *Detective Lovelorn—The Antman—Mask under Mask* (2000–2002).

Walter G. Hall

British-American Art Director

Worked on D. W. Griffith's *Intolerance*'s Babylonian sets in 1916. Developed and patented Hall Trick (in 1921): In front of the camera lens, cutouts and drawings were positioned to fill in the life-size sets.

Sol Halperin (1902–1977)

American Process Cinematographer

Brother of director Victor Halperin (*White Zombie*). Sometimes credited as Sol Halprin. Uncle of cinematographer Richard H. Kline. Had a lifelong association with Fox Studios. Operated Grandeur camera on *The Big Trail* (1930).

For many years he was in charge of transparencies and background photography: *Dante's Inferno* (1935), *Think Fast, Mr. Moto* (1937), *Stanley and Livingstone* (1939), *The Rains Come* (1939), *A Yank in the R.A.F.* (1941), *Lifeboat* (1944), *Captain Eddie* (1945), *Sentimental Journey* (1946). 3D technology: *Inferno* (1953), *Gorilla at Large* (1954).

Edwin Hammeras (1902–????)

American Effects and Process Photographer

Born in Minneapolis, Minnesota, the younger brother of cinematographer Ralph Hammeras was educated (grade school and high school) in Los Angeles. Started at Realart, film laboratory, immediately on leaving school, remaining two years. Assistant cameraman one year, then one year in title department at Realart, photographing titles. Two years at Ince Studio, photographing trick work. Eventually became cameraman at

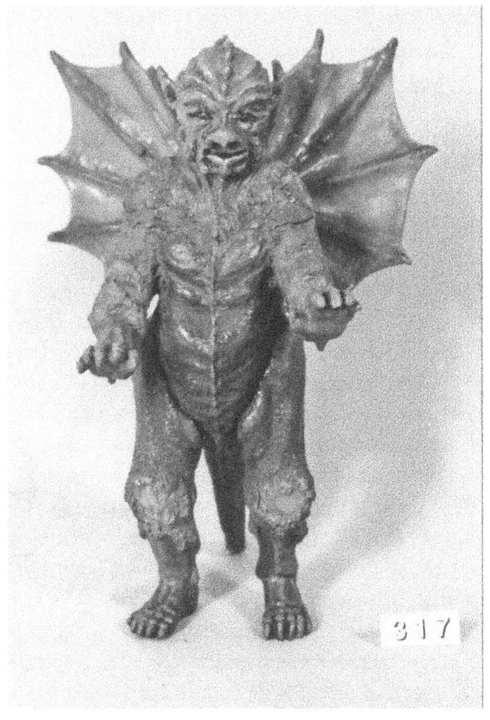

Der Drache Daniel, model of a very human-like, winged dragon for a DEFA children's film produced at Babelsberg Studios in 1989. On the Babelsberg lot they used the Schüfftan process up until German reunification (courtesy Rolf Giesen Collection, Deutsche Kinemathek Berlin).

First National East and West Coast Studios, photographing miniatures, matte and glass shots, double exposures, etc. Together with his brother and Willis O'Brien he created camera effects for Arthur Conan Doyle's dinosaur epic *The Lost World* (1924–25). Matte photography: *The Private Life of Helen of Troy* (1926). Six years at Fox assisting his brother on *Just Imagine* (1929–30), *Helldorado* (1935), *Under Two Flags* (1936) and other notable productions. Spent one year in Europe photographing background scenes for many productions, and for the stock film library of the studio. Subsequently at 20th Century–Fox involved in *Laura* (1944), *A Tree Grows in Brooklyn* (1945) and *The Shocking Miss Pilgrim* (1947). In the 1960s, according to Jim Danforth, he was process projectionist for Carroll L. Shepphird at MGM Studios in Culver City.

Ralph Oscar Hammeras
(1894–1970)

American Director of Photography, Miniature Photographer and Matte Artist

Ralph Oscar Hammeras was born in Minneapolis, Minnesota; the family is of Norwegian origin. Attended Seward grade school as far as the third grade, then accompanied his sick mother and a brother to Norway where he continued his education for three years. At sixteen he was educated at Society of Fine Arts of Minneapolis where he had his first formal training in the arts. Interior decorator in Minneapolis and later Seattle. At eighteen he found a mentor in the muralist Edwin H. Blaisfield. He did murals and decorated buildings in St. Paul, Minnesota, Sioux Falls, South Dakota and Seattle, Washington. Attended John Butler Arts Institute of Seattle, College of Fine Arts — University of Southern California, Occidental College — Los Angeles. Entered motion pictures in June 1915 as scenic artist with Realart as well as Hobart Bosworth and Pallas Pictures Corp. Became an expert in illustrating art-titles. Learned film photography from James O. Taylor while he did title art, then (starting with *Skin Deep*, a Milton Sills picture) photographed miniatures and glass shots for Thomas Ince (Triangle), Famous Players Lasky, Joseph M. Schenck, Selznick, and Mike

Levee (1920–1924). Between 1924 and 1929 he supervised trick shots for First National East and West Coast Studios in New York and Burbank: *The Lost World* (1924–25, with Willis O'Brien animating dinosaurs), *Clothes Make the Pirate* (1925), *The Patent Leather Kid* (1927). Academy Award nomination for Technical Effects in 1928: *The Private Life of Helen of Troy* (1927, directed by Alexander Korda). (Hammeras held a patent for glass shots: #1,540,213.) When the Burbank lot was sold to Warners, Hammeras left for Fox Studios where he and his associate George J. Teague not invented but at least originated background projection:

> [I]t was on [1929's *Divine Lady*] that I got the idea for a new photographic method that would eliminate a lot of locations with the stars and cast, and also allowed fine automobile traveling shots to be made on stage. It came about one afternoon as I was running the daily rushes with [director Frank] Lloyd. He had selected a scene from high up in the hills of Naples, Italy, from the stock library — but he wasn't satisfied with it entirely, as he wanted a foreground tree with hanging branches to frame the whole scene. As I sat there watching, Mr. Lloyd took a cane he was carrying and walked up to the screen, pointing out on the projected scene with his cane just where he wanted me to paint the tree he had in mind. As he stood in front of the screen, the projector lighted him up and he looked as though he was standing there in the picture overlooking Naples. He blended right into the scene. I was struck with the thought that right on our own stages in the studio, I could put any of the stars in any city or town in the world — maybe have them go up the elevator of the Eiffel Tower, or have them stand at the rail of an ocean liner overlooking a stormy sea, without any danger to them [*Cinefex* number 15, p. 59].

At Fox he was involved in the making of *As Good as Married* (1929), *The Sky Hawk* (1929), *Just Imagine* (1929–30, a second Academy Award nomination for creating 1980 New York City in a huge miniature complete with futuristic aircraft flown above the streets on wires), *Body and Soul* (1931), *A Connecticut Yankee* (1931), *Chandu the Magician* (1932), *Helldorado* (1935), *Way Down East* (Henry King's 1935 remake of D.W. Griffith's ice floe sequence), *Dante's Inferno* (1935, a ten-minute tour through the depths of Hell). At 20th Century–Fox: *Ali Baba Goes to Town* (1936), *In Old Chicago* (1938), *Suez* (1938), *Four Men and a Prayer* (1938). In 1940 he left

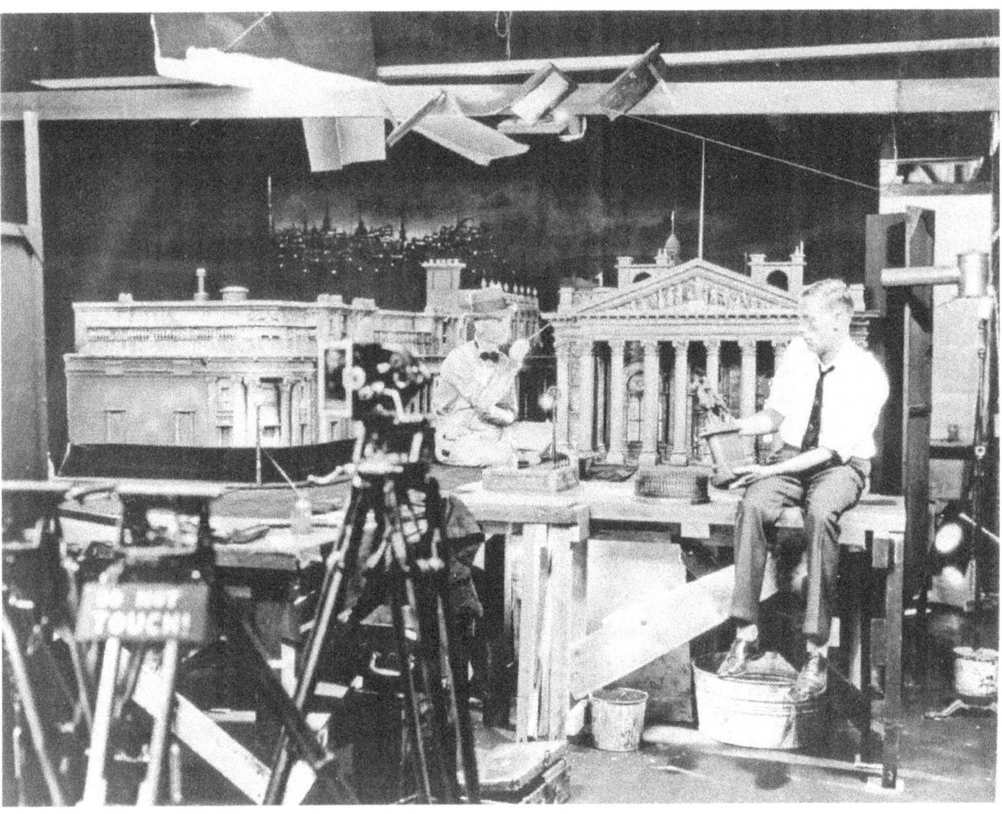

The Lost World's miniatures as supervised by Ralph Hammeras (courtesy Deutsche Kinemathek Berlin).

Fox and joined producer Mario Castegnaro under the Techniprocess and Special Effects Corporation banner to create visual dramatizations of popular songs for jukeboxes. Then he did *The Great Dictator* (1940) for Charles Chaplin. Returned to 20th Century–Fox in the early 1940s as assistant to Fred Sersen and his successor Ray Kellogg, photographing miniatures: *How Green Was My Valley* (1941), *A Yank in the R.A.F.* (1941), *Belle Starr* (1941), *Charley's Aunt* (1941), *This Above All* (1942), *Jitterbugs* (1943), *The Dancing Masters* (1943), *Winged Victory* (1944), *The Keys of the Kingdom* (1944), *Where Do We Go from Here?* (1945), *Captain Eddie* (1945), *A Bell for Adano* (1945), *Billy Rose's Diamond Horseshoe* (1946), *The Dolly Sisters* (1945), *Dragonwyck* (1946), *Anna and the King of Siam* (1946), *Deep Waters* (1948, Academy Award nomination for sea storm sequence), *The Robe* (1953, first CinemaScope picture). Loaned out with other Fox personnel to Walt Disney Productions to super-

vise *Nautilus* miniature photography for *20000 Leagues Under the Sea* (1953–54), the second CinemaScope picture to go into production. *Journey to the Center of the Earth* (1959) was Hammeras' next Jules Verne feature. In between he did freelance jobs on low-budget productions: silly outer space giant turkey effects for Columbia's *The Giant Claw* (1956–57), filmed in Mexico, and the Ray Kellogg-directed *The Giant Gila Monster* (1959) and *My Dog, Buddy* (1960). Retired from the business after 45 years with some miniature airplane photography for *The Longest Day* (1962) and a matte painting of ancient Rome for *Cleopatra* in 1963. In *International Photographer*, June 1935, Hammeras reviewed his miniature work under the title "An American cameraman in American studios." In his leisure time he made painting trips to the High Sierras and the desert between Palm Springs and Banning.

Robert [Bob] Hansard

American Process Specialist

Started Hansard Process Company. Worked on *One Too Many* (1950), *Master of the World* (1960–61), *The Beach Girls and the Monster* (1965). His son Bill later took over what became a family business.

William [Bill] Hansard

American Process Specialist

The son of Bob Hansard, he supervised rear screen and front projection service: *The Time Travelers* (1964), *Thunder Alley* (1967), *Skyjacket* (1972), *The Neptune Factor* (1973), *Sleeper* (1973), *Breakheart Pass* (1975), *Silver Streak* (1976), *Black Sunday* (1977), *Exorcist II: The Heretic* (1977), *New York, New York* (1977), *The Manitou* (1977–78), *Coma* (1978), *Damien: Omen II* (1978), *Star Trek: the Motion Picture* (1978–79), *Blow Out* (1981), *Buddy Buddy* (1981), *One from the Heart* (1982), *Annie* (1982), *Dead Men Don't Wear Plaid* (1982), *Zelig* (1983), *Scarface* (1983), *Unfaithfully Yours* (1984), *Gremlins* (1984), *Falling in Love* (1984), *Rainbow War* (1985), *Explorers* (1985), *The Boy Who Could Fly* (1986), *Innerspace* (1986–87), *Bird* (1988), *Christmas Vacation* (1989), *Narrow Margin* (1990), *Hudson Hawk* (1991), *Just a Cause* (1995), *Beyond Rangoon* (1995), *The Tuskegee Airmen* (1995), *Fly Away Home* (1996), *Deconstructing Harry* (1997), *The Game* (1997), *The Odd Couple II* (1998), *Lethal Weapon 4* (1998), *The Parent Trap* (1998), *Blast from the Past* (1999), *In the Bedroom* (2001), *Kill Bill: Vol. 1* (2003), *Kill Bill: Vol. 2* (2004).

Henry Harris

(1899–1971)

British Special Effects Cinematographer

Born London, he was a cameraman beginning in the 1920s. In the early 1940s he focused on photographing effects: *Atlantic Ferry* (1941), *This Was Paris* (1942), *Flying Fortress* (1942), *Sabotage Agent* (1943). Participated in Rank's special effects program: *A Matter of Life and Death* (U.S.: *Stairway to Heaven*, 1946), *Fame Is the Spur* (1947), *Uncle Silas* (1947), *Hamlet* (1948, directed by Laurence Olivier). With Bill Warrington on *Quatermass 2* (U.S.: *Enemy from Space*, 1957).

Fred Harryhausen (18??–1964?)

American Machinist

His son Ray asked him to machine the armatures for most of his (Ray's) films, including the awesome skeletons for *The 7th Voyage of Sinbad* (1957–58) and *Jason and the Argonauts* (1961–63). The last film he worked on was *First Men in the Moon* in 1963–64. Died in Los Angeles.

Ray Harryhausen (1920–)

American Stop-Motion Animator and Creator of Visual Effects

Born in Los Angeles, the son of Fred Harryhausen and his wife Martha born Reske. Family roots of both parents lead to Germany where

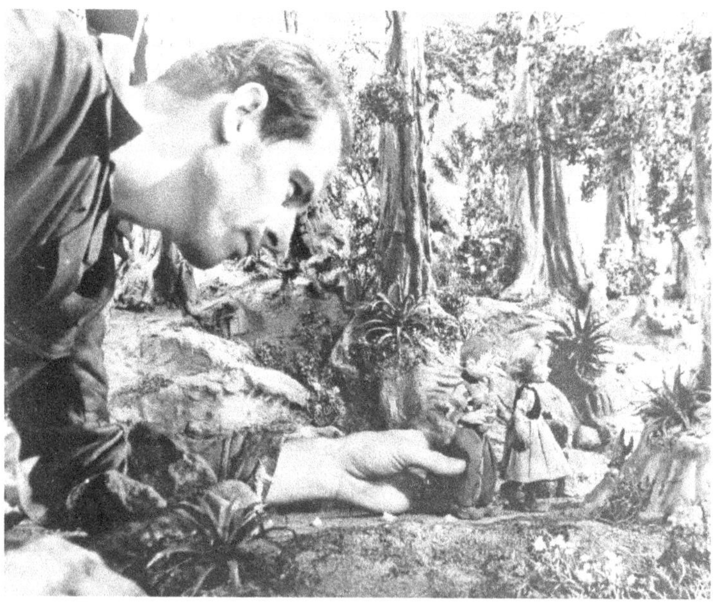

A young Ray Harryhausen at work on one of his fairy tales (courtesy Ray Harryhausen and Deutsche Kinemathek Berlin).

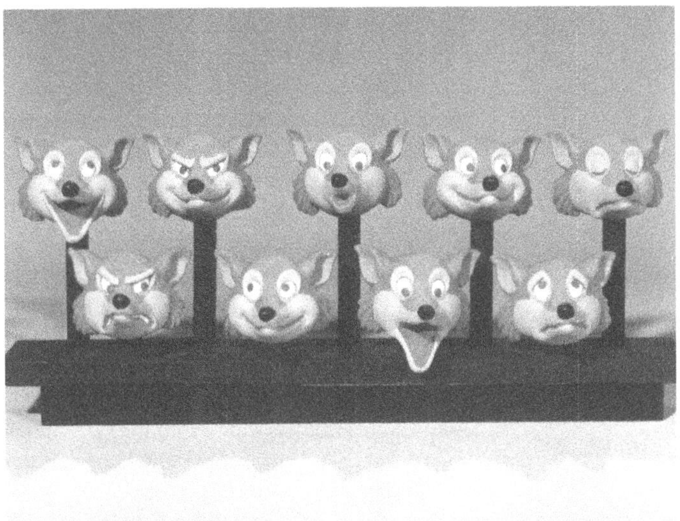

Ray Harryhausen became the first visual effects artist known to a larger audience for his unique achievements in stop-motion animation. He started experimenting in his garage in the late 1930s before becoming a professional animator with George Pal and Willis O'Brien. Replacement heads of the Fox character from *The Tortoise and the Hare* (courtesy Ray and Diana Harryhausen Collection as displayed by Deutsche Kinemathek Berlin).

Harriehausen is a common name. It is supposed that the Harriehausens came from the area of Hanover. Raymond Frederick (Ray) Harryhausen attended Audubon Junior High School and Manual Arts High School. In his youth he was inspired by the La Brea dinosaur tar pits of Los Angeles and by seeing the dinosaur movies *The Lost World* and *King Kong*; he saw the latter at Grauman's Chinese Theatre when he was 12. "I have never been the same since," he confessed later. "I came out of the theatre stunned and haunted. I knew [the creatures inhabiting Skull Island] couldn't be real — although maybe in the back of my mind I hoped they were." Gradually he found out about the stop-motion process

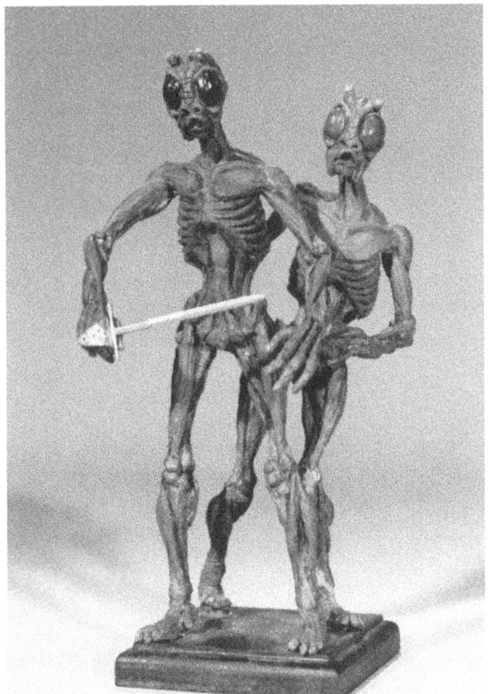

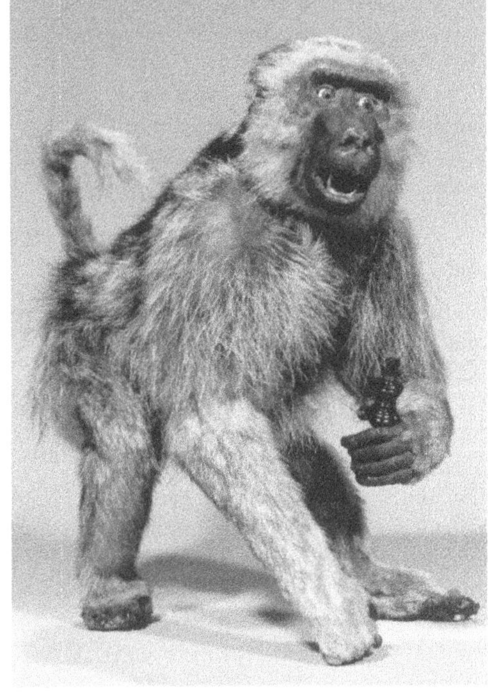

Left: The ghouls from *Sinbad and the Eye of the Tiger*; *right:* the baboon from *Sinbad and the Eye of the Tiger* (both courtesy Ray and Diana Harryhausen Collection as displayed by Deutsche Kinemathek Berlin).

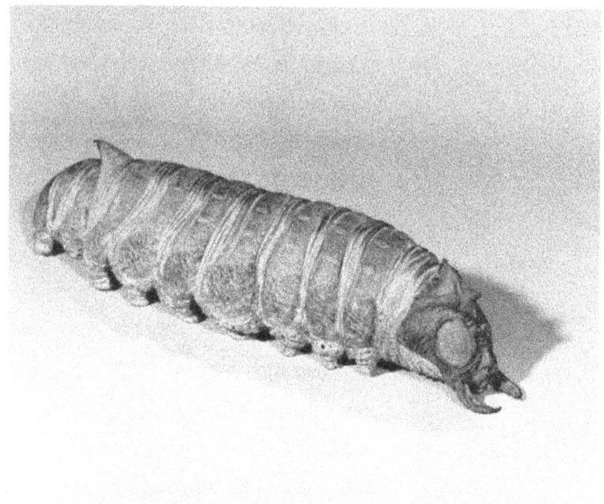

The Moon Calf from *First Men in the Moon*.

of animation, began experimenting in 16mm, attended exhibitions with the models of Willis O'Brien on display and met the master animator in 1939 while O'Brien was preparing his ill-fated *War Eagles* at MGM. The same year, Harryhausen enrolled at the Los Angeles City College and studied dramatics, photography and sculpture as well as art direction and film at the University of Southern California. First professional job was with George Pal Productions and the *Puppetoons* in 1940: *Western Daze, Dipsy Gypsy, Hoola Boola, The Gay Knighties, Jasper and the Watermelons, Sky Princess, Jasper and the Haunted House, Tulips Shall Grow*, and *Bravo, Mr. Strauss*. On *Jasper's Choo-Choo*, Ray had the pleasure of jointly animating with O'Brien, who left the studio after a short while. But they stayed in touch. Ray visited O'Brien when he (O'Brien) was trying to sell *Gwangi* to RKO. In 1942, during the war, Harryhausen was drafted into the U.S. Army and, due to his animation skills, was assigned to Frank Capra's Army Signal Corps assisting cinematographer Joseph Biroc and doing training films. Right after the war, Harryhausen, who always wanted to see the pyramids of Chichen Itza, "took a Greyhound bus down to Miami, then a plane over to Cuba. Then I flew to the Yucatan Peninsula, going through

Chichen Itza and Ouschmal." When he returned to Hollywood he set up a small studio in his garage and was going to do some shorts on his own again. At that time he received a phone call from O'Brien, who asked him to come to RKO and assist him on *Mighty Joe Young* (1946–49). It turned out that Ray was the fastest and best of all animators, and so he did about 85 percent of the stop-frame animation. *Mighty Joe Young* got O'Brien an Academy Award in 1950. Harryhausen remained with O'Brien and helped him and producer Jesse Lasky with a project called *Valley of the Mist*. A lifelong friendship with Lasky's son, Jesse Jr., who wrote the screenplay, evolved but, alas, no production. Harryhausen left O'Brien; they only collaborated once more, on the dinosaur prologue of Irwin Allen's Technicolor documentary *The Animal World* in 1956. Harryhausen did several 16mm fairy-tale shorts and was contracted to do stop-motion work for the low-budget *The Beast from 20,000 Fathoms* in 1952. As he knew that he couldn't use O'Brien's expensive animation-in-depth technique which called for extensive miniature sets, backdrops, foreground glasses

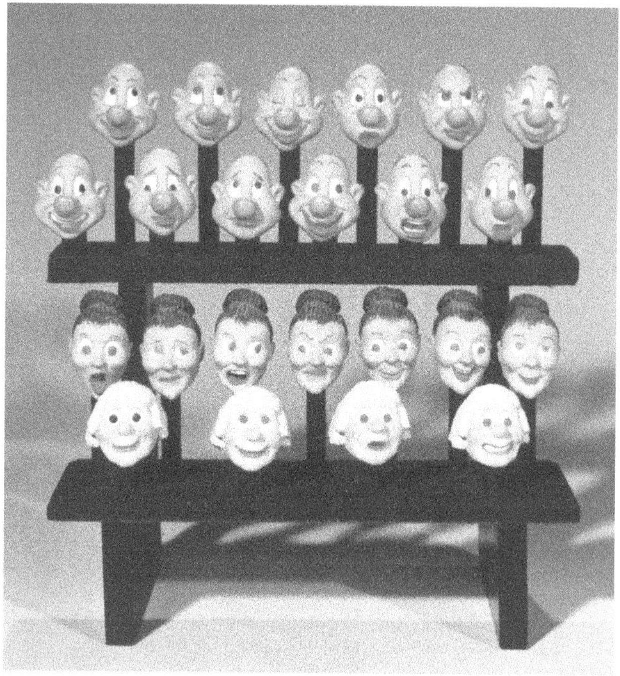

A set of replacement "Mother Goose Stories" heads (both courtesy Ray and Diana Harryhausen Collection as displayed by Deutsche Kinemathek Berlin).

and miniature projection, he asked a low price and the additional money to buy necessary equipment (one of the miniature rear process projectors built by Harry Cunningham for *Mighty Joe Young*). With that he devised stop-frame plates that would sandwich by split screen the stop-motion model of a "Rhedosaurus" right into the picture. After that an army friend recommended Harryhausen to another B picture producer, Charles H. Schneer, who was looking for someone to create a giant octopus for the Sam Katzman feature *It Came from Beneath the Sea* (1954–55). Schneer became the producer for most of Ray's subsequent feature films: *Earth vs. the Flying Saucers* (1955–56), *20 Million Miles to Earth* (1956–57, with locations shifted from Chicago to Rome) and the color fantasy classic *The 7th Voyage of Sinbad* (1957–58) with fresh locations found in Spain. When Schneer and Harryhausen were offered a *Gulliver* project by Jack Sher, they decided to go to Britain as Hollywood lacked sufficient traveling matte techniques for color process. At Rank, Victor Margutti had developed the yellow screen process which was used extensively on *The 3 Worlds of Gulliver* (1959–60). Harryhausen settled and married (Diana Livingstone) in Britain and did *Mysterious Island* (1961–62) from a leftover Columbia adaptation of Jules Verne's work (which he

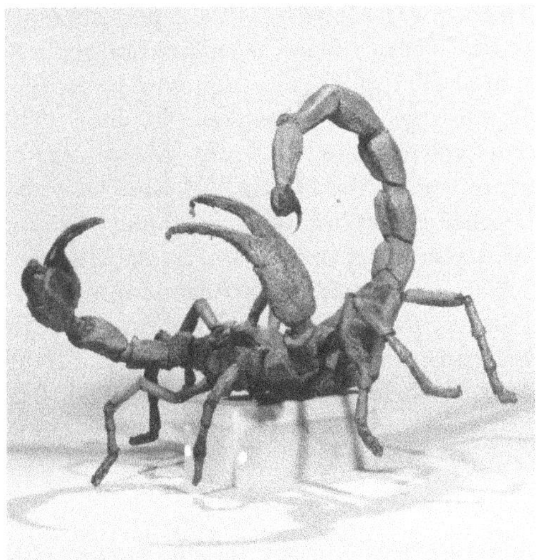

Replacement heads of the Hare character from *The Tortoise and the Hare*.

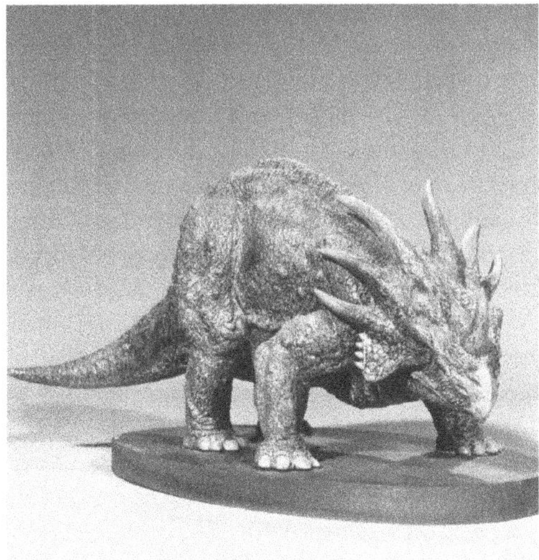

Left: One of the three scorpion models from *Clash of the Titans*; *right:* the Styracosaurus mock-up from *The Valley of Gwangi* (all three courtesy Ray and Diana Harryhausen Collection as displayed by Deutsche Kinemathek Berlin).

enriched with some giant creatures), *Jason and the Argonauts* (1962–63, with the seven skeletons coming to life his best animation), *First Men in the Moon* (1964–65), *One Million Years B.C.* (1965–66, for Hammer Films), *The Valley of Gwangi* (1967–69, O'Brien's aborted project), *The Golden Voyage of Sinbad* (1972–73), *Sinbad and the Eye of the Tiger* (1976–77), and *Clash of the Titans* (1979–80, adapting the myth of Perseus and Medusa). In 1992 Harryhausen received the Gordon A. Sawyer Award from the Academy of Motion Picture Arts and Sciences and a star on Hollywood Boulevard.

Byron Haskin (1899–1984)

American Cinematographer, Special Effects Supervisor and Director

Born in Portland, Oregon, he attended the University of California at Berkeley. He was a cartoonist for the *San Francisco Daily News* and later an advertising man, traveling and taking industrial pictures. His screen career began as cameraman for Pathe and International Newsreel. In 1920 he worked as assistant director with Selznick and assistant cameraman for films directed by Marshall Neilan, Sidney Franklin and Raoul Walsh. In 1923 he was first cameraman for Alan Holubar and at Warner Bros. the favorite cinematographer of John Barrymore. With Barrymore he did *Don Juan* (1926) and others. For director Roy Del Ruth he photographed *Wolf's Clothing* (1927) which involved a montage of trick shots. In 1926 he directed *Ginsberg the Great* and *the Siren*. In the early 1930s he joined the special effects department (*42nd Street*, 1932–33; *As the Earth Turns*, 1934; Max Reinhardt-William Dieterle's *A Midsummer Night's Dream*, 1935). When Fred W. Jackman left, Haskin became head of the entire department: *Slim* (1937), *Submarine D-1* (1937), *The Dawn Patrol* (1938), *The Roaring Twenties* (1939), *We Are Not Alone* (1939), *The Private Lives of Elizabeth and Essex* (1939), *The Sea Hawk* (1940), *Castle on the Hudson* (1940), *Torrid Zone* (1940), *Brother Orchid* (1940), *They Drive by Night* (1940), *City for Conquest* (1940), *A Dispatch from Reuter's* (1940), *The Sea Wolf* (1940–41), *High Sierra* (1941), *Arsenic and Old Lace* (1941–44),

Desperate Journey (1942), *Captains of the Clouds* (1942, directing second unit for Michael Curtiz, involving Hudson bombers, Hurricanes, and shots of convoys leaving the harbor), *Action in the North Atlantic* (1943), *Mission to Moscow* (1943). Helped to design triple background process work. According to Haskin, the Warner Bros. special effects department was virtually a studio within a studio. "Almost every department of the studio had its counterpart in the special effects organization. We had our own designers, art directors, and set-building facilities, our own camera and electrical equipment, personnel and stage crews generally. The department also had its own film laboratory, cutting facilities, business office and even its own writers."

In the late 1940s Haskin joined former Warner producer Hal B. Wallis at Paramount and became a film director, repeatedly helming sfx productions: George Pal's *The War of the Worlds* (1952–53), *The Naked Jungle* (1954) and *Conquest of Space* (1955). Others include *From the Earth to the Moon* (1958), the Munich-made *Captain Sindbad* (1962–63), for which he did many effects in-camera himself, and *Robinson Crusoe on Mars* (1964). He was associate producer of the TV series *The Outer Limits*.. Scientific or Technical Award, Class III: For pioneering the development and for the first practical application to motion picture production of the triple head background projector. *Journal SMPTE*, March 1940, published his article "The development and practical application of the triple-head background projector." In *American Cinematographer*, November 1939 and January 1940, he wrote "Making matte shots" and in the March 1943 issue he wrote "Special effects and wartime production." In 1984, shortly before his death, an oral history of Haskin (conducted by Joe Adamson) was published by the Directors Guild of America. His nickname was Bunny (according to Jim Danforth, spelled Buni).

Arthur Hayward

British Sculptor

When Ray Harryhausen came to London, he often hired Hayward, who had worked for the

Museum of Natural History in London, to sculpt creatures for his stop-motion epics: *Mysterious Island* (1961–62), *Jason and the Argonauts* (1962–63), *First Men in the Moon* (1964), *One Million Years B. C.* (1965–66) and *The Valley of Gwangi* (1968–69). Hayward was also credited for creature work on Hammer's *The Lost Continent* (1968). In the August 1969 issue of *Animals: The International Wildlife Magazine,* Hayward had an article titled "Making Fossils Live":

> My profession is the preparation of museum exhibits. I have no training in cine animation, as it is called, nor access to the elaborate and expensive apparatus of the film studios; but I became so obsessed with the idea of making dinosaurs walk and eat and fight on the screen that I decided to try my hand at it.... All that was needed, I told myself, was to place the model in the foreground of the set, suitably lighted, and then move the legs a little at a time, making an exposure between each movement. As pictures are projected onto the screen at a rate of 24 every second, I had a lot of movements and single-frame exposures to perform, a matter of many hours work. However, it was done at last and the film sent off for processing.

According to the article, when the film came back from the laboratory, Hayward realized that the model slithered and jerked about all over the place; "Obviously, I still had a lot to learn." Eventually Hayward had six films ready, each 50 feet long, starring a Stegosaurus and a Ceratosaurus eating a Diplodocus, and finally a short film emerged, *The Age of the Dinosaurs.* No mention of Harryhausen is made in the article, which puzzled fans, but on the cover the Allosaurus from *the Valley of Gwangi* is prominently featured within a diorama.

John Hench (1908–2004)
German-American Animation and Effects Supervisor

Born in Cedar Rapids, Iowa. Lifelong association with Walt Disney in production and background art (starting with animated feature films). Designed many effects including the giant squid for *20000 Leagues Under the Sea* (1953–54). Became Disney's right hand man in developing rides for Disneyland. Albert Whitlock, who for some time was associated with Disney, remembered Hench in a letter dated April 18, 1985, as "a nice and most generous person.... He is of German origin (we called him the baron!)." 1966: on the board of WED. 1972: chief operations officer. 1980: senior vice-president. Died in Burbank (heart attack).

Cecil Hepworth
British Producer

Became interested in trick films early on: *The Explosion of a Motor Car* (1900), *How It Feels to Be Run Over* (1900), and *Alice in Wonderland* (1903): "The film is composed of 16 scenes, dissolving very beautifully from one to another" (catalogue advertisement).

Helmut Herbst (1939–)
German Experimental and Animation Filmmaker

Did lots of animation and effects for TV. Founder, Cinegrafik, Hamburg. Herbst also directed the sci-fi *Die phantastische Welt des Matthew Madson* (1974, in collaboration with Klaus Wyborny) and the sfx documentary *Synthetischer Film oder Wie das Monster King Kong von Phantasie und Präzision erzeugt wurde* (1975). As professor, he teaches filmmaking.

David L. Hewitt
American Special Effects Supervisor and Director

David Lee Hewitt did effects for ultra low-budget films: *The Time Travelers* (1964), *Horror of the Blood Monsters* (*Vampire Men of the Lost Planet,* 1970), *The Devonsville Terror* (1983). Also directed the C pictures *The Wizard of Mars* (1965), *Journey to the Center of Time* (1967), *Dr. Terror's Gallery of Horrors* (1967), *The Mighty Gorga* (1968). In later years he was involved in *Superman IV: The Quest for Peace* (1987), *Willow* (1989), *Honey, I Shrunk the Kids* (1989), *Millennium* (1989) and *Dark Future* (1994).

Arthur Higgins
Australian Special Effects Supervisor

In the 1930s he developed an optical printer and introduced sfx techniques to the Australian film industry.

Clyde Hill

American Matte Artist

Did matte paintings for Warner Bros.

Henri Hillinck (1901–1959)

American Matte Artist

At RKO he painted mattes for the original *King Kong* (1932–33) and *Kentucky Kernels* (1934). Later joined MGM's matte department for films like *Forbidden Planet* (1956) and *Raintree County* (1957). Died in Los Angeles.

Ho Look-Ying

Chinese Cinematographer

In the early Hong Kong film industry he was a pioneer in developing special effects through superimposition and calculated lighting.

Robert R. Hoag (1908–1987)

Canadian-American Optical Cinematographer

Born in Nova Scotia, Canada. Emigrated to the United States at the age of 13. Started in the film lab at Universal City Studios. Later employed at the Roy Davidge Lab in Hollywood where he helped to execute optical photography, then as assistant cameraman at MGM (*Ben-Hur, The Single Standard, College Days, Sequoia* et al.). Assigned to MGM effects in February 1929. In 1934, as second cameraman, became the assistant of Irving G. Ries, head of MGM's optical department. In 1950 he was appointed director of photography. Became the head of the department when Ries retired. Hoag supervised dissolves, montages, split screens and matte shots for *Annie Get Your Gun* (1950), *The Toast of New Orleans* (1950), *Scaramouche* (1952), *The Prisoner of Zenda* (1952), *The Sheepman* (1958), *Ben-Hur* (1959), *The Big Circus* (1959), *Ask Any Girl* (1959), *Green Mansions* (1959), *Home from the Hill* (1960), *Cimarron* (1960), *Atlantis, the Lost Continent* (1961), *The Wonderful World of the Brothers Grimm* (1962–63, in three-strip Cinerama), *Mutiny on the Bounty* (1962–63), *The Birds* (1963, additional optical effects), *The Prize* (1963), *7 Faces of Dr. Lao* (1963–64), *The Great-*

est Story Ever Told (1963–64), *Ice Station Zebra* (1968), *Soylent Green* (1973). Died in Los Angeles. Son Robert, Jr. worked as technician in the MGM laboratories.

Winton C. Hoch (1905–1979)

American Cinematographer

The future Academy Award-winning cameraman was born in Iowa. Was a research physicist at the California Institute of Technology. One of the foremost specialists in Technicolor photography. Started with Technicolor as laboratory technician. Occasionally got assignments to shoot effects scenes in color: *Gone with the Wind* (1939, his dual-screen fire sequence was deleted from final release prints) as well as *The Black Swan* (1942) and *Crash Dive* (1943) for Fred Sersen at 20th Century–Fox. Did some color matte photography for Warren Newcombe at MGM. Director of Photography: *Dr. Cyclops* (1939–40, directed by Ernest B. Schoedsack), *Joan of Arc* (1948), *Darby O'Gill and the Little People* (1959) for Walt Disney, *The Lost World* (1960), *Voyage to the Bottom of the Sea* (1961), *Robinson Crusoe on Mars* (1964) and some notable westerns for John Ford. Also photographed scores of episodes of the Irwin Allen TV series *Voyage to the Bottom of the Sea, Lost in Space* and *The Time Tunnel.*

Roswell A. Hoffman (1905–2001)

American Matte and Optical Cinematographer

The Rhode Island-born Hoffman had a lifelong association with Universal City Studios. Assisted Jerome H. Ash. Assistant cameraman, *The Invisible Man* (1933). Optical effects for *The Invisible Ray* (1935–36), *The Invisible Woman* (1940), *Invisible Agent* (1942), *Abbott and Costello Meet the Invisible Man* (1951), *It Came from Outer Space* (1953), *This Island Earth* (1954–55), *Tarantula* (1955), *The Incredible Shrinking Man* (1956–57), *The Land Unknown* (1957), *Pillow Talk* (1959), *Spartacus* (1959), *The Brass Bottle* (1964). Became Albert Whitlock's matte photographer: *The Birds* (1962–63), *Captain Newman; M.D.* (1963), *Island of the Blue Dolphins* (1964), *Marnie* (1964), *Shenandoah* (1965), *The War Lord* (1965), *That Funny Feeling* (1965),

Beau Geste (1966), *Munster, Go Home!* (1966), *Torn Curtain* (1966), *Tobruk* (1967), *The War Wagon* (1967), *Hellfighters* (1968), *Colossus: The Forbin Project* (1969), *Topaz* (1969), *Slaughterhouse-Five* (1972), *Frenzy* (1972). Hoffman's last film was *Earthquake* (1973–74). He died in Beverly Hills.

Walter Hoffman

American Explosives Expert

Spent a lifetime at Paramount Studios: *For Whom the Bell Tolls* (1942), *Unconquered* (1947), *The War of the Worlds* (1952–53, atomic blast).

Tom Holland

American Stop-Motion Animator

Actor-turned-puppeteer. At Project Unlimited: *The Time Machine* (1959–60), *Dinosaurus!* (1960, animating Brontosaurus), *Goliath and the Dragon* (1960–61, assisted Marcel Delgado in creating big dragon head), *Jack the Giant Killer*

(1960–62), *The Wonderful World of the Brothers Grimm* (1962–63). Had a later career as a sculptor of fine-art bronzes.

Antonín Horák

Czech Effects and Animation Photographer

Started as apprentice in the mid–30s in the puppet film studio in Zlín (later Gottvaldov). Lensed 2D and 3D animation. Joined Karel Zeman's unit and, technically speaking, introduced composite photography to *Cesta do praveku* (1954) and *Vynález zkázy* (*The Fabulous World of Jules Verne*, 1958) by using the original camera negative for double and multiple exposure.

Willi Horn

German Art Director and Miniature Supervisor

One of those unsung creative forces who contributed in the 1920s to the Shuftan process. At Deutsche Spiegeltechnik Company he worked

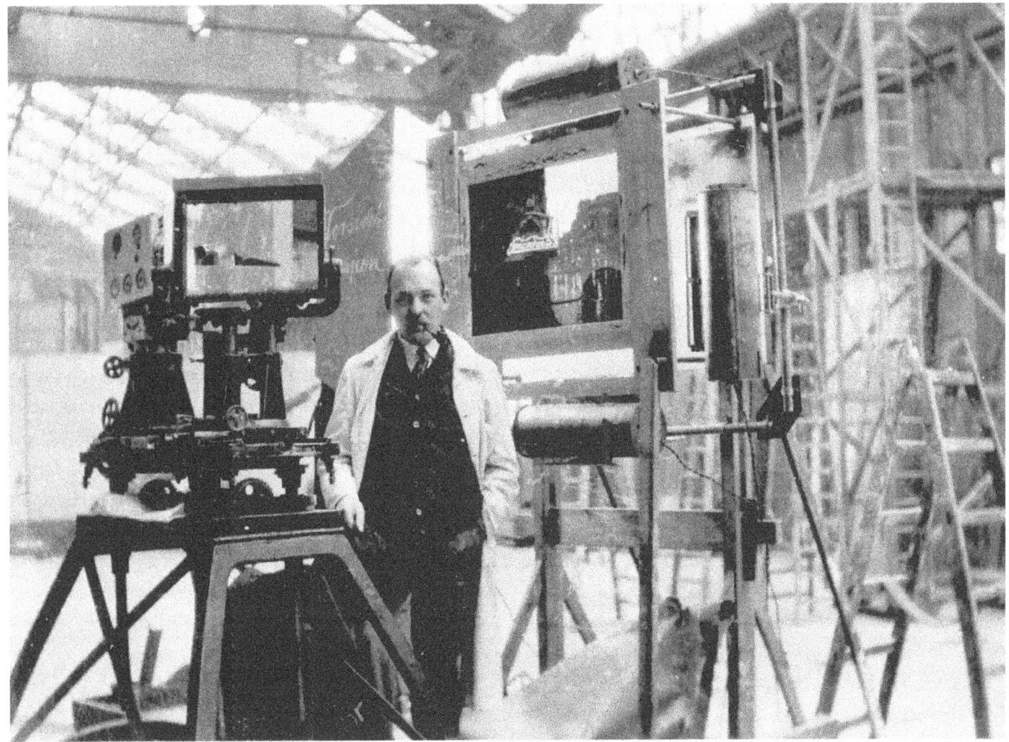

Willi Horn, a set designer who worked in the Schüfftan unit during the 1920s (courtesy Fritz Maurischat Collection, Deutsche Kinemathek Berlin).

closely with Fritz Maurischat in designing model shots. Later became an art director on feature films such as *Die Martinsklause* (1951).

David S. Horsley (1906–1976)
American Effects Cinematographer and Supervisor

David Stanley "Stan" Horsley was a child actor in silent films produced by his father, who was one of the founders of Universal. Worked at the Morosco Film Lab, later became camera assistant at Universal Studios: *The Hunchback of Notre Dame* (1922–23). Camera operator at Metro-Goldwyn-Mayer: *Ben-Hur* (1925), *Freaks* (1932). In 1934, John P. Fulton invited him to become his assistant in the Universal special photography department: *Bride of Frankenstein* (1935), *Werewolf of London* (1935), *The Invisible Ray* (1935–36), *The Invisible Man Returns* (1939–40), *The Boys from Syracuse* (1940), *The Wolf Man* (1941), *The Invisible Woman* (1940), *The Ghost of Frankenstein* (1942), *Invisible Agent* (1942). During World War II he was master sergeant at Fort Roach (Roach Studios) lensing Army training films. After the war, he became head of the Universal effects department: *Canyon Passage* (1946), *The Killers* (1946), *Mexican Hayride* (1948), *Abbott and Costello Meet Frankenstein* (1948), *Mr. Peabody and the Mermaid* (1948), *Abbott and Costello Meet the Killer, Boris Karloff* (1949), *Francis* (1949), *Mystery Submarine* (1950), *Abbott and Costello in the Foreign Legion* (1951), *Abbott and Costello Meet the Invisible Man* (1951), *The Lady Pays Off* (1951), *The World in His Arms* (1952), *The Black Castle* (1952), *Against All Flags* (1952), *Francis Goes to West Point* (1952), *It Came from Outer Space* (1953, known on the lot as "Horsley's project"; developed 3D equipment), *Francis Covers the Big Town* (1953), *Abbott and Costello Meet Dr. Jekyll and Mr. Hyde* (1953), *The Glass Web* (1953, 3D), *Wings of the Hawk* (1953, 3D technology), *Creature from the Black Lagoon* (1953–54, 3D technology), *Taza, Son of Cochise* (1953–54, 3D technology), *Francis Joins the Wacs* (1954), *Magnificent Obsession* (1954), *Revenge of the Creature* (1955, 3D technology), *Tarantula* (1955, preproduction only). Horsley: "This was a totally different period from the days when I was changing Lon Chaney, Jr. into the Wolf Man or making Vincent Price invisible. Television was in competition with the movies and the cost of making pictures was going up. I had caught hell by going over budget on *Abbott and Costello Go to Mars*, 1953] so they were keeping an eye on me, but I would do my experimenting at home since they told me I couldn't have any new equipment. I never paid them any attention though, and went ahead and built what I needed, then I'd call it something else on the reports, and they never caught on until the end" (interview with Philip J. Riley). Due to the cost overruns of *City Beneath the Sea* (1953, with sequences shot dry for wet with foreground mattes) and *This Island Earth* (1955), Horsley's contract wasn't renewed and he was forced to freelance again. Title cards photographed for *The Ten Commandments* (1956). Second unit: *Around the World in 80 Days* (1956). Blue screen consultant. *The Longest Day* (1961–62), *The Jolly Genie* (1963). Director of photography: *Jack the Giant Killer* (1961–62). Wes Thompson got him out of retirement for *Midway* (1975–76). Scientific or Technical Award, Class III in 1954 for a portable remote control device for process projectors.

Tom Howard (19??–1985)
British Optical Cinematography Expert

The son of an electrical mechanical engineer, Thomas "Tom" Howard joined Alexander Korda around Christmas of 1934 as darkroom assistant. Korda had just left Elstree and moved his operation to Isleworth. Howard assisted Jack Thomas, one of Ned Mann's American experts, on the optical printer for a year and became an expert in that complicated piece of machinery. Eventually he ran Elstree's optical department and became an expert in blue screen shots which were introduced by special effects director Larry Butler: *The Thief of Bagdad* (1939–40), *Love on the Dole* (1941), *In Which We Serve* (1942), *Thunder Rock* (1943). Spent World War II part-time with the R.A.F. First Academy Award for color effects on director David Lean's *Blithe Spirit* (1945). In 1946 he was appointed head of the optical and effects department at MGM British Studios Borehamwood: *Idol of Paris* (1948), *The Guinea Pig* (1948), *Edward, My Son* (1948), *Conspirator* (1949), *The Miniver Story* (1950), *Quo Vadis* (1950–51, photographing Peter Ellenshaw matte paintings and blue screen composites), *Calling Bulldog Drummond* (1951), *Ivanhoe* (1952), *The Hour of 13* (1952), *Knights of the Round Table* (1953, Howard's first CinemaScope picture), *Mogambo* (1953), *Time Bomb* (1953), *Seagulls Over Sorrento* (1954), *Betrayed* (1954), *Beau Brummell* (1954), *The Adventures of Quentin Durward* (1955), *The Man Who Never Was* (1956), *Bhowani Junction* (1956), *Invitation to the Dance* (1956), *The Gamma People* (1956), *The Barretts of Wimpole Street* (1957), *Tarzan and the Lost Safari* (1957), *The Little Hut* (1957), *Action of the Tiger* (1957), *Sea Wife* (1957), *tom thumb* (1958, second Academy Award for George Pal production), *The Scapegoat* (1959), *Libel* (1959), *Suddenly, Last Summer* (1959), *Gorgo* (1959–61, King Bros. monster movie), *The Day They Robbed the Bank of England* (1960), *Village of the Damned* (1960), *Murder She Said* (1961), *A Matter of Who* (1961), *The Secret Partner* (1961), *The Green Helmet* (1961), *Il ladro di Bagdad* (*The Thief of Bagdad*, 1961), *Invasion Quartet* (1961), *Village of the Daughters* (1962), *Light in the Piazza* (1962), *I Thank a Fool* (1962), *Kill or Cure* (1962), *Postman's Knock* (1962), *Captain Sindbad* (1962–63), *Children of the Damned* (1963), *Come Fly with Me* (1963), *The Haunting* (1963), *Murder at the Gallop* (1963), *The V.I.P.s* (1963), *633 Squadron* (1964), *The Yellow Rolls-Royce* (1964), *Operation Crossbow* (1965), *Battle Beneath the Earth* (1967), *Where Eagles Dare* (1968). Developed front projection system for use in apeman prologue of Stanley Kubrick's *2001: A Space Odyssey* (1965–68). After leaving MGM, he did freelance work: *The Man Who Haunted Himself* (1970), *Young Winston* (1972), *Digby, the Biggest Dog in the World* (1973), *The Legend of Hell House* (1973), *The Little Prince* (1974), *Professor Popper's Problem* (1974). Appeared in the BBC documentary *How on Earth Did They Do It.* Died in Hertfordshire, England.

Alan Hume (1924–)

British Cinematographer

Worked on the TV series *The Avengers*, several James Bond films and *Star Wars Episode VI: Return of the Jedi* (1983) as director of photography. Frequent photographic assignments on sfx productions: *Captain Nemo and the Underwater City* (1969–70), *The Land That Time Forgot* (1975), *At the Earth's Core* (1976), *Gulliver's Travels* (1977), *The People That Time Forgot* (1977), *Warlords of Atlantis* (1978), *Arabian Adventure* (1979), *Caveman* (1981), *Lifeforce* (1985), Michael Anderson's TV version of *20,000 Leagues Under the Sea* (1997). For some years he was matte cameraman for Peter Ellenshaw on Disney's early British feature films: *Robin Hood and His Merrie Men* (1952), *Rob Roy the Highland Rogue* (1953), *The Sword and the Rose* (1953). With Gareth Owen wrote *Memoirs of a Film Cameraman: A Life Through the Lens.*

Paul Huston

American Model Maker and Matte Artist

Attended the University of Colorado architectural school. One of his teachers there was James Shourt, who knew John Dykstra and recommended Huston to the *Star Wars* (1975–77) unit. At Industrial Light & Magic he started as storyboard artist, then got into modelmaking. Assisted Doug Smith in shooting models onstage. During the making of *Return of the Jedi* (1982–83) he joined ILM's matte painting department. For *Indiana Jones and the Temple of Doom* (1983–84) he went to Sri Lanka to shoot reference photos for the matte and model shop.

Gerhard Huttula (1902–1996)

German Cinematographer, Expert in Animation and Special Effects Photography

The Berlin-born Huttula started as trick photographer for his former drawing master, Wolfgang Kaskeline, in 1922 and worked mainly on Ufa commercials. He was the first German technician to work with the Truca, a crude optical printer manufactured by Debrie: *Ekstase* (1932). Cinematographer in Argentina, located in Buenos Aires (under the name Gerardo Huttula). In 1937 he returned to Germany and took over the Ufa process department in Babelsberg from veteran cinematographer Guido Seeber: *Spiel im Sommerwind* (1938; part of that holiday car ride was filmed on the process stage), *Die Geliebte* (1939), *Diesel* (1942; the Ufa demo reel

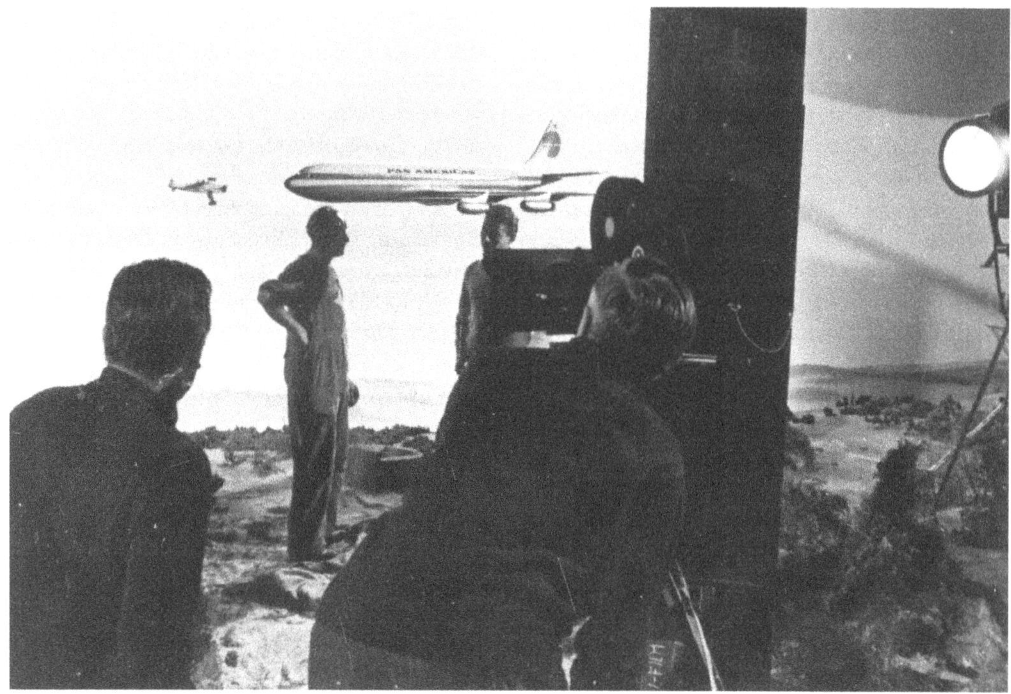

Gerhard Huttula sets up model airplanes for a commercial made at UFA Studios in Berlin-Tempelhof. In the 1940s, Huttula was in charge of miniatures and process for propaganda films like *Stukas* and *Die grosse Liebe* (courtesy Gerhard Huttula and Deutsche Kinemathek Berlin).

contains a shot with actors in front of a huge machine, actually a rear-projected model, which is not in the released version of the movie), *Hab' mich Lieb* (1942). Frequently worked with NS film producer-director Karl Ritter: *Die Hochzeitsreise* (1938), *Bal Paré* (1939), *Jud Süss* (1940; Huttula was involved with only one or two process shots), *Über alles in der Welt* (1941), *Stukas* (1941), *GPU* and Ritter's unfinished production *Das Leben geht weiter* (1945), directed by Wolfgang Liebeneiner. A specialist in model aircraft, he created scenes for *Kongo-Express* (1939), Heinz Rühmann's comedies *Quax der Bruchpilot* (1941) and *Quax in Fahrt* (1943–44), Roger von Norman's *Himmelhunde* (1942) and the most successful film of the NS era, *Die grosse Liebe* (1943) starring Zarah Leander. Created the miniature train disaster for another Leander vehicle, *... Damals* (1942–43), Hans Albers' rear-projected cannonball ride for *Münchhausen* (1942–43), a motor launch ride through the docks of Hamburg for another Albers Agfacolor production, *Grosse Freiheit Nr. 7* (1943–44), and a vaudeville scene for *Die Frau meiner Träume*

(1944) with Hungarian dancing queen Marika Rökk. Second camera: Veit Harlan's propaganda epic *Kolberg* (1944). After the war, served as Agfacolor consultant on West Germany's first color feature, *Schwarzwaldmädel* (1950), and photographed Fritz Genschow's fairy tales *Rotkäppchen* (1953), *Hänsel and Gretel* (1954), *Frau Holle* (1954), and *Aschenputtel* (1955). Supervised virtually hundreds of commercials for Ufa Werbefilm in Berlin-Tempelhof. In 1960 he was consultant for the TV show *Achtung! Hochspannung!—Tricks und Sensationen im Film*, revealing some tricks of his trade. Lectured at Fachhochschule für Optik in Berlin. Died in the home of his daughter in Düren.

Illusion Arts, Inc.
American Matte Art Company

Founded by two Albert Whitlock collaborators, artist Syd Dutton and matte cinematographer Bill Taylor, after Universal disbanded their matte department. Illusion Arts specialized in high-quality matte paintings.

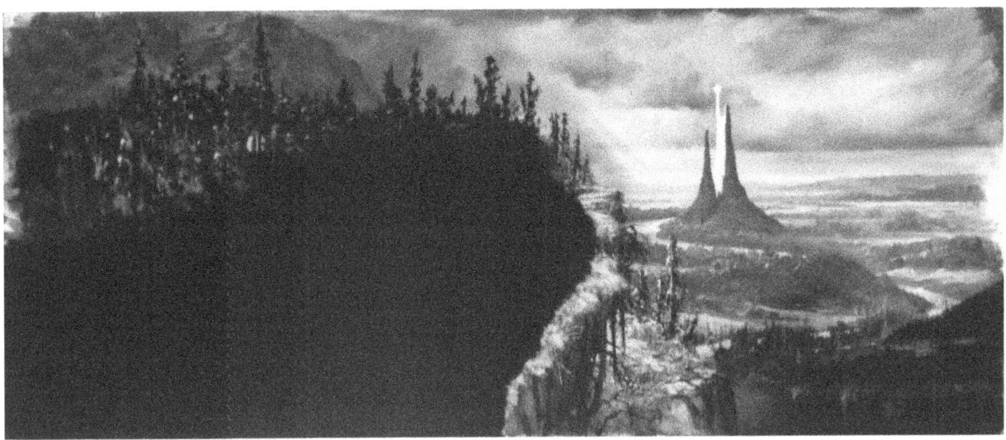

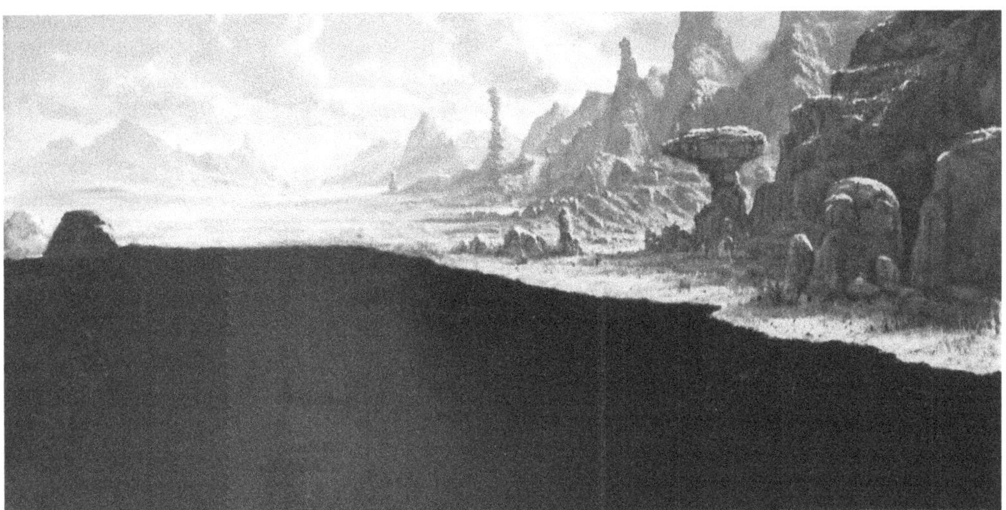

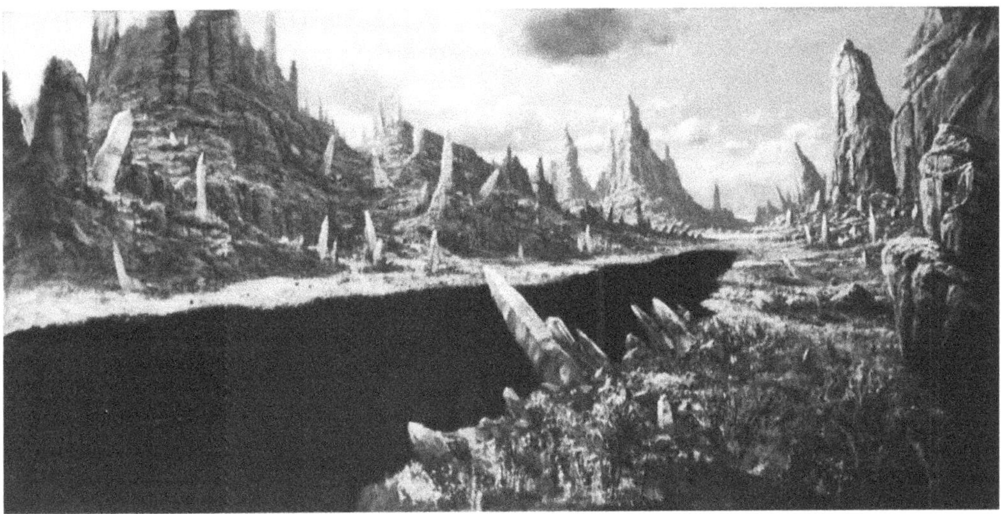

Various glass and matte paintings for *Die unendliche Geschichte II (The NeverEnding Story II)*, supervised by Albert Whitlock. The plates were shot at Bavaria Studios in Munich, painted by Syd Dutton and photographed by Bill Taylor at Illusion Arts in Van Nuys (courtesy Deutsche Kinemathek Berlin).

Henry Imus

British Blue Screen Cinematographer

Technicolor technician: *The Thief of Bagdad* (1939–40), *Week-end in Havana* (1941, second unit).

Industrial Light & Magic

American Visual Effects Company

The effects arm of Lucasfilm, at certain times almost a monopolist for expensive effects. After *Star Wars* (1976–77), the George Lucas-owned company relocated in San Rafael, Marin County, and worked with directors Steven Spielberg, Martin Scorsese, Wolfgang Petersen, Robert Zemeckis, James Cameron, Jan De Bont, Tim Burton, Brian De Palma et al. (and, of course, Lucas): *The Empire Strikes Back* (1979–80), *Raiders of the Lost Ark* (1980–81), *Dragonslayer* (1980–81), *Poltergeist* (1982), *Star Trek II: The Wrath of Khan* (1982), *E.T. the Extra-Terrestrial* (1982), *The Dark Crystal* (1982), *Return of the Jedi* (1982–83), *Twice Upon a Time* (1983), *Indiana Jones and the Temple of Doom* (1983–84), *Star Trek III: The Search for Spock* (1984), *Die Unendliche Geschichte* (*The Neverending Story*, 1984), *The Ewok Adventure* (1984, TV special), *Starman* (1984), *The Goonies* (1985), *Cocoon* (1985), *Back to the Future* (1985), *Explorers* (1985), *Mishima* (1985), *Amazing Stories* (1985), *Ewoks: Battle for Endor* (1985, TV special), *Enemy Mine* (1985), *Young Sherlock Holmes* (1985), *Out of Africa* (1985), *Here Comes Santa Claus* (1985, 3D), *The Money Pit* (1986), *Labyrinth* (1986), *Howard the Duck* (1986), *Captain Eo* (1986, 3-D special exclusively made for Disneyland and Disney World), *Star Trek IV: The Voyage Home* (1986), *The Golden Child* (1986), *Star Tours* (1987, simulator film ride for Disney), *The Witches of Eastwick* (1987), *Harry and the Hendersons* (1987), *Innerspace* (1987), **batteries not included* (1987), *Star Trek: The Next Generation* (1987, TV), *Empire of the Sun* (1987), *Willow* (1988), *Star Trek Attraction* (1988, brief film segment for Universal Studios Tour), *Who Framed Roger Rabbit* (1988, mixing cartoon and live action), *The Last Temptation of Christ* (1988), *Caddyshack II* (1988), *Cocoon: the Return* (1988), *the 'Burbs* (1989),

Skin Deep (1989), *Body Wars* 1989, simulator ride for Disney's Epcot Center), *Field of Dreams* (1989), *Indiana Jones and the Last Crusade* (1989), *Ghostbusters II* (1989), *The Abyss* (1989), *Back to the Future II* (1989), *Always* (1989), *Joe Versus the Volcano* (1990), *The Hunt for Red October* (1990), *Back to the Future Part III* (1990), *Die Hard 2: Die Harder* (1990), *Akira Kurosawa's Dreams* (1990), *Ghost* (1990), *The Godfather—Part III* (1990), *The Doors* (1991), *Switch* (1991), *Hudson Hawk* (1991), *Backdraft* (1991), *The Rocketeer* (1991), *Terminator 2: Judgment Day* (1991), *Space Race* (1991, simulator ride film with Showscan), *Star Trek VI: The Undiscovered Country* (1991), *Hook* (1991), *Memoirs of an Invisible Man* (1991–92), *Death Becomes Her* (1992), *Alien Encounter* (1992), *Jurassic Park* (1992–93), *Alive* (1993), *The Nutcracker* (1993), *Fire in the Sky* (1993), *Last Action Hero* (1993), *Rising Sun* (1993), *Manhattan Murder Mystery* (1993), *Meteorman* (1993), *Schindler's List* (1993), *The Hudsucker Proxy* (1994), *Maverick* (1994), *The Flintstones* (1994), *Wolf* (1994), *Baby's Day Out* (1994), *Forrest Gump* (1994), *The Mask* (1994), *Radioland Murders* (1994), *Star Trek Generations* (1994), *Disclosure* (1994), *In the Mouth of Madness* (1995), *Casper* (1995), *Village of the Damned* (1995), *Congo* (1995), *The Indian in the Cupboard* (1995), *The American President* (1995), *Sabrina* (1995), *Jumanji* (1995–96), *Twister* (1996), *Mission: Impossible* (1996), *Dragonheart* (1996), *Eraser* (1996), *The Trigger Effect* (1996), *Sleepers* (1996), *Star Trek: First Contact* (1996), *101 Dalmatians*

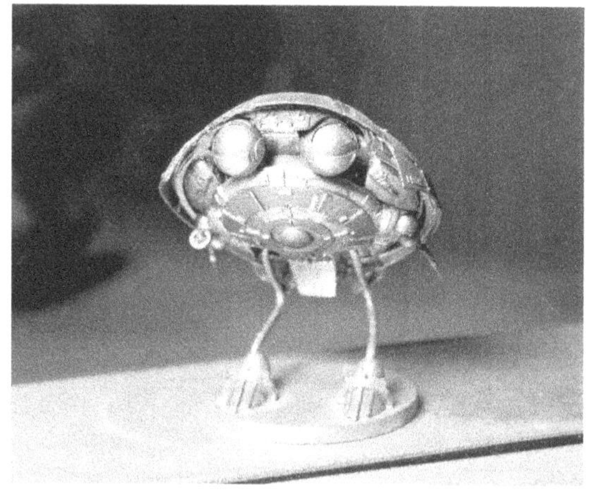

***batteries not included** (courtesy Paul Swendsen and Deutsche Kinemathek Berlin).

(1996), *Daylight* (1996), *Mars Attacks!* (1996), *The Lost World: Jurassic Park* (1997), *Speed 2: Cruise Control* (1997), *Men in Black* (1997), *Contact* (1997), *Spawn* (1997), *Deconstructing Harry* (1997), *Titanic* (1997), *Starship Troopers* (1997), *Flubber* (1997), *Midnight in the Garden of Good and Evil* (1997), *Amistad* (1997), *Deep Rising* (1998), *Mercury Rising* (1998), *Deep Impact* (1998), *Small Soldiers* (1998), *Saving Private Ryan* (1998), *Snake Eyes* (1998), *Celebrity* (1998), *Reach the Rock* (1998), *The Last Days* (1998), *Meet Joe Black* (1998), *Jack Frost* (1998), *Mighty Joe Young* (1998, remake), *Stars Wars: Episode I–The Phantom Menace* (1998–99), *Keep Clear* (1999), *October Sky* (1999), *The Mummy* (1999), *Wild Wild West* (1999), *The Haunting* (1999), *Deep Blue Sea* (1999), *Sweet and Lowdown* (1999), *Snow Falling on Cedars* (1999), *Bringing Out the Dead* (1999), *Sleepy Hollow* (1999), *The Green Mile* (1999), *Magnolia* (1999), *Galaxy Quest* (1999), *Mission to Mars* (2000), *The Adventures of Rocky & Bullwinkle* (2000), *The Perfect Storm* (2000), *Space Cowboys* (2000), *Pollock* (2000), *Pay It Forward* (2000), *Work in Progress* (2000), *Pearl Harbor* (2000–01), *The Pledge* (2001), *The Mummy Returns* (2001), *AI Artificial Intelligence* (2001), *Jurassic Park III* (2001), *Planet of the Apes* (2001), *Harry Potter and the Sorcerer's Stone* (2001), *The Majestic* (2001), *Star Wars: Episode II—Attack of the Clones* (2001–02), *Impostor* (2002), *Manassas: End of Innocence* (2002), *The Time Machine* (2002), *Big Trouble* (2002), *Punch-Drunk Love* (2002), *The Bourne Identity* (2002), *Minority Report* (2002), *Men in Black II* (2002), *K-19: The Widowmaker* (2002), *Signs* (2002), *Blood Work* (2002), *Harry Potter and the Chamber of Secrets* (2002), *Gangs of New York* (2002), *Tears of the Sun* (2002), *Dreamcatcher* (2003), *The Hunted* (2003), *Hulk* (2003), *Pirates of the Caribbean: The Curse of the Black Pearl* (2003), *Terminator 3: Rise of the Machines* (2003), *The League of Extraordinary Gentlemen* (2003), *Let's Go* (2003), *Master and Commander: The Far Side of the World* (2003), *Timeline* (2003), *Peter Pan* (2003), *Stuck on You* (2003), *Oedipus* (2004), *Along Came Polly* (2004), *Morphine* (2004), *Hidalgo* (2004), *Twisted* (2004), *Van Helsing* (2004), *The Day After Tomorrow* (2004), *Harry Potter and the Prisoner of Azkaban* (2004), *The Chronicles of Riddick* (2004), *The Bourne Supremacy* (2004), *The Village* (2004), *Eros* (2004),

Sky Captain and the World of Tomorrow (2004), *Lemony Snicket's A Series of Unfortunate Events* (2004), *Star Wars: Episode III—Revenge of the Sith* (2004–05), *War of the Worlds* (2004–05), *Are We There Yet* (2005), *Son of the Mask* (2005), *The Pacifier* (2005), *The Amityville Horror* (2005), *xXx: State of the Union* (2005), *The Adventures of Sharkboy and Lavagirl 3-D* (2005), *Herbie Fully Loaded* (2005), *The Island* (2005), *Chicken Little* (2005), *Jarhead* (2005), *Harry Potter and the Goblet of Fire* (2005), *Rent* (2005), *The Chronicles of Narnia: The Lion, the Witch and the Wardrobe* (2005), *Cheaper by the Dozen 2* (2005), *Munich* (2005). *Eight Below* (2006), *Mission: Impossible III* (2006), *The Fast and the Furious: Tokyo Drift* (2006), *Pirates of the Caribbean: Dead Man's Chest* (2006), *Lady in the Water* (2006), *Eragon* (2006), *Pirates of the Caribbean: At World's End* (2007), *Evan Almighty* (2007), *Transformers* (2007), *Harry Potter and the Order of the Phoenix* (2007), *Next* (2007), *Red Tails* (2008), *Jurassic Park IV* (2008), *Indiana Jones 4* (2008), *The Spiderwick Chronicles* (2008), *Iron Man* (2008), *The Curious Case of Benjamin Button* (2008), *Star Trek XI* (2008). TV series: *The Young Indiana Jones Chronicles* (1992–93)

Yasuyuki Inoue

Japanese Special Effects Art Director

Assistant of Akira Watanabe on Toho's special effects films (the original *Gojira/Godzilla, King of the Monsters!* in 1954 and many more). When Watanabe retired, it became Inoue's chore to supervise monsters and miniatures.

Ub Iwerks (1901–71)

American Cartoonist, Animator and Optical Technique Expert

Born Ubbe Eert Iwwerks, the son of Friesian-American parents. As a cartoonist and commercial artist he met Walt Disney in his native Kansas City and joined forces with him in 1919. Iwerks was one of the organizers of United Film Advertisers in Kansas City, making animated advertising films. They rejoined in 1923 when Disney had opened a cartoon film factory in Los

Angeles (and produced the *Alice* series combining a live-action girl with animation). Iwerks animated almost single-handedly the first *Mickey Mouse* cartoons (in fact he invented Mickey!) and *Silly Symphonies* (*Plane Crazy, The Gallopin' Gaucho, Steamboat Willie, The Barn Dance, The Opry House, The Skeleton Dance, Hell's Bells*) but then left for a contract with Disney's former distributor Pat Powers. During the next years, under his own Ub Iwerks Studio and Animated Pictures Corp. banner, he did some minor cartoon series in black-and-white (*Flip the Frog, Willie Whopper*) and some fairy tales in bi-pack Cinecolor (*Comicolor Classics,* including a few early horizontal multiplane shots). When his series failed to rival Disney's product, Iwerks returned to his former partner as technician, engineer, and inventor. As head of the process and optical printing department, Iwerks introduced all sorts of camera effects to Disney's feature-length cartoons (*Victory Through Air Power,* 1943, *The 3 Caballeros,* 1945, and *Song of the South,* 1948, mixing animation with live-action segments; *Alice in Wonderland,* 1950–51; *Melody in 3D,* 1953, *3-D Jamboree,* 1956; *Peter Pan,* 1953; *Sleeping Beauty,* 1956–58; *One Hundred and One Dalmatians,* 1960–61, which made full use of Ub's *xerography* process), so-called *True Life* documentaries: *The Living Desert* (1953), *The Vanishing Prairie* (1955) and feature films: *20000 Leagues Under the Sea* (1953–54), *Davy Crockett, King of the Wild Frontier* (1955), *The Absent Minded Professor* (1960–61), *The Parent Trap* (1961), *Mary Poppins* (1964), *The Three Lives of Thomasina* (1964). On loan-out to Universal he performed traveling matte/sodium vapor consulting duties on Alfred Hitchcock's *The Birds* (1962–63). In 1953 he mainly took care of the special research division at Disney's and installed miracles like *the* Haunted House at Disneyland. Also did some work for Walt Disney World. Academy Awards for technical contributions to the film industry in 1959–60 and 1965 which included a double-headed optical printer, the liquid optical printer (wetgate) to eliminate scratches in 16mm footage blown up to 35mm, the refinement of Rank's sodium vapor process, and Circarama. Sons Don and Dave Iwerks worked in motion pictures, too. Died in Burbank, California (heart attack).

Fred Jackman (1881–1959)

American Cinematographer and Visual Effects Supervisor

Born in Iowa, Frank Woodruff Jackman had an early job as a projectionist. Bought his own camera in 1913 and got a job with Essanay in Chicago, then moved to Los Angeles where he worked for Pathe and Triangle, with Harold Lloyd at Hal Roach's and most notably with Roach's competitor Mack Sennett (who once called Jackman "the greatest action cameraman"). For Sennett he organized the first trick department in Hollywood: "It is no longer a trade secret that the stunts and wild gyrations of the comedy production performers have been accomplished through expert manipulation in the hands of the cinematographer. In my seven years' experience as chief cinematographer for Mack Sennett, we have never had a serious accident and all of our leading comedians, bathing girls, animals and other performers are still intact, although the public time and again has seen them in terrible automobile crashes, falls from high rooms, in horseback jumps over wide gaps at altitudes of hundreds of feet, in dashes in front of trains traveling 60 miles an hour, and in fights with clubs on the wings of tossing aeroplanes, etc. etc." ("Comedy 'kicks' require courage and skill," *American Cinematographer*, December 1922). Photographed a few of Harold Lloyd's more famous comedies, including special photography for *A Small Town Idol* (1921). Founding member and part-time president of ASC. In 1924–25 he supervised effects and split-screen photography for *The Lost World* with assistant cinematographers Hans F. Koenekamp and Vernon L. Walker. Directed a version of Jack London's *Call of the Wild* in 1923 and several Rex, the Wild Horse entries for Hal Roach (*The King of Wild Horses* in 1924, the Stan Laurel-scripted *The Devil Horse* in 1926, and *No Man's Law* in 1927), then in charge of special effects production at Warner Bros. (*The Jazz Singer,* 1927) and the Warner-owned First National Pictures in Burbank. There he built a studio within a studio: the famous Stage 5. Didn't do creative work, just collected the money to keep the operation going with effects directors like William Mc-Gann and cinematographers Koenekamp, Byron

Haskin, Ed DuPar, son Fred Jackman, Jr., and others: *Noah's Ark* (1929), *The Isle of Lost Ships* (1929), *Moby Dick* (1930), *The Dawn Patrol* (1930), *Outward Bound* (1930), *The Lost Flight* (1930), *Svengali* (1931), *Doctor X* (1932), *A Midsummer Night's Dream* (1935), *Captain Blood* (1935), *The Petrified Forest* (1936), *The Green Pastures* (1936), *Isle of Fury* (1936), *China Clipper* (1936), *The Charge of the Light Brigade* (1936), *Anthony Adverse* (1936), *On Such a Night* (1937), *Paradise Isle* (1937) and *The Crowd Roars* (1937–38). In 1937 left Warners and founded own Jackman Process Company: Boris Karloff's *Mr. Moto* series for Monogram, *Forced Landing* (1941). Tried to resurrect *Lost Atlantis* film project from First National days with stop-motion dinosaurs in 1938 in association with producer Trem Carr and even photographed two reels of animation but failed.

Fred Jackman, Jr.   (1913–1982)
American Director of Photography and
*   Process Cinematographer*

Son of Fred W. Jackman. As a child actor he worked under his father's direction in the Hal Roach Western *The Devil Horse* in 1926. Entered Stage 5 at Warner Bros.-First National, which became his father's domain, and did process shots: *Doctor X* (1932), *The Case of the Curious Bride* (1935), *Bullets or Ballots* (1936), *Two Against the World* (1936), *Fugitive in the Sky* (1936), *Black Legion* (1937), *Green Light* (1937), *The Great O'Malley* (1937). With his father he left Warners and later became production cameraman: *Unknown Island* (1948), *Earth vs. the Flying Saucers* (1956), *Julie* (1956, Doris Day playing a stewardess is able to pilot and land an airplane thanks to Jackman process shots). Aerial photography: *Jungle Flight* (1947). Many TV series were photographed or directed by Jackman, Jr. Died Los Angeles.

Jan W. Jacobsen   (19??–1998)
Norwegian Camera Constructor and
*   Inventor*

Became well-known in Britain for developing scope lenses (Hammerscope, Ultrascope) and special cameras (Technirama camera for *Sparta-*cus, Cinemiracle camera for *Windjammer*, 3D equipment used by Hifi Stereo 70 and first Imax camera that went to outer space). Chief constructor for producer Harry Saltzman. For Saltzman's *The Battle of Britain* (1968) and later for *Superman* (1977–78), the latter in association with Wally Veevers, he created lightweight front projection equipment. Invented dual screen process which was recognized by the Academy with an Oscar (originally the Academy wanted to award Introvision until they found out that Jacobsen's earlier process was equal). Jacobsen went to Germany where he handled a front projection service with Theodor Nischwitz, who was eager to contribute his organizing skills: Hans Jürgen Syberberg's *Hitler—Ein Film aus Deutschland* (1977), Billy Wilder's *Fedora* (1977–78), Mark Robson's *Avalanche Express* (1979), Rainer Werner Fassbinder's TV series *Berlin Alexanderplatz* (1979–80), Wolfgang Petersen's *Das Boot* (*The Boat*, 1980–81), Hans W. Geissendörfer's *Der Zauberberg* (1981), Delbert Mann's *Night Crossing* (1981–82, Disney picture). In Italy *L'umanoide* (*The Humanoid*, 1979), in Spain *Super Sonicman* (1979). Died in Augsburg, Germany.

Donald A. Jahraus
American Model Maker and Miniature
*   Supervisor*

In charge of RKO's model shop: *Danger Lights* (1930), *The Case of Sergeant Grischa* (1930), *The Lost Squadron* (1932), *Flying Devils* (1933), *Ace of Aces* (1933), *Bird of Paradise* (1932), *The Most Dangerous Game* (1932), *Flying Down to Rio* (1933). In 1937 to MGM: *Test Pilot* (1938), *The Wizard of Oz* (1939), *Stand by for Action* (1943), *A Guy Named Joe* (1943), *Thirty Seconds Over Tokyo* (1943), *They Were Expendable* (1945), *The Green Years* (1946), *Green Dolphin Street* (1947), *Quo Vadis* (1950–51), *Plymouth Adventure* (1952).

Gregory Jein
American Model Maker

"In effect, we're toymakers," admits Gregory "Greg" Jein, a native of Los Angeles. "We build the toys and give them to someone else to play with. But I try to make them not so toylike. I try to give them the breath of life." Degree in fine arts from Los Angeles State College. His ability in Fiberglassing got him his first job with Bill Hedge in a small shop in Santa Monica. When Hedge became involved in *Flesh Gordon* (1971–74) he asked Jein to build a miniature

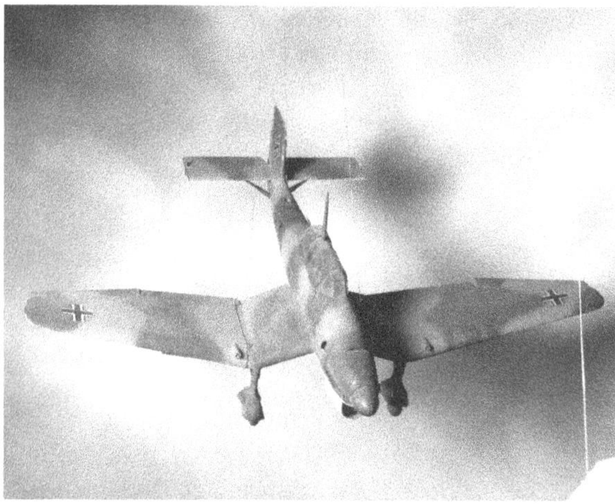

Science fiction films turned the images of World War II into outer space and thus helped to "popularize" the *Star Wars* idea. A model airplane (Stuka) from *A Yank in the R.A.F.* (courtesy Gregory Jein and Deutsche Kinemathek Berlin).

"Flying Phallus" rocketship. After that, Jein did another spaceship model (designed by Ron Cobb) for a "student movie" by John Carpenter and Dan O'Bannon which turned out to be *Dark Star* (1974). Jobbed at places like Cascade Pictures and the 20th Century–Fox Model Shop. When Douglas Trumbull happened to see the *Dark Star* model on display at a *Star Trek* convention, he contracted Jein (who did some TV shows in the meantime, like the *Wonder Woman* pilot and *The UFO Incident*) to do the model work on Steven Spielberg's *Close Encounters of the Third Kind* (1975–77), especially the model Devil's Tower and the extraterrestrial mothership (from a design by Ralph McQuarrie). Spielberg re-hired him for *1941* (1979). Miniatures for: *Laserblast* (1978), *Star Trek: The Motion Picture* (1978–79), *The Day Time Ended* (1980), *Fukkatsu no hi* (*Virus*, 1980), *One from the Heart* (1982, directed by Francis Ford Coppola, re-creating the entire downtown Premont Street intersection of Las Vegas on a scale no larger than a Lionel

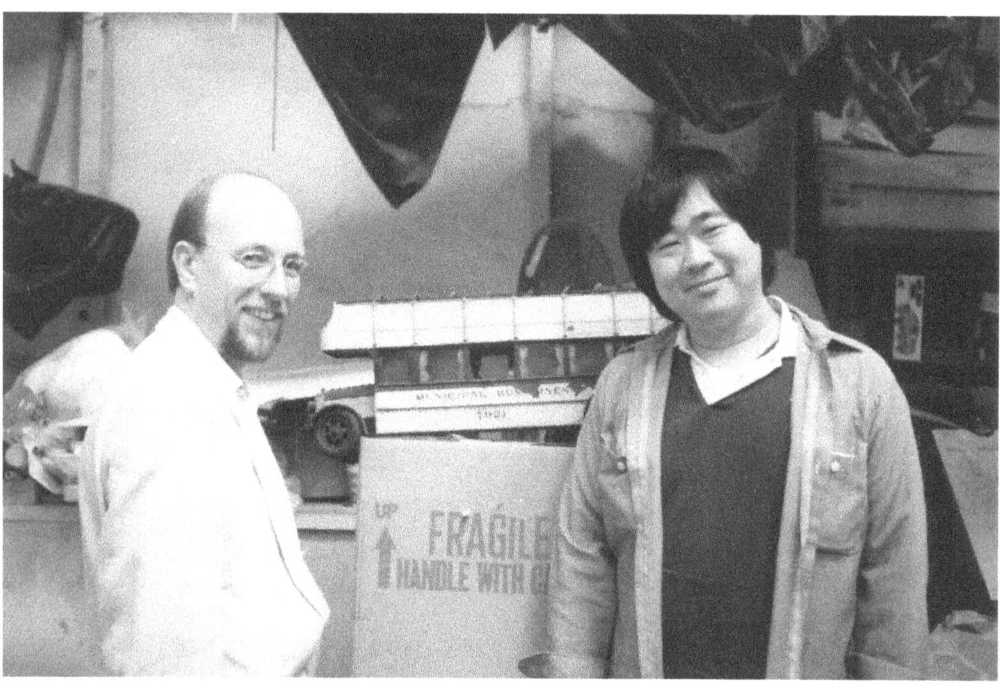

Gregory Jein (with the author) in front of the miniature bus used in the Laurel & Hardy feature *The Dancing Masters*. Not only was Jein one of Hollywood's most prominent model makers but also a great collector of World War II movie props and miniatures.

train set), *The Adventures of Buckaroo Banzai* (1984), **batteries not included* (1987), *Star Trek V: The Final Frontier* (1989), *The Hunt for Red October* (1990), *Star Trek VI: The Undiscovered Country* (1991), *Stargate* (1994), *Star Trek: Insurrection* (1998). *Showscan: Let's Go* (1985, supervised by Trumbull). TV: *V* (1983), *V: The Final Battle* (1984), *Star Trek: The Next Generation* (1987), *Star Trek: Deep Space Nine* (1993). Jein had a great collection of war time and Fox models which, unfortunately, he was forced to sell or auction.

Devereaux Jennings (1885–1952)
American Cinematographer and Visual Effects Cameraman

Joseph Devereaux "Dev" Jennings was the brother of Gordon Jennings. Expert silent (since 1915) and early sound cinematographer, lighting for Rudolph Valentino, Harry O. Hoyt (*The Lost World*, 1924–25), Buster Keaton (*The General*, 1926), and James Cagney (*The Public Enemy*, 1931). In 1933 he joined his brother in Paramount's special effects department. He multiplied two miniature galleys into a fleet by use of parallel mirrors for *Cleopatra* (1934, Cecil B. DeMille), created a war montage for *The Crusades* (1935, DeMille again), a shipwreck for *Souls at Sea* (1937), and a waterfall for DeMille's *Unconquered* (1947). Also: *Practically Yours* (1944), *Two Years Before the Mast* (1946), *The Dark Mirror* (1946, directed by Robert Siodmak), *Blaze of Noon* (1947), *The Greatest Show on Earth* (1952, DeMille), Academy Award for *Spawn of the North* (1938, a trawler collides with an iceberg). Founding member of ASC.

Gordon Jennings (1896–1953)
American Cinematographer and Special Effects Supervisor

Cecil B. DeMille called Jennings the best special effects man he was ever privileged to work with. Born in Salt Lake City, Utah, and educated in Salt Lake City and Europe. Attended University of Utah to continue engineering studies. Worked as an engineer until landing a job as assistant cameraman in 1919 with the Lois Weber production company. Did title credits and camerawork. From 1933 up to his death, he was head of the special effects and title printing departments at Paramount in Hollywood: *Island of Lost Souls* (1933), *Alice in Wonderland* (1933), *The Midnight Club* (1933), *This Day and Age* (1933), *One Sunday Afternoon* (1933), *The Scarlet Empress* (1934, directed by Josef von Sternberg), *Cleopatra* (1934), *The Crusades* (1935), *Peter Ibbetson* (1935), *Hollywood Extra Girl* (1935), *Annapolis Farewell* (1935), *Every Night at Eight* (1935), *Shanghai* (1935), *Smart Girl* (1935), *The Big Broadcast of 1936* (1936), *Give Us This Night* (1936), *The General Died at Dawn* (1936), *Rhythm on the Range* (1936), *The Plainsman* (1936), *The Big Broadcast of 1937* (1937), *Wells Fargo* (1937), *The Big Broadcast of 1938* (1938), *Men with Wings* (1938), *Spawn of the North* (1938), *If I Were King* (1938), *St. Louis Blues* (1939), *Union Pacific* (1939, DeMille), *Rulers of the Sea* (1939), *Dr. Cyclops* (1939–40), *Typhoon* (1940), *North West Mounted Police* (1940, DeMille), *Aloma of the South Seas* (1941), *The Mad Doctor* (1941), *I Wanted Wings* (1941), *Reap the Wild Wind* (1942), *The Great Man's Lady* (1942), *This Gun for Hire* (1942), *Wake Island* (1942), *I Married a Witch* (1942, directed by René Clair), *Road to Morocco* (1942), *No Time for Love* (1943), *China* (1943), *So Proudly We Hail!* (1943), *Dixie* (1943), *For Whom the Bell Tolls* (1943), *Hostages* (1943), *The Uninvited* (1944), *Lady in the Dark* (1944), *The Story of Dr. Wassell* (1944), *Going My Way* (1944), *The Hour Before the Dawn* (1944), *Till We Meet Again* (1944), *Our Hearts Were Young and Gay* (1944), *Rainbow Island* (1944), *Frenchman's Creek* (1944), *Here Come the Waves* (1944), *Practically Yours* (1944), *A Medal for Benny* (1945), *Sally O'Rourke* (1945), *Murder, He Says* (1945), *Incendiary Blonde* (1945), *Love Letters* (1945), *Duffy's Tavern* (1945), *Kitty* (1945), *Hold That Blonde* (1945), *The Lost Weekend* (1945, directed by Billy Wilder), *Masquerade in Mexico* (1945), *The Stork Club* (1945), *Road to Utopia* (1946), *Two Years Before the Mast* (1946), *To Each His Own* (1946), *The Virginian* (1946), *The Bride Wore Boots* (1946), *The Well-Groomed Bride* (1946), *O.S.S.* (1946), *The Searching Wind* (1946), *Monsieur Beaucaire* (1946), *Blue Skies* (1946), *California* (1946), *Ladies' Man* (1947), *My Favorite Brunette* (1947), *Calcutta* (1947), *Blaze of Noon* (1947), *The Trouble with Women* (1947), *The Perils of Pauline* (1947), *Desert Fury*

(1947), *Golden Earrings* (1947), *Variety Girl* (1947), *Unconquered* (1947), *Where There's Life* (1947), *Road to Rio* (1947), *Saigon* (1948), *The Big Clock* (1948), *The Sainted Sisters* (1948), *The Emperor Waltz* (1948), *Hazard* (1948), *Dream Girl* (1948), *A Foreign Affair* (1948, Billy Wilder), *Sorry, Wrong Number* (1948), *Isn't It Romantic?* (1948), *Sealed Verdict* (1948), *Miss Tatlock's Millions* (1948), *Whispering Smith* (1948), *The Paleface* (1948), *The Accused* (1949), *My Own True Love* (1949), *A Connecticut Yankee in King Arthur's Court* (1949), *Bride of Vengeance* (1949), *Sorrowful Jones* (1949), *The Great Gatsby* (1949), *Rope of Sand* (1949), *Top O' the Morning* (1949), *My Friend Irma* (1949), *The Heiress* (1949), *Song of Surrender* (1949), *Samson and Delilah* (1949, crashing huge miniature of stone idol for De-Mille), *The Great Lover* (1949), *The File on Thelma Jordon* (1950), *Paid in Full* (1950), *No Man of Her Own* (1950), *Captain Carey, U.S.A.* (1950), *My Friend Irma Goes West* (1950), *Fancy Pants* (1950), *Sunset Blvd.* (1950, Billy Wilder), *The Furies* (1950), *September Affair* (1950), *Let's Dance* (1950), *Peking Express* (1950), *A Place in the Sun* (1951), *Rhubarb* (1951), *When Worlds Collide* (1951, produced by George Pal), *Here Comes the Groom* (1951), *Submarine Command* (1951), *My Favorite Spy* (1951), *The Greatest Show on Earth* (1952, last time with DeMille), *Sailor Beware* (1952), *Aaron Slick from Punkin Crick* (1952), *My Son John* (1952), *The Atomic City* (1952), *Jumping Jacks* (1952), *Son of Paleface* (1952), *Somebody Loves Me* (1952), *The Savage* (1952), *The Turning Point* (1952), *Come Back, Little Sheba* (1952), *The Stooge* (1953), *Off Limits* (1953), *The Stars Are Singing* (1953), *The Girls of Pleasure Island* (1953), *Botany Bay* (1953), *Shane* (1953), *Scared Stiff* (1953), *Stalag 17* (1953, Billy Wilder), *Houdini* (1953), *Forever Female* (1953), *Little Boy Lost* (1953), *Here Come the Girls* (1953). Won two Academy Awards. Suffered a heart attack on the golf course right after the time-consuming, award-winning work for George Pal's *The War of the Worlds* (1952–53) for which he supervised the attack of wire-suspended Martian war machines. Scientific or Technical Award, Class II (shared with S. L. Stancliffe) in 1951 for the design, construction and application of a servo-operated recording and repeating device (originally used for the climax of *Samson and Delilah*).

Brian Johnson
British Special Effects Supervisor

Worked under the names Brian Johnson and Brian Johncock. After public school he worked in a laboratory. His career took off in 1958 with Bowie Films, where he did physical as well as photographic effects and miniatures for Anglo Scottish Pictures, first as a helper, then as a camera assistant, by which time he had joined the union. After that he did some work for a commercial company before serving in the Royal Air Force for two years (from the end of 1959 to 1961). Eventually rejoined Bowie: *The Day the Earth Caught Fire* (1961) and Hammer's *Captain Clegg* (1961–62), *The Phantom of the Opera* (1961–62), *The Kiss of the Vampire* (1962/64). Les Bowie recommended him to Stanley Kubrick for *2001: A Space Odyssey* (1965–68, equipping the space wheel with Bell & Howell 16mm rear-projection systems) and to producer Gerry Anderson for the TV series *Thunderbirds* (1964–65) and *Space: 1999* (1975; "The thing I've tried to do with the series, is to shoot it almost like a documentary. You very often see special effects sets on the screen and because they've been set up by somebody who's fairly artistically minded, they're often more composed than a genuine shot would be. In other words, there's always a nice little tree over on the left hand side of the shot, balancing that on the right is a lump of rock. And in the background in the valley is a city, and the sky balances the whole thing. I maintain that you don't necessarily have to do that. You should shoot something which people will not instantly take as a model..."). Working again for Hammer Films, Johnson did *Taste the Blood of Dracula* (1970) and assisted Jim Danforth in setting up *When Dinosaurs Ruled the Earth* (1968–71, creating the solar eclipse and birth-of-the-moon shots). With Bowie he did *Mosquito Squadron* (1969). *SFX* supervisor: *The Tamarind Seed* (1974), *Glitterball* (1977), *The Medusa Touch* (1977–78, airplane model crashing into skyscraper, 25 years before 9/11), *Revenge of the Pink Panther* (1978), *Alien* (1978–79, Academy Award), *The Empire Strikes Back* (1979–80, Academy Award), *Dragonslayer* (1980–81), *The Pirates of Penzance* (1983), *Die unendliche Geschichte* (*The Neverending Story*, 1983–84, filmed in Munich at Bavaria Geiselgasteig Stu-

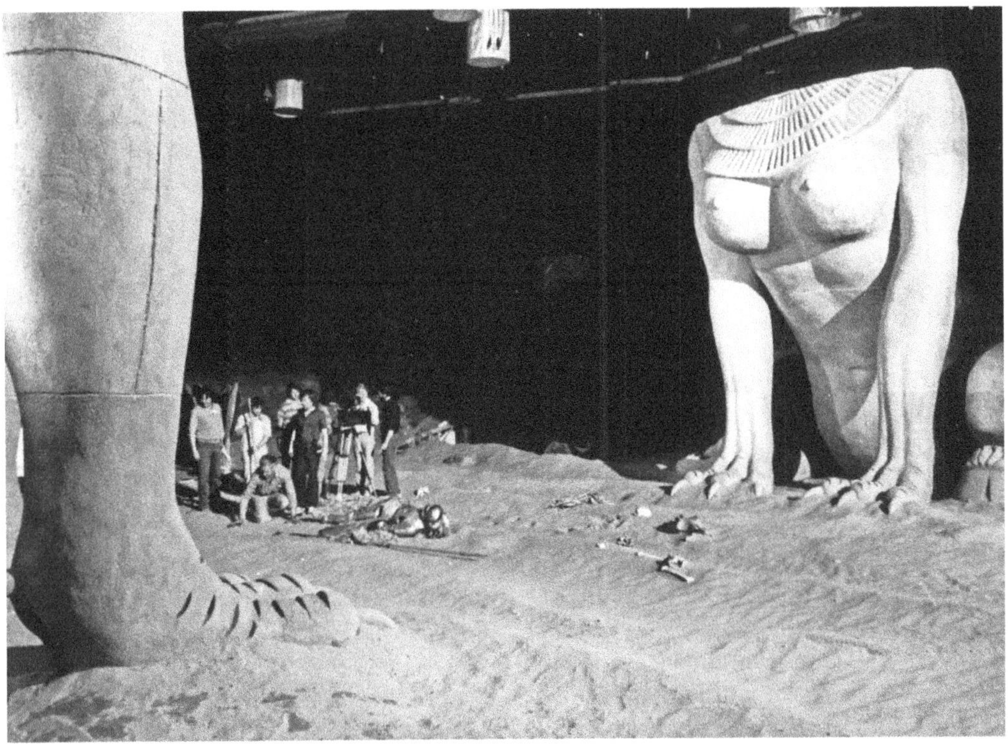

A British FX crew under the supervision of Brian Johnson at work at Munich's Bavaria Studios on *The NeverEnding Story* (1983–84) (courtesy Deutsche Kinemathek Berlin).

dios), *Spies Like Us* (1985), *Aliens* (1986), *Slipstream* (1989), *Highlander III: The Sorcerer* (1994), *Dragonheart* (1996), *Space Truckers* (1996). Television special: *Into Infinity* (1976). His goal to become a film director (project *Telepathy*) apparently failed.

Elmer R. Johnson

Swedish Model Maker

Worked in the Universal model shop and manufactured the odd spacecraft used in the original *Flash Gordon* serial of 1936.

J. MacMillan Johnson

(1912–1990)

American Art Director, Illustrator and Visual Effects Artist

Born in Los Angeles, J. MacMillan Johnson graduated in Architecture from USC, then attended Art Center School. Regularly working in the art department, he illustrated or designed including David Selznick's *Gone with the Wind* (1939), *Duel in the Sun* (1946), *The Paradine Case* (1947) and the effects sequence for *Portrait of Jennie* (1948). Art Also worked for Paramount, MGM and other companies: *The Jungle Book* (1942), *Rear Window* (1954), *Conquest of Space* (1955), *One-Eyed Jacks* (1961) and *Mutiny on the Bounty* (1962). At MGM he was in charge of special effects after the retirement of A. Arnold Gillespie, with whom he had worked on *The Wizard of Oz* in 1939: *Billy Rose's Jumbo* (1962), *A Ticklish Affair* (1963), *The Prize* (1963), *Advance to the Rear* (1964), *The Unsinkable Molly Brown* (1964), *The Outrage* (1964), *Signpost to Murder* (1964), *The Greatest Story Ever Told* (1965), *Joy in the Morning* (1965), *When the Boys Meet the Girls* (1965), *The Glass Bottom Boat* (1966), *Hold On!* (1966), *7 Women* (1966), *Spinout* (1966), *Hot Rods to Hell* (1967), *Point Blank* (1967), *La Bataille de San Sebastian* (1968), *Ice Station Zebra* (1968), *The Power* (1968), *Where Were You When the Lights Went Out?* (1968), *The Extraordinary Seaman* (1969), *The Gypsy Moths*

(1969), *Marlowe* (1969). TV: *Earth II* (1971, with Jim Danforth). Died in Napoopoo, Kona, Hawaii.

Joe Johnston (1950–)
American Storyboard Artist and Director

Joseph "Joe" Johnston was born in Fort Worth, Texas. After graduating from college, he did preliminary sketches of Yoda, snow walkers, Ewoks and speeder bikes for the *Star Wars* saga. Storyboard sketches for *Battlestar Galactica* (1978), *Raiders of the Lost Ark* (1981) and *Indiana Jones and the Temple of Doom* (1984), then enrolled in the University of Southern California (USC) Film School to become a director: *Honey, I Shrunk the Kids* (1989), *The Rocketeer* (1991), *The Pagemaster* (1994), *Jumanji* (1995–96), *October Sky* (1999), *Jurassic Park III* (2001), *Hidalgo* (2004). Second unit director: **batteries not included* (1987). Associate producer: *Willow* (1988). Academy Award for *Poltergeist* (1982).

Koichi Kawakita (1942–)
Japanese Special Effects Director

Entered Toho's special effects division in 1962 when they did *Yosei Gorasu* (*Gorath*) and *Kingukongu tai Gojira* (*King Kong vs. Godzilla*). Focused on composites and optical effects: *Zero faita dai kusen* (1966), *Kingukongu no gyakushu* (*King Kong Escapes*, 1967). Directed episodes for the *Urutoraman* (*Ultraman*) and *Ryusei Ningen Zon* (*Zone Fighter*) TV series (1973). Chief assistant director to Teruyoshi Nakano: *Nosutoradamasu no daiyogen* (*Catastrophe 1999: The Prophecies of Nostradamus*, 1974), *Gojira tai Mekagojira* (*Godzilla vs. Mechagodzilla*, 1974), *Tokywan enjo* (*Tokyo Gulf Burns*, 1975), *Wakusei daisenso* (*The War in Space*, 1977). Also assisted Teisho Arikawa on *Xing xing wang* (*Colossus of Congo*) in 1977. On his own he supervised effects for *Sayonara, Jupeta* (*Sayonara Jupiter*,1984), *Zerosen moyu* (*Zero Fighter Burns*, 1984) and *Ai: Tabidachi* (*Love: Take Off*, 1985). On the strength of his sci-fi entry *Ganheddo* (*Gunhed*, 1989) and a *Making Of* he had created for the new *Gojira*, he was appointed director of effects for the Godzilla series: *Gojira tai Biorante* (*Godzilla Vs. Biollante*, 1989), *Gojira tai Kingu Gidora* (*Godzilla vs. King Ghidorah*, 1991), *Gojira tai Mosura* (*Godzilla vs. Mothra*, 1992), *Gojira VS Mekagojira* (*Godzilla vs. Mechagodzilla II*, 1993), *Godzilla vs. Spacegodzilla* (1994), *Gojira VS Desutoroia* (*Godzilla vs. Destroyah*, 1995), *Mosura* (*The Rebirth of Mothra*, 1996), *Mosura 2: Kaitei kessan* (*Rebirth of Mothra II*, 1997). In 2003 he supervised effects for the TV series *Choseijin Guranseiza* (*Super Star God Gransazar*).

W. Wallace Kelley
American Cinematographer

Spent most of his professional life at Paramount Studios. Photographed process plates for *Dr. Cyclops* (1939–40), *Aloma of the South Seas* (1941), *I Wanted Wings* (1941), *Reap the Wild Wind* (1941–42), *The Story of Dr. Wassell* (1944), *Incendiary Blonde* (1945), *Unconquered* (1947), *Samson and Delilah* (1949), *Red Mountain* (1951), *Something to Live for* (1952), *Sangaree* (1953, 3D), *Those Redheads from Seattle* (1953, 3D), *Botany Bay* (1953), *Jivaro* (1953–54, 3D), *Alaska Seas* (1954), *Elephant Walk* (1954), *The Bridges at Toko-Ri* (1954–55), *Vertigo* (1958), *The Buccaneer* (1958). Miniature photography: *The War of the Worlds* (1952–53). Aerial photographer: *Wake Island* (1942). Second unit camera: *The Greatest Show on Earth* (1952), *The Ten Commandments* (1953–56), *Living It Up* (1954), *To Catch a Thief* (1955), *Pardners* (1956), *Hollywood or Bust* (1956), *Houseboat* (1958), *The Trap* (1959), *Alias Jesse James* (1959), *The Five Pennies* (1959), *But Not for Me* (1959), *One-Eyed Jacks* (1961), *Blue Hawaii* (1961), *Marooned* (1969). Jerry Lewis made him a director of photography on his comedies (*The Ladies Man* and *The Errand Boy* in 1961, *The Nutty Professor* and *Who's Minding the Store?* in 1963) and recently called Kelley the best cameraman who ever worked in Hollywood (see: bonus on DVD edition of *The Nutty Professor*).

Philip A. Kellison (19??–2005)
American Stop-Motion and Effects Cinematographer

Philip A. "Phil" Kellison was a fan of Willis O'Brien's. Began with 16mm amateur films. Began professionally as an animation cameraman on George Pal's *Puppetoons*. After that he worked on many commercials. Photographed the main titles for Michael Todd's *Around the World in 80 Days* (1956), was involved in Ziv TV's sci-fi series *Men in Space* and served as cameraman and optical printing technician for companies like Jack Rabin (*The Giant Behemoth*, 1958–59) and Howard A. Anderson (*The Black Scorpion*, 1956–57, *The Time Machine*, 1959–60). For Anderson and Project Unlimited, where he had already animated the steam-shovel that pushed the T.Rex from the cliff in *Dinosaurus!* (1960), he was first unit camera operator on (and then did the stop-motion photography for) *Jack the Giant Killer* (1960–62). At some time in his career Kellison was associated with oldtimers Ned H. Mann and Leonard Pickley. Later worked as a supervisor at Cascade Pictures and Coast Special Effects with Roy Seawright. Miniature photography for *Airplane II: The Sequel* (1982).

Ray Kellogg (1919–1981)

American Special Effects Supervisor, Second Unit Director, Director

E. R. [Ray] Kellogg was right-hand man to Fred M. Sersen, head of the special effects department at 20th Century–Fox. Also an expert matte artist: *The Rains Came* (1939), *The Blue Bird* (1940), *A Yank in the R.A.F.* (1941), *Wilson* (1944), *Captain Eddie* (1945), *Deep Waters* (1948), *Down to the Sea in Ships* (1949), *Slattery's Hurricane* (1949), *You're in the Navy Now* (1951), *Fourteen Hours* (1951), *The Day the Earth Stood Still* (1951), *The Desert Fox: The Story of Rommel* (1951). In 1952, when Sersen retired, Kellogg took charge of the department: *Phone Call from a Stranger* (1952), *Five Fingers* (1952), *Deadline—U.S.A.* (1952), *With a Song in My Heart* (1952), *Belles on Their Toes* (1952), *Wait Till the Sun Shines, Nellie* (1952), *We're Not Married!* (1952), *Lure of the Wilderness* (1952), *Don't Bother to Knock* (1952), *Dreamboat* (1952), *Les Misérables* (1952), *The Snows of Kilimanjaro* (1952), *What Price Glory* (1952), *Monkey Business* (1952), *My Pal Gus* (1952), *Pony Soldier* (1952), *Stars and Stripes Forever* (1952), *My Cousin Rachel* (1952), *The I Don't Care Girl* (1953), *Niagara* (1953), *The Silver Whip* (1953), *Call Me Madam* (1953), *Ti-*

tanic (1953), *The Desert Rats* (1953), *The Glory Brigade* (1953), *The Girl Next Door* (1953), *The President's Lady* (1953), *Pickup on South Street* (1953), *White Witch Doctor* (1953), *Gentlemen Prefer Blondes* (1953), *The Kid from Left Field* (1953), *Vicki* (1953), *The Robe* (1953, first CinemaScope feature), *A Blueprint for Murder* (1953), *How to Marry a Millionaire* (1953), *Beneath the 12-Mile Reef* (1953, underwater scenes including the attack of an overgrown octopus), *King of the Khyber Rifles* (1953), *Hell and High Water* (1954), *Prince Valiant* (1954), *River of No Return* (1954), *Demetrius and the Gladiators* (1954, sequel to *The Robe*), *Garden of Evil* (1954), *Broken Lance* (1954), *The Egyptian* (1954), *Black Widow* (1954), *Desirée* (1954), *There's No Business Like Show Business* (1954), *Prince of Players* (1955), *The Racers* (1955), *Untamed* (1955), *A Man Called Peter* (1955), *Daddy Long Legs* (1955), *Soldier of Fortune* (1955), *The Seven Year Itch* (1955), *House of Bamboo* (1955), *The Virgin Queen* (1955), *How to Be Very, Very Popular* (1955), *Love Is a Many-Splendored Thing* (1955), *The Left Hand of God* (1955), *Seven Cities of Gold* (1955), *The Girl in the Red Velvet Swing* (1955), *Good Morning, Miss Dove* (1955), *The Rains of Ranchipur* (1955, remake of *The Rains Came*), *The Tall Men* (1955), *The Bottom of the Bottle* (1956), *Carousel* (1956), *On the Threshold of Space* (1956), *The Man in the Grey Flannel Suit* (1956), *Hilda Crane* (1956), *23 Paces to Baker Street* (1956), *D-Day the Sixth of June* (1956), *The Proud Ones* (1956), *The King and I* (1956), *Bigger Than Life* (1956), *Bus Stop* (1956), *The Last Wagon* (1956), *Between Heaven and Hell* (1956), *Teenage Rebel* (1956), *Love Me Tender* (1956), *The Girl Can't Help It* (1956), *Three Brave Men* (1956), *The True Story of Jesse James* (1957), *Heaven Knows, Mr. Allison* (1957), *Boy on a Dolphin* (1957), *Desk Set* (1957), *The Way to the Gold* (1957). In 1957 he left 20th Century–Fox and directed some low-budget efforts involving inexpensive effects: *The Giant Gila Monster* and *The Killer Shrews* (1959, the first with a lizard on miniature sets, the second with dogs-turned-giant rats, both for producer Ken Curtis, who for some time was John Ford's son-in-law), and *My Dog, Buddy* (1960). Kellogg was an acknowledged expert in outdoor shooting and combat scenes (in World War II he had been a member of John Ford's field photo division, was promoted to commander and was responsible for the editing of a documentary, *The Nazi Plan,* to be shown during the Nuremberg War Crimes Trials in 1945 which he covered on film in *That Justice Be Done*). He became a sought-after second unit director: *Cleopatra* (1962–63), John Ford's *Cheyenne Autumn* (1965), *Stagecoach* (the 1966 remake of John Ford's classic), *Batman* (1966), *Way ... Way Out* (1966), *Chuka* (1967), *Castle Keep* (1969), *Tora! Tora! Tora!* (1969–70), *The Revengers* (1972). Co-directed the dubious Vietnam drama *The Green Berets* (1968) with John Wayne. For TV he produced *The Red Pony* (1973). Died in Sherman Oaks, California.

George Kenyon

American-Australian Visual Effects Supervisor

Left the United States to direct effects department of Cinesound Studios in Sydney. George Heath was his cinematographer, Stuart Ralston did the background projection. They worked on the Australian productions *Lovers and Luggers* and *Tall Timbers* (both 1937).

Erich Kettelhut (1893–1979)

German Art Director

A former scenic painter, Kettelhut, with associates Otto Hunte and Karl Vollbrecht, created the sets for Fritz Lang's *Doktor Mabuse, der Spieler* in 1921–22, *Die Nibelungen* in 1922–24 and *Metropolis* in 1925–26. His involvement in these grand productions (as well as his first encounter with Lang on *Das wandernde Bild* in 1920) introduced him to trick shots. For the epic *Nibelungen*, a fire-breathing dragon had to be unleashed. Originally, a living lizard was considered, enlarged by miniature sets, but director Fritz Lang decided against that proposal and ordered a full-scale mechanical dragon. Kettelhut contributed the technical designs. The dragon's long neck was assembled with gradually enlarging iron rings, as was the tail. The neck's curve was created using stabilizing beechwood frames which were fastened vertically into the ring forms. Wire tackles made it maneuverable. In all, the beast measured approximately fifty feet and was mounted on wheels. Inside its hollow body, a man manipulated the eyes and mouth. Other technicians, hidden beneath the dragon in a trench, provided motivation for the legs. In the monster's giant head was a petrol can with a hose leading to a pair of bellows concealed within the torso. On the other side of the can was a hole, and in front of that a little basin filled with acetylene fuel. Through the creature's open mouth, the can was filled with lycopodium powder in motion over the flame, which in turn produced a fiery burst twenty to thirty feet long. *Metropolis* was the technological culmination of German effects photography of the day. For various shots the City of the Future was painted by Kettelhut, who called this technique *Maltrick* (painted effect). Also a huge miniature was built, complete with tiny airplanes and ground vehicles which would be painstakingly animated using stop-motion. According to Kettelhut, "The aeroplanes had to be animated .6 inch after a single frame of film was exposed, the high-speed rail cars .4 inch, the automobiles about .3 inch and the pedestrians just minimally to get fluid movement in a believable tempo. An animation team was assembled by Edmund Ziehfuss, the resident model maker. Each man was assigned to a specific job. A blue light signaled the move. Cars, trains and pedestrians had to be animated conscientiously and for exactly the required distance. The aeroplanes were animated with the aid of wires. The work had to be done sometimes in uncomfortable positions since frontages and railway bridges and lamp sockets hindered our efforts enormously. When everybody had done his requested animation, the gaffer switched on full shooting light and another frame of film was exposed."

Jack Kevan

American Makeup Expert

Whenever a photographer showed up at Universal to cover one of their monster makeup creatures, Bud Westmore, the head of the department, posed besides the creature, but often there was another man seen with him. This was the guy who handled the actual makeup concept. Kevan had already done fantasy stuff for *The Wizard of Oz* (1939) and a Frankenstein monster for MGM's 3D short *Third Dimensional Murder* (1940), which certainly qualified him to

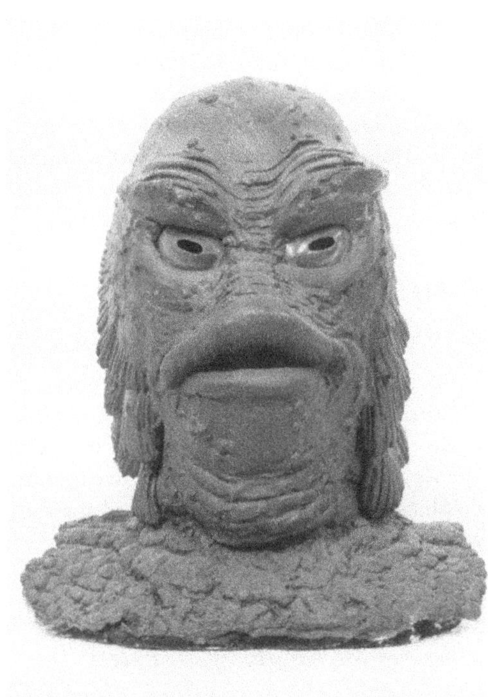

A replica of the creature from the *Black Lagoon* (the original was by Jack Kevan) (courtesy Deutsche Kinemathek Berlin).

try his hand on Glenn Strange as the Monster in *Abbott and Costello Meet Frankenstein* (1948). Other Universal horrors: *Abbott and Costello Meet Dr. Jekyll and Mr. Hyde* (1953), *It Came from Outer Space* (1953, 3D), *Creature from the Black Lagoon* (1954, 3D) and sequel *Revenge of the Creature* (1955, 3D), the Metaluna Mutant from *This Island Earth* (1955), *Tarantula* (1955), dinosaurs for *The Land Unknown* (1957), *The Mole People* (1956), the Lon Chaney "biographical" picture *Man of a Thousand Faces* (1957) starring James Cagney, *Monster on the Campus* (1958). In 1958, he independently co-produced *The Monster of Piedras Blancas*.

Otto Anton Kiechle

German-American Matte Artist

Painter of stained glass windows. Moved from Missouri to Hollywood where he found a niche in early movies painting background sets. Became a matte artist for Warren A. Newcombe at MGM in Culver City. His son, Edgar Kiechle, did backgrounds for Ub Iwerks and Walter Lantz cartoons before he joined Universal's art department as production illustrator (*Spartacus*).

Peter Kleinow

American Stop-Motion Animator

Got a contract from Project Unlimited: *7 Faces of Dr. Lao* (1963–64) and another George Pal film, *The Power* (1967–68). Animator for Fantasy II (Gene Warren, Jr.) and other companies: *Caveman* (1980), *Goliath Awaits* (1981, TV), *Spacehunter: Adventures in the Forbidden Zone* (1983), *Gremlins* (1984), *The Terminator* (1984), *Santa Claus* (1985), *The Puppetoon Movie* (1987, additional animation), *Leonard Part VI* (1987), *RoboCop 2* (1990), *Stephen King's It* (1990, TV), *Terminator 2: Judgment Day* (1991), *Nemesis* (1993), *Army of Darkness* (1993).

Pavel Vladimirovich Klushantsev (1910–99)

Soviet-Russian Director

Born in St. Petersburg, the son of a physician. Enrolled in the Photo-Cinema-Technical Secondary School and finished in 1930 as a cameraman. Started making popular science and educational films. His skill in solving mechanical challenges and creating photographic effects led to a career in special effects in 1938 with a workshop called Lennauchfilm (Lensciencefilm) Studio. In 1943 he made military instructional films in Novosibirsk, Siberia. After the war he impressed with *Northern Lights* (1946), *Meteory* (1947–48) and *Kosmos* (*The Universe*, 1951). Later joined Lenfilm Studios and, around the time Sputnik was launched, directed space films *Doroga k zvezdam* (*Way to the Stars/Road to the Stars*, 1957), about a trip to the Moon, and *Planeta bur* (*Planet of Storms*, 1962), a journey to Venus, for which he devised outstanding special effects. (In the United States, footage from it was cannibalized for 1965's *Voyage to the Prehistoric Planet*). In 1965, in *Luna* (*The Moon*), he presented a colonized lunar surface with workers and their families living in a city designed by science fiction artist Yuri Shvets, and in 1968's *Mars*, he set foot on the red planet. Klushantsev retired in 1972. Robert F. Skotak, a fan of Klushantsev's work, devoted a post-mortem documentary, *The Star Dreamer* (2002), to his work.

Lloyd W. Knechtel (1907–1971)

Canadian-American Effects and Second Unit Cinematographer

Born in Southampton, Ontario, Canada. In 1923 he started in a laboratory in Detroit. 1926: Pathe News, Hollywood. In 1927 he assisted Fred W. Jackman on the *Rex, the Wild Horse* series. In 1929 he built up RKO's camera effects department with artist Paul Detlefsen and assistant Linwood G. Dunn: *Ringside* (1929), *Rio Rita* (1929), *Night Parade* (1929), *Jazz Heaven* (1929), *Girl of the Port* (1930), *Second Wife* (1930), *The Cuckoos* (1930), *Conspiracy* (1930), *Danger Lights* (1930, train wreck in 65mm), *Leathernecking* (1930), *Hit the Deck* (1930), *Dixiana* (1930), *Cimarron* (1931), *Beau Ideal* (1931), *Three Who Loved* (1931), *The Sin Ship* (1931), *What Price Hollywood?* (1932), *Are These Our Children?* (1931), *The Lost Squadron* (1932), *Bird of Paradise* (1932), *The Most Dangerous Game* (1932), *The Conquerors* (1932), *The Monkey's Paw* (1932–33). Left Hollywood in 1933 and went to Britain to introduce background projection to George Humphries & Co. Pictures: *Jack Ahoy* (1934), *Emil and the Detectives* (1935, distortion effects), *Last Journey* (1936), *It's Love Again* (1936), *Secret Agent* (1936), *Non-Stop New York* (1937), *O.H.M.S.* (1937). Shot process plates in Britain and Europe for *David Copperfield* (MGM), *A Yank at Oxford* (MGM), *Angel* (Paramount), *Artists and Models* and *Bluebeard's Eighth Wife* (Paramount), *Algiers* (Walter Wanger). Returned to the United States. Second unit photographer for Alfred Hitchcock's *Rebecca* (1940) and for *Tarzan's Secret Treasure* (1941, MGM, in Wakulla Springs, Florida). Was assigned to film Bikini underwater atomic test with crew (Paul and Harry Perry, Tom Tutwiler, Gilbert Warrenton): "With the United States Army and Navy cooperating to the utmost, it will stand in history as one of the greatest demonstrations and shows of all time in the propaganda for peace in this world." In 1951 he did optical effects for Lou Bunin's puppet version of *Alice in Wonderland*. Cinematographer: *The Mortal Storm* (1940, uncredited), *Naked Youth* (1960). Effects photographer: *I, the Jury* (1953, Mike Hammer in 3D), *The Angry Red Planet* (1959). Last assignment as director of photography: *Wilbur and the Baby Factory* (1970). Article in *American Cinematographic Annual* II, American Society of Photographers, 1931: "Optical Printing." Died in Long Beach, California.

John Knoll

American Visual Effects Supervisor

Started as motion-control camera operator. Credits include *Star Trek IV: The Voyage Home* (1986), *Innerspace* (1987), *Willow* (1988). With *The Abyss* (1989) he turned entirely to computer graphics and digital effects. Invented the software program Photoshop.

Fred Knoth

American Mechanical Effects Expert

Attended University of Colorado. In 1922 he came to California and helped to build the Venice Pier Rollercoaster. Found a job with Hal Roach Studios in Culver City and created mechanical effects for Our Gang and Laurel & Hardy comedies: *Pardon Us* (1931), *Swiss Miss* (1938). Feature film work for Roach included the *Topper* series and the dinosaur epic *One Million B.C.* (1939–40) with an allosaurus costume and a miniature volcano. In 1942 he joined Universal Studios: *The Ghost of Frankenstein*. In charge of mechanical and technical effects and special props at Universal since 1948: *Abbott and Costello Meet Frankenstein* (1948), *Creature from the Black Lagoon* (1953–54), *Revenge of the Creature* (1955), *This Island Earth* (1955), *Tarantula* (1955), *The Deadly Mantis* (1957), *The Land Unknown* (1957), *The Incredible Shrinking Man* (1956–57), *Hellfighters* (1968, with burning oil fields and a heroic John Wayne). Scientific or Technical Award Class III in 1954 (with Orien Ernest): for the development of a hand portable, electric, dry oil-fog machine.

Hans F. Koenekamp (1891–1992)

American Visual Effects Cinematographer

Byron Haskin once called Koenekamp "the greatest effects man of them all." He was born in

Denison, Iowa; his parents were immigrants from Oldenburg, Germany. In 1911 he came to Hollywood and began as a projectionist. In 1913 he became a pioneer cameraman at Mack Sennett's Keystone Studios where his first task was to build a submersible camera housing for some undersea scenes with famous comedienne-actress Mabel Normand. He also photographed Charles Chaplin (*Mabel's Strange Predicament*, 1914; at least part of *Tillie's Punctured Romance*, 1914), Wallace Beery, Gloria Swanson, the Keystone Cops and the Sennett Bathing Beauties. After a stint with Fox Studios in 1917 and the epic *Civilization* in 1918 at Inceville, he joined Vitagraph and became Larry Semon's favorite cinematographer (*Wizard of Oz*, 1925, with Semon as the Scarecrow and Oliver Hardy as the Tin Man). Assisted his former Sennett colleague, Fred W. Jackman, in photographing visual effects (*The Lost World*, 1924–25) and second unit and started an unparalleled career which lasted for about 30 years after Warners eventually had occupied the First National lot in Burbank: two versions of *Isle of Lost Ships* (1923 and 1929), *Noah's Ark* (1929), *Moby Dick* (1930), *Svengali* (1931), *I Am a Fugitive from a Chain Gang* (1932), *42nd Street* (1932–33), *A Midsummer Night's Dream* (1935, additional photography), *Earthworm Tractors* (1936), *Isle of Fury* (1936), *The Charge of the Light Brigade* (1936), *China Clipper* (1936, aerial photography), *Black Legion* (1937), *Green Light* (1937), *The Great O'Malley* (1937), *San Quentin* (1937), *Submarine D-1* (1937), *Wings of the Navy* (1939), *The Private Lives of Elizabeth and Essex* (1939), *We Are Not Alone* (1939), *Virginia City* (1940), *Torrid Zone* (1940), *The Sea Hawk* (1940), *They Drive by Night* (1940), *Santa Fe Trail* (1940), *The Sea Wolf* (1940–41), *High Sierra* (1941), *The Wagons Roll at Night* (1941), *Manpower* (1941), *Navy Blues* (1941), *Wings of the Eagle* (1942), *Captains of the Clouds* (1942), *Air Force* (1943), *Mission to Moscow* (1943), *Thank Your Lucky Stars* (1943), *Roughly Speaking* (1945), *God Is My Co-Pilot* (1945), *The Horn Blows at Midnight* (1945), *Conflict* (1945), *That Way with Women* (1947), *Cheyenne* (1947), *Deep Valley* (1947), *Dark Passage* (1947; the first half-hour of this mystery story with Humphrey Bogart escaping from San Quentin and undergoing plastic surgery is shown from Bogart's point of view: "I had him roll down a hill in a barrel, cross the Golden Gate Bridge, fight with a guy, romance Lauren Bacall, etc."), *The Treasure of the Sierra Madre* (1948), *My Girl Tisa* (1948), *Winter Meeting* (1948), *The Big Punch* (1948), *June Bride* (1948), *Fighter Squadron* (1948), *Colorado Territory* (1949), *The Fountainhead* (1949), *It's A Great Feeling* (1949), *White Heat* (1949), *The Story of Seabiscuit* (1949), *The Lady Takes a Sailor* (1949), *Chain Lightning* (1950), *The Daughter of Rosie O'Grady* (1950), *Pretty Baby* (1950), *Operation Pacific* (1951), *Strangers on a Train* (1951), *Fort Worth* (1951), *On Moonlight Bay* (1951), *The Big Trees* (1952), *Mara Maru* (1952), *The Winning Team* (1952), *South Sea Woman* (1953), *A Star Is Born* (1954), *The Silver Chalice* (1954), *Young at Heart* (1954), *The Sea Chase* (1955), *Sincerely Yours* (1955), *The Court-Martial of Billy Mitchell* (1955), *Sayonara* (1957), *Lindbergh* (1957), *The Old Man and the Sea* (1958). He considered *The Beast with Five Fingers* (1946–47, with a disembodied hand playing piano and strangling Peter Lorre) his best work. Father of cinematographer Fred J. Koenekamp and two daughters. Invented an interlocking motor that synchronized background projector and camera and was widely used. Died in Northridge, California.

Willi Koerner

German Process Technician

Koerner assisted cameramen Guido Seeber and Gerhard Huttula at Ufa Studios' Process Stage in Babelsberg: *Über alles in der Welt* (1940), *Stukas* (1941), *Münchhausen* (1942–43). When the Babelsberg Studios were transformed into DEFA after World War II, Koerner remained in charge of background projection. In the 1950s he was sent to China to build up a process department at Shanghai Film Studios. Remained active until the 1960s.

Shigeru Komatsuzaki

Japanese Mechanic Designer and Illustrator

Studied physics and electronics. During World War II he became part of a team experimenting with laser technology. Worked on projects for the Japanese Navy. After the war, he got assignments from Eiji Tsuburaya to design fanciful Marcalite guns and bizarre alien costumes for *Chikyu boeigun* (U.S.: *The Mysterians*, 1957), ray guns and the flying undersea battleship *Gohten-go* for *Kaitei gunkan* (U.S.: *Atragon*, 1963; he contributed the story element of Mu Empire as well), from a novel he had illustrated as a children's book in 1955. Also did comic book art (Manga).

Emil Kosa, Jr. (1903–1968)

French-American Matte Artist

Born in Paris. His father had smuggled the young child from Czechoslovakia in a potato sack into the United States. In 1933 he entered Fred Sersen's matte department at Fox Studios as assistant: *Crash Dive* (1943), *The Razor's Edge* (1946), *Deep Waters* (1948), *The Day the Earth Stood Still* (1951). For a short time in the 1940s he was with Warren Newcombe and MGM. Besides winning prizes for his regular paintings, in 1952 he became head of 20th Century–Fox's matte department: *The Robe* (1953, in CinemaScope), *Hell and High Water* (1954), *The Rains of Ranchipur* (1955), *The Gift of Love* (1958), *Journey to the Center of the Earth* (1959), *North to Alaska* (1960), *The Story of Ruth* (1960), *Snow White and the Three Stooges* (1961), *Tender Is the Night* (1962), *Five Weeks in a Balloon* (1962), *Take Her, She's Mine* (1963), *Shock Treatment* (1964), *Fate Is the Hunter* (1964), *Goodbye Charlie* (1964), *Our Man Flint* (1965), *Morituri* (1965), *Dear Brigitte* (1965), *The Agony and the Ecstasy* (1965), *John Goldfarb, Please Come Home* (1965), *Von Ryan's Express* (1965), *The Sound of Music* (1965), *The Sand Pebbles* (1966), *Fantastic Voyage* (1966), *Stagecoach* (1966), *Way ... Way Out* (1966), *In Like Flint* (1967), *Caprice* (1967), *A Guide for the Married Man* (1967), *The St. Valentine's Day Massacre* (1967), *The Flim Flam Man* (1967), *Doctor Dolittle* (1967), *Planet of the Apes* (1967–68), *Bandolero!* (1968), *The Sweet Ride* (1968), *Star!* (1968). Academy Award for *Cleopatra* (1963).

Neil J. Krepela

American Matte Cinematographer

Photographed animation for an experimental film company in San Francisco. Happened to be the first cinematographer behind the matte camera of Industrial Light & Magic when they moved to San Rafael: *The Empire Strikes Back* (1979–80), *Raiders of the Lost Ark* (1981). When Richard Edlund returned to Hollywood, Krepela joined him at Boss Films: *Ghostbusters* (1983–84), *2010: The Year We Make Contact* (1984), *Cliffhanger* (1993). In 2000 he supervised effects for Disney's digital *Dinosaurs*.

Ernst Kunstmann (1898–1995)

German Effects Photographer

Born in Babelsberg (Nowawes). Started there at the pioneering Bioscop company in 1918. Specialized in miniatures and trick shots (*Der müde Tod*, 1921, *Der letzte Mann*, 1923–24). In 1923 he became assistant to Eugen Schüfftan (Eugene Shuftan), with whom he developed the Shuftan Process and worked on *Metropolis* (1925–27). For a short period he accompanied Schüfftan to Hollywood and Universal City where in 1926 they did trick and mirror shots for Paul Leni's *Love Me and the World Is Mine*. At that time he also was involved in *The Love Thief, Into Her Kingdom, Prisoners of the Storm* and *The Fourth Commandment*. Member of the Ufa-controlled Deutsche Spiegeltechnik G.m.b.H. & Co.: *Madame Pompadour* (1927), *Die Liebe der Jeanne Ney* (1927), *Königin Luise* (1927). Special photography: *Frau im Mond* (*Woman in the Moon/By Rocket to the Moon*, 1928–29), *Berge in Flammen* (1931), *F.P.1 antwortet Nicht* (*Secrets of F.P.1*, 1932), *Das Testament des Dr. Mabuse* (1932, forbidden Fritz Lang film), *Gold* (1933–34), *Triumph des Willens* (1934–35, Leni Riefenstahl), *Amphitryon* (1935), *Leichte Kavallerie* (1935), *Der Bettelstudent* (1936), *Ewiger Wald* (1936), *Stadt Anatol* (1936), *Olympia* (1936–38, Riefenstahl). From 1937 to 1945 he was in charge of photographic effects at Tobis Studios in Berlin-Johannisthal: *Die Fledermaus* (1937), *Der Tiger von Eschnapur* (1937), *Das indische Grabmal* (1937), *Fahrendes Volk* (1938), *Robert Und Bertram* (1939), *Die 3 Codonas* (1940), *Traummusik* (1940), *Ritorno* (1940), *D III 88* and *Kampfgeschwader Lützow* (1940–41, airplane miniatures), *Mein Leben für Irland* (1940–41), *Annelie—Die Geschichte einer Liebe* (1941), *Die Entlassung* (1942), *Meine Frau Teresa* (1942), *Titanic* (1942–43), *Fritze Bollmann wollte angeln* (1943), *Herr Sanders lebt gefährlich*

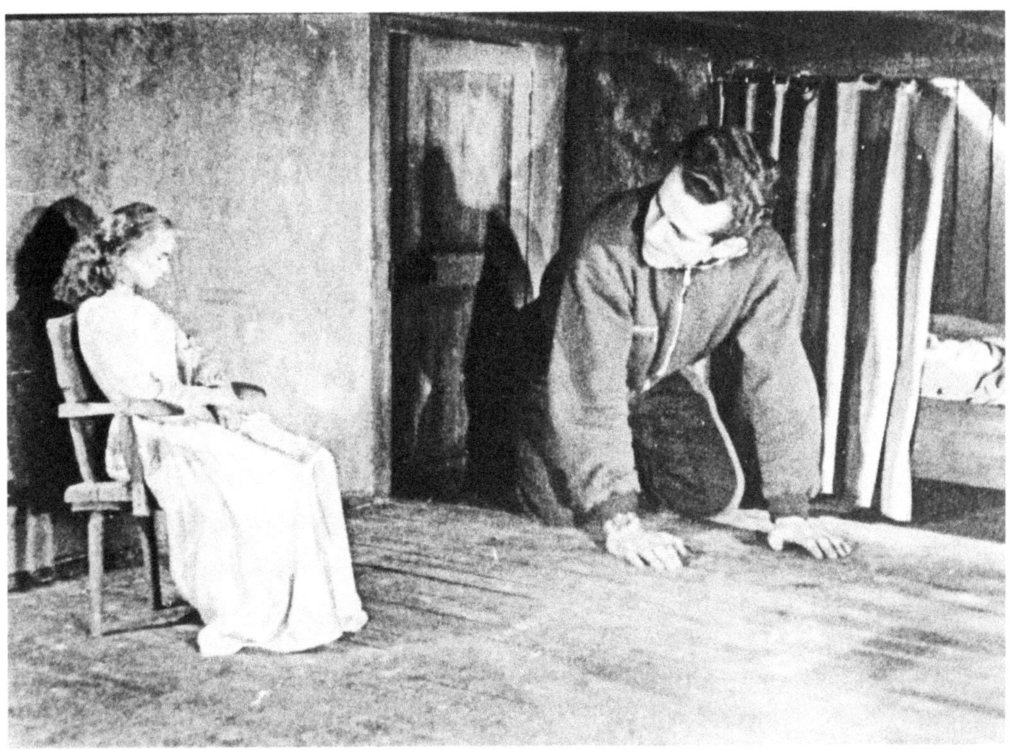

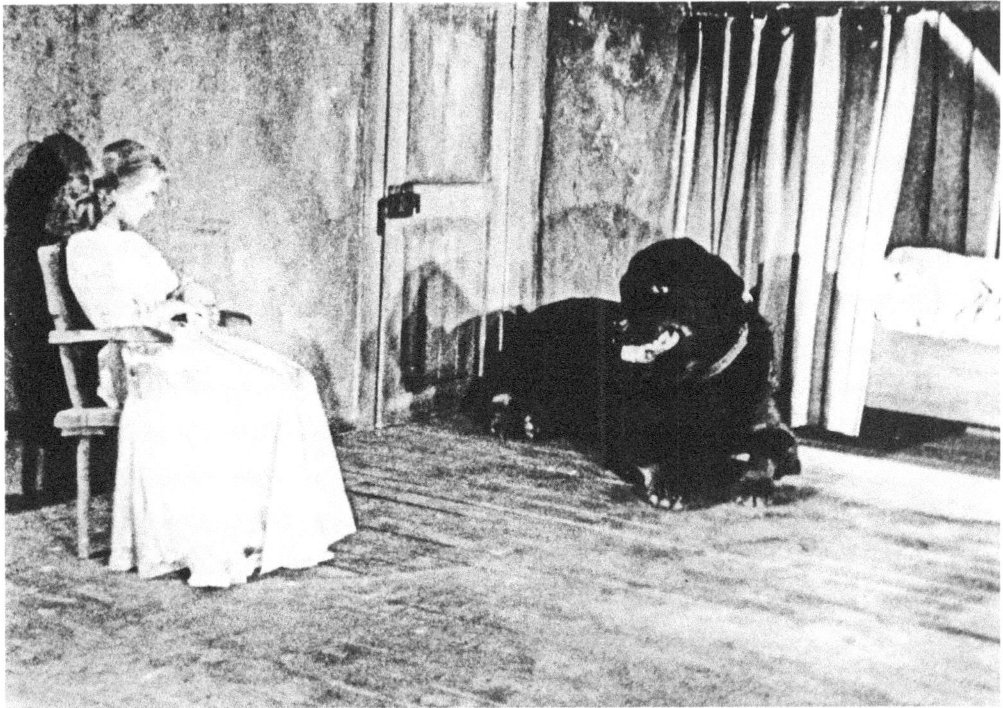

Ernst Kunstmann's assistant prepares a Shuftan shot. Final result without technician but with dog in *Das Feuerzeug* (*The Tinder Box*, 1958) from a fairy-tale by Hans Christian Andersen (courtesy Deutsche Kinemathek Berlin).

(1943), *Das kleine Hofkonzert* (1944–45). Was hired to create a special sequence for Ufa's 25th anniversary production *Münchhausen* film (1942–43). After the war, in 1947, he joined East German DEFA at the former Ufa Studios in Ba-

belsberg. Among his many credits were *Ehe im Schatten* (1947), *Chemie und Liebe* (1947–48), *Und wieder 48* (1948), *Träum nicht, Annette!* (1948), *Die Buntkarierten* (1948–49), *Rotation* (1948–49), *Der Rat Der Götter* (1949–50), *Fam-*

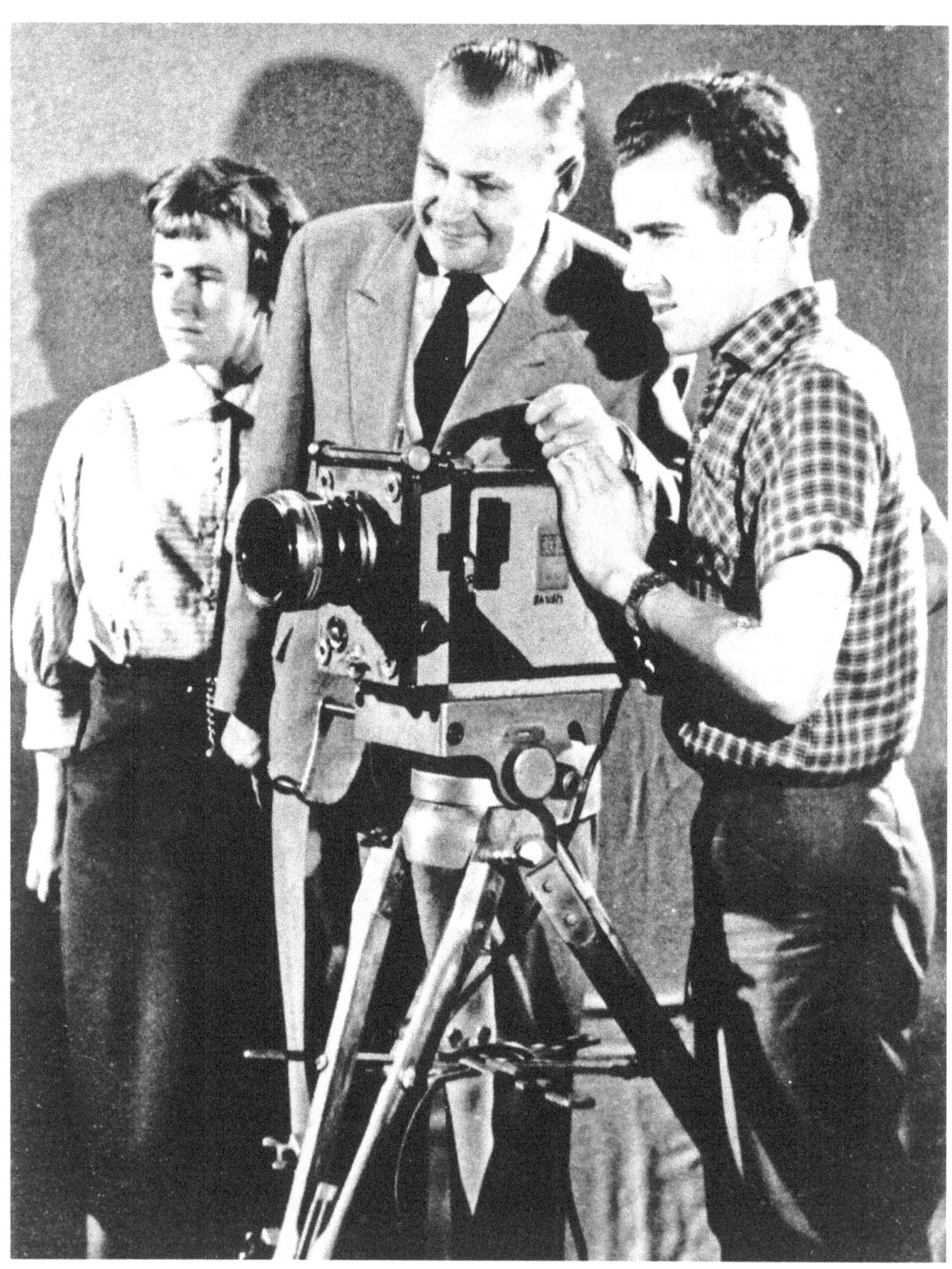

Ernst Kunstmann (center) with assistants, daughter Vera Kunstmann and Günter Gericke (courtesy Deutsche Kinemathek Berlin).

ilie Benthin (1950), *Das verurteilte Dorf* (1951), *Karriere in Paris* (1951–52), *Roman einer Jungen Ehe* (1951–52), *Schatten über den Inseln* (1951–52), *Sein grosser Sieg* (1951–52), *Geheimakte Solvay* (1952), *Anna Susanna* (1952), *Die Unbesiegbaren* (1952–53), *Das kleine und das grosse Glück* (1953), *Gefährliche Fracht* (1953–54), *Ernst Thälmann—Sohn seiner Klasse* (1953–54), *Das geheimnisvolle Wrack* (1953–54), *Hexen* (1953–54), *Stärker als die Nacht* (1954), *Carola Lamberti—Eine vom Zirkus* (1954), *Pole Poppenspäler* (1954), *Der Ochse von Kulm* (1954), *Wer seine Frau lieb hat* (1954), *Du und mancher Kamerad* (1954–56), *Einmal ist keinmal* (1954–55), *Ein Polterabend* (1954–55), *Ernst Thälmann—Führer seiner Klasse* (1954–55), *Das Fräulein von Scuderi* (1955), *Robert Mayer—Der Arzt aus Heilbronn* (1955), *Der Teufelskreis* (1955), *Friedrich Schiller* (1955), *Der Fackelträger* (1955), *Mich dürstet* (1955–56), *Das Traumschiff* (1955), *Der Hauptmann von Köln* (1956), *Die Fahrt nach Bamsdorf* (1956), *Die Abenteuer des Till Ulenspiegel* (1956), *Schlösser und Katen* (1956), *Tinko* (1956), *Lissy* (1956–57), *Berlin—Ecke Schönhauser* (1957), *Spur in die Nacht* (1957), *Tatort Berlin* (1957), *Jahrgang 21* (1957), *Abenteuer in Bamsdorf* (1957), *Sonnensucher* (1957–58), *Meine Frau macht Musik* (1957–58), *Sie kannten sich alle* (1957–58), *Der Prozess wird vertagt* (1958), *Das Lied der Matrosen* (1958), *Reportage 57* (1958–59), *Simplon-Tunnel* (1958–59), *Sas 181 antwortet nicht* (1958–59), *Weisses Blut* (1959), *Das russische Wunder* (1959–63, two-part documentary), *Leute mit Flügeln* (1959–60), *Fünf Tage—Fünf Nächte* (1960), *Der Traum des Hauptmann Loy* (1961), *Tempel des Satans* (1961), *Die schwarze Galeere* (1961–62), *Die Glatzkopfbande* (1962). His aircraft miniatures for *Geschwader Fledermaus* (1958) were criticized as old-fashioned. Several Agfacolor fairy tales which included extensive use of Shuftan Process, models, forced perspective and hanging miniatures became his heritage: *Das kalte Herz* (*A Heart of Stone*, 1950), *Die Geschichte vom Kleinen Muck* (1953), *Das Feuerzeug* (1956), *Das singende, klingende Bäumchen* (1957), *Die goldene Jurte* (1960–61), and *Vom König Midas* (1962), his last picture. For one of these fairy tales, *Der Teufel vom Mühlenberg* (1954), Kunstmann had to virtually petrify a villain, the *Mühlmann* (a miller played by Willy A.

Kleinau) of the title: "For this scene we had to build two identical landscape sets in the studio. Each rock, and even the outlines of the mountains had to be absolutely alike in both sets. In the set on the camera's left, the boulder in the shape of the miller-turned-to-stone was built. In front of the camera we had a large 45-degree mirror. The silvering was partially scraped away so that it reflected only the boulder and a few millimeters of the left set. In the camera's eyepiece, I could see the set in front, but not the actor who was masked by the boulder's reflection. The mirror with the contours was then pulled down until I could see the actor. At first, I filmed the set with the real miller. Then my assistant slowly drew up the mirror with the contours of the miller turned to stone. The moment the silvering reached the actor's feet it began to reflect the boulder on the left set until the actor had totally turned into stone." In 1959, assisted by his daughter Vera, Günter Gericke and Kurt Marks, he did some effects and model work for the first G.D.R. sci-fi epic, *Der schweigende Stern/Milczaca gwiazda*, released in the U.S. as *First Spaceship on Venus*. Occasionally he was loaned out by DEFA for West German and Austrian productions: *Feuerwerk* (1954), *Des Teufels General* (1954–55), *Hanussen* (1955), *Bonjour Kathrin* (1955–56), Walter Felsenstein's version of *Fidelio* (1956), *Ein Mann geht durch die Wand* (1959) starring Heinz Rühmann, *Herrin der Welt* (1959–60), and *Division Brandenburg* (1960). In 1956 he was awarded the National Prize 3rd Class. Kunstmann retired in 1963 and died in Potsdam-Babelsberg.

Erwin Lange (1913–1982)
German Explosives Expert

Born in Berlin. From 1931, he focused on mechanical effects and explosives for propaganda films: *Pour le Mérite* (1941), *Stukas* (1941), *Quax der Bruchpilot* (1941), *Kolberg* (1944) and the unfinished *Das Leben geht weiter* (1945). After World War II he was still involved in war films: *Der Stern von Afrika* (1957), Stanley Kubrick's *Paths of Glory* (1957, starring Kirk Douglas), *Die grünen Teufel von Monte Cassino* (1958), *Hunde, wollt ihr ewig leben?* (1959), *Die Brücke* (1959), *Division Brandenburg* (1960). Staff member of Kirk Douglas' *The Vikings* (1958) as well as *Cleopatra* (1962–63) in Italy. In the 1960s he worked on a highly successful series of Yugoslavian-made Karl May westerns, beginning with *Der Schatz im Silbersee* (1962) and *Winnetou* (1963), both starring former "Tarzan" Lex Barker and Pierre Brice. He died in Munich.

Michael Lantieri

American Mechanical Effects Supervisor

Supervised mechanical effects for *Jurassic Park* (1992–93) and received an Academy Award for his work. For *Hook* (1991) he created a hydraulic rig to rock and tilt the pirate ship set. Involved in: *Indiana Jones and the Temple of Doom* (1984), *Star Trek IV: The Voyage Home* (1986), *Who Framed Roger Rabbit* (1988), *Back to the Future Part II* (1989), *Back to the Future Part III* (1990), *Death Becomes Her* (1992), *Bram Stoker's Dracula* (1992), *The Flintstones* (1994), *Casper* (1995), *Congo* (1995), *Mars Attacks!* (1996) and *Mousehunt* (1997).

Juan Larrinaga

Mexican-American Matte and Glass Artist

Joined his brother Mario at RKO (*King Kong*, 1932–33, *The Son of Kong*, 1933) and Warner Bros.-First National Pictures.

Mario Larrinaga

Mexican-American Matte and Glass Artist and Production Illustrator

In 1916 he was technical artist at Universal Studios, painting miniatures, backgrounds and cycloramas. Silent film work on glass mattes for Douglas Fairbanks' *The Gaucho* (1928). Joined Willis O'Brien at RKO: the ill-fated *Creation* project (1930–31), *King Kong* (1932–33), *The Son of Kong* (1933), *The Last Days of Pompeii* (1935). Other RKO work: *Cimarron* (1931), *The Most Dangerous Game* (1932), *She* (1935), *Gunga Din* (1939), *The Hunchback of Notre Dame* (1939), *Citizen Kane* (1940–41). Head of art effects department at Warner Bros.–First National in Burbank. Semi-retired to Taos, New Mexico in 1951. Eventually with Cinerama: prologue paintings for *This Is Cinerama* (1952) and *Seven Wonders of the World* (1956).

Emile LaVigne

American Makeup Artist

One of many makeup artists working at MGM on *The Wizard of Oz* in 1939. Later collaborated at Universal on some Frankenstein films, such as 1948's *Abbott and Costello Meet Frankenstein* (transforming Lon Chaney Jr. into the Wolf Man). Also made-up the mutants for *World Without End* (1956).

Russell E. Lawson

American Matte Artist

Worked with Fred Sersen in the matte department of Fox Studios. Was hired to paint mattes for disaster spectacle *Deluge* in 1933. Joined forces with Jack Cosgrove on Columbia, Universal and Chesterfield–Invincible pictures: *The Black Cat* (1934), *Bride of Frankenstein* (1935), *The Invisible Ray* (1935–36), *Death from a Distance* (1936). When Cosgrove left, Lawson stayed at Universal in charge of matte work: *Tower of London* (1939), *Arabian Nights* (1942), *Phantom of the Opera* (1943, Technicolor), *The Imposter* (1944), *Dressed to Kill* (1946), *This Island Earth* (1955), *Spartacus* (1959–60). Received screen credit for *Taras Bulba* (1962). When he inherited a fortune, he left the department in the hands of Albert Whitlock in 1963 with the words, "You can have it all."

Lee LeBlanc (1913–1988)

American Matte Artist

Born in Powers, Michigan. Attended LaFrance Art Institute, Philadelphia; Art Students League, New York; Chiunard School of Art and Jepsen Art School in Los Angeles. Commercial artist until 1939, then took a job with Walt Disney. In 1941 with Fred M. Sersen (and Ray Kellogg) at 20th Century–Fox: *The Day the Earth Stood Still* (1951), *The Robe* (1953), *Prince Valiant* (1954). After Warren A. Newcombe retired in 1956, LeBlanc was invited to head the MGM matte department: *This Could Be the Night* (1957), *Don't Go Near the Water* (1957), *Cat on a Hot Tin Roof* (1958), *The Brothers Karamazov* (1958), *Party Girl* (1958), *The Law and Jake Wade* (1958), *Ben-Hur* (1959), *The World, the*

Flesh and the Devil (1959), *North by Northwest* (1959), *Green Mansions* (1959), *The Wreck of the Mary Deare* (1959), *Tarzan, the Ape Man* (1959), *Never So Few* (1959), *Bells Are Ringing* (1960), *The Subterraneans* (1960), *Where the Boys Are* (1960), *Cimarron* (1960), *Ada* (1961), *King of Kings* (1961), *Atlantis the Lost Continent* (1961), *The Honeymoon Machine* (1961), *Two Loves* (1961), *The Four Horsemen of the Apocalypse* (1961), *Sweet Bird of Youth* (1962), *Mutiny on the Bounty* (1962–63). At MGM he was associated with former Fox matte photographer Clarence Slifer. Retired from the movie industry in 1963. Illustrated children's wildlife books and did illustrations for magazines.

Daniel [Danny] Lee (1919–?)
American Mechanical Effects Expert

Son of mechanic Carl Lee. Worked at Lockheed Corporation after he returned from service in World War II. Mechanical effects technician on *Around the World in 80 Days* (1956). Cars, wire effects and explosives for *It's a Mad Mad Mad Mad World* (1962–63), *The Great Race* (1965), *Murderers' Row* (1966), *What Did You Do in the War, Daddy?* (1966), *Bonnie and Clyde* (1968), *The Ambushers* (1968), *The Secret of Santa Vittoria* (1969–70), *Pussycat, Pussycat, I Love You* (1970). Many years at Walt Disney Studios and Disneyland: *Darby O'Gill and the Little People* (1958–59), *Swiss Family Robinson* (1960), *The Absent Minded Professor* (1960–61), *Mary Poppins* (1964; he was the one to fly Julie Andrews), *The Love Bug* (1968–69, creating the original VW Herbie). In 1971 was appointed head of the special effects department at Disney: *Bedknobs and Broomsticks* (1971), *Snowball Express* (1972), *Now You See Him, Now You Don't* (1972), *Escape to Witch Mountain* (1975), *The Island at the Top of the World* (1974), *The Shaggy D.A.* (1976), *Herbie Rides Again* (1974), *Herbie Goes to Monte Carlo* (1977), *Pete's Dragon* (1977), *The Cat from Outer Space* (1978), *Return from Witch Mountain* (1978), *The Black Hole* (1979, manufactured robots), *The World's Greatest Athlete* (1979), *Herbie Goes Bananas* (1980), *Last Flight of Noah's Ark* (1980), *Dragonslayer* (1981). Left Disney and opened his own shop in Glendale. In 1984 he was commissioned by Deutsche Kinemathek Berlin to produce a miniature replica of his *Mary Poppins* flying rig. Appeared in the German-Austrian TV documentary *Special Effects* (February 1985).

Paul K. Lerpae (1900–1989)
American Optical Cinematographer

Paul Karl Lerpae was born in Mexico City. Started in the industry as laboratory technician at Standard Film Laboratories, Metro-Goldwyn and Paramount Pictures, then became an assistant cameraman. At Paramount he did camera effects for *Dr. Jekyll and Mr. Hyde* (1931, transforming Fredric "Dr. Jekyll" March into the hideous Mr. Hyde), *Cleopatra* (1933–34), *Death Takes a Holiday* (1934), *The Crusades* (1935), *The Jungle Princess* (1936), *The General Died at Dawn* (1936), *The Plainsman* (1936), *Hollywood Boulevard* (1936), *The Texas Rangers* (1936), *Champagne Waltz* (1937), *The Big Broadcast of 1937* (1937), *Forgotten Faces* (1937), *Artists & Models* (1937), *Her Jungle Love* (1938). Later was in charge of the optical department and optical printing: both versions of *The Buccaneer* (1938 and 1958), *Spawn of the North* (1938), *Union Pacific* (1939), *The Cat and the Canary* (1939), *Dr. Cyclops* (1939–40), *The Ghost Breakers* (1940), *Typhoon* (1940), *Road to Singapore* (1940) and subsequent *Road* pictures, *Aloma of the South Seas* (1941), *I Wanted Wings* (1941), *So Proudly We Hail* (1943), *Lady in the Dark* (1944), *The Story of Dr. Wassell* (1944), *The Woman in the Window* (1944), *Murder, He Says* (1945), *The Dark Mirror* (1946), *Unconquered* (1947), *Samson and Delilah* (1949), *The Greatest Show on Earth* (1952), *The War of the Worlds* (1952–53), *Flight to Tangier* (1953, 3D), *Those Redheads from Seattle* (1953, 3D), *Jivaro* (1953–54, 3D), *Money from Home* (1954, 3D), *The Bridges at Toko-Ri* (1954–55), *The Ten Commandments* (1953–56), *Conquest of Space* (1955), *Hatari!* (1962), *Donovan's Reef* (1963), *The Nutty Professor* (1963), *Red Line 7000* (1965), *The Greatest Story Ever Told* (1965), *Boeing, Boeing* (1965), *The Family Jewels* (1965), *Johnny Reno* (1966), *The Last of the Secret Agents?* (1966), *The Spirit Is Willing* (1967), *El Dorado* (1967–68), *The Odd Couple* (1968), *Project X* (1968). Scientific or Technical Award, Class III in 1944 for the design and construction of the Paramount traveling matte projection and photographing device. In the optical department he was assisted by, among others, his brother Carl. Retired in 1971. Died in his Palm Springs home.

Helmar [Hjalmar] Lerski
(1871–1956)

German Effects Cinematographer

Born in Strasburg, he was the son of Polish-Jewish immigrants. In 1910 he learned to become a still photographer. Went to Milwaukee, Wisconsin. In 1915 he returned to Europe and joined the film industry in Berlin. 1917–18: chief technician at Deutsche Bioscop. Cooperation with inventor Eugen Schüfftan in developing the Shuftan process. 1925–27: chief technician at Deutsche Spiegeltechnik G.m.b.H. & Co.: *Ein Walzertraum* (1925), *Die Brüder Schellenberg* (1925–26), *Metropolis* (1925–26), *Die Boxerbraut* (1926), *Dagfin* (1926), *Die Czardasfürstin* (1926–27), *Madame Pompadour* (1927). Director of photography: *Der heilige Berg* (1925–26),

Sprengbagger 1010 (1929). He first went to Palestine in 1931, was exiled there in 1933, and returned to Europe (Zurich) in 1949.

Louis Lichtenfield

American Matte Artist

In 1937, Lichtenfield came to Hollywood with his portfolio. Hired by production designer William Cameron Menzies, he was brought to Selznick International where he assisted Jack Cosgrove on *Gone with the Wind* (1939). After World War II service, he worked at various studios (Columbia, RKO) studying different techniques of photographing painted mattes. Assistant to Fitch Fulton on the glass paintings for RKO's *Mighty Joe Young* (1946–49). In 1949 he worked on *The Fountainhead* (1949) at Warners and in 1951 on *An American in Paris* at *MGM*. Eventually became head of painted mattes and photographic effects at Warner Bros., where he would team with John P. Fulton, Vern Taylor,

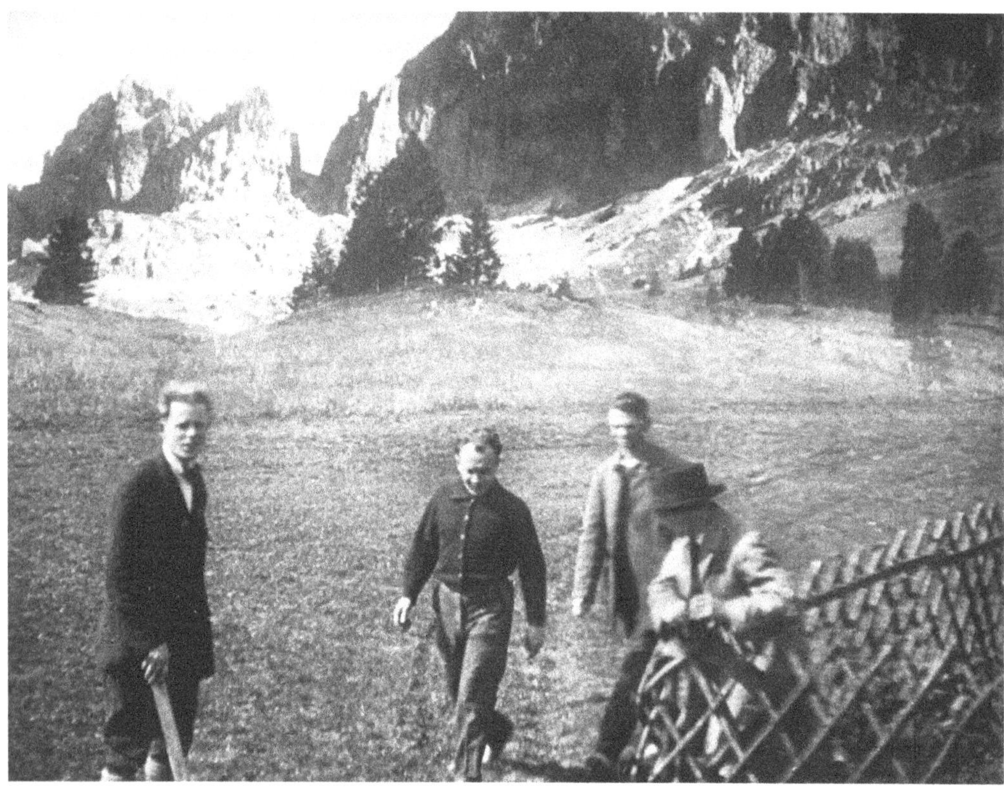

Schüfftan photographer Helmar Lerski, art director Heinrich Weidemann and unknown crew members on location (courtesy Fritz Maurischat Collection, Deutsche Kinemathek Berlin).

Jack Shaw, Cliff Silsby and eventually would bring back Jack Cosgrove: *The Silver Chalice* (1954), *Helen of Troy* (1955), *The Spirit of St. Louis* (1957), *No Time for Sergeants* (1958). Came out of retirement (and to Van der Veer Photo Effects) for Dino DeLaurentiis' *King Kong* remake (1976), *Flash Gordon* (1980) and *Never Say Never Again* (1984).

Edwin G. Linden (1896–1956)
American Cinematographer

Edwin G. "Eddie" Linden was director of photography of live-action and stop-motion on *King Kong* (1932–33) and *The Son of Kong* (1933). An expert technician, he was no great aesthete and often flooded miniature sets with light. Later worked on programmers and did effects shots for *The Lost City* (1935, serial in 12 chapters). He was with Larry Butler for *That Hamilton Woman* (1941, Korda), *The Adventures of Mark Twain* (1944), and *Crime by Night* (1944).

Harold Lipstein (1898–1974)
American Effects Cameraman and Director of Photography

At MGM: *Plymouth Adventure* (1952).

Laine Liska
American Stop-Motion Technician

Crew member on *Flesh Gordon* (1971–74), *The Day Time Ended* (1980), *Caveman* (1981), *Dolls* (1987), *Honey, I Shrunk the Kids* (1989), *Oblivion* (1994).

Lo Ki-Ping
Chinese Effects Expert, Set and Props Designer

Started as stage designer in Shanghai. In the 1950s went to Hong Kong and became a set and prop designer in the movie industry. Created weird creatures, apes, giant birds and gimmick-like weapons for martial arts pictures: "At that time there were no art directors. Nobody designed the creatures and it's wholly a work out of my own imagination. We got some inspiration from foreign science-fiction movies, such as *Frankenstein*." Much-needed inspiration also came from Japanese films. In 1961 a superimposition was created to have Fung Bo-bo talk with a giant in *Magic Cup*. In 1965 Lo did a Classic Cantonese fantasy, *The Furious Buddha's Palm*, which had its roots in the 1928 Shanghai production *The Burning of Red Lotus Temple*.

George Lofgren
American Taxidermist and Model Maker

At MGM, where he manufactured horses' backs for westerns, he met Willis O'Brien and began "feathering" miniature eagles for the (later aborted) *War Eagles* project. O'Brien called him to RKO as assistant for *Mighty Joe Young* (1946–49) for which he received screen credit. Perfected a method of rubberizing animal fur which was used on *Mighty Joe*: "Lofgren could embed any type of animal fur in a flexible latex rubber skin which could be worked with easily" (*Cinefex*, January 1982, p. 54). Joined Ray Harryhausen on *Earth vs. the Flying Saucers* (1955–56), *20 Million Miles to Earth* (1956–57) and *The 7th Voyage of Sinbad* (1957–58, screen credit). Collaborated on animals for Disneyland.

Brian Loftus
British Effects Technician

Crew member on *2001: A Space Odyssey* (1965–68) and *Mackenna's Gold* (1968).

Bruce Logan
British Cinematographer

Animation artist: *2001: A Space Odyssey* (1967–68). Second unit photography/miniature and optical effects: *Star Wars* (1975–77). Additional photography. *Star Trek: The Motion Picture* (1978–79). Visual effects supervisor: *Avalanche Express* (1979), *The Incredible Shrinking Woman* (1981). Process cinematography: *Firefox* (1982), *Bird* (1988). Director of effects photography: *Airplane!* (1980), *Batman Forever* (1995). Second unit director in charge of effects: *Deal of the Century* (1983).

August J. [Augie] Lohman

*American Mechanical Effects and
   Explosives Expert*

Credits include: *Bowery Buckaroos* (1947), *Fall Guy* (1947), *Drums in the Deep South* (1951), *Lost Continent* (1951), *Mutiny* (1952), *The Maze* (1953), *The Bowery Boys Meet the Monsters* (1954), *Friendly Persuasion* (1955–56), *The Monster That Challenged the World* (1957), *The Rebel Set* (1959), *The Horse Soldiers* (1959, directed by John Ford), *The Last Voyage* (1960), *Jack the Giant Killer* (1960–62, blowing up Pendragon's castle), *Major Dundee* (1964, directed by Sam Peckinpah). As Lohman was represented by the Paul Kohner Agency in Hollywood, he sometimes was connected with another client, director John Huston: *Moby Dick* (1954–56), *La Bibbia/The Bible ... in the Beginning* (1965–66, working on the Creation sequence at Dinocittà in Rome). For several years was assigned to pictures in Europe: *The Longest Day* (1960–61), *Escape from East Berlin* (1962), *Cleopatra* (1962–63), *Captain Sindbad* (1962–63), *Se Tutte Le Donne Del Mondo* (1966), *Barbarella* (1967), *Doctor Faustus* (1968, directed by Richard Burton), *Candy* (1968). Returned to the United States: *Soylent Green* (1972), *Pat Garrett & Billy the Kid* (1973), *Three Days of the Condor* (1975), *The Shootist* (1976, directed by Don Siegel), *Murder by Death* (1976), *From Noon Till Three* (1976), *The Cheap Detective* (1978), *California Suite* (1978), *Winter Kills* (1979), *The Electric Horseman* (1979, with Robert Redford).

Eugène Lourié (1903–1991)

*Russian-French-American Production
   Designer, Art Director, Miniature Effects
   Supervisor and Director*

Born in Kharkov, Russia, he had an early interest in theatre and cinema. Came to France in 1921. Started as scenery painter at Albatross studios. Studied painting and design. Got to know fellow Russian art directors Minine and Wilke, who introduced him to the technique of hanging miniatures. Worked with models in *Les Yeux noirs* (1935, built Russian street in miniature) and Marcel L'Herbier's adaptation of Tolstoy's *Nuits de feu* (1937, Russian setting with Imperial Opera as hanging miniature). Eventually became art director for Jean Renoir on *Les Bas Fonds* (1936), *La grande illusion* (1937), *La Bête humaine* (1938) and *La Règle du jeu* (1938) as well as working for Marc Allegret, Robert Siodmak, Max Ophuls and René Clair. In 1942 he came to Hollywood (and several times to Britain) where, besides doing production design (including Charles Chaplin's 1952-*Limelight*) he directed a couple of monster-on-the-loose pictures: Ray Harryhausen's first solo feature *The Beast from 20,000 Fathoms* (1952–53) for Mutual Productions of California, *The Colossus of New York* (1958) for Paramount, *The Giant Behemoth* (1958–59) with live-action footage filmed in London and *Gorgo* (1959–61) made by the King Bros. at MGM British Studios in Borehamwood. Originally was chosen to direct *The Black Scorpion* (1956–57) but left after some preliminary work with Willis O'Brien. Returned to Europe and worked as art director on productions that involved effects sequences and miniatures: *Adventures of Captain Fabian* (1951, model ships and hanging miniatures filmed in Nice), *Crack in the World* (1965), *Battle of the Bulge* (1965), *Custer of the West* (1966), *Krakatoa, East of Java* (1969, volcanic eruption). TV work: *Captain Nemo's Return* (1977), *Supertrain* (1979), *A Whale for the Killing* (1980). In 1962 he collaborated with the Daiei special effects department on the shooting of the Japanese-filmed *Flight from Ashiya* (with some additional studio tank work farmed out to Cinecittà, Rome). "Basically, here are some situations where miniatures can be used: (1) purely miniature scenes, where everything you see on the screen is miniature, such as views of volcanoes, ships in raging seas, fires, automobile accidents, and battlefields; (2) miniatures combined with live action, shot simultaneously on the same negative. These can be either hanging miniatures or miniature backgrounds; and (3) miniatures optically combined with live action, where the live action is shot separately and combined later through photography. This allows the scenes to be shot in different places and at different times" (Lourié, *My Work in Films*, p. 179).

Cecil D. Love (1900–1995)
American Optical Cinematographer

Optical effects for *Hell's Angels* (1930), then to RKO Radio Pictures for films from *King Kong* (1932–33) up to *The French Line* (1953, Jane Russell in 3D). During World War II he was with the United States Navy Photo Science Laboratory in Anacostia. With RKO colleague Linwood G. Dunn he designed the Acme-Dunn Special Effects Optical Printer (Scientific or Technical Award, Class III in 1944 and Award of Merit in 1980) and co-founded Film Effects of Hollywood: *West Side Story* (1961), *It's a Mad Mad Mad Mad World* (1962–63), *The Great Race* (1965), *Hawaii* (1965).

George Lucas (1944–)
American Producer and Director

When he started the *Star Wars* saga in 1975, he decided to build his own effects company, Industrial Light & Magic, which became the leading sfx plant. Had enrolled in the University of Southern California (USC) film school. Made short film *THX 1138*. Became associated with Francis Ford Coppola as production assistant (*The Rain People*). After *American Graffiti* (1973) he founded Lucasfilm.

Eustace Arden Lycett (1914–2006)
British-American Visual Effects Supervisor

Born Stroke-on-Trent, Stratfordshire, Britain, on Christmas Eve. Studied engineering and graduated from Cal Tech with an engineering degree. In 1937 he joined Walt Disney Productions in Hollywood as mechanical engineer, assigned to redesign camera equipment. Was involved in multiplane shots for *Snow White and the Seven Dwarfs* (1937). Slowly drifted into effects. Assisted Ub Iwerks in building up Disney's process laboratory: *20000 Leagues Under the Sea* (1953–54), *3-D Jamboree* (1956), *Sleeping Beauty* (1956–58). When Iwerks was hospitalized after a heart attack, Lycett was made head of the department in 1957 (Iwerks reportedly never spoke to him again): *Darby O'Gill and the Little People* (1958–59), *The Absent Minded Professor* (1960–61, first screen credit), *One Hundred and One Dalmatians* (1960–61), *Babes in Toyland* (1961), *Bon Voyage* (1962), *Moon Pilot* (1962), *Savage Sam* (1963), *Son of Flubber* (1963), *Summer Magic* (1963), *Mary Poppins* (1964), *The Monkey's Uncle* (1965), *That Darn Cat* (1965), *Those Calloways* (1965), *Lt. Robin Crusoe, U.S.N.* (1966), *The Ugly Dachshund* (1966), *The Adventures of Bullwhip Griffin* (1967), *The Gnome-Mobile* (1967), *The Happiest Millionaire* (1967), *Blackbeard's Ghost* (1968), *Never a Dull Moment* (1968), *The Love Bug* (1968–69), *Rascal* (1969), *The Boatniks* (1970), *Bedknobs and Broomsticks* (1971), *Now You See Him, Now You Don't* (1973), *Herbie Rides Again* (1974), *The Island at the Top of the World* (1974), *Herbie Goes to Monte Carlo* (1977), *Pete's Dragon* (1977), *The Cat from Outer Space* (1978), *Return from Witch Mountain* (1978), *The Black Hole* (1979). Since 1971, after Iwerks' death, also director of research. Retired in 1979. Died in Fullerton, California.

Howard J. Lydecker (1911–1969)
American Miniature Effects Supervisor

Howard J. "Babe" Lydecker was born in Havana, Cuba. For family background see the writeup on his brother Theodore H. Lydecker. Howard, the younger brother, began in the Mack Sennett and Mascot Studios under Jack Coyle: *The Fighting Marines* (1935) and *The Phantom Empire* (1935). With Theodore he coordinated all the stunning model sequences that became the highlight of Republic Pictures' serials and features. Republic credits include: *Darkest Africa* (1936), *Undersea Kingdom* (1936), *SOS Coast Guard* (1937), *Women in War* (1940), *Drums of Fu Manchu* (1940), *Mysterious Doctor Satan* (1940), *Adventures of Captain Marvel* (1941), *Flying Tigers* (1942), *G-Men vs. the Black Dragon* (1943), *Captain America* (1944), *The Crimson Ghost* (1946), *Macbeth* (1948, directed by Orson Welles), *King of the Rocket Men* (1949), *Rio Grande* (1950, directed by John Ford), *Zombies of the Stratosphere* (1952), *Tobor the Great* (1954). Part of the reason the Lydeckers' miniatures looked so realistic is that they were shot outdoors. Loaned to Disney to consult on *20000 Leagues Under the Sea* (1953–54, rigging the *Nautilus* model). After Republic stopped active production in 1959, Howard freelanced on *Sink the Bismarck!* (in Britain), *The Underwater City,* *HMS Defiant* and the massive comedy *It's a Mad Mad Mad Mad World,* then became a regular miniature supervisor at 20th Century–Fox: *Fantastic Voyage* (1965–66), *Flight of the Phoenix* (1965), *Doctor Dolittle* (1967) and TV work for producer Irwin Allen. Died during the preparation of the ship models for *Tora! Tora! Tora!* (1969).

Theodore H. Lydecker
(1908–1990)
American Miniature Effects Supervisor

Theodore H. [Ted] Lydecker was born in Inglewood, New Jersey. John Howard Lydecker, his father, moved the family to Havana, Cuba, where as head engineer he helped to raise the battleship *Maine.* Then the family settled in Balboa, California. Theodore started in the movies as an assistant to famed art director William Cameron Menzies on the 1924 *Thief of Bagdad.* During the Depression days, Ted moved as a cowboy to Idaho but his younger brother Howard called him back to Hollywood and asked to join him on all miniature work at Republic's serial factory. Republic credits include: *Darkest Africa* (1936), *Undersea Kingdom* (1936), *Adventures of Captain Marvel* (1941, a papiermache dummy that measured seven feet, suspended on a cable), *Flying Tigers* (1942), *King of the Rocket Men* (1949), *Sands of Iwo Jima* (1949) et al. His son George recalls the working relationship between the two brothers: "Dad took care of the shop while Howard did the politics, like dealing with the brass from the front office. And that could get a little bit crazy! The executives were always on them for budget, and when they'd view the special effects rushes, some of the producers would ask why they had to waste so much film at the beginning of the shot before the actual stunt happened. This was a simple problem that the two of them overcame with the help of the editors. The reality was that those old Mitchell cameras took a while to come up to speed, so there was always dead film that wasn't leader before the effect took place. Since the execs at Republic couldn't understand why film was being wasted, the two of them went to the editors and made sure that the dailies were edited of the excess film at the beginning and

ends, thereby fooling the brass, who had no technical understanding of special effects" (*Cult Movies* #13, p. 46). In the 1960s Ted went to work for Universal: *The Birds* (1962–63), *The Andromeda Strain* (1970).

Warren E. Lynch
Special Effects Cinematographer

Still photographer: Erich von Stroheim's *Greed* (1923). Production cameraman: *The Iron Mask* (1929). Staff member of Stage 5, Warner Bros.: *The Petrified Forest* (1936), *Julie* (1944), *The Very Thought of You* (1944), *The Horn Blows at Midnight* (1945), *Pillow to Post* (1945), *Of Human Bondage* (1946), *The Big Sleep* (1946).

Robert A. MacDonald
American Mechanical Effects Supervisor

Staff member of A. Arnold Gillespie's effects crew at MGM: *They Were Expendable* (1945), *Forbidden Planet* (1956). Rigged the chariot race of *Ben-Hur* (1959). Went on his own and later founded an effects company: *The Longest Day* (1961–62), *Paris brule-t-il?* (*Is Paris Burning?,* 1966), *The Charge of the Light Brigade* (1968), *A Flea in Her Ear* (1968), *Alfred the Great* (1969), *Ryan's Daughter* (1970), *What's Up, Doc?* (1972), *Report to the Commissioner* (1975), *Doc Savage: The Man of Bronze* (1975, for producer George Pal), *The Outlaw Josey Wales* (1976), *March or Die* (1977), *Heaven Can Wait* (1978), *Superman* (1977–78, effects in New Mexico), *When Time Ran Out* (1980), *Yes, Giorgio* (1982), *Gremlins* (1984), *Enemy Mine* (1985, filmed at Bavaria Studios in Munich), *Explorers* (1985), *Howard the Duck* (1986). Television: *Cover Girls* (1977).

John Mackey
British Matte and Optical
Cinematographer

At Shepperton he assisted Wally Veevers. In 1964 he joined Les Bowie and Bowie Films to help with camera and optical work: *She* (1965), *City Under the Sea* (1965), *One Million Years B.C.* (1965–66), *The Deadly Bees* (1967), *Dracula Has Risen from the Grave* (1968), Hired by Stanley Kubrick for matte shots of the excavated pit on the moon and traveling shots of moonscape in *2001: A Space Odyssey* (1965–68). With Bob Cuff he formed Abacus Productions and made commercials. In 1968 he went to America to supervise plates made for *Mackenna's Gold.*

Alan Maley (1931–1995)
British-American Matte Artist

At age 17 he entered Denham Studios where his uncle, Cyril Lamont, had been a sign painter. Started at Shepperton Studios in Britain under Wally Veevers. In 1964, having worked on some of Disney's British productions, he decided to go to America. Matte paintings mostly for Walt Disney Studios: *The Love Bug* (1968–69), *The Horse in the Gray Flannel Suit* (1968), *Bedknobs and Broomsticks* (1971, winning an Academy Award), *The Island at the Top of the World* (1974). Matte paintings for the James Bond adventure *The Spy Who Loved Me* (1977). Left Disney to pursue fine arts like many matte artists did. Returned as matte consultant to Industrial Light & Magic: *Raiders of the Lost Ark* (1980–81), *Dragonslayer* (1980–81).

Ray Mammes
American Optical Expert

Invented an early composite reduction process that allowed the blending of a living lion into the MGM trademark.

Ned Herbert Mann (1893–1967)
American Special Effects Director

Born in Redkey, Indiana, Mann was educated in St. Louis and studied art at Washington U. Early occupations included professional auto racer and roller skater and stage actor and director. In 1923 he entered motion pictures as an actor. Eventually jobbed in a plaster shop and decided on a career in models and hanging miniatures for Douglas Fairbanks, United Artists and other companies: *The Thief of Bagdad* (1923–24, Bagdad miniatures and flying carpet), *Don Q, Son of Zorro* (1925), *Camille* (1926), *The Bat* (1926), *The Winning of Barbara Worth* (1926), *Two Arabian Nights* (1927), *Alibi* (1929),

Noah's Ark (1929, miniature train wreck and flood sequence), *The Bat Whispers* (1930), *Madame Satan* (1930), *Dirigible* (1931), *Deluge* (1933). Alexander Korda invited him and selected crew members (Larry Butler, Harry Zech, Edward Cohen, Jack Thomas, Ross Jacklin) to London Films: *The Private Life of Don Juan* (1934), *The Scarlet Pimpernel* (1934–35), *The Ghost Goes West* (1935), *Rembrandt* (1935), *Things to Come* (1935–36), *Men Are Not Gods* (1936), *The Man Who Could Work Miracles* (1936), *Fire Over England* (1937), *Thunder in the City* (1937), *Dark Journey* (1937), *Storm in a Teacup* (1937), *Knight Without Armour* (1937), *Dinner at the Ritz* (1937), *The Divorce of Lady X* (1938). At the outbreak of the war he returned to the United States: *Beyond Tomorrow* (1940). After World War II he went back to Korda: *Frieda* (1947), *Bonnie Prince Charlie* (1948), *Anna Karenina* (1948), *The Fallen Idol* (1948), *Miracolo a Milano* (*Miracle in Milan*, 1951, with director Vittorio de Sica in Italy). Last film work: *Around the World in 80 Days* (1956) with producer Michael Todd.

Yoichi [Yukio] Manoda
Japanese Special Effects Cinematographer

Assistant cameraman on the original *Gojira* (U.S.: *Godzilla, King of the Monsters!*, 1954), *Gojira no gyakushu* (U.S.: *Gigantis, the Fire Monster*, 1955), *Chikyu boeigun* (U.S.: *The Mysterians*, 1957), *Uchu daisenso* (U.S.: *Battle in Outer Space*, 1959–60). Full-fledged effects and optical cameraman: *Daitozoku* (U.S.: *The Lost World of Sinbad*, 1963), *Zero faita dai kusen* (*Zero Fighters*, 1966), *Kingukongu no gyakushu* (U.S.: *King Kong Escapes*, 1967), *Kaiju soshingeki* (U.S.: *Destroy All Monsters*, 1968), *Kureji no daibakuhatsu* (1969), *Nihonkai daikaisen* (*Battle of the Japan Sea*, 1969), *Konto gojugo-go: Uchu daiboken* (1969). Chief cameraman: *Gezora, Ganime, Kameba: Kessen! Nankai no daikaiju* (U.S.: *Yog: Monster from Space*, 1970), *Gojira tai Hedora* (U.S.: *Godzilla vs. the Smog Monster*, 1971), *Mekagojira no Gyakushu* (U.S.: *Terror of Mechagodzilla/The Terror of Godzilla*, 1975). Collaborated with Akira Watanabe on the effects of Toei's *Gamma sango uchu daisakusen* (U.S.: *The Green Slime*, 1968).

Antonio Margheriti (1930–2001)

Italian Director

Born in Rome, Margheriti studied in Verona. Involved in documentaries since 1950. Low-budget science-fiction and effects films under pseudonyms Anthony Daisies and Anthony Dawson: *Space Men* (1960), *Il planeta degli uomi spenti* (1961), *I criminali della galassia* (1965), *I diafiboidi portano la morte* (1966), *Missione planeta errante* (1966), *Operazione Goldman/Operación Goldman* (1966), *L'inafferrabile invincibile Mr. Invisible* (1973), *Killer Fish* (1979), *Tornado* (1982), *The Hunter from the Future* (1983). Production manager and in charge of special effects: *Perry Rhodan—SOS aus dem Weltall* (*Operation Stardust/Mission Stardust*, 1966), *L'umanoide* (*The Humanoid*, 1979).

Victor L. A. [Vic] Margutti

British Traveling Matte Supervisor

Involved with Les Bowie in the company Bowie-Margutti: *Spaceways* (1952–53), *The Quatermass Xperiment* (U.S.: *The Creeping Un-*

known, 1954), *The Dam Busters* (1954–55); after that, in charge of all traveling matte and sodium process work at Rank's Pinewood Studios and as consultant for various foreign pictures: *One Wish Too Many* (1956), *Der Stern von Afrika* (1957, matte consultant for German production in cooperation with K. L. Ruppel), *The 3 Worlds of Gulliver* (1959–60, first film with producer Charles Schneer and Ray Harryhausen), *Soldatensender Calais* (1960, matte consultant for German production, patented reduced matte process with K. L. Ruppel), *Mysterious Island* (1960–61), *Konga* (1961), *Nils Holgersson* (1961, consultant for Swedish production), *Sodoma e Gomorra* (*Sodom and Gomorrha*, 1963), *Dr. Strangelove or: How I Learned to Stop Worrying and Love the Bomb* (1963–64), *The Golden Voyage of Sinbad* (1971–72), *Dunderklumpen* (1973).

Kurt Marks (1933–)

German Visual Effects Cinematographer

Born in Altdamm near Stettin (now Szczecin Dabie in Poland). Studied at Staatliche

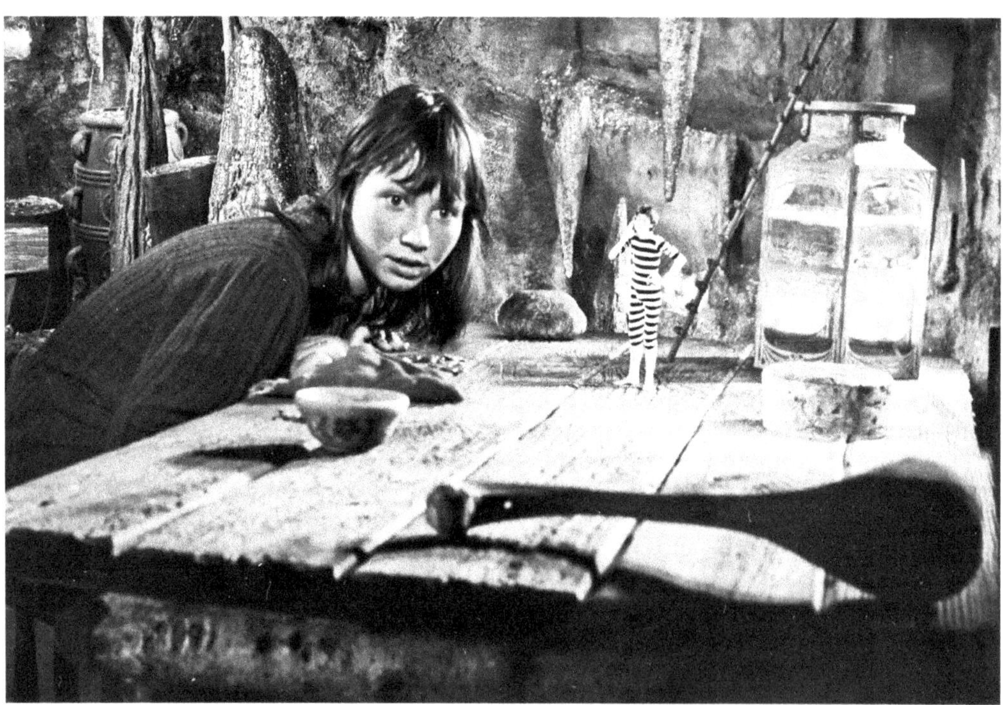

Shuftan shot by Kurt Marks for the East German TV production *Die Geschichte vom goldenen Taler* (1985) (courtesy Uwe Fleischer and Deutsche Kinemathek Berlin).

Hochschule für Film und Fernsehen, GDR (German Democratic Republic), and joined East-German Defa Studios as assistant to Ernst Kunstmann: *Der schweigende Stern* (U.S.: *First Spaceship on Venus*, 1959). Expert in Shuftan mirror and miniature shots: *Die Glatzkopfbande* (1962), *Die gefrorenen Blitze* (1963–64), *Karbid und Sauerampfer* (1964), *Alaskafüchse* (1964), *Signale—Ein Weltraumabenteuer* (1969–70), *Anflug Alpha 1* (1971, front projection), *Eolomea* (1971–72, 70mm), *Orpheus in der Unterwelt* (1973, 70mm), *Schneeweisschen und Rosenrot* (1978), *Spuk unterm Riesenrad* (1978, TV series), *Spuk im Hochhaus* (1981, TV series), *Gritta von Rattenzuhausbeiuns* (1984), *Die Geschichte vom goldenen Taler* (1985, TV), *Die Geschichte von der Gänseprinzessin und ihrem treuen Pferd Fallada* (1988), *Olle Hexe* (1990). TV: *Die schwarze Mühle* (1975). Retired after German reunification.

Robert A. Mattey
American Mechanical Effects Expert

As a crew member of *King Kong* (1932–33) he became interested in mechanical props and monsters. For *Tarzan* producer Sol Lesser he created water-spying turtle and radio-controlled alligator. Made the octopus for John Wayne's *Wake of the Red Witch* (1948) which got him a job with Walt Disney to mechanize the giant squid for *20000 Leagues Under the Sea* (1953–54). Stayed with Disney: *The Absent Minded Professor* (1961), *Babes in Toyland* (1961), *Mary Poppins* (1964), *Son of Flubber* (1963), *The Gnome-Mobile* (1967), *Blackbeard's Ghost* (1968, with Peter Ustinov playing the title character), *The Love Bug* (1968–69). Consultant: *The Guns of Navarone* (1960–61) and *The Lost Continent* (1968) in Britain. TV: *The Outer Limits*. On the strength of his giant squid, Steven Spielberg hired him to work on *Jaws* (1974–75) and *Jaws 2* (1978).

Artur Georg Fritz Maurischat
(1893–1988)
German Art Director

Scenic artist Maurischat was born in Berlin. In 1922 he had his first film experience with art director Martin Jacoby-Boy. For Paul Leni he designed 1923's *Das Wachsfigurenkabinett* (*Waxworks*). A year later, Maurischat was involved in testing the Shuftan process with its inventor Eugen Schüfftan. They produced a short demo reel. A few years later, Schüfftan asked him to become a supervisor at Deutsche Spiegeltechnik G.m.b.H. & Co.: *Eine Dubarry von heute* (1926, directed by Alexander Korda), *Klettermaxe* (1926–27), *Der Zigeunerbaron* (1926–27), *Die Czardasfürstin* (1926–27), *Am Rande der Welt* (1927), *Die weisse Spinne* (1927), *Svengali* (1927), *Bigamie* (1927), *Das tanzende Wien* (1927), *Der Geisterzug* (1927), *Die Liebe der Jeanne Ney* (1927, directed by G.W. Pabst), *Die Stadt der tausend Freuden* (1927, directed by Carmine Gallone), *Die Sandgräfin* (1927), *Königin Luise* (1927–28, two parts), *Die Sache mit dem Schorrsiegel* (1928), *Haus Nr. 17* (*Number Seventeen*, 1928), *Geschlecht in Fesseln* (1928), *Durchs Brandenburger Tor* (1929), *Narkose* (1929, directed by Alfred Abel), *Das Schiff der verlorenen Menschen* (1929, directed by Maurice Tourneur), *Sprengbagger 1010* (1929). In the mid–30s Maurischat brought his former Shuftan colleague Ernst Kunstmann to Tobis Studios. In 1942–43 he designed *Titanic* which included some notable miniature work (the model shots were reused by Roy Baker in *A Night to Remember* in 1958). After World War II he collaborated on the design of the fantastic *Die seltsame Reise des Brandner Kaspar/Das Tor zum Paradies* (1949) with Rudolf Pfenninger.

Michael J. McAlister
American Visual Effects Cinematographer

At Industrial Light & Magic: *Indiana Jones and the Temple of Doom* (1984), *Howard the Duck* (1985–86). Later worked for Cinesite: *X-Men* (2000).

William C. McGann (1893–1977)
American Special Effects and Second Unit Director

Born Pittsburgh, Pennsylvania, and educated at the University of California at Berkeley, McGann began his career as cameraman in 1915 and worked on Buster Keaton's *The Three Ages* (1923). Eventually he turned to film directing but mainly won fame as special effects director on

Warner's Stage 5 in Burbank: *The Horn Blows at Midnight* (1945), *A Stolen Life* (1946), *The Beast with Five Fingers* (1947), *Cheyenne* (1947), *The Woman in White* (1948), *The Treasure of the Sierra Madre* (1948), *The Fountainhead* (1949), *Chain Lightning* (1950), *Fort Worth* (1951), *On Moonlight Bay* (1951). He was also the head of Warner's camera department. Died in Woodland Hills, Los Angeles.

Luis McManus
American Illustrator and Matte Artist

Did art titles for Hal Roach Studios (including Laurel & Hardy's 1933 *Busy Bodies*) and assisted Roy Seawright on the effects work for *Swiss Miss* (1938). Matte art for *Joan of Arc* (1948, interior of French cathedral). Matte paintings for TV series such as *The Untouchables* commissioned by the Howard A. Anderson Company. For Anderson, McManus also designed the stop-motion models and did additional paintings for *Jack the Giant Killer* (1960–62).

Jack McMasters
American Mechanical Effects Expert

In 1935 he joined the MGM staff as a laborer. Special props and effects for *The Wizard of Oz* (1939) and *Forbidden Planet* (1956). At Universal he worked on *Earthquake* (1973–74).

Ralph McQuarrie (1929–)
American Design and Matte Artist

During the 1960s McQuarrie was with Boeing and Litton Industries. He was introduced to George Lucas by Hal Barwood and Matthew Robbins even before Lucas had completed his first solo project, *THX 1138*. Did conceptual artwork on the first *Star Wars* films. While there, he studied the technique of matte paintings and painted mattes for *Star Wars* (1975–77), *Battlestar Galactica* (1978), *The Empire Strikes Back* (1979–80) and *Raiders of the Lost Ark* (1981). Designed the spaceships for *Close Encounters of the Third Kind* (1975–77), *E.T. the Extra-Terrestrial* (1982) and **batteries not included* (1987).

Joshua [Josh] Meador
American Expert for 2D Effects Animation

An animator at Disney Studio (including 1937's *The Old Mill*), then headed the effects animation department on animated feature films, *True Life* adventures and live-action: *Fantasia* (1940), *20000 Leagues Under the Sea* (1953–54, although most of his work, deep sea fish and *Nautilus*, couldn't be used), *Forbidden Planet* (1956, on loan-out to MGM), *Sleeping Beauty* (1956–59), *Darby O'Gill and the Little People* (1958–59).

Phil Meador
American Visual Effects Supervisor

The son of Joshua Meador, he worked for some years as head of the visual effects department at Disney Studios in Burbank.

Derek Meddings (1931–1995)
British Miniature and Effects Supervisor

London-born Meddings joined London Films in the late 1940s as a lettering artist and soon found himself working in the matte department. He learned to help out with all kinds of effects photography but his first love was always miniatures: "Sometimes when you talk with the director whose responsibility it is to turn out a good film, you get some very strange looks when you say that you are going to do an effect with a miniature. This is because although they are experienced as directors, the only thing they can remember is the worst miniature shot they have ever seen — and they can imagine it in their film. When you start on a picture, your intention, after reading the script, is to do a certain amount with miniatures. But there are times when you do not have to give so much thought, because it is down in the script in such a way that you know you are going to do it for real" (*The BKSTS Journal*, October 1984). Worked for Les Bowie and Bowie Films in Slough: *The Evil of Frankenstein* (1963), *First Men in the Moon* (1964–65). In 1965, Bowie recommended him to do miniature work for Gerry Anderson's puppet and live-action TV series: *Thunderbirds, Joe 90, UFO*. Also did feature film work for Anderson: *Thun-

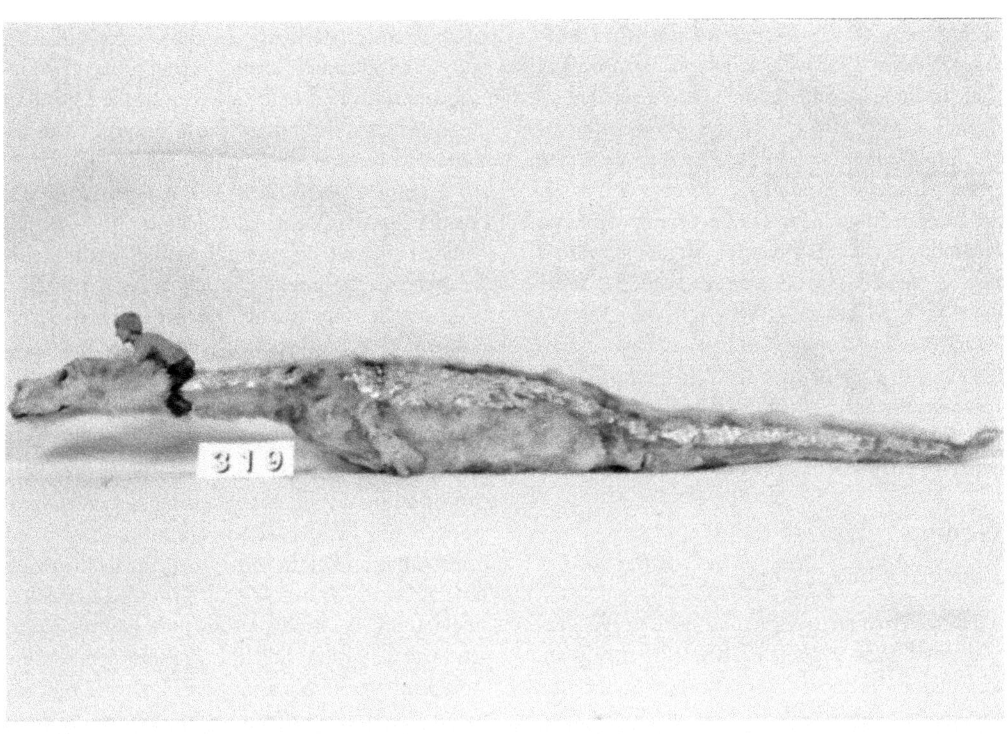

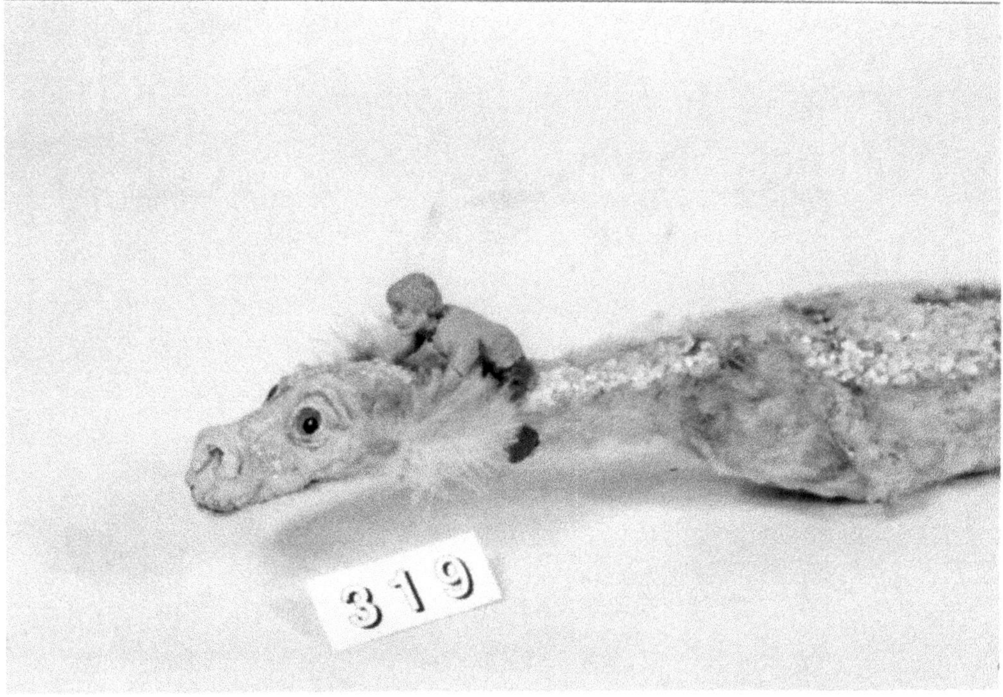

A model of Bastian Balthasar Bux riding Falkor the luck dragon in *The NeverEnding Story II*. Effects supervised by Derek Meddings in Bavaria Studios, Munich, and Shepperton Studios, London (1989) (courtesy Deutsche Kinemathek Berlin).

derbirds Are Go (1966), *Thunderbird 6* (1968), *Doppelgänger* (1969). Took over miniature effects for the James Bond series: *The Man with the Golden Gun* (1974), *The Spy Who Loved Me* (1977), *Moonraker* (1979), *For Your Eyes Only* (1981). Academy Award for *Superman* (1977–78). Founder of Magic Camera Company which was located on the Shepperton lot: *Superman II* (1980), *Krull* (1983), *Superman 3* (1983), *Supergirl* (1984), *Santa Claus* (1984–85), *Mio Min Mio* (1987), *Batman* (1988–89), *High Spirits* (1988–89), *Die unendliche Geschichte II* (*The Neverending Story II*, 1989–90, in Munich) and *III* (1992, in the former Ufa/Defa studios in Babelsberg). *Golden Eye* (1995) was his last film.

Georges Méliès (1861–1938)

French Trickfilm Pioneer

"I was born an artist in my soul, very skilled with my hands, capable of inventing things and a comedian by nature. I was at once an intellectual and a manual worker." Born at 29 Boulevard Saint-Martin, Paris, the third son of a wealthy manufacturer, Méliès received his baccalauréat on July 20, 1880, then served in the military. Visiting London, he began to frequent the Egyptian Hall, a magic theater run by John Nevil-Maskelyne and George Alfred Cook. Méliès was eager to become a painter and to enter the École des Beaux-Arts; his father objected. So Georges turned to overseeing the familiar factory machinery. In 1888, when his father retired, Méliès sold his share to his older brothers, Henri and Gaston, and acquired the leading magical stage of Paris, the Théatre Robert-Houdin. Méliès (quoted by biographers Maurice Bessy and Lo Duca): "Robert-Houdin had planned and equipped his theater with extreme care, solely for prestidigitation. The resulting amenities were superb and facilitated any trick that depended on more than sleight of hand. If the facilities are not at hand for marvels that involve dexterity, mechanics, electricity, levers, pulleys, trap doors, and the help of an invisible assistant, then these splendid wonders cannot be. For this reason, some fine illusions and tricks were to be seen only at the Robert-Houdin." Méliès knew the

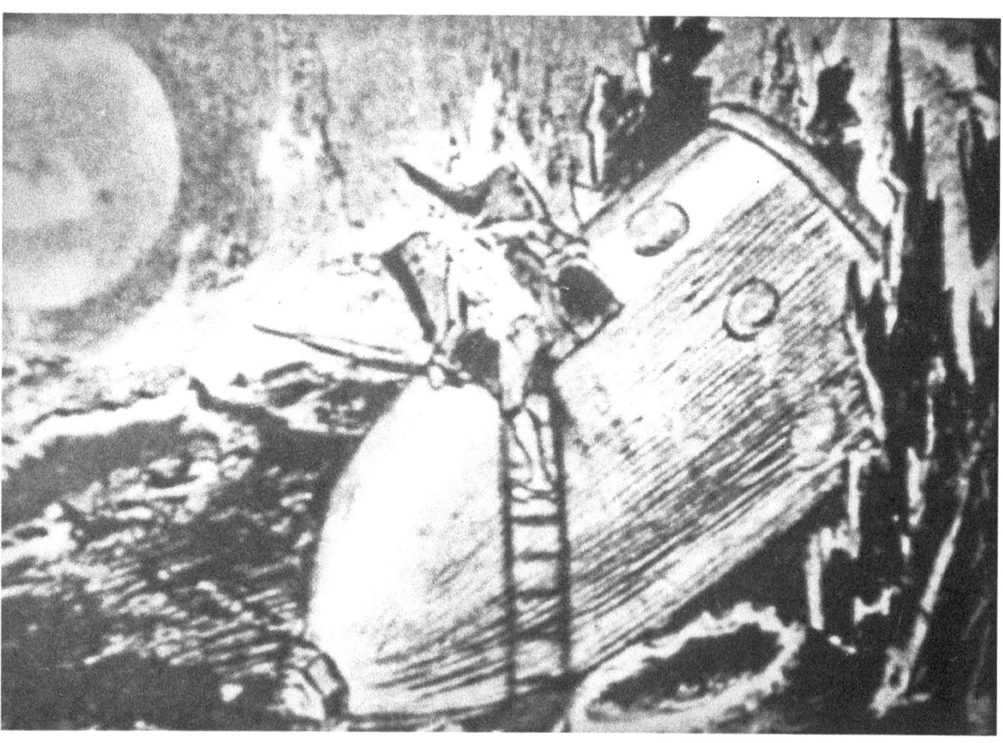

Preproduction art by Georges Méliès for *Le Voyage dans la Lune* (1902), inspired by Jules Verne and H. G. Wells (courtesy Deutsche Kinemathek Berlin).

Brothers Lumière, who invited him to a screening of moving images at the Grand Café in late 1895. Méliès went to London to acquire a projector from Robert William Paul, modified it and started to produce trick films for which he used floor effects known from the stage as well as in-camera effects. Under the Star Film banner, a specially equipped glass stage was opened at Montreuil-sous-Bois in 1897: "Pretty soon, wishing to obtain certain fantastic effects belonging really to the mechanical contrivances of the theater, Méliès had a pit three meters deep dug in the entire area where the stage was to be. The floor was modified and set up like the stage for fairy plays, with ramps, trap doors, slots, set banks, elevator traps for apparitions, star traps, traps called 'the tomb' and winches placed not above the stage as it is done in the theater but rather outside the studio which was then too narrow to put them inside" (Maurice Noverre, *Le Nouvel Art cinématographique*, No. 3, 2nd series, July 1929, translated by Susan F. Frazer). Méliès' operators were Leclerc and Michaut (the latter remained with him for many years), Lallemand and Astaix (who left in 1903 to form a distribution company), Lucien Tainguy, Lucien Bardou, Henri Gallet, Georges Hatot, Victorin Jasset, and his own daughter Georgette. Titles include: *Une Nuit terrible* (*A Terrible Night*, 1896), *Escamotage d'un Dame chez Robert-Houdin* (*The Vanishing Lady*, 1896, stop-substitution), *Le Manoir du Diable* (*The Devil's Castle/The Haunted Castle*, 1896), *L'hallucination de l'alchimiste* (*A Hallucinated Alchemist*, 1897), *Le Cabinet de Mephistopheles* (*Laboratory of Mephistophélès*, 1897), *Faust et Marguerite* (*Faust and Marguerite*, 1897), *Magie Diabolique* (*Black Art/Devilish Magic*, 1898), *Quais de la Havane* (*The Blowing Up of the Maine in Havana Harbor*, 1898), *Visite de l'epave du Maine* (*A View of the Wreck of the Maine*, 1898) and *Visite sous-marin du Maine* (*Divers at Work on the Wreck of the Maine*, 1898, filming dry-for-wet by placing a large fish tank in front of the camera), *Le Magicien* (*The Magician*, 1898), *Illusions Fantasmagoriques* (*The Famous Box Trick*, 1898), *La Lune à une Mètre/L'homme dans la Lune* (*The Astronomer's Dream*, 1898, a forerunner of 1902's *A Trip to the Moon*), *La Danse du Deu* (*Haggard's "She"—the Pillar of Fire*, 1899), *Le Portrait Mystérieux* (*A Mysterious Portrait*, 1899, employing matte and counter-matte), *Le Miroir du Cagliostro* (*Cagliostro's Mirror*, 1899), *Neptune et Amphitrite* (*Neptune and Amphitrite*, 1899), *Le Christ marchant sur les flors* (*Christ Walking on the Water*, 1899), *Cendrillon* (*Cinderella*, 1899), *La Statue de Neige* (*The Snow Man*, 1899), *L'homme Orchestre* (*The One-Man Band*, 1900, multiple exposure), *L'illusioniste double et la Tete vivante* (*The Triple Conjuror and the Living Head*, 1900), *L'homme aux cent trucs* (*The Conjuror with a Hundred Tricks*, 1901), *Guguste et Belzebuth* (*The Clown Versus Satan*, 1901), *Mésaventures d'un Aèronaute* (*The Ballonist's Mishap*, 1901), *Bouquet d'illusions* (*The Triple-Headed Lady*, 1901), *L'homme à la tete de Caoutchouc* (*The Man with the Rubber Head*, 1902; thanks to double-exposure and a pulley-operated chair—with Méliès seated on it—that was pulled toward the camera over a ramp, Georges was able to create the illusion of his head exploding), *Le Diable Géant ou le Miracle de la Madonne* (*The Devil and the Statue/The Gigantic Devil*, 1902), *L'armoire des Frères Davenport* (*The Cabinet Trick of the Davenport Brothers*, 1902), *Eruption volcanique à la Martinique* (*The Eruption of Mount Pelee/The Terrible Explosion of Mount Pelee and Destruction of St Pierre, Martinique*, 1902, explosive diorama), *Le Voyage dans la Lune* (*A Trip to the Moon*, released August 1902, adapting both Jules Verne, as illustrated by Alfred de Neuville, and H. G. Wells with his fantasy of Selenites titled "*The First Men on the Moon*," which required 18 sets and cost 10,000 francs to produce), *Les Trésors de Satan* (*The Treasures of Satan/The Devil's Money Bags*, 1902), *Le Voyage de Gulliver à Lilliput et chez les Géants* (*Gulliver's Travels Among the Lilliputians and the Giants*, 1902), *Le Cake-walk infernal* (*The Cake Walk Infernal/The Infernal Cake Walk*, 1903), *La Statue animée* (*The Drawing Lesson or, the Living Statue*, 1903), *La Flamme merveilleuse* (*The Mystical Flame*, 1903), *Le Sorcier* (*The Witch's Revenge/The Sorcerer's Revenge*, 1903), *Le Portrait spirite* (*A Spiritualistic Photographer*, 1903), *Le Mélomane* (*The Melomaniac*, 1903, multiple exposure: Méliès playing a music master who repeatedly removes his head and throws it up to the musical staff of five telegraph wires where the heads form lively notes), *Le Monstre* (*The Monster*, 1903), *Le Royaume des Fées* (*Fairyland or, the Kingdom of the Fairies*, 1903), *Le Chaudron infernal* (*The Infernal Cauldron and the Phantasmal Vapours*, 1903), *Illusions funambulesques* (*Extraordinary Illusions/ The 20th Century Illusionist*, 1903), *L'enchanteur Alcofrisbas* (*Alcofrisbas, the Master Magician/ The Enchanter*, 1903), *Jack et Jim* (*Jack and Jim/ Comical Conjuring*, 1903), *La Lanterne Magique* (*The Magic Lantern*, 1903), *Faust aux enfers/ La Damnation de Faust* (*The Damnation of Faust/ The Condemnation of Faust*, 1903), *Siva l'invisible* (*The Invisible Silvia*, 1904), *Le Coffre enchanté* (*The Bewitched Trunk*, 1904), *Les Transmutationes imperceptibles* (*The Imperceptible Transmutations*, 1904), *Damnation du Docteur Faust* (*Faust and Marguerite/ Faust*, 1904), *La Sirène* (*The Mermaid*, 1904), *Les Costumes animés* (*The Animated Costumes*, 1904), *Le Voyage à travers l'Impossible* (*An Impossible Voyage/ Whirling the Worlds*, 1904; a train en route to the Sun, budgeted at 37,500 francs), *La Grotte aux surprises* (*The Grotto of Surprises*, 1905), *Les Cartes vivantes* (*The Living Playing Cards*, 1905), *Le Diable noir* (*The Black Imp*, 1905), *Le Palais des Mille et Une Nuits* (*The Palace of the Arabian Nights*, 1905), *Le Raid Paris-Monte Carlo en 2 heures* (*An Adventurous Automobile Trip*, 1905), *L'ile de Calypso. Ulysse et le Géant Polyphème* (*The Mysterious Island*, 1905, an encounter with Homer's one-eyed cyclops), *La Légende de Rip Van Winkle* (*Rip's Dream*, 1905), *Le Cauchemar du Pêcheur ou L'escarpolette fantastique* (*The Angler's Nightmare, or a Policeman's Troubles*, 1905), *Le Dirigeable fantastique ou le Cauchemar d'un Inventeur* (*The Inventor Crazybrains and His Wonderful Airship*, 1906), *La Magie à travers les Àges* (*Old and New Style Conjurors*, 1906), *Les 400 Farces du Diable* (*The Merry Frolics of Satan*, 1906), *La Fée Carabosse ou le Poignard fatal* (*The Witch*, 1906), *Le Carton fantastique* (*A Mischievous Sketch*, 1907), *Deux cent mille lieues sous les mers ou le Cauchemar d'un Pêcheur* (*Under the Seas*, 1907, Jules Verne's *20,000 Leagues Under the Sea* filmed for the first time), *Le Tunnel sous la Manche ou le Cauchemar franco–anglais* (*Tunnelling the English Channel*, 1907), *Satan en prison* (*Satan in Prison*, 1907), *La Gènie du feu* (*The Genii of Fire*, 1908), *La Poupée vivante* (1908), *Les Illusions fantaisistes* (1910), *L'homme aux mille inventions* (1910), *Les Hallucinations de Münchausen* (1911), *Le Vitrail diabolique* (1911), *À la Conquête du Pole* (*Conquest of the Pole*, 1912, defeating a snow giant and thus copying a 1903 R.W. Paul production, *Voyage of the Arctic*), *Le Chevalier des Neiges* (1912). As Méliès was not willing to submit to new distribution techniques, he was forced out of business even before World War I: "Financial problems were the major reason for Méliès' decline. His later work shows no sign of artistic deterioration when he was personally involved with a production. On the other hand, his work showed little sign of change. His idea of cinema was too close to a certain kind of theater for him to succeed in getting out of his own closed universe with its visions, its demons, and its captive princesses. Audiences began to dismiss Méliès as a relic of the past. The general cultural climate of France was changing from the cheerful buoyancy of the Belle Epoque toward a new worldliness and cynicism. The twentieth century had arrived and Méliès was no longer in his century" (John Frazer, *Artificially Arranged Scenes: The Films of Georges Méliès*, p. 53). His last performance in the Theatre Robert-Houdin took place in 1920. He and his second wife, former actress Jehanne d'Alcy, whom he married in 1925, fell on hard times thereafter. They rented a little shop in the Gare Montparnasse (Confiserie et Jouets) where they sold candy and toys. Eventually Méliès was rediscovered. On December 16, 1929, a retrospective of his surviving work was organized in the Salle Pleyel in Paris. At a grand banquet in 1931 he was acknowledged as the "creator of cinematographic spectacles" and awarded the Legion of Honor by Louis Lumière. Alas, an ambitious plan to build a museum and shrine to the movies to be called *Notre Dame du Cinema* didn't come to fruition. Neither did some ideas to introduce the old man to moviemaking again. In 1932 Marcel Carné planned the film project *The Phantom of the Métro* with Méliès as technical advisor, and Dada filmmaker Hans Richter asked for his contribution on a new version of *Baron Munchausen,* but nothing came out of it. Méliès only appeared in two publicity shorts for La Régie des Tabacs. He died of cancer at the Hopital Léopold-Bellan in Paris, and was buried at Père Làchaise cemetery.

Peter Melrose (1930–)
British Matte Artist

Born in the Royal and Ancient County of Berkshire, Melrose knew from a very early age that he wanted to be an artist and, against strong opposition from his parents, he eventually took the entrance examination and went to Art College. At that time he had absolutely no idea of a career in films; in fact, he was aiming very much towards a career in advertising. But at the end of his art course, his work was noticed at an exhibition by a man who worked in films. The result was that Melrose landed a job in the title department of the J. Arthur Rank Organization. After about a year and a half of doing this, he joined the scenic artists, meeting and assisting Albert Whitlock with foreground glasses. Finally he came to know Wally Veevers, who was in charge of the small but prestigious Shepperton Studios matte department and desperately needed a new artist. Melrose's first matte for Veevers was a coast guard tower in the waters off Hong Kong for *Lord Jim* (1965). Then came *The Blue Max* (1966) and *The Battle of Britain* (1968–69). Over the years Melrose contributed matte and glass art for *Dracula Has Risen from the Grave* (1968, Hammer Films), *The Lion in Winter* (1968), *Fiddler on the Roof* (1971), *Nicholas and Alexandra* (1971), *Macbeth* (1971), *Jesus Christ Superstar* (1973) and *Frankenstein: the True Story* (1973). His most prominent effect was for Roman Polanski's *Dance of the Vampires* (U.S.: *The Fearless Vampire Killers*, 1967): "For the opening shot, Roman wanted the longest zoom shot ever attempted. It was to start with a close-up on a crater on the moon. The lens pulls slowly back to reveal the whole moon, then back further to see the moon in the sky; pulling back still further; now coming back over the tops of the mountains with the moon still in the sky; back over the tree tops into the snowy landscape of Transylvania where we see our two heroes coming towards us in a horse-drawn sleigh…. I started by shooting close-up on a 6 ft. diameter model of the moon revolving slowly and tracked back and zoomed back, simultaneously stop-framing for a smooth shot. I then repeated the process with a 1 ft. 6 in. diameter model of the moon and combined the two shots so as to appear as one very long zoom back off the moon. To obtain the effect of coming over the mountaintops, I painted a series of glasses each depicting a perspective plane, i.e., distant mountains, near mountains, trees and snowy landscape, each glass behind the other. Running the film through the camera in reverse, I tracked up to the first glass, then removed it in order to track up to the next one and so with all the painted glasses. With the film running normally, this gave the effect of coming back over the mountains and through the tree tops" (*Little Shoppe of Horrors*, Number 10/11). Melrose also did many foreground glasses for TV shows.

Ray Mercer (1896–1981)
American Effects Cinematographer and Supervisor

Born in Pennsylvania, he founded Ray Mercer & Company which specialized in low-budget optical effects, titles and inserts: *Frontier Days* (1934), *Timber Terrors* (1935), *The New Adventures of Tarzan* (1935 serial), *Revolt of the Zombies* (1936), *The Drag-Net* (1936), *Return of the Ape Man* (1944), *Fuzzy Settles Down* (1944), *White Pongo* (1945), *Behind the Mask* (1946), *Tumbleweed Trail* (1946), *The Mask of Diijon* (1946), *Suspense* (1946), *The Feathered Serpent* (1948), *The Mozart Story* (1948), *16 Fathoms Deep* (1948), *Treasure of Monte Cristo* (1949), *Zamba* (1949), *The Return of Jesse James* (1950), *Lost Continent* (1951), *Pier 23* (1951), *FBI Girl* (1951), *Superman and the Mole-Men* (1951), *Savage Drums* (1951), *Bomba and the Jungle Girl* (1952), *Mesa of Lost Women* (1953), *Safari Drums* (1953), *Jail Bait* (1954), *Highway Dragnet* (1954), *Riot in Cell Block 11* (1954), *The Golden Idol* (1954), *Port of Hell* (1954), *Lord of the Jungle* (1955), *Spy Chasers* (1955), *Jail Busters* (1955), *Dig That Uranium* (1956), *Untamed Mistress* (1956), *Kentucky Rifle* (1956), *Naked Gun* (1957), *Crashing Las Vegas* (1956), *Plan 9 from Outer Space* (1958–59), *Gorgo* (1961, additional optical effects), *Master of the World* (1960–61), *The L-Shaped Room* (1962), *Flesh Gordon* (1974), *Star Wars* (1975–77, additional optical effects). TV: *The Adventures of Superman*, *Topper*, *The Outer Limits*. Died in Orange County, California.

John J. Mescall (1899–1962)
American Director of Photography and Effects Cinematographer

Born in Litchfield, Illinois, John Joseph Mescall started in the laboratory, became an assistant cameraman, then second cameraman. Began as first cameraman with the Goldwyn Company. Worked on tests for MGM in Europe for eight months. Trick and process photography for Warner Bros., then Universal. Miniature photography: *The Invisible Man* (1933). Director of photography: *Bride of Frankenstein* (1935). Last feature film credit was *Not of This Earth* (1957). In private life he was a world-class golfer. Spent his last years in obscurity, and died in Los Angeles County.

Henry E. [Hal] Millar

American Mechanical Effects Technician

Started as a laborer at MGM. With *The Wizard of Oz* (1939) he became involved in special effects there: *Forbidden Planet* (1956), *Ice Station Zebra* (1968, Academy Award nomination). With Burt Lancaster he made a polit thriller filmed in Munich: *Das Ultimatum* (U.S.: *Twilight's Last Gleaming*, 1977).

Hiroshi Mukoyama [Mukaiyama]

Japanese Optical Cinematographer

At Toho Studios he was in charge of opticals, matte photography and composites for Eiji Tsuburaya and Teisho Arikawa: *Taiheyo no washi* (*Eagle of the Pacific*, 1953), *Hana no naka no musumetachi* (1953), *Tomei ningen* (*The Invisible Man*, 1954), *Gojira* (*Godzilla, King of the Monsters!*, 1954), *Ju jin yukio Otoko* (1955), *Gojira no gyakushu* (*Gigantis, the Fire Monster*, 1955), *Byaku fujin no yoren* (*Madame White Snake*, 1956), *Sora no daikaiju Radon* (*Rodan*, 1956), *Bijo to ekitainingen* (*The H-Man*, 1958), *Daikaiju Baran* (*Varan the Unbelievable*, 1958), *Uchu daisenso* (*Battle in Outer Space*, 1959), *Sensuikan I-57 kofuku sezu* (*Submarine I-57 Will Not Surrender*, 1959), *Nippon tanjo* (*The Three Treasures*, 1959), *Sun Go Ku* (*The Adventures of Sun Wu Kong*, 1959), *Denso ningen* (*The Telegian*, 1960), *Hawai Middouei daikakusen: taiheyo no arashi* (*I Bombed Pearl Harbor*, 1960), *Osaka jo monogatari* (*Devil in the Castle*, 1961), *Mosura* (*Mothra*, 1961), *Sekai daisenso* (*The Last War*, 1961), *Gen to fudomyo-o* (*The Youth and His Amulet*, 1961), *Kurenai*

no umi (*Blood on the Sea*, 1961), *Yosei Gorasu* (*Gorath*, 1962), *Kingukongu tai Gojira* (*King Kong vs. Godzilla*, 1962), *Taiheyo no tsubasa* (*Kamikaze*, 1963), *Matango* (*Matango: Fungus of Terror*, 1963), *Chintao yosai bakugeki meir ei* (*Siege at Fort Bismarck*, 1963), *Daitozoku* (*The Lost World of Sinbad*, 1963), *Kaitei gunkan* (*Atragon*, 1963), *Shikonmado—Dai tatsumaki* (*Whirlwind*, 1964), *Mosura tai Gojira* (*Godzilla vs. the Thing*, 1964), *Uchu daikaiju Dogora* (*Dagora, the Space Monster*, 1964), *San daikaiju: Chikyu saidai no kessen* (*Ghidrah, the Three-Headed Monster*, 1964), *Kureiji no daiboken* (*Crazy Adventure/Don't Call Me a Crime Man*, 1965), *Kaiju daisenso* (*Invasion of the Astro-Monsters*, 1965), *Taiheyo kiseki no sasuken: Kisuka* (*Miraculous Military Operation in the Pacific*, 1965), *Furankenshutain no kaiju: Sanda tai Gaira* (*The War of the Gargantuas*, 1966), *Gojira, Ebira, Mosura: Nankai no daiketto* (*Godzilla vs. the Sea Monster*, 1966), *Kingukongu no gyakushu* (*King Kong Escapes*, 1967), *Kaiju soshingeki* (*Destroy All Monsters*, 1968), *Rengo kantai shirei chokan: Yamamoto Isoroku* (*Admiral Yamamoto*, 1968), *Nihonkai daikaisen* (*Battle of the Japan Sea*, 1969).

Dennis Muren (1946–)

American Special Effects Cinematographer and CGI Supervisor

Born in Glendale, California. A pre-teen Muren became very interested in the stop-motion work of Ray Harryhausen after seeing *Earth vs. the Flying Saucers* (1956) and especially *The 7th Voyage of Sinbad* (1958), the latter about eight times when it was originally released: "I had to figure out what I was seeing, how an effect was done and how it fit into the whole picture" (*Industrial Light + Magic: Into the Digital Realm*, p. 280). A neighbor, Phil Kellison, took the young 8mm film amateur to Project Unlimited so that he (Muren) could watch them work on *Jack the Giant Killer* (1960–62). After graduation, Muren's professional job was with Kellison and Cascade Pictures on Pillsbury Doughboy commercials. With $8,000 and the help of stop-motion-oriented friends David Allen and Jim Danforth, Muren produced the 16mm *Equinox* (1966) which became the basis for Jack H. Har-

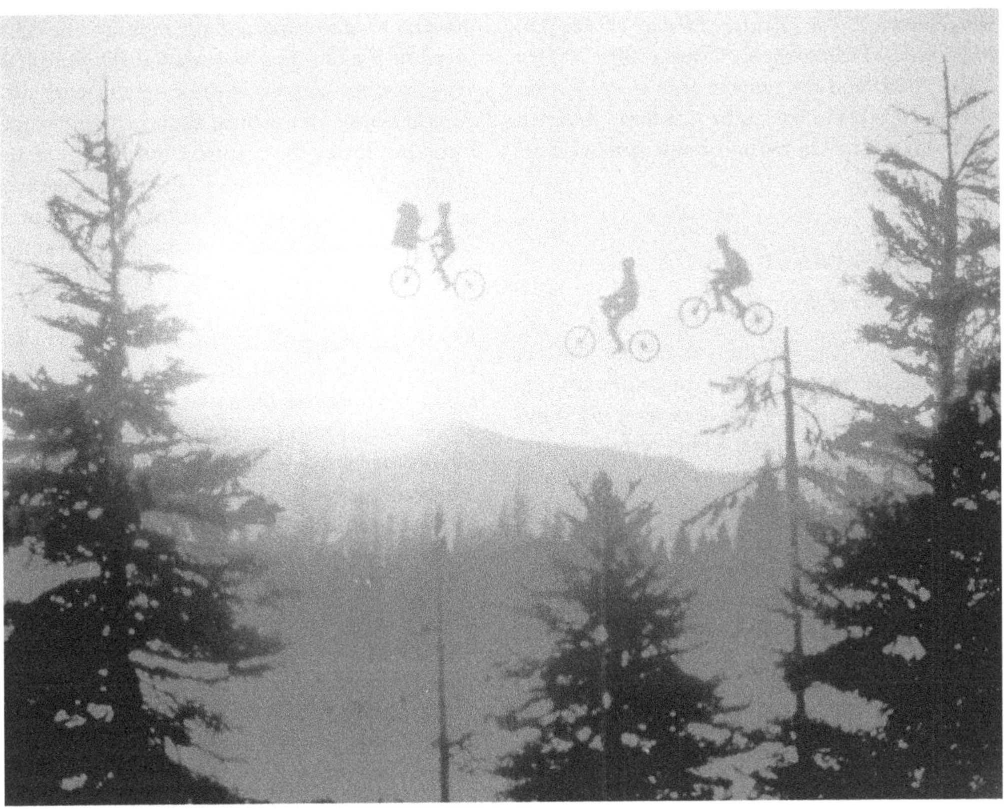

Stop motion animation for _E.T._ (1982), photographed by Dennis Muren at ILM (courtesy Deutsche Kinemathek Berlin).

ris' theatrical release in 1971. Muren also assisted Allen (and Danforth, who was slightly involved) on the perennially unfinished project _The Primevals_ and on _Willy Wonka and the Chocolate Factory_ (1970), then photographed the stop-motion scenes for an infamous erotic sci-fi spoof, _Flesh Gordon_ (1971–74). Applied for a job with John Dykstra and worked on the first _Star Wars_ (1975–77) and _Close Encounters of the Third Kind_ (1975–77, for Douglas Trumbull and Richard Yuricich). After _Battlestar Galactica_ (1978), another Dykstra project, Muren became a staff member at Industrial Light & Magic in San Rafael, Marin County, and (after Richard Edlund left) their principal cinematographer: _The Empire Strikes Back_ (1978–80), _Dragonslayer_ (1981–82), _E.T. the Extra-Terrestrial_ (1982), _The Return of the Jedi_ (1982–83), _Indiana Jones and the Temple of Doom_ (1984), _The Ewok Adventure: Caravan of Courage_ (1984), _Innerspace_ (1987), _Willow_ (1988), _Ghostbusters II_ (1989). With _Young Sherlock Holmes_ (1986, stained glass

window knight coming to life, done in cooperation with Pixar's John Lasseter and Bill Reeves), _The Abyss_ (1989, pseudopod sequence), _Terminator 2: Judgment Day_ (1991), _Jurassic Park_ (1992–93), _Casper_ (1995), _Jumanji_ (1995) and _Twister_ (1996), he specialized in CGI: "I knew all the traditional tools and how something could be best done traditionally. I just started getting bored with that toward the mid–1980s — I thought we [had] hit a wall. All we were doing was variations on stuff, and it couldn't get any better, and digital had always been sort of a promise" (_Industrial Light + Magic_, p. 280). Muren's interest in computer graphics had begun around the time they were finishing up on _The Empire Strikes Back_: "Somebody sent over a test film that was done by Triple-I [Information International, Inc.] of five X-wings flying around. It was all CG. It had its flaws and there was no motion blur, but the potential was there...." Muren eventually became senior effects supervisor at ILM. Directed CGI sequences for _Star_

Wars Episode I: The Phantom Menace (1998–99) and *Episode II: Attack of the Clones* (2001–2002), *Hulk* (2003) and the remake *War of the Worlds* (2004–2005). He has eight Academy Awards and a star on the Hollywood Boulevard Walk of Fame.

Fumio Nakadai

Japanese Wire Effects Expert

Member of Eiji Tsuburaya's effects unit at Toho Studios. Supervised the dinosaur's tail for *Gojira* (*Godzilla, King of the Monsters!*, 1954) by support of overhead wires. Other films (as special effects or wire manipulator) which involved flying monsters, airplanes or UFOs: *Hana no naka no musmetachi* (1953), *Sora no daikaiju Radon* (*Rodan*, 1956), *Chikyu boeigun* (*The Mysterians*, 1957), *Uchu daisenso* (*Battle in Outer Space*, 1959–60), *Uchu daikaiju Dogora* (*Dagora, the Space Monster*, 1964), *Furankenshutain tai chitei kaiju Baragon* (*Frankenstein Conquers the World*, 1965), *Kaiju daisenso* (*Invasion of the Astro Monsters*, 1965), *Furankenshutain no kaiju: Sanda tai Gaira* (*The War of the Gargantuas*, 1966), *Zero faita dai kusen* (*Zero Fighters*, 1966), *Gojira, Ebira, Mosura: Nankai no daiketto* (*Ebirah, Horror of the Deep*, 1966), *Kingukongu no gyakushu* (*King Kong Escapes*, 1967), *Kaijuro no kessen: Gojira no musuko* (*Son of Godzilla*, 1967), *Kaiju soshingeki* (*Destroy All Monsters*, 1968), *Rengo kantai shirei chokan: Yamamoto Isoroku* (*Admiral Yamamoto*, 1968), *Ido Zero daisakusen* (*Latitude Zero*, 1969), *Nihonkai daikaisen* (*Battle of the Japan Sea*, 1969), *Gojira-Minira-Gabara: Oru kaiju daishingeki* (*Godzilla's Revenge*, 1969), *Chikyu mogeki Meirei: Gojira tai Gaigan* (*Godzilla on Monster Island*, 1972).

Haruo Nakajima (1929–)

Japanese Monster Actor

Yamagata-born stunt man and bit player at Toho Studios. With his "portrayal" of *Gojira* (*Godzilla, King of the Monsters!*) in 1954 he became the favorite "monster suit" actor (until 1972): "There were three cables coming out of the back of the costume. Two were for the operation of the eyes and one was for the operation of the mouth. Eizo Kaimai was responsible for the movement of the eyes and the mouth. The ASA speed of the film that was used at the time was very slow, so the set had to be very brightly lit. Another actor complained that the lights made it too hot inside the costume, but I never complained" (*Cult Movies* No. 17, p. 56). In the early days of his career, he would commonly lose over 20 pounds while shooting. Nakajima continued to play Godzilla in *Gojira no gyakushu* (*Gigantis, the Fire Monster*, 1955), *Kingukongu tai Gojira* (*King Kong vs. Godzilla*, 1962), *Mosura tai Gojira* (*Godzilla vs. the Thing*, 1964), *San daikaiju chikyu saidai no kessen* (*Ghidrah, the Three-Headed Monster*, 1964), *Kaiju daisenso* (*Invasion of the Astro-Monsters*, 1965), *Gojira, Ebira, Mosura: Nankai no daiketto* (*Ebirah, Horror of the Deep*, 1966), *Kaijuro no kessen: Gojira no musuko* (*Son of Godzilla*, 1967), *Kaiju soshingeki* (*Destroy All Monsters*, 1968), *Gojira-Minira-Gabara: Oru kaiju daishingeki* (*Godzilla's Revenge*, 1969), *Gojira tai Hedora* (*Godzilla vs. the Smog Monster*, 1971), *Gojira kogeki meirei: Gojira tai Gaigan* (*Godzilla on Monster Island*, 1972). Other costumed and *kaiju eiga* monster parts: *Tomei ningen* (*The Invisible Man*, 1953), *Sora no daikaiju Radon* (*Rodan*, 1956), *Chikyu boeigun* (*The Mysterians*, 1957, as Moguera the mole-like giant robot), *Daikaiju Baran* (*Varan the Unbelievable*, 1958), *Gasu ningen dai ichigo* (*The Human Vapor*, 1960, as transitional vapor man), in *Mosura* (*Mothra*, 1961, as head part of Mothra larva), *Yosei Gorasu* (*Gorath*, 1962, as giant walrus; cut from American prints), *Furankenshutain tai chitei kaiju Baragon* (*Frankenstein Conquers the World*, 1965, as Baragon), *Furankenshutain no kaiju: Sanda tai Gaira* (*The War of the Gargantuas*, 1966, as Gaira), *Kingukongu no gyakushu* (*King Kong Escapes*, 1967, as Kong), *Ido Zero Daisakusen* (*Latitude Zero*, 1969, as winged lion and giant rat), *Gezora, Ganime, Kameba: Kessen! Nankai no daikaiju* (*Yog: Monster from Space*, 1970, as tentacled Gezora). Also as actor and instructor with Tsuburaya Productions: *Urutoraman* (*Ultra Man*).

Minoru Nakano (1939–)

Japanese Visual Effects Supervisor

Nakano was a 19-year-old freshman at Nippon University when he met Eiji Tsuburaya for the first time in December 1958, but declined his invitation to join Toho Studios' Special Technique Department as an apprentice because he wanted to finish his film studies. Eventually he came on board when they made *Kingukongu tai Gojira* (*King Kong vs. Godzilla*, 1962) for which he even did a few seconds of stop-frame animation of Kong kicking his antipod Godzilla. After finishing *Mosura tai Gojira* (*Godzilla vs. the Thing*, 1964) he worked on all TV series for Tsuburaya Productions. Visual effects consultant: *Saigo no kyoryu* (U.S.: *The Last Dinosaur*, 1977), *Uchu no messeji* (*Message from Space*, 1978), *Akira Kurosawa's Dreams* (1990), *Gamera—Daikaiju kuchu kessen* (*Gamera—the Guardian of the Universe*, 1995).

Teruyoshi Nakano (1935–)
Japanese Special Effects Director

Born in Manshu, Korea. Graduated from Nippon University's film department (where he had met Ishiro Honda) in 1959. That same year he entered Toho Studios as an assistant director: *Nppon tanjo* (*The Three Treasures*, 1959), *Uchu daisenso* (*Battle in Outer Space*, 1959), *Denso ningen* (*The Telegian*, 1960), *Hawai Middouei daikaikusen: Taiheiyo no arashi* (*I Bombed Pearl Harbor/ Storm Over the Pacific*, 1960), *Osaka jo monogatari* (*Devil in the Castle*, 1961), *Sekai daisenso* (*The Last War*, 1961). While assisting on *Sensuikan I-57 kofuku sezu* (*Submarine I-57 Will Not Surrender*, 1959) he became interested in traveling mattes and effects work. He eventually joined Tsuburaya's special technique department: *Yosei Gorasu* (*Gorath*, 1962), *Kingukongu tai Gojira* (*King Kong vs. Godzilla*, 1962), *Matango* (*Attack of the Mushroom People/ Matango: Fungus of Terror*, 1963), *Kaitei gunkan* (*Atragon*, 1963). He was promoted to first assistant director and worked on the war film *Taiheiyo no tsubasa* (*Attack Squadron!/ Wings Over the Pacific*) in 1963 and *Mosura tai Gojira* (*Godzilla vs. the Thing*) in 1964. He assisted on *San daikaiju: Chikyu saidai no Kessen* (*Ghidrah, the Three-Headed Monster*, 1965), *Furankenshutain tai chitei kaiju Baragon* (*Frankenstein Conquers the World*, 1965), *Kaiju daisenso* (*Invasion of the Astro-Zombies*, 1965), *Furankenshutain no kaiju: Sanda tai Gaira* (*The War of the Gargantuas*, 1966), *Gojira, Ebira, Mosura: Nankai no daiketto* (*Ebirah, Horror of the Deep*, 1966), *Kai-*

juro no kessen: Gojira no musuko (*Son of Godzilla*, 1967), *Kaiju soshingeki* (*Destroy All Monsters*, 1968), *Ido Zero daisakusen* (*Latitude Zero*, 1969), *Gezora, Ganime, Kameba: Kessen! Nankai no daikaiju* (*Yog: Monster from Space*, 1970). Assisted Ishiro Honda in finishing new effects sequences for the compilation *Gojira-Minira-Gabara: Oru kaiju daishingeki* (*Godzilla's Revenge*, 1969). Some time after Tsuburaya died, Nakano was put in charge of the whole department: *Gojira tai Hedora* (*Godzilla vs. the Smog Monster*, 1971), *Chikyu kogeki meirei: Gojira tai Gaigan* (*Godzilla on Monster Island*, 1972), *Gojira tai Megara* (*Godzilla vs. Megalon*, 1973), *Gojira tai Mekagojira* (*Godzilla vs. Mechagodzilla*, 1974), *Mekagojira no gyakushu* (*Terror of Mechagodzilla/ The Terror of Godzilla*, 1975). The Japanese film industry was currently facing a deep depression, so he had to keep the costs low on his Godzilla and sci-fi releases: "I was a 'poor director,' because I had to continue making the [Godzilla] films during this difficult time. I hated [relying on stock footage], but there was no choice. Of course it hurt me when I had to re-use those scenes, but there was no other way — we did not have the time or the money" (*Monsters Are Attacking Tokyo!*, p. 112). His biggest success as a special effect director was the massive *Nippon chiubotsu* (*Tidal Wave*, 1973) dealing with the submersion of Japan. Also: *Esupai* (*Espy*, 1974), *Wakusei daisenso* (*The War in Space*, 1977, a cheap-looking *Star Wars* rip-off), *Nosutoradamusu no daiyogen* (*Catastrophe 1999: The Prophecies of Nostradamus*, 1979), *Imperial Navy* (1981), *Kaguya* (*Princess of the Moon*, 1987). Television series: *Ryusei Ningen Zon* (*Zone Fighter*, 1971–73). His last Godzilla feature was *Gojira* (1984, released in the U.S. as *Godzilla 1985*). Later helped to create effects-oriented rides for theme parks (including Space World in Kyushu) and lectured.

Edward Nassour (1911–1962)
American Producer

Born in Colorado Springs. With his brother he founded Nassour Studios and produced low-budget projects like Abbott & Costello's *Africa Screams* (1949). His interest in stop-motion animation led him to think about *Lost Atlantis*, an abandoned Willis O'Brien project that failed a second time, first with effects pioneer Fred Jackman, then with Walter Lantz animators and Columbia, and let him buy several of O'Brien's story properties. Only one was released during O'Brien's lifetime, *The Beast of Hollow Mountain* (1956, announced as filmed in the Regiscope System). Nassour, however, didn't hire OBie for the effects as he considered him too slow (and perhaps too costly). He supervised the stop-frame and replacement animation by Henry Lion and Jay Bard himself. He also directed stop-motion sequences for the low-budget *Lost Continent* (1951). Another O'Brien project, *Ring Around Saturn*, based on the story *Emilio and His Magical Bull,* was filmed in 1953 but due to copyright problems not released until 1975. Edward Nassour died in Sherman Oaks.

Józef [Joseph] Natanson
(1909–2003)
Polish Illustrator and Matte Artist

Born in Cracow, Poland, he started a career in Surrealist painting. When he went to Great Britain he became involved in trick and matte work. Added pictorial effects to Powell & Pressburger's color production *The Red Shoes* (1948). With Technicolor setting up a plant in Rome, Natanson was repeatedly sent to Italy and decided to settle there. He contributed considerably to the films of Federico Fellini, Vittorio De Sica, Pier Paolo Pasolini and Franco Zeffirelli as well as to bread-and-butter sandal epics: *Femmina* (1954), *Casta Diva* (1954), *Erode il Grande* (*Herod the Great,* 1958), *Nel segno di Roma* (1959), *Giuseppe Venduto dai fratelli* (1960), *La contessa azzurra* (1960), *La regina delle Amazzoni* (*Colossus and the Amazon Queen,* 1960), *La ciociara* (1960), *Il gigante di Metropolis* (1961), *Maciste nella terra dei Ciclopi* (1961), *Francis of Assisi* (1961), *Arrivano i titani* (*The Titans/U.S.: My Son, the Hero,* 1961–62), *Giulio Cesare, il conquistadore delle Gallie* (*Julius Caesar the Conqueror,* 1962), *La sette folgori di Assur* (1962), *Cleopatra* (1963), *L'eroe di Babilonia* (1963), *La belle famiglie* (1964), *La Bibbia/ The Bible* (1965) *La montagna di luce* (1965), *Sette contro la morte* (1965), *Se tutte le donne del mondo* (1966), *Mark Donen Agente Zeta 7* (1966), *Caccia alla volpe* (*After the Fox,* 1966), *Cast a Giant Shadow* (1966), *The Cavern* (1966), *Arriva Dorellik* (1967), *Arabella* (1967), *La cintura di Castita'* (1967), *Il fischio al naso* (1967), *Tre passi nel delirio* (1967), *Satyricon* (1968), *Histoires extraordinaires* (1968, segment "Toby Dammit"), *The Witches* (1969), *I guerrieri dell'anno* 2072 (1984), *The Name of the Rose/Der Name der Rose* (1986) by Jean-Jacques Annaud. Died in Rome.

Warren A. Newcombe
(1894–1960)
American Matte Artist

Started in art titles and did pastel artwork on castles in the clouds for *The Enchanted City,* an experimental film made in 1922. He was hired by MGM studio manager Eddie Mannix to head the matte department, where matte and glass shots were called "Newcombe shots": *American* (1924), *Where East Is East* (1928), *The Mask of Fu Manchu* (1932), *Tarzan the Ape Man* (1932), *Tarzan and His Mate* (1934), *Mark of the Vampire* (1934–35), *China Seas* (1935), *Marie Antoinette* (1938), *Tarzan Finds a Son!* (1939), *The Wizard of Oz* (1939), *Dr. Jekyll and Mr. Hyde* (1940–41), *Tarzan's Secret Treasure* (1941), *Two-Faced Woman* (1941), *The Feminine Touch* (1941), *Billy the Kid* (1941), *Smilin' Through* (1941), *Rio Rita* (1942), *Tarzan's New York Adventure* (1942), *A Yank at Eton* (1942), *Tennessee Johnson* (1942), *Reunion in France* (1942), *Mrs. Miniver* (1942), *Tortilla Flat* (1942), *I Married an Angel* (1942), *Madame Curie* (1943), *Lassie Come Home* (1943), *Du Barry Was a Lady* (1943), *The Cross of Lorraine* (1943), *Above Suspicion* (1943), *A Guy Named Joe* (1943), *The White Cliffs of Dover* (1943), *Stand by for Action* (1943), *Cry "Havoc"* (1943), *Thirty Seconds Over Tokyo* (1944), *Mrs. Parkington* (1944), *Dragon Seed* (1944), *Gaslight* (1944), *Kismet* (1944), *Lost in a Harem* (1944), *They Were Expendable* (1945), *Yolanda and the Thief* (1945), *Week-end at the Waldorf* (1945), *The Valley of Decision* (1945), *Son of Lassie* (1945), *The Sailor Takes a Wife* (1945), *Adventure* (1945), *The Clock* (1945), *Her Highness and the Bellboy* (1945), *The Yearling* (1946), *Keep Your Powder Dry* (1945), *Till the Clouds Roll by* (1946), *My Brother Talks to Horses* (1946), *The Hoodlum Saint* (1946), *The Romance of Rosy Ridge* (1947), *If Winter Comes* (1947), *The Hucksters* (1947), *High Wall* (1947), *High Barbaree* (1947), *Cass Timberlane* (1947), *The Beginning or the End* (1947), *The Sea of Grass*

(1947), *Green Dolphin Street* (1947), *The Three Musketeers* (1948), *Tenth Avenue Angel* (1948), *The Sun Comes Up* (1948), *A Southern Yankee* (1948), *Hills of Home* (1948), *B.F.'s Daughter* (1948), *Easter Parade* (1948, first use of the Dupy Duplicator invented by O. L. Dupy for motion control matte shots), *Take Me Out to the Ball Game* (1949), *The Stratton Story* (1949), *The Secret Garden* (1949), *On the Town* (1949), *Madame Bovary* (1949), *In the Good Old Summertime* (1949), *Malaya* (1949), *Little Women* (1949), *The Barkleys of Broadway* (1949), *Challenge to Lassie* (1949), *The Bribe* (1949), *The Yellow Cab Man* (1950), *Crisis* (1950), *Three Little Words* (1950), *The Tall Target* (1951), *The Strip* (1951), *Shadow in the Sky* (1951), *The Red Badge of Courage* (1951), *The Painted Hills* (1951), *No Questions Asked* (1951), *The Light Touch* (1951), *The Law and the Lady* (1951), *Angels in the Outfield* (1951), *Show Boat* (1951), *Three Guys Named Mike* (1951), *The Great Caruso* (1951), *The People Against O'Hara* (1951), *Go for Broke!* (1951), *Royal Wedding* (1951), *Texas Carnival* (1951), *Across the Wide Missouri* (1951), *An American in Paris* (1951), *It's A Big Country* (1951), *Washington Story* (1952), *Talk About a Stranger* (1952), *The Prisoner of Zenda* (1952), *Pat and Mike* (1952), *The Girl in White* (1952), *Desperate Search* (1952), *The Belle of New York* (1952), *The Bad and the Beautiful* (1952), *Singin' in the Rain* (1952), *Scaramouche* (1952), *Above and Beyond* (1952), *Plymouth Adventure* (1952), *The Merry Widow* (1952), *Young Bess* (1953), *Remains to Be Seen* (1953), *Give a Girl a Break* (1953), *Escape from Fort Bravo* (1953), *Cry of the Hunted* (1953), *The Band Wagon* (1953), *Julius Caesar* (1953), *The Naked Spur* (1953), *The Actress* (1953), *Dream Wife* (1953), *Kiss Me Kate* (1953), *The Story of Three Lovers* (1953), *Arena* (1953), *Valley of the Kings* (1954), *Her Twelve Men* (1954), *Green Fire* (1954), *Executive Suit* (1954), *Brigadoon* (1954), *Seven Brides for Seven Brothers* (1954), *Rose Marie* (1954), *The Long, Long Trailer* (1954), *Deep in My Heart* (1954), *Trial* (1955), *The King's Thief* (1955), *I'll Cry Tomorrow* (1955), *The Glass Slipper* (1955), *Guys and Dolls* (1955), *Love Me or Leave Me* (1955), *It's Always Fair Weather* (1955), *The Teahouse of the August Moon* (1956), *Somebody Up There Likes Me* (1956), *The Opposite Sex* (1956), *Meet Me in Las Vegas* (1956), *Forbidden Planet* (1956), *Designing Woman* (1957), *Raintree Country* (1957). Artists who worked under him were called Newcombe Men: Henri Hillinck, Howard Fisher, Otto Anton Kiechle, Ray Schlagenhauser, Oscar Medlock, Albert Ashworth, George Chittenden, Vernon Mangold, Hernando Villa, Sigmund Nesselroth, Joe Duncan Gleason, Rufus Harrington, Jack Shaw, Irving Block, Emil Kosa, Jr., Matthew Yuricich and others. His main cinematographer was Mark Davis. Other cameramen were Winton Hoch and Tom Tutwiler. At the time the highly eccentric and equally protective Newcombe retired, he was deeply involved in a love affair with the wife of the Mexican ambassador which turned into a political scandal. He died under mysterious circumstances in Mexico.

Bruce Nicholson
American Optical Cinematographer

Joined Industrial Light & Magic as optical camera assistant in the final stages of *Star Wars* (1976–77), and eventually became head of the optical department.

Theodor (Theo) Nischwitz
(1913–1994)
German Visual Effects Supervisor

The Berlin-born son of film director Heinrich Nischwitz-Lisson had a 1930 apprenticeship at that city's Ufa-controlled Afifa Laboratories. In 1931 he began working in optical effects at Afifa, trained by Gerhard Huttula on the crude optical printing machine "Truca" (Debrie), and taking over after Huttula left for Argentine: *Bomben auf Monte Carlo* (1931), *Der Kongress tanzt* (*The Congress Dances*, 1931), *F.P.1 antwortet nicht* (*Secrets of F.P.1,* 1932), *Ekstase* (1932), *Flüchtlinge* (1933), *Gold* (1933–34), *Maskerade* (1934), *Liebe, Tod und Teufel* (1934), *Das Stahltier* (1934, forbidden film), *Amphitryon* (1935), *Königswalzer* (1935), *Mazurka* (1935), *Stadt Anatol* (1936), *Capriccio* (1938), *Die Hochzeitsreise* (1938–39), *Es war eine rauschende Ballnacht* (1939), *Bal Paré* (1940), *Stukas* (1941), and *Münchhausen* (1942–43). During World War II he was an army newsreel cameraman. Effects cinematographer: *Besatzung Dora* (1942–43), which wasn't released officially although it was directed by Karl Ritter, a prominent Nazi. In 1948, Nischwitz left Berlin and went to Munich to work at Bavaria Studios: *Der Herr vom anderen Stern* (1948–49), *Der Apfel ist ab* (1948), *Wohin Die Züge Fahren* (1949), *Nachtwache* (1949), *Hallo, Fräulein!* (1949), *Königskinder* (1949), *Das doppelte Lottchen* (1950), *Herbstgedanken* (1950), *Verzauberte Bergwelt* (1950), *Nachts auf den Strassen* (1951), *Ich heisse Niki* (1952), *Sauerbruch—Das war mein Leben* (1953–54), *Stählerne Adern* (1956), *Geliebte Bestie* (1958–59), *Die Nackte und der Satan* (*The Head*, 1959), *Ein Mann geht durch die Wand* (1959), *Nacht fiel über Gotenhafen* (1959–60), *Das Spukschloss im Spessart* (1960, double-exposures of greenish ghostly images), *Das Wunder des Malachias* (1960–61), *Hitler—Ein Film aus Deutschland* (1977). Later joined forces with Jan W. Jacobsen, supervising and managing front projection shots for *Ludwig—Requiem für einen jungfräulichen König* (1972), *Karl May* (1974), *Der amerikanische Freund* (1976–77), Billy Wilder's *Fedora* (1977–78), *Avalanche Express* (1979), Wolfgang Petersen's *Das Boot* (*The Boat*, 1980–81), *Der Zauberberg* (1981), *Night Crossing* (1981–82, a Disney picture). TV: the sci-fi mini-series *Raumpatrouille* (1966, assisted by Werner Hierl et al.), *Frau Luna* (1975), *Carmina Burana* (1975), *Berlin Alexanderplatz* (1979–80, by Rainer Werner Fassbinder), *Hänsel und Gretel* (1980–81), *Der Flug zum Mond* (1983–84), *Das Gespenst* (1983–84), *Flucht nach Afrika* (1984), *Das Rätsel der Sandbank* (1984–85). 1984: Bundesfilmpreis (German Film Prize).

Barry Nolan

American Optical Cinematographer

The chief technician at Van der Veer Photo Effects, he took over after Frank Van der Veer's demise: *King Kong* (1976), *Flash Gordon* (1980), *Conan the Barbarian* (1982), *Dune* (1983–84).

Gustaf M. Norin (1905–1988)

Swedish-American Prosthetics Technician and Makeup Artist

Born in Malmö, Sweden. With his father, Josef Norin, he joined MGM (*The Wizard of Oz,*

1939) and helped to transform Charles Laughton into Quasimodo for RKO's 1939 *The Hunchback of Notre Dame*. They also did *Cyrano de Bergerac* (1950, with José Ferrer). Gustaf Norin worked on *Tomorrow Is Forever* (1946), *High Noon* (1952) and two Jules Verne pictures, *20000 Leagues Under the Sea* (1953–54) and *Around the World in 80 Days* (1956). Did Marlene Dietrich's special makeup for *Witness for the Prosecution* (1957). Remained active up to 1981: *History of the World, Part I*.

Josef A. Norin (1882–1954)

Swedish-American Prosthetics Sculptor

Born in Sweden. Josef and son Gustaf joined the MGM makeup department in 1935 and specialized in bald caps and appliances for movies such as *The Good Earth* (1937) and *The Wizard of Oz* (1939). Loaned out to Perc Westmore and RKO to create Charles Laughton's makeup prosthetics for *The Hunchback of Notre Dame* (1939). Also on *Cyrano de Bergerac* in 1950.

Lester Novros (1909–2000)

American Animator and Effects Supervisor

Veteran Disney animator: *Snow White and the Seven Dwarfs* (1937), *Fantasia* (1940, assisting Bill Tytla on the "Night on Bald Mountain" sequence). Founded Graphic Films and produced training films and documentaries for the U.S. Air Force and NASA, sometimes on large formats: *To the Moon and Beyond* (1964), *Universe* (1976), *Tomorrow in Space* (1982). Hired promising young talent like Douglas Trumbull, Con Pederson, John Dykstra and Robert Abel. Did preliminary designs for Stanley Kubrick's *2001: A Space Odyssey* (1965–68).

Willis H. O'Brien (1886–1962)

American Stop-Motion Pioneer and Illustrator

"A scene that flashes before your eyes on the screen for a few seconds may have required several weeks of concentrated preparation and work. Often a day's work of twenty-five feet of finished film is shown in about one-third of a minute on the screen" (O'Brien, *Miniature Effects*

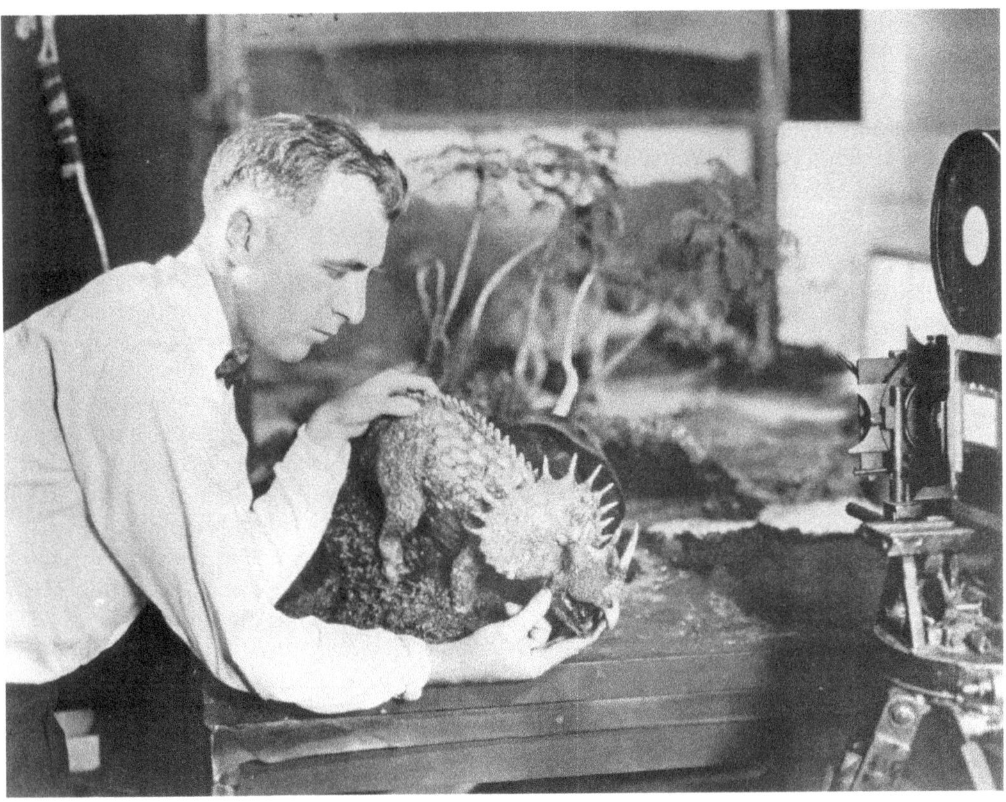

Willis O'Brien animating *The Lost World* (courtesy Deutsche Kinemathek Berlin).

Shots). Willis Harold O'Brien was born in Oakland, California. His parents were William Henry O'Brien, an etymologist who operated a military academy and a hotel at times, and Minnie Gregg; the family came from Ireland. Willis' started his career as a newspaper cartoonist. In 1914 he pioneered stop-motion and dinosaur films in a series of short puppet films for Edison Company: *The Dinosaur and the Missing Link* (1915), *Morpheus Mike* (1915–16), *Birth of a Flivver* (1915–16), *Curious Pets of Our Ancestors* (1917), *In the Villain's Power* (1917), *Nippy's Naughty Nightmares* (1917), *Mickey and the Goat* (1917), *Prehistoric Poultry* (1917), *Sam Lloyd's Famous Puzzles/ The Puzzling Billboard* (1917, based on the Sam Lloyd Puzzle Books, then very popular in Britain), *Rural Delivery 10,000 A.D./RFD 10,000 B.C.* (1917). Mixed stop-motion and live-action footage in the scientifically more serious and ambitious *The Ghost of Slumber Mountain* (1919) for Major Herbert M. Dawley. *Ghost* got favorable reviews when it was released by World Pictures. From a May 10, 1919, statement by G.

Clyde Fisher, Ph. D., of the American Museum of Natural History, as told to Dawley: "Last Saturday evening I saw *The Ghost of Slumber Mountain* at the Rivoli and I was greatly pleased. It is astonishing how lifelike those old dinosaurs and the giant bird, Diatryma, were. You are to be congratulated, not only upon the realistic restorations, but also upon the attractive introductions and settings; the whole thing was extremely well done." We see the Diatryma devouring a ten-foot snake and watch a fight to the death between a Tyrannosaurus Rex and a Triceratops. In his next installment, Dawley tried to introduce "full-grown human beings in the scenes with the ancient beasts" (maybe by use of split-screens) but by then he had lost O'Brien to an equally innovative rival producer: Watterson R. Rothacker of the Rothacker Mfg Co. (Rothacker made his first contact with the motion picture industry as a journalist. In 1910, he established a production company in association with Carl Laemmle and R. H. Cochrane, specializing in advertising and educational films. He was also active in war films.) From an August 9, 1919, World statement by Rothacker:

> It was in 1914 in San Francisco I first heard of Mr. O'Brien's work. He was working on a roof making his first plastic pictures, the result being a picture 75 feet in length, featuring a brontosaurus and a dinosaur. In the latter part of 1915, Mr. O'Brien made a reel of prehistoric animals entitled *The Dinasaurus* [sic] *and the Missing Link*, and then made two novelty pictures, entitled *Morphous* [sic] *Mike* and *The Birth of a Flivver*. In 1916, Mr. O'Brien went to New York City to make pictures for Edison's Conquest program. For this purpose, Manikin Films Inc. was formed.... When the Conquest program was discontinued, Mr. O'Brien was asked to edit a weekly [newsreel] in which the educational feature was to be a series of prehistoric animals. In order to make these scientifically correct, Mr. O'Brien went to the American Museum of Natural History and consulted with Dr. Brown of the museum. Much of the action appearing in *The Ghost of Slumber Mountain* was the suggestion of Dr. Brown. While with the Edison Co., Mr. O'Brien made *Curious Pets of Our Ancestors, Rural Delivery 2,000,000 B.C.* (released as *R.F.D. 1,000,000 B.C.*), *Power* [sic], *Mickey and the Goat, Sam Lloyd Puzzle Picture* and *Nippy's Nightmare*. In the last production, human characters were used with the manikins and it was the picture that convinced Mr. O'Brien that his previous pictures were lacking in human interest. When the Edison Co. sold out to Lincoln & Parker, the plan to make educational pictures a chapter of the weekly was abandoned. It was about at that time that O'Brien met Herbert Dawley, who had been working along some special experimental lines, and had, as a result, a small book in which he had pasted a large number of exposures of the plastic dinosaur. Mr. O'Brien entered into some arrangement with Mr. Dawley, and *The Ghost of Slumber Mountain* was started. The work on this was all done by Mr. O'Brien. His manikins were used and the entire production was made by him without any scenario, the only material being a sheet of titles. *The Ghost of Slumber Mountain* was originally about 3000 feet in length and was cut to present proportions for obvious reasons.... Since then an attempt has been made to create the impression that the work was not done by him, which, of course, is contrary to the facts of the case.... We have already finished with Mr. O'Brien 3 or 4 subjects far superior to anything he has ever produced.

These three or four shorts don't seem to have survived the passage of time but there was leftover footage from *Ghost* incorporated by Dawley, who was about to usurp O'Brien's process, into *Along the Moonbeam Trail* (1920). Rothacker, in the meantime, joined an agreement with First National Pictures (he became vice-president and managing director of First National Productions) and co-produced the dinosaur epic *The Lost World* (1924–25) in West and East Coast Studios. The climax of that picture showed a brontosaurus (brought from the Amazon to London) on the rampage in that city, then escaping via the River Thames. *The Lost World* became the model for all monster-on-the-loose stories to come. When other projects (*Atlantis* and *Frankenstein*) failed at First National (which was in the process of being absorbed by Warner Bros.), O'Brien went with Ralph Hammeras and George J. Teague over to Fox Studios, studying process shots and inventing miniature projection, then got a call from Harry O. Hoyt, *Lost World*'s director, to come to RKO Radio Pictures for a dinosaur sound film, *Creation*. With the arrival of a new studio regime in 1931, *Creation* was shelved, but O'Brien's staff and techniques were saved for Merian C. Cooper's brainchild *King Kong* (1932–33). For this O'Brien used miniature rear projection, which he had developed in 1930, for the first time in connection with tabletop sets and stop-motion animation. Cooper saw that O'Brien got his share of publicity too (*Hollywood-On-The-Air* on NBC on the night of Friday, February 10, 1933):

> COOPER: Our thanks also go to Willis O'Brien, Hollywood's most noted technical expert.... Mr. O'Brien is here in the studio with us. He is a scholar on the subject of anthropology and has spent more than 20 years in the study of prehistoric life. I want you to meet this man who has labored for more than two years in making *King Kong* become a reality. Mr. O'Brien!
>
> O'BRIEN: Thank you, Mr. Cooper. I left the projection room here at the studio a few minutes ago where I saw our completed handiwork—*King Kong*. In the near future, it will be showing in your city. It will take you about two hours to see it. Two hours! Into that finished product of two hours, we have crammed many years of hard work in an effort to bring to you something entirely new—the conflict of prehistoric creatures with modern man and civilization. Speaking for myself, *King Kong* represents the goal of more than 20 years. For that long a time—and that is a long time in motion pictures—I have delved

into bygone periods, studied the life of animals long before the descent of man, preparing myself for the day when someone would dare to reproduce on the screen the giant beasts that once ruled the world. Without knowing it, I was waiting for *King Kong*. That is the picture for which I have studied 20 years. I feel it has been worth the long years of research. And I hope you, too, will feel the same way after seeing *King Kong*.

(Why didn't O'Brien mention *The Lost World?* Well, all circulating prints of that earlier effort had been withdrawn by then to avoid any competition with *Kong.*) O'Brien remained with Cooper and worked on *The Son of Kong* (1933), *The Last Days of Pompeii* (1934–35), *The Dancing Pirate* (1936, glass paintings in Technicolor), *The War Eagles* (1939, aborted project at MGM where O'Brien was treated like an intruder), and *Mighty Joe Young* (1946–49) for which he received a long overdue Academy Award. As his techniques were considered too costly (because of overheads on *Mighty Joe*) and time-consuming, he didn't find work easily thereafter and finally was reduced to overseeing low-budget efforts: Irwin Allen's *The Animal World* (1956), *The Black Scorpion* (1956–57) and *The Giant Behemoth* (1958–59). Sold original idea for *The Beast of Hollow Mountain* (1956–57) and *Ring Around Saturn* (not released until 1975) to the Nassour Brothers (and other, unfilmed story properties: *The Last of the Labyrinthodons, Below the Bottom, The Vines of Ceres, The Devil's Slide*). His stop-motion concepts for Irwin Allen's 1959–60 remake of *The Lost World* were changed to live lizard footage and his project *King Kong vs. Frankenstein,* bought by producer John T. Beck, changed into the Japanese *Kingukongu tai Gojira* (U.S.: *King Kong vs. Godzilla,* 1962–63) without O'Brien's consent. Other story ideas that remained unfilmed include *The New Adventures of King Kong* (planned in the Cinerama process), *Umbah, the Last of the Oso-Si Papu,* and *Baboon: A Tale About a Yeti.* O'Brien married twice. While he was occupied with *The Son of Kong,* his first wife, Hazel, desperately ill with tuberculosis, killed their two sons, William and Willis, Jr., and then tried to commit suicide. In November 1934, after Hazel's death, he married Darlyne Prenett. O'Brien died of a heart attack during preproduction for the stop-motion climax of *It's a Mad Mad Mad Mad World.* Ray

Harryhausen filmed his *Valley of Gwangi* several years later (1967–69).

Fuminori Ohashi

Japanese Special Effects Supervisor

Ohashi was once an assistant to Yasujiro Ozu at Shochiku. In 1938, a few years after the Japanese release of *King Kong*, he created special costumes and effects for *Edo ni arawareta Kingukongu* (*King Kong Appears in Edo*) with the giant ape tearing up sections of ancient Tokyo. Eiji Tsuburaya, who was aware of this pioneering effort, called him in after World War II (and a stint at Disneyland preproduction offices) to help him with *Gojira* (*Godzilla, King of the Monsters!*, 1954) and *Kingukongu tai Gojira* (*King Kong vs. Godzilla,* 1962). Apparently he worked as consultant on the American *Planet of the Apes* (1968). Television series: *Agon* (1968). Special technical advisor for the atrocious *Kyoryu—Kaicho no densetsu* (*The Legend of the Dinosaurs,* 1977) in which a plesiosaur fought it out with a pterodactyl.

Les Ostinelli

British Effects Cinematographer and Technical Director

Started in the Camera Department at Denham Studios in 1935 and subsequently joined the Special Effects Department. During the war years, he served as a cameraman in the AFPU after which he worked freelance, then worked at MGM British Studios as a special effects cameraman for seven years. More recently he represented a number of major laboratories and, as a result of his photographic background, gained a unique reputation for his ability to liaison between filmmakers and particularly the cameramen and the laboratory. In 1974 he rejoined Technicolor Ltd. as Director of Producers Services and was appointed Technical Director in 1978.

John Oxberry

British Engineer

Designed an optical printer that was named after him.

David Pal (1937–)

American Stop-Motion Animator

Born Eindhoven, Noord-Brabant, Netherlands, David (real name: George Siels Pal) was the son of George and Zsoka Pal. After the Pals moved to Hollywood, David attended Los Angeles schools, including the Hollywood Professional School. At age 16 he changed his name to George David Pal. He worked for some time as an animator at Project Unlimited (and subsequent enterprise controlled by Gene Warren and Wah Chang) on films produced by his father George Pal: *The Time Machine* (1959–60), *The Wonderful World of the Brothers Grimm* (1962–63, elf sequence in three-strip Cinerama) and *The Power* (1967–68). Of his work on *Brothers Grimm*, Jim Danforth says, "There is a scene of the 'blue' elf dancing in a pair of human-size shoes which I think is the best scene of its type that has ever been done by anyone." David also worked on *Dinosaurus!* (1960, some scenes involving the Tyrannosaurus Rex), *Jack the Giant Killer* (1960–62) and the original *Outer Limits* and *Star Trek* TV series. He later turned to wide-screen processes and ultra-high speed photography: assistant head of the photographic department at Cinerama, head of the photographic department at Cinemiracle, camera department member at Walt Disney Studios and CBS Studio Center. As an art director he worked for MGM-Europe and returned to the Netherlands to assist his father's former partner, stop-motion animator Joop Geesink, on Philips Cavalcade's *History of Music*, then became a third partner in Excelsior Films. In the mid–1970s he left the film business to specialize in furniture and interior design. David was interviewed for a documentary on the Cinerama process.

George Pal (1908–1980)

Hungarian-American Producer, Director and Animator

Born in Hungary as György Pál Marczincsák, he studied at the Budapest Academy of Art. Starting as an animator in Budapest, in 1931 he came to Berlin and supervised Ufa's cartoon and commercial department for some time before going independent and producing a cigarette short for Oberst Tobacco with 3D-replacement animation in his own studio, Pal & Wittke, located in Berlin's Nürnberger Strasse (Nuremberg Street). In 1933, with the advent of the Nazis, Pal left Germany, set up Palstudio in the Netherlands and got a contract to produce puppet commercials for Philips Radio in Eindhoven. In the Kohner Agency files of the Berlin Cinematheque, there is a July 15, 1936, letter which Pal had written to Paul Kohner, then with MGM:

I have been in the film business for about seven years now, after working for a short while in Budapest, I went to Berlin, where I became manager of the UFA trick film department very soon, which position I held for two years, during which time I produced a great number of animated cartoons, and was able to improve my technique considerably. Although these films were very favorably commented upon by the press and the leading critics, I personally was really never satisfied with the work I turned out, because I felt that with the enormous resources the American trick film production could put behind their films, I would never be able to successfully compete with such productions. Plans, therefore, ripened in my mind to produce cartoons in the third dimension. Being an architect and interior decorator, it was not difficult for me to design suitable décors and figures for such a film. So in the course of 1932 I produced my first film in the new process in my own studio. This film was about 500 feet long and it took me five months to produce it with six assistants. This short film had an unprecedented success in Germany. For a number of years I produced advertising films for large European concerns, using and improving at the same time the process of animated dolls, which I believed to have a great future, it being an entire novel and comic presentation of the trick film. During the time I worked and experimented for myself, many new inventions and improvements were made, and I gradually overcame the difficulties of showing only a few dolls in motion at the same time. I do not think it is necessary for me here, to go into details about the difficulties I had to overcome. I take it that you can quite well realize yourself what the difficulties were…. About three years ago I left Germany and I produced some films in Prague for the Schicht Margarine Concern in Aussig, through the intermediary of the A-B Film and in Paris. At that time the Gasparcolor company developed a new colored film process, which gave quite new possibilities of this new development, induced me to come to Holland, guaranteeing enough films to make it worth my while to install a new studio in Eindhoven, where for the past two years I have produced a great number of films for the Philips company, who are, as you may be aware the largest radio and incandescent lamp manufacturers of Europe. Apart from some black-and-white and colored animated cartoons, all those films were done in the plastic puppet treatment, including among others, *The Ship of the Ether, Magic Atlas, In Lamplight Land* and *The Ether Symphony*. Of last year's film, *The Magic Atlas*, a 600-foot film, over 160 copies were circulated in practically all parts of the world, with the exception of the United States and Canada, where the Philips company does not do any business. At an International Advertising Film Show in Berlin last year, two of my films were sent down and they both got first and second place respectively. During the past two years in Holland, I have been able to gradually improve my studio, so that I may say, that today I have the largest and best equipped trick film studio on the Continent, employing about twenty people regularly. In the meantime I have produced films also for the Horlick's Malted Milk Co. through the intermediary of the Walter Thompson Company of New York and London. Of course, I am somewhat hampered here in Europe with the production of my films, because I have to concentrate chiefly on advertising films, where it is not always possible, as you will appreciate, to follow one's own ideas from an artistic point of view. Before all, the advertising message must be put across, and sometimes the artistic value suffers. It is, however, utterly impossible to compete in Europe with the American production of animated cartoons for entertainment purposes only. The Disney [product is] sold so cheaply over here, that it is practically impossible to put anything against it. However, never being satisfied with my own work, I produced such a film last year at my own risk, based on material from the Thousand and One Night stories. This film, *Ali Baba and the Forty Thieves*, was a first attempt in this direction and has been successfully shown all over Europe. Personally I was not very enthusiastic about this particular film. My greatest difficulty over here is to find the right manuscripts and I did not consider the Ali Baba manuscript particularly brilliant. This is one of the reasons why I have not continued to finish the stories of the Arabian Nights of which I had originally planned six films. Besides, you must not forget, that when producing advertising films I get my money immediately, whereas, when producing entertainment films I have to wait very long before I get anything in return. As obviously, the cost of my productions is rather high (for *Ali Baba* I had to make about 50,000 exposures!), it is also hard to induce film renters to buy such films, because they can get American productions at very much lower prices. Besides, I am at present so occupied with several new films I still have to make,

that I have no time left to bother much about it right now. It may interest you to know after my experiments had been successful, the UFA several times tried to engage me again and get the exclusive rights for my process. However, as I am very satisfied with the result I have obtained so far, I have always turned down their offers.... My work has been widely publicized all over Europe, also thanks to the efforts of the Philips Company, and especially the last few months I have received numerous inquiries from America. If I can get away at all, I am planning a trip to the United States in the Fall, and in that case I shall be particularly charmed if you would allow me to pay you a visit, as undoubtedly I could give you a better impression of my work personally than I can ever hope to give you by letter.

With the outbreak of World War II, Pal came to Hollywood, set up a shop for replacement animation and produced the Technicolor *Puppetoons* and *Madcap Models* series for Paramount release. In 1943 the Academy of Motion Picture Arts and Sciences acknowledged Pal with a Special Award (Plaque) for the development of novel methods and techniques in the production of his Puppetoons. Among the animators and artists employed at his studio at various times were Ray Harryhausen, Willis O'Brien (working on only one short, *Jasper's Choo-Choo*), Gene Warren, Wah Chang, Bob Baker, Duke Goldstone, Phil Kellison and cameraman Paul Sprunck. Late in the 1940s, Pal withdrew from short subjects and started making feature films involving animation and special effects. Eagle-Lion releases: *The Great Rupert* (1949–50), *Destination Moon* (1949–50). Paramount releases: *When Worlds Collide* (1951), *The War of the Worlds* (1952–53), *Houdini* (1953), *The Naked Jungle* (1954) and *Conquest of Space* (1955). MGM releases, some directed by himself: *tom thumb* (1957–58), *The Time Machine* (1959–60), *Atlantis the Lost Continent* (1960–61), *The Wonderful World of the Brothers Grimm* (1962–63, in three-strip Cinerama), *7 Faces of Dr. Lao* (1963–64) and *The Power* (1967–68). Warner Bros. release: *Doc Savage, the Man of Bronze* (1975; his original concept which could have been something along the lines of Indiana Jones was virtually destroyed by the production company). Some of the special effects technicians involved in his features received Academy Awards or nominations: Lee Zavitz, Gordon

Jennings, Tom Howard, Gene Warren, Tim Baar, Jim Danforth and makeup artist William Tuttle.

Michael Angelo Pangrazio

American Matte Artist

At Industrial Light & Magic from 1978 to 1985. For *The Empire Strikes Back*'s(1979–80) stop-motion sequence (photographed by Dennis Muren), Pangrazio painted Hoth backdrops, then joined the matte department. "[He was the] first painter to project pictures onto his easel as a reference. Pangrazio also utilized the 'cut-and-paste' technique pioneered by earlier matte artists, a shortcut in which actual photographs, blown up to the appropriate size, could be attached to a painting's surface to save time and add to the overall realism" (*Industrial Light & Magic: Into the Digital Realm*, pp. 90–91). Other productions include *Raiders of the Lost Ark* (1981), *Poltergeist* (1982), *Return of the Jedi* (1982–83), *The Shadow* (1994).

Charles E. Parker (1910–1977)

Canadian-British Makeup Artist

Born in Nova Scotia, Canada. Besides doing regular makeup jobs on big-budget productions like *Quo Vadis* (1950–51), *Ben-Hur* (1958–59) and *King of Kings* (1961), Parker repeatedly turned to special effects makeup work: *Moby Dick* (1956, consultant for whale model), *tom thumb* (1958), *2001: A Space Odyssey* (1965–68), *Trog* (1970), *The Devils* (1971) and *Star Wars* (1975–77, cantina sequence). Died in Watford, Hertfordshire, Britain.

Richard Parker

American Mechanical Effects Supervisor

Rigged *The Ten Commandments* (1956), went to Africa for *Hatari!* (1962), went to Europe for *Circus World* (1963), *Those Magnificent Men in Their Flying Machines* (1965) and *Monte Carlo Rally* (1969) and to Morocco for *The Man Who Would Be King* (1975).

Robert William Paul

(1869–1943)

British Inventor and Producer

Manufactured scientific instruments and early cinematographique equipment when in 1894 two Greek showmen asked him to produce six duplicates of an Edison and Dickson Kinetoscope which they had acquired. Georges Méliès bought a projector from him, too. When Edison refused to supply movies, Paul went on to produce his own "animated photographs" or trick films: *The Last Days of Pompeii* (1897), *A Railway Collision* (1900, miniature train wreck), *The Haunted Curiosity Shop* (1901), *The Magic Sword* (1902), *Voyage of the "Arctic," or How Captain Kettle Discovered the North Pole* (1903, 11 scenes including a snow giant that was later copied by Méliès in *À la conquête du Pole*, 1912), *The ? Motorist* (1906, an automobile travels into outer space and back to earth), *The Butterfly* (1910).

Kenneth D. Peach (1903–1988)

American Director of Photography and Effects Cinematographer

Born in El Reno, Oklahoma, Peach entered the motion picture business when he was 20. In 1926 he became first cameraman. He specialized in composite processes, miniatures, montages and matte shots at Tiffany Pictures and, with Fred Jackman's technical effects department, at Warner Bros.-First National. Then for two years he was with various independents and for one year with Columbia Pictures. In late 1931 he joined the camera effect department at RKO, did matte shots for *The Most Dangerous Game* (1932) and alternated with Eddie Linden on *King Kong* (1932–33). In 1933 he became a first cameraman at Hal Roach Studios (*Sons of the Desert*). In World War II he joined the U.S. Navy: "Upon my release I did the special effects and process photography on several independent pictures. I went to work at RKO Studio in June 1946 as a director of photography, shooting process and second unit material for many features — including *I Remember Mama* — and aerial sequences for *Jet Pilot*." In 1950 he turned independent again and was involved in many features and numerous television shows (*Lassie, Sea Hunt,* the original *Outer Limits*). Peach remained active until 1984.

Sydney Pearson
British Mechanical Effects Expert

Did effects for *Black Narcissus* (1946), then worked at Ealing Studios: *Scott of the Antarctic* (1948), *Whisky Galore!* (1949), *Kind Hearts and Coronets* (1949), *Cage of Gold* (1950), *The Lavender Hill Mob* (1951), *The Man in the White Suit* (1951), *The Titfield Thunderbolt* (1952), *The Cruel Sea* (1952), *Meet Mr. Lucifer* (1953), *The Maggie* (1954), *The Ladykillers* (1955). His Hammer films include *The Steel Bayonet* (1956–57), *The Snorkel* (1957), *Dracula* (U.S.: *Horror of Dracula*, 1957–58, disintegrating vampire Christopher Lee at the climax), *I Only Arsked* (1958), *The Hound of the Baskervilles* (1958–59), *The Brides of Dracula* (1960), *The Gorgon* (1963–64, rigging the snake-head of a none-too-convincing Gorgon by creating a plastic skull-cap with a wig from which protruded nine artificial snakes), *The Secret of Blood Island* (1964–65), *Fanatic* (1964–65), *The Brigand of Kandahar* (1964–65), *Creatures the World Forgot* (1970).

Con Pederson
American Animation Effects Expert

Worked for Lester Novros and Graphic Films on *To the Moon and Beyond* (1964). Stanley Kubrick hired him for *2001: A Space Odyssey* (1965–68) to run space animation and related effects at MGM British. Later was at Robert Abel & Associates and MetroLight.

Zoran Perisic (1940–)
Yugoslavian-British Rostrum Cameraman and Front Projection Expert

Born in Prokuplje, Serbia. Studied at both Belgrade and Birmingham Universities. Did rostrum and animation work as a special effects rostrum cameraman for *2001: A Space Odyssey* (1965–68). In 1968 he built up the animation department for Yorkshire Television. Since 1970, worked on 500 TV and cinema commercials and several documentaries. Wrote and directed the animated TV series *The Magic Fountain* and *Captain Cook's Travels*, co-produced by his own company, Courier Films Ltd. and Halas and Batchelor. In the mid–1970s he developed Zoptic (Zoom optic) front projection process for *Superman* (1977–78), for which he received an Academy Award for Outstanding Visual Effects as well as the BAFTA Michael Balcon award. "The key feature of this unique, patented system is the use of interlocked zoom lenses on both camera and projector which creates an apparent 'movement in depth.' In addition it features a 3-axis capability making it possible to *pan*, *tilt* and *rotate* (360 degrees) the camera/projector unit." The system helped to create effects for *The Thief of Bagdad* (1978), *Superman 2* (1980), *Greatest American Hero* (1981), *Megaforce* (1982), *Superman III* (1983), *Deal of the Century* (1983), *High Road to China* (1983) and Disney's *Return to Oz* (1983). Perisic controlled the Zoptic patent in his own company Merlin. Directed *Sky Bandits* (*Gunbus*, 1986) and *Phoenix and the Magic Carpet* (1995). The Zoptic Front Projection has also been used on TV commercials for Bendix, Levi's, 7-Up, Kellogg's, Volkswagen, Visa, British Airways and more. Perisic wrote several books, including the 1980 book *Special Optical Effects*. Technical Achievement Award in 1979 for the Zoptic Special Optical Effects Device for motion picture photography.

Harry F. Perry (1888–1985)
American Cinematographer and Aerial Photographer

Born at Idana, Kansas. His older brother Paul, who was already a first cameraman, got Harry a job with Famous Players-Lasky. In 1921 Harry was promoted to first cameraman. Chief cinematographer on Paramount's *Wings* (1927) and Howard Hughes' similar *Hell's Angels* (1930), about aerial warfare in World War I. He later acted as photographic supervisor of the Camera Division of the U.S. Air Force and photographed the aerial shots of the underwater atomic blast at Bikini in 1946. Retired in 1957. Died at the Motion Picture Hospital at Woodland Hills.

Lorne Peterson (1944–)

American Miniature Supervisor

One of the oldest staff members at Industrial Light & Magic, Peterson was involved in all parts of the *Star Wars* saga, *Space Cowboys* (2000) and *Wild, Wild West* (2002). He became chief model maker on *The Empire Strikes Back* (1979–80), and was eventually in charge of ILM's model shop, then ILM model shop project supervisor until shop was closed. Academy Award for *Indiana Jones and the Temple of Doom* (1983–84).

Peter Peterson (19??–1961)

American Stop-Motion Animator

A grip at RKO Studios, Petersen was assigned to Willis O'Brien unit for *Mighty Joe Young* (1946–49) and volunteered to do stop-motion animation. He later animated two other O'Brien projects, *The Black Scorpion* (1956–57) and *The Giant Behemoth* (1958–59). Peterson unsuccessfully tried to launch two projects of his own, *The Las Vegas Monster* and *The Beetlemen*. Victim of multiple sclerosis for about a decade. Phil Kellison (interviewed by Paul Mandell), who saw him animate *The Giant Behemoth*: "I don't know how badly crippled he was at that time. I thought he had to animate sitting down only because the sets were built so low." Peterson died of kidney cancer.

Lewis Wood Physioc (1879–1972)

American Matte Artist and
* Cinematographer*

Born in South Carolina. In 1914 he was the scenic artist on *When Rome Ruled*. Later worked for Goldwyn Studios in Culver City. For Columbia he painted mattes for *The Blood Ship* (1927). Other credits include: *The Viking* (1928), *Along the Navajo Trail* (1945), *Traffic in Crime* (1946), *The Inner Circle* (1946).

Jack P. Pierce (1889–1968)

Greek-American Makeup Artist

Born in Valdetsyou, Greece (real name, Janus Piccoulas). Projectionist for Harry Culver, founder of Culver City. In 1915 he started a career in the movies by playing bit parts. Makeup-wise, early credits included Fox's *The Monkey Talks* (1927, directed by Raoul Walsh) and some uncredited work which he apparently did for the always secretive Lon Chaney. For almost twenty years he was in charge of the makeup department at Universal City Studios and was responsible for most of the classic movie monsters: Conrad Veidt in *The Man Who Laughs* (1929), Bela Lugosi in *Dracula* (1930–31), *Murders in the Rue Morgue* (1931–32) and the independently produced *White Zombie* (1932), Boris Karloff in *Frankenstein* (1931), *The Old Dark House* (1932) and *The Mummy* (1932); Karloff and Lugosi in *The Black Cat* (1934), *The Raven* (1935) and *The Invisible Ray* (1935–36), Karloff and Elsa Lanchester in *Bride of Frankenstein* (1935), Henry Hull as *WereWolf of London* (1935), Karloff as the Frankenstein Monster and Lugosi as Ygor in *Son of Frankenstein* (1938–39), Karloff in *Tower of London* (1939) and *Black Friday* (1939–40), Tom Tyler in *The Mummy's Hand* (1940); Lon Chaney Jr. in *Man Made Monster* (1941), *The Wolf Man* (1941), *The Ghost of Frankenstein* (1942), *The Mummy's Tomb* (1942), *The Mummy's Ghost* (1944) and *The Mummy's Curse* (1944); Chaney Jr. and Lugosi in *Frankenstein Meets the Wolf Man* (1942–43), Claude Rains in *Phantom of the Opera* (1943), Acquanetta in *Captive Wild Woman* (1943), David Bruce in *The Mad Ghoul* (1943), Chaney Jr. and Glenn Strange in *House of Frankenstein* (1944) and *House of Dracula* (1945), many more. When his methods (he did horror makeups with Egyptian cotton, spirit gum, collodion and lens paper, among other ingredients) were criticized by the front office as old-fashioned and too time-consuming, Pierce was released and had to work on potboilers like *Master Minds* (1949), *Teenage Monster* (1958), *The Brain from Planet Arous* (1958), *Giant from the Unknown* (1958), *The Devil's Hand* (1961), *Beauty and the Beast* (1963) and *The Creation of the Humanoids* (1963). TV work include the series *You Are There* and the ever-popular *Mr. Ed*. Died in Hollywood.

Roy J. Pomeroy (1892–1947)

American Effects Supervisor

Born in India. Chief technician at Paramount Studios: *The Ten Commandments* (1923, parting the Red Sea), *Feet of Clay* (1924), *Peter Pan*

(1924), *Old Ironsides* (1926). Improved the Dunning Process (making it the Dunning-Pomeroy Process) by combining the technique with the advantages of glass painting. Received an Academy Award for Engineering Effects for *Wings* (1927). As Paramount's new sound director he acted like a tyrant while handling voice tests and finally was dismissed.

Edwin S. Porter (1870–1941)

American Producer, Director and
Cinematographer

This member of the Edison Company was born in Connellsville, Pennsylvania. He used trick photography (mattes, miniatures, and stop-motion) in his pioneering silents: *Uncle Jack at the Picture Show* (1902), *Jack and the Beanstalk* (1902), the groundbreaking western *The Great Train Robbery* (1903, using the matte and counter-matte system, for one scene in a window to show that train passing outside, the other through an open door of a baggage car), *Dream of a Rarebit Fiend* (1906), six stop-motion *Teddy Bears* (1907), and *The Eagle's Nest* (1907, using a mechanical eagle). Died in New York City.

Don Post (1902–1979)

American Special Makeup and Mask
Expert

Founded a commercial mask studio and distributed Frankenstein and Star Wars rubber masks. Involved in feature film production as supplier: *20000 Leagues Under the Sea* (1953–54), *Invasion of the Body Snatchers* (1956), *From Hell It Came* (1957), *The Great Race* (1965), Dino DeLaurentiis' *King Kong* remake (1976), more.

Project Unlimited

American Effects and Stop-Motion Studio

Founded by George Pal alumni Gene Warren and Wah Chang with former Universal miniaturist Tim Baar. (Their previous company, Centaur, had folded; at Centaur they had handled assignments from stage producers and amusement and theme parks): George Pal's *tom thumb* (1958, Puppetoons sequence), *The Time Machine*

(1959–60), *Atlantis, the Lost Continent* (1960–61), *The Wonderful World of the Brothers Grimm* (1962–63, in three-strip Cinerama), and *7 Faces of Dr. Lao* (1963–64). Also: *Spartacus* (1959–60, forced perspective shot of slain rebels after battle), *Dinosaurus!* (1960), *Goliath and the Dragon* (1960–61, additional stop-motion animation), *Master of the World* (1960–61, *Albatross* model shots), *Jack the Giant Killer* (1960–62), *Flight of the Lost Balloon* (1961), *Journey to the 7th Planet* (1962), *Around the World Under the Sea* (1965). TV: *The Twilight Zone, The Outer Limits*. Other workers: William and Barbara Brace, Martha Armstrong, Don Sahlin, David and Peter Pal (George's sons), Jim Danforth, Tom Holland, Ralph Rodine, Peter Kleinow, Paul LeBaron, Paul Pattee, Al Hamm, Howard Weeks, Marcel and Victor Delgado, Blanding Sloane, Phil Kellison. The company, which was located on Sunset Boulevard in Hollywood, disbanded in 1965.

Francisco Prosper

Spanish Miniature Designer

Created model landscapes and hanging miniatures. Repeatedly worked with Emilio Ruiz del Rio and Ray Harryhausen, such as *The Golden Voyage of Sinbad* (1972–73). Other credits: *Mr. Arkadin* (*Confidential Report*, 1955), *Spartacus*

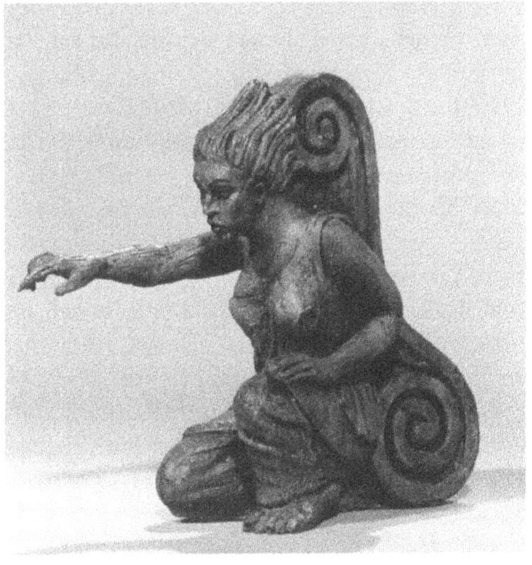

A figurehead (prop) from *The Golden Voyage of Sinbad* (courtesy Ray and Diana Harryhausen Collection as displayed by Deutsche Kinemathek Berlin).

(1959–60), *Cromwell* (1976), *Robin and Marian* (1976), *Viaje del centro de la tierra* (1978), *Conan the Barbarian* (1981–82), *Dune* (1983–84).

Alexander L. Ptushko
(1900–1973)
Russian Director and Effects Supervisor

Born in Lugansk, he studied in Kiev (architecture) and Moscow (Institute of Economics). In 1927 he started in animation and puppet films (*kukolny film*). For Mosfilm he produced and directed the first feature–length live-action-puppet animation film, *Novy Gulliver* (1933–1935, a.k.a. *The New Gulliver*) with a live actor and virtually hundreds of Lillipuppets. In 1936 Ptushko was in charge of Sojusmultfilm animation studio. A year later he produced the first Russian color film, *Skazka o rybake i rybke,* from a poem by Aleksandr Pushkin (*The Tale of the Fisherman and the Fish*). In 1938 he did the live-action-effects feature film *Zolotoy klyuchik* (*The Golden Key*). During World War II he was special effects supervisor at Alma-Ata studios, a tradition he had started with model airplanes created for *Aerograd* (1935) and *Deti Kapitana Granta* (1936, from Jules Verne's *The Children of Captain Grant*). Other films done at that time: *Batyri stepey* (1942), *Paren iz nashego goroda* (1942), *Sekretar Raykoma* (1942), *Front* (1943), *Nebo Moskvy* (1944), *Zoya* (1944), *Nashe sertse* (1946). After the war he directed several fairy tales: *Kamenny tsvetok* (*The Stone Flower*, 1946, the Soviet Union's first three-color feature in the German Agfacolor process), *Sadko* (1952), *Ilya Muromets* (U.S.: *The Sword and the Dragon*, 1955–56, the first Russian Scope picture), *Sampo* (U.S.: *The Day the Earth Froze*, 1959, a Soviet-Finish co-venture illustrating the Kalevala myth), *Alye Parusa* (1961), *Skazka o poteryannom vremen* (1964), *Skazka o Tsare Saltane* (1966, his second adaptation of a Pushkin work), *Ruslan e Lyudmila* (1972). Co-directed *Tri Vstrechi* (1950) with V. Pudovkin and S. Yutkevich. Special effects for Nikolai Gogol adaption of *Vij* (1967).

Jack Rabin (1914–1987)
American Optical Effects Supervisor

"My whole thing had been restrained budgets," Rabin lamented retrospectively. "I never had the luxury of big bucks and I didn't care a lot about it. It's the challenge of illusion — would a piece of string look like a pine tree, or a ball of tin foil look like a meteor?" (*American Cinematographer*, November 1951) In 1937 Rabin started at Selznick International Studios. Under Jack Cosgrove he worked on matte shots, miniature design and opticals.. Then he was with Warner Bros. (four years on the Burbank lot meeting Chesley Bonestell and other matte artists) and 20th Century–Fox until, with Irving Block, he founded an independent effects company, Studio Film Service, on the Eagle-Lion lot. They were joined by title artist Louis DeWitt and for some time by David Commons: *I Killed Geronimo* (1947), *T-Men* (1947), *Northwest Stampede* (1948), *The Amazing Mr. X* (1948), *He Walked by Night* (1948), *Adventures of Casanova* (1948), *Rocketship X-M* (1950, competing with George Pal's *Destination Moon*), *The Man from Planet X* (1950–51), *Invasion U.S.A.* (1951, Cold War gets hot: the Russians bomb New York on the screen for a minuscule effects budget of $10,000), *Unknown World* (1951), *Flight to Mars* (1951), *Captive Women* (1952), *Port Sinister* (1952–53), *Invaders from Mars* (1953), *The Neanderthal Man* (1953), *Robot Monster* (1953, in 3D), *I, the Jury* (1953, in 3D), *Cat-Women of the Moon* (1953–54, also co-producer, shot in five days in 3D), *Top Banana* (1953–54, 3D), *The Big Combo* (1955), Charles Laughton's *The Night of the Hunter* (1955), *The Black Sleep* (1956), *Around the World in 80 Days* (1956, process service for producer Michael Todd), Stanley Kubrick's *The Killing* (1956), *The Brave One* (1956), *The Beast of Hollow Mountain* (1956–57), *Pharaoh's Curse* (1957), *Kronos* (1957), *The Invisible Boy* (1957), *The Saga of the Viking Women and Their Voyage to the Waters of the Great Sea Serpent* (1957), *Daughter of Dr. Jekyll* (1957), *Voodoo Island* (1957), *Monster from Green Hell* (1957), *War of the Satellites* (1958), *Fort Bowie* (1958), *The Giant Behemoth* (1958–59, joining forces with supervising stop-motion creator Willis O'Brien), *The 30-Foot Bride of Candy Rock* (1959, Lou Costello's final film appearance), *The Atomic Submarine* (1959), *Blacula* (1972, bat effects), *Death Race 2000* (1975), Bert I. Gordon's *The Food of the Gods* (1975–76), *The Bees* (1978), *Deathsport* (1978), *Hollywood*

Boulevard (1978), *Airplane!* (1980). In the 1980s Jack Rabin and Associates handled the opticals for all films produced by Roger Corman's company, such as *Galaxy of Terror* (1981) and *Saturday the 14th* (1981). In 1951, for the *Adventures of Superman* TV series starring George Reeves, Rabin made hundreds of flying shots. Other TV credits: *The Pied Piper of Hamelin* (1957), *Men into Space* (1959, short-lived Ziv series), Hanna-Barbera's *Jack and the Beanstalk* (1967, with Gene Kelly), Munich Olympic Games logo for ABC. For $60,000 he made a pilot for the proposed TV series *Outpost in Space* using the flying saucer from *The Atomic Submarine*; this "science fiction *Gunsmoke*" never got off the ground.

Ken Ralston (1953-)
American Visual Effects Supervisor

Was at Industrial Light & Magic right from the beginning: *Star Wars* (1975–77), *The Empire Strikes Back* (1979–80), *Dragonslayer* (1980–81), *Poltergeist* (1982), *Return of the Jedi* (1983), *Cocoon* (1985), *The Golden Child* (1986), *Who Framed Roger Rabbit* (1988), *Back to the Future Part II* (1989), *The Rocketeer* (1991), *Death Becomes Her* (1992), *Forrest Gump* (1994), *The Mask* (1994–95), *Jumanji* (1995), *Phenomenon* (1996), *Contact* (1997). Over the years, he was one of many talents involved in the making of the unfinished *The Primevals*.

Carlo Rambaldi (1923 or 1925-)
Italian Prop and Mechanical Effects Artist

In Italy, Rambaldi (born Vigarano Mainarda) did the mechanical dragon for *Sigfrido* (1956), transformed Kronos into Goliath for *David e Golia* (1959), was involved in *Cleopatra* (1962–63), created another dragon and Medusa for *Perseo l'invincibile* (1963), did effects for Federico Fellini's *Giulietta degli spiriti* (*Juliet of the Spirits*, 1965) and Luchino Visconti's *Ludwig* (1973), and worked on *Carne per Frankenstein* (*Flesh for Frankenstein/Andy Warhol's Frankenstein*, 1973–74, in 3D), *Possession* (1981) and TV's *Le Avventure du Ulisse/L'odissea* (1968). Dino De-Laurentiis, for whom he had worked on *La Bibbia/the Bible … in the Beginning* (1965–66), brought him to the United States for his remake of *King Kong* (1976) and the inevitable sequel, *King Kong Lives* (1986). Rambaldi produced extraterrestrials for *Close Encounters of the Third Kind* (1976–77), *Alien* (1979) and *E.T. the Extraterrestrial* (1982). In 1995 he produced *Decoy*. His main assistant was Carlo de Marchis.

Harry Redmond, Jr.
American Mechanical Effects Expert

At RKO Studios: *The Most Dangerous Game* (1932), *King Kong* (1932–33), *The Last Days of Pompeii* (1935). In the 1950s he freelanced on *Donovan's Brain* (1953) and Ivan Tors' sci-fi productions *Riders to the Stars* (1953–54) and *Gog* (1954, 3D).

Fred Reese (1896–1971)
American Mechanical Effects Expert

The Wyoming-born Reese joined the technical staff at RKO Radio Pictures, helped Willis O'Brien construct the giant *King Kong* bust (1932–33) and also was involved in the shooting of *The Son of Kong* (1933). After leaving RKO he worked on many westerns for Warner Bros. Died in Lompoc, California (heart attack).

William Reinhold
American Visual Effects Cameraman

Started as assistant cameraman on feature films like *The Public Enemy* (1931). At RKO he became involved in effects photography: *King Kong* (1932–33), *Gunga Din* (1939), *The Hunchback of Notre Dame* (1939). Screen credit for *The Captive City* (1952) and the low-budget sci-fi *Kronos* (1957). At Film Effects of Hollywood: *It's a Mad Mad Mad Mad World* (1962–63). While working at Joseph Westheimer's place, he met young Richard Edlund, who invited him over to *Star Wars* (1975–77) to help them set up blue screen shots.

Milt Rice
American Mechanical Effects Expert

Special props for *Seven Angry Men* (1955), *Invasion of the Body Snatchers* (1955–56), *World Without End* (1956), *Voodoo Island* (1957), *Queen of Outer Space* (1958), *The Magnificent Seven* (1960), *The Magic Sword* (1962, working on a two-headed fire-breathing dragon for producer Bert I. Gordon), *Grand Prix* (1966), *Maya* (1966), *Villa Rides!* (1968), *Damnation Alley* (1977). Billy Wilder's favorite effects and props expert: *The Apartment* (1960), *One, Two, Three* (1961), *Irma La Douce* (1963, creating artificial fruit), *Kiss Me, Stupid* (1964), *Buddy Buddy* (1981).

Cliff Richardson (1905–1985)
British Mechanical Effects and Explosives Expert

Richardson entered the film industry in 1923 and joined the staff of Stirling Films, a company that turned out Grand Guignol quickies, and later Barker's Motion Photography Company as a prop assistant. Developed an interest in firearms and gun powder. In 1926 he became a specialist in pyrotechnics for British International Pictures (BIP) at Elstree and contributed to war films such as *The Poppies of Flanders* (1927?). In 1932 he went to Ealing Studios where he opened a model shop with Ray Kellino and for 17 years handled fog, rain, snow and wind machines: *Dead of Night* (1945). In 1947 he was the assistant of Ned Mann at Korda's Shepperton Studios. When his contract with Korda expired, he became an independent effects man: *Captain Horatio Hornblower R.N.* (1951), *The African Queen* (1951), *The Red Beret* (1955), *Zarak* (1956), *Alexander the Great* (1956), *Exodus* (1960), *Lawrence of Arabia* (1962), *Tarzan's Three Challenges* (1963), *Lord Jim* (1965), *Help* (1965), *Judith* (1965), *A Funny Thing Happened on the Way to the Forum* (1966), *The Dirty Dozen* (1966), *The Lost Continent* (1967–68), *Casino Royale* (1968), *The Battle of Britain* (1968), *Duffy* (1968), *The Private Life of Sherlock Holmes* (1969), *Zeppelin* (1971), *Young Winston* (1972), *The Day of the Jackal* (1973), *The Mackintosh Man* (1973), *Rosebud* (1975).

John Richardson (1940–)
British Mechanical, Miniature and Visual Effects Supervisor

The son of explosives expert Cliff Richardson, he joined his father in the family business on *Ex-*

odus (1960), *Lord Jim* (1965), *The Lost Continent* (1967–68, for Hammer Films-Seven Arts), *Casino Royale* (1968) and *The Battle of Britain* (1968). Mechanical effects for *The Devils* (1971), *Young Winston* (1972), *The Little Prince* (1974), *Rosebud* (1975), *The Omen* (1976), *A Bridge Too Far* (1977), *Superman* (1977–78), *North Sea Hijack (ffolkes,* 1979), *Raise the Titanic!* (1980), *Ladyhawke* (1985). Considers himself an all-rounder. He took over all effects work for James Bond pictures with *Moonraker* (1979).

Irving G. Ries (1890–1963)
American Visual Effects and Optical Cinematographer

Born in Akron, Ohio, he started as janitor in a nickelodeon. In 1907 he acquired his own movie camera. In 1927 he created an effect of Louise Fazenda riding an ostrich for an MGM picture and subsequently became head of all optical tricks at MGM: *The Mysterious Island* (1928), *Tarzan the Ape Man* (1932), *Tarzan and His Mate* (1934), *The Canterville Ghost* (1944), *The Barkleys of Broadway* (1949, dancing shoe sequence), *Annie Get Your Gun* (1950), *Toast of New Orleans* (1950), *Singin' in the Rain* (1952), *The Belle of New York* (1952), *Scaramouche* (1952), *Dangerous When Wet* (1953), *Forbidden Planet* (1956), *Invitation to the Dance* (1957, supervised compositing of live-action dance scenes and Hanna-Barbera cartoon footage). Built 3D camera for *Metroscopix.* Retired in 1958.

Günther Rittau (1897–1971)
German Director of Photography

Studied at Technical University in Berlin. Decla-Bioscop company hired him to devise the technical means for photographing scientific films. Did some special photography for Fritz Lang's *Doktor Mabuse, der Spieler* (1921–22). Second camera and all effects work for Fritz Lang's *Die Nibelungen* (1922–24) and *Metropolis* (1925–27). Director Lang later stated that Rittau contributed enormously to *Metropolis,* creating a city of the future, cloning a robot by light rings that encircled the automaton and transformed it into a *femme fatale.* For *Metrop-*

olis Rittau also did some early miniature background projection: When the master of Metropolis (Alfred Abel) communicates with the televised image of a foreman (Heinrich George), the television set was in fact a small rear-projection screen. To accomplish this scene, Rittau installed a mechanical linkage which synchronized the shutter movements of a background projector with those of the camera. Rittau later photographed Emil Jannings and Marlene Dietrich in *Der Blaue Engel* (U.S.: *The Blue Angel*, 1929–30). Directed a submarine propaganda feature *U-Boote westwärts* (1941).

Arthur S. Roades

American Mechanical Effects Expert

At Warner Bros. was involved in *Captain Horatio Hornblower R.N.* (1951) and the mechanical close-up dinosaurs for *the Animal World* (1956–57).

Irmin Roberts

American Special Effects and Matte Cameraman and Technician

Member of Paramount's Special Effects Photography staff on *Spawn of the North* (1938), *Union Pacific* (1939), *Dr. Cyclops* (1939–40), *Aloma of the South Seas* (1941), *I Wanted Wings* (1941), *Reap the Wild Wind* (1941–42), *For Whom the Bell Tolls* (1943), *Unconquered* (1947), *the Great Gatsby* (1949), George Pal's productions of *When Worlds Collide* (1951), *War of the Worlds* (1952–53) and *The Conquest of Space* (1954–55), *The Ten Commandments* (1956), *The Court Jester* (1956). Often did matte shots with artist Jan Marinus Domela. Second Unit: *Elephant Walk* (1954), *It's a Mad, Mad, Mad, Mad World* (1962–63), *Fun in Acapulco* (1963). In Alfred Hitchcock's *Rear Window* (1954) the instance of Jeff comparing the height of the zinnias in Thorwald's flower bed to their height in the 35mm transparencies he had taken previously was accomplished by rigging the camera with a device designed by Roberts, which used prisms, short-range projection, and quick focus changes.

Glen E. Robinson

American Mechanical and Miniature Effects Expert

Assistant to A. Arnold Gillespie at Metro-Goldwyn-Mayer Studios: *The Wizard of Oz* (1939), *Forbidden Planet* (1956), *Ben-Hur* (1959). Supervised miniature alien space craft for *The Bamboo Saucer* (1960) and model aircraft for *The Battle of Britain* (1968–69). For *Earthquake* (1973–74) duplicated Hollywood Dam in miniature, created a model airship *Hindenburg* (1974–75) and helped Dino DeLaurentiis build his version of *a King Kong* robot in 1976. Consultant: *Meteor* (1979), *Flash Gordon* (1980), *Dead Men Don't Wear Plaid* (1982).

Edgar [Edward?] Charles Rogers

British Director and Effects Pioneer

A set designer and scenic artist who came from the stage, he was hired in 1911 by producer Charles Urban to work as art director and devise effects techniques for the studio's product such as the glass shot. Rogers also developed the Kinemacolor technology. Painted backdrops for *The Poppies of Flanders* (1927).

Scott Ross

American Visual Effects Supervisor

Oversaw production at Industrial Light & Magic, then co-founded (with James Cameron and Stan Winston) the effects company Digital Domain.

Emilio Ruiz Del Rio (1923–)

Spanish Model, Hanging Miniature and Glass Shot Supervisor

The Madrid-born Del Rio was a leading expert in hanging miniatures who started in 1942 for producer Sigfrido Burman and worked on many American and international films that were done in Spain (repeatedly associated with art director Francisco Prosper): *Mister Arkadin* (*Confidential Report*, 1955, directed by Orson Welles), *Solomon and Sheba* (1959, directed by King

Vidor), several Samuel Bronston pictures including *El Cid* (1960), *King of Kings* (1960), *55 Days at Peking* (1963), and *The Fall of the Roman Empire* (1964), *Lawrence of Arabia* (1961–62, directed by David Lean), *Cleopatra* (1962–63), *Crack in the World* (1965), *Doctor Zhivago* (1965, David Lean), *Patton* (1969), *The Royal Hunt of the Sun* (1969, with Eugène Lourié as designer), *Nicholas and Alexandra* (1971), *The Golden Voyage of Sinbad* (1972–73), *Super Sonicman* (1979), *L'umanoide* (*The Humanoid*, 1979), *Conan the Barbarian* (1981–82), *Dune* (1983, directed by David Lynch), *Red Sonja* (1985), *Conan II* (1985), *Maximum Overdrive* (1987). All in all, he contributed to more than 450 films.

Karl Ludwig Ruppel (1913–1993)
German Traveling Matte Expert

In the 1930s, Ruppel became a cameraman for Tobis Director's Studio. He also did film work for National Socialist *Deutsche Arbeitsfront*, for instance on board the doomed *Kraft-durch-Freude* ship *Wilhelm Gustloff*. In the 1940s, together with editor Carl Otto Bartning, Ruppel created model aircraft for the amazing propaganda film *Front am Himmel* (*Front in the Sky*), which (although never released in full) led to his postwar activities in the field of visual effects. While working on traveling mattes for *Der Stern von Afrika* in 1956, he became an associate of British expert Victor Margutti: "Our first tests for that picture were done with a foreign laboratory. When Alfred Weidenmann, the director, saw the rushes, he asked, 'Could I have this scene perhaps without matte lines?' Indeed we had made every mistake possible. So we called in Victor Margutti, the traveling matte expert from Rank in England. He immediately came with his set of filters and helped us to manage our problems." Margutti held a patent for black-and-white traveling mattes produced on Eastmancolor negative stock photographed in front of a selective blue backing. In 1960, Margutti and Ruppel invented an additional traveling matte process for *Soldatensender Calais*. The plates for that war picture were shot in VistaVision and then reduced to ordinary 35mm to guarantee a better quality of image and composites by shrinking the matte lines. Ruppel's other film credits include *U 47—Kapitänleutnant Prien* (1958), *Ein Lied geht um die Welt* (1958), *Die grünen Teufel vom Monte Cassino* (1958), *Ein Mann geht durch die Wand* (1959), *Das Totenschiff* (1959), *Drillinge an Bord* (1959), *Abschied von den Wolken* (1959), *Der Frosch mit der Maske* (1959), *Die Brücke* (1959–60), *Der rote Kreis* (1959–60), *Die Bande des Schreckens* (1960), *Wilhelm Tell* (1960–61, made in Switzerland), *Mörderspiel* (1961), *Kohlhiesels Töchter* (1961), *Der Traum von Lieschen Müller* (1961), *Die unsichtbaren Krallen des Dr. Mabuse* (1962), *Moral 63* (1963), *Tonio Kröger* (1964), *DM-Killer* (1964–65), the *Raumpatrouille* TV series (1965–66) and the *G-Man Jerry Cotton* films (mid–1960s) with New York process plates. Ruppel also found himself a niche in some British productions: *Fiend Without a Face* (1957, starring stop-motion brain creatures animated by Flo Nordhoff), *I Was Monty's Double* (1958), *First Man into Space* (1959), *Armored Command* (1961) and the Spanish *La isla de la muerte* (1967).

Kazuo Sagawa
Japanese Special Effects Director

Selected by Eiji Tsuburaya to supervise TV series at Tsuburaya Productions: *Urutoraman* (*Ultraman*, 1966), *Yasuyoshi ito Yasuji Morita* (*Mighty Jack*, 1968). Second unit director of special effects: *Kaitei gunkan* (*Atragon*, 1963). Effects director for the U.S.-Japanese co-production *Saigo no kyoryu* (*The Last Dinosaur*, 1977).

Don Sahlin (193?–197?)
*American Puppeteer and Stop-Motion-
Animator*

Born in Stratford, Connecticut, Sahlin was introduced to the art of puppetry at age 11, when he saw a production of the New York Marionette Guild. He became the apprentice of puppeteer Rufus Rose and, in 1946, joined Martin and August Stevens. In 1949 he went to Hollywood and worked with Bob Baker, then returned home and designed his own puppet show, *St. George and the Dragon*. When he got out of the Army he was hired as an animator on Michael Myerberg's Technicolor puppet version of *Hansel and Gretel* (1953, released through RKO). With fellow animator Kermit Love Sahlin unsuccessfully tried to set up a London shop to execute stop-motion sequences for a proposed feature film version of Beatrix Potter's *Tailor of Gloucester.* He became a regular with Project Unlimited in Hollywood: *tom thumb* (1958), *The Time Machine* (1959–60), *Dinosaurus!* (1960, animating the T-Rex), *Jack the Giant Killer* (1960–62, test animation of two-headed Galligantua and an earlier version of the tentacled sea monster whose head resembled that of a parrot), *The Wonderful World of the Brothers Grimm* (1962–63). Left to join Jim Henson in New York and, up to his death, made all the famous puppets and creatures for *Sesame Street* and *The Muppet Show.*

Tom St. Amand

American Stop-Motion Technician

An alumnus of Cascade Pictures, he mainly designed and machined stop-motion armatures: the uncompleted *Timegate* and the equally ill-fated *the Primevals,* as well as for *The Day Time Ended* (1979). Then he worked at ILM on *The Empire Strikes Back* (1979–80), *Raiders of the Lost Ark* (1981), *Dragonslayer* (1982), *E.T. the Extraterrestrial* (1982), *Return of the Jedi* (1983), *Indiana Jones and the Temple of Doom* (1984), *Star Trek III* (1984), *Cocoon* (1985), *Ewoks: the Battle for Endor* (1985), *The Golden Child* (1986), *Howard the Duck* (1986), *Young Sherlock Holmes* (1986), **batteries not included* (1987), *RoboCop* (1987), *Who Framed Roger Rabbit* (1988), *Willow* (1988), *Honey, I Shrunk the Kids* (1989), and for Tippett Studios: *RoboCop 2* (1990), *The Rocketeer* (1991), *Jurassic Park* (1993), *RoboCop 3* (1993). Feature-length puppet films: *The Nightmare Before Christmas* (1993) and *James and the Giant Peach* (1996).

George Samuels

British Matte Artist

With his brother Ted he worked at Shepperton Studios and entered the matte department run by Percy Day and Wally Veevers. Painted mattes for *The Lady with a Lamp* (1951), *Gift Horse* (1952), *The Story of Gilbert and Sullivan* (1953), *The Green Man* (1956), *The Smallest Show on Earth* (1957), *The Pure Hell of St. Trinian's* (1960) and *The Guns of Navarone* (1960–61).

Ted Samuels

British Special Effects Supervisor

With his brother George, who painted mattes, he joined Alexander Korda's staff (*The Thief of Bagdad,* 1939–40), working in Percy Day's department. Later he was in charge of all effects work at Shepperton Studios: *Road to Hong Kong* (1961), *The War Lover* (1962), *Dr. Terror's House of Horrors* (1964), *The Tomb of Ligeia* (1964), *The Skull* (1965), *Das Geheimnis der weissen Nonne/ The Trygon Factor* (1967), *When Dinosaurs Ruled the Earth* (1968–71), *The Best House in London* (1969), *Macbeth* (1970), *The Asphyx* (1972–73), *The Beast Must Die* (1974).

Tom Savini (1946–)

American Effects Makeup Artist and Director

"Tom Savini's interest in makeup was initiated by the [1957] film *Man of a Thousand Faces,* which starred James Cagney as the legendary Lon Chaney.... With this inspiration at the young age of twelve, Tom could be found in the bathroom 'doing grotesque things' to his face while the other kids were outside playing football. It was this fascination with the magic of movie-making which helped [him] launch his own motion picture career in the early 1970s after numerous appearances on stage and a tour of duty as combat photographer in Vietnam" (*Grande Illusions*). The almost ghastly Vietnam experience eventually led to a career in horror and splatter films for the Pittsburgh-born Savini. After *Deathdream* (1972) and *Deranged* (1974), a successful association with Pittsburgh-based filmmaker George Romero evolved: *Martin* (1978), *Dawn of the Dead* (1979), *Creepshow* (1982). Savini's screen credits also include *Friday the 13th* (1980), *Maniac* (1980), *Eyes of a Stranger* (1981), *The Burning* (1981), *The Prowler* (1981) and *Necronomicon* (1994). In George Romero's Arthurian epic *Knightriders* (1981), Savini was seen as Morgan, the Black Knight. Co-directed *Night of the Living Dead* (1990) and *Chill Factor: House Call* (2004).

Stanley W. Sayer (1917–2000)

*British Cinematographer and Blue Screen
  Expert*

Consultant on most British blue screen releases from *The Thief of Bagdad* (1939–40) up to
Star Wars (1975–77), *Superman* (1977–78), *The
Empire Strikes Back* (1979–80), *Return of the Jedi*
(1982–83), *Dune* (1984), *Brazil* (1985), *Return
to Oz* (1985), *The Adventures of Baron Munchausen* (1988–89), *Alice* (1990) and *Year of the
Comet* (1992). 3D: *Royal River* (1951). Also camera operator and second unit photographer. Died
in Hillingdon, Middlesex.

Eugen Schüfftan (1893–1977)

*German Artist, Inventor and
  Cinematographer*

A.k.a. Eugene Shuftan. After World War I,
the Breslau-born artist became interested in ex-
pressionism, then turned to movies, developing
and patenting the Shuftan process. Schüfftan was
one to strongly emphasize space and depth of
field. He had been dissatisfied with contempo-
rary cinematography because it failed to convey
depth. The overlapping of images on shop windows inspired him to superimpose scenes by
using mirrors. Not only did this create a multi-
layered space but also partly solved the problem
of suggesting depth. Supervised Shuftan shots
for *Varieté* (*Variety*, 1925), *Metropolis* (1925–27,
hall of the workers, Moloch, sports stadium,
head sculpture of Hel et al.) and the American
Love Me and the World Is Mine (1927), filmed at
Universal Studios. Also did the storm sequence
miniatures for Abel Gance's imposing *Napoleon*
(1926–27). Became a regular cinematographer
in 1928 when he supported Robert (and Curt)
Siodmak, Rochus Gliese, Edgar Ulmer and Billy
Wilder in photographing *Menschen am Sonntag*
(1928–29). In 1933 he left Germany for France.
According to assistant Henri Alékan, Schüfftan
knew every camera trick. In 1940 he came to
America. Academy Award for *The Hustler* (1962).

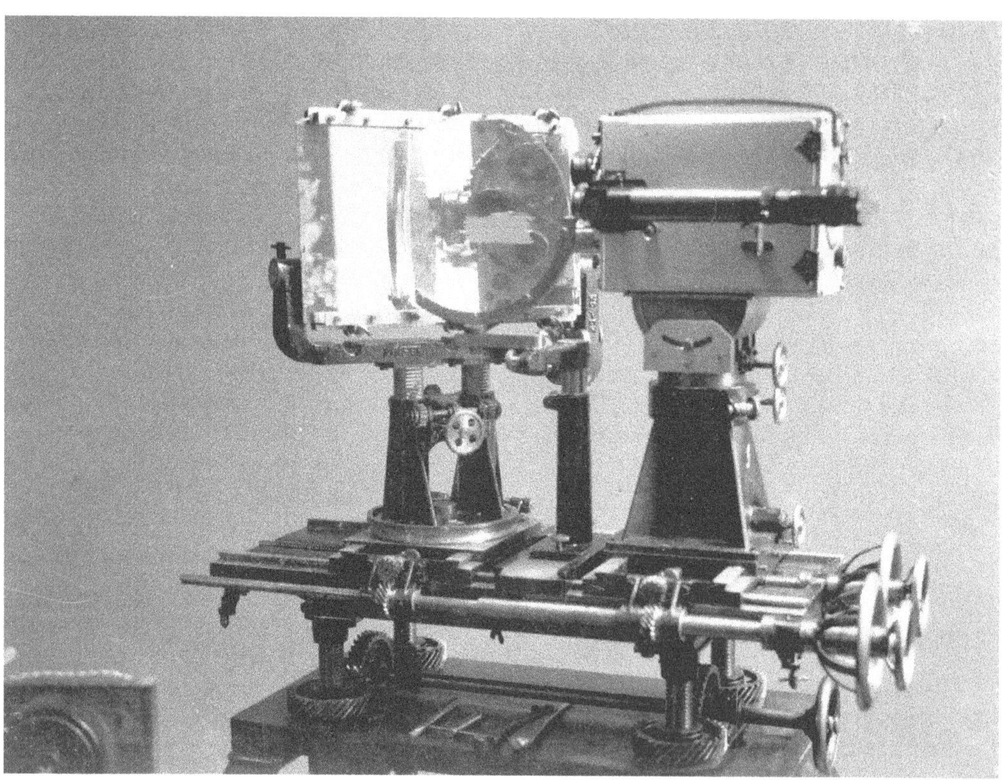

**Original Schüfftan setup with mirror and camera (courtesy Fritz Maurischat Collection, Deutsche Kine-
mathek Berlin).**

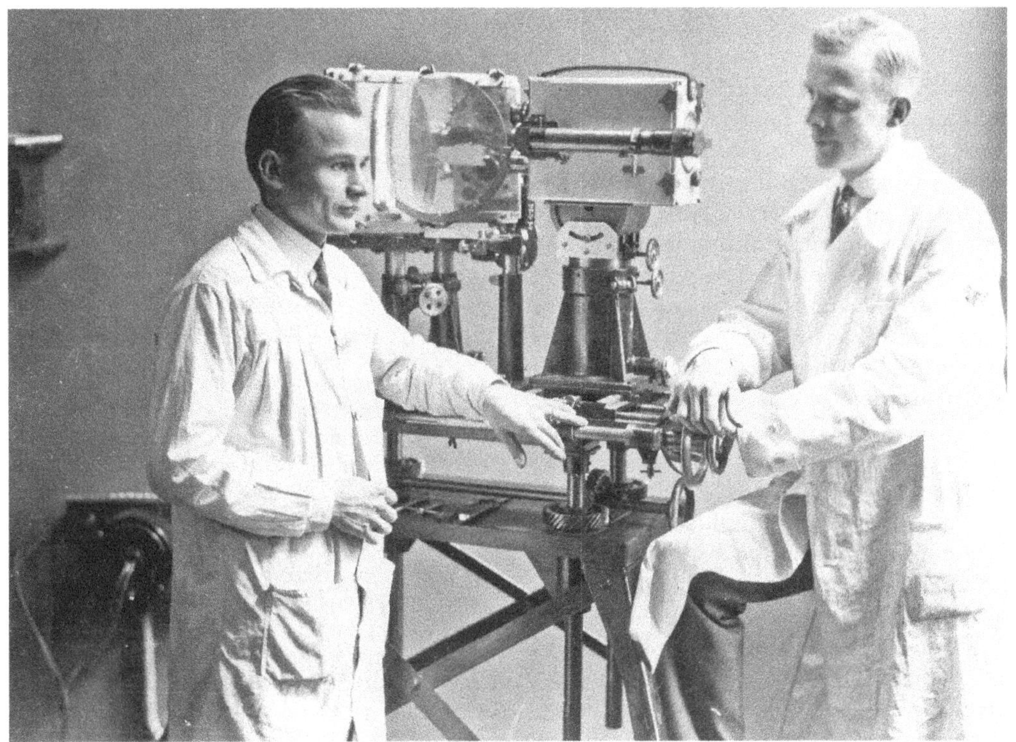

In European cinema of the 1920s and early 1930s, the Schüfftan Process was the most popular way of compositing miniatures and live-action right in the camera. Two Schüfftan technicians operate the setup.

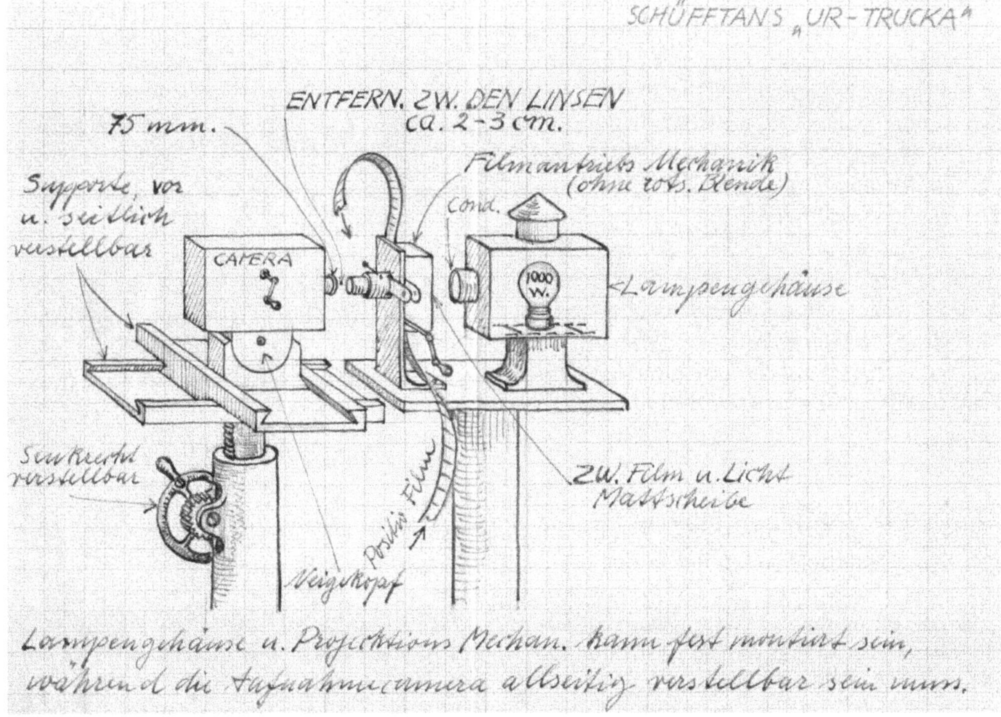

Original blueprint for the Schüfftan compositing setup described as early Truca (which was a forerunner of the optical printer) (both courtesy Fritz Maurischat Collection, Deutsche Kinemathek Berlin).

After World War II he supervised the effects work on *Ulysses* (1953–54) in Rome where he blended mirror shots of the Trojan Horse and cyclops Polyphem (Umberto Silvestri) being challenged by title role actor Kirk Douglas. In 1958 he saw a chance to contribute effects to *Gulliver's Travels*, at that time planned at Universal City by writer-director Jack Sher. (The fantastic images of Swift's novel, rather than the mundane set extension it was finally used for, were the reason for Schüfftan's invention but he failed to convince German producer Guido Bagier to continue producing *Ein moderner Gulliver* [*A Modern Gulliver*] in 1924 at E.F.A. Studios at Berlin Zoo.) Schüfftan and Sher had a meeting of the minds in New York City. On April 21, 1958 Sher wrote to Shuftan, "It seems we are going to go ahead on the Gulliver's Travels picture; and after talking with the head of the Studio and the head of the Production department, they both have evinced great interest in your process. Unfortunately, as I said in New York, nobody with any technical understanding of these things has had an opportunity of talking to you. Just as soon as you clear your patents, I wish that you would write me all the information on your process, because I am certain that if it will save us money, some sort of deal can be made between yourself and the Studio" (*Paul Kohner Files*, Deutsche Kinemathek Berlin). But then Universal backed out, and in 1959 Sher signed a deal with producer Charles H. Schneer. That meant: Schüfftan was out and Ray Harryhausen was in for the project became *The 3 Worlds of Gulliver* in SuperDynamation. Schüfftan was hired as director of photography for the Munich-made *Captain Sindbad* (1962–63) but was fired after several days by director Byron Haskin and the King Bros. He died in New York City.

where they filmed the first replacement cigarette commercial.

I became acquainted with George Pal at UFA Werbefilm where I was responsible for model animation photography and for the photographic quality of the cartoons. In 1932, when he decided to leave UFA and establish his own company, Pal asked if I was interested in joining him. He told me that he had in mind something really unusual and that he wanted to equip his new studio in a very up-to-date manner. Always interested in experiments, I accepted. Our first commission was an advertising film for Oberst Cigarettes. Pal didn't want to have it drawn frame by frame in the common cartoon fashion, but to do it instead with dimensional animation. A blade of tobacco would fold up by itself, glide into a paper husk, stand up, get legs and a head and so on. Then the twenty cigarettes from one package would form a squadron, with an *Oberst* (colonel) commanding in front, and march through a futuristic setting which consisted of cigarette packages. The main street of our set was about thirty feet long and ran the whole length of the studio. The cigarettes for each animation step were mounted on boards. All in all, we had approximately sixteen or eighteen boards with squadrons of cigarettes in various walking positions to complete one single walking step which, repeatedly used, resulted in a walking cycle. Once this principle was decided upon, we thought it rather tedious showing the march of the cigarettes without camera movement, so I constructed an overhead telescope-like lift to move the camera frame by frame.

Schulze later used a transfocator lens to great advantage on Leni Riefenstahl's *Olympia* films (1936–38), did the inventive educational short *Raum im kreisenden Licht* with animated camera movements following light streaming through the windows of a church, and turned out model shots of burning oil fields for a wartime propaganda effort, *Aufruhr in Baku* (1941). After the war he founded Infafilm.

Hugo O. Schulze (1905–19??)
German Cinematographer

Hugo Otto Schulze started as a trainee at Ufa. He was Günther Rittau's camera assistant on *Metropolis* (1925–27), for which he executed trick shots such as the transformation of the robot and some miniatures. Schulze was George Pal's cameraman at Ufa Werbefilm and at Pal & Wittke

Ian Scoones
British Effects Technician

One of Les Bowie's boys, frequently assigned to Hammer productions: *Taste of Fear* (1960–61), *The Shadow of the Cat* (1960–61), *The Damned* (U.S.: *These Are the Damned*, 1961/63), *The Pirates of Blood River* (1961–62), *Captain Clegg* (1961–62), *The Old Dark House* (1962; while pushing a statue from a pillar at the gates of the old house, Scoones' arm is seen but director William Castle left it in as a joke), *Paranoiac* (1962), *The Kiss of the Vampire* (1962/64, helped to make frames of chicken wire and string up rubber bats on nylon thread and also worked on the castle model seen at the climax), *The Scarlet Blade* (1963), *The Devil-Ship Pirates* (1963–64), *The Evil of Frankenstein* (1963–64), *She* (1964–65), *One Million Years B.C.* (1965–66), *Frankenstein Created Woman* (1965–66), *The Mummy's Shroud* (1966–67), *First Men in the Moon* (1963–64) and, more recently, *A Prayer for the Dying* (1987). Television series: *Thunderbirds, Doctor Who, Blake's 7*.

Roy W. Seawright (1905–1991)
American Special Effects Supervisor

Born in Los Angeles County. His father died while working on the construction of Hal Roach Studios in 1919. Roach himself took the young boy under his wings. Seawright started as Roach's office boy, worked in the prop department and finally, in 1927, was given a job as cartoonist (*Flying Elephants*). Eventually he became head of Roach's photographic effects department. He regularly was involved in Laurel & Hardy's shorts: He did the art titles for *Busy Bodies* (1933) incorporating an animated buzzsaw; did the split-screen shots for *Twice Two* (1933) showing the comedians as husbands and wives respectively; and he enabled the comedians to play their own small sons in the oversized sets of *Brats* (1930): "You just had the original set, and built the second one three times scale, exactly. After that, it's just a case of positioning your camera. If it's six feet from the wall to the camera with your normal-sized set, then you multiply the distance three times and make it 18 feet for your oversized set. Everything's tripled...." Also did effects for L&H's feature films: *Babes in Toyland* (1934), *Bonnie Scotland* (1935, an animated bee swarm), *Our Relations* (1935, *Doppelgänger*), *Way Out West* (1936, background projection for dance routine), *Swiss Miss* (animated bubbles, miniature chasm and glass shots), *Block-Heads* (1938) and *A Chump at Oxford* (1940). Other work included *Mister Cinderella* (1936), *Of Mice and Men* (1939), *Captain*

Fury (1939), *Zenobia* (1939), *Road Show* (1941), *The Devil with Hitler* (1942), *Taxi, Mister* (1943), *Calaboose* (1943), *Learn and Live* (1943), *Carnegie Hall* (1947), *The Hal Roach Comedy Carnival* (1947), *The Fabulous Joe* (1947), *The Gangster* (1947), *Who Killed Doc Robbin?* (1948), *Here Comes Trouble* (1948), *Two Knights from Brooklyn* (1949), *The Big Cat* (1949), *Reign of Terror* (a.k.a. *The Black Book*, 1949). Best-known for supervising the *Topper* series (*Topper*, 1937; *Topper Takes a Trip*, 1939; *Topper Returns*, 1941) and the lizards of *One Million B.C.* (1939–40). Became a pioneer in TV commercials and co-founded Cascade Pictures and Coast Special Effects. Died in Torrance, California.

Joy Seddon
British Matte Artist

Worked with Stanley Kubrick on *2001: A Space Odyssey* (1966–68), then on *Mackenna's Gold* (1968). The wife of matte process cameraman Paul Cuff.

Guido Seeber (1879–1940)
German Cinematographer

Born in Chemnitz, he apprenticed in his father's photo shop. In 1896 Clemens Seeber and his son saw what the Brothers Lumière did in France and immediately they acquired a camera. Guido became the operator and studied the mechanics of the various shooting techniques. When he came to Berlin, he was already sort of a veteran cinematographer. Frequently experimented with trick shots (*Die geheimnisvolle Streichholzdose* with animated matches in 1909–10; *Prosit, Neujahr 1910!*) and became supervising cinematographer of Deutsche Bioscop company. He was the one to discover the Neubabelsberg spot which eventually became Germany's leading film lot. Employed in-camera split-screen technique to duplicate actor Paul Wegener for *Der Student von Prag* (*The Student of Prague*), a popular horror fantasy of 1913. During World War I he created the means for aerial photography. Trick shots for Wegener's Tibetan fantasy *Lebende Buddhas* (*Living Buddhas*) in 1923; in one shot, Wegener's Buddha head rises gigantically at the horizon and guides an ocean liner

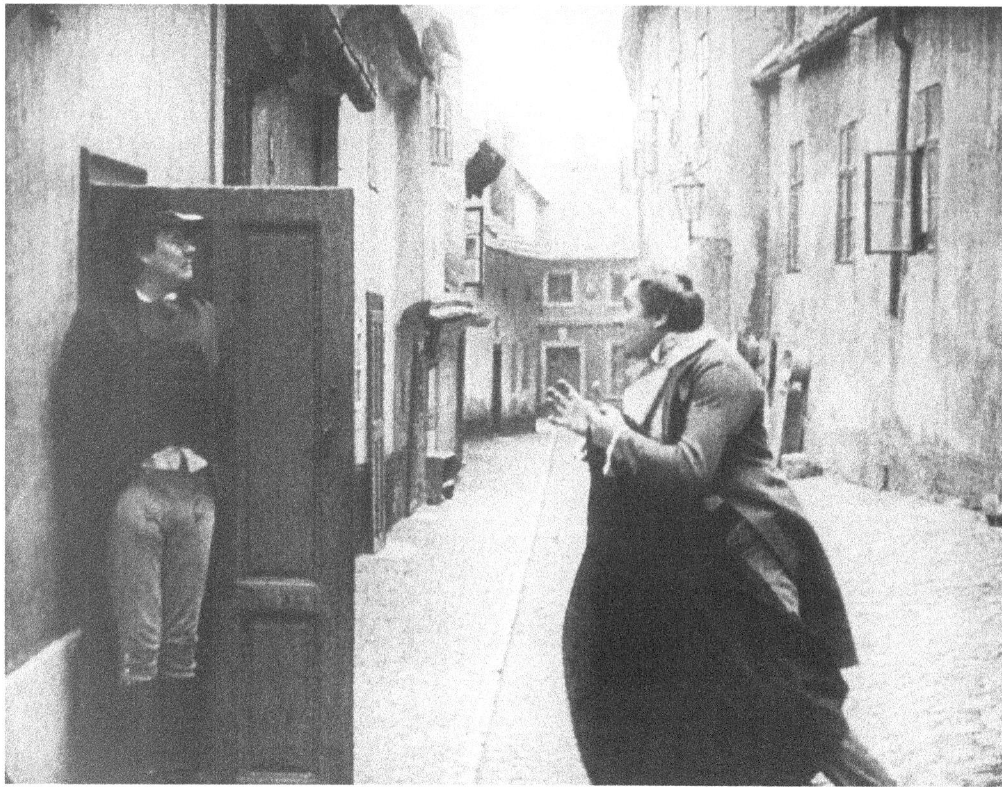

Paul Wegener and his Doppelgänger: *The Student of Prague*, photographed in 1913 by German effects pioneer Guido Seeber (courtesy Deutsche Kinemathek Berlin).

with the power of his eyes. In his 1927 book *Der Trickfilm in seinen grundsätzlichen Möglichkeiten*, Seeber described the process:

> For the execution of this problem, a method was used which was already described in French literature early in 1912. A person garbed in dark clothes is filmed against an entirely white background. From this shot a positive is printed which shows a dark person in front of an entirely transparent background. If this master positive is placed directly in front of a dupe negative — emulsion-to-emulsion, with both strips running in bipack fashion through the camera — in addition to the objects of the now-filmed scene, the scene of the positive is also copied onto the dupe negative. In our case the sailing ship was filmed as it crossed against a cloudless sky. From this shot, a clean and as transparent a negative as possible was printed. Buddha's head was supposed to arise at the horizon line. To accomplish this, there was a white background which consisted of two parts. One was only as high as the horizon line of the previously filmed sea picture, which was useful for hiding the body of the actor rising in the rear. About two and a half feet behind that was the second white background which — as seen from the front — formed with the other part one big, equally white plain. This white background was illuminated considerably from the front to achieve, by reflection of strong light, the printing of the bipack-run master positive. When the liner appeared in the positive, behind the lower white wall, the actor's head arose looking upon the crossing ship.

Seeber also created a Freud-inspired dream sequence for G. W. Pabst's *Geheimnisse einer Seele* (1925–26). In 1925, with producer Julius Pinschewer, he turned out a remarkable short about early cinematography employing all possibilities of double-exposure and trick photography: *Du musst zur Kipho/Kino- und Photo-Ausstellung 1925*. After suffering a stroke he withdrew from active cinematography in 1932. In October 1935 he became head of special photographic effects at Ufa in Babelsberg, supervising titles and background projection.

Fred M. Sersen (1890–1962)

American Visual Effects Supervisor and Matte Artist

As Fox art director, title artist, production illustrator and cinematographer, he pioneered matte shots in the early 1920s. Painted mattes and conceptual art for *The Red Dance* (1928), *The Big Trail* (1930), *A Connecticut Yankee* (1931), *Chandu the Magician* (1932), *Dante's Inferno* (1935) and *Under Two Flags* (1936). Eventually he became head of the 20th Century–Fox special photographic effects department and nominally was in charge for their entire output of films up to 1952: *In Old Chicago* (1938), *Suez* (1938), *The Rains Came* (1939), *Young People* (1940), *The Blue Bird* (1940), *Little Old New York* (1940), *Brigham Young, Frontiersman* (1940), *A Yank in the R.A.F.* (1941), *How Green Was My Valley* (1941), *The Black Swan* (1942), *Claudia* (1943), *The Moon Is Down* (1943), *Hello Frisco, Hello* (1943), *They Came to Blow Up America* (1943), *Coney Island* (1943), *Jitterbugs* (1943), *Bomber's Moon* (1943), *Heaven Can Wait* (1943), *Holy Matrimony* (1943), *Wintertime* (1943), *Sweet Rosie O'Grady* (1943), *Paris After Dark* (1943), *Guadalcanal Diary* (1943), *Happy Land* (1943), *Stormy Weather* (1943), *The Dancing Masters* (1943), *The Song of Bernadette* (1943), *The Gang's All Here* (1943), *The Fighting Lady* (1944 documentary), *Lifeboat* (1944), *The Lodger* (1944), *The Sullivans* (1944), *Jane Eyre* (1944), *The Purple Heart* (1944), *Four Jills in a Jeep* (1944), *Buffalo Bill* (1944), *Tampico* (1944), *Pin Up Girl* (1944), *The Bermuda Mystery* (1944), *The Eve of St. Mark* (1944), *Ladies of Washington* (1944), *Home in Indiana* (1944), *Take It or Leave It* (1944), *Wing and a Prayer* (1944), *Roger Touhy, Gangster* (1944), *Wilson* (1944), *Sweet and Low-Down* (1944), *In the Meantime, Darling* (1944), *The Big Noise* (1944), *Greenwich Village* (1944), *Laura* (1944), *Irish Eyes Are Smiling* (1944), *Something for the Boys* (1944), *Sunday Dinner for a Soldier* (1944), *The Keys of the Kingdom* (1944), *Winged Victory* (1944), *Doll Face* (1945), *Hangover Square* (1945), *A Tree Grows in Brooklyn* (1945), *A Royal Scandal* (1945), *Diamond Horseshoe* (1945), *The All-Star Bond Rally* (1945 short), *The Bullfighters* (1945), *Where Do We Go from Here?* (1945), *Molly and Me* (1945), *Don Juan Quilligan* (1945), *Nob Hill* (1945), *Junior Miss* (1945), *Captain Eddie* (1945), *A Bell for Adano* (1945), *The Caribbean Mystery* (1945), *Within These Walls* (1945), *State Fair* (1945), *The House on 92nd Street* (1945), *Thunderhead—Son of Flicka* (1945), *Fallen Angel* (1945), *Three Little Girls in Blue* (1945), *The Dolly Sisters* (1945), *Leave Her to Heaven* (1945), *The Spider* (1945), *Shock* (1946), *Colonel Effingham's Raid* (1946), *Behind Green Lights* (1946), *Claudia and David* (1946), *Sentimental Journey* (1946), *Johnny Comes Flying Home* (1946), *The Dark Corner* (1946), *Dragonwyck* (1946), *Cluny Brown* (1946), *Strange Triangle* (1946), *Do You Love Me* (1946), *Somewhere in the Night* (1946), *Anna and the King of Siam* (1946), *Smoky* (1946), *Centennial Summer* (1946), *It Shouldn't Happen to a Dog* (1946), *If I'm Lucky* (1946), *Home, Sweet Homicide* (1946), *Margie* (1946), *The Razor's Edge* (1946), *Wake Up and Dream* (1946), *My Darling Clementine* (1946), *The Shocking Miss Pilgrim* (1947), *13 Rue Madeleine* (1947), *The Brasher Doubloon* (1947), *Boomerang!* (1947), *The Late George Apley* (1947), *Carnival in Costa Rica* (1947), *The Homestretch* (1947), *Miracle on 34th Street* (1947), *Moss Rose* (1947), *The Ghost and Mrs. Muir* (1947), *Thunder in the Valley* (1947), *Kiss of Death* (1947), *I Wonder Who's Kissing Her Now* (1947), *The Foxes of Harrow* (1947), *Nightmare Alley* (1947), *Forever Amber* (1947), *Gentleman's Agreement* (1947), *Daisy Kenyon* (1947), *Captain from Castile* (1947), *You Were Meant for Me* (1948), *Call Northside 777* (1948), *Sitting Pretty* (1948), *Scudda Hoo! Scudda Hay!* (1948), *Fury at Furnace Creek* (1948), *Give My Regards to Broadway* (1948), *The Iron Curtain* (1948), *The Street with No Name* (1948), *Deep Waters* (1948), *The Walls of Jericho* (1948), *That Lady in Ermine* (1948), *The Luck of the Irish* (1948), *Road House* (1948), *Cry of the City* (1948), *Apartment for Peggy* (1948), *The Snake Pit* (1948), *When My Baby Smiles at Me* (1948), *That Wonderful Urge* (1948), *Unfaithfully Yours* (1948), *Chicken Every Sunday* (1948), *A Letter to Three Wives* (1949), *Yellow Sky* (1949), *Down to the Sea in Ships* (1949), *Mother Is a Freshman* (1949), *The Fan* (1949), *Mr. Belvedere Goes to College* (1949), *The Beautiful Blonde from Bashful Bend* (1949), *It Happens Every Spring* (1949), *You're My Everything* (1949), *House of Strangers* (1949), *Come to the Stable* (1949), *Sand* (1949), *Slattery's Hurricane* (1949), *I Was a Male War Bride* (1949), *Pinky* (1949), *Father Was a*

Fullback (1949), *Thieves' Highway* (1949), *Everybody Does It* (1949), *Prince of Foxes* (1949), *Oh, You Beautiful Doll* (1949), *Whirlpool* (1949), *Dancing in the Dark* (1949), *Twelve O'Clock High* (1949), *When Willie Comes Marching Home* (1950), *Three Came Home* (1950), *Mother Didn't Tell Me* (1950), *Under My Skin* (1950), *Wabash Avenue* (1950), *Cheaper by the Dozen* (1950), *The Big Lift* (1950), *A Ticket to Tomahawk* (1950), *Love That Brute* (1950), *Panic in the Streets* (1950), *The Gunfighter* (1950), *Where the Sidewalk Ends* (1950), *Stella* (1950), *Broken Arrow* (1950), *No Way Out* (1950), *Mister 880* (1950), *I'll Get By* (1950), *Two Flags West* (1950), *All About Eve* (1950), *The Jackpot* (1950), *American Guerrilla in the Philippines* (1950), *For Heaven's Sake* (1950), *Halls of Montezuma* (1951), *The 13th Letter* (1951), *Call Me Mister* (1951), *I'd Climb the Highest Mountain* (1951), *You're in the Navy Now* (1951), *Fourteen Hours* (1951), *Bird of Paradise* (1951), *Rawhide* (1951), *I Can Get It for You Wholesale* (1951), *On the Riviera* (1951), *Follow the Sun* (1951), *Half Angel* (1951), *The House on Telegraph Hill* (1951), *The Frogmen* (1951), *Take Care of My Little Girl* (1951), *Mr. Belvedere Rings the Bell* (1951), *As Young as You Feel* (1951), *The Secret of Convict Lake* (1951), *David and Bathsheba* (1951), *Meet Me After the Show* (1951), *The Guy Who Came Back* (1951), *People Will Talk* (1951), *The Day the Earth Stood Still* (1951), *Love Nest* (1951), *The Desert Fox: The Story of Rommel* (1951), *Anne of the Indies* (1951), *Golden Girl* (1951), *Let's Make It Legal* (1951), *Fixed Bayonets!* (1951), *Elopement* (1951), *The Model and the Marriage Broker* (1951), *Red Skies of Montana* (1952), *Viva Zapata!* (1952), *5 Fingers* (1952), *With a Song in My Heart* (1952), *The Pride of St. Louis* (1952), *Lydia Bailey* (1952), *Down Among the Sheltering Palms* (1953), *The Farmer Takes a Wife* (1953). Academy Award for the submarine movie *Crash Dive* (1943). Sersen's closest collaborators during his time as department head were: Ralph Hammeras (miniature photographer), Ray Kellogg (matte painter and second unit director), James B. Gordon (director of effects photography), L. B. Abbott (effects photographer), Sol Halperin (process photographer). Uncredited consultant at Lake Sersen, Fox's studio tank (named after him): *20000 Leagues Under the Sea* (1953–54) and *Around the World in 80 Days* (1956). Articles:

"Making Matte Shots" (*Cinematographic Annual II*, American Society of Photographers, 1931); "Special Photographic Effects" (*The Technique of Motion Picture Production*, New York: Interscience Publishers, 1944).

Jack Shaw (19??–1956)
American Matte and Glass Artist

Took assignments from MGM (the abandoned *War Eagles* with supervising animator Willis O'Brien and, possibly, *The Wizard of Oz* in 1939), Selznick International (*Gone with the Wind*, 1939, and *Since You Went Away*, 1944), Hal Roach (*Swiss Miss*, 1938, and *One Million B.C.*, 1939–40, painting backdrops for dinosaur lizards), Eagle-Lion (*Bad Man of Tombstone*, 1949). Willis O'Brien hired him for preproduction glass paintings for his doomed *Gwangi* project and for *Mighty Joe Young* (1948–49). Shaw also worked with Louis Lichtenfield at Warner Bros. (he might have worked with Lichtenfield on 1955's *Helen of Troy*. Committed suicide by jumping off the Pasadena Bridge during the making of *The Animal World* (1956). Ray Harryhausen remembers him as being very fast and efficient.

Carroll L. Shepphird
American Process Supervisor

While "Shep" Shepphird was working in the RKO art department, Willis O'Brien asked him to supervise camera positions, focal lenses and miniature back projection of *King Kong* (1932–33), *The Son of Kong* (1933) and *The Last Days of Pompeii* (1935). (O'Brien: "If people were to be photographed or matted in the set, a complete drawing for that part of the set would be necessary, so that they would take their place in the miniature in the correct perspective and create a convincing picture.") Shepphird later went to MGM, where he was put in charge of background projection: *Plymouth Adventure* (1952), *Valley of the Kings* (1954), *Ben-Hur* (1958–59), *North by Northwest* (1959), *The Prize* (1963), *When the Boys Meet the Girls* (1965), *The Glass Bottom Boat* (1966), *Spinout* (1966), *The Venetian Affair* (1967), *Hot Rods to Hell* (1967), *Marlowe* (1968), *The Gypsy Moths* (1969), *Ice Station*

Zebra (1970). TV: *Earth II* (1970). Jim Danforth recalls that Shepphird's projectionist at MGM was Edwin Hammeras.

Clifford Shirpser (1906–1977)
American Camera Operator and Effects Photographer

Native Californian Shirpser started as a camera assistant in the early 1920s: *The Hunchback of Notre Dame* (1922–24), *The Thief of Bagdad* (1923–24). Joined MGM: *Ben-Hur* (1924–25), *Mutiny on the Bounty* (1935), *The Wizard of Oz* (1939). As camera operator for Technicolor, he specialized in process and matte work: *Samson and Delilah* (1949), *When Worlds Collide* (1951), *The War of the Worlds* (1952–53), *Soldier of Fortune* (1955), *The Rains of Ranchipur* (1955), *On the Threshold of Space* (1956), *Jet Pilot* (1957, aerial photography), *The Wayward Bus* (1957). Rejoined MGM: *Run Silent Run Deep* (1958), *Torpedo Run* (1958), *Ben-Hur* (1958–59), *Never So Few* (1959), *Green Mansions* (1959), *North by Northwest* (1959), *Mutiny on the Bounty* (1962), *The Unsinkable Molly Brown* (1964), *The Greatest Story Ever Told* (1965). He died in Los Angeles.

Robert Short
American Mechanical Effects Expert

Created special props for *E.T. the Extraterrestrial* (1982, heartbeep), *Splash* (1984, fishtail), *Beetle Juice* (1988).

James Shourt
American Optical Effects Technician

"Jamie" Shourt contributed to *The Andromeda Strain* (1971), *Star Wars* (1975–77) and *Altered States* (1980). Title designer: *Halloween II* (1981).

Don Siegel (1912–1991)
American Montage Supervisor and Special Effects Director

Before the Chicago-born Siegel became a director (*Invasion of the Body Snatchers*, *Dirty Harry*), he worked on Stage 5, Warner Bros.-First National Studios Burbank, as head of the insert department under Byron Haskin. With his cameraman Archie Dalzell, cinematographer Robert Burks and editor Jim Leicester, Siegel created many fine montage sequences and did second unit work for *Dark Victory* (1939), *Confessions of a Nazi Spy* (1939), *The Roaring Twenties* (1939), *Knute Rockne, All American* (1940), *Blues in the Night* (1941), *They Died With Their Boots On* (1941), *Flight from Destiny* (1941), *Yankee Doodle Dandy* (1942), *Mission to Moscow* (1943), *The Adventures of Mark Twain* (1944), *Passage to Marseilles* (1944) and *Saratoga Trunk* (1945). He died in Nipoma, California.

Cliff Silsby
American Matte Artist

A staff member of the matte department at 20th Century–Fox under Fred Sersen and at Warner Bros. under Louis Lichtenfield. Already an oldtimer when he contributed matte art for *It's a Mad Mad Mad Mad World* (1962–63) at Film Effects of Hollywood.

Thol O. [Si] Simonson
American Miniature and Mechanical Effects Expert

In 1930 Simonson began as painter and propmaker at MGM. A short time later he joined RKO and worked on the New York miniature buildings for *King Kong* (1932–33) and was in floor effects for *Swiss Family Robinson* (1940). In the process department he collaborated with cameraman Harold Stine rigging foreground objects. He met actor George Reeves while at Paramount for *So Proudly We Hail!* (1943), and later joined him for TV's *Adventures of Superman* series in 1951. Became an expert in breakaway walls and explosives. Mechanical effects for American-International and other companies: *The Bonnie Parker Story* (1958), *Earth vs the Spider* (1958), *Escape from Hell Island* (1963), *Voice of the Hurricane* (1964), *The Klansman* (1974). Television series: *Men into Space* (1959), *The Outer Limits* (1963), *The Fugitive* (1963).

Albert Maxwell Simpson
(1893–1980)

American Matte Artist

Started by painting backdrops for vaudeville theatres. In 1915 he joined the film business specializing in glass and matte art. Was involved pm D. W. Griffith's *The Birth of a Nation* (1914) for which he executed glass paintings, Cecil B. DeMille's *The Ten Commandments* (1923) and *In Old Arizona* (1923, the first Fox talkie filmed on location). At RKO he did mattes for the original *King Kong* (1932–33) and later (after Mario Larrinaga had left for Warners) for *Swiss Family Robinson* (1940), *The Devil and Daniel Webster* (1942), *The Enchanted Cottage* (1945), *Bedlam* (1946), *Crack Up* (1946), *Sister Kenny* (1946) and John Wayne's ill-fated Genghis Khan epic *The Conqueror* (1956). Jack Cosgrove also relied on Simpson's services: *The Prisoner of Zenda* (1937), *Gone with the Wind* (1939), *Rebecca* (1940, painting of the mansion Manderley), *Meet John Doe* (1941), *The Pride of the Yankees* (1942) and *Duel in the Sun* (1946). In the 1950s, Simpson did mattes for *Dementia* (1953, released in 1955) and Byron Haskin's *From the Earth to the Moon* (1958). He re-joined Linwood G. Dunn at Film Effects of Hollywood for *The Great Race* (1965) and *Hawaii* (1966). Simpson served as president and v.p. of Local 790 Motion Picture Illustrators and Matte Artists.

Dennis Skotak (1943–)

American Visual Effects Supervisor

Born in Detroit, Michigan. With his brother Robert, he worked on *Battle Beyond the Stars* (1980), *Escape from New York* (1981), *Galaxy of Terror* (1981), *The Aftermath* (1982), *Aliens* (1986), *The Abyss* (1989), *Terminator 2: Judgment Day* (1991), *Batman Returns* (1992), *Tank Girl* (1995), *Titanic* (1997), *Hard Rain* (1998) and *X2* (2003). Miniature consultant: *Captain Ron* (1992), *Bio-Dome* (1996).

Robert F. Skotak (1948–)

American Visual Effects Supervisor

Younger brother of Dennis Skotak. Robert was inspired by *This Island Earth* and *The Angry Red Planet* as well as Russian space films directed by Pavel Klushantsev and later researched and wrote about these movies. The Skotak brothers created effects for *Battle Beyond the Stars*, 1980), *Escape from New York* (1981), *Galaxy of Terror* (1981), *The Aftermath* (1982), *Aliens* (1986), *The Abyss* (1989), *Terminator 2: Judgment Day* (1991), *Batman Returns* (1992), *Tank Girl* (1995), *Titanic* (1997), *Hard Rain* (1998) and *X2* (2003). On his own, Robert was involved in the production of *Jaws 3-D* (1983), *Lords of the Deep* (1989), *Mars Attacks!* (1996), *Mousehunt* (1997) and *House on Haunted Hill* (1999).

Clarence W.D. Slifer (1904–1986)

American Matte Photographer

Born in Kansas City, he had a lifelong enthusiasm for photography: "My interest in photography was wide and varied, from 16mm and 28mm substandard motion picture formats to Autochrome and Agfa color plates. While studying at Washington University I decided to make photography my vocation rather than my hobby." In 1924 he established himself as a portrait photographer and in 1927 won *Screenland*'s Pev Marley Contest for a chance as assistant cameraman. He worked with Marley on the 1929 *Godless Girl* by Cecil B. DeMille. Assisted renowned cinematographer Arthur Miller at Pathe-DeMille Studios. In 1932 he joined the camera effects department at RKO Studios, assisting in matte photography: *Me and My Gal* (1932), *A Woman Commands* (1932), *The Most Dangerous Game* (1932), *King Kong* (1932–33), *The Son of Kong* (1933), *The Last Days of Pompeii* (1935), and *She* (1935). In 1936 he moved to Technicolor, then became a photographer for Jack Cosgrove at Selznick (and on loan-out business). Stayed at Selznick International until 1953: *The Garden of Allah* (1936), *The Prisoner of Zenda* (1937), *The Young at Heart* (1938), *Gone with the Wind* (1939, for which he designed a special optical printer to add moving elements such as smoke to conventional matte shots), *Rebecca* (1940), *Since You Went Away* (1944), *Spellbound* (1945), *Duel in the Sun* (1946), *The Paradine Case* (1947); received an Academy Award for Selznick's *Portrait of Jennie* (1948). When Selznick had to reduce his production activities during World War II, Slifer operated the department on a special agreement for other companies. He was especially occupied then with productions for Samuel Goldwyn: *The North Star* (1943), *Up in Arms* (1944), *The Princess and the Pirate* (1944). Director of effects photography for Samuel Goldwyn's production *Hans Christian Andersen* (1952) starring Danny Kaye. In 1953 at 20th Century–Fox (under Ray Kellogg, working with artists Emil Kosa, Jr. and Lee LeBlanc): *The Robe* (1953), *Prince Valiant* (1954). In 1957 he went with Lee LeBlanc to MGM: *Ben-Hur* (1959), *The World, the Flesh and the Devil* (1959), *North by Northwest* (1959). He received screen credit on *The Greatest Story Ever Told* (1965) and *Ice Station Zebra* (1968). As an expansion of the idea of the printer he designed for *Gone with the Wind*, he later created an aerial-image matte camera that permitted moving shots to be made, in which live and painted elements moved in perfect synchronization, without the need to incorporate repeater moves in the original photography. These became known as "Slifer Shots." In 1975 he retired to San Diego. Died of cancer.

Dick Smith (1922–)

American Character Makeup Artist

Richard Emerson Smith was born in New York and attended Yale University. Fascinated by Charles Laughton in *The Hunchback of Notre Dame* (1939) and by Spencer Tracy in *Dr. Jekyll and Mr. Hyde* (1941) he got hold of a copy of Ivard Strauss' book *Paint, Powder and Makeup*. After World War II he worked sporadically with small theatre groups and at the Museum of Natural History. After being turned down by virtually every movie studio, Smith went to work in the new medium of television. 1945–1959: early latex and plastics work at NBC-TV in New York City. For television he aged Claire Bloom for *Victoria Regina* (1957); created a terrifying dummy head for the climax of *The Picture of Dorian Gray* (1961); transformed Lee J. Cobb in *Don Quixote/Don Kikhot* (1957) and Laurence Olivier into the whiskey-sipping priest of Graham Greene's *The Power and the Glory* (1961). In 1963 he turned to movie special makeup for *It's a Mad Mad Mad Mad World*, *The Cardinal* (replacing Maurice Seiderman, the makeup artist who had done *Citizen Kane*), *The World of Henry*

Orient (1964), *Les Fabuleuse Aventures du Marco Polo* (U.S.: *Marco the Magnificent*, 1964, transforming Anthony Quinn into Kublai Khan), *Midnight Cowboy* (1969), *Little Big Man* (1969–70, starring 32-year-old Dustin Hoffman as a 121-year-old), *House of Dark Shadows* (1970), *The Godfather* (1971–72, Marlon Brando's Don Vito Corleone makeup), *The Exorcist* (1972–73, assisted by Rick Baker), *The Godfather Part II* (1973–74), *The Stepford Wives* (1974), *The Sunshine Boys* (1975), *Taxi Driver* (1976), *Burnt Offerings* (1975), *Marathon Man* (1975–76), *The Sentinel* (1976–77), *Exorcist II: The Heretic* (1976–77), *The Fury* (1977), *Altered States* (1978–79), *Nighthawks* (1981), *Dogs of War* (1981), *Scanners* (1980–81), *The Fan* (1981), *Amadeus* (1983, called in to age F. Murray Abraham), *Starman* (1984). For TV's *The Strange Case of Dr. Jekyll and Mr. Hyde* (1967) he turned Jack Palance into Hyde. Emmy Award for Hal Holbrook's five-hour makeup for *Mark Twain Tonight* (1967).

George Albert Smith (1864–1959)

British Inventor

Smith came from portrait photography and transferred several of its technologies on film. In 1897 he patented double exposure and used it for *Doppelgänger* shots in his film *The Corsican Brothers* the same year. An early exponent of glass shots, he became an associate of producer Charles Urban in 1900. He was also active in early color film (Kinemacolor).

Steven Spielberg (1946–)

American Director

In his childhood he made amateur films. In 1969 he entered Atlanta Film Festival with the short film *Amblin'* which led to a contract with Universal Studios. Directed pilot episode of *Night Gallery* and took directorial assignments on *Columbo* and *Marcus Welby, M.D.* First feature film: the made-for-TV *Duel* (1972). Many of his features contain an outstanding percentage of mechanical effects, miniatures, animation and CGI usually executed by Industrial Light & Magic: *Jaws* (1975), *Close Encounters of the Third Kind* (1975–77), *Raiders of the Lost Ark* (1981),

E.T. the Extraterrestrial (1982), *Indiana Jones and the Temple of Doom* (1984), *Indiana Jones and the Last Crusade* (1989), *Hook* (1991), *Jurassic Park* (1992–93), *The Lost World* (1997), *War of the Worlds* (2004–2005).

Paul G. Sprunck (1892–1963)

American Effects and Stop-Motion Cameraman

Maryland-born Sprunck was a technical engineer involved in the shooting of *The King of Kings* (1927) and *The Godless Girl* (1929). Joined George Pal and photographed a lot of Technicolor *Puppetoons* in the 1940s. Miniatures and low-budget effects for *Untamed Women* (1952) and *Brightest Night* (1952). Director: *The Adventures of Sam Space* (1955). Ray Harryhausen acquired from him distortion glasses that he used to create the force fields for *Earth Vs. the Flying Saucers* (1956) and *The 7th Voyage of Sinbad* (1958, Cyclops on the beach sequence). Sprunck also photographed 3D stills of puppets (sculptures) for Viewmaster stereoscopic discs. Died in Los Angeles.

Scott Squires

American Visual Effects Technician

Held jobs as projectionist, TV stringer, industrial filmmaker and newspaper photographer. In 1975 he came to Hollywood. Was referred to Future General and met Douglas Trumbull, who offered him a position as assistant. In 1976, for Steven Spielberg's *Close Encounters of the Third Kind*, Squires helped to develop Cloud Tank Effect to create spectacular cloud formations. Technical director on *Willow* (1987) and *Who Framed Roger Rabbit* (1988). Co-founder of Dream Quest Images and served as their president from 1979 to 1995. Eventually turned to video and digital technology. Academy Award nominations: *The Mask* (1994) and *Dragonheart* (1996).

Charles D. Staffell (19??–2000)

British Process Technician

Started as a transparency projectionist for Rank: *A Canterbury Tale* (1944), *I Know Where I'm Going!* (1945), *Sleeping Car to Trieste* (1948), *Warning to Wantons* (1948), *Stop Press Girl* (1949), *Prelude to Fame* (1950). Eventually in charge of back projection at Pinewood Studios, London: *The Clouded Yellow* (1951), *Appointment with Venus* (1951), *The Purple Plain* (1954), *Simba* (1955), *The Prince and the Showgirl* (1957), *The Hellfire Club* (1961). One of the first to try front projection technique. Worked on *Masquerade* (1965), *Bunny Lake Is Missing* (1965), *Charlie Bubble* (1967), *Fahrenheit 451* (1967), *Barbarella* (1968), *The Man Who Haunted Himself* (1970), *Young Winston* (1972), *Murder on the Orient Express* (1974), *Zardoz* (1974), *The Ghoul* (1975), *The Human Factor* (1975), *The Land That Time Forgot* (1975), *Legend of the Werewolf* (1975), *At the Earth's Core* (1976), *The People That Time Forgot* (1977), *Valentino* (1977), *Superman* (1977–78), *Warlords of Atlantis* (1978), *Arabian Adventure* (1979), *Ragtime* (1981), *Nineteen Eighty-Four* (1984), *Dune* (1984), *Santa Claus* (1984–85), *Murder Elite* (1985), *The Holcroft Covenant* (1985), *Aliens* (1986), *Batman* (1989), *Hudson Hawk* (1991, in Rome), *Kafka* (1991), *Mercy Mission: The Rescue of Flight 771* (TV, 1993), *Eyes Wide Shut* (1999), and some of the movies in the Bond series: *Live and Let Die* (1973), *Octopussy* (1983), *A View to a Kill* (1985). Often did not receive screen credit. Consultant on the prologue for Stanley Kubrick's *2001: A Space Odyssey* (1965–68). In 1968, with Philip V. Palmquist of Minnesota Mining and Manufacturing Company, and Dr. Herbert Meyer of the Motion Picture and Television Research Center, he shared a Scientific or Technical Award, Class I, for the development of a successful embodiment of the reflex background projection system for composite cinematography.

John Stears (1934–1999)

British Mechanical Effects Expert

Trained as a silversmith; Bill Warrington employed him as a model maker. Assisted Warrington on *The Guns of Navarone* (1960–61) at Shepperton Studios. Supervised mechanical effects for the James Bond series up to *Diamonds Are Forever* (1971). Handled mechanical effects for *Outland* (1981). Academy Awards for *Thunderball* (1965) and *Star Wars* (1975–77). Other credits include *The Thief of Bagdad* (1978, magic carpet), *The Bounty* (1984), *F/X* (1986), *The Mask of Zorro* (1998). TV: *The Martian Chronicles, Babylon 5, The Gathering.*

Mark A. Stetson
American Model Maker

Miniatures for: *Star Trek: The Motion Picture* (1978–79), *Blade Runner* (1982), *The Right Stuff* (1983), *2010* (1984, models of the *Leonov* and *Discovery* spaceships), *The Fifth Element* (1997), *Total Recall* (1990), Peter Jackson's *The Lord of the Rings* trilogy (2001–2003), *Superman Returns* (2006).

David Stewart
American Model Photographer

Originally with Robert Abel and Associates. Hired by Future General (Douglas Trumbull, Richard Yuricich) to operate motion tracking system and photograph the miniature U.F.O.s for Spielberg's *Close Encounters of the Third Kind* (1976–77). Stayed with Trumbull and Yuricich for *Star Trek: The Motion Picture* (1978–79) and worked with Richard Edlund (Boss Film) on *2010* (1984).

Peter Stich
American Painting Technician

Sometimes phonetically spelled Peter Stitch. Stand-by painter: Charles Chaplin's *The Gold Rush* (1925). Painted miniature backdrops for Willis O'Brien: *King Kong* (1932–33), *The Son of Kong* (1933) and *Mighty Joe Young* (1946–49).

Clifford R. Stine (1906–1986)
American Director of Photography and
Visual Effects Cinematographer

Born in California. With his brother Harold, he grew up on the Irvine Ranch overlooking the Pacific. Watched movies being made at an early age and was fascinated with cameras. Eventually his brother got 18-year old Cliff a job in the movies. In the course, Cliff Stine became assistant to famed cinematographers Peverell Marley and Arthur Miller at Pathe-DeMille Studios in Culver City. With the arrival of the talkies, Stine turned to sound recording for a year, but in 1929 turned to cinematography again and joined RKO. Assistant to Vernon L. Walker, new head of camera effects. Until 1949, only interrupted by four years service in the U.S. Air Force, he stayed in the RKO camera effects department: *King Kong* (1932–33), *The Son of Kong* (1933), *The Gay Divorcee* (1934), *Gunga Din* (1939), *The Hunchback of Notre Dame* (1939), *Citizen Kane* (1940–41), *Step by Step* (1946), *The Miracle of the Bells* (1948), *The Clay Pigeon* (1949), *Once a Thief* (1950), *Never a Dull Moment* (1950). Director of photography at Universal since 1949: *It Came from Outer Space* (1953, 3D), *Abbott and Costello Go to Mars* (1953), *Wings of the Hawk* (1953, 3D), *The Glass Web* (1953, additional 3D photography), *Creature from the Black Lagoon* (1953–54, additional 3D photography), *This Island Earth* (1955). In charge of special photography and process department at Universal for five years (the department closed down after Revue took over the studio): *The Purple Mask* (1955), *The Second Greatest Sex* (1955), *Tarantula* (1955), *Abbott and Costello Meet the Mummy* (1955), *The Square Jungle* (1955), *The Price of Fear* (1956), *Raw Edge* (1956), *The Creature Walks Among Us* (1956), *Congo Crossing* (1956), *I've Lived Before* (1956), *Away All Boats* (1956), *Walk the Proud Land* (1956), *The Unguarded Moment* (1956), *Written on the Wind* (1956), *The Mole People* (1956), *Battle Hymn* (1956), *Francis in the Haunted House* (1956), *The Deadly Mantis* (1956), *Outside the Law* (1956), *The Incredible Shrinking Man* (1956–57), *Four Girls in Town* (1957), *Istanbul* (1957), *The Tattered Dress* (1957), *Kelly and Me* (1957), *The Deadly Mantis* (1957), *The Midnight Story* (1957), *Night Passage* (1957), *The Land Unknown* (1957), *Slaughter on Tenth Avenue* (1957), *The Monolith Monsters* (1957), *Man of a Thousand Faces* (1957), *Mister Cory* (1957), *The Female Animal* (1958), *The Lady Takes a Flyer* (1958), *Touch of Evil* (1958, additional photography), *Love Fast, Die Young* (1958), *A Time to Love and a Time to Die* (1958), *Twilight for the Gods* (1958), *Voice in the Mirror* (1958), *Kathy O'* (1958), *Step Down in Terror* (1958), *Once Upon a Horse ...* (1958), *The Restless Years* (1958), *The Perfect Furlough* (1958), *Monster on the Campus* (1958), *The Tarnished Angels* (1958),

Run Silent Run Deep (1958, Hecht-Hill-Lancaster production), *A Stranger in My Arms* (1959), *Imitation of Life* (1959), *The Wild and the Innocent* (1959), *This Earth Is Mine* (1959), *Pillow Talk* (1959), *Operation Petticoat* (1959). Second unit photography (in Spain): *Spartacus* (1959–60). Effects Photography: *The Creeping Terror* (1964). Came out of retirement to supervise miniature photography: *Earthquake* (1973), *The Hindenburg* (1974), *The Legend of King Kong* (only some lamentable tests in 1975), *The Concorde: Airport '79* (1979). Died in Clairmont, California.

Harold E. Stine (1903–1977)
American Director of Photography and Process Expert

Born in Chino, California, the brother of cinematographer Clifford Stine. Started at Harry Garson Studios in Edendale as assistant to L. William O'Connell. Was boom operator on *King Kong* (1932–33). As a full-fledged director of photography he took charge of RKO's process department in the 1940s: *Without Reservations* (1946), *Berlin Express* (1948), *Mighty Joe Young* (1946–49), *The Thing from Another World* (1950–51), *On Dangerous Ground* (1952), *A Girl in Every Port* (1952). Television: *Adventures of Superman* (1953–54; the last season was in color so Stine had to turn to blue screen matte shots). Photographed TV series, then the feature films *M*A*S*H* (1970) and *The Poseidon Adventure* (1972).

David Stipes
American Visual Effects Cinematographer

Amateur-turned-pro during the making of 16mm *Equinox* in the late 1960s. Other credits include *The Stuff* (1985) and TV's *V* and *Star Trek: Deep Space Nine*.

Walter Stone
American Mechanical Effects Expert

At Walt Disney Studios (under Robert A. Mattey's supervision) he handled wireworks: *The Absent Minded Professor* (1960–61), *Mary Poppins* (1964).

Kenneth Strickfaden (1896–1984)
American Electrical Effects Technician

Became interested in electrical effects and built laboratories and gadgets for Frankenstein films: *Frankenstein* (1931), *Bride of Frankenstein* (1935), *Son of Frankenstein* (1938–39), *Dracula vs. Frankenstein* (1971), *Blackenstein* (1973) and Mel Brooks' *Young Frankenstein* (1974). Other films include: *Just Imagine* (1929–30), *The Mask of Fu Manchu* (1932), *Chandu the Magician* (1932); the serials *The Lost City* (1935), *The Phantom Empire* (1935), *Flash Gordon* (1936), *Undersea Kingdom* (1937), *Buck Rogers* (1939), and *Mysterious Doctor Satan* (1940); *The Wizard of Oz* (1939), *The War of the Worlds* (1952–53), *Monstrosity* (1964). Also contributed to the "I Was a Teenage Monster" episode of TV's *The Monkees* and provided sound effects for *Tron* and *Frankenweenie*.

Paul Swendsen (1953-)
American Matte Artist and Illustrator

Born in San Francisco, he studied fine arts. Entered Colossal Pictures for commercials, painted murals for Francis Ford Coppola's *Tucker* (1988) and joined the matte department at Industrial Light & Magic: *Willow* (1988), *Who Framed Roger Rabbit* (1988), *The 'Burbs* (1989), *The Abyss* (1989), *Kurosawa's Dreams* (1990, conceptual art), *Ghost* (1990), *Jacob's Ladder* (1990, preproduction conceptual design), *The Doors* (1991, concept paintings). Lorne Peterson from ILM recommended Paul to Rolf Giesen. Right after German reunification, Giesen helped to build up a matte department for CineMagic at the former East-German Babelsberg Studios. Together they did *Die Tigerin* (*The Tigress*, 1992) and various commercials. After that, Paul went to Paris. At Excalibur he did *Der Freischütz* (1994), *Giorgino* (1994), *Mina Tanenbaum* (1994), *L'emigré* (1994) and *Antartida* (1995); at Ex Machina *Marie de Nazareth* (1994), *Une femme francaise* (1994), *Rimbaud-Verlaine* (1996), *Tout doit disparaitre* (1996), *Le huième Jour* (1996), *Witch Way Love* (1997), *Washington Square* (1997), *Assassin(s)* (1997), *La Femme du Cosmonaute* (1997) and *Le Bossu* (1998); at L'est: *Babel* (1998) and *Vercingetorix* (1999). Occasionally illustrated covers for Arthur C. Clarke's books.

Bill Taylor

American Visual Effects Cinematographer and Blue Screen Expert

Taylor's lifelong interest in stage magic and sleight of hand combined with Ray Harryhausen's miraculous effects in *Jason and the Argonauts* (1963) to inspire Bill to seek parallel careers in visual effects for film and illusion design for the stage. He spent ten years as an optical cameraman specializing in blue screen compositing, working with Petro Vlahos and Linwood G. Dunn. Helped with optical effects of *Dark Star* (1974). After Roswell Hoffman's retirement, Taylor became Albert Whitlock's matte photographer: *The Hindenburg* (1974–75), *The Prisoner of Zenda* (1979; Whitlock: "Bill Taylor's optical work was his best for my choice of all he did during Universal days"), *History of the World, Part 1* (1981), *Ghost Story* (1981). When Universal closed down the department in 1985, Taylor and Whitlock's assistant matte artist Syd Dutton founded Illusion Arts, Inc. They have credits on more than 160 films, including *Red Sonja* (1985), *Die unendliche Geschichte 2* (*The Neverending Story II*, 1989–90), *Dragonheart* (1996) and *The Mask of Zorro* (1998). Bill's most successful film as visual effects supervisor is *Bruce Almighty*. More recent credits include two films directed by Lasse Hallstrom: *Casanova* (2005) and *The Hoax* (2006). Along with membership in the American Society of Cinematographers, he is a founding board member of the Visual Effects Society.

James O. Taylor

American Director of Photography

According to Ralph Hammeras, it was J. O. Taylor from whom he learned the basics of film photography. Hammeras later hired him to do photograph process plates for *Dante's Inferno* (1935). At RKO he was involved in the shooting of *King Kong* (1932–33) and *The Son of Kong* (1933). Process photography: *The Monkey's Paw* (1932–33), *The Silver Cord* (1933), *Sentimental Journey* (1946).

George J. Teague (1893–1985)

American Process Technician

Born Pomona, California, educated at St. Vincent's College. Was telephone technician, still photographer, mechanical engineer and designer before he entered the moving picture industry. From 1913–1914, with D. W. Griffith,

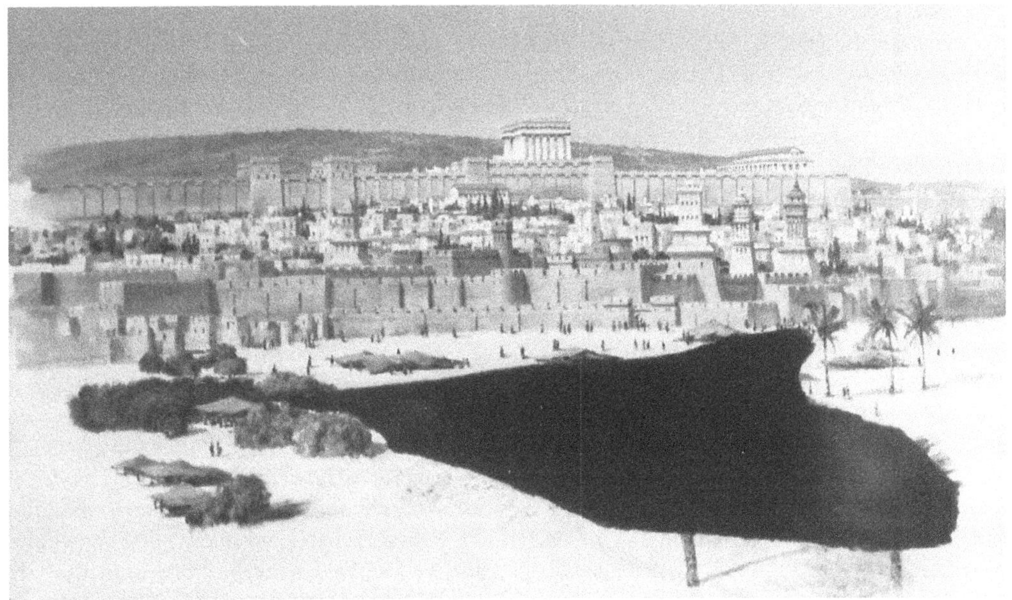

Jerusalem painted by Albert Whitlock and photographed by Bill Taylor for the mini-series *Masada* (courtesy Deutsche Kinemathek Berlin).

Biograph, Reliance, Majestic, Fine Arts-Majestic, as assistant cameraman. Engineered special effects for Griffith's favorite cinematographer, G.W. Bitzer, including *Macbeth* with Constance Collier and Sir Herbert Tree. Worked on animated cartoon equipment, then joined First National Pictures for technical and camera effects. Built equipment for *The Lost World* (1924–25) on which he collaborated with Willis O'Brien and Ralph Hammeras. When Hammeras left and went to Fox, Teague accompanied him. At Fox he developed methods of process projection, 1929–1935, on the productions *Just Imagine* (1930), *Liliom* (1930), *State Fair* (1933) and *Catspaw* (1933). Went to England to bring projection process to Alexander Korda (*Sanders of the River*, 1933; *The Scarlet Pimpernel*, 1934; *Things to Come*, 1935–36), then returned to the U.S. where he did process work for producer Walter Wanger's *Shanghai* (1935) at General Service Studios as well as *Sweetheart of the Navy* (1937) and for a short time was in charge of effects at Universal (*Tower of London*, 1939). Processed Chaplin's *The Great Dictator* (1940, with associate Ralph Hammeras) and finally ended up at Eagle-Lion Studios, which united the filmmaking of railroad magnate Robert Young's PRC and British film czar J. Arthur Rank: *Born to Speed* (1947), *It's A Joke, Son!* (1947), *The Devil on Wheels* (1947), *Lost Honeymoon* (1947), *Philo Vance Returns* (1947), *The Big Fix* (1947), *Out of the Blue* (1947), *Repeat Performance* (1947), *Stepchild* (1947), *Heartaches* (1947), *The Red Stallion* (1947), *Philo Vance's Secret Mission* (1947), *Railroaded!* (1947), *Bury Me Dead* (1947), *Love from a Stranger* (1947), *T-Men* (1947), *Man from Texas* (1948), *The Noose Hangs High* (1948), *The Cobra Strikes* (1948), *Raw Deal* (1948), *Assigned to Danger* (1948), *Mickey* (1948), *Canon City* (1948), *The Amazing Mr. X* (1948), *Hollow Triumph* (1948), *Behind Locked Doors* (1948), *In This Corner* (1948), *He Walked by Night* (1948), *Let's Live a Little* (1948). In the 1950s he organized an independent process service for *La ilusión viaja en tranvía* (1954) and for Sam Katzman's low-budget productions at Columbia (*It Came from Beneath the Sea*, 1954–55, *Earth Vs. the Flying Saucers*, 1955–56 and *20 Million Miles to Earth*, 1956–57, with Ray Harryhausen effects; *The Giant Claw*, 1956–57, with Ralph

Hammeras). Article: "Ingenious accessories simplify making of spezial effects shots," *American Cinematographer*, October 1938. Died in Iola, Kansas.

Ellis J. [Bud] Thackery
(1903–1990)

American Effects Cinematographer

Ellis J. "Bud" Thackery was born in Shawnee, Oklahoma and educated at Chaffee Junior College, Ontario, California. He worked with the U.S. Agricultural Department, and in 1923 joined First National, working at various jobs. Beginning in 1924 he was an assistant glass artist and assistant cameraman with Warner Bros. In 1927 he worked on *The Jazz Singer*. When Warners took over the First National lot in Burbank, Thackery became a full-time member of the special effects department, focused on in-camera split screen photography and assisted matte artist Paul Grimm on *Noah's Ark* (1929). Process departments Fox, Universal. In 1930–31 he was with The Dunning Process Company: *Just Imagine* (1930), *Dirigible* (1931), *Subway Express* (1931), *Mr. Robinson Crusoe* (1932). At RKO: *The Most Dangerous Game* (1932), *King Kong* (1932–33) and others. Studied Willis O'Brien's miniature projection and transferred the technique to Mascot Pictures which had established itself on the former Mack Sennett lot for the serial *The Phantom Empire* (1935). On *Kong* "we had used miniature rear projection for the first time to place live people into the little sets with the ape and dinosaurs" (*American Cinematographer*, April 1994). Worked on other serials for Mascot and Republic where he became chief cameraman in 1941 (*Darkest Africa*, *SOS Coast Guard*, *House of a Thousand Candles*, *The Fighting Marines*, *Women in War*, *Flying Tigers*, *Dick Tracy*, *Dick Tracy Returns*, *Jesse James Rides Again*, *The Black Widow*, *Federal Agents vs. Underworld, Inc.*, *Down Dakota Way*, *Ghost of Zorro*, *The Invisible Monster*, *Desperados of the West*, *the Sea Hornet*, *Flight Nurse*, *the Wild Blue Yonder*). Later did many television shows and was active in the business until the late 1960s.

Harry Thomas (1909–1996)

American Makeup Expert

Background in art. Started at Hal Roach Studios. Extra in Laurel & Hardy's *Pardon Us* and Marlene Dietrich's *Morocco* (he was cut out of the latter). Eventually turned to makeup and landed a job as an assistant in the MGM makeup department under Jack Dawn. On various occasions he assisted Jack P. Pierce, whom he describes as "a little, feisty man." On more prestigious assignments, Thomas helped to transform Orson Welles in *Macbeth* (1948) and age Charlton Heston in Cecil B. DeMille's *The Ten Commandments* (1953–56). Better known (and therefore more notorious), however, for his countless low-budget efforts: *Glen or Glenda?* (1952–53, directed by Edward D. Wood, Jr.), *Port Sinister* (1953), *Killers from Space* (1954, directed by W. Lee Wilder, Billy's brother), *The Unearthly* (1957), *Voodoo Woman* (1957), *From Hell It Came* (1957), *The Bride and the Beast* (1958, from a screenplay by Wood), *Plan 9 from Outer Space* (1958–59, Wood), *Frankenstein's Daughter* (1959), *The Little Shop of Horrors* (1960), *Night of the Ghouls* (1960, Wood), *The Navy vs. the Night Monsters* (1966, made up radiation-burn victim). Also: *Logan's Run* (1976), *The Hand* (1981). TV: *The Adventures of Superman*, *The Munsters*, *Star Trek*. Died in Los Angeles.

Wes Thompson

American Effects Technician and Production Executive

At Universal Studios he worked under both John P. Fulton and David S. Horsley. Credits include *It Came from Outer Space* (1953), *This Island Earth* (1955) and many more. Revamped miniature background projectors, originally machined by Harry Cunningham for *Mighty Joe Young*, for use with color film stock in *Jack the Giant Killer* (1960–62) on behalf of Howard A. Anderson Company and David Horsley, director of photography. Returned to Universal as production executive. Thompson got the retired Horsley to come back one last time as consultant on *Midway* (1976).

Phil Tippett (1951–)

American Stop-Motion Animator and CGI Supervisor

Fan-turned-pro. Assisted Jim Danforth and David Allen on stop-motion animation for *The Crater Lake Monster* (1977), *Timegate* (unfinished Danforth project), *The Primevals* (unfinished Allen project). Did some stop-motion cuts for *Piranha* (1978) and joined Industrial Light & Magic: *Star Wars* (1975–77), *The Empire Strikes Back* (1979–80), *Dragonslayer* (1982, Go-Motion animation), *Return of the Jedi* (1983), *Indiana Jones and the Temple of Doom* (1984), *The Ewok Adventure: Caravan of Courage* (1984), *Ewoks: The Battle for Endor* (1985), *The Golden Child* (1986), *Howard the Duck* (1986), *Willow* (1988), *Ghostbusters II* (1989). Freelanced on *House II* (1986), *RoboCop* (1987) and *Honey, I Shrunk the Kids* (1989) and opened his own effects house in Berkeley and progressed from traditional model animation to CGI: *RoboCop 2* (1990), *Coneheads* (1993), *Jurassic Park* (1992–93, D.I.D. input), *RoboCop 3* (1993), *Dragonheart* (1996), *Tremors II: Aftershocks* (1996), *Starship Troopers* (1997), *The Haunting* (1999), *Hollow Man* (2000). Directed *Komodo* (1999).

Louis H. Tolhurst

American Optical Effects Technician

Did process for MGM's *The Mysterious Island* (1929). For Hal Roach's *One Million B.C.* (1939–40) he devised a technique he termed miniature foreground projection similar to the one employed by Willis O'Brien in *King Kong*, "...a rear projection process that did not use a transparency screen, instead an ingenious use of lens achieved a sharp focus on two or more planes, one of which was the projected image" (John Brosnan, *Movie Magic*, p. 75).

Sokei Tomioka

Japanese Effects Cinematographer

Effects co-photographer of *Gojira* (*Godzilla, King of the Monsters!*, 1954), *Mosura tai Gojira* (*Godzilla vs. the Thing*, 1963), *San daikaiju: chikyu saidai no kessen* (*Ghidrah, the Three-Headed Monster*, 1964) under sfx director Eiji

Tsuburaya. Director of effects photography: *Kaiju soshingeki* (*Destroy All Monsters*, 1968) under Teisho Arikawa, *Gojira-Minira-Gabara: Oru kaiju daishingeki* (*Godzilla's Revenge*, 1969) under Ishiro Honda, *Mekagojira no gyakushu* (*Terror of Mechagodzilla/The Terror of Godzilla*, 1975) under Teruyoshi Nakano.

Teizo Toshimitsu

Japanese Model Maker

For many years he created Toho Studios' monster suits, from *Gojira* (*Godzilla, King of the Monsters*, 1954) up to *Gezora Ganime Kamera: Kessen nankai no daikaiju* (1970). Graduated from art college in Osaka. Approached producer Tomoyuki Tanaka with his dream of becoming an actor. As a result he got a job in the effects department under Eiji Tsuburaya. For the original *Godzilla* he sculpted various test models in clay before supervising the construction of the actual monster suit. (The first one proved too large and clumsy to wear.)

Herman E. Townsley

American Mechanical Effects and Miniature Expert

Destination Moon (1949–50, wirework), *Suddenly* (1954), *House on Haunted Hill* (1959), *The Angry Red Planet* (1959), *Tormented* (1960), *Ring of Fire* (1961), *The Boy and the Pirates* (1962), *Village of the Giants* (1965), *Tobruk* (1966), *The Hellfighters* (1969), *The McMasters* (1970), *Soldier Blue* (1970). TV: *My Favorite Martian*.

Boris T. Travkin

Russian Effects Photographer

At Mosfilm Studios he was involved in *Ilya Muromets* (U.S.: *The Sword and the Dragon*, 1955–56, first Soviet scope production), *Soy Cuba/Ya Kuba* (1964), *Lenin v Polshe* (1966), *Kochajmy Syrenki* (1967), *Solaris* (1972), *Moltschanije Doktora Iwensa* (1973), *Zwyozdnyy Inspektor* (1980) and *Lunnaya Raduga* (1984). His article "Chemical mixtures for creating special effects cinematography" appeared in *American Cinematographer*, August 1974, and referred to his work on the science fiction film *Eolomea*

(East-German co-production, 1972) and similar projects (experimental film *Space, Earth, Space,* 1970):

It is difficult to conceive the existence of cinematography without the achievements of chemistry which, as far back as a hundred years ago, laid down the foundations of photographic art. Chemistry is used in all branches of cinematography, beginning with raw stock manufacture and ending with construction of plastic sets. And in such a variety of cinematographic art as the technique of special effects, chemistry also continues to take up new positions. There exists a number of methods for shooting special effects. Some of them, such as model shots, painted elements and traveling mattes, are in constant use at our studios, others are being assimilated and introduced.... It has been observed that some solutions of chemical substances, mixed under certain conditions, show an unexpected and curious pattern. For instance, when putting into water a drop of tooth elixir, the latter does not merely disappear in the mass of liquid but results in a dynamic splash of a peculiar pattern.... [I]t should be noted that the described method of producing the motion picture effect also ensures a considerable economy, since it permits us, in quite a simple way, to present on a screen very interesting composite scenes, which either would be shot using rather complex and expensive means or not shot at all [Translated from the journal *Technika Kino i Televidenija* No 11, November 1972].

Conrad Tritschler

American Matte Artist

He was obviously of German origin. Albert Whitlock was very fond of him although he (Tritschler) seems to have only two screen credits: *Flowing Gold* (1924) and the Bela Lugosi vehicle *White Zombie* (1932). But from a Whitlock statement it might be assumed that Tritschler did some work at Universal, maybe painting the vampire's (Bela Lugosi) Transylvanian castle for the original *Dracula* (1930–31); it stylistically resembles the work in the other Lugosi pictures.

Donald [Don] Trumbull

American Engineer

Started early in the film industry and was a special effects rigger on MGM's *The Wizard of Oz* (1939). For his son Douglas he co-designed

70mm moving plate front projection machine for *Close Encounters of the Third Kind* (1975–77). Constructed equipment for *Star Wars* (1975–77) and became a partner of John Dykstra in Apogee Productions, Inc. In 1984 he shared a Scientific and Engineering Award (for design and development of the "Blue Max" high power blue-flux projector for traveling matte composite photography) with Jonathan Erland, Stephen Fog and Paul Burk.

Douglas Trumbull (1942–)

American Visual Effects Designer, Inventor and Director

The Los Angeles-born son of Donald Trumbull studied architecture at El Camino College in Torrance, California, but left to become an artist. Landed a job with Lester Novros and Graphic Films and helped to produce promotional films for NASA. One of these, *To the Moon and Beyond*, was seen by Stanley Kubrick at the 1964 World Fair in New York. Kubrick got in touch with Graphic Films and brought Trumbull and colleague Con Pederson to London to work on *2001: A Space Odyssey* (1965–68). In September 1965 Trumbull started to work on planet animation (producing all readouts astronomical backgrounds of stars, Earth, moon, Jupiter, etc., and all rotoscoped mattes). He organized the model detailing department and supervised the photography of some moon terrain shots. Later devised David Bowman's cosmic ride, the Stargate Corridor of Light, through slit-scan photography. In Jan Harlan's 2001 documentary *Stanley Kubrick: A Life in Pictures,* Trumbull said of that sequence:

> There was a lot of evolution to the concept of how you would be transported from one dimension to another; it was never really solved in the screenplay. I had remembered knowing of an experimental filmmaker (John Whitney) who was exploring this whole idea of long time exposures; while the camera shutter was open he would move all kinds of art work or slits around in front of the camera to scan colored objects onto the film in a rather unusual way. And I thought, if you took what he was doing, you could create this streak exposure — a streak exposure is like a time exposure of car headlights become a streak of light. It occurred to me that there might be some way to apply that to the Stargate sequence.

Trumbull returned to California and created effects for *Candy* (1968), *The Andromeda Strain* (1970), *Close Encounters of the Third Kind* (1975–77) and *Blade Runner* (1982). He directed *Silent Running* (1970–71) and *Brainstorm* (1983). In conjunction with Paramount, he founded Future General Corporation (right after directing *Silent Running*) to jointly develop new film processes such as Showscan, then Left Future General and founded Entertainment Effects Group (EEG). In 1985 he became the first CEO of Showscan Film Corporation. (In the Showscan process, 70mm films are shot and projected at 60 frames per second to bring 150 percent more visual information.) Trumbull himself shot a couple of shorts in that process: *New Magic* (1984) and *Leonardo's Dream* (1989). Four years later he left Showscan and moved to Lenox, Massachusetts, to establish the Berkshire Motion Picture Corporation and its subsidiary, Berkshire Ridefilm Corp. (changed in 1992 to Trumbull Company, Inc., and Ridefilm Theaters Corp.). He has also designed rides for theme parks, among them the *Back to the Future* attraction on the Universal City Studios Tour.

Kostantin Tschet [Cetverikov] (1902–1977)

*After adoption became: **Konstantin Irmen-Tschet** / Russian-German Cinematographer*

Born in Moscow. In the early 1920s he came to Berlin and did effects photography for *Metropolis* (1925–27) and *Frau im Mond* (1928–29). Director of photography at Ufa Studios. He did the in-camera effects for Ufa's anniversary color film *Münchhausen* (1942–43).

Eiji Tsuburaya (1901–1970)

Japanese Special Technique Director and Cinematographer

Master of *Tokusatsu* (Japanese special effects). According to Henry G. Saperstein, who co-produced several of Toho's science fiction entries: "He was *the* master of special effects. Everything from rear-screen projection, front screen projection, to miniaturization, to articulated models — that was all Tsuburaya. I worshipped the man. I used to love to just sit and listen to him and look at what he was doing. Steven Spielberg and George Lucas have said in print many times, their inspiration in special effects was all the work of Tsuburaya. There wouldn't be *Terminator 2* and all that if it hadn't been for Tsuburaya and the Godzilla films" (*Monsters Are Attacking Tokyo!*, p. 53). Tsuburaya was born in Sukagawa City, Fukushima Prefecture, the first son of Isamu and Sei Tsuburaya. His mother died when he was four years old. By 1908 he had entered the Sugagama-Chori-Deiichi-Jinjyo-hi Elementary School. Became interested in photography; as quoted in a 1964 issue of *Famous Monsters of Filmland*: "When I was a youngster I 'borrowed' coins from my father's shop to buy a movie projector I had seen in a store window. I realized that if I were caught with the camera I would be punished, so I took it apart, examined it and threw it away. Then I built my own." Also enthusiastic about aviation. In 1910 he made model airplanes his hobby. In 1911 he saw his first movie. In 1914 entered high school and graduated in 1916. In 1917 he went to Tokyo and got a job with the Stukisima Iron Factory. After six months he quit and joined the Japanese Airplane School in Haneda. A year later he entered the Kendo Electronic School. In 1919 he was offered a job as assistant cameraman by Yoshiro Edamasa of the Tenkatsu Film Company in Kyoto, which then was the Hollywood of Japan. Between 1921 and 1923 he was off to war with the correspondence staff. Then back to Kyoto and film production. In 1926, was with Shochiku Kyoto Studios and with Shin Kankaku-Ha Eiga Ren-mei (Teinosuke Kinugasa's 1926 *Kurutta ippeiji/A Page of Madness*), then with Tennenshoku Katsudo Shashin Company, Kokkatsu, Ogasawara Productions, Kinegasa Eiga Renmei. In 1927 became a full fledged cameraman with director Chojiro Hayashi. By 1930, with *Chohichiro matsudaira*, his interest already had turned to photographic effects such as slow-motion and double-exposure. The same year he married 19-year-old Musuno Araki. In November 1932 with Nikkatsu-Taihei Studios. Two years later entered Taihei-Hassei Studio; in 1935, at the time his second son was born, joined J. O. Studios. For his effects work he was nicknamed "Smoke Tsuburaya." When *King Kong* (1933) came to Kyoto, he became even more intrigued

with film tricks: "That inspired me. At that time, Japanese trick photography was very backward."

Tsuburaya's career accelerated in 1935 when he was hired by JO Studios in Kyoto, where studio head Yoshio Osawa encouraged him to develop his talents for film trickery. In *Princess of the Moon*, a fantasy based on "The Tale of the Bamboo Cutter," a Japanese folk story, Tsuburaya photographed a miniature model of the city of Kyoto, superimposed a crowd and a cow-drawn carriage in the foreground, and he devised an effect to simulate angels descending from the sky [*Japan's Favorite Mon-Star*, p. 45].

After that 1936 film, originally titled *Koutareki*, he had his first experience with process on a big scale on the German-Japanese co-production *Die Tochter des Samurai/ Atarashiki tsuchi* (*The New Earth*, 1936–37), directed by Arnold Fanck. Soon production supervisor Iwao Mori invited him over to Tokyo and Toho to built up a new department. "When I started to work in Toho it was 1939," Tsuburaya recalled. "At that time I was the only person in the special techniques department. Not only that, but tricks were considered to be top secret, so I couldn't get any help with special effects. There was no one to depend on except myself. The traditional people in the studio were indifferent toward me. I had to get into the studio secretly. Only Iwao Mori was helpful, because he understood the situation" (*Shukan Bunshun*, August 3, 1961). With World War II that slight feeling of antagonism changed for special techniques enhanced, among others, some highly important war films: *Tsubasa no gaika* (*A Triumph of Wings*, 1942), the massive *Hawai Marè oki kaisen* (*The War at Sea from Hawaii to Malaya*, 1942, depicting the attack on Pearl Harbor; Tsuburaya was awarded the Gijutsu Kenkyu Award), *Ahen senso* (*The Opium War*, 1943), *Kato Hayabusa sento-tai* (*Colonel Kato's Flying Squadron*, 1944, at the time his third son was born), *Torpedo Squadrons Move Out* and others. After the war, he was not allowed to work at the studios. He experimented with various camera devices such as the automatic snap and later opened a small company of his own, Tsuburaya Laboratory, where he sporadically handled effects assignments from Toho, Toei, Shintoho and Daiei: *Toho senichi-ya* (*A Thousand and One Nights with Toho*, 1947), *Hana Kurabe tanuki-*

goten (1949), *Tomei ningen arawaru* (*The Transparent Man*, 1949), *Musashino Fujin* (1951), *Nangoku no hada* (*The Skin of the South*, 1952), *Ashi ni sawatta onna* (1952), *Minato e kita otoko* (1952), *Seishun zenigata heiji* (1953). Officially returned to Toho in 1952 and supervised effects for war films like *Taiheyo no washi* (*Eagle of the Pacific*, 1953, for the first time with director Ishiro Honda), Josef von Sternberg's *Anatahan* (*Saga of Anatahan*, 1953–54), *Taiheyo no tsubasa, Saraba Rabauru* (*Farewell Rabaul*, 1954) and *Miyamoto musashi* (1954). Then, besides war films, came science fiction epics, fantasy yarns and particularly monster-suit movies: *Tomei ningen* (*The Invisible Man*, 1953–54), *Gojira* (U.S.: *Godzilla King of the Monsters!*, 1954, clearly inspired by the American release *The Beast from 20,000 Fathoms*, starring a radioactively awakened hybrid of T. Rex and Stegosaurus; Tsuburaya would have preferred a giant octopus), the inevitable sequel *Gojira no gyakushu* (*Godzilla Raids Again*/U.S.: *Gigantis, the Fire Monster*, 1955), *Ju Jin Yuki Otoko* (U.S.: *Half Human: The Story of the Abominable Snowman*, 1955), *Meoto zenzai* (1955), *Byaku Fujin no yoren* (*Madame White Snake*, his first horror film in Agfacolor), *Sora no daikaiju Radon* (U.S.: *Rodan*, 1956, again in Agfacolor), *Chikyu boeigun* (U.S.: *The Mysterians*, the first Tohoscope release), scenes of the wandering Spider's Web Forest for Akira Kurosawa's *Kumonosu jo* (U.S.: *Throne of Blood*, 1957), *Bijo to ekitainingen* (U.S.: *The H-Man*, 1958), *Daikaiju Baran* (U.S.: *Varan the Unbelievable*, 1958–59), *Nippon tanjo* (*The Three Treasures*, 1958–59, creating a multiple-headed monster which attacked Toshiro Mifune, a storm at sea and an earthquake for the mythological story of the Birth of Japan), *Son Go Ku* (*The Adventures of Sun Wu Kong*, 1959, a famous Chinese myth about the Monkey King), *Sensuikan I-57 kofuku sezu* (*Submarine I-57 Will Not Surrender*, 1959), *Uchu dai senso* (U.S.: *Battle in Outer Space*, 1959–60), *Denso ningen* (*The Telegian*, 1960, with director Jun Fukuda who had been an assistant on *Radon*), *Hawai Middouei daikaikusen: Taiheyo no arashi* (*I Bombed Pearl Harbor*, 1960), *Gasu ningen dai ichigo* (*The Human Vapor*, 1960), *Osaka jo monogatari* (*Osaka Castle Story*, 1961), *Mosura* (U.S.: *Mothra*, 1961), the first time that a basically positive giant creature was featured in a Toho production, *Sekai daisenso* (*The Last War*, 1961), *Kurenai no umi* (*The Crimson Sea*, 1961), *Gen to fudomyo-o* (*The Youth and His Amulet*, 1961), *Yosei Gorasu* (U.S.: *Gorath*, 1962), *Korenai no sora* (1962), *Kingukongu tai Gojira* (U.S.: *King Kong vs. Godzilla*, 1962–63, with King Kong giving lots of comedy relief), *Chuchingura—Hana no maki yuki no maki, Taiheyo no tsubasa* (*Wings Over the Pacific*, 1963), *Chintao Yosai Bakugeki Meir Ei* (*Siege of Fort Bismarck*, 1963), *Matango* (U.S.: *Matango: Fungus of Terror/Attack of the Mushroom People*, 1963, introducing a new optical printer, the "Oxberry 1200" to Toho Studios to do almost seamless composite shots), *Daitozoku* (U.S.: *The Lost World of Sinbad*, 1963), *Kaitei gunkan* (U.S.: *Atragon*, 1963, about a Flying Supersub left over from World War II saving the world from the sunken Kingdom of Mu), *Shikonmado—Dai tatsumaki* (1964), *Kyomo ware ozorami ari* (1964), *Mosura tai Gojira* (U.S.: *Godzilla vs. the Thing*, 1964), *Uchu daikaiju Dogora* (U.S.: *Dagora, the Space Monster*, 1964), *San daikaiju: Chikyu saidai no kessen* (U.S.: *Ghidrah, the Three-Headed Monster*, 1964), *None But the Brave* (1965, directing special effects and World War II ships at sea for a Frank Sinatra production), *Taiheyo Kiseki no sakusen: kisuka* (1965), *Furankenshutain tai chitei kaiju Baragon* (U.S.: *Frankenstein Conquers the World*, 1964–65), *Kureji no daiboken* (*Don't Call Me a Crime Man*, 1965), *Kaiju daisenso* (U.S.: *Invasion of the Astro-Monsters*, 1965, including some stock footage from the original *Radon*), *Hyappatsu hyakuchu* (*Ironfinger*, 1965), *Furankenshutain no kaiju: Sanda tai Gaira* (U.S.: *The War of the Gargantuas*, 1966), *Zero faita dai kusen* (1966), *Kingukongu no gyakushu* (U.S.: *King Kong Escapes*, 1967). In the 1960s he divided his activities and in 1964 established his own Tsuburaya Productions (grown out of Tsuburaya Special Effects Productions, founded in April 1963) for tokusatsu TV series like the 28-episode *Ultra Q* (which premiered in January 1966) and *Urutoraman* (*Ultraman*, premiered in July 1966). For these he created bizarre creatures with outlandish names like Crazygon, Eleking, Gamma-Kujita, Booksa, Metronian (Man from Planet Metron), Godorian (Man from Planet Godorah), Dodonga, Chamegon, Zaragass, Villiam (Monster from Planet Villa), Vanilla, Jeronimo, Gango, Jamira, Cyigo, Pester, Zarabian, Jirarse, Gander, Mikrus, Gillandras, Garamon,

Packy, Kangeon, Utom, Gigose, Antler and Goldon. Sometimes for these creatures he refurbished old monster-suits from Toho where he continued to supervise effects films up to his demise. In 1963 he visited the World Expo and created effects for the Mitsubishi Pavilion. In 1968 he established a merchandising company, Tsuburaya Enterprises. In 1969 he developed the "Holi-Mirror" for the Mitsubishi Pavilion of the World Expo in Japan. In Toho entries of the 1960s, he shared supervisor credit with co-creator Sadamasa Teisho Arikawa: *Gojira, Ebira, Mosura: Nankai no daiketto* (U.S.: *Godzilla vs. the Sea Monster*, 1966), *Kaijuro no kessen: Gojira no musuko* (U.S.: *Son of Godzilla*, 1967), *Kaiju Shoshingeki* (U.S.: *Destroy All Monsters*, 1968, as sort of an anniversary movie with most of Toho's monster squadron on display). Out of respect for his work he received screen credit for *Gojira-Minira-Gabara: Oru Kaiju Daishingeki* (U.S.: *Godzilla's Revenge*, 1969) but wasn't involved due to illness. An overworked Tsuburaya, who had been baptized into the Catholic Church in 1960, passed away from pneumonia and a heart attack shortly after supervising *Rengo kantai shirei chokan: Yamato Isoroku* (*Admiral Yamamoto*, 1968), *Kureji no daibakuhatsu* (1969), *Ido Zero daisakusen* (U.S.: *Latitude Zero*, 1969) and *Nihonkai daikaisen* (*Battle of the Japan Sea*, 1969) and during preproduction of *Gezora, Ganime, Kameba: Kessen! Nankai no daikaiju* (U.S.: *Yog: Monster from Space*, 1970). Teruyoshi Nakano: "In Japanese society, we tend to divide people into two categories. There are the scientific people, and ones who are more like poets, artistic types. I would describe Mr. Tsuburaya as someone who was both. He was scientific and artistic as well" (*Monsters Are Attacking Tokyo!*, p. 53).

Hajime Tsuburaya (1931–1973)

Japanese Effects Producer

First son of Eiji Tsuburaya. Volunteered under his father's watchful supervision at Toho while they made *Gojira* (*Godzilla, King of the Monsters!*, 1954). Co-founded Tsuburaya Productions and with his father supervised the *Urutoraman* (*Ultraman*) TV series in the mid–1960s.

Yonesaburo Tsukiji

Japanese Effects Cinematographer and Director

At Daiei he co-directed effects for *Gamera* and *Majin* series (a giant, Golem-like stone statue): *Dai Majin* (*Majin*, effects director: Yoshiyuki Kuroda), *Dai Majin gyakushu* (*Majin Strikes Again*), *Dai Majin ikaru* (*The Return of the Giant Majin*, all in 1966).

Thomas E. Tutwiler (1905–1984)

American Effects, Aerial and Second Unit Cinematographer

In his own words, Tutwiler "always made pictures the hard way, under difficult and dangerous conditions." He was born in Leakey, Texas, and for two years attended Texas A&M, then went to California and found extra jobs at MGM, for instance as a beer-drinking student in Ernst Lubitsch's *The Student Prince* (1926). Seven months later he found himself a niche in the film loading department, then became assistant cameraman. In 1929 he was assigned to the matte (Warren Newcombe) and process (Paul Eagler) departments. Director of photography since 1933. Effects work for the *Tarzan* series (*Tarzan Escapes* et al.), *Mutiny on the Bounty* (1935), *The Devil Doll* (1935–36), *The Good Earth* (1937). In 1942 he joined the photographic effects department at Warner Bros.; in February 1943 the Army Air Force. In 1946 he shot aerial scenes of the first two atomic bomb tests in the Pacific which led to his becoming a specialist for aerial photography and second unit work in Thailand and the Far East: *The Bridges at Toko-Ri* (1953), *Strategic Air Command* (1954), *The Spirit of St. Louis* (1957), *Jet Pilot* (1957) and *The Hunters* (1958). Also photographed the shark and marlin sequences of *The Old Man and the Sea* (1958). Later did many TV shows. Retired in 1975.

Yusei Uesugi

American Matte Artist

Conventional and digital matte paintings at Industrial Light & Magic. In 1990 he painted Neverland to be scanned and textured onto a 3D model for Steven Spielberg's *Hook*. Also on *Back to the Future Part II* (1989), *Ghostbusters 2* (1989), *The Doors* (1991), *Jurassic Park* (1992–93), *Star Wars Episode 1—The Phantom Menace* (1999), *Peter Pan* (2003), *Harry Potter and the Goblet of Fire* (1995).

Charles Urban (1871–1942)
American Producer

Came to Britain and managed the London office of the Edison Company. Developed his own projector and left Edison. Produced several trick-films including *Possibilities of War in the Air* (1906) and *The Airship Destroyer* (1909). In association with a chemist he spearheaded Kinemacolor process and returned to the United States in 1912.

Armando Valcauda
Italian Stop-Motion Animator

A fan of Ray Harryhausen. Tried his hand at several Italian low-budget fantasies: *L'umanoide* (*The Humanoid*, 1979), *Starcrash* (1979), *Hercules* (1983).

Frank Van Der Veer (1921–1982)
American Optical Cinematographer

The son of cameraman William Van der Veer, he was one of the youngest newsreel cameramen of the United States. 1950–1956: staff member of effects department at 20th Century–Fox: *The Robe* (1953, first CinemaScope feature). 1956–1962: Warner Bros. Studios. In 1962 he founded Van der Veer Photo Effects. Got equipment from John P. Fulton to create effects for Fulton's pet project *The Bamboo Saucer* (eventually released in 1968). Other credits: *The Towering Inferno* (1974, additional opticals), *Logan's Run* (1976, additional visuals), *King Kong* (1976 DeLaurentiis remake), *Star Wars* (1975–77, additional opticals), *Logan's Run* (1976, additional visuals), *Orca* (1977), *The Spy Who Loved Me* (1977), *Exorcist II: The Heretic* (1977), *Superman* (1977–78, additional opticals), *The Manitou* (1977–78), *1941* (1979, blue screen consultant), *The Empire Strikes Back* (1979–80, additional opticals), *Flash Gordon* (1980), *Clash of the Titans* (1980–81, additional opticals for Ray Harry-

hausen), *Conan the Barbarian* (1982). TV: original *Star Trek* series, *Killer Bees* (1974), *The Return of Captain Nemo* (1978).

Willard Van Enger (1901–1946)
American Special Effects Cinematographer

Born New York City. Brother of cinematographer Charles Van Enger. At Warner Bros.–First National Pictures as assistant cameraman and operator, then joined the effects department as director of photography: *Casablanca* (1942), *A Stolen Life* (1946), *The Big Sleep* (1946).

Wally Veevers (1917–1983)
British Visual Effect, Miniature and Matte Cinematographer

According to Con Pederson, who worked with Veevers on *2001: A Space Odyssey*, "[He] was an old time special effects director. He went way back to Hitchcock (sic) as one of the most preeminent special effects directors in England. He knew everything about movies you needed to know to get things moved around. He was really terrific" (1999 interview). Veevers spent two years at Regent Street Polytechnic in London, where he learned all about cinematography. He was one of four trainees to work under Ned Mann for Alexander Korda on *Things to Come* (1936). Learned the craft of hanging miniatures from Mann's assistant Ross Jacklin and provided such shots for *The Thief of Bagdad* (1939–40). Percy Day's photographer in the Shepperton Studios matte department: *Anna Karenina* (1948), *The Winslow Boy* (1948), *Bonnie Prince Charlie* (1948), *The Last Days of Dolwyn* (1949), *The Elusive Pimpernel* (1950), *The Black Rose* (1950), *Gone to Earth* (1950), *The Mudlark* (1950), *Pandora and the Flying Dutchman* (1951), *Outcast of the Islands* (1952), *The Wild Heart* (1952). Took over after Day retired (working with artists George Samuels, Albert Julian, Bob Cuff, Joseph Natanson, Judy Jordan, Ivor Beddoes, Alan Maley and later Peter Melrose): *Hobson's Choice* (1953), *Devil Girl from Mars* (1954), *Richard III* (1955), *Three Men in a Boat* (1956), *A Killer in Korea* (1956), *Satellite in the Sky* (1956), *Alexander the Great* (1956), Charles Chaplin's *A King in New York* (1956–57), *The Smallest Show on*

Earth (1957), *The Admiral Crichton* (1957), *Silent Enemy* (1958), *I Was Monty's Double* (1958), *Carlton Brown of the F.O.* (1958), *Room at the Top* (1958), *Night of the Demon* (U.S.: *Curse of the Demon*, 1958), *I'm All Right Jack* (1959), *Expresso Bongo* (1959), *Too Hot to Handle* (1960), *The Guns of Navarone* (1960–61), *Mysterious Island* (1960–61), *The Longest Day* (1961–62), *The War Lover* (1962), *Summer Holiday* (1962), *The Day of the Triffids* (1962–63), *Lawrence of Arabia* (1962–63), *The Victors* (1963), *Havens Above* (1963), *Sodoma e Gomorra* (*Sodom and Gomorrha*, 1963), *Lord Jim* (1964), *Monster of Terror* (1964–65, U.S.: *Die, Monster, Die!*). After Veevers did *Dr. Strangelove or: How I Learned to Stop Worrying and Love the Bomb* (1963–64), for which he projected an enlarged photograph of the Earth as seen from a plane behind Major King (Slim Pickens) riding a bomb), its director Stanley Kubrick had him do all the complicated rigging for *2001: A Space Odyssey* (1965–68). Veevers continued with *The Battle of Britain* (1968–69), *The Private Life of Sherlock Holmes* (1970), *Diamonds Are Forever* (1971, with matte artist Albert Whitlock), *The Man Who Would Be King* (1975, with Whitlock), *Superman* (1977–78, front projection with Jan W. Jacobsen) and *Excalibur* (1981). His last films were *Saturn 3* (1980) and *The Keep* (1983).

Marcel Vercoutere

American Effects Technician

Involved in the miniature shooting of *It's a Mad Mad Mad Mad World* (1962–63) at Film Effects of Hollywood, *Support Your Local Sheriff!* (1969), *McCabe & Mrs. Miller* (1971), *Deliverance* (1972), *The Exorcist* (1973–74), *Convoy* (1978).

Joseph Viskocil

American Explosives Expert

Miniature explosions for: *Star Wars* (1975–77), *The Day Time Ended* (1980), *The Terminator* (1984), *The Abyss* (1989), *Batman Returns* (1992), *True Lies* (1994), *Johnny Mnemonic* (1995), *Apollo 13* (1995), *Independence Day* (1996), *Alien: Resurrection* (1997), *Godzilla* (1997–98), *Armageddon* (1998), *Battlefield Earth* (2000), *Panic Room* (2002).

Petro Vlahos

American Blue Screen Expert

Staff member in MGM's optical department when they made *Ben-Hur* (1959). With Wadsworth E. Pohl and Ub Iwerks, he shared a Scientific or Technical Award, Class I in 1964 for the conception and perfection of techniques for Color Traveling Matte Composite Cinematography. Eventually turned to electronics and devised the efficient Ultimatte process.

Heinz von Jaworsky (1912–2000)

Austrian-German Aerial Cinematographer

Born in Vienna. Specialist in aerial and second unit cinematography: *Wunder des Fliegens—Der Film eines deutschen Fliegers* (1935), *Gewitterflug zu Claudia* (1937), *D III 88* (1939), *Feldzug in Polen* (1940), *Kampfgeschwader Lützow* (1940–41), *Quax der Bruchpilot* (1941), the unfinished *Das Leben geht weiter* (1945). In 1936 he did special camera work for Leni Riefenstahl's *Olympia* films. Died in New York City.

Menrad Von Mulldorfer

American Matte Artist

Capable of both matte painting and animation. At 20th Century–Fox: *Kronos* (1958, only screen credit), *Journey to the Center of the Earth* (1959), *Cleopatra* (1963), *Von Ryan's Express* (1964, animating rocket).

Slavko Vorkapich (1895–1976)

Yugoslavian-American Montage Effects Artist

Studied painting in Belgrad, Budapest and Paris. In 1920 he came to Hollywood and entered the industry as a set designer. Did tabletop miniatures for *The Life and Death of a Hollywood Extra* (1928), an experimental short by Robert Florey and Gregg Toland. 1928–34: directed visual effects, then specialized in montage sequences for RKO, Paramount, Columbia, Warner and especially MGM: *Viva Villa!* (1934), *Crime Without Passion* (1934), *David Copperfield* (1935), *A Tale of Two Cities* (1935), *The President Vanishes* (1935), *Romeo and Juliet* (1936), *The*

Good Earth (1937), *Maytime* (1937), *Broadway Melody of 1938* (1937), *Boy's Town* (1938), *Marie Antoinette* (1938), *Mr. Smith Goes to Washington* (1939), *The Howards of Virginia* (1940), *Meet John Doe* (1941). Vorkapich on the art of montages (according to Don Siegel, *A Siegel Film: An Autobiography*, p. 56):

> Montage literally means the placing of one picture on to another. Eisenstein used it as a form of editing: taut, precise, sometimes a matter of frames. Generally, it gets over a lapse of time. But when one considers that montage is the single section of film that gives the audience credit for creative intelligence, the importance of montage transcends the mundane film as a whole. The use of symbolism stirs the imagination of the viewer. One can show the invisible or intangible by means of visible impressions. The whole film can be made more vivid and given more pace by the proper use of montage technique.

In 1938 Vorkapich lectured at the Museum of Modern Arts in New York City. 1949–51: head of film department, University of Southern California. 1952–56: lecture tour through Europe. 1955: did a picture in his native Yugoslavia, *Hanka*.

Vernon L. Walker (1894–1948)
American Effects Cinematographer and Supervisor

Born in Detroit, Michigan. Education: high school, East Denver. Cameraman, seven years, News Weekly Gaumont, Mutual and Selig Tribune; production cameraman, two years, Fox Studios, two years, Pathe serials, five years, Mack Sennett comedies. Assistant to Fred W. Jackman on the silent *The Lost World* (1924–25); for two years at Warner Bros.–First National Pictures in Burbank and at Columbia Pictures. Then came to RKO, as assistant of Lloyd W. Knechtel, eventually becoming department head, process and photo effects in 1933: *The Most Dangerous Game* (1932), *The Conquerors* (1932), *King Kong* (1932–33, process photography), *The Silver Cord* (1933), *Lucky Devils* (1933), *Christopher Strong* (1933), *The Monkey's Paw* (1933), *Melody Cruise* (1933), *Ace of Aces* (1933), *Flying Down to Rio* (1933), *Ann Vickers* (1933), *The Son of Kong* (1933), *Kentucky Kernels* (1934), *Hips, Hips, Hooray!* (1934), *Finishing School* (1934),

Stingaree (1934), *Of Human Bondage* (1934), *Cockeyed Cavaliers* (1934), *Down to Their Last Yacht* (1934), *The Gay Divorcee* (1934), *By Your Leave* (1934), *Anne of Green Gables* (1934), *The Silver Streak* (1934), *The Little Minister* (1934), *Romance in Manhattan* (1935), *Murder on a Honeymoon* (1935), *Captain Hurricane* (1935), *She* (1935), *Top Hat* (1935), *The Three Musketeers* (1935), *The Last Days of Pompeii* (1935), *The Rainmakers* (1935), *Another Face* (1935), *I Dream Too Much* (1935), *Follow the Fleet* (1936), *Love on a Bet* (1936), *Mary of Scotland* (1936), *Swing Time* (1936), *Walking on Air* (1936), *Without Orders* (1936), *Smartest Girl in Town* (1936), *Winterset* (1936), *Don't Tell the Wife* (1936), *Sea Devils* (1937), *The Man Who Found Himself* (1937), *The Soldier and the Lady* (1937), *The Woman I Love* (1937), *Shall We Dance* (1937), *Behind the Headlines* (1937), *There Goes My Girl* (1937), *New Faces of 1937* (1937), *Super-Sleuth* (1937), *The Toast of New York* (1937), *Flight from Glory* (1937), *The Life of the Party* (1937), *Annapolis Salute* (1937), *Music for Madame* (1937), *Danger Patrol* (1937), *A Damsel in Distress* (1937), *High Flyers* (1937), *Pacific Liner* (1938), *Crashing Hollywood* (1938), *Radio City Revels* (1938), *Bringing Up Baby* (1938), *Maid's Night Out* (1938), *Go Chase Yourself* (1938), *Joy of Living* (1938), *Having Wonderful Time* (1938), *Sky Giant* (1938), *Mother Carey's Chicken* (1938), *I'm from the City* (1938), *Carefree* (1938), *Fugitives for a Night* (1938), *Gunga Din* (1939), *Boy Slaves* (1939), *Twelve Crowded Hours* (1939), *Love Affair* (1939), *They Made Her a Spy* (1939), *The Story of Vernon and Irene Castle* (1939), *Fixer Dugan* (1939), *Panama Lady* (1939), *Five Came Back* (1939), *Bachelor Mother* (1939), *Way Down South* (1939), *In Name Only* (1939), *Nurse Edith Cavell* (1939), *Reno* (1939), *The Hunchback of Notre Dame* (1939), *The Saint's Double Trouble* (1940), *Swiss Family Robinson* (1940), *Abe Lincoln in Illinois* (1940), *Millionaire Playboy* (1940), *Primrose Path* (1940), *Irene* (1940), *Tom Brown's Schooldays* (1940), *Millionaires in Prison* (1940), *Cross-Country Romance* (1940), *Lucky Partners* (1940), *Stranger on the Third Floor* (1940), *Wildcat Bus* (1940), *Dance, Girl, Dance* (1940), *Men Against the Sky* (1940), *I'm Still Alive* (1940), *Too Many Girls* (1940), *They Knew What They Wanted* (1940), *Mexican Spitfire Out West* (1940), *You'll Find Out* (1940), *Little Men* (1940),

No, No, Nanette (1940), *Kitty Foyle: The Natural History of a Woman* (1940), *Citizen Kane* (1940–41), *The Saint in Palm Springs* (1941), *Play Girl* (1941), *Mr. and Mrs. Smith* (1941), *A Girl, a Guy, and a Gob* (1941), *Repent at Leisure* (1941), *The Devil and Miss Jones* (1941), *They Met in Argentina* (1941), *Sunny* (1941), *Tom Dick and Harry* (1941), *Hurry, Charlie, Hurry* (1941), *My Life with Caroline* (1941), *Parachute Battalion* (1941), *Unexpected Uncle* (1941), *The Devil and Daniel Webster* (1941), *Suspicion* (1941), *Look Who's Laughing* (1941), *Playmates* (1941), *Four Jacks and a Jill* (1941), *Call Out the Marines* (1942), *Obliging Young Lady* (1942), *Valley of the Sun* (1942), *Sing Your Worries Away* (1942), *The Tuttles of Tahiti* (1942), *Syncopation* (1942), *My Favorite Spy* (1942), *Powder Town* (1942), *The Magnificent Ambersons* (1942), *The Big Street* (1942), *Here We Go Again* (1942), *Army Surgeon* (1942), *The Navy Comes Through* (1942), *Once Upon a Honeymoon* (1942), *Seven Days' Leave* (1942), *Cat People* (1942), *The Great Gildersleeve* (1942), *Hitler's Children* (1943), *I Walked with a Zombie* (1943), *Fight for Freedom* (1943), *Journey into Fear* (1943), *This Land Is Mine* (1943), *Bombardier* (1943), *Mr. Lucky* (1943), *The Sky's the Limit* (1943), *Behind the Rising Sun* (1943), *A Lady Takes a Chance* (1943), *The Fallen Sparrow* (1943), *Gangway for Tomorrow* (1943), *The Falcon and the Co-eds* (1943), *Around the World* (1943), *The Ghost Ship* (1943), *Tender Comrade* (1943), *Mademoiselle Fifi* (1944), *Government Girl* (1944), *Passport to Destiny* (1944), *Action in Arabia* (1944), *Seven Days Ashore* (1944), *Days of Glory* (1944), *Marine Raiders* (1944), *Gildersleeve's Ghost* (1944), *Step Lively* (1944), *Bride by Mistake* (1944), *The Falcon in Mexico* (1944), *Youth Runs Wild* (1944), *My Pal Wolf* (1944), *Tall in the Saddle* (1944), *None but the Lonely Heart* (1944), *Heavenly Days* (1944), *Girl Rush* (1944), *The Woman in the Window* (1944), *The Falcon in Hollywood* (1944), *Murder, My Sweet* (1944), *Experiment Perilous* (1944), *The Enchanted Cottage* (1945), *Betrayal from the East* (1945), *Pan-Americana* (1945), *Having Wonderful Crime* (1945), *Two O'Clock Courage* (1945), *The Brighton Strangler* (1945), *Back to Bataan* (1945), *The Falcon in San Francisco* (1945), *Radio Stars on Parade* (1945), *First Yank into Tokyo* (1945), *The Spanish Main* (1945), *George White's Scandals* (1945), *Man Alive* (1945), *A Game of Death* (1945), *The Bells of St. Mary's* (1945), *Johnny Angel* (1945), *The Spiral Staircase* (1945–46), *Riverboat Rhythm* (1946), *From This Day Forward* (1946), *Deadline at Dawn* (1946), *Bedlam* (1946), *The Truth About Murder* (1946), *Without Reservations* (1946), *Sunset Pass* (1946), *The Bamboo Blonde* (1946), *Notorious* (1946), *Sister Kenny* (1946), *Genius at Work* (1946), *Sinbad the Sailor* (1947), *Mourning Becomes Electra* (1947), *Tycoon* (1947), *Variety Time* (1947–48). Articles: "Use of miniatures in process backgrounds," *American Cinematographer*, August 1934, "Rhythmic optical effects for musical pictures," *American Cinematographer*, December 1936. Died on Balboa Island, Los Angeles.

Fred Waller, Jr. (1886–1954)
American Effects Expert and Inventor

The Brooklyn-born Waller did art titles and film effects for Paramount's East Coast Studio: *If Women Only Knew* (1921), *Modern Matrimony* (1923), *Puritan Passions* (1923), *Youthful Cheaters* (1923), *The Sorrows of Satan* (1926). Developed Cinerama process, first used basically at New York World Fair, then as gunnery trainer for the U.S. Air Force, in the 1950s as roadshow attraction starting with *This Is Cinerama*. Died in Huntington, Long Island, New York.

Harry Walton
American Stop-Motion Animator

Under the supervision of Gene Warren he did *The Legend of Hillbilly John* (1973) and *Black Sunday* (1977). Also involved on: *Laserblast* (1978), *Never Say Never Again* (1983), *The Puppetoon Movie* (1987, additional animation for Fantasy II), *RoboCop* (1987), *RoboCop 2* (1990), *RoboCop 3* (1993). At Industrial Light & Magic: *Ewoks: Battle for Endor* (1985), *The Golden Child* (1986), *Howard the Duck* (1986), *Young Sherlock Holmes* (1986), *Innerspace* (1987), *Who Framed Roger Rabbit* (1988), *Willow* (1988), *Ghostbusters II* (1989). Animator on: *Honey, I Shrunk the Kids* (1989), *The Nightmare Before Christmas* (1993), *Dragonworld* (1994), *James and the Giant Peach* (1996).

Gene Warren (1916–1999)

American Stop-Motion Animator

Started as an animator with George Pal's *Puppetoons*. Feature film work includes *Variety Girl* (1947, George Pal sequence), *The Twonky* (1953), *Tarantula* (1955), *Kronos* (1957). With Wah Chang and Tim Baar, he founded Project Unlimited, Inc., supervised and coordinated miniature and stop-motion work for all of George Pal's MGM features: *tom thumb* (1958), *The Time Machine* (1959–60, Academy Award), *Atlantis, the Lost Continent* (1960–61), *The Wonderful World of the Brothers Grimm* (1962–63, three-strip Cinerama), *7 Faces of Dr. Lao* (1963–64, only slightly involved); outside of Projects: *The Power* (1968). Other work includes *Monster from Green Hell* (1958), *Dinosaurus!* (1960), *Goliath and the Dragon* (1960–61), *Master of the World* (1960–61), *Flight of the Lost Balloon* (1961), *Jack the Giant Killer* (1960–62), *Journey to the Seventh Planet* (1962), and *Around the World Under the Sea* (1965–66) with scenes of a miniature submarine, a live and a miniature eel. TV: *The Outer Limits, Star Trek*. After working with Projects, Warren founded Excelsior! Animated Moving Pictures Studios and did the TV series *Land of the Lost* and *Man from Atlantis* and the feature films *The Legend of Hillbilly John* (1973) and *Black Sunday* (1977) with animator Harry Walton. After the death of his wife, he left the film business. Son Gene Jr. continues the family tradition.

Gene Warren, Jr.

American Stop-Motion Animator

Assisted his father Gene on TV series *Land of the Lost*. Founded Fantasy II Film Effects: *Goliath Awaits* (1981, TV movie), *Spacehunter: Adventures in the Forbidden Zone* (1983), *Gremlins* (1984), *The Terminator* (1984), *Moving Violations* (1985), *Flight of the Navigator* (1986), *Killer Klowns from Outer Space* (1987), *The Puppetoon Movie* (1987, additional animation), *Captain America* (1989), *Fright Night Part II* (1989), *Cyborg* (1990), *Stephen King's It* (1990), *Terminator 2: Judgment Day* (1991), *Nemesis* (1992).

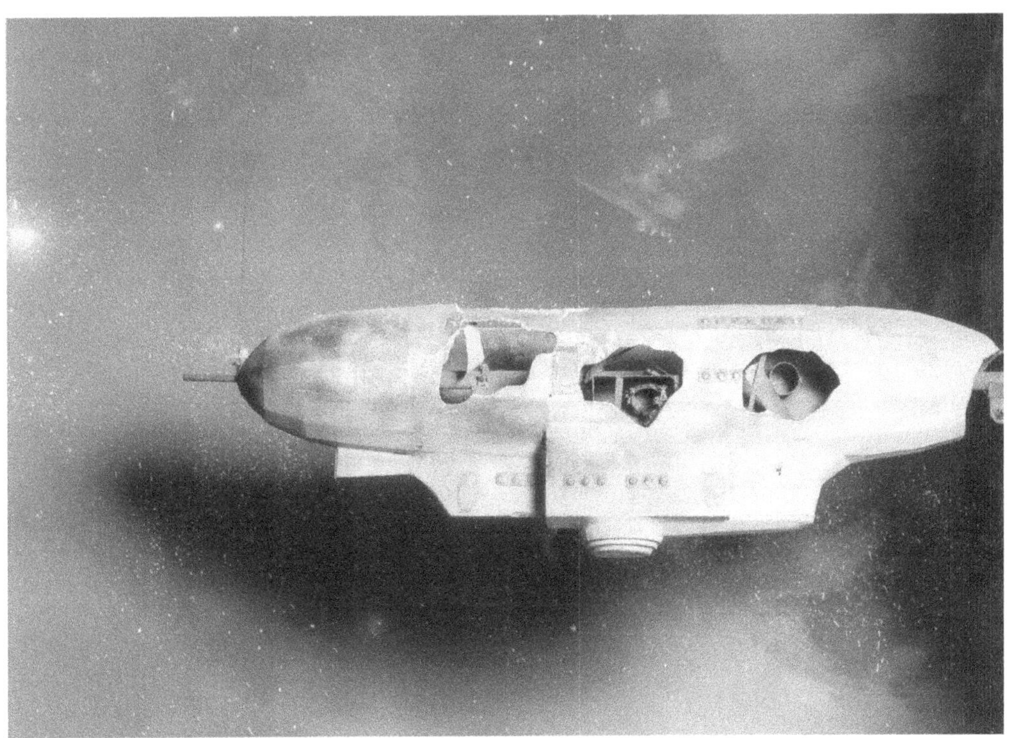

Master of the World's airship Albatross (one of several models, this one used for the destruction scene) (courtesy Deutsche Kinemathek Berlin).

William H. [Bill] Warrington
(1910–1981)
British Special Effects Supervisor

Started his career as a model maker and was familiar with the Shüfftan Process which quite often used transparencies that were blended into a life-sized set or models; "We used to make [the models] with a special type of paper because the grain and finish of timber wasn't fine enough in texture and so on" (John Brosnan, *Movie Magic*, p. 95). He was soon a full-fledged special effects man at Elstree. After World War II he joined Rank, who had decided to build the biggest effects department at Denham and later at Pinewood for what was called the Independent Frame method. Warrington physically organized the whole show: *The Way Ahead/ The Immortal Battalion* (1944), *Caesar and Cleopatra* (1945), *Odd Man Out* (1947), *So Long at the Fair* (1949), *Trio* (1950), *Hotel Sahara* (1951), *Malta Story* (1953), *The Net* (1953), *Up to His Neck* (1954), *The Purple Plain* (1954), *Simba* (1955), *Above Us the Waves* (1956), *Reach for the Sky* (1956), *The Prince and the Showgirl* (1957), *An Alligator Named Daisy* (1957), *The Battle of the River Plate* (1957), *A Night to Remember* (1958), *Sink the Bismarck!* (1959–60). Too late he realized that he could make more money by becoming independent. He left Rank to start freelancing and became an explosives expert: *Quatermass 2* (U.S.: *Enemy from Space*, 1956), *Yesterday's Enemy* (1959, accidentally almost burned off the roof of a soundstage at Shepperton with explosive charges during a scene in which Japanese troops blew up a village), *The Mummy* (1959), *Swiss Family Robinson* (1959), *La Fayette* (1961), *The Scarlet Blade* (1963), *The Long Ships* (1963–64), *Genghis Khan* (1965), *The Heroes of Telemark* (1965), *Twist of Sand* (1968), *The Password Is Courage* (1969), *The Desperados* (1969), *Cromwell* (1970), *Gold* (1974), *Journey into Fear* (1975). Consultant on *Raiders of the Lost Ark* (1980–81). Academy Award for *The Guns of Navarone* (1960–61).

Ronnie Wass (1925–)
British Rostrum Cameraman

London-born Wass worked as a rostrum and aerial cinematographer from 1939 until 1988: *The Dam Busters* (1954–55), *Summer Holiday* (1963), *A Hard Day's Night* (1964, titles), *Battle of Britain* (1968–69), *Superman IV: The Quest for Peace* (1987, titles).

Akira Watanabe
Japanese Special Effects Art Director

Met Eiji Tsuburaya for the first time in 1931 at Shochiku Studios and did some war films with him (including *Hawai Mare–oki kaisen* [*The War at Sea from Hawaii to Malaya*, 1942]); later rejoined Tsuburaya's operation as head of the art department (*Anatahan/ The Saga of Anatahan*, 1954), designing monster suits and supervising model aircraft and other miniatures: *Taiheyo no washi* (*Eagle of the Pacific*, 1953), *Gojira* (U.S.: *Godzilla, King of the Monsters!*, 1954), *Gojira no gyakushu* (*Godzilla Raids Again/* U.S.: *Gigantis, the Fire Monster*, 1955), *Sora no daikaiju Radon* (U.S.: *Rodan*, 1956), *Chikyu boeigun* (U.S.: *The Mysterians*, 1957), *Bijo to ekitainingen* (U.S.: *The H-Man*, 1958), *Daikaiju Baran* (U.S.: *Varan the Unbelievable*, 1958), *Nippon tanjo* (*The Three Treasures*, 1959), *Uchu dai senso* (U.S.: *Battle in Outer Space*, 1959–60), *Osaka jo monogatari* (*Osaka Castle Story/ Daredevil in the Castle*, 1961), *Mosura* (U.S.: *Mothra*, 1961), *Sekai Daisenso* (*The Last War*, 1962), *Yosei Gorasu* (U.S.: *Gorath*, 1962), *Kingukongu tai Gojira* (U.S.: *King Kong vs. Godzilla*, 1962), *Daitozoku* (U.S.: *The Lost World of Sinbad*, 1963), *Kaitei gunkan* (U.S.: *Atragon*, 1963), *Mosura tai Gojira* (U.S.: *Godzilla vs. the Thing*, 1964), *Uchu daikaiju Dogora* (U.S.: *Dagora, the Space Monster*, 1964), *San daikaiju: Chiyku saidai no kessen* (U.S.: *Ghidrah, the Three-Headed Monster*, 1964), *Furankenshutain tai chitei kaiju Baragon* (U.S.: *Frankenstein Conquers the World*, 1965), *Kaiju daisenso* (U.S.: *Invasion of the Astro-Monsters*, 1965). On his own, he directed the effects sequences of *Supa Jyaiantsu* (*Starman* series, 1957–58, Shintoho), *Dai kyoju Gappa* (U.S.: *Monster from a Prehistoric Planet*, 1968, Nikkatsu) and *Gamma Sango Uchu Daisakusen* (U.S.: *The Green Slime*, 1968, Toei). Produced *Urusei yatsura: Haato o tsukane*. Last assignment was design of the monster Gigan for *Chikyu Kogeki Meirei: Gojira tai Gaigan* (*Godzilla on Monster Island*, 1971–72).

Don W. Weed

American Optical Cinematographer

Co-founder of Film Effects of Hollywood with Linwood G. Dunn and Cecil D. Love: *It's a Mad Mad Mad Mad World* (1962–63), *The Great Race* (1965), *Airport* (1970). Resumed company activities with Film Effects International, Inc., and promoted Dynavision, a 65mm process, both in flat format and 3D.

Howie Weed

American Model Maker

Miniatures for Industrial Light & Magic: *Innerspace* (1987), *Bram Stoker's Dracula* (1992).

Howard Weeks

American Model Maker

Miniatures for *Sky Lines* (1949), *The Man from Planet X* (1951), *Project Moon Base* (1953), *The Angry Red Planet* (1959), *Master of the World* (1960–61, *Albatross* model), *Jack the Giant Killer* (1960–62) and *The Wonderful World of the Brothers Grimm* (1962–63).

Paul Wegener (1874–1948)

German Actor

Popular on the stage under Max Reinhardt. In films since 1913. Was very interested in trick-film and effects and believed in a totally artificial film medium. Cameraman Guido Seeber doubled Wegener for his *Doppelgänger* part in *Der Student von Prag* (*The Student of Prague*) in 1913. Wegener was the original Golem (in 1914 and 1920–21). In *Rübezahls Hochzeit* (1916) he played a legendary giant from the mountains who transforms himself into a steward intent on playing a trick on his master, the count. As the count prepares to cut up a tasty pike, Rübezahl (Old Nip) restores the fish to life and lets it swim through the air. In another film made the same year, *Der Yoghi*, Wegener again appeared in a dual role, as a scientist and as a yogi, who is able to render himself invisible by magic. Doors open and close automatically, footsteps appear in the sand and, at the end, drops of blood spill from the mortally wounded invisible man. It was Wegener

who asked young Lotte Reiniger to animate rats and create silhouette art titles for his version of the story of the Pied Piper of Hamelin, *Der Rattenfänger von Hameln* (1918), thus starting her career in animated films such as *Die Abenteuer des Prinzen Achmed* (1923–26). He also asked Guido Seeber to pull out all stops for *Lebende Buddhas* in 1923.

Heinrich Friedrich Jakob Weidemann (1889–1982)

German Visual Effects Expert and Art Director

Born in Schwerin. Assisted Eugen Schüfftan, Ernst Kunstmann and others in blending miniatures and live-size sets by use of mirrors in *Metropolis* (1925–27), *Amphitryon* (1935) and the NS propaganda film *Ewiger Wald* (1936) in which he transformed the trees of German forest into cathedrals. Later became an art director and remained active until 1969. Died in Berlin.

Alex C. Weldon

American Mechanical Effects and Explosives Expert

Weldon originally wanted to become a basketball player but thanks to his father, a prop man for Douglas Fairbanks, he ended in movies. Low-budget work: *Phantom from Space* (1953), *Invasion of the Saucer Men* (1957). Went to Europe (*The Longest Day*, 1960–61) and to Spain to work for Samuel Bronston, who got the funds to open a huge studio in Madrid: *El Cid* (1961), *King of Kings* (1961), *55 Days at Peking* (1962), *Circus World* (1963), *The Battle of the Bulge* (1965), *Krakatoa—East of Java* (1969), *Patton* (1969). Returned to the United States for *Lost Horizon* (1972), *Oklahoma Crude* (1973), *Star Trek: The Motion Picture* (1978–79).

Harold E. Wellman (1905–1992)

American Effects Cinematographer

Born in Colorado Springs. In 1928 he started as a grip, prop man and electrician at Inspiration Pictures (*She Goes to War*), Tec-Art and Paramount. Specialized in miniatures, second unit and process. In 1929 he became assistant cameraman at Paramount, then followed cinematographer Edward Cronjager to RKO. Did some aerial scenes for *The Lost Squadron* (1932). Eventually became a member of the camera effects department, with Lloyd Knechtel, then Vernon L. Walker. Remained with RKO until 1957. Stop-motion photography: *Creation* (1931, unfinished predecessor to *Kong*), *King Kong* (1932–33), *The Son of Kong* (1933), *The Animal World* (Irwin Allen production for Warner Bros., 1956). Process, mattes, second unit, miniatures and photographic effects for *Cimarron* (1930), *The Monkey's Paw* (1933), *The Hunchback of Notre Dame* (1939), *Citizen Kane* (1941), *Days of Glory* (1944), *Sinbad the Sailor* (1947), *The Big Steal* (1949), *The White Tower* (1950), *The Thing from Another World* (1950–51, second unit shot), *Jet Pilot* (1950 but held back until 1957), *His Kind of Woman* (1951), *Macao* (1952), *Blackbeard, the Pirate* (1952), *The Las Vegas Story* (1952), *Clash by Night* (1952), *The Hitch-Hiker* (1953), *Split Second* (1953), *Dangerous Mission* (1954, 3D). Second unit photography for MGM: *Ben-Hur* (1959), *Mutiny on the Bounty* (1962–63), *The Prize* (1963). For United Artists release: *What Did You Do in the War, Daddy?* (1966). Director of photography: *The Invisible Boy* (1957), *Watusi* (1959), *Atlantis, the Lost Continent* (1960–61). Emmy Award for front projection on TV special *Hemo the Magnificent*. Involved in process and blue screen shots for the *Adventures of Superman* TV series. Effects supervisor on *Catch-22* (1970), *King Kong* (1976 DeLaurentiis remake) and *Beyond the Poseidon Adventure* (1979). Retired in June 1982.

Kit West
British Effects Expert

Les Bowie's cameraman on the blue screen shots and other effects for *The Damned* (U.S.: *These Are the Damned*, 1961–63), *The Pirates of Blood River* (1961–62), *Jason and the Argonauts* (1961–63), *The Old Dark House* (1962), *Paranoiac* (1962), *Nightmare* (1962–63), *The Scarlet*

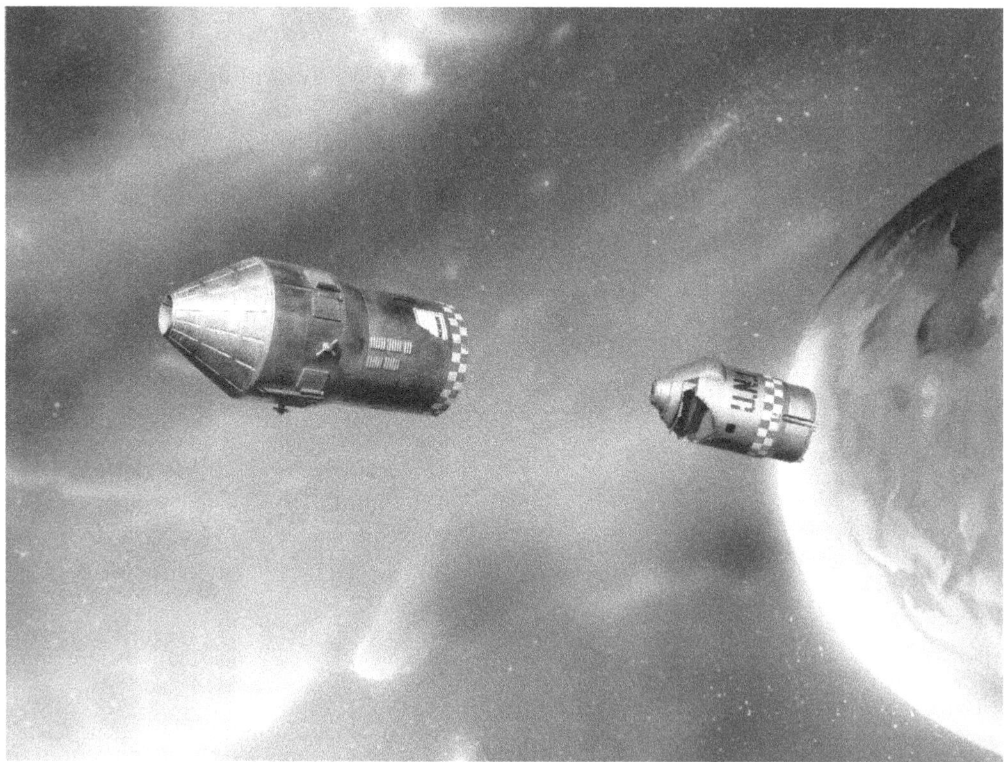

A Harryhausen spaceship from ***First Men in the Moon*** (courtesy Ray and Diana Harryhausen Collection as displayed by Deutsche Kinemathek Berlin).

Blade (1963), *The Devil-Ship Pirates* (1963–64), *The Evil of Frankenstein* (1963–64), *First Men in the Moon* (1963–64, assisting Ray Harryhausen), *She* (1964–65), *Moon Zero Two* (1970). On Hammer's *The Kiss of the Vampire* (1962–64), "The bats coming in through windows and flying through the set and past camera were shot by me. I actually went onto the floor after they had finished shooting on the same set. We had all our guys up in the gantry puppeteering them all, and I photographed all that" (*Hammer Films: The Bray Studios Years*, p. 260). Independent mechanical effects supervisor on: *The Battle of the Bulge* (1965), *The Wild Geese* (1978), *Lion of the Desert* (1979–80), *The Big Red One* (1980), *Raiders of the Lost Ark* (1980–81), *Return of the Jedi* (1982–83), *Dune* (1983), *Young Sherlock Holmes* (1985), *Empire of the Sun* (1987), *Universal Soldier* (1992), *1492: Conquest of Paradise* (1992), *Stargate* (1994), *Enemy at the Gates* (2000–2001).

Joseph Westheimer (1916–1998)
American Visual Effects Supervisor

Born in Los Angeles. At age 15 he worked at Warner Brothers as a studio messenger, then in the prop department. Graduated as electrical engineer from California Institute of Technology (class of '38) and returned to Warners, hired by Byron Haskin who was in charge of Special Effects Stage 5 on the Burbank lot. Designed projection process screens and rear-projection equipment. In World War II: newsreel cameraman at the U.S. Air Force. After the war he joined the special effects unit at Eagle-Lion operating in the Fine Arts Studio on Sunset Boulevard. In 1949: opticals and insert photography for Consolidated Film Industries. In 1955 he founded the Westheimer Company and was involved in effects and inserts for the TV series *The Outer Limits, Twilight Zone, Star Trek, Amos Burke—Secret Agent, The Big Valley, Honey West, The Smothers Brothers, Lassie, Branded, Dynasty* and *Shogun*. Additional effects and titles for the features *Drango* (1957), *The Glory Guys* (1965), *Cyborg 2087* (1966), *Dimension 5* (1966), *The Scalphunters* (1968), *The Heart Is a Lonely Hunter* (1968), *Sam Whiskey* (1969), *Who Is Harry Kellerman and Why Is He Saying Those Terrible Things About Me?* (1971), *Phantasm* (1979), *The Muppet Movie* (1979), *The Empire Strikes Back* (1979–80). Mentor of Richard Edlund. Academy Class III Scientific or Technical Award "for the development of a device to obtain shadowed titles on motion picture film" (1975). Died from Alzheimer's disease.

Albert J. Whitlock (1913–1999)
British-American Matte Artist

In making a composite matte painting shot, the live action insert is always shot first, and I'm always actually on the set when it is being filmed. The area that is to be a painting is blacked out, so that only the live action area is recorded on the first pass through the camera. Being there during this live action filming gives me the opportunity to visualize the complete final scene and make sure that we are getting a composition that will work [*American Cinematographer*, November 1974, p. 133I].

Born in London, Whitlock entered the film industry in 1929. "Because of the Depression I quit school and went to work to help out the family." He said that at the studios he was called a "fetch and carry fellow," which meant he was asked to do all sorts of chores for just about everyone on the lot. Part of the work was as an actor playing pages, newspaper boys and sundry other parts. Other duties: disguising nitrate film so he could carry it across London on a bus, picking up costumes, assisting electricians, cameramen and scenic artists, moving lights, painting sets, building scenery and models, working as an office boy and as art director Alfred Junge's assistant (*Non-Stop New York*, 1936), sign painting, assisting in modelmaking (Alfred Hitchcock's *The Man Who Knew Too Much*, 1934), doing title cards, and working as a glass and matte artist at Gaumont Lime Grove Studio and Gainsborough (painting the title card for the Gainsborough Lady logo). He eventually settled on matte and glass shots. First screen credit as A. J. Whitlock on *Christopher Columbus* in 1949. At Pinewood Studios he worked under the supervision of Les Bowie: *Quartet* (1949), *Give Us This Day* (working title: *Christ in Concrete*, 1949), *So Long at the Fair* (1949), *Trio* (1950), *Outpost in Malaya* (1952), *The Malta Story* (1953), *Genevieve* (1953), *Romeo and Juliet* (1953), *The Seekers* (1954). Assisted Peter Ellenshaw on Disney's

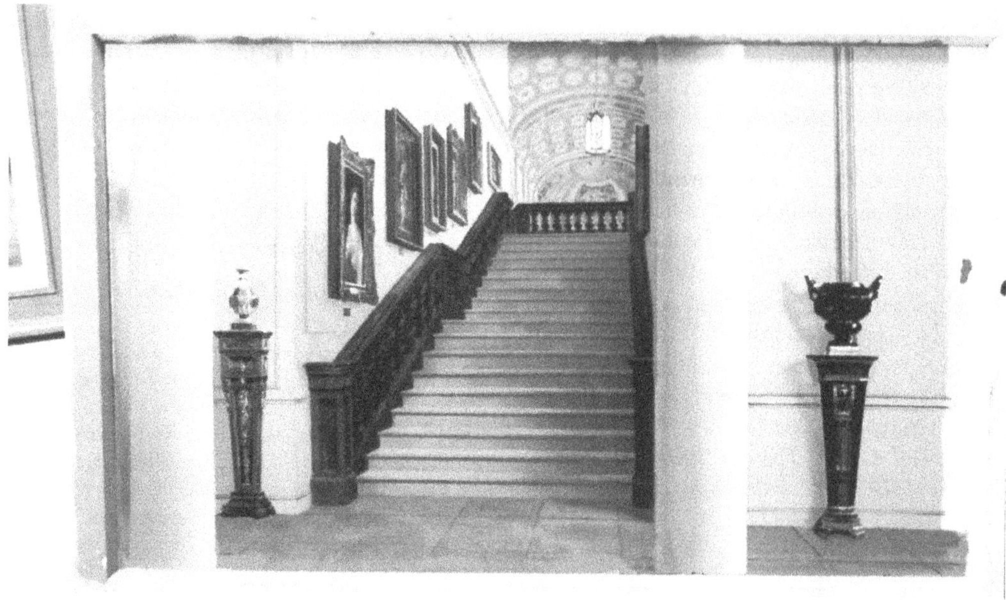

Matte art by Albert Whitlock for an East Berlin museum scene in Alfred Hitchcock's *Torn Curtain* (1966) (courtesy Deutsche Kinemathek Berlin).

British productions *The Sword and the Rose* (1953) and *Rob Roy, the Highland Rogue* (1953) for which he also designed the titles. Left Britain in 1954 and applied at Walt Disney Studios, but there were no openings at the time. Whitlock and family went to San Francisco where he painted murals and billboards. When he was ready to return to Britain, he got a call from Disney's: Ellenshaw had recommended him to design the main titles for *20000 Leagues Under the Sea* (1954). Stayed at Disney's matte department under Ellenshaw's supervision: *Davy Crockett* (TV), *Mickey Mouse Club* (TV), *Zorro* (TV), *The Great Locomotive Chase* (1956), *Westward Ho the Wagons* (1956), *Perri* (1958, art titles), *Tonka* (1958), *Darby O'Gill and the Little People* (1958–59, suggesting perspective effects), *Ten Who Dared* (1960), *Third Man on the Mountain* (1960), *Grand Canyon* (1960 short), *Daniel Boone* (1960, TV mini-series), *Greyfriar's Bobby* (1961), *The Absent Minded Professor* (1961), *The Parent Trap* (1961). Also was involved with some of the basic concepts at Disneyland and painted the Main Street Theatre. Walt Disney himself asked Whitlock to stay, offering him a lifelong position, but Whitlock, eager for a new chance, left for Universal in 1961 following an invitation from George Golitzen whom he knew from Dis-

ney's. Renewed his association with Hitchcock by doing pictorial designs and 13 matte paintings for *The Birds* (1962–63). Freelanced in his spare time for other effects companies such as Butler-Glouner Inc. (the AIP Poe films) and Howard A. Anderson Company (*Jack the Giant Killer*, 1960–61, *Taras Bulba*, 1962). After Russ Lawson retired in 1963, Whitlock was put in charge of Universal's matte department and also was loaned out several times to other studios: *That Touch of Mink* (1962), *Captain Newman, M.D.* (1963), *The Thrill of It All* (1963), *The Ugly American* (1963), *I'd Rather Be Rich* (1964), *Marnie* (1964), *Island of the Dolphins* (1964), *Father Goose* (1964), *Wild and Wonderful* (1964), *Ship of Fools* (1965), *Shenandoah* (1965), *Mirage* (1965), *That Funny Feeling* (1965), *The War Lord* (1965), *Blindfold* (1965), *Beau Geste* (1966), *Munster, Go Home!* (1966), *The Rare Breed* (1966), *Torn Curtain* (1966), *The King's Pirate* (1967), *The War Wagon* (1967), *The Reluctant Astronaut* (1967), *The King's Pirate* (1967), *The Way West* (1967), *Rough Night in Jericho* (1967), *Thoroughly Modern Millie* (1967), *The Ballad of Josie* (1967–68), *Funny Girl* (1968), *P.J.* (1968), *Counterpoint* (1968), *Madigan* (1968), *In Enemy Country* (1968), *Hellfighters* (1968), *The Shakiest Gun in the West* (1968), *The

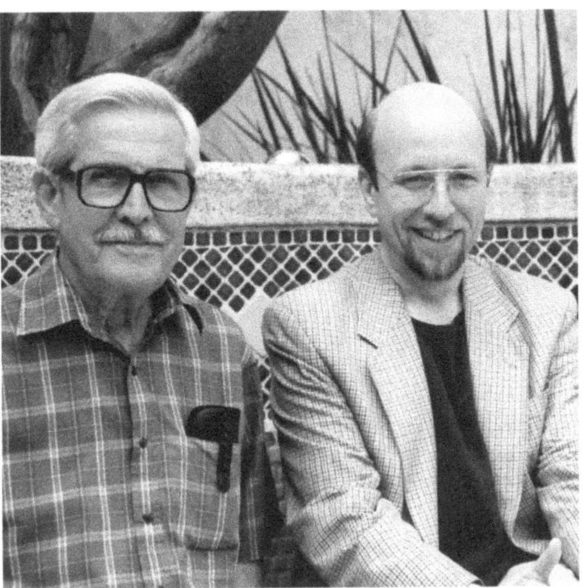

Albert Whitlock watched Schüfftan people operate in Britain. Whitlock became very interested in trick photography and focused on glass and matte art. Albert Whitlock (left) and the author in the 1980s at the Whitlock Residency in Santa Barbara.

Learning Tree (1969), *Gaily, Gaily* (1969), *Colossus: the Forbin Project* (1970), *Topaz* (1969), *Skullduggery* (1970), *Catch-22* (1970), *Two Mules for Sister Sara* (1970, called in as consultant by director Don Siegel), *Raid on Rommel* (1971), *The Andromeda Strain* (1971), *Big Jake* (1971), *One More Train to Rob* (1971), *Diamonds Are Forever* (1971, James Bond picture), *Slaughterhouse-Five* (1972), *Frenzy* (1972), *The Sting* (1972–73), *Cahill. United States Marshal* (1973), *The Day of the Dolphins* (1973), *That Man Bolt* (1973), *The Train Robbers* (1973), *Showdown* (1973), *Papillon* (1972–73), *Oklahoma Crude* (1973), *The Girl from Petrovka* (1974), *Mame* (1974), *Funny Lady* (1974–75), *The Day of the Locust* (1974–75), *The Man Who Would Be King* (1975), *Two Minute Warning* (1976), *W. C. Fields and Me* (1976), *Bound for Glory* (1976, duplicating a dust storm by using three discs of cotton rolling over a painting), *Swashbuckler* (1976), *The Front* (1976), *Family Plot* (1976), *The Sentinel* (1977), *The Last Remake of Beau Geste* (1977), *MacArthur* (1977), *Exorcist II: The Heretic* (1977), *The Car* (1977), *Airport '77* (1977), *The Wiz* (1978), *I Wanna Hold Your Hand* (1978), *Dracula* (1979), *The Prisoner of Zenda* (1979, Whitlock: "The shot of

Sellers taking himself out of the basket was good. I did it with a double to get the contacting arm and then we got rid of the double by covering him with the other Sellers character"), *The Island* (1980), *Cheech & Chong's Next Movie* (1980), *The Blues Brothers* (1980), *In God We Trust* (1980), *Heartbeeps* (1981), *Ghost Story* (1981), *Cat People* (1982), *The Best Little Whorehouse in Texas* (1982), *Missing* (1982), *Victor/Victoria* (1982), *The Thing* (1982), *The Wicked Lady* (1983), *Psycho II* (1983). Academy Award nomination: *Tobruk* (1967). Academy Awards: *Earthquake* (1974, with a total of 44 matte shots) and *The Hindenburg* (1975). With Mel Brooks he did *High Anxiety* (1977, in which he had a bit part as Madeline Kahn's father) and *History of the World, Part 1* (1981). Other credits: *The Sting II* (1983), *Greystoke: The Legend of Tarzan, Lord of the Apes* (1983–84), *The Lonely Guy* (1984), *Dune* (1984), *Clue* (1985), *Red Sonja* (1985), *Dragnet* (1986), *Critical Condition* (1987), *Spaceballs* (1987, Mel Brooks), *Funny Farm* (1988), *Coming to America* (1988), *Cry Freedom* (1989), *Millennium* (1989), *Gremlins 2: The New Batch* (1990), *Chaplin* (1992). Additional TV work: *Star Trek* (1966 sci-fi series), *Gunsmoke* (western series), *The Birdmen* (1971), *Vanished* (1971), *Female Artillery* (1972), *Short Walk to Daylight* (1972), *Hec Ramsey* (1972), *The Questor Tapes* (1974), *Killdozer* (1974), *The Log of the Black Pearl* (1975), *Masada, A.D.* (1985, mini-series). "It was actually on-the-job training," Whitlock said. "We are involved in painting realism on film, therefore, I did not find it unusual to make clouds move, have smoke float up into the air, have waves in water and see flames in a fire flicker." Whitlock was asked by John Landis if he would like to play an English butler in *Beverly Hills Cop III* (1994), "which was amusing and flattering. Very brief and only two spoken words!" Unfortunately, the scene landed on the cutting room floor. At the invitation of producer Dieter Geissler and Rolf Giesen, Whitlock came to Germany to supervise matte shots for *Die unendliche Geschichte II* (*The Neverending Story II*, 1989–90), one of his last jobs. He was also in the Austrian documentary *Der*

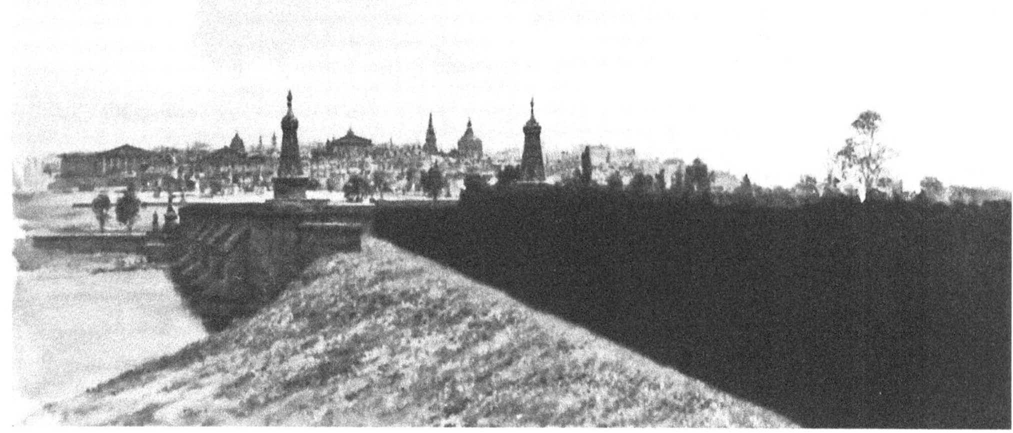

From the movie *History of the World Part I*, a matte painting of Paris by Albert Whitlock (courtesy Deutsche Kinemathek Berlin).

Zauberer von Hollywood (1989). His pet project, *The Lost World* (in the early stages, Jim Danforth was involved too), which he was going to produce, never materialized. Whitlock often mentioned the original *King Kong* and wanted to enhance the aesthetics of his *Lost World* with lots of painted mattes. In doing the preproduction work, he was clearly influenced by the work of German-born Albert Bierstadt (1830–1902), one of the most industrious American artists of the 19th century. For some of the bigger scenes Whitlock envisioned locations in New Zealand (eventually used by Peter Jackson for his 2005 *King Kong* remake). A victim of Parkinson's disease, Whitlock died in Santa Barbara. One of his sons, Mark, also worked as a matte artist. The other was a paramedic with the Los Angeles Fire Department.

Philip H. [Phil] Whitman
(c. 1893–1935)

American Effects Cinematographer

Born New York. Handled glass shots, hanging miniatures and fever dream sequence) in Lon Chaney's *The Hunchback of Notre Dame* (1922–23) and the flying horse effects in Douglas Fairbanks' *The Thief of Bagdad* (1923–24). In 1926 he collaborated with American director Rex Ingram in a Nice studio on the submarine film *Mare Nostrum*. Eventually Whitman switched to directing and screenwriting.

Nicolas [Nicholas Wilke] Wilcké
Russian Art Director and Miniature Expert

Went from Russia to Berlin, where he designed impressive Arabian Nights hanging miniatures for *Geheimnisse des Orients* (1927). Then he went to Paris where he did miniatures for Abel Gance's *Napoléon* (1927) and later introduced young Eugéne Lourié to this technique. Lourié wanted to bring Wilcke back for *Gorgo* (1959) but, alas, nothing came out of it. Supervised miniature work for *Untel Père et Fils* (1943), *Corridor of Mirrors* (1948), *L'auberge Rouge* (1951), *Le Plaisir* (1952), *Le Rouge est mis* (1952), *Lucrèce Borgia* (1953, panning from huge miniature of 16th century Rome to live-action set and back), *Madame du Barry* (1954), *Les Evadés* (1955), *The Ambassador's Daughter* (1956).

Frank D. Williams (1893–1961)
American Cinematographer and Traveling Matte Expert

Born in Nashville, Missouri, Williams was a photographer at Mack Sennett's Keytone and was involved in Charles Chaplin's early films: *Making a Living* (1914), *Kid Auto Races at Venice* (1914, also appearing as the cameraman), *The Rounders* (1914), *His Prehistoric Past* (1914) and especially *Tillie's Punctured Romance* (1914). In 1916, Chaplin brought him over to Lone Star

Studios for some Mutual shorts as well: *The Floorwalker, The Fireman, The Vagabond*. From 1916 to 1918, Williams developed a traveling matte process named after him. A patent was granted in 1923 (which was in court for some time and expired in 1940). In his own studio, Williams did composite shots for *The Lost World* (1924–25), *Ben-Hur: A Tale of the Christ* (1925), *Sunrise* (1926), Universal pictures like *The Invisible Man* (1933) and *The Invisible Ray* (1936), and RKO's *King Kong* (1932–33), depicting Kong breaking through the big gate and creating havoc in the native village. *Kong* used the Williams Double-Matting Process, invented by cameraman Joseph B. Walker and sold to Williams' laboratory, which adapted a blue backing as an aid to producing a matte (although not on color film stock).

William N. [Billy] Williams
(?–1976)
American Cinematographer

For 12 years he photographed some 60 comedies for Mack Sennett. 1929–31: with Multicolor Films, Inc., then competing with Technicolor. For some time he worked with Fred W. Jackman at Warner Bros.-First National. Independent effects photography: *Deluge* (1933). Then he joined the process department at RKO as head process cameraman. Second unit photography: *Around the World in 80 Days* (1956).

Paul Wilson
British Effects and Miniature Cinematographer

Favorite cameraman of Derek Meddings: *Superman* (1977–78), *The Dark Crystal* (1983), *Krull* (1983), *Supergirl* (1984), *Santa Clause— The Movie* (1984–85), *High Spirits* (1988). Did many James Bond films. Meddings: "...Wilson is very skilled in lighting miniatures to make them look convincing. He has to copy in miniature exactly the same lighting conditions as existed on the full sized set. For example, exterior shots must never have shadows crossing over each other, and of course the shadows must fall in exactly the same place" (*The BKSTS Journal*, October 1984). Wilson started in the film industry in 1942 at Gaumont-British studios as trainee and clapper boy in the camera department. Joined the Royal Navy in 1943 and was given extensive photographic training. When Gaumont closed in 1949, he became a freelance camera assistant on such films as *Sound Barrier* (*Breaking the Sound Barrier*, 1952) and John Huston's *Moby Dick* (1956). In 1958 he started operating. He became a lighting cameraman in 1973 with second units.

Rex Wimpy (1899–1972)
American Effects and Second Unit Cinematographer

At Warner Bros.-First National: *42nd Street* (1932–33), *Mystery of the Wax Museum* (1933), *Dodge City* (1939), *Dive Bomber* (1941), *Captains of the Clouds* (1942), *Air Force* (1943), *To Have and Have Not* (1944), *Passage to Marseille* (1944), *The Man Who Cheated Himself* (1950). Effects photography: *Spellbound* (1945), *Darling Lili* (1970). Second unit: Hitchcock's *Psycho* (1959–60), *The Misfits* (1961).

Stan Winston (1946–2008)
American Special Makeup/Prosthetics and Mechanical Effects Expert

At the University of Virginia, Winston studied painting and sculpture. In 1968, he moved to Hollywood to become an actor. Apprentice in the makeup department of Disney Studios. In 1972 he landed a job making creatures for the TV movie *Gargoyles* for which he won an Emmy. Second Emmy for 1974 TV movie *The Autobiography of Miss Jane Pittman* making actress Cicely Tyson look 110 years old. 1981 Academy Award nomination for *Heartbeeps*. Received a total of four Academy Awards. Became involved in puppet work and props on *The Terminator* (1984), *Aliens* (1986) for which he did the alien queen monster, *Terminator 2: Judgment Day* (1990–91) and the full-size dinosaurs of Steven Spielberg's *Jurassic Park* (1992–93). Together with Scott Ross, once with ILM, and director James Cameron, he founded the CGI company Digital Domain in order to pay tribute to the age of the computer. In his own Stan Winston Studios in Van Nuys, he employs more than 100 artists and technicians: *Starman* (1984), *Invaders from Mars* (1986), *Predator* (1987), *Batman Returns* (1992), *Small Soldiers* (1998), *End of Days* (1999).

Louis J. Witte

American Mechanical Effects Expert

Lifelong association with William Fox Studios and 20th Century–Fox: *What Price Glory?* (1925), *Chandu the Magician* (1932), *Dante's Inferno* (1935), *In Old Chicago* (1937), *The Rains Came* (1939), *A Yank in the R.A.F.* (1941), *The Song of Bernadette* (1943). Scientific or Technical Award, Class II (shared with Nick Kalten) in 1948 for a process of preserving and flame-proofing foliage.

Douglas Woolsey

British Miniature Expert

Did ship models and model aircraft for films like *Convoy* (1940), *One of Our Aircraft Is Missing* (1942), *In Which We Serve* (1942). Joined the Rank Organization: *Caesar and Cleopatra* (1945), *A Matter of Life and Death* (1946), *Great Expectations* (1946).

Egil S. Woxholt

British Underwater and Second Unit Cinematographer

Involved in *Mysterious Island* (1960–61), *The Heroes of Telemark* (1965), *Clash of the Titans* (1979–80) and *Das Boot* (U.S.: *The Boat*, 1980–81).

Dewey Wrigley (1898–1950)

American Second Unit and Plate Cinematographer

Organized a trick department at Pathe Studio, then joined Paramount and usually photographed process plates for Farciot Edouart's transparency department and location work, such as the Holy Land footage for *Samson and Delilah* (1949). Other work for Cecil B. DeMille: *The Crusades* (1935), *The Plainsman* (1936) and *Union Pacific* (1939). In a tank at Malibu Beach he did scenes with a 20-foot mechanical squid for DeMille's *Reap the Wild Wind* (1942); a tentacle destroying a ladder in a sunken ship done by

"back-cranking" (wrapping the tentacle around the ladder, pulling it away and screening the scene in reverse). Shot process plates for Billy Wilder's *A Foreign Affair* (1948) in the destroyed city of Berlin. His son, Dewey Wrigley, Jr., was with Paul K. Lerpae in Paramount's optical department.

Nobuyuki Yasumaru

Japanese Sculptor and Model Maker

Coming from the mountainous Toyama area, he was interested in wood carving. Studied sculpture at the Musashino Art School. Started at Toho in the Plaster Section building miniatures when *Mosura* (U.S.: *Mothra*, 1960) was underway. Other credits: *Kingukongu tai Gojira* (U.S.: *King Kong vs. Godzilla*, 1962), *Kaitei gunkan* (U.S.: *Atragon*, 1963), *Furankenshutain tai chitei kaiju Baragon* (U.S.: *Frankenstein Conquers the World*, 1965). When a monster suit (the allosaurus-like Gorosaurus) they had ordered for *Kingukongu no gyakushu* (U.S.: *King Kong Escapes*, 1967) didn't prove satisfactory, Yasumaru volunteered (to Eiji Tsuburaya's delight) and from then on he did suits and monsters for other Toho releases: *Gojira tai Hedora* (*Godzilla vs. the Smog Monster*, 1971), *Chikyu kogeki meirei: Gojira tai Gaigan* (*Godzilla on Monster Island*, 1972), *Gojira* (*Godzilla 1985*, 1984), *Gojira tai Biorante* (*Godzilla Vs. Biollante*, 1989).

Hoyt H. Yeatman, Jr.

American Visual Effects Supervisor

Was on Steven Spielberg's *Close Encounters of the Third Kind* (1975–77), Coppola's *One from the Heart* (1982), David Cronenberg's *The Fly* (1987) and also *The Blob* (1988). Co-founded Dream Quest Images: *E.T.: The Extra-Terrestrial* (1981–82, additional effects), *Crimson Tide* (1995), *The Abyss* (1989), *Armageddon* (1998), *Mighty Joe Young* (1998), *Mission to Mars* (2000).

Frank H. Young

American Effects Cinematographer and Inventor

After World War I he was with Hal Roach. In 1927, with his brother Elmer Young, a pioneering animator, he opened Kinex Studio and produced 48 puppet films. For Universal he photographed the first miniature in Technicolor, the New York City of *Broadway* (1930), and stayed at that studio for a year and a half. Later returned to Roach to install an optical printer and background projector. Involved in Roach's production of *One Million B.C.* (1939–40).

Jack H. Young (1910–1992)

American Makeup Artist

For many years he was a member of the MGM makeup department. Made up Margaret Hamilton for her role as the Witch in *The Wizard of Oz* (1939). Later freelanced on independent productions. For producer-director Bert I. Gordon, he transformed Dean Parkin into the title characters in *The Cyclops* (1957) and *War of the Colossal Beast* (1958). Did several horror films: *Skullduggery* (1970), *Murders in the Rue Morgue* (1971), *Ben* (1972), *Terror in the Wax Museum* (1973), *The Reincarnation of Peter Proud* (1975), *The Evil* (1978, prosthetics makeup artist), *The Brood* (1979), *Salem's Lot* (1979). Also involved in the production of *Apocalypse Now* (1979).

Noriaki Yuasa (1933–2004)

Japanese Director

The son of a stage actor, he began as a child actor himself. In 1955, after graduation, he joined Daiei Studios as assistant director. Directed the early entries of the Gamera series: *Daikaiju Gamera* (U.S.: *Gammera the Invincible*, 1965), *Daikaiju kuchesen Gamera tai Gaosu* (U.S.: *The Return of the Giant Monsters*, 1967), *Gamera tai uchu kaiju Bairasu* (U.S.: *Destroy All Planets*, 1968), *Gamera tai daikaiju Giron* (U.S.: *Attack of the Monsters*, 1969), *Gamera tai maju Jaiga* (U.S.: *Gamera vs. Monster X*, 1970), *Gamera tai shinkai Jigura* (*Gamera vs. Zigra*, 1971), and *Uchu kaiju Gamera* (*Super Monster*, 1980, recycling old footage in a new but very cheap frame). Also directed the effects sequences for *Daikaiju ketto Gamera tai Barugon* (U.S.: *War of the Monsters*, 1966). Later mainly worked in television. Died of a stroke.

Matthew J. [Matt] Yuricich

American Matte Artist

Born in Lorain, Ohio. Early on he loved to draw and to paint, and after the service he wanted to pursue a fine arts career. Attended Miami University of Ohio, then did postgraduate work at the University of California. In 1950, rather accidentally, he became an assistant matte artist at 20th Century–Fox. *The Day the Earth Stood Still* (1951), *The Robe* (1953), *Prince Valiant* (1954). In 1954 he went to MGM: *Forbidden Planet* (1956), *Raintree County* (1957), *Ben-Hur* (1959), *The World, the Flesh and the Devil* (1959), *North by Northwest* (1959), *Atlantis, the Lost Continent* (1960–61), *Mutiny on the Bounty* (1962), *Ice Station Zebra* (1968), *Point Blank* (1968), *Soylent Green* (1973), *Logan's Run* (1976). Did the Statue of Liberty for Fox's *Planet of the Apes* (1967–68). Independent work: *Young Frankenstein* (1974). On the recommendation of his brother Richard Yuricich, he was hired by Douglas Trumbull and Richard Edlund et al. for *Close Encounters of the Third Kind* (1975–77), *Damnation Alley* (1977), *The Deer Hunter* (1978), *The China Syndrome* (1979), *Star Trek: The Motion Picture* (1978–79), *1941* (1979), *The Last Chase* (1981), *Blade Runner* (1982), *Yes, Giorgio* (1982), *My Favorite Year* (1982), *Strange Brew* (1983), *Brainstorm* (1983), *Ghost Busters* (1984), *2010: Odyssey 2* (1984), *Fright Night* (1985), *Poltergeist II: The Other Side* (1986), *The Boy Who Could Fly* (1986), *Solarbabies* (1986), *Masters of the Universe* (1987), *Die Hard* (1988), *Field of Dreams* (1989), *Dances with Wolves* (1990), *Harley Davidson and the Marlboro Man* (1991). TV: *V* (1983).

Richard Yuricich

American Visual Effects Cinematographer

Younger brother of matte artist Matthew Yuricich. Came to England for the finishing touches of *2001: A Space Odyssey* (1968). With Douglas Trumbull on *Close Encounters of the Third Kind* (1975–77), *Star Trek: The Motion Picture* (1978–79), *Blade Runner* (1982), *Brainstorm* (1983). Did *Dark Territory: Under Siege II* (38 minutes of digital rear projection), *Mission: Impossible* (1996), *Event Horizon* (1997), *Mission Impossible II* (2000).

Lee Zavitz

*American Mechanical Effects and
    Explosives Expert*

Assisted Louis Witte on *What Price Glory?* and *Seas Beneath*. Helped to create effects for *The Hurricane* in 1937. Burned Atlanta in *Gone with the Wind* (1939). Other credits: *Rebecca* (1940), *Foreign Correspondent* (1940), *Captain Kidd* (1945), *The Diary of a Chambermaid* (1946), *Abbott and Costello Meet Captain Kidd* (1952), *Apache* (1954), *The Snow Creature* (1954, directed by W. Lee Wilder, Billy's brother), *Around the World in 80 Days* (1956), *From the Earth to the Moon* (1958), *On the Beach* (1959), *The Alamo* (1960), *Captain Sindbad* (1962–63), *Sodom e Gomorra* (*Sodom and Gomorrha*, 1962–63), *The Train* (1965), *Viva Maria!* (1965), *Castle Keep* (1969), *La Bataille de San Sebastian* (1968). Academy Award for *Destination Moon* (1949–50).

Harry Alvin Zech (18??–1944)

*American Effects and Process
    Cinematographer*

In 1929 and '30 he was on *Alibi, Border Romance, Peacock Alley, Under Montana Skies, Charley's Aunt* and *Hell's Angels*. Went with Ned Mann to Britain for *Things to Come* (1934–36). Returned to United States and Warner Bros.

Josef Zeman

Czech Puppet Animator

Joined his brother Karel Zeman on several of his live-action feature films such as *Cesta do praveku* (U.S.: *Journey to the Beginning of Time*, 1954) and *Vynalez zkázy* (U.S.: *The Fabulous World of Jules Verne*, 1958).

Karel Zeman (1910–1989)

Czech Director and Puppet Animator

An animator with Hermina Tyrlova in Zlin. Later competed with Tyrlova and turned out his own *Pan Prokouk* series. Directed well-known Jules Verne and fantasy combinations of live-action, effects and animation. In his *Cesta do praveku* (U.S.: *Journey to the Beginning of Time*, 1954), four young boys entered the age of dinosaurs (stop-motion), were attacked by pterodactyls and witnessed a fight between a Tyrannosaurus and a Stegosaurus. *Vynalez zkázy* (U.S.: *The Fabulous World of Jules Verne*, 1958) depicted an Invention of Destruction. *Baron Prasil* (*Baron Munchausen*, 1961) sent the baron up on a cannonball to the moon. *Na Komete* (*On the Comet*, 1970) was another Jules Verne tale. Later Zeman returned to inexpensive cut-out animation.

Edmund Ziehfuss

German Model Maker

Was in charge of miniature construction for Fritz Lang's *Metropolis* (1925–27). From behind-the-scenes stills found in the collection of the late art director Fritz Maurischat, we know that Ziehfuss remained with the Schüfftan crew and was in charge of models and miniatures for films like *Die Brüder Schellenberg* (1926).

Stuart Ziff

American Effects Technician

In 1981 he shared a Technical Achievement Award with Dennis Muren for the development of a Motion Picture Figure Mover for stop-motion photography. This referred to the so-called Go-Motion Technique to provide for a greater fluency in stop-motion animation in *Dragonslayer* (1982). Worked on *The China Syndrome* (1979).

The Filmography

1913

Der Student von Prag Romantisches Drama in vier Akten. Deutsche Bioscop, Germany. Filmed at Bioscop Studios Neubabelsberg

Director: Stellan Rye. *Cinematographer and Visual Effects:* Guido Seeber.

Split screen shots depict actor Paul Wegener as "Doppelgänger" killing his own shadow image in a duel. Directed by Danish filmmaker Stellan Rye and written by the infamous Hanns Heinz Ewers, the story had Wegener as a poor student, Balduin, who sells his mirror reflection to a devilish sorcerer in exchange for love and wealth — and with this unwise act he also relinquishes his soul. The mirror image, called forth from the glass, leads a demonic life of its own that eventually results in tragic consequences. When Balduin finally tries to destroy his troublesome double, the gunshot fired at the apparition results only in his own death.

1914

Cabiria Visione Storica del Terzo Secolo A.C. Itala Film, Italy.

Director: Giovanni Pastrone. *Camera Effects — Visual Effects Creator:* Segundo de Chomón.

This monumental film version of the Emilio Salgari novel *Carthago in Flames* includes trick shots of an erupting Vesuve and the siege of Carthago (including early glass shots).

1923

The Ten Commandments Famous Players-Lasky/Paramount, U.S.A.

Director: Cecil B. DeMille. *Photographic Effects — Photographic Effects Supervisor:* Roy J. Pomeroy. *Assistant:* Fred Moran. *Traveling Matte Process:* Frank D. Williams.

The parting of the Red Sea: "In the film the divided sea appears to resemble two lumps of quivering jelly covered with running water" (John Brosnan, *Movie Magic*, p. 31). "The Red Sea Sequence offered a challenge to Pomeroy, who was noted for his clever miniature work. He used the Williams Traveling Matte Process to combine footage of fleeing Israelites shot at Guadalupe Sand Dunes with reverse-printed slow-motion footage of a flood of water cascading over gelatin mounds that represented the walls of the Red Sea" (Robert S. Birchard, *American Cinematographer*, October 1992).

1923–24

The Thief of Bagdad Douglas Fairbanks (for United Artists release), U.S.A.

Director: Raoul Walsh. *Art Department — Production Designer:* William Cameron Menzies. *Assistants:* Anton Grot, Theodore H. Lydecker. *Photographic Effects — Effects Cameraman:* Philip H. (Phil) Whitman. *Miniatures — Hanging Miniatures:* Ned H. Mann. *Mechanical Effects — Mechanical Effects Director:* Hampton Del Ruth. *Special Effects:* Coy Watson, Sr.

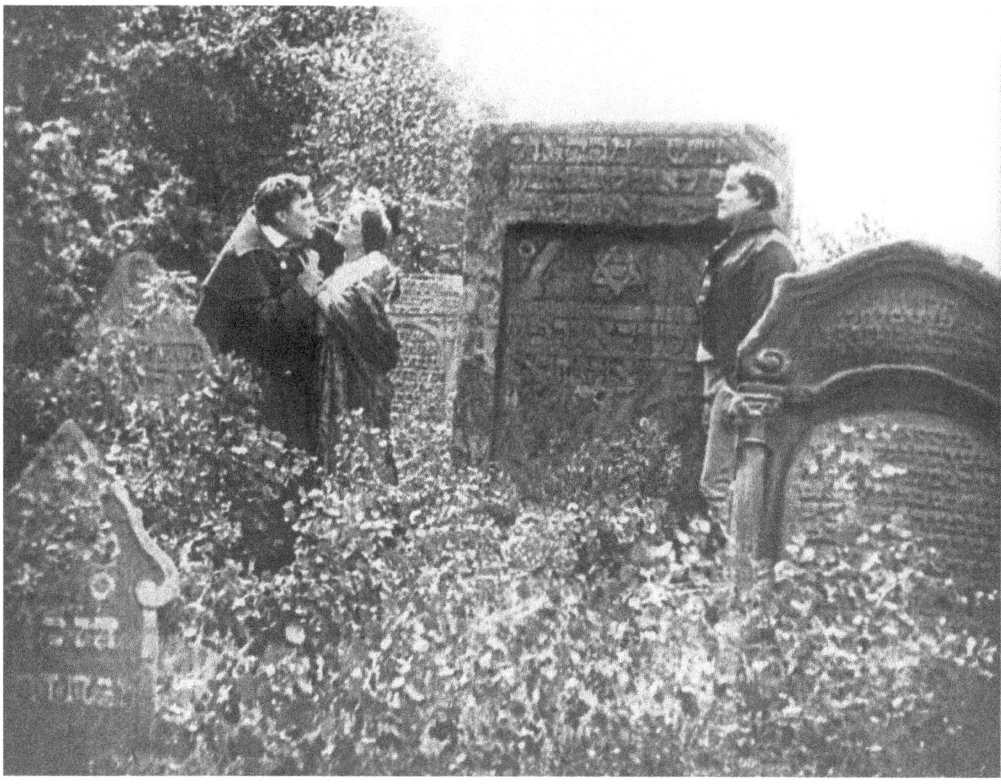

Paul Wegener and his Doppelgänger: *The Student of Prague*, photographed in 1913 by German effects pioneer Guido Seeber (courtesy Deutsche Kinemathek Berlin).

The marvels of the Arabian Nights. Douglas Fairbanks on both flying horse and flying carpet (in close-up supported by overhead wires and flown around by a crane, in long shots as double exposure), fighting a dragon and a deep sea spider, calling for a magic army out of wonderful seeds obtained in the Citadel of the Moon to protect the monumental gates and towers of Bagdad (which are hanging miniatures) from an approaching Mongolian enemy. "There were some kinky problems facing the technical director when the plans to film this fantasy were first unveiled in the Fairbanks studio.... The Flying Horse upon which the Thief rides to the Citadel of the Moon is mystifying, to say the least, until the simplicity with which the scene was made, is explained. The horse and rider were taken against a black background and then the film was rewound and clouds painted on a moving canvas were taken. When developed, a composite view resulted.... There is a terrible monster made by harnessing horns to a

crocodile ... and taking an exposure at six feet. 'Doug' is then taken on the same film at twenty feet. The distances gives the monstrous size" (From the pages of *Science and Invention* for May 1924). There is some unverified rumor (inspired by director Fritz Lang) that Fairbanks went so far as to acquire the American distribution rights to a recent German Lang film, *Der müde Tod* (*Destiny*, 1920–21), just to copy some of the photographic effects including a sequence with a flying carpet. In an interview, director Raoul Walsh told Peter Bogdanovich that they had special effects personnel trained at Mack Sennett's (supervisor Hampton Del Ruth, brother of Roy Del Ruth, had worked with Sennett in various capacities since the days of *Tillie's Punctured Romance* in 1914). In his memoirs *Each Man in His Time: The Life Story of a Director* (New York: Farrar, Straus and Giroux, 1974), Walsh wrote about the flying carpet:

We had shot it all except the end scenes — the battle for the palace, and the ousting of the rival princess while the thief and the princess made their getaway. *Arabian Nights* readers will remember that the escape called for a magic carpet, which could fly through the air as its owner desired.... I found the answer while watching a construction job at the corner of Highland and Hollywood Boulevard. The steelworkers were topping out, and one of them was riding a load of girders up from the ground level, hoisted by a large crane. That gave me the clue. If he could ride the steel, then the thief and the princess could ride the flying carpet. I would stretch it over a framework of supporting cables and find some way to avoid showing the support.... Getting hold of a suitable crane was not difficult. The question was where to put it. The story had them floating away through a palace window and out over the rooftops of Bagdad. Short of inducing hypnotic levitation, I did not know how I was going to get them off the chamber floor. I finally solved that problem by installing an overhead pulley and a hand winch (both off camera) and using a burly extra to wind the crank. The result was better than I had expected. The carpet had a steel frame and steel cross-strapping underneath. When the drum winch began to turn, the whole thing, with Fairbanks and Miss Johnston sitting cross-legged on it, rose before the eyes of the suitably astonished spectators and thin wires pulled it toward the window.... I cut the action when the contraption reached the open window and the cameras picked it up again after we connected the carpet to the crane outside the palace. The crane I settled for had an eighty-foot boom, long enough to swing the eloping lovers over the city.

1924–25

The Lost World First National in association with Watterson R. Rothacker, U.S.A.

Director: Harry O. Hoyt. *Stop-Motion — Stop-Motion Animation, Effects and Research:* Willis H. O'Brien. *Stop-Motion Models:* Marcel Delgado. *Additional Stop-Motion Animation:* Joseph Leeland Roop. *Process Operator:* Jim Pratt. *Miniature Photography and Glass Art Unit — Miniature Supervisor and Glass Shots:* Ralph Ham-

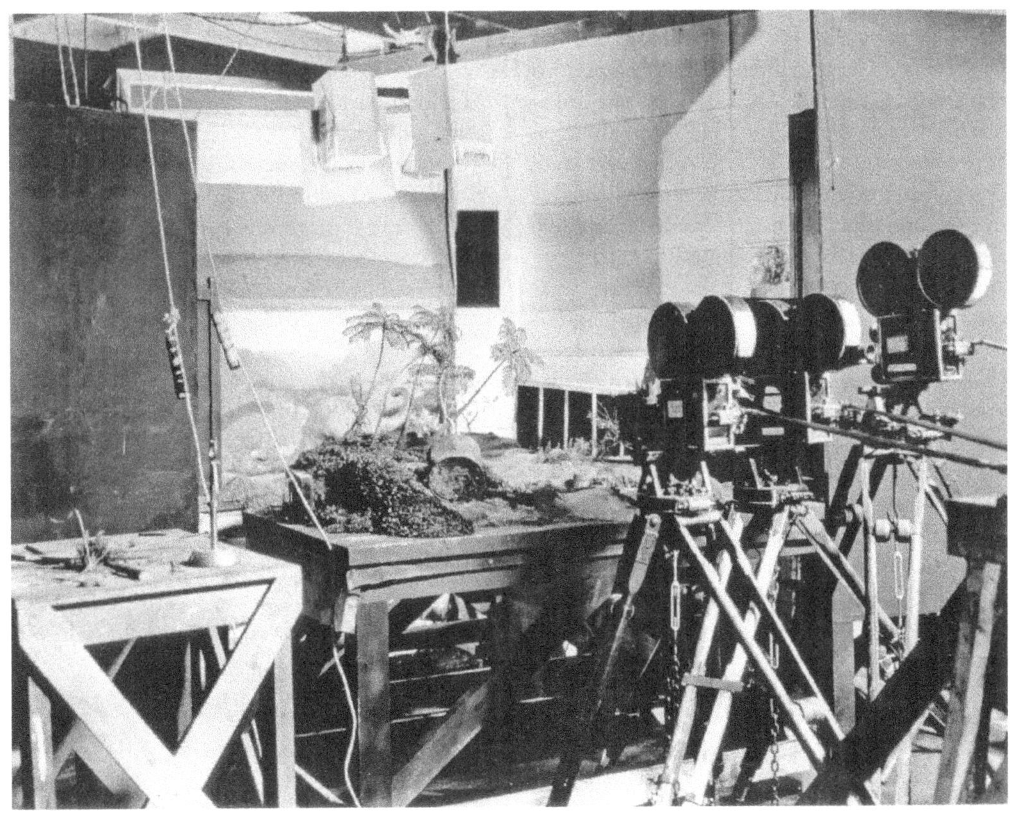

A miniature set-up for the original *The Lost World* (courtesy Deutsche Kinemathek Berlin).

meras. *Effects Photography, Hammeras Unit:* Edwin Hammeras. *Process Equipment, Hammeras Unit:* George J. Teague. *Member of Miniature Crew:* Charles Baker. *Photographic Effects Unit— Photographic Effects and Split Screen Supervisor:* Fred W. Jackman. *Effects Photography, Jackman Unit:* Hans F. Koenekamp, Vernon L. Walker. *Assistant Cameraman:* Bert Willis. *Williams Process Shots:* Frank D. Williams.

Almost 50 foam rubber dinosaurs with jointed armatures were prepared to populate prehistoric dioramas representing an Amazonian plateau. One brontosaurus brought to London by Professor Challenger (Wallace Beery) created some havoc before it escaped in the Thames and reached the open sea. Outtakes prove that O'Brien worked with several animators and didn't do stop-motion animation all by himself. One animator was a sculptor named J.L. Roop, born in 1869 in Louisville, Kentucky, who passed away in 1932. Roop also did a spoof on *The Lost World* titled *The Savage* (1926) starring an affable dinosaur which pursues the hero back to New York. During *Lost World* production, famous visitors to the set included Charles Chaplin and German director Fritz Lang on his first trip to the United States: "They saw brontosauri which were a foot high and towered above miniature forests. Twelve cameras were employed in taking one frame at a time of this picture, and often the director only made a few feet a week, each slightest movement of the animal miniatures having to receive the most careful technical attention. Mr. Lang referred to this production as a technical masterpiece" (*New York Times*). "This photoplay, which was presented last night at the Astor Theatre before a gathering in which there were a number of the heads of the film industry and screen celebrities, is a unique production which will create a lot of talk, as some of the scenes are as awesome as anything that has ever been shown in shadow form" (*New York Times*, February 9, 1925).

1924–25

Ben-Hur MGM, U.S.A./Italy.
Director: Fred Niblo. *Glass Art— Glass Paintings:* Ferdinand Pinney Earle. *Photography — Second Unit Cinematography:* Paul E. Eagler. *Art Department— Assistant Art Director and Hanging Miniature Supervisor:* A. Arnold Gillespie. *Travelling Mattes—Williams Process Shots:* Frank D. Williams.

Filming of this epic started in Rome and wrapped in Culver City. Long shots of the Circus Maximus where the chariot race takes place were created by use of a hanging miniature populated with ten thousand mechanically moved and raised dolls. The collapsing senate building crushing people was created by use of the Williams process.

1924–25

Wunder der Schöpfung Kultur-Abteilung der Ufa and Colonna-Film G.m.b.H., Germany.
Director: Hanns Walter Kornblum. *Trick Photography and Animation — Staff:* Hermann Boehlen, Otto von Bothmer, Wera Cleve, Bodo Kuntze, E. M. Schumacher. *Art Department— Art Directors:* Gustav Henning, Hans Minzloff, Walter Reimann, Carl Stahl-Urach.

Extraordinary feature-length educational about the history of astronomy which leads to a fictitious space trip to the Moon and Beyond (at a time when Pluto yet wasn't even known). At the end there is some visual speculation about Earth and Mankind being destroyed by asteroids. Some footage was incorporated into the American *Our Heavenly Bodies*. A print was rediscovered by Filmmuseum Munich in Finland.

1925

Maciste all'inferno Olympia, Italy.
Director: Guido Brignone. *Visual Effects:* Segundo de Chomón.

Muscleman Bartholomeo Pagano, a former laborer working in the harbors, famous for his part as Maciste in *Cabiria*, returns to fight the devils and demons of an underworld right out of *Dante's Inferno*.

1925–27

Metropolis Erich Pommer/Universum Film A.G. (Ufa), Germany. Filmed at Ufa Studios

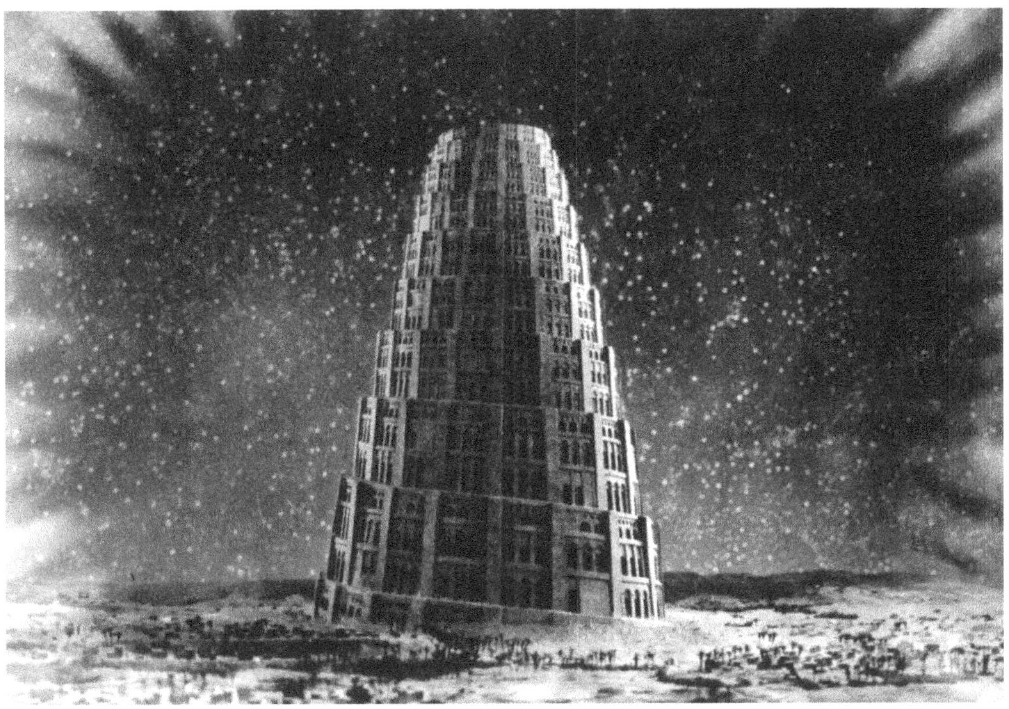

A miniature of the Tower of Babel, designed by Erich Kettelhut and photographed by Günther Rittau for *Metropolis* (1925–27) (courtesy Deutsche Kinemathek Berlin).

Neubabelsberg and Filmwerke Staaken (a former Zeppelin hangar)

Director: Fritz Lang. *Photographic Effects — Photographic Effects and Second Camera:* Günther Rittau. *Assistant Operator:* Hugo O. Schulze. *Additional Effects Photography:* Konstantin Irmen-Tschet. *Art Effects — Painting Technician and Effects Art Director:* Erich Kettelhut. *Schüfftan Miniature Unit — Schüfftan Process Supervisor:* Eugen Schüfftan. *Schüfftan Photography:* Helmar Lerski, Ernst Kunstmann, Heinrich Weidemann. *Miniature Foreman:* Edmund Ziehfuss. *Model maker:* Willy Muller.

In a city of the future (the film is set in the year 2000), a mad scientist clones a robot and makes it a female seducer. Working with art directors Otto Hunte, Erich Kettelhut and Karl Vollbrecht, director Fritz Lang ordered a huge miniature of the city and the central New Tower of Babel, complete with tiny airplanes and ground vehicles which would be painstakingly animated by stop-motion technicians. "From our tests," Kettelhut recalled, "we knew that the aeroplanes had to be animated .6 inch after a single frame of film was exposed, the high-speed

rail cars .4 inch, the automobiles about .3 inch and the pedestrians just minimally to get fluid movement in a believable tempo. An animation team was assembled by Edmund Ziehfuss, the model maker. Each man was assigned a specific task. A blue light signaled the move. Cars, trains and pedestrians had to be animated conscientiously and for exactly the required distance. The aeroplanes were animated with the aid of wires. The work had to be done sometimes in uncomfortable positions since frontages and railway bridges and lamp sockets hindered our efforts considerably. When everybody had done his requested animation, the gaffer switched on full shooting light and another frame of film was exposed."

For certain scenes featuring the New Tower of Babel, oil paintings were prepared by Kettelhut. Sweeping searchlight beams were laboriously animated using glycerine paint on a large pane of glass positioned in front of the tower. Between each single-frame exposure, the glass was wiped clean and the beam repainted in its next sequential position.

The most challenging task, however, was the

transformation of the heroine Maria (Brigitte Helm) into an automaton. When Maria's flesh is transferred onto the metallic body by mad scientist Rotwang (Rudolf Klein-Rogge), the automaton is encircled by glittering concentric light rings and electric flashes. Lap-dissolves made it possible to change the robot's face into Maria's. The rings and flashes were executed during postproduction in a blackened barrack on Ufa's backlot in Neubabelsberg. In front of a rigidly mounted Mitchell camera, a plywood silhouette of the robot — garbed in black velvet for matte purposes — was carefully positioned. Just over the silhouette, a simple lift was erected to maneuver two parallel rings attached to three fine wires. The rings themselves were made of a special grease-proof paper that dispersed light. To further diffuse the imagery, a sheet of glass smeared with thin layers of grease was placed in front of the camera. After running some test footage, each ring was double-exposed several times onto the original negative. Also some electrical flashes were added. (According to another source, quoted by Patrick McGilligan in his otherwise very readable and highly recommendable book *Fritz Lang: The Nature of the Beast*, "Rittau achieved this effect by photographing a small, rapidly whirling silver ball against a backdrop of black velvet. The impression of expanding and contracting rings, ascending and descending, was obtained by raising and lowering the camera on this single silver ball.")

Metropolis was a technical marvel and the culmination of German effects cinematography of the day. Yet, oddly enough, no one thought of assembling all the talented people, who had created those effects, into one cohesive trick department at Ufa studios as they would have done in the United States. After the picture was completed, the crew dispersed, except for the Schüfftan unit. *Metropolis*, rumored to have cost more than five million marks to produce, was a financial failure for Ufa. After its premiere, the disgruntled studio (and later its American distributor Paramount) shortened (butchered!) the picture until it was incomprehensible, and despite subsequent efforts to salvage the excised footage, some of it is lost forever.

1926–29

The Mysterious Island   MGM, U.S.A.

Director: Lucien Hubbard. *Additional Directors:* Maurice Tourneur, Benjamin Christensen. *Miniatures — Technical Effects Director:* James Basevi. *Composite Photography — Camera Effects:* Louis H. Tolhurst, Irving G. Ries. *Special Service — Underwater Photography:* James Ernest Williamson.

Ninety percent Technicolor (two-color), with hastily added sound effects, starring Lionel Barrymore as Jules Verne's Count Dakkar, complete

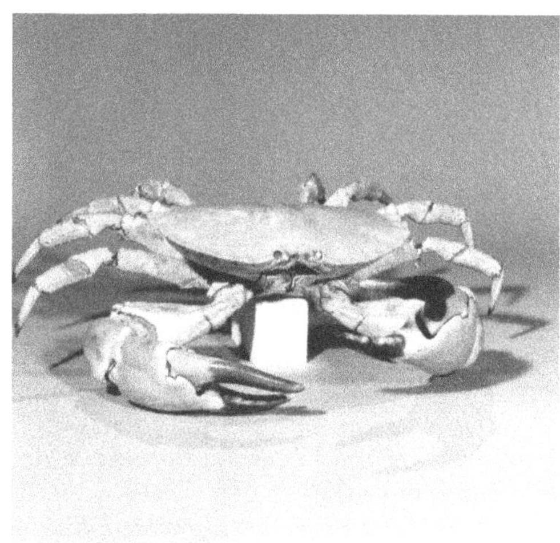

The giant crab from *Mysterious Island* (1961).

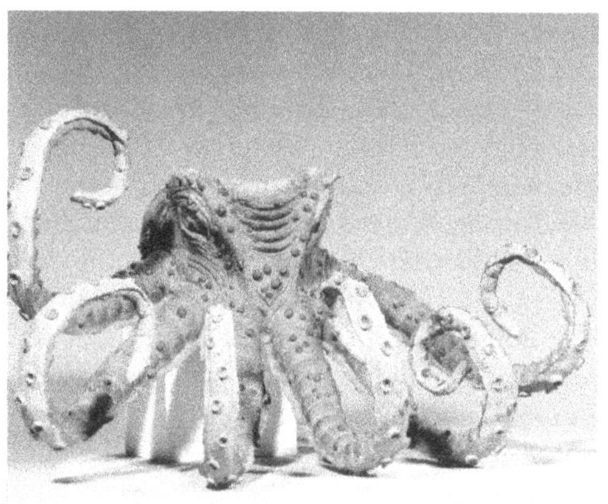

The giant mollusk (shell missing) from *Mysterious Island* (1961) (both courtesy Ray and Diana Harryhausen Collection as displayed by Deutsche Kinemathek Berlin).

with *Nautilus,* a giant sea serpent and an enormous octopus released by the dwarf-like inhabitants of an underwater city. According to the A. W. Strickland-Forrest J Ackerman book *A Reference Guide to American Science Fiction Films,* the film "received a great deal of notoriety and public acclaim for an exquisite feature. It is unfortunate that the picture took so long to make that it was plagued with problems even after completing the script and getting the final okay in mid–1926. Enormous obstacles still lay in the way of its completion. The film crew's journey from California to Florida was a fatiguing ordeal with many becoming ill along the way. Their final leg of the trip led them to the Bahamas to Williamson's underwater film laboratory. As fate would have it, within weeks after the crew's arrival a hurricane (September, 1926) descended upon the small island chain, totally destroying their boats and much of their precious film equipment. All of this required nearly ten months to eventually overcome and finally begin filming the epic. Within two months of the first shooting, one of the executives decided he would like to see some drastic changes in some of the film's structure. Obviously this required a great deal of additional shooting and several more rewrites, all totally unexpected."

1928–29

Frau im Mond   [U.S.: *By Rocket to the Moon*] Fritz Lang Film/Universum Film A.G. (Ufa), Germany. Filmed at Ufa Studios Neubabelsberg

Director: Fritz Lang. *Photographic Effects— Camera Effects:* Oskar Fischinger. *Miniature Unit— Miniature Photography:* Konstantin Tschet, Ernst Kunstmann. *Art Effects— Art Technician:* Josef Danilowatz.

This film, about a rocketship trip to the moon in search of gold deposits, blended state-of-the-art science with time-worn melodrama. Among the technical consultants were German rocket pioneers Hermann Oberth and Rudolf Nebel.

1929

Noah's Ark   Warner Bros.–First National, U.S.A.

Director: Michael Curtiz. *Photographic Effects — Special Photographic Effects Supervisor:* Fred W. Jackman. *Special Effects Photography:* Hans F. Koenekamp, Vernon L. Walker. *Miniatures — Miniature Supervisor:* Ned H. Mann. *Painted Mattes — Glass Paintings:* Paul Grimm. *Assistant:* Ellis J. "Bud" Thackery. *Optical Cinematography — Optical Effects:* William Butler. *Assistant:* Lawrence W. Butler.

In a flashback, the Biblical story is retold with the use of miniatures and glass paintings. Several stuntmen were killed while filming the flood sequence.

1929–30

Just Imagine   Fox, U.S.A.

Director: David Butler. *Miniatures — Miniature Photography Supervisor:* Ralph Hammeras. *Effects Photographer:* Edwin Hammeras. *Model maker:* Marcel Delgado. *Effects Consultant:* Willis H. O'Brien. *Process — Process Equipment:* George J. Teague. *Dunning Process:* Dunning Process Co. *Dunning Photography:* Ellis J. "Bud" Thackery. *Additional Service — Electrical Properties:* Kenneth Strickfaden.

Just imagine: a miniature townscape of futuristic New York City of 1980 (!) with enormous skyscrapers supposed to be 250 storeys high, all built in a zeppelin hangar at a cost of $250,000. The movie is an example of early process cinematography.

1930

Hell's Angels   Howard Hughes (for United Artists release), U.S.A.

Director: Howard Hawks. *Photographic Effects—Process and Miniature Cinematography:* E. Roy Davidson. *Effects Photographers:* Harry Zech, Cecil D. Love. *Special Photography—Additional Aerial Photography:* Elmer G. Dyer.

World War I aerial combats: two sequences mixing live-action and miniatures.

1932

Airmail   Universal, U.S.A.

Director: John Ford. *Photographic Effects—Miniature and Process Cinematography:* John P. Fulton. *Additional Aerial Photography:* Elmer G. Dyer. *Miniatures—Miniature Supervisor:* Charles Baker.

Aerial miniatures. The shooting took five months on a new process stage built at Universal Studios: "One of the scenes involved the flying of a plane through a blizzard. For this Fulton constructed a regulation cockpit with all the controls, but instead of controlling a real plane, it directed the movements of a miniature. The cockpit was hung from overhead tracks on the roof of the studio. Beneath the cockpit hung the miniature plane. By operating the controls in the regulation manner the tiny plane underneath could be made to dip, veer, twist from side to side — anything that a real plane might do in heavy weather" (John Brosnan: *Movie Magic*, p. 69).

1932–33

King Kong   Merian C. Cooper/RKO, U.S.A.

Executive Producer: David O. Selznick. *Directors:* Merian C. Cooper, Ernest B. Schoedsack. *Stop-Motion and Miniatures—Stop-Motion Animation, Art and Visual Effects Supervisor, Chief Technician:* Willis H. O'Brien. *Additional Stop Motion Animation and Model Work:* Elgen Brooks Gibson, Orville Goldner. *Stop-Motion Models:* Marcel Delgado. *Additional Puppet Work:* Charles Christadoro. *Woodwork:* John Cerisoli. *Miniature Sets:* W. G. "Gus" White. *Special Effects Mechanic:* Fred Reese. *Miniature Crew and Propmen:* Juan Larrinaga, Victor Delgado, Zachary Hoag, Thol (Si) Simonson, Robert A. Mattey. *Conceptual Art, Glass and Matte Paintings Art Technicians, Conceptual Art and Glass Paintings:* Mario Larrinaga, Byron L. Crabbe. *Additional Conceptual Art:* Ernest Smythe. *Painting Technician/Backdrops:* Peter Stich. *Matte Artists:* Henri Hillinck, Albert Maxwell Simpson. *Assistant Matte Photography:* Clarence W.D. Slifer. *Photographic Effects—Director of Photography (Live Action and Miniature Unit):* Edward (Eddie) Linden. *Stop Frame Pho- tography:* Bert Willis, Clifford R. Stine, Harold E. Wellman, William Reinhold. *Process Cinematography:* Vernon L. Walker, James O. Taylor, Kenneth Peach. *Miniature Process Projection Equipment and Stop Motion Armatures:* H.G. (Harry) Cunningham. *Process Screens:* Sidney Saunders. *Optical Cinematography:* Linwood G. Dunn, Cecil D. Love, William Ulm. *Optical Printing Engineer:* Bill Leeds. *Process Service—Dunning Process:* C. Dodge and Carroll H. Dunning, Dunning Process Co. *Dunning Photography:* Ellis J. "Bud" Thackery. *Williams Process:* Frank D. Williams, Williams Composite Laboratories. *Production Effects—Mechanical Effects:* Harry Redmond, Jr.; *Lighting Gaffer:* Orville Beckett.

Collector Forrest J Ackerman holds a Triceratops model conceived for the ill-fated production *Creation* (1931). It was intended for re-use in *King Kong* (1932–33) but was not seen in that film's final cut (photograph by Hans Helmut Prinzler, courtesy Deutsche Kinemathek Berlin

"King Kong"!

Who is he? What is he? How were the scenes of so great and terrifying an imaginary monster made to appear so realistic? These and a hundred other questions are asked by persons when they hear that *King Kong*, the sensation of several years ago, returns to the screen in a re-enactment of his exploits with Fay Wray, Robert Armstrong and Bruce Cabot as his human contrasts.

How did Merian C. Cooper and Ernest B. Schoedsack, the producers of this RKO Radio picture, so skillfully maneuver King Kong, tall as a four story building, into scenes of the streets of New York, to say nothing of his jungle combats with other giant prehistoric creatures? On this point the producers are silent, allowing their production miracle to speak for itself. The method used to depict King Kong climbing the Empire State Building tower with Fay Wray in the palm of his hand is perhaps the most intriguing of their methods that baffle solution.

However, King Kong does not ride to public favor simply because of camera or production technique. While he definitely is a novel star, the chief claim to fame is that he is a "thriller's thriller." In other words, Dracula, Frankenstein's Monster, and other creepy characters of the past, actually tremble at the mere mention of King Kong, who would totally ignore such fancy-pants shenanigans as werewolves, spooks and what have you.

Imagine a giant ape, a lovely but frightened girl of whom he is enamored lying at his great feet, making his last stand against civilized man from atop the tallest building in the world!

Said to be stranger than any fiction ever written and more fantastic than the wildest dream, *King Kong is* truly the Eighth Wonder of the World! [From *RKO Radio Pictures: FLASH* Vol. 1— No. 1, 1952 reissue].

On foggy Skull Island, dinosaurs (stegosaurus, brontosaurus, Tyrannosaurus, elasmosaurus, pteranodon), a left-over from RKO's ill-fated *Creation* project, and a giant gorilla are discovered by Carl Denham (Robert Armstrong) and the sailors of the *Venture*. Shamelessly exhibited in New York City, Kong breaks loose holding aspiring starlet Ann Darrow (Fay Wray) in his paws. He is killed by Navy biplanes atop the recently built Empire State Building but actually, says Denham, "It was Beauty killed the Beast."

Almost all effects techniques known until then (1932–33) were used, and others, such as miniature projection, were invented to repaint a drama along the lines of Samson and Delilah. *Kong*, originally titled *The Beast* (and *King Ape*), mainly was the brainchild of writer-producer Merian Cooper and stop-motion pioneer Willis O'Brien. There was a low-budget movie released by RKO in 1931, *Ingagi*, with Charles Gemora in his gorilla suit trying to "rape" a black female extra. Cooper intended to have someone like Gemora fight Komodo dragons (*Varanus Komodoensis*) but then on the RKO lot he met O'Brien and was sold on the use of animation throughout the entire picture. According to Ronald Haver, "Since Kong (as a model) was eighteen inches high and was supposed to be eighteen feet high, O'Brien wanted to scale down everything else proportionately. Cooper was a great believer in using sleight of hand with Kong's height; sometimes he was eighteen feet tall, in other scenes he was sixty feet tall." As Cooper said: "This broke every rule that O'Bie and his animators had ever worked with. But I felt confident that if the scenes moved with excitement and beauty, the audience would accept any height that fit into the scene. If Kong had been eighteen feet high on top of the Empire State Building, he would have been lost, like a little bug. So I continually shifted his height to fit the settings and illusions. He was different in practically every shot. After all, who knows how tall a tree is?"

Some stop-motion, however, was cut by Cooper: "The film was previewed in San Bernardino in late January 1933. The picture played exactly as Cooper knew it would, with one exception. As Kong shook the men off the log and they fell into the ravine below, they were set upon by huge, slimy insects and snakes and were eaten alive. The screaming on screen was matched by the screaming from the audience, a great many of whom left, and those who stayed kept up a buzz of conversation for the next few minutes, making it difficult to keep up with the continuing story. 'It stopped the picture cold,' said Cooper, 'so the next day back at the studio, I took it out myself. O'Bie was heartbroken, he thought it was the best work he'd done, and it was, but it worked against the picture so out it came'" (Ronald Haver: *Merian C. Cooper: The Man Who Was King Kong*, brochure edited for special screenings on July 22 and 24, 1977, at the Los Angeles County Museum of Art).

Ray Bradbury claimed that as a young boy he

went to that San Bernardino preview, and when a photo of the lost spider pit sequence appeared in the pages of a fan magazine, *Famous Monsters of Filmland*, it became a cult among aficionados. Eventually, Peter Jackson in a DVD release tried to reconstruct it from stills and preproduction art and proved that maybe Cooper was right. In fact, the newly added sequence slows down the action.

In the continuity (as quoted from pages found in the Ackerman Collection), the original scenes are described as follows:

> *Ext. Ravine Bottom Long Shot Day*—The men at the bottom of the ravine are attacked by giant insects who come out of caves & fissures to eat them.
>
> *Ext. Ravine Bottom Close up Day*—The surprised face of a sailor lying in the mud as he sees this.
>
> *Ditto*— Face of another sailor staring up in horror from the mud.
>
> *Ditto*— Face of a third sailor in the mud, horrified as he sees —
>
> *Medium Shot*— An insect with octopus arms takes a man. (Projection)
>
> *Semi Close up*— Its arms wind about the struggling man.
>
> *Bit*— Two men on their backs staring up at a spider who attacks them. (Proj.)

Interestingly enough, with its reissue, *Kong* became even more successful:

> *King Kong*
> *Mighty Monster*
> *Eighth Wonder of the World!*
> *Sensational Thrill to Startle Millions*
> *King Kong* Returns in Amazing Screen Classic
> When the primitive mastodonic ape, King Kong, made his debut in the spectacular imaginative motion picture of that name a few years ago to crash to a spectacular death from the highest building in New York after finally releasing a beautiful girl to her rescuers, audiences all over the world gasped at the daring conception which made a studio "prop" a thing of such realistic animation.
>
> *King Kong* now returns to the screen after a retirement of several years to thrill the public again, as vigorous and awe-inspiring as ever. All the technical skill and resources which the motion pictures can command were called into play to create the many imaginative scenes in the epic Merian C. Cooper and Ernest B. Schoedsack production featuring Fay Wray, Robert Armstrong and Bruce Cabot. King Kong and the other pre-historic animals, made to perform in mammoth size by the

clever technical methods of the producers and their staffs, amazed all beholders of this highly popular picture. Not only was the ape shown in fifty-foot stature, but also, in corresponding proportions, such monsters of past eons as a tyrannosaurus, giant sea serpents, huge pterodactyls or flying reptiles, and a brontosaurus.

The unique film was produced from a story conceived by Merian C. Cooper and the late Edgar Wallace and was personally directed by Cooper and Ernest B. Schoedsack, with Willis J. [*sic*] O'Brien as Chief Technician. David O. Selznick was Executive Producer [*RKO Radio Pictures: FLASH* Vol. 1, No. 1, 1952 re-release].

1933

The Invisible Man   Universal, U.S.A.
Director: James Whale. *Photographic Effects— Visual Effects and Process Supervisor:* John P. Fulton. *Assistant:* Bill Heckler. *Williams Process:* Frank D. Williams, Williams Composite Laboratories. *Assistant Cinematographer:* Roswell A. Hoffman. *Miniatures—Miniature Photography:* John Joseph Mescall. *Miniatures and Footprint Effects:* Charles A. Baker. *Miniature Sequence:* Donald Jahraus. *Production Effects—Mechanical Effects/Wire Effects:* Al Johnson, Bob Laszlo. *Special Makeup:* Jack P. Pierce.

Ten writers attempted a screen adaptation of H.G. Wells' *The Invisible Man*; there was even a rejected version by Preston Sturges. Some effects were done with invisible wires, others involved an actor (doubling for Claude Rains) in black velvet tights, black gloves and wearing a black headpiece that didn't reflect any light acting partly costumed, in front of a completely black, non-reflective velvet set. This image was used to print onto another set and create invisibility by traveling mattes. In an article for *American Cinematographer* (June 1934), Fulton talked about the shooting of the scene in which the Invisible Man stood in front of a mirror and unwrapped his bandaged head: "[T]he shot had to show the man himself (from the rear) and his reflection in the mirror. Ordinarily, this would be simple enough — but when you add to it the difficulties incident to showing the unwrapping of an invisible head, you have some rather complicated problems to solve! This required the making of four separate 'takes,' which were combined, by the traveling-matte printing system, into a single picture. First, there was the shot of the wall and the mirror, with the mirror itself masked out by black velvet, next, a separate shot of the opposite wall of the room, as reflected in the mirror, thirdly, the shot of the invisible man, from the rear, unwrapping his bandages, and lastly, the reflection of him, from the front, doing the same act."

1933

Deluge   KBS-Admiral Productions (released by RKO), U.S.A.

Director: Felix E. Feist. *Miniatures—Miniature Effects Supervisor:* Ned H. Mann. *Photographic Effects—Special Effects Cinematographer:* William N. Williams. *Camera Department Supervisor:* Edward Tiffany. *Process Service—Composite Shots:* Dunning Process Co. *Mechanical Effects—Effects Technicians:* Al Cohen, Donald Donaldson. *Matte Paintings_Matte Artist:* Russell E. Lawson.

In an early scene, we see the destruction of a huge model of Manhattan. The disaster was filmed high speed at 240 frames per second. "This is probably one of the largest, and certainly the most intricate, job of miniature work ever done in any production. Principal specification was for an exact replica of the city of New York, its waterfront and downtown district. An earthquake and tidal wave bring about complete destruction of the waterfront, ships, docks and the city itself, all with amazing reality," Ned Mann wrote in the *Brulatour Bulletin*, a newsletter of the West Coast distributor of Eastman motion picture films. "For the earthquake effect on the skyscrapers in the downtown business district we built a platform of approximately 100 feet square, and this was cut into eight sections. Each of these sections was mounted on rollers upon separate undulating tracks, similar to a roller coaster structure. Springs were operated electrically to produce a desired effect. We took no chances in missing any part of the action from any angle. When the time came for the actual photographic and sound recording of this part of the picture, I had eight cameras on the set. The motors were started on the cameras and on the

platforms. Slight vibrations developed into severe jolts and shocks. Sections of the platform separated, opening large crevices in the earth's foundation. The entire platform moves towards the cameras. The buildings shake and crumble. The destruction was as dramatic as it was complete."

1934–35

The Last Days of Pompeii   Merian C. Cooper/RKO, U.S.A.

Director: Ernest B. Schoedsack. *Miniatures and Matte Art—Miniature Effects Supervisor:* Willis H. O'Brien. *Art Technician/Matte and Glass Shots:* Byron L. Crabbe. *Production Illustrator:* Mario Larrinaga. *Miniature Projection Process:* Carroll L. Shepphird. *Special Props:* Marcel Delgado. *Photographic Effects and Process—Director of Photography:* Edwin G. Linden. *Process Cinematography:* Vernon L. Walker. *Miniature Sets:* W. G. "Gus" White. *Matte Photography:* Clarence W. D. Slifer. *Optical Cinematography:* Linwood G. Dunn. *Production Effects—Pyrotechnics:* Harry Redmond, Jr.

Married in 1933, honeymooning producer Merian Cooper and actress Dorothy Jordan made a world tour lasting nearly a year. In Pompeii, Cooper became interested in a motion picture about the eruption of Mount Vesuvius. It was originally planned in the Technicolor process but eventually filmed in black-and-white. A trade ad proclaimed, "A Flaming Panorama of Excitement Hurled to the Screen with a Surging Power That Will Storm the Hearts of Thrill-Hungry Millions of Today! Behold the wonders of the biggest show in 2,000 years!"

1934–36

Things to Come   Alexander Korda/London Film Productions (for United Artists release), Great Britain

Director: William Cameron Menzies (who also joined Vincent Korda and László Maholy-Nagy in designing the futuristic sets). *Miniatures and Process—Special Effects and Miniature Director:* Ned H. Mann. *Assistant:* Lawrence W. Butler. *Hanging Miniatures:* Ross Jacklin. *Photographic*

Effects—Miniature Photography: Edward Cohen. *Process Photography:* Harry Zech. *Process Technique:* George J. Teague. *Optical Cinematography:* Jack Thomas. *Traveling Mattes:* Paul Morell. *Assistant:* Wally Veevers. *Matte Paintings—Supervising Matte Artist:* Walter Percy Day. *Assistant Matte Artist:* Peter Ellenshaw. *Matte Photography:* Thomas Sydney Day.

H.G. Wells' prophesy of the impending World War II and a doomed society rebuilt on the belief in modern science culminating in space gun and space flight. A feast of miniatures and, for its time, clever composites.

1935

Amphitryon — Aus den Wolken kommt das Glück   Universum-Film A.G. (Ufa), Germany, Filmed at Ufa Studios Neubabelsberg

Director: Reinhold Schünzel. *Effects Cinematography—Effects and Process Photography:* Werner Bohne. *Miniature Photography—Miniature and Mirror Shots:* Ernst Kunstmann, Heinrich Weidemann. *Opticals—Optical Cinematography (Truca):* Theodor Nischwitz.

This "Doppelgänger" tale of the amorous affairs of Jupiter (played by Willy Fritsch) marked the reintroduction of trick shots in a big way in Germany. To duplicate actors Fritsch (as Jupiter) and Paul Kemp (as Hermes), background projection was installed.

1935

Dante's Inferno   Fox, U.S.A.

Director: Harry Lachman. *Visual Effects—Visual Effects Design:* Fred Sersen. *Miniatures and Process—Miniature and Process Cinematography:* Ralph Hammeras, Edwin Hammeras. *Process Supervisor:* Sol Halperin. *Additional Photography:* James O. Taylor. *Mechanical Effects—Mechanical Effects Supervisor:* Louis Witte. *Technicians:* William O'Neal, James Donnelly.

A dream sequence revives Gustave Doré's *Dante's Inferno* illustrations with lots of miniatures, painted mattes, process photography and pyrotechnics. Ray Harryhausen told this writer that there is no reason to see this early Spencer Tracy vehicle except the elaborate nightmare.

1935

Bride of Frankenstein   Carl Laemmle, Jr./ Universal, U.S.A.

Director: James Whale. *Visual Effects—Photographic Effects:* John P. Fulton. *Assistant:* David Stanley Horsley. *Williams Process:* Frank D. Williams, Williams Composite Laboratory. *Miniatures—Miniature Supervisor:* Charles A. Baker. *Matte Paintings—Matte Artists:* Russell A. Lawson, Jack Cosgrove. *Special Services—Electrical Properties:* Kenneth Strickfaden. *FX Makeup—Special Makeup:* Jack P. Pierce. *Associate:* Otto Lederer.

The Monster (Karloff) demands a Bride (Elsa Lanchester). A rare thing in film history: A sequel that matches the original (*Frankenstein* was filmed in 1931) and segment-wise even surpasses it, especially in the sinister scenes with the macabre Dr. Pretorius (Ernest Thesiger). The effects include excellent miniatures, masterful lighting, controlled pyrotechnics and high-speed photography. "Virtuoso effects depict Pretorius' seven miniature homunculi in their glass jars. Fulton and Horsley were on the set for two days during live-action filming. Careful measurements were made of camera elevations, distances and angles, as well as the sizes of the jars and other props. The little people — a queen, a king, a bishop, a ballet dancer, a baby, a devil who resembles Pretorius, and a mermaid — were photographed separately in large-scale jars and matted into the small jars. The composites are flawless, including a scene in which the king escapes and Pretorius picks him up by the scruff of the neck and pops him into a jar" (Jan A. Henderson and George E. Turner in *American Cinematographer*, January 1998). The homunculi were played by A. S. Byron (King), Joan Woodbury (Queen), Norman Ainsley (Archbishop), Peter Shaw (Devil), Kansas DeForest (Ballerina), Josephine McKim (Mermaid), and Billy Barty (Baby).

1935

A Midsummer Night's Dream   Warner Bros.–First National, U.S.A.

Directors: Max Reinhardt, William Dieterle. *Photographic Effects—Visual Effects Cinematographer:* Byron Haskin. *Visual Effects Producer:* Fred W. Jackman. *Additional Photography:* Hans F. Koenekamp. *Equipment—Engineer:* Bill Thomas. *Mechanical Effects—Wireworks:* Glen Beldt.

For one scene in this filmization of Shakespeare's famous tale, a scherzo, effects photographer Byron Haskin (then a member of Fred Jackman's unit) had to shoot fairies who materialize dancing out of the grass: "My engineer, Bill Thomas, and I put a huge plate glass on the set, staked down in front of a test camera. We marked where every girl would be on the glass. We took the glass back to the shop and he spent a day grinding out hollow places so that the girls would appear to materialize.... The optical glass was thick. Thomas ground it out in channels — indentations in the glass which became distortion lenses for each girl's areas. The girls crouched down before appearing, then stood up on signal, slowly appearing through the little distortion lenses into clarity, coming to pause just above it" (Byron Haskin interviewed by Joe Adamson, p. 118).

1935–36

Flash Gordon   Universal, U.S.A.

Director: Frederick (Fritz) Stephani. *Photographic Effects—Director of Photography/Miniature Cinematography:* Jerome H. (Jerry) Ash. *Miniatures—Special Properties and Models:* Elmer R. Johnson. *Special Service—Electrical Properties:* Norman Dewes, Kenneth Strickfaden, Raymond Lindsey. *Effects Mechanic:* Robert A. Mattey.

13-chapter serial version of Alex Raymond's science fiction comic strip depicts Flash Gordon's adventures on Planet Mongo and his encounter with Ming the Merciless.

1936

San Francisco   MGM, U.S.A.

Special Effects—Special Effects Supervisor: James Basevi. *Special Effects Art Director:* A. Arnold Gillespie. *Photographic Effects—Miniature Photography:* Maximilian Fabian. *Additional Photography:* Russell A. Cully. *Assistant Camera:* Loyal Griggs. *Special Service—Effects Editor:* John Hoffman.

The climax, of course, depicts that city's 1906 earthquake. None of the 400 extras was injured during production.

1938

Spawn of the North   Paramount, U.S.A.

Director: Henry Hathaway. *Photographic Effects—Photographic Effects Supervisor:* Gordon Jennings. *Effects Cinematographers:* Devereaux Jennings, Irmin Roberts. *Optical Cinematography:* Paul K. Lerpae. *Matte Paintings—Matte Artist:* Jan Domela. *Miniatures—Chief Model maker:* Art Smith. *Process—Process Supervisor:* Farciot Edouart. *Process Cinematography:* Loyal C. Griggs.

Academy Award (Honorary Award): Gordon Jennings, Jan Domela, Devereaux Jennings, Irmin Roberts, Art Smith, Farciot Edouart, Loyal Griggs.

A drama with Canadian deep sea fishermen. One of their trawlers (miniature) collides with an iceberg.

1938–39

Gone with the Wind   David O. Selznick in association with MGM, U.S.A. Technicolor.

Directors: Victor Fleming, George Cukor, David O. Selznick, William Cameron Menzies. *Matte Paintings—Supervising Matte Artist:* Jack Cosgrove. *Matte Artists:* Fitch Fulton, Albert Maxwell Simpson, Jac Shaw. *Assistant Artist:* Louis Lichtenfield. *Preliminary Matte Concept:* Byron L. Crabbe. *Matte Photography:* Clarence W.D. Slifer. *Special Sequence—Special Montage Sequence:* Peter Ballbusch. *Additional Effects Footage Photographers:* William Neumann, Russell Hoover, Bert Willis. *Mechanical Effects—Pyrotechnics:* Lee Zavitz. *Special Services—Additional Cinematography (dual-screen fire sequence not used in final version):* Winton C. Hoch. *Tech-

nicolor Technicians: Rube Boyce, John Hamilton, Dave Jordan, Nelson Cordes. *Process Equipment:* George J. Teague. *Process Projectionist:* Bob Creso.

One hundred matte paintings of Tara and the Civil War fall of the doomed Old South. In the Atlanta fire scene, the big wall of the native village from *King Kong* was burned. In a 1956 letter to William Paley of CBS (quoted in *The Invisible Art*), producer David O. Selznick revealed: "Forgive me if I say that one of the many fields in which the Selznick International pictures were ahead of the rest of the business was in their common use of matte shots, optical effects.... When *Gone with the Wind* came along, it became even more apparent to me that I could not even hope to put the picture on the screen properly without an even more extensive use of special effects than had ever before been attempted in the business...."

1938–39

The Wizard of Oz   Mervyn LeRoy, Arthur Freed/MGM, U.S.A. Technicolor (Kansas scenes in black-and-white).

Directors: Victor Fleming and (uncredited) Mervyn LeRoy, Richard Thorpe (footage not used), King Vidor (Kansas scenes), George Cukor (tests). *Special Effects and Miniatures— Miniature Effects Supervisor:* A. Arnold Gillespie. *Miniature Photography:* Maximilian Fabian. *Camera Operator:* Jack Smith. *Special Effects Supervisor:* Edwin Bloomfield. *Assistant Miniature Design.* J. McMillan Johnson. *Miniature Shop Supervisor:* Donald A. Jahraus. *Model Technician (Flying Ape Sequence):* Marcel Delgado. *Special Effects Technicians:* Jack McMasters, Franklin E. Milton, Glen Robinson, Hal Millar, Tim Baar. *Special Effects Rigger:* Donald Trumbull. *Propmaker Foreman:* Jack Gaylord. *Set Dresser (Trees):* A. D. Flowers. *Matte Paintings—Supervising Matte Artist:* Warren A. Newcombe. *Matte Cinematography:* Mark R. Davis. *Matte Artist (Castle):* Candelario Rivas. *FX Makeup:—Special Character Makeup:* Jack Dawn. *Makeup Department Head:* Cecil Holland. *Makeup Artists:* Jack H. Young, Lyle Dawn, Emile LaVigne, Norbert Miles, Web Overlander, Fred B. Phillips, Robert J. Schiffer, Charles H. Schram, Lee Stanfield. *Assistant Makeup Artists:* Del Armstrong, Holly Bane, Don L. Cash, Jack Kevan, Lou LaCava, George Lane, Eddie Polo, Howard Smit, William Tuttle. *Prosthetic Technician:* Gustaf Norin. *Prosthetic Sculptor:* Josef Norin. *Body Makeup Artists:* Betty Masure, Edith Wilson. *Wig Supervisor:* Max Factor. *Wig Designers:* Fred Frederick, Bob Roberts. *Hairstyles:* Sydney Guilaroff.

In black-and-white, a miniature tornado was made from muslin. In Technicolor, hordes of miniature monkeys were built and puppeteered on 1100 wires.

1939

The Hunchback of Notre Dame   Pandro S. Berman/RKO, U.S.A.

Director: William (Wilhelm) Dieterle. *Photographic Effects—Camera Effects Supervisor:* Vernon L. Walker. *Special Effects and Process Cinematography:* Clifford R. Stine, Harold E. Wellman, William N. Williams. *Optical Cinematography:* Linwood G. Dunn, Cecil D. Love. *Matte Paintings—Matte Artists:* Mario Larrinaga, Chesley Bonestell, Walter Percy Day. *FX Makeup:— Makeup Supervisor:* Perc Westmore. *Prosthetic Technician:* Gustaf Norin. *Prosthetic Sculptor:* Josef Norin.

The cathedral of Notre Dame was a miniature and , in the final scene, a matte painting. Harold Wellman: "[L]ike *King Kong*, [*Hunchback*] made extensive use of background projection, stop-motion, miniatures and process. One shot, for instance, pulls back from a 2' x 2' background image of Laughton, sitting by a gargoyle, to a long shot including the entire facade of the Cathedral of Notre Dame."

1939

The Rains Came   Darryl F. Zanuck/20th Century–Fox, U.S.A.

Director: Clarence Brown. *Photographic Effects and Mattes—Effects Supervisor:* Fred M. Sersen. *Matte Artist:* Ray Kellogg. *Assistant Matte Artist:* Emil Kosa, Jr. *Camera Effects:* James B. Gordon.

Camera Operator: L. B. Abbott. *Mechanical Effects—Mechanical Effects Supervisor:* Louis Witte. *Academy Award:* Fred Sersen.

An earthquake was shot with extensive use of miniatures and painted mattes. Remade in 1955 in CinemaScope as *The Rains of Ranchipur.*

1939–40

The Thief of Bagdad   Alexander Korda/ London Films (for United Artists release), Great Britain and U.S.A. Technicolor.

Directors: Dr. Ludwig Berger, Michael Powell, Tim Whelan. *Additional scenes directed by* William Cameron Menzies, Zoltan Korda. *Visual Effects—Visual Effects Supervisor:* Lawrence W. Butler. *Optical Cinematography:* Tom Howard. *Miniatures—Hanging Miniatures:* Johnny Mills. *Hanging Miniatures Photography:* Wally Veevers. *Matte Paintings—Supervising Matte Artist:* Walter Percy Day. *Matte Photography:* Thomas Sydney Day. *Assistant Matte Artist:* Peter Ellenshaw. *Assistant Technician:* Arthur George Day. *Blue Screen—Blue Screen Cinematography:* Henry Imus, Wilkie Cooper (tests). *Blue Screen Consultant:* Stanley W. Sayer. *Mechanical Effects—Effects Technician:* Ted Samuels. *U.S. Crew—Aerial Photography:* Elmer G. Dyer. *Additional Model Work:* Chris Mueller, Jr. *Spider Sequence Photography:* Edward Cohen. *Academy Award:* Lawrence Butler.

A lavish Arabian Nights fantasy in Technicolor starring Sabu. The Djinn played by Rex Ingram and the flying horse ridden by Miles Malleson and villain Conrad Veidt represented the beginning of the blue screen process. There were 55 blue backing shots used in 99 cuts, according to Jim Danforth. There are matte paintings using the Latent Image Technique and excellent hanging miniatures of Basra and Bagdad. "[T]he tricks, with a few exceptions, are convincing and exciting. The magical scenes are very satisfactory. The enormous Djinn trying to stamp on the diminutive form of Sabu, who is no bigger than his big toe, the sudden storm summoned by the Vizier to wreck the hero's boat, and the terrifying toy which does a Siva-like dance before stabbing the Sultan to

death — all these are the true stuff of fairy tales" (Basil Wright, *Spectator,* December 1940). Production was started at Denham Studios in London and finished at General Service Studios in Hollywood.

1939–40

One Million B.C.   Hal Roach Studios (for United Artists release), U.S.A.

Directors: Hal Roach, Hal Roach, Jr. *Consultant:* D.W. Griffith. *Visual Effects—Visual Effects Supervisor:* Roy Seawright. *Effects Cinematographer:* William V. Draper. *Process—Miniature Projection:* Louis H. Tolhurst. *Optical and Process Equipment:* Frank William Young. *Art Effects—Background and Matte Artist:* Jack Shaw. *Mechanical Effects—Mechanical Effects Supervisor:* Fred Knoth. *Special Service—Animal Supervisor:* Charles Oelze.

Iguanodon, lizards and a baby alligator fight to their death in miniature and back projection. A pretty bad allosaurus costume was mostly hidden by bushes while fighting with star Victor Mature.

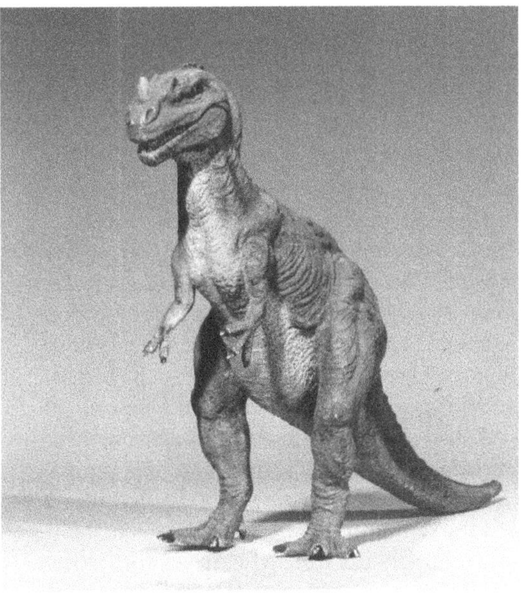

The Ceratosaurus mock-up from *One Million Years B.C.* (1966) (courtesy Ray and Diana Harryhausen Collection as displayed by Deutsche Kinemathek Berlin).

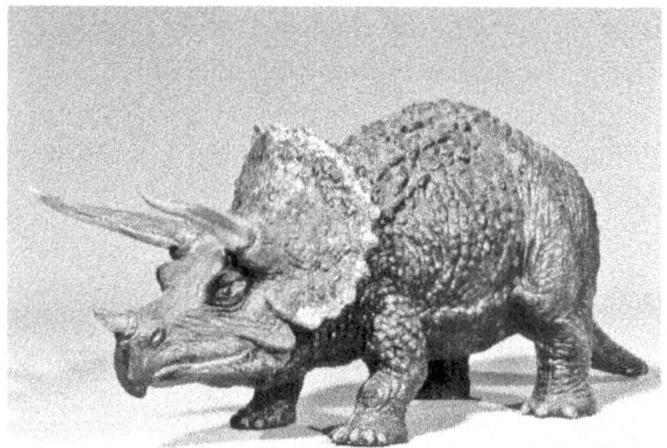

The Triceratops mock-up from *One Million Years B.C.* (1966) (courtesy Ray and Diana Harryhausen Collection as displayed by Deutsche Kinemathek Berlin).

1939–40

The Great Dictator   Chas. Chaplin Film Co. (for United Artists release), U.S.A.

Director: Charles Chaplin. *Mattes—Supervising Matte Artist:* Jack Cosgrove. *Process and Miniatures—Process Service:* George J. Teague. *Miniature Photography:* Ralph Hammeras.

Model airplane with Chaplin puppet, back projection and hailing masses made of popcorn.

1939–40

Dr. Cyclops   Paramount, U.S.A. Technicolor.

Director: Ernest B. Schoedsack. *Process—Process Supervisor:* Farciot Edouart. *Process Photography:* W. Wallace Kelley. *Photographic Effects—Photographic Effects Supervisor:* Gordon Jennings. *Effects Cinematographer:* Irmin Roberts. *Optical Cinematography:* Paul K. Lerpae. *Matte Paintings—Matte Artist:* Jan Domela.

A mad scientist reduces people in size with the help of Paramount's triple-head rear projection system: "By projecting reduced-size images of actors onto miniature process screens built into normal-size sets in which actor Albert Dekker performed, extremely convincing composites were achieved which showed miniature people interacting with a normal-size man," says Jim Danforth. "In other scenes, the projection

procedure was reversed. A gigantic image of Albert Dekker was projected onto a large screen positioned behind the actors portraying the miniaturized people. In these scenes, the disparity in quality between the original image of the actors and the projected image of Dr. Cyclops became quite apparent."

1940–41

Citizen Kane   Orson Welles, George Schaefer/Mercury/RKO, U.S.A.

Director: Orson Welles. *Photographic Effects—Camera Effects Supervisor:* Vernon L. Walker. *Process Cinematography:* Russell A. Cully, Harold E. Wellman. *Optical Cinematography:* Linwood G. Dunn. *Optical Printing Technicians:* Cecil D. Love, Bill Leeds. *Matte Paintings—Matte Artists:* Chesley Bonestell, Mario Larrinaga, Fitch Fulton. *Machine Shop—Machine Shop Foreman:* H. G. (Harry) Cunningham. *Special Service—Montage Effects:* Douglas Travers.

It was editor Robert Wise who introduced Orson Welles to the miracles of the optical printer and compositing. The picture contains all (invisible) tricks of the book: miniatures and process photography and lots of matte paintings of Kane's Castle Xanadu.

1941

A Yank in the R.A.F.   Darryl F. Zanuck/ 20th Century–Fox, U.S.A.

Director: Henry King. *Photographic Effects—Special Effects Supervisor:* Fred M. Sersen. *Camera Effects:* James B. Gordon. *Camera Operator:* L. B. Abbott. *Miniatures-Miniature Photography:* Ralph Hammeras. *Process—Process Supervision:* Sol Halperin. *Mattes—Matte Artist:* Ray Kellogg. *Mechanical Effects—Explosives:* Louis Witte.

American pilots defend British co-pilots at Dunkirk.

1941–42

The Jungle Book   Alexander Korda (for United Artists release), U.S.A. Technicolor.

Director: Zoltan Korda *Photographic Effects—Special Effects Director:* Lawrence W. Butler. *Matte Paintings—Matte Artist:* Fitch Fulton.

Full-size mechanical replicas of cobra and alligator, the burning of a lost (miniature) city in the jungle and several matte paintings make this film adaptation of Rudyard Kipling work.

1942

Hawai Marè okikaisen   [*The War at Sea from Hawaii to Malaya*], Toho, Japan

Director: Kajiro Yamamoto. *Miniature Photography—Technical Effects Supervisor:* Eiji Tsuburaya. *Effects Art Department—Miniature Art Director:* Akira Watanabe.

This tale of a naval cadet from boot camp to Pearl Harbor "marked the greatest use of special effects and miniature work ever seen in a Japanese film up to that time," Joseph Anderson and Donald Richie wrote in their book *The Japanese Film.* "It was gigantic in every sense of the word and cost over $380,000 to make, when the average first-class film was budgeted for $40,000." The late Noriaki Yuasa called it "a golden shining tower in the Japanese special effects movie history" and emphasized that "no one has since made a film of that scale" (*Monsters Are Attacking Tokyo!,* p. 54). U.S. military authorities originally mistook some miniature scenes for actual newsreel footage.

1942–43

Münchhausen   Eberhard Schmidt/Universum Film (Ufa), Germany, Filmed at Ufastadt Babelsberg, Agfacolor

Director: Josef von Baky. *Photographic Effects—In-Camera Effects:* Konstantin Irmen-Tschet. *Process—Process Supervisor:* Gerhard Huttula. *Process Technicians:* Willi Körner, Ewald Krause. *Process Projection:* Joop Huisken. *Special Sequence—Mirror Sequence:* Ernst Kunstmann. *Opticals—Optical Cinematography (Truca):* Theodor Nischwitz. *2D Animation—Effects Animation:* Hans Held.

The story of an 18th-century baron (played by Hans Albers) noted for his tall tales was made to celebrate the silver anniversary of Germany's leading film company, Ufa. Before production on this extravaganza commenced, agents of Dr. Joseph Goebbels — Hitler's minister of propaganda, who oversaw all films turned out by the Third Reich — procured such films as Alexander Korda's Technicolor epic *The Thief of Bagdad* and others by Walt Disney for careful study as this fantastic fable, photographed in Agfacolor, would require numerous special effects. In the relatively short span of ten months, such illusions as the baron's cannonball ride into the fortress of Ostrakov (background projection and wireworks) and a montgolfiere trip to the moon were mostly rendered in-camera by Konstantin Irmen-Tschet.

1944

Thirty Seconds Over Tokyo   MGM, U.S.A.

Special Effects—Miniature Effects Supervisor: A. Arnold Gillespie. *Miniatures—Miniature Photography:* Maximilian Fabian. *Miniature Shop Supervisor:* Donald A. Jahraus. *Miniature Technician:* Marcel Delgado. *Mechanical Effects—Explosives:* A. D. Flowers. *Matte Paintings—Supervising Matte Artist:* Warren A. Newcombe. *Matte Cinematography:* Mark Davis. Academy Award: A. Arnold Gillespie.

The movie begins with a short but technically impressive miniature sequence of bombing raids on Japan. The footage was re-used in the prologue of *Midway* (1976).

1945

The Horn Blows at Midnight   Warner Bros., U.S.A.

Director: Raoul Walsh. *Photographic Effects—Special Effects Directors:* Lawrence W. Butler, William C. McGann. *Department Head Stage 5:* Byron Haskin. *Effects Cinematographers:* Robert Burks, Warren E. Lynch. *Miniature Photography:* Hans F. Koenekamp. *Matte Paintings—Matte Artists:* Paul Detlefsen, Chesley Bonestell.

Jack Benny plays an angel sent down to destroy Earth with a blast from Gabriel's horn.

1946–49

Mighty Joe Young   Merian C. Cooper and John Ford/Argosy–RKO (An ARKO Production), U.S.A.

Director: Ernest B. Schoedsack *Stop-Motion—Visual Effects and Stop-Motion Designer and Supervisor:* Willis H. O'Brien. *First Assistant/Stop-Motion Animation:* Ray Harryhausen. *Second Assistant/Stop-Motion Animation:* Peter Peterson. *Stop-Motion Models:* Marcel Delgado. *Taxidermist* and *Miniaturist:* George Lofgren. *Miniature Projectors and Armatures:* H.G. (Harry) Cunnigham. *Effects Animation:* Scott Witticker. *Additional Stop-Motion and Test Animation:* Willis H. O'Brien, Marcel Delgado, Victor Delgado, Elgen Brooks Gibson. *Photographic Effects—Stop-Motion Photography:* Bert Willis. *Process Photography:* Harold E. Stine. *Optical Cinematography:* Linwood G. Dunn. *Matte Paintings—Glass and Matte Paintings:* Fitch Fulton. *Assistant Matte Artist:* Louis Lichtenfield. *Special Art:* Jack Shaw. *Painting Technician/Backdrops:* Peter Stich. *Mechanical Effects—Production Effects:* Jack Lannon. Academy Award: Willis O'Brien.

During an expedition to Africa to capture lions for the new Hollywood nightclub, The Golden Safari, master showman Max O'Hara (Robert Armstrong) and a group of cowboys right out of John Ford's movies rope a 12-foot-tall gorilla, the pet of sweet Jill Young (Terry Moore), who raised him from infancy. Joe and Jill perform superbly on stage in Hollywood, but after a few weeks Joe becomes a clown for the audience. Joe is teased and given liquor by three drunks. The gorilla goes mad and destroys the nightclub but finally proves a hero when he saves a little girl from the roof of a burning orphanage. O'Brien wanted a stronger climax of two gorillas fighting it out in San Francisco atop a cablecar (and used this idea for his ill-fated *King Kong vs. Frankenstein* project). "The star of this film is a Mr. Willis O'Brien, who is described as its technical Creator, and is therefore, I take it, the man responsible for the ingenious trick photography and the manipulation of this huge [*sic!*] puppet. He has done his work well" (Fred Majalany, *Daily Mail*, London, October 14, 1949).

1947

The Beast with Five Fingers   Warner Bros., U.S.A.

Director: Robert Florey. *Visual Effects—Visual Effects Cinematography:* Hans F. Koenekamp. *Visual Effects Director:* William C. McGann.

Veteran effects cinematographer Koenekamp considered the dream sequence with a live human hand playing piano the best work of his entire career.

1949–50

Destination Moon   George Pal Productions Inc./Eagle-Lion, U.S.A. Technicolor.

Director: Irving Pichel. *Mechanical Effects—Mechanical Effect Supervisors:* Lee Zavitz. *Wire Effects:* Herman Townsley. *Art Effects—Astronomical Art:* Chesley Bonestell. *Stop-Motion—Stop-Motion Photography:* John S. Abbott. *Stop-Motion Animation:* Fred Madison. *Stop-Motion Technicians:* Dale Tholen, Miles E. Pike. *2D Animation—Woody Woodpecker Sequence:* Walter Lantz Productions. Academy Award: Lee Zavitz.

The first moon landing as brainchild of the Cold War. Originally producer George Pal wanted to do all effects in his own Puppetoons studio. Some stop-motion scenes of astronauts walking outside on the rocketship were done there. The control room set of the spaceship was built so that it could be tilted, rigged by mechanical effects supervisor Lee Zavitz. It was "a special rig three storeys high to enable the control room set to be rotated. Carpenters built a platform around it and the camera was mounted on a giant boom, the latter being so impressive that Cecil B. DeMille himself visited the studio to see it" (John Brosnan: *Movie Magic*, pp. 189–190).

1949–50

Samson and Delilah   Cecil B. DeMille Productions Inc./Paramount, U.S.A. Technicolor.

Director: Cecil B. DeMille. *Photographic Effects—Special Photographic Effects Supervisor:* Gordon Jennings. *Effects Cinematography:* Devereaux Jennings. *Special Camera Equipment (Mo-*

tion Control): S. R. Stancliffe, Jr., Frank Butler. *Optical Cinematography:* Paul K. Lerpae. *Matte Paintings—Matte Artist:* Jan Domela. *Matte Photography:* Irmin Roberts. *Miniatures—Miniature Foreman:* Ivyl Burks. *Process Photography—Process Supervisor:* Farciot Edouart. *Process Plates:* W. Wallace Kelley.

For the climax, in which blinded Samson (Victor Mature) destroys a giant statue of the Philistines' idol god Dagoth, a very big miniature set was used and a motion control technique devised to crush extras believably in the composites. The temple was 37 feet high and the statue 17 feet.

1951

When Worlds Collide George Pal/Paramount, U.S.A. Technicolor.

Director: Rudolph Maté. *Photographic Effects—Special Photographic Effects Supervisor:* Gordon Jennings. *Effects Cinematography:* Devereaux Jennings. *Rocketship Miniature Sequences Director:* Harry Barndollar. *Optical Cinematography:* Paul K. Lerpae. *Technicolor Camera Operator:* Clifford Shirpser. *Miniatures—Miniature Foreman:* Ivyl Burks. *Assistant Model maker:* Tim Baar. *Matte Paintings—Matte Artist:* Jan Domela. *Matte Photography:* Irmin Roberts. *Special Astronomical Art:* Chesley Bonestell. *Process—Process Photography Supervisor:* Farciot Edouart. Academy Award: Gordon Jennings (with Paul K. Lerpae, Devereaux Jennings, Irmin Roberts, Harry Barndollar, Jan Domela, Chesley Bonestell, Ivyl Burks).

When the Earth is going to be destroyed by collision with a passing planet, a Space Ark is built, a selected few board and it is successfully launched via a huge ramp. The Edwin Balmer-Philip Wylie novel on which the movie was based was originally acquired for Cecil B. DeMille. The film version was to be titled *The End of the World* ("There has NEVER been any picture like *The End of the World*") but, as with *The War of the Worlds*, DeMille "spared" it for George Pal. Pal commissioned Chesley Bonestell with whom he had previously worked on *Destination Moon,* to prepare a series of sketches of the cataclysm and to design the Space Ark. Some scenes are impressive, some are not. In one of the dis-

aster highlights, New York's Times Square is flooded. Pal and the trick staff took a scene from an old Samuel Goldwyn production and froze the frame. Then they built a replica of black, dumped water in from two tanks, rotoscoped the result frame by frame and did hand-painted mattes.

1951

Lost Continent Sigmund Neufeld Productions/Lippert Pictures, U.S.A. Mountaintop sequences tinted green.

Director: Samuel Newfield. *Stop-Motion—Stop-Motion Supervisor:* Edward Nassour. *Mechanical Effects—Mechanical Effects Supervisor:* Augie Lohman. *Opticals—Optical Effects:* Ray Mercer & Company.

Low-grade but amusing stop-motion dinosaurs threaten an expedition exploring a mountaintop plateau. "The animation is peculiarly unrealistic. Only one section of a model seems to move at a time — one leg, the head, the tail, etc. instead of all of them moving a little bit most of the time, as is usual in better stop-motion films.... [T]he ceratopsians look more like reptilian parrots than anything else, and are rather cute" (Bill Warren, *Keep Watching the Skies! Volume I*, p. 37).

1951

Miracolo a Milano [U.S.: *Miracle in Milan*], Soc. Prod. De Sica in association with l'Enic (Executive Producer: Sir Alexander Korda), Italy.

Director: Vittorio De Sica. *Miniatures and Effects—Special Effects Director:* Ned H. Mann. *Photography—Effects Cinematography:* Vaclav Vich, Enzo Barboni. *Technical Department—Effects Technicians:* Sid Howell, Dave Matture, Martia Triznya.

Toto the Good brings joy and laughter to the poor in the slums outside of Milan. Aided by the old lady who raised him as a child and rejoins him after death, he works magic and makes the poor ride on broomsticks over the Cathedral. Alexander Korda, Britain's film czar, who was involved in financing this production, sent his American effects director Ned Mann to Rome to stage miniatures and background projection.

1952–53

The Beast from 20,000 Fathoms Jack Dietz and Hal E. Chester/Mutual Films of California for Warner Bros., U.S.A.

Director: Eugene Lourié. *Stop-Motion—Stop-Motion Animation and Miniature Process:* Ray Harryhausen. *Stop-Motion Armature:* Fred Harryhausen. *Taxidermist:* George Lofgren. *Additional Miniatures:* Willis Cook. *Process Photography—Process Service:* Paul E. Eagler.

Ray Harryhausen's first solo credit involves a radioactively awakened dinosaur. After an Arctic Circle atomic test, nuclear scientist Tom Nesbitt (Paul Christian) catches sight of a gigantic, dragonlike monster, but back in New York City nobody is willing to believe what they call his traumatic hallucinations. Then, off Newfoundland, in the Grand Banks area of the North Atlantic, a fishing boat is sunk by something described as a big sea serpent and, off the coast of Maine, a lighthouse is demolished. Nesbitt is sure that the beast, now identified as a prehistoric Rhedosaurus, was freed from more than a hundred million years of icy hibernation by the bomb. He is proven right when the dinosaur, weighing close to 500 tons, shows up in New York's Hudson River and goes on a rampage through Manhattan. When the beast is wounded by a bazooka shot, big drops of blood spot the streets and cause a virulent plague. The monster is the carrier of an unknown disease. In order to destroy the creature without spilling blood, Nesbitt fires a radioactive isotope in the monster's wound, while it is wrecking the roller coaster at the Coney Island amusement park.

The Beast was a rip-off of *Kong,* which had been re-released to enormous success in 1952. As Harryhausen financially was not able to employ Willis O'Brien's system of animation-in-depth complete with miniature projection, model landscapes, painted backdrops and foreground glass paintings, he would experiment with split-screen miniature projection which he had used ever since. When Japanese producer Tomoyuki Tanaka saw the result, he got the idea for *Godzilla.*

1952–53

The War of the Worlds George Pal/Paramount, U.S.A. Technicolor.

Director: Byron Haskin. *Photographic Effects—Special Photographic Effects Supervisor:* Gordon Jennings. *Special Effects Cinematography:* W. Wallace Kelley. *Technicolor Camera Operator:* Clifford Shirpser. *Optical Cinematography:* Paul K. Lerpae. *Optical Printing:* Aubrey Law, Jack Caldwell. *Effects Design—Special Effects Art Director:* Albert Nozaki. *Miniatures—Miniature Supervisor:* Ivyl Burks. *Model makers:* Albert Silva, Marcel Delgado. *Matte Paintings—Astronomical Art:* Chesley Bonestell. *Matte Artist:* Jan Domela. *Matte Photography:* Irmin Roberts. *Process—Process Supervisor:* Farciot Edouart. *Mechanical Effects—Mechanical Effects Foremen:* George Ulrick, Lee Vasque. *Effects Technicians:* Romaine Brickmeyer, Charles Davis, Soldier Graham, Royal Lowe, Milt Olsen, Chester Pate, Bob Springfield, Eddie Sutherland, Bud Thomp-

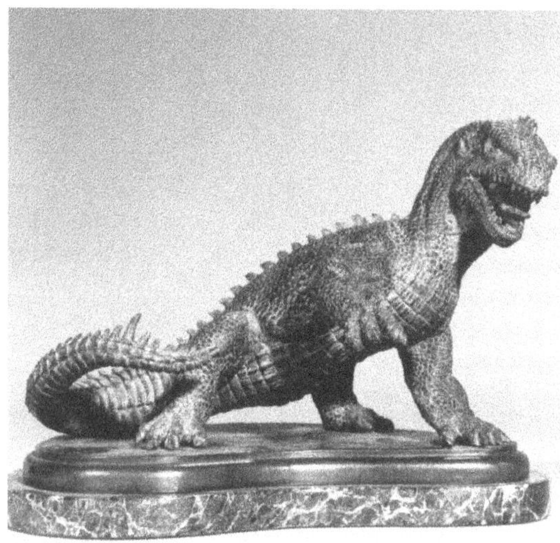

The Beast from 20,000 Fathoms **Rhedosaurus recreated in bronze (courtesy Ray and Diana Harryhausen Collection as displayed by Deutsche Kinemathek Berlin).**

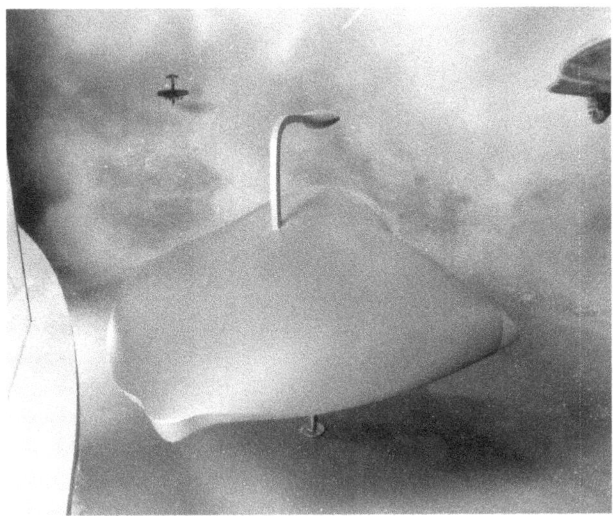

A Gregory Jein-made replica of the Martian war machine from George Pal's *The War of the Worlds* (courtesy Deutsche Kinemathek Berlin).

son. *Electrical Properties:* Kenneth Strickfaden. *Pyrotechnics/Powder Man (atom bomb):* Walter Hoffman. *Special Makeup—Special Martian Suit designed and worn by* Charles Gemora. Academy Award: Gordon Jennings (with W. Wallace Kelley, Paul K. Lerpae, Irmin Roberts, Jan Domela, Chesley Bonestell, Ivyl Burks, George Ulrick, Lee Vasque)

The film rights to the original H. G. Wells story had been purchased by Cecil B. DeMille for Paramount in 1925 and were even offered as a hot property to Russian filmmaker Sergei Eisenstein when he visited Hollywood in 1930. Orson Welles transformed it into a much acclaimed Halloween radio broadcast in October 1938 which won him a Hollywood contract. When Welles quoted the fact in his own *F Is for Fake*, he used clips from Ray Harryhausen's *Earth Vs. the Flying Saucers*. Harryhausen himself badly wanted to make it after World War II and even did some stop-motion tests in color but it needed the U.F.O. craze, the success of *Destination Moon* and producer George Pal to realize its potential. "*The War of the Worlds* was no longer as ancient as Wells had once believed. With all the talk about flying saucers, it had become especially timely. And that is one of the reasons we updated the story to the present and placed it in California — the other being the obviously limited budget and the

costliness of a London period film" (*Cinefantastique* Volume 5 Number 4, p. 9).

Director Byron Haskin (interviewed by Joe Adamson, p. 207) agreed with Pal's vision: "Even without the Martian shots, it was potentially a great war picture. God willing that it'd never happen, but if Russia and the United States had started hostilities, you could have substituted the Russian invasion and have a hell of a war film." Three manta ray-shaped Martian war machines, designed by Albert Nozaki, 42 inches in diameter, were made of copper and "flown" and supported by fifteen wires each; according to George Pal, this resulted in marionette theater in the grand style. "As originally planned this was to go to 3-D for the last reel, beginning where the cast puts on goggles prior to the atomic blast, and indeed the film appears to have been shot stereoscopically from that point on" (R. M. Hayes, *3-D Movies*, p. 364).

The movie was remade by Steven Spielberg in 2005, this time using the giant tripod concept that Wells had envisioned for the Martian war machines. But that entry created only boredom as Tom Cruise walked around ILM-engineered disaster.

1953–54

20000 Leagues Under the Sea Walt Disney Productions, U.S.A. CinemaScope, Technicolor.

Director: Richard Fleischer. *Special Design* Nautilus *Designer:* Harper Goff. *Special Effects Design:* John Hench. *Miniature Photography Unit—Miniature Effects Unit Supervisor/Effects Photography:* Ralph Hammeras. *Director of Special Effects Photography:* Charles Bovel. *Miniature Technicians:* Warren Ray Hamilton, Les Wharburton. *Special Effects Assistant:* Jim Donnelly. *Special Effects Technician:* Lou Gray. *Background Projection:* Andy Lane. *Fox Studios Supervisor (Sersen Lake):* Fred M. Sersen. *Special*

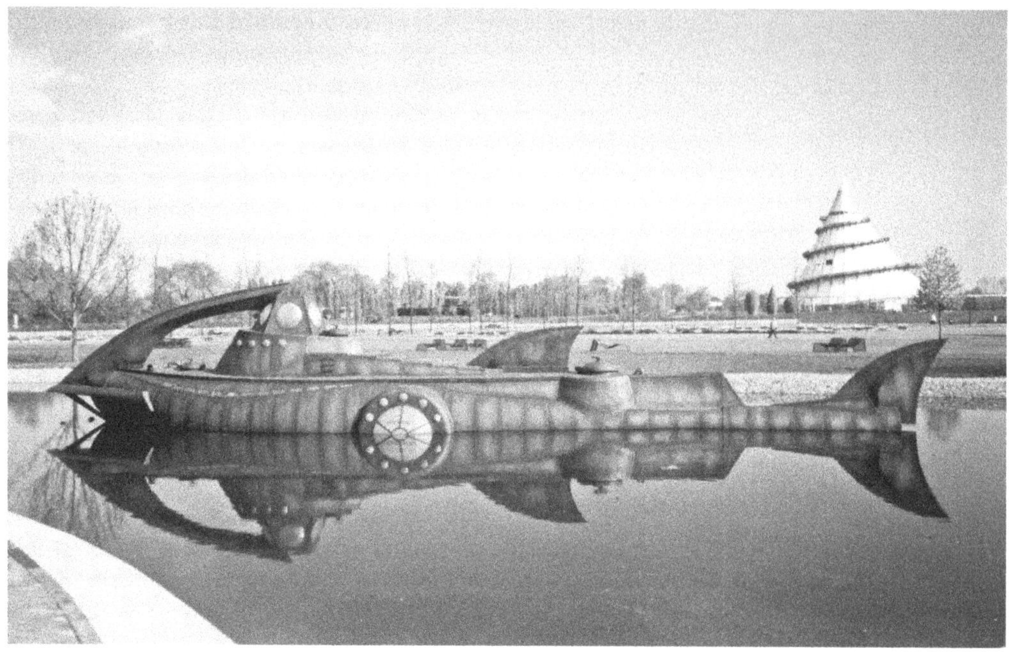

20000 Leagues Under the Sea? No, it's not. This *Nautilus,* very similar to Harper Goff's design for Disney's 1954 production, was seen at Bundesgartenschau in Magdeburg in 1999 (photograph by Dr. Ralf Bülow, courtesy Deutsche Kinemathek Berlin).

Effects/Miniature Effects Consultants/Suspending of Nautilus *Miniature:* Howard J. and Theodore H. Lydecker. *Optical Effects—Special Visual Effects/Special Processes:* Ub Iwerks. *Visual Effects/ Process Assistant:* Eustace A. Lycett. *Optical Printer Technician:* Art Cruickshank. *Matte Paintings—Matte and Glass Art:* Peter Ellenshaw. *Title Art:* Albert J. Whitlock. *2D Animation—Effects Animation Supevisor:* Joshua Meador. *Mechanical Effects Unit—Giant Squid Sequence Director:* James C. Havens. *Giant Squid Mechanics:* Robert A. Mattey. *Giant Squid Sculptor:* Chris Mueller. *Giant Squid Technician/Sculptor:* Marcel Delgado. *Special Action Props:* Don Post Studios. *Special Service—Second Unit Photography:* Edward Colman. Academy Award: Ralph Hammeras or Ub Iwerks.

This, the second CinemaScope picture to go into production, was originally intended to be an animated feature. The fight with a giant squid was filmed twice. In the first try, shot on a calm sea lit by the setting sun, the wires that supported the kapok-filled tentacles were clearly visible. Screenwriter Earl Felton suggested filming the sequence on a stormy sea. A second squid was built and manipulated by upwards of 50 technicians. Interestingly enough, the script has two squids attacking: the first smaller, then the second larger one takes over where the first one has failed. (It even might have been filmed that way but in the finished film there only seems to be one squid around.)

1953–56

The Ten Commandments   Motion Picture Associates Inc./Paramount, U.S.A. VistaVision, Technicolor.

Director: Cecil B. DeMille. *Photographic Effects—Special Photographic Effects Supervisor:* John P. Fulton. *Optical Cinematography:* Paul K. Lerpae. *Optical Printing:* Frank Stanley, Jack Caulfield, Aubrey Law, Carl Lerpae. *Miniatures—Miniature Supervisor:* Ivyl Burks. *Matte Paintings—Matte Artist:* Jan Domela. *Matte Photography:* Irmin Roberts. *Process Photography— Process Supervisor:* Farciot Edouart. *Second Unit Photography:* W. Wallace Kelley. *Special Art—Effects Animation:* Joe Alves. *Title Photography:* David Stanley Horsley. *Mechanical Effects—Me-*

chanical Effects Supervisor: Richard Parker. Academy Award: John P. Fulton

"Forget the script," says Martin Scorsese, "you've got to concentrate on the special effects, the texture, the color. The Angel of Death killing the firstborn in green smoke, the Red Sea, the lamb's blood of the Passover, the parting of the waters. DeMille put a dreamlike quality on film that was so real, it excited me as a child and stuck with me for life."

The sequence in which Moses (Charlton Heston) parted the Red Sea in VistaVision took six months to film. The contents of a huge tank (360,000 gallons of water) were released in ten minutes and filmed at high speed: In order to film this sequence in summer 1955, they even had to tear down the fence that separated Paramount from the neighboring RKO lot. "Built on one-fifth scale, the wall-of-water image was formed on the *bottom* of a tilted ramp. The ramp stood 32 feet high and 80 feet long, adjacent to Paramount's Western street, with water supplied from an elevated tank through 15 manually controlled, hydraulically operated slit valves. This allowed a long stretch of water to cascade down in a thin sheet, dip, then 'surf up' into a turbulent mass and spill over the rim. Built over the bottom 'hump' was a network of wooden riffles which helped break up the flow, into thick currents" (Paul Mandell, *Cinemagic* Issue #31, p. 47). Thus effects supervisor John P. Fulton and his unit were able to get enough violent water action plummeting downward and to photographically control the currents. The splashing water footage was optically reversed to create the final walls of water. Matte Artist Jan Domela added painted elements of rock formations for the exposed sea bottom. 600 extras were multiplied by split-screen mattes into a crowd of 1,800 marching through the area.

The Ten Commandments contain lots of blue screen as well as ordinary rear-projection shots. To execute these, Farciot Edouart's process department got a Mitchell VistaVision projector.

1954

Gojira [U.S.: *Godzilla, King of the Monsters!*] Tomoyuki Tanaka/Toho Co., Ltd., Japan

Director: Ishiro Honda. *Technical Effects—Technical Effects Director:* Eiji Tsuburaya. *Technical Effects Assistant Director:* Masakatsu Asai. *Volontary:* Hajime Tsuburaya. *Production Assistant:* Yasuaki Sakamoto. *Art Department—Special Effects Art Director:* Akira Watanabe. *First Assistant Art Director:* Yasuyuki Inoue. *Second Assistant Art Director:* Yoshio Irie. *Prop Masters:* Kintaro Makino, Yoshikazu Tanaka. *Backdrop Artist:* Fukutaro Suzuki. *Photographic Effects—Special Effects Photography:* Teisho (Sadamasa) Arikawa, Sokei Tomioka, Yoichi Manoda, Yukio Kabayama. *Lighting Supervisor:* Kuichiro Kishida. *Lighting Technicians:* Shinji Akiichi, Hideo Hata. *Grips:* Mitsukazu Toshibukuro, Hajime Takayama. *Matte and Optical Cinematography—Optical Cinematography/Composites and Matte Photography:* Hiroshi Mukoyama. *Matte Paintings:* Takao Yuki, Tadao Izuka. *Monster Costumes and Miniatures—Wire Effects:* Fumio Nakadai, Shoji Ogawa. *Gojira Suit:* Teizo Toshimitsu, Koei Yagi, Kanji Yagi, Eizo Kaimai, Yoshio Suzuki. *Plasters:* Yukio Odagiri, Mitsuo Tomigashi, Sakai Terui. *Consultant:* Fuminori Ohashi. *Godzilla Played by* Haruo Nakajima and Katsumi Tezuka.—*Gojira* was inspired by *The Beast from 20,000 Fathoms*. Originally the idea was to use stop-motion animation but it was ultimately decided to speed up the production process by using specially designed monster suits (for bit player Haruo Nakajima) and (for close-ups) a mechanically operated head as well as a traditional hand puppet. It was effects director Tsuburaya's idea to use a gigantic octopus as Harryhausen did in *It Came from Beneath the Sea* but he was overruled in favor of a Tyrannosaurus-Stegosaurus hybrid.

On April 4, 1956, an Americanized version that added footage with actor Raymond Burr was successfully launched in the United States. Breathless commentary from the sensational theatrical trailer made up by Trans World:

> *Godzilla—King of the Monsters!*
> Alive! Surging up from the depths of the sea on a tidal wave of terror to wreak vengeance on mankind!
> *Godzilla—King of the Monsters!*
> It's alive! A gigantic beast! Stalking the Earth! Crushing all before it in a psychotic cavalcade of electrifying horror! Raging through the streets on a rampage of total destruction!

Godzilla—King of the Monsters!

Incredible titan of terror! Wiping out a city of six million in a holocaust of flame! Jet planes cannot destroy it! Bombs cannot kill it! All modern weapons fail! Is this the end of our civilization? Can the scientists of the world find a way to stop this creature?

For the answer, see *Godzilla—King of the Monsters!*

You may wish to deny it, but your eyes tell you it's true! A tale to stun the mind! More fantastic than any ever written by Jules Verne! More terrifying than any ever shown on the screen! Awesome! Incredible! Unbelievable! A story beyond your wildest dreams!

Dynamic Violence! Savage Action! Spectacular Thrills!

Godzilla—King of the Monsters!

Fantastic beyond comprehension! Gripping beyond compare! Astounding beyond believe!

See *Godzilla—King of the Monsters!*

1954–55

The Dam Busters   Associated British Picture Corporation, Ltd., Great Britain

Director: Michael Anderson. *Miniatures—Miniature Supervisor:* George Blackwell. *Photographic Effects—Matte Effects and Traveling Mattes:* Les Bowie, Victor L. A. Margutti (Bowie-Margutti). *Effects Photography:* Gilbert Taylor. *Rostrum Camera/Rotoscope Mattes:* Ronnie Wass. *Director of Photography/Aerial Photography:* Erwin Hillier.

R.A.F. bombers attack Nazis and blow up Ruhr dam. Some scenes became the blueprint for the Deathstar attack in *Star Wars*. Made at Elstree Studios.

1954–55

This Island Earth   William Alland/Universal, U.S.A, Technicolor.

Director: Joseph Newman. *Art Department—Conceptual Art:* Fransiscus L.A.M. Baron van Lamsweerde. *Photographic Effects—Special Photography:* David Stanley Horsley. *Director of Photography and Additional Miniature Photography:* Clifford R. Stine. *Optical Cinematography:* Roswell A. Hoffman. *Special Effects Grip:* Wes Thompson. *Miniatures—Miniatures Supervisor:* Charles A. Baker. *Matte Paintings—Supervising Matte Artist:* Russell A. Lawson. *Mechanical Effects—Mechanical Effects and Explosives:* Fred Knoth. *Effects Technicians:* Evan Baldwin, Eddie Stein, Ralph Howle, Cecil Swartz, Frank Tipper. *FX Makeup—Makeup Supervisor:* Bud Westmore. *Makeup Creator (Metaluna Mutant):* Jack Kevan. *Sculptor (Metaluna Mutant):* Chris Mueller. *Assistant Makeup:* Bob Hickman.

Earth scientists get involved in the interplanetary war between Zahgon and Metaluna and are kidnapped to support Metaluna but too late they arrive on the doomed planet. In the days before motion control, the spaceship models had to do all the traveling, not the camera. Stan Horsley: "In doing miniature work of this kind, I would always arrange it so that gravity was working for me rather than against me. Gravity is one of the dependable, useful forces that is at our disposal. Whenever possible, this effect of gravity was utilized. When miniatures are suspended on wires—fine steel piano wires for the most part—these wires are like springs. When you try to accelerate the object, the wires stretch, and when you cease to accelerate, they spring back into the other position, introducing a tendency known as 'wire wobble.' Now you can avoid this by sloping the wires in such a way that gravity lends a hand. Very often a set can be tilted or even erected vertically in such a way that an object can fall through it as though it were flying through it, with the camera on its side. For example, on the Metaluna set, we would lift the saucer out of the set by increasing the pull on the wires as we went. It would be gaining speed as it left the surface; consequently, the wires would not be slacked off, and it would not have the tendency to bobble. We could bring it in smoothly to a perfect landing by running a shot of this kind in reverse" (Interview with Philip J. Riley). During production there was friction between Horsley and the Front Office. He blew his top, left the set—and when he returned, his position was given to somebody else. Typical Hollywood gratitude....

1955

Tarantula   William Alland/Universal, U.S.A.
Director: Jack Arnold. *Photographic Effects—Special Photography:* Clifford R. Stine. *Prepro-

duction: David Stanley Horsley. *Optical Cinematography:* Roswell A. Hoffman *Miniatures—Miniature Supervisor:* Charles A. Baker. *Miniature Technician:* Tim Baar. *Spider Model (for close-ups):* Wah Ming Chang, Gene Warren. *FX Makeup—Makeup Supervisor:* Bud Westmore. *Makeup Creator:* Jack Kevan.

Due to scientific experiments, a tarantula starts to grow to immense size and attacks a desert town. It is killed by napalm rockets fired from a plane by uncredited bit player Clint Eastwood. Live tarantulas are effectively superimposed in the scenes, walking around like nightmarish traveling mattes (in fact, they are).

1955

Gojira no gyakushu [U.S.: *Gigantis, the Fire Monster*], Tomoyuki Tanaka/Toho Co., Ltd., Japan

Director: Motoyoshi Oda. *Technical Effects—Technical Effects Director:* Eiji Tsuburaya. *Technical Effects Assistant Director:* Masakatsu Asai. *Art Department—Special Effects Art Director:* Akira Watanabe. *First Assistant Special Effects Art Director:* Yasuyuki Inoue. *Second Assistant Special Effects Art Director:* Yoshio Irie. *Photographic Effects—Special Effects Photography:* Teisho (Sadamasa) Arikawa, Sokei Tomioka, Yoichi Manoda. *Assistant Cameraman:* Koichi Takano. *Lighting Effects:* Masao Shirota. *Matte and Optical Cinematography—Optical Cinematography/Composite and Matte Photography:* Hiroshi Mukoyama. *Monster Costumes and Miniatures Wire Effects:* Fumio Nakadai. *Monster Suits:* Teizo Toshimitsu, Koei Yagi, Kanji Yagi, Eizo Kaimai. *Miniatures:* Yukio Odagiri, Mitsuo Tomiguchi. *Godzilla Played by* Haruo Nakajima. *Angirasu Played by* Katsumi Tezuka.

An often overlooked, certainly underestimated minor "suitmation" classic, released in Japan six months after the original *Gojira*. The first of Toho's "monster vs. monster" films: "They'll make you scream twice as loud!" A second dinosaur of the same radioactive species as the premier *Gojira* turns up in Osaka and destroys lots of miniatures including Osaka Castle (they had to build it twice as it didn't break satisfactorily the first time) while fighting Angirasu (Angilas), a spike-laden quadruped beast identified by on-screen scientists (Takashi Shimura is back as Dr. Yamane) as sort of an Ankylosaurus. While shooting the miniature fights, one of the three recording cameras accidentally shot slow (18 fps) instead of high speed. As cinematographer Teisho Arikawa remembers, "It was ordinary to shoot Godzilla at high speed. But camera C wasn't set in high speed. I don't know if he meant to do it, or he forgot to set it, we still don't know. But when we saw the dailies, cameras A and B were on the right setting, but camera C's Godzilla moved quicker than A and B" (*Japan's Favorite Mon-Star*, p. 63). Nevertheless, effects supervisor Eiji Tsuburaya seemed to have been impressed enough by the result to order more scenes of this type for now the two creatures appeared to engage themselves in fierce, mortal combat. The surviving creature, Gojira (who else?), escapes and eventually is located on a snow-covered island where it is buried under the explosions of icy slopes thanks to Japanese jet planes.

1955–56

Forbidden Planet Nicholas Nayfack/MGM, U.S.A. CinemaScope, Eastmancolor. Prints by Metrocolor.

Director: Fred McLeod Wilcox. *Special Effects—Special Effects Supervisor:* A. Arnold Gillespie. *Miniatures—Miniature Cinematographer:* Maximilian Fabian. *Miniature Technician:* Glen Robinson. *Mechanical Effects—Mechanical Effects Foreman and Explosives:* A. D. Flowers. *Special Effects Technicians:* Logan Frazee, Dean Pearson, Joe Zomar, Jack McMasters, Robert A. MacDonald, Max Gebinger, Earl McCoy, Chuck Frazier, Dion Hanson, Eddie Fisher. *Matte Paintings—Supervising Matte Artist:* Warren A. Newcombe. *Matte Artists:* Howard Fisher, Henri Hillinck. *Assistant Matte Artist:* Matthew J. Yuricich. *Matte Photography:* Dwight Carlisle. *Optical Cinematography—Optical Cinematography Supervisor:* Irving G. Ries. *Walt Disney Unit/Effects Animation—Supervising Effects Animation (Courtesy of Walt Disney Productions):* Joshua Meador. *Optical Consultant:* Ub Iwerks. *Effects Animation:* Joseph Alves, Ron Cobb. *Effects Animation Design:* Ken Hultgren. *Effects Animation Photography:* Art Cruickshank.

Science-fiction variation of Shakespeare's *The Tempest* and Sigmund Freud's idea of the Id. Conceived by Allen Adler and matte artist Irving A. Block, who locate their story on Altair-4 where the members of United Planets Cruiser C-57-D not only encounter Prof. Morbius (Walter Pidgeon), his robot servant Robby and his beautiful daughter Altaira (Anne Francis), who has never seen another man before, but also the monsters from the Id that destroyed the once-powerful Krel civilization. Originally Adler and Block suggested invisible monsters but MGM went for the obvious and asked Disney to visualize and animate a two-legged lion head.

1955–56

Ilya Muromets [U.S.: *The Sword and the Dragon*], Mosfilm, USSR., Sovscope, Sovcolor.
Director Aleksandr L. Ptushko. *Photographic Effects—Director of Photography:* Fyodor Provorov. *Camera Effects:* Aleksei Renkov. *Optical Effects:* Boris T. Travkin. *FX Makeup—*

Makeup Artist: Yevgeni Svidetelev. *Mechanical Effects—Dragon Gorynych Constructed by* V. Smirnov.

For this, the Soviet Union's first anamorphic widescreen picture (2.5:1 ratio), Aleksandr Ptushko, the premier Russian expert in film fantasy, adapted ancient folk tales (*bylini*) into a coherent storyline. Ilya Muromets (played by Boris Andreyev) is a typical Russian hero larger than life, a Goliath or Samson, who fights Khan Kalin and his invading Tugars who in the end unleash the winged dragon creature Gorynych against the City of Kiev.

Ptushko on the "wonders of the camera":

Hundreds of *bylini* have been written about Ilya Muromets. They all basically revolve around the same pivot — Ilya Muromets sat at home for 33 years and then was cured of his lameness, rose to his feet, and carried out a number of patriotic deeds. These individual tales, however, could not by themselves serve as material for a film. They would be a series of interesting vignettes, lacking dramaturgical cohesiveness. To solve this problem was no easy matter, but I believe that M. Kochnev's script succeeded in doing so.... The epic scope of the events that were to be shown in our

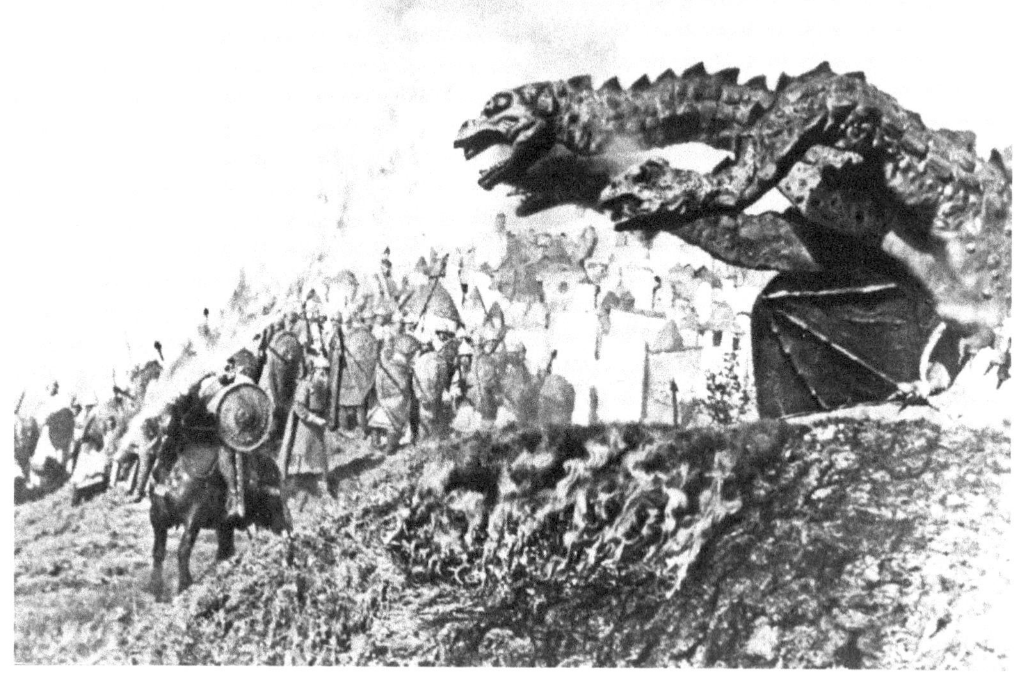

The three-headed fire-breathing dragon Gorynych built by V. Smirnov for Alexander Ptushko's epic *Ilya Muromets* (1956), the first Russian scope picture (courtesy Deutsche Kinemathek Berlin).

film compelled us to rely upon the very latest film technology. Naturally this meant, above all, the capabilities of the wide screen, but special effects were also extremely important in our film, like never before, model constructions and other effects were applied: the countless hordes like locusts, the huge dragon Gorynych, the horses standing on their hind legs running "through" the enemy, and other similar shots. These tasks were brilliantly realized by the special effects cameramen A. Renkov, B. Travkin, and the constructor V. Smirnov [published in a collection of Mosfilm: Articles, Publications, Visual Materials in 1959, translated by Alan Upchurch for *Video Watchdog* No. 9, Jan.-Feb. 1992].

Mirrors were used to multiply the members of the advancing Tugar army. Different models were made to show the three-headed, fire-breathing dragon Gorynych fly; oversized heads and wings to show him on the ground ready to be killed by Muromets and his brave son.

1956–57

The Incredible Shrinking Man   Albert Zugsmith/Universal, U.S.A. CinemaScope.

Director: Jack Arnold. *Photographic Effects— Special Photography:* Clifford R. Stine. *Process Cinematography:* Tom McCrory. *Optical Cinematography:* Roswell A. Hoffman. *FX Editing— Effects Editor:* Everett H. Broussard. *Miniatures— Miniature Supervisor:* Charles A. Baker. *Mechanical Effects—Mechanical Effects Foreman:* Fred Knoth. *Mechanicial Effects Technician:* Ben "Whitey" MacMahon. *Technical:* Jack Tait. *Special Sets and Props:* Ed Keyes, Roy Neal, Russ Gausman, Floyd Farrington.

During a boat ride, Scott Carey (played by Grant Williams) sails into a radioactive cloud and starts to shrink. As a modern-day tom thumb, he has to fight many obstacles in the vastness of his own cellar. The climax involves a fight with a spider. Dozens of tarantulas were used under the hot studio lights and "directed" by means of puffs of air, with Williams' action meticulously timed to the beats of a metronome before both segments were combined in an optical printer.

1956

Earth vs. the Flying Saucers   Charles H. Schneer and Sam Katzman/Clover/Columbia, U.S.A.

Director: Fred F. Sears. *Stop-Motion—Stop-Motion Animation and Visual Effects:* Ray Harryhausen. *Aluminum Saucers:* Fred Harryhausen. *Special Effects Prop Man:* George Lofgren. *Visual Effects and Process—Visual Effects Consultant and Second Unit Director:* Lawrence W. Butler. *Process Service:* George J. Teague. *Director of Photography:* Fred Jackman, Jr. *Mechanical Effects—Mechanical Effects Supervisor:* Jack Erickson.

The residents of a dying planet, fragile metal-encased aliens, want to settle on Earth. They give us 60 days to surrender. If world governments refuse, they will be seized by force. Dr. Russell Marvin (Hugh Marlowe) a missile expert, starts work on a weapon designed to unbalance the flying saucers' gyroscopic stability. His anti-spaceship guns finally save Washington D.C. from the inevitable flying saucer attack. For animation purposes, Ray Harryhausen designed the models "so that the outer rim of the craft and the center were independent of the inner revolving section. These rims were decorated with parallel lines that give the saucers, when animated, a strange stroboscopic effect." Footage from *Flying Saucers* was used in *The Giant Claw, The 27th Day,* and Orson Welles' *F for Fake.*

1956–57

The Giant Claw   Sam Katzman/Clover/Columbia, U.S.A./Mexico, Miniatures filmed at Churubusco Studios

Director: Fred F. Sears. *Process—Second Unit Director:* Lawrence W. Butler. *Process Service:* George J. Teague. *Miniatures—Director of Miniature Photography:* Ralph Hammeras. *Miniatures:* Churubusco Studios Prop Shop.

A bomb of a giant turkey: "That bird is extra-terrestrial. It comes from outer space. From some godforsaken anti-matter galaxy, millions and millions of light years from the Earth. No other explanation is possible." An enigma to everyone who has seen it. How could it happen that they dared to turn loose such a hair-rising marionette flapping through cheap miniature landscapes and towering above skyscraper models? Ray Harryhausen was offered the job but turned it down. Two or three years earlier, when Harryhausen presented his concept for an animated octopus (*It Came from Beneath the Sea*) to low-budget producer Sam Katzman, he was told that it didn't look like what the executive had envisioned. Katzman took a piece of paper and drew what he considered a *real* octopus: a big *balloon* with tentacles attached. Harryhausen: "It looked like something out of a Popeye cartoon." Apparently in *The Giant Claw,* Katzman got what he wanted. George Teague, process supervisor, suggested Ralph Hammeras, an old and experienced — but obviously rather weak-willed — pro. To cut costs, the effects scenes in *Giant Claw* were filmed at Churubasco Studios in Mexico. "It's just a bird. A big bird. Guns, cannons, rockets — it's just a bird."

1956–57

The Black Scorpion   Frank Melford and Jack Dietz/Amex (released by Warner Bros.), U.S.A./Mexico, Filmed at Churubusco Studios

Director: Edward Ludwig. *Stop-Motion—Stop-Motion Design and Supervisor of Special Effects:* Willis H. O'Brien. *Stop-Motion Animation:* Peter Peterson. *Effects Consultant and Painter:* Ralph Hammeras. *Postproduction—Optical Effects:* Howard A. Anderson Company. *Optical Effects Supervisor:* Howard A. Anderson, Jr. *Optical Cinematography:* Philip Kellison. *Special Props (Closeup Scorpion Model):* Wah Ming Chang.

Giant-bug-on-the-loose picture begun in Mexico, where all of the action takes place, and finished in a garage back in Glendale. "With its sprightly special effects by Willis O'Brien ... this is considerably more lively than most of the recent examples of eccentric zoology" (*Monthly Film Bulletin*, December 1958). Ralph Hammeras, while working on that literal turkey *The Giant Claw*, had suggested to O'Brien to set up a shop at Churubusco Studios in Mexico.

1956–57

20 Million Miles to Earth   Charles H. Schneer/Morningside Productions/Columbia, U.S.A. Many exteriors filmed in Italy.

Director: Nathan Juran. *Stop-Motion—Creator of Technical Effects/Stop-Motion Animation:* Ray Harryhausen. *Armature:* Fred Harryhausen. *Assistant Model maker/Taxidermist:* George Lofgren. *Process—Second Unit Director (Italy):* Lawrence W. Butler. *Process Service:* George J. Teague.

When an American spaceship returning from the initial manned flight to Venus crashes into the sea off Sicily, a small canister, which contains a jellylike Venusian egg, washes ashore. A tiny humanoid reptile hatches, growing at an alarming rate in Earth's alien atmosphere. Brought to a lab at the Rome Zoo, the creature, now over 20 feet tall and sedated by a constant flow of electricity, is able to smash its chains during a power outage, and destroys some of the ancient ruins such as the Temple of Saturn. The creature is killed by tanks firing while it climbs the Coliseum. Originally Harryhausen envisioned a satyr-like creature invading Chicago but changed his mind as he was interested in seeing a little bit of Europe. When they filmed in Rome, a director had not yet been selected. Larry Butler, in charge of Columbia's effects department, volunteered and took that job. This is one of three Harryhausen features which have recently been digitally colorized.

1956–57

Kronos   Robert L. Lippert/Regal Films (20th Century–Fox), U.S.A. Regalscope.

Director: Kurt Neumann. *Photographic Effects—Optical Company:* Studio Film Service. *Optical Cinematography, Animation and Co-Production:* Jack Rabin, Louis DeWitt. *Art Department—Special Effects Art Director:* Irving A. Block. *Matte Paintings—Matte Artist:* Menrad Von Mulldorfer. *Stop-Motion—Stop-Motion Model:* Wah Ming Chang. *Stop-Motion Animation:* Gene Warren.

Kronos is a most interesting low-budget effort co-produced by the cheaply notorious effects trio of Rabin, DeWitt and Block (the latter also wrote the story). Two models of Kronos, a box-like giant robot deposited on Earth by flying saucer, were used, one larger for all major effects and also a six-inch version. Jack Rabin: "We had the little one as a kind of stand-in model. If we'd used the big one for some of the far shots, the background would get pretty damned big.... When it became a box it was done through a se-ries of dissolves — we never had a totally collapsi-ble model. What we couldn't do with either model was done by animation. When Kronos is disintegrating in the end, we put a sheet of glass in a door frame. Atop that we put aluminum powder. We heated it up so it started to melt, to run. Everything else, the lightning etc., was an-imation put on top of that. The powder wouldn't run fast enough so we really heated it up — we got pyrex glass to withstand the heat so that the stuff would crack and 'do its thing.'" (*Fantascene* Vol. 1 No. 2)

1957

Chikyu boeigun [U.S.: *The Mysterians*], Tomoyuki Tanaka/Toho Co., Ltd., Japan, TohoScope, Eastmancolor.

Director: Ishiro Honda. *Technical Effects—Technical Effects Director:* Eiji Tsuburaya. *Technical Effects Assistant Director:* Masakatsu Asai. *Art Department—Special Effects Art Director:* Akira Watanabe. *First Assistant Art Director:* Yasuyuki Inoue. *Second Assistant Art Director:* Yoshio Irie. *Special Technical Designs (Marcalite Ray Guns et al.):* Shigeru Komatsuzaki. *Photographic Effects—Special Effects Cinematography:* Sadamasa (Teisho) Arikawa, Hidesaburo Araki. *Lighting Effects:* Masao Shirota. *Composite and Matte Photography:* Hiroshi Mukoyama. *Miniatures—Wire Effects:* Fumio Nakadai. *Miniatures:* Yukio Odagiri, Mitsuo Tomiguchi. *Mogera the Mole-Like Giant Robot Played by* Haruo Nakajima.

"Electronic War Erupts from Outer Space." Earth Defense Forces unite under Japanese command to fight off an attack of invaders from outer space in Tohoscope. The Mysterians, Strontium-90-infected survivors of an extraterrestrial atomic war, threaten to destroy the Earth

if not given human females. Two grand battles, although overlong, fill the narrative with minia-tures, explosives and rotoscoped rays.

1957–58

The 7th Voyage of Sinbad Charles H. Schneer/Morningside Productions/Columbia, U.S.A./Britain, Filmed in Spain, Photographed in Eastmancolor. Prints by Technicolor. Selected Prints in Megascope. *Special Process:* Dynamation.

Director: Nathan Juran. *Stop-Motion — Visual Effects and Stop-Motion Animation Created by* Ray Harryhausen. *Taxidermist and Miniature Technician:* George Lofgren. *Stop-Motion Armatures:* Fred Harryhausen. *Photographic Effects—Director of Photography, Blue Screen and Process Plate Photography:* Wilkie Cooper. *Camera Effects:* Lawrence W. Butler, Donald C. Glouner. *Blue Screen Service:* Technicolor London. *Additional Service—Fencing Instructor (Skeleton Sequence):* Enzo Musumeci-Greco. *Main Titles:* Robert Gill.

"*The 7th Voyage of Sinbad* started when I made one sketch of a skeleton going up a staircase. Outside of a dream sequence the only acceptable way would be to have a sort of Arabian Nights fantasy. So I started reading the Arabian Nights stories and realized then how lacking in fantasy the other movies on the subject had been." With these words, Ray Harryhausen especially refers to RKO's Technicolor *Sinbad the Sailor* in which Douglas Fairbanks, Jr., in the beginning talks about the giant bird Roc but it isn't shown on screen. Influenced by *Kong* and the artwork of Gustave Doré, Harryhausen made a dozen or so sketches and presented them to various producers, such as Merian C. Cooper, Jesse Lasky and Edward Small, but nothing came out of it. Finally, the work was seen by Charles H. Schneer, who was looking for a follow-up to *20 Million Miles to Earth.*

The story was developed jointly by Harry-hausen (receiving no story credit) and screen-writer Kenneth Kolb: During a stop on the shores of monster-ridden Colossa Island, Sinbad the Sailor (Kerwin Mathews) rescues a magician,

Sokurah (Torin Thatcher), from a satyr-like cyclops. In an effort to force Sinbad to return with him to Colossa and aid him in obtaining a magic lamp, which now is in the cyclops' cavelike "treasure trove," Sokurah miniaturizes the sailor's fiancée, Princess Parisa (Kathryn Grant), claiming that her normal size can only be restored by a potion prepared from an eggshell of the two-headed Roc, a gigantic bird nesting on the peaks of Colossa Island. In the course of various adventures, Sinbad blinds the one-eyed ogre, finds the eggshell which eventually restores doll-sized Parisa and learns the secret of the magic lamp's boy genie Barani (Richard Eyer). To recover the lamp, Sokurah revives a skeleton warrior, then leads the fire-breathing watchdog of his murky underground castle, a dragon that just has overwhelmed and killed a second cyclops, against Sinbad and his men. But Sinbad succeeds in killing the creature with the huge shaft of a giant crossbow.

1958

tom thumb   George Pal/Galaxy Films, Inc./MGM, Great Britain/U.S.A. Metroscope, Metrocolor. *Process:* Automotion.

Director: George Pal. *Photographic Effects—Optical Cinematography:* Tom Howard (MGM British). *Stop-Motion Sequence—Stop-Motion Animation:* Project Unlimited, Inc. *Sculptor:* Wah Ming Chang. *Stop-Motion Animation:* Gene Warren, Don Sahlin, Herbert Johnson. *Additional Puppet Work:* Bob Baker. Academy Award: Tom Howard

Grimm's fairy tale about the boy who is not bigger than your thumb. Instead of reducing the actor's image (as suggested by Tom Howard and other specialists), Pal insisted on shooting the scenes with tom thumb (played by the very acrobatic Russ Tamblyn) on a black stage sometimes from 90 feet away to get the proper proportions and the image softness for such a tiny character. In fact, they even had to cut a hole in the studio roof on the MGM British lot. In one sequence, done back in Hollywood by Project Unlimited, tom thumb encounters George Pal's Puppetoons.

1957–58

Vynález zkázy   [*The Invention of Destruction*/U.S.: *The Fabulous World of Jules Verne*], Czechoslovensky, SSR, Filmed at Studio Gottvaldov, Zlín

Director: Karel Zeman. *Photographic Effects—Effects Photography:* Antonín Horák. *Cinematography:* Jirí Tarantík, Bohuslav Pikhart. *Art Department—Settings:* Zdenek Rozkopal. *Miniature Effects and Animation—Animation Unit:* Josef Zeman, Arnost Kupik, Jindrich Liska, Frantisek Krcmar. *Art Effects:* Zdenek Ostrocil. *Special Effects Assistants:* Jan Cep, Vlastas Slamenova.

A visually inspired combination of puppets, submarine models and stop-motion, dry-for-wet shots, two-dimensional drawings and foreground glass effects with fine horizontal lines that resemble the engravings and black-and-white etchings of the original Jules Verne books by Bennett and Riou. The movie looks like it was made in the 19th century. Director Karel Zeman: "I have stylized the smallest details."

> One of the central problems in the acceptance of films such as this is that Americans have trained Hollywood to give them films with lots of special effects, and Hollywood has responded with films in the mode of stylization called "realism." That is, effects that always are *supposed* to look as if they were happening in reality. Actually, that's not quite what it is: Hollywood gives us heightened, interpreted "reality": spaceships that roar in the airless vacuum of space and bank like fighter planes against the resistance of air that isn't there; floods that tower above buildings like waves instead of welling up around them; waves at sea that are higher than ships; dinosaurs that behave like crabby lizards.... What Karel Zeman did in *The Fabulous World of Jules Verne* was simple, yet rejected by many moviegoers: he tried to bring to life on screen the style of illustrations that accompanied the first editions of Verne's works. These were generally done in woodcuts (some sources say steel engravings, but the original illustrations were wood-engraving or line block reproductions), and as a result, there were many horizontal lines in the finished picture [Bill Warren, *Keep Watching the Skies!* Volume II, pp. 511–512].

According to trick cameraman Antonín Horák, there was not only an aesthetic but a technical reason for it. All effects had to be done latent image with a Slechta camera (named after its engineer, Josef Slechta) on the original negative. The composites therefore were jiggling but the horizontal lines make it look better as nobody noticed the technical faults then. "This complicated marriage of live-action, drawings and puppet-like models meant that the same film often went through the camera three and four times, for example, for some scenes cartoons were first drawn of the outdoor backgrounds. Then a weird, 12-propeller flying machine — actually a two-foot long plastic miniature — was photographed via the puppet stop-action method, superimposed over the same film. Then live actors, filmed in appropriate perspective, went through their paces, and this was superimposed again over the drawings and puppet-type miniatures" (Aline Mosby, *American Cinematographer,* October, 1958). "As a result, the black-and-white film lies far from our notions of "realism," and so the rejection by some U.S. moviegoers" (Warren, p. 512).

1958–59

Ben-Hur: A Tale of the Christ   Sam Zimbalist/MGM, Italy/U.S.A. Filmed at Cinecittà Studios, Rome. MGM Camera 65 (65mm), Technicolor.

Director: William Wyler. *Miniatures—Special Effects and Studio Tank Supervisor:* A. Arnold Gillespie. *Effects Technicians:* Glen Robinson, A. D. Flowers. *Matte Paintings—Supervising Matte Artist:* Lee LeBlanc. *Matte Artist:* Matthew J. Yuricich. *Matte Cinematography:* Clarence W. D. Slifer, Clifford Shirpser. *Optical Cinematography—Optical Cinematograph Supervisor:* Robert R. Hoag. *Optical Technician:* Petro Vlahos. *Process—Process Supervisor:* Carroll L. Shepphird. *Chariot Race Effects—Mechanical Effects Chariot Race:* Robert A. MacDonald. *Second Unit Photographer:* Harold E. Wellman. Academy Award: A. Arnold Gillespie, Robert MacDonald

In contrast to the silent *Ben-Hur* (1925), A. Arnold Gillespie and his team "did the entire sea galley sequence in miniature except for full-size sections of the galley that were filmed on the sound stage and blended in with process backgrounds and a few traveling mattes." Not all went well during shooting: "Unfortunately,

when they put the film together the ships were so slow and cumbersome that their scenes ruined the tempo of the film and as a result only a few short cuts of the miniatures appeared in the final picture" (L.B. Abbott, *Special Effects: Wire, Tape and Rubber Band Style*, p. 119).

1958–59

Darby O'Gill and the Little People   Walt Disney Productions, U.S.A, Technicolor.

Director: Robert Stevenson. *Photographic Effects—Director of Photography:* Winton C. Hoch.—*Special Consultants:* Ub Iwerks, Bob Otto. *Matte Paintings—Matte Artist and Effects Consultant:* Peter Ellenshaw. *Assistant Matte Artist:* Albert J. Whitlock. *Art Department—Consultant:* Don DaGradi. *Optical Cinematography—Optical Cinematography Supervisor:* Eustace A. Lycett. *Optical Technicians:* Art Cruickshank, Robert Broughton. *Effects Animation—Effects Animation Supervisor:* Joshua Meador. *Effects Animator:* Don MacManus. *Mechanical Effects—Mechanical Effects Technician:* Danny Lee.

Intriguing trick perspective shots, used to great effect, show actor Albert Sharpe (as cunning Darby O'Gill) and elfish leprechauns in the same frame. Albert Whitlock, who knew the Shuftan process from his days in Britain was the first to suggest this time- and energy-consuming (many lights) but highly effective system to the Disney people. With engineer Bob Otto, the inventive Ub Iwerks devised a nodal-point perspective camera to shoot the forced perspective effects.

1958–59

North by Northwest   MGM, U.S.A. VistaVision, Metrocolor.

Director: Alfred Hitchcock. *Special Effects—Special Effects Supervisor:* A. Arnold Gillespie. *Process Photography—Process Supervisor:* Carroll L. Shepphird. *Matte Paintings—Supervising Matte Artist:* Lee LeBlanc. *Assistant Matte Artist:* Matthew J. Yuricich. *Matte Cinematography:* Clarence W.D. Slifer, Clifford Shirpser. *Additional Service—Main Titles:* Saul Bass.

Two big effects sequences: Cary Grant is shot

at from an airborne crop duster; climax involves transparencies and numerous matte shots of Mt. Rushmore.

1959

Journey to the Center of the Earth   20th Century–Fox Film Corp. in association with Cooga Mooga Productions, Inc. and Joseph M. Schenck Enterprises, U.S.A, CinemaScope, DeLuxe Color.

Director: Henry Levin. *Photographic Effects — Photographic Effects Supervisor:* L. B. Abbott. *Effects Cinematography:* James B. Gordon. *Matte Paintings—Supervising Matte Artist:* Emil Kosa, Jr. *Assistant Matte Artists:* Menrad Von Mulldorfer. *Miniature Unit—Miniature Photography:* Ralph Hammeras. *Prop Miniature Foreman:* Herb Cheek. *Mechanical Effects—Mechanical Effects Foreman:* Frank O'Connor.

This film version of Jules Verne's expedition to our planet's core (*Voyage au Centre de la Terre*, first published in 1864) brings us live lizards (iguanas) optically blown up to dimetrodon size, a magnetic storm on the interglobal ocean (a.k.a. Sersen Lake on the Fox backlot, 260 feet wide and 300 feet long) and the discovery of the miniaturized Lost City of Atlantis eventually destroyed by an earthquake (built on platforms supported on springs, the earthquake caused by electric motors). In charge of photographic effects was L. B. Abbott: "To show the dimetrodon being hit by the alpenstock, we built a small set and just off camera left we placed a 4'x8' plywood panel with a hole in it. Behind the board we placed a prop miniature man with a blow gun. The missile was a stick from a lollipop with a tiny metal barb on the end. As I recall, this was the only shot on the entire project where we really lucked out. The monster was on its stark mark, arc on tail, man at hole with loaded blow gun; the monster began to pant, the camera rolled, the monster made two slow steps forward, the blowgun was fired, the missile lodged in the upper portion of the monster's mouth, and the monster turned its head sharply to the left and froze. By optically rocking back and forth the five frames of head-turning action we had on film, we were able to make it appear that the monster shook its head" (*Special Effects: Wire, Tape and Rubber Band Style*, p. 75).

1959

Nippon tanjo   [U.S.: *The Three Treasures*], Sanezumi Fujimoto, Tomoyuki Tanaka/Toho Co., Ltd., Japan, Agfacolor.

Director: Hiroshi Inagaki. *Technical Effects—Technical Effects Director:* Eiji Tsuburaya. *Technical Effects Assistant Director:* Masakatsu Asai. *Art Department—Special Effects Art Director:* Akira Watanabe. *First Assistant Special Effects Art Director:* Yasuyuki Inoue. *Photographic Effects—Special Effects Cinematography:* Teisho (Sadamasa) Arikawa. *Optical Photography:* Hidesaburo Araki. *Lighting Effects:* Kuichiro Kishida. *Composite and Matte Photography:* Hiroshi Mukoyama. *Miniatures—Wire Effects:* Fumio Nakadai.

The birth of Japan and the origins of Shinto, as based on the legends "Kojiki" and "Nihon Shoki." One of the most ambitious Japanese fantasy films, the Japanese equivalent of Cecil B. DeMille's *The Ten Commandments*, *Nippon tanjo* stars Toshiro Mifune as Prince Yamato Takeru. There are three special effects sequences: a storm at sea, a seven-headed dragon (a forerunner of both Harryhausen's *Jason and the Argonauts* Hydra and Tsuburaya's own Ghidrah) and the final eruption of Mt. Fuji: Tsuburaya: "A fifteen-foot replica of the mountain was built in the studio pool, the only area large enough for it in the cramped back lot. After the top was blown off with gunpowder, vats of molten lead were poured over the crater to simulate lava. The eruption and subsequent lava flow were picked up in slow motion with several cameras to obtain a variety of angles at one shooting. 'In such work as this, which calls for extreme slow motion, I often use a Debrie camera turning at 240 frames per second" (Clifford V. Harrington, *American Cinematographer*, Vol. 41, No. 8).

1959

Uchu daisenso [U.S.: *Battle in Outer Space*], Tomoyuki Tanaka/Toho Co., Ltd., Japan, TohoScope, Eastmancolor

Director: Ishiro Honda. *Technical Effects—Technical Effects Director:* Eiji Tsuburaya. *Technical Effects Assistant Director:* Masakatsu Asai. *Art Department—Special Effects Art Director:* Akira Watanabe. *First Assistant Special Effects Art Director:* Yasuyuki Inoue. *Second Assistant Special Effects Art Director:* Yoshio Irie. *Special Technical Design:* Shigeu Komatsuzaki. *Photographic Effects—Special Effects Cinematography:* Teisho (Sadamasa) Arikawa. *Optical Photography:* Hidesaburo Araki. *Lighting Effects:* Kuichiro Kishida. *Composite and Matte Photography:* Hiroshi Mukoyama. *Miniatures Wire Effects:* Fumio Nakadai. *Model makers:* Yukio Odagiri, Mitsuo Tamiguchi.

This was meant to be a sequel to *The Mysterians* (1957): When explorers arrive on the Moon, they discover an alien base operated by militarists from Planet Natal. The aliens' mothership and flying saucers immediately attack the major cities of the Earth. "The film's highlight comes with the jaw-droppingly impressive climax where Tokyo is literally sucked up into the sky. The scene with the meteor falling on New York lasts but a few seconds, but special effects director Eiji Tsuburaya's crew managed to recreate a huge and reasonably accurate Manhattan skyline" (Stuart Galbraith IV, *Japanese Science Fiction, Fantasy and Horror Films*, p. 46). "Far and away the most attractive thing about this Toho production is the decor — the clean, bright color and a fetching assortment of obvious, but effective, miniature settings and backgrounds. Some of the art work is downright nifty.... The Japanese have opened a most amusing and beguiling bag of technical tricks" (Howard Thompson, *New York Times*).

1959

Der schweigende Stern/Milczaca gwiazda [U.S.: *First Spaceship on Venus*], DEFA/Film Polski, German Democratic Republic/Poland,

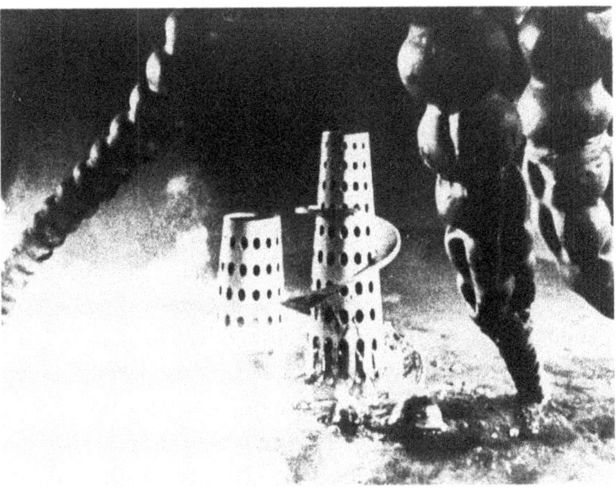

Ernst Kunstmann model shot for the spectacular East-German/Polish co-production *Der schweigende Stern* (1959), released in the United States as *First Spaceship on Venus* (courtesy Deutsche Kinemathek Berlin).

Filmed at DEFA Studios Babelsberg, Totalvision, Agfacolor.

Director: Kurt Maetzig. *Miniature Photography Unit—Miniature Photography:* Ernst Kunstmann. *Assistants:* Vera Kunstmann, Günter Gericke, Kurt Marks. *Photographic Effects—German Effects Cinematographer:* Helmut Grewald. *Polish Effects Cinematographer:* Jan Olejniczak. *Stop-Motion—Model Animation:* Erich Günter, Herbert K. Schulz.

The first East German outer space mission (*Kosmokrator I*) discovers that Venusian aggressors ready to attack Earth had been wiped out by their own atomic warfare instruments. On the ground, the *Kosmokrator* was mostly a huge miniature built in perspective. Almost surrealistic miniature scenes and double exposure depict the graveyard on Venus. According to Kurt Marks, who came fresh from East German film school to assist on the movie, there was some disagreement between German and Polish effects people.

1959–60

The Angry Red Planet Sid Pink/Sino, U.S.A. Filmed at Hal Roach Studios, Culver City. Eastmancolor. Cinemagic Process.

Director: Ib J. Melchior. *Effects Concepts—Special Effects Conceptual Art (in "Cinemagic"):* Norman Maurer. *Storyboard Artist:* Alex Toth.

Miniatures and Mechanical Effects—Effects Properties: Herman Townsley. *Model makers:* Howard Weeks, Herb Switzer, Jack Schwartz. *Puppeteer (Marionette):* Bob Baker. *Process and Effects Photography—Process Service:* Howard A. Anderson, Jr. (Howard A. Anderson Company). *Additional Effects Photography:* Lloyd W. Knechtel. *FX Makeup—Creature Shop:* Paul Blaisdell.

Low-budget space opera in a process called Cinemagic (a special lens developed by Norman Maurer, a former comic book artist who previously had done some artwork in 3D using respectively red/green tinted glasses). Made on rented sound stages of the Hal Roach Studios and originally titled *Invasion of Mars*: On Mars, astronauts encounter a bat-rat-spider crab marionette, a giant amoeba with rotating cyclops eye (instead of "two roughly circular nuclei, *almost* like 'eyes' in its center, which revolve constantly," as described by screenwriter-director Ib Melchior) and a Martian civilization. According to *Variety,* Cinemagic "is a kind of photographic trick that produces the effect of a negative. Shown in pinkish-colored tones, shadings are reverse, light's dark, dark's light. While it may take considerable ingenuity to produce this effect, the result isn't really worth it...."

Innocent kids, of course, couldn't withstand the showmanship of the promotion expertly handled by its distributor, American International Pictures:

> See the Strange Mile-High City of Mars!
> See the Gigantic Bat-Rat-Spider!
> See the Dead River Where Only the Monster Amoeba Can Live!
> Spectacular Adventure Beyond Time and Space ... as the Startling New Screen Process
> Cinemagic takes you on man's first visit to ...
> *The Angry Red Planet.*

1959–60

The 3 Worlds of Gulliver Charles H. Schneer/Morningside Worldwide Pictures–Columbia, Great Britain, Eastmancolor by Pathe. *Special Process:* SuperDynamation.

Director: Jack Sher. *Visual Effects and Stop-Motion—Visual Effects and Stop Motion Created by* Ray Harryhausen. *Sculptor:* Arthur Hayward. *Spanish Art Director/Miniature Sets:* Gil Par-

rondo. *Photographic Effects—Director of Photography and Process Plates:* Wilkie Cooper. *Traveling Matte Process:* Victor L. A. Margutti [*J. Arthur Rank Organization*]. *Additional Service—Fencing Master:* Enzo Musumeci-Greci.

Dr. Lemuel Gulliver's fantastic eighteenth-century adventures in Lilliput and Brobdingnag, land of the giants. A giant in Lilliput, Gulliver stops the small nation's silly war with the neighboring island of Blefuscu. A dwarf in Brobdingnag, reunited with his fiancée Elizabeth (June Thorburn), he is accused of witchcraft by court alchemist Makovan (Charles Lloyd Pack) and has to fight a huge crocodile to prove that he is no disciple of the black arts. Finally, he and Elizabeth are rescued by giant girl Glumdalclitch (Sherri Alberoni) who helps them return to England.

As Hollywood didn't have sufficient traveling matte laboratories, producer Charles Schneer and Ray Harryhausen decided to go to Britain where they would have the advantage of the Rank laboratories at Pinewood and their sodium vapor process. Schneer had obtained the original screenplay from Sher and Arthur Ross which first was offered to Universal Studios (and Eugen Schüfftan, who already was prepared to check his patents). They were going to hire Jack Lemmon for the title role but had to be content with Kerwin Mathews, who at least had some experience in working with Harryhausen.

1959–60

The Time Machine George Pal/Galaxy Films Inc.–MGM, U.S.A. Wide Screen, Metrocolor.

Director: George Pal. *Photographic Effects and Miniatures—Photographic Effects and Miniature Service:* Project Unlimited, Inc. *Effects and Miniature Supervisors:* Wah Ming Chang, Gene Warren, Tim Baar. *Art Effects and Matte Paintings:* William Brace. *Stop-Motion—Stop-Motion Animation:* David Pal, Don Sahlin, Tom Holland. *Effects Technician:* Jim Danforth. *Optical Cinematography—Optical Effects:* Howard A. Anderson Company. *Optical Cinematography Photographer:* Philip A. Kellison. *Optical Cinematography Supervisor:* Howard A. Anderson, Jr. Academy Award: Gene Warren, Tim Baar.

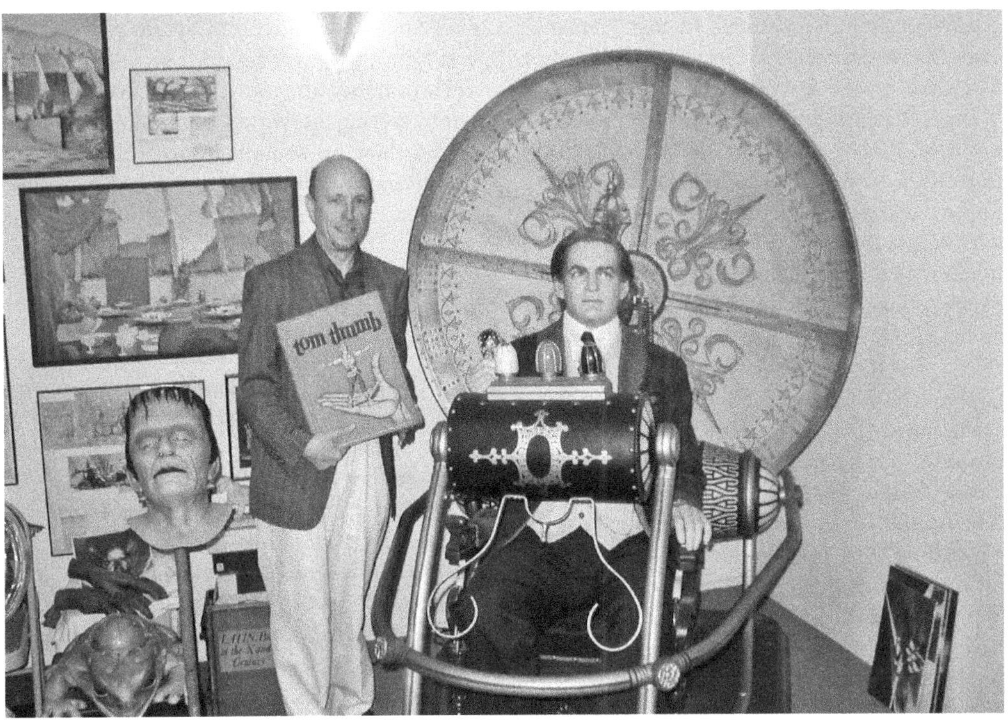

In the home of Hollywood collector Bob Burns, the author is allowed to pose beside the reconstructed Time Machine.

For his film version of H.G. Wells' story of an inventor who is able to travel into the distant future, George Pal hired Project Unlimited to do some time-lapse, stop-motion, effects illustration and miniatures. Pal later tried to get funds for a sequel and even offered the effects of *Time Machine II* to Jim Danforth but nothing came out of it.

1959–61

Gorgo King Bros. Productions/MGM, Great Britain/U.S.A. Technicolor.

Director and Miniature Effects Designer: Eugène Lourié. *Photographic Effects—Optical Cinematography:* Tom Howard [MGM British]. *Additional Service—Blue Screen:* Technicolor London. *Additional Optical Work (Postproduction):* Ray Mercer & Company.

Giant dinosaur (120') follows its motherly instincts and invades London to save its infant (36') which is exhibited in a circus in the amusement area of Battersea Park. Cleverly staged *Godzilla* rip-off, originally scheduled to be filmed in Japan under the working title *Kuru Island* (most obviously with Toho Company which instead turned out *Varan the Unbelievable*), then rewritten for London locations. Unlike director Lourié's previous efforts in the genre, *The Beast from 20,000 Fathoms* and *The Giant Behemoth*, *Gorgo* employs no stop-motion, instead utilizing a rubber monster suit and breakaway duplicates of Tower Bridge, Big Ben and central London streets: "I also decided that only one miniature beast would be used for both monsters, however different in size. For scenes with the 'baby' monster, the action was staged on a miniature set scaled down relative to the monster's size. But scenes with the giant 'mother' beast were shot with much smaller miniatures sized proportionally to the beast's size" (Lourie, *My Work in Films*, p. 244).

1960

Dinosaurus! Jack H. Harris/Fairview–Universal, U.S.A. CinemaScope, DeLuxe Color.

Director: Irvin S. Yeaworth, Jr. *Stop-Motion—Stop-Motion Sequences:* Project Unlimited. Inc. *Stop-Motion and Miniature Supervisors:* Gene Warren, Wah Ming Chang, Tim Baar. *Stop-Motion Models:* Marcel Delgado. *Armatures and Machine Work*: Victor Delgado, Paul LeBaron. *Stop-Motion Animation:* Don Sahlin, David Pal (Tyrannosaurus Rex), Tom Holland (Brontosaurus), Philip A. Kellison (steam shovel, earth digger). *Consultant to Producer Jack H. Harris:* Willis H. O'Brien. *Mechanical Effects—Special Effects Technicians:* Roscoe S. Cline, George Schlicker, George E. Peckham.

"Leave my friend alone, you bad old Tyrannosaurus!" On a remote island (location work: St. Croix, Virgin Islands), two deep-frozen dinosaurs and a Neanderthal Man are revived by a lightning bolt. The Tyrannosaurus is finished off by an earth digger similar to the one that Willis O'Brien's ill-fated *Gwangi* project would have had. No wonder: OBie was involved in this production as story consultant and visited Project Unlimited during shooting. The total budget was about $450,000. The brontosaurus model also appeared in *a Twilight Zone* episode ("The Odyssey of Flight 33").

1960–61

Mysterious Island   Charles H. Schneer/Ameran Films–Columbia, Great Britain
Eastmancolor.
Director: Cy Endfield. *Stop-Motion—Visual Effects Creator/Stop-Motion Animation:* Ray Harryhausen. *Models Sculpted by* Arthur Hayward. *Armatures:* Fred Harryhausen. *Photographic Effects—Director of Photography/Background Plates:* Wilkie Cooper. *Traveling Matte Consultant:* Victor L. A. Margutti. *Matte Paintings—Matte Photographer:* Wally Veevers. *Additional Service—Main Titles:* Robert Gill.

A leftover screenplay for a Jules Verne movie was enriched by adding (originally) prehistoric stop-motion creatures. During the siege of Richmond in 1865, three Union soldiers and a Northern newspaper correspondent escape from a Confederate prison in an observation balloon. Blown by a storm, they land on an uncharted South Pacific island, where they are joined by two shipwrecked English ladies. They encounter giant animal life and meet Captain Nemo (Herbert Lom), who is responsible for mutating animals in hopes of eliminating the root cause of war by solving the world's food problems. When pirates show up and a volcano erupts, our heroes escape but Nemo is trapped in the *Nautilus* and goes down with the island.

1960–61

The Guns of Navarone   Carl Foreman–Open Road Films Ltd./Highroad/Columbia, Great Britain. CinemaScope, Eastman Color. Processed by Technicolor.
Director: J. Lee Thompson. *Special Effects, Explosives and Miniatures—Special Effects and Pyrotechnical Supervisor:* William H. (Bill) Warrington. *Effects Cinematographer:* Ted Moore. *Miniature Technician:* John Stears. *Matte Paintings—Matte Photography:* Wally Veevers. *Matte Artists:* George Samuels, Bob Cuff. *Additional Service—Effects Consultant:* Robert A. Mattey. *Additional Optical Effects:* Butler-Glouner, Inc. *Maps:* Halas & Batchelor Cartoon Films Ltd. Academy Award: Bill Warrington.

A German mountain fortress in the Aegeis is equipped with two heavy radar-controlled German guns, the product of Shepperton Studios effects and matte crews.

1960–61

The Absent Minded Professor   Walt Disney, Bill Walsh/Walt Disney Productions, U.S.A.
Director: Robert Stevenson. *Matte Paintings—Matte Artist:* Peter Ellenshaw. *Assistant Matte Artist:* Albert J. Whitlock. *Optical Cinematography—Optical Cinematography Supervisor:* Eustace A. Lycett. *Assistant Optical Cinematography/Optical Printer Operator:* Art Cruickshank. *Optical Consultant:* Ub Iwerks. *Optical Photography Coordinator:* Robert Broughton. *Sequence Consultant:* Don DaGradi. *Mechanical Effects—Mechanical Effects Supervisor/Wirworks:* Robert A. Mattey. *Mechanical Effects Technicians:* Danny Lee, Walter Stone.

Prof. Ned Brainard (Fred MacMurray) invents

a substance he calls "Flubber," which makes his college's basketball team and his old Ford Model T car fly. "The many scenes of the flying Model T were accomplished in several ways. Peter Ellenshaw supervised the miniature car for scenes of it flying in and out of clouds, looping around a church steeple, and so forth.... By far the most impressive flying-car scenes are those involving a lightweight but full-sized Model T raised off the ground by invisible wires fastened to what must have been a colossal crane" (Bill Warren, *Keep Watching the Skies! Volume II*, p. 490).

1960–61

Master of the World   James H. Nicholson-Samuel Z. Arkoff-Anthony Carras/Alta Vista for American International Pictures, U.S.A.

Director: William Witney. *Miniatures—Modelshop:* Project Unlimited, Inc. *Miniature Supervisors:* Tim Baar, Wah Ming Chang, Gene Warren. *Model and Prop Makers:* Howard Weeks, Marcel Delgado, Victor Delgado. *Mold Maker:* Paul LeBaron. *Miniature Technician:* Jim Danforth. *Photographic Effects— Camera Effects and Model Photography:* Ray Mercer (Ray Mercer & Company). *Special Color Processes:* Modern Film Effects. *Matte Shots—Matte Painting Photography:* Butler-Glouner, Inc. *Process and Aerial Photography—Process Service:* Bob Hansard. *Aerial Cinematography:* Kay Norton. *Mechanical Effects—Special Props and Special Effects:* Patrick A. Dinga.

American International's answer to Disney's *20000 Leagues Under the Sea.* Producer Jim Nicholson's pet project involved an imaginative miniature aircraft, the *Albatross,* manned by Vincent Price and his crew. The movie was based on the Jules Verne novels *Robur le Conquérant* (1886) and *Maitre du Monde* (1904). "The featured player in effect is the flying craft, which as in most recent film derivations from 19th century Verne's conceptions, combines the futuristic and the archaic, looks like a Zeppelin with an oil refinery mounted on top, stained glass windows in the control cabin and various interior appurtenances mildly Victorian in style.... One can't help wondering if a younger generation that

takes for granted the likely invasion of the moon will be suitably impressed by the mechanical ingenuity or amused by the archaic decor" (*New York Herald-Tribune*). AIP delivered the picture to the Academy for an Effects Oscar nomination but to no avail.

1960–62

Jack the Giant Killer   Edward Small/Zenith (for United Artists release), U.S.A. Technicolor. *Special Process:* Fantascope.

Director: Nathan Juran. *Photographic Effects—Special Photographic Effects:* Howard A. Anderson Co. *Effects Supervisor:* Howard A. Anderson, Jr. *Director of Photography:* David Stanley Horsley. *Miniature Process Technician:* Wes Thompson. *Stop-Motion Camera, First and Second Unit Photography:* Philip A. Kellison. *Matte Paintings—Matte Artist:* Albert J. Whitlock. *Special Effects Design and Additional Matte Art:* Luis McManus. *Effects Animation—Effects Animators:* Lloyd L. Vaughan, Boyd Vaughan, Don MacManus. *Rotoscope Technician:* Nancy Van Rensaeller. *Production Effects—Explosions:* August J. Lohman. *Stop-Motion and Miniatures—Stop-Motion Animation and Miniatures:* Project Unlimited, Inc. *Stop Motion Sculptor:* Wah Ming Chang. *Stop-Motion Supervisor:* Gene Warren. *Miniature Supervisor:* Tim Baar. *Title Art and Effects Art:* William Brace. *Jack Puppet:* Martha Armstrong. *Armatures and Miniatures:* Victor Delgado, Paul LeBaron. *Additional Puppet and Miniature Work:* Marcel Delgado, Howard Weeks, Blanding Sloane. *Stop-Motion Animators:* Jim Danforth, David Pal, Tom Holland. *Test Animation:* Don Sahlin. *Stop-Motion Camera and Model Technician:* Ralph Rodine. *Production—Secretary at Project Unlimited:* Marion Young.

When Ray Harryhausen's *The 7th Voyage of Sinbad* proved the box-office sleeper of 1958, producer Edward Small decided to copy it with a fairy-tale from Cornwall. A farmer's son, Jack (Kerwin Mathews), fights ogres and other creatures turned loose by evil sorcerer Pendragon (Torin Thatcher), who wants to take the throne of Cornwall. Cormoran, the evil 20-foot giant who kidnaps Princess Elaine (Judi Meredith), sporting a horn, is almost a copy of Harryhausen's cyclops. As a substitute for the *7th Voy-*

age fight cyclops vs. dragon, *Jack* pits Galligantua, a two-headed giant, against a sea monster that during production mutated from lizard (in Luis MacManus' original design) and multi-tentacled parrot (in the test footage) to an octopus creature with the head of a Tyrannosaurus. At the end, Pendragon transforms into a winged Harpy that Jack manages to slay in mid-air.

1961

Mosura/Daikaiju Mosura   [U.S.: *Mothra*], Tomoyuki Tanaka/Toho Co., Ltd., Japan (in cooperation with Columbia Pictures), Toho-Scope, Eastmancolor

Director: Ishiro Honda. *Technical Effects— Technical Effects Director:* Eiji Tsuburaya. *Technical Effects Assistant Director:* Masakatsu Asai. *Art Department—Special Effects Art Director:* Akira Watanabe. *First Assistant Special Effects Art Director:* Yasuyuki Inoue. *Second Assistant Special Effects Art Director:* Yoshio Irie. *Photographic Effects—Special Effects Cinematography:* Teisho (Sadamasa) Arikawa. *Lighting Effects:* Kuichiro Kishida. *Optical Cinematography:* Hiroshi Mukoyama. *Miniatures—Wire Effects:* Fumio Nakadai. *Model makers:* Yukio Odagiri, Mitsuo Tamiguchi, Noboyuki Yasumaru.

Stuart Galbraith IV, an enthusiast of Japanese film fantasy, rates this as one of that country's best fantastic films. Mothra is a gigantic caterpillar making her way to Tokyo Tower, where she builds an enormous cocoon in order to emerge from it as a giant moth flown on wires: "The wire works crew performs one of the most difficult and demanding tasks, giving life to inanimate objects such as monster tails, props, miniature vehicles, etc. Since suspended objects are rather heavy, piano wire is normally used because of its tensile strength and relatively narrow width.... When large props like Mothra or King Ghidorah ... are operated and flown around the set, a mobile crane with an aerial brace is used to suspend the model by wires" (*The Illustrated Encyclopedia of Godzilla*, p. 156). "Japanese and American moviegoers watch films in different ways. In Japan, the so-called realism of its story and special effects mattered little, so long as the story was one worth telling and the special ef-

fects work was visually appealing.... I had the good fortune to watch these pictures with the innocence of childhood. I never believed at any time that what I was seeing was actually happening, but when the storytellers said, 'Here's our premise,' I was happy to accept their launching point, however absurd it might be in the real world. If I wanted the real world, I'd watch a Fredrick Wiseman movie. I was a kid, and I wanted films like *Mothra*" (Galbraith IV, *Japanese Science Fiction, Fantasy and Horror Films*, pp. 70–71).

1961–62

The Longest Day   Darryl F. Zanuck Productions/20th Century–Fox, France/U.S.A. CinemaScope.

Directors: Ken Annakin, Andrew Marton, Bernhard Wicki, Gerd Oswald, Darryl F. Zanuck, Elmo Williams. *Matte Paintings—Matte Photographer:* Wally Veevers. *Matte Artists:* George Samuels, Bob Cuff. *Blue Screen—Blue Screen Consultant and Photographic Effects Controller (at Studios Bois de Boulogne):* David Stanley Horsley. *Cinematographer:* Jean Fouchet. *Effects Department Supervisor:* L. B. Abbott. *Miniatures—Additional Miniature Photography:* Ralph Hammeras. *Models:* Henri Assola. *Pyrotechnics—Mechanical Effects and Explosives:* Karl Baumgartner, Pedro Coronadolar, Basilio Cortijo, Karl Helmer, August J. Lohman, Robert A. MacDonald Sr., Alex C. Weldon. Academy Award: Robert MacDonald

This story of D-Day opens with a matte shot of the fleet attacking the Germans at the Normandy shore. A huge glass shot depicts the Allied fleet seen from the shore of Normandy. There are lots of pyrotechnical effects when the troops storm the German fortifications. Zanuck, however, wasn't satisfied with some of the shots that the French technicians had executed and asked L.B. Abbott to take that footage back to Hollywood and complete it on the Fox lot. Among those were a few aerial miniatures.

1962–63

The Wonderful World of the Brothers Grimm George Pal/MGM and Cinerama, Cinerama, Technicolor.

Directors: Henry Levin, George Pal (Fairy Tales). *Stop-Motion and Miniatures—Stop-Motion Animation:* Project Unlimited, Inc. *Sculptor, Project Coordinator and Stop-Motion Supervisor for "The Cobbler and the Elves":* Wah Ming Chang. *Project Coordinator and Stop-Motion Supervisor for "The Singing Bone":* Gene Warren. *Miniature Supervisor:* Tim Baar. *Effects Art Director:* William Brace. *Storyboard Artist:* Dick Kelsey. *Stop-Motion Animators:* David Pal, Don Sahlin, Jim Danforth, Peter Von Elk. *Stop-Motion Photographer:* Ralph Rodine. *Camera Assistants and Camera Riggers:* Peter Pal, Bob Ray. *Armatures:* Howard Weeks, Paul LeBaron, Milt Ballard. *Molds supplied by* Glendale Mold Shop (Ben Hubbard). *FX Editing—Editing Layout:* Edward "Red" Schryver. *Production—Secretary at Project Unlimited:* Marion Young. *Optical Effects—Optical Cinematogaphy Supervisor:* Robert R. Hoag (MGM).

The fanciful, overly sentimental biography of Wilhelm and Jakob Grimm (played by Laurence Harvey and Karlheinz Böhm) offers three fairy-tale segments, two of them containing stop-motion segments: singing elves helping a shoemaker (Harvey again) and a jeweled, fire-breathing comic dragon versus Terry Thomas and Buddy Hackett. Although filmed in Cinerama three-strip, the production went on rather smoothly as Jim Danforth recalls, due to the careful planning and set-up by Gene Warren and Wah Chang. Danforth: "We had the original Fred Waller camera, with 3.28mm lenses, but for the animation, Photosonics, which is the company that makes Acme animation equipment, built three wrap-over Cinerama aperture cameras, in other words, one camera, one lens, and it was on a very precision machined base-plate with stops, three position stops and you had like a trigger in the back, like a pistol grip, and you pulled on the pistol grip and it released the lock position and you could pan the camera from A panel to B panel and lock it in any of those positions, so usually I work alone, but in that case we had an assistant do the camerawork because in some cases we were shooting alternate frame mattes, had six exposures to make for each frame. We had A panel front light, B panel front light, C panel front light, A panel back light, B panel back light, C panel back light and then we'd animate and do the whole thing again. We tried whenever possible to keep the animation in one or two panels, in other words, if there was no animation in the third panel, then we had no matte set up and we didn't shoot the third panel, and that speeded things up.... Bob Hoag, who put the stuff together had horrendous problems with the logistics of skip-framing all that out. If you think about it, it's all on one long piece of film, six frames for one frame on the movie, and you've got to set the printer up to go through and pick out which frames you want" (*Fantasy Film Journal* Volume 1, Number 2 Summer 1978).

1961–63

Cleopatra Walter Wanger, Darryl F. Zanuck/MCL Films-Walwa Films and 20th Century–Fox, Italy/U.S.A. Filmed at Cinecittà Studios, Rome. Miniatures filmed on the 20th Century–Fox lot. Todd-AO, Color by DeLuxe.

Director: Joseph L. Mankiewicz. *Matte Paintings—Supervising Matte Artist:* Emil Kosa, Jr. *Matte Designs:* John DeCuir. *Additional Matte Art:* Ralph Hammeras, Menrad Von Mulldorfer. *On-location Glass Artist:* Joseph Natanson. *Miniature Photography—Special Photographic Effects and Miniature Supervisor:* L.B. Abbott. *Miniature Technicians:* Bill Mittlestedt, Herb Cheek, Frank O'Connor. *Additional Miniatures:* Emilio Ruiz del Rio. *Mechanical Effects—Mechanical Effects:* August J. Lohman, Gerald Endler, Carlo Rambaldi, Erwin Lange, Academy Award: Emil Kosa Jr.

An ill-fated, extremely costly production, originally started by director Rouben Mamoulian in London, then transferred to Rome where Joseph L. Mankiewicz resumed directing chores. *Cleopatra*'s box office failure almost ruined the studio, which was forced to sell real estate that eventually became Century City. It took several years to break even. Some of the visual effects are splendid. Emil Kosa's enormous matte paintings catch Alexandria and the ancient world. It was not intended to film the sea battle of Actium but when Darryl F. Zanuck returned to helm the operation, he decided that such a spectacle had to be seen by audiences, not just talked about. So a new tank had to be built on the remaining Fox lot (the old one went with Century City) where the action was filmed with lots of model ships.

1961–63

Jason and the Argonauts

Charles H. Schneer/Morningside Worldwide Pictures–Columbia, Great Britain/Italy, Eastman Color, *Process:* Dynamation-90.

Director: Don Chaffey. *Stop-Motion—Visual Effects and Stop-Motion Animation Created by* Ray Harryhausen. *Director of Photography/Background Plates:* Wilkie Cooper. *Sculptor:* Arthur Hayward. *Armatures:* Fred Harryhausen. *Blue Screen—Blue Screen Service:* Bowie Films. *Blue Screen Supervisor:* Les Bowie. *Additional Blue Screen Photography:* Kit West. *Stunts—Stunt Coordinator (Skeleton Sequence):* Fernando Poggi. *Titles—Main Titles:* James Wines.

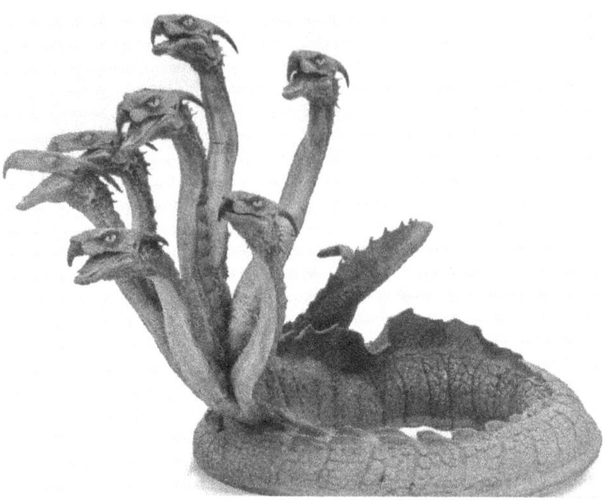

The seven-headed Hydra from *Jason and the Argonauts.*

On their voyage in search of the wonder-working Golden Fleece, the Argonauts are pursued by Talos, the bronze titan. At the island of Phrygia, they free blind seer Phineas (Patrick Troughton) from troublesome flying Harpies. Grateful Phineas gives his liberators directions to Colchis, the legendary land of the Fleece. There Jason (Todd Armstrong) slays the seven-headed, two-tailed Hydra, guardian of the Fleece. Out of the Hydra's teeth grow seven sword-wielding skeletons.

1962–63

The Birds

Universal, U.S.A. Widescreen. Technicolor.

Director: Alfred Hitchcock. *Cinematography—Director of Photography:* Robert Burks. *Matte Paintings Matte Artist and Conceptual Art:* Albert J. Whitlock. *Matte Photography:* Roswell A. Hoffman. *Traveling Mattes—Traveling Matte Consultant:* Ub Iwerks (Walt Disney Studios). *Assistant:* Robert Broughton. *Composites—Optical Cinematography:* L.B. Abbott (crow attack on school), Robert R. Hoag (Bodega Bay scenes), Linwood G. Dunn (Tippi Hedren attacked by birds in Brenner attic). *Effects Animation Supervisor:* David Fleischer. *Mechanical Effects—Mechanical Effects Supervisors:* Lawrence A. Hampton, Theodore H. Lydecker. *Mechanical Birds:* George Lofgren, Marcel Delgado. *Ad-*

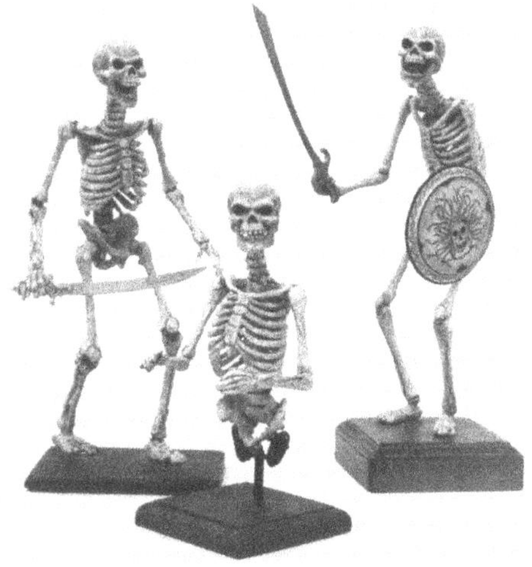

Three of the seven skeleton warriors seen in *Jason and the Argonauts* (both courtesy Ray and Diana Harryhausen Collection as displayed by Deutsche Kinemathek Berlin).

ditional Photography: Jon Hall. *Special Services— Bird Trainer:* Ray Berwick. *Associate Editor:* Bud Hoffman. *Credit Sequence:* James S. Pollak. *FX Makeup—Makeup Artist:* Howard Smit.

The bird attack on Bodega Bay entailed 412 optical effects shots. According to assistant editor Bud Hoffman, a former member of the special effects department at 20th Century–Fox, tests were done using mechanical birds which looked rather phony: "In one test, they put some young people on a treadmill to simulate the crow attack in the picture. Then they released these strange-looking creatures that looked like model airplanes with wings that moved up and down. There was also a glider type of bird which came down on wire that was just about as laughable" (*Cinefantastique* Volume 10 Number 2, p. 16). So Hitchcock and his effects-experienced cinematographer Robert Burks (a veteran of Warner Bros.' Stage 5 in the '40s) turned to optical effects. Hitchcock hired Disney's Ub Iwerks to supervise sodium traveling matte process but there were so many shots (and according to Albert Whitlock Iwerks seemed to lose interest during production, even went for a congress to Berlin) that they had to postpone the original release date (Thanksgiving 1962) and other effects departments had to be subcontracted as well.

1962–63

Captain Sindbad   King Bros. Productions, U.S.A. in Association with Bavaria Studios, West Germany, Filmed at Geiselgasteig Studios in Munich. Eastmancolor.

Director: Byron Haskin. *Effects Cinematography—Visual Effects Supervisor:* Byron Haskin. *Director of Photography:* Günther Senftleben. *Preliminary Cinematographer:* Eugen Schüfftan. *Miniature Photography (Studio Tank):* Ernst Wild. *Mechanical Effects—Mechanical Effects Supervisors:* Lee Zavitz, August J. (Augie) Lohman. *Explosives:* Karl Baumgartner. *Optical and Matte Cinematography—Optical, Process and Matte Supervisor:* Tom Howard (MGM British). *Planning:* MGM Optical Department, Culver City, U.S.A. *Additional Opticals:* Theodor Nischwitz.

No great competition for the *Sinbad* entries of Ray Harryhausen. An Arabian Nights tale

clearly inspired by the *Firebird* concept, with Pedro Armendariz as an Oriental Tyrant with his heart safely stored in a tower far away from Baristan and Guy (Zorro) Williams as the daring hero. Byron Haskin: "I was assured that there were all kinds of facilities in the Bavaria studios, everything you wanted. I got there and it was absolutely Mack Sennett, 1917. Nothing there. One rear-projection machine, without even flame carbons, so the background was all-over blue. Their optical machine was not much. No modern facilities for special effects at all. I thought, 'What the hell am I going to do?' So, having been pretty good at tricks in my youth as a cameraman, I decided to make all the effects in the camera" (Byron Haskin, interviewed by Joe Adamson, p. 246–247).

Lee Zavitz built a miniature dragon, guardian of the tower, that had nine heads (on wires) and barked like a dog. An invisible monster had a cameo, as did some giant birds that tried to sink Sinbad's ship (filmed in a pool at Bavaria Studios). For most of the in-camera effects, Haskin ordered a transmission mirror which allowed to shoot of the action while another part was reflected from a right angle offstage. As cinematographer, the King Brothers hired old-timer Eugene Shuftan (Schüfftan), who originally came from Germany, but found him too old and dismissed him after a few days.

1962–63

It's a Mad, Mad, Mad, Mad World   Stanley Kramer (for United Artists release), U.S.A. Cinerama (70 mm), Technicolor.

Director: Stanley Kramer. *Mechanical Effects—Mechanical Effects Supervisor:* Danny Lee. *Photographic Effects and Stop-Motion Sequence—Photographic Effects:* Film Effects of Hollywood. *Supervisors:* Linwood G. Dunn, Cecil D. Love. *Effects Cinematography:* James B. Gordon. *Miniatures and Stop-Motion—Miniature Supervisor:* Howard Lydecker. *Stop-Motion Designer:* Willis H. O'Brien. *Stop-Motion Models:* Marcel Delgado. *Stop-Motion Animation:* Jim Danforth, Marcel Vercoutere. *Stop-Motion Technician:* Marcel Vercoutere. *Matte Paintings—Matte Artists:* Howard Fisher, Cliff Silsby. *Process Cin-*

ematography—Process Service: Paramount Studios. *Process Supervisor:* Farciot Edouart; *Lighting Gaffer:* Orville Beckett.

Overblown comedy with dozens of famous screen and TV actors who, substituted by stop-motion puppets, are seen swinging on and thrown off a fire truck's ladder in the climax. In an interview conducted by the late George Turner, Marcel Delgado claimed that he not only built the miniatures but animated them as well. Linwood Dunn didn't use these shots, however, and ordered Jim Danforth to redo them. That might have been so; Delgado's claim that the original footage was better is doubtful.

1963

Kaitei Gunkan [*Atoragon*/U.S.: *Atragon*], Tomoyuki Tanaka/Toho, Ltd., Japan, Tohoscope, Eastmancolor.

Director: Ishiro Honda. *Technical Effects—Technical Effects Director:* Eiji Tsuburaya. *Second Unit Director:* Kazuo Sagawa. *Technical Effects Assistant Director:* Teruyoshi Nakano. *Art Department—Special Mechanic Designs:* Shigeru Komatsuzaki. *Special Effects Art Director:* Akira Watanabe. *First Assistant Art Director:* Yasuyuki Inoue. *Second Assistant Art Director:* Yoshio Irie. *Effects Photography—Special Effects Cinematography:* Sadamasa (Teisho) Arikawa, Sokei Tomioka. *Lighting Effects:* Kuichiro Kishida. *Composite and Matte Photography:* Hiroshi Mukoyama. *Wireworks—Scene Manipulation:* Fumio Nakadai. *Miniatures—Model makers:* Tadao Izuka, Nobuyuki Yasumaru. *Additional Models:* Gunyi Model Craft, Toda Warehouse. *Miniature Explosions:* Tadaaki Watanabe.

Two story ideas projected into one hybrid movie: The original (propaganda) novel by Shunro Oshikawa, *Kaitei Gunkan*, was written in 1899, 33rd year of the Meiji era, and dramatized the Russo-Japanese War; the element of an underwater empire (as a substitute for Russia) came from mechanics designer and gifted illustrator Shigeru Komatsuzaki (*Kaitei Okoku*). The underwater empire of Mu, sunken in the Pacific Ocean 10,000 years ago, rises again and is destroyed by Captain Shinguji (Jun Tazaki), an old-time militarist, and his highly equipped "Undersea Battleship" (*Kaitei Gunkan*). Eiji

Tsuburaya had nearly 200 employees finish the effects sequences in great haste (three months) to meet the Christmas–New Year's holiday prime box office release date. Five different scales of miniature subs were constructed and ten different size models for a not-too-convincing sea serpent, guardian of the Mu Empire, named Manda, as seemingly no Toho sci-fi picture of that era could do without a giant monster. *Variety:* "[The special effects] are consistently excellent, including futuristic weapons, inevitable monsters, underwater explosions and fine miniature work depicting an earthquake which levels part of Tokyo."

1963–64

Mary Poppins Walt Disney Productions, U.S.A. Technicolor.

Director: Robert Stevenson. *Matte Paintings—Matte Artist:* Peter Ellenshaw. *Assistant Matte Artist:* Constantine Ganakes. *Optical Cinematography and Traveling Mattes—Optical Cinematography Supervisor:* Eustace A. Lycett. *Effects Consultant:* Ub Iwerks. *Special Photography/Sodium Process:* Art Cruickshank. *Optical Coordinator:* Robert Broughton. *2D Animation Sequence—Animation Director:* Hamilton S. Luske. *Mechanical Effects—Mechanical Effects Supervisor:* Robert A. Mattey. *Wire Effects:* Danny Lee. *Mechanical Effects Technicians:* Walter Stone, Marcel Delgado. Academy Award: Peter Ellenshaw.

Great matte art by Ellenshaw illustrating London. The sodium process was used to put Julie Andrews, Dick Van Dyke and two kid actors into some cartoon action.

1963–64

7 Faces of Dr. Lao George Pal/Galaxy Films, Inc./Scarus/MGM, U.S.A. Metrocolor.

Director: George Pal. *Stop-Motion and Miniatures—Stop-Motion and Special Effects Sequences:* Project Unlimited, Inc. *Sculptures:* Wah Ming Chang, Jim Danforth (Loch Ness monster), Martha Armstrong (additional Loch Ness monster heads). *Stop-Motion Animation and Miniature Supervisor:* Jim Danforth. *Stop-Motion Photography:* Ralph Rodine. *Additional Animation:*

Peter Kleinow. *Special Effects Art Director:* William Brace. *Miniature Shop Supervisor:* Tim Baar. *Optical Cinematography—Optical Cinematography Supervisor:* Robert R. Hoag (MGM). *Titles and Opticals:* MGM Laboratories. *Mechanical Effects—Mechanical Effects:* Paul B. Byrd. *FX Makeup—Special Makeup Effects:* William Tuttle, Charles Schram. Academy Award (for Special Makeup): William Tuttle.

In the Western town of Abilene, the Circus of Dr. Lao (Tony Randall) arrives. Lao transforms into several mythological creatures. The film's highlight is a growing Loch Ness monster which, at the end, shrinks in the rain. Scenario, based on Charles G. Finney's novel *The Circus of Dr. Lao*, was by the late, lamented Charles Beaumont with uncredited polish by the famous scriptwriting team of Ben Hecht and Charles Lederer. Jim Danforth: "On the subject of *Dr. Lao*, I also had a sequence which I felt could have been funnier and more exciting and aid in furthering a story point: The Loch Ness Monster would have chased the cowboys in their model 'B' Ford through town to the box canyon from which emerged the crumbling aqueduct mentioned in the film as the town's precarious water supply. The chase would have climaxed with a 'roundy-roundy between the pilings of the aqueduct trestle, the automobile finally crashing into the structure, destroying it and bringing water cascading down onto the Loch Ness Monster to shrink him back to his small size" (*Fantascene* Vol. 1 No. 2).

1963–64

First Men in the Moon   Charles H. Schneer/ Ameran Films–Columbia, Great Britain, Panavision, Eastmancolor ("Lunacolor").

Director: Nathan Juran. *Stop-Motion—Creator of Special Visual Effects and Stop-Motion Animation:* Ray Harryhausen. *Model Sculpture:* Arthur Hayward. *Armatures:* Fred Harryhausen. *Paintings and Miniatures—Studio:* Bowie Films. *Effects Supervisor:* Les Bowie. *Effects Photographer:* Kit West. *Optical Effects:* John Mackey. *Painting Technicians and Mattes:* Ray Caple, Bob Cuff. *Miniature Technicians:* Derek Meddings, Ian Scoones.

Harryhausen and Schneer rented the shop of Bowie Films as base for the effects work for *First Men*, which was shot in what they called Lunacolor. On the moon, United Nations astronauts come across a British flag and a receipt dated 1899 and bearing the name of Arnold Bedford.

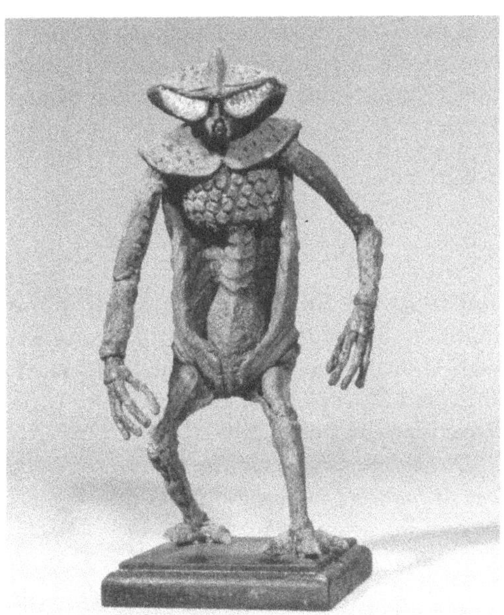

A discarded Selenite version from *First Men in the Moon.*

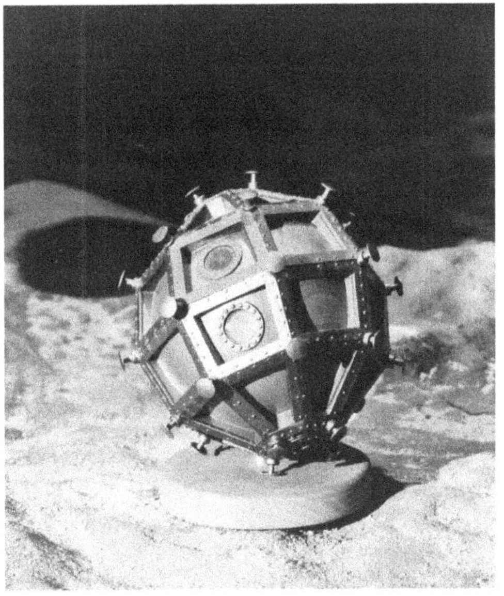

The First Men in the Moon Moon sphere, recreated by a fan and given to Harryhausen as a gift (both courtesy Ray and Diana Harryhausen Collection as displayed by Deutsche Kinemathek Berlin).

Bedford (Edward Judd), now an elderly gentleman, is located in a nursing home in England and claims that in the late nineteenth century he made the first lunar trip. To get there, Professor Cavor (Lionel Jeffries) invented "Cavorite," a substance that nullified the force of gravity. Bedford and Cavor encountered mooncalves, mountain-sized centipedes, an underground civilization of insect-like Selenites and their Grand Lunar.

1965

Battle of the Bulge   Milton Sperling and Philip Yordan/Sidney Harmon in association with United States Pictures, Inc., Cinerama, Inc., and Warner Bros., Spain/U.S.A. Ultra Panavision, Technicolor.

Director: Ken Annakin. *Art Department—Art and Miniature Director:* Eugène Lourié. *Miniatures—Chief Model maker:* Charles-Henri Assola. *Mechanical Effects:—Mechanical Effects Supervisor:* Alex C. Weldon. *Special Effects:* Basilio Cortijo, Richard Parker.

The last German offensive of World War II, which took place in the Ardennes, Belgium, in December 1944, was here recreated in miniature sequences. Eugène Lourié: "My miniature tanks were about three feet long with two-horsepower motors, and had numerous electric commands to advance, retreat, turn the turret, and shoot the guns. They had realistic recoiling guns and were perfect reproductions of real tanks, down to the smallest detail. All the scenes that were difficult or impossible to achieve with real tanks were performed by miniatures" (Lourie, *My Work in Films*, p. 278–79).

1965–66

Fantastic Voyage   Saul David/20th Century–Fox, U.S.A. CinemaScope, DeLuxe Color.

Director: Richard Fleischer. *Visual Effects—Visual Effects Supervisor:* L.B. Abbott. *Visual Effects Cinematographer:* Art Cruickshank. *Matte Paintings—Supervising Matte Artist:* Emil Kosa, Jr. *Art Department—Effects Design:* Harper Goff,

Dale Hennesy. *Miniatures—Miniature Supervisor:* Howard Lydecker. *Puppets:* Marcel Delgado. *Miniature Technician:* Roy Arbogast, *Prop Shop Supervisor:* Gail Brown. *Mechanical Effects—Mechanical Effects Technician:* Bob Chesler. *Wire Effects:* Peter Foy. *Gaffer:* Frank O'Connor Academy Award: Art Cruickshank

A microsized medical team boards a minisubmarine, *Proteus,* and is injected into a patient. Disney's Ub Iwerks recommended Art Cruickshank as effects cinematographer; Cruickshank won an Oscar for his work.

1965–66

Raumpatrouille   Bavaria Studios, West Germany. Filmed at Geiselgasteig Studios in Munich.

Directors: Theo Mezger, Michael Braun. *Effects Supervisors—Effects Creator:* Werner Hierl. *Effects Coordinator:* Theodor Nischwitz. *Effects Photography—Oxberry High-Speed Cam:* Klaus Schumann, Vinzenz Sandner, Jörg Michael Kunsdorff, Michael Böhr, Peter Hilpert. *Camera Operators:* Dieter Liphardt, Peter Harrer, Robert Salvagnac. *16mm test footage:* Georg Kramer. *Miniatures—Model makers:* Hans Wiesenberger, Florian Fux von Nordhoff, Hal Clay, Werner Hierl, Götz Weidner, Hans Nothof. *Animation—Rostrum Operators (Oxberry and Crass equipment):* Peter Hilpert, Robert Salvagnac, Peter Dolp, Mark Decker, Michael Peters. *Blue Screen—Blue Screen Supervisor:* Karl Ludwig Ruppel. *Compositing—Oxberry Technicians:* Gustav Witter, Jörg Michael Kunsdorff, Alice Francevics, Georg Kramer. *Negative Editing—Operators:* Bernd Schlichting, Gisela Dietzler, Alice Francevics, Karin Moderegger, Ralf Schulmeister.

A seven-part sci-fi series, it was first broadcast on German TV in the mid–1960s, then following an initiative of Dr. Rolf Giesen, Deutsche Kinemathek, it was released theatrically in the 1980s. Extraterrestrials, called "Frogs," attack future mankind. Very similar in concept to *Star Trek* (with a multicultural crew on board spaceship *Orion*), which was developed around the same time.

1965–68

2001: A Space Odyssey Hawk Films Ltd./ MGM, Great Britain, Cinerama, Super Panavision (70mm), Color by Technicolor and Metrocolor.

Director: Stanley Kubrick. *Miniature and Special Effects Photography—Supervising Visual Effects Director, Miniature Cinematography and Special Effects Rigging:* Wally Veevers. *Animation and Photographic Effects—Animation and Visual Effects Supervisors:* Con Pederson, Douglas Trumbull. *Special Art Elements:* Roy Naisbitt, John Rose. *Front Projection—Front Projection (Prologue Sequence)/Special Effects Supervisor:* Tom Howard. *Photographic Effects—Special Photographic Effects and Animation Unit:* Colin J. Cantwell, Bryan Loftus, Frederick Martin, Bruce Logan, Tony Masters, David Osborne, John (Jack) Malick. *Visual and Matte Effects—Director of Photography:* David Osborne. *Additional Effects and Matte Cinematography:* Richard Yuricich. *Matte Camera Printer Technicians:* Jim Budd, Ron Wooster, Jack Spooner. *Airbrush Artist:* William C. Davies. *Special 16mm Projectors:* Brian Johncock (Johnson). *Camera Operator, Visual Effects Unit:* Martin Kelly. *Visual Effects Floor Camera Department:* Brian Bennett, Martin Brody, Bernard Ford, Peter Harman, Bob Rickerd. *Moon Sequence—Moonscape Artist:* Bob Cuff. *Moonscape Miniatures:* Joyce Seddon, Roger Dicken. *Miniatures—Model Maker:* Douglas Potts. *Mechanical and Special Effects Unit—Mechanical Effects Supervisor:* Ron Ballanger. *Special Effects Coordinator:* Colin Brewer. *Special Effects Engineer:* Ted Creed. *Special Effects Supervisor:* Denis Hall. *Special Effects Coordinator:* George Pollack. *Special Effects:* Jimmy Harris, Fred Heather, Garth Inns, Curly Nelhams, Jimmy Ward. *Special Effects Assistants:* Hilary Ann Pickburn. *Special Effects Stills Painter:* Graham Hooper. *Special Effects Stills Printer:* Dan McGowen. *Special Effects Maintenance:* Tom Welford. *Special Effects Department Secretaries:* Valerie Kent, Delia Tindall. *Special Effects Runner:* Tori Traynor. *Animation Unit—Rostrum Camera Technicians, Animation Stand and Technical Animation:* Zoran Perisic, James R. Dickson, Edward Gerald, Martin Goldsmith, Dennis Hall, Jaiseet Singh. *Blob Art—Blob Artists:* Herbert Bailey, Peter Biggs, Jenny Foster, John Grant, Caird Green, Andy Griffiths, Fran Guye, Paul Haywood, John Horton, Sarah Katz, Bob Nadkami, David Peterson, Catherine Philby, William Plampton, Hapugoda Premaratne, Hilary Randall, Livia Rolandini, Clive Sheperd, James Simpson, Gary Sinclair, Dennis Smith, David Temple, Roger Turner, Nigel Walter, David Watkinson, James Wilkins, Brian Wilsher. *Consultants—Preproduction Set-up:* Wally Gentleman. *Consultants:* Les Bowie, Charles Staffell (Front Projection). Linwood G. Dunn (Film Effects of Hollywood, Background Plates). *Preliminary Research:* Lester Novros, Graphic Films (Los Angeles). *FX Makeup—Supervising Makeup Artist (Prologue):* Stuart Freeborn. *Special Ape Masks:* Colin Arthur. *Makeup Artist:* Graham Freeborn. *Assistant Makeup Artist:* Kay Freeborn. *Makeup Consultant:* Charles E. Parker. Academy Award: Stanley Kubrick (credited as Special Effects Designer and Director)

A journey beyond the stars to meet our alien ancestors. *Journey Beyond the Stars* was the project's working title, announced in a press release issued by MGM on Tuesday, February 25, 1965: "*Journey Beyond the Stars* is an epic story of adventure and exploration, encompassing the Earth, the planets of our Solar System, and a journey light-years to another part of the Galaxy. It is a scientifically based yet dramatic attempt to explore the infinite possibilities that space travel now opens to mankind. The great biologist J. B. S. Haldane said: "The Universe is not only stranger than we imagine; it is stranger than we *can* imagine.' When you consider that in our Galaxy there are a hundred *billion* stars, of which our Sun is a perfectly average specimen, and that present estimates put the number of Galaxies in the visible Universe at a hundred *million*, Haldane's statement seems rather conservative."

In May 1966, Kubrick finished shooting with the cast on the soundstages of MGM's British Studios in Borehamwood, outside London, and spent another year and a half creating a total of 205 innovative effects shots. Wally Gentleman from Canada did the general set-up before he left the production, Wally Veevers did all the complicated camera rigging and supervised miniature shooting, Tom Howard turned to the front-projection prologue, Con Pederson and Doug Trumbull (two American youngsters) made stars and planets work (Trumbull devised the slit-scan Stargate ride which involved a pattern of streaky dots), but Kubrick claimed the Oscar for himself as the Academy then had to follow certain rules (the number of names on the ballot was limited to three). So it was no ego thing on Kubrick's part but necessary. Ernest Farino: "The visual effects would have been disqualified and otherwise would not have been acknowledged at all. In 1998, Con Pederson worked at Metrolight, a company I hired to do some of the work on *From the Earth to the Moon*, and he verified to me that this was a conscious and aboveboard effort by Kubrick to ensure recognition for the effects on behalf of the SFX team."

1965–66

One Million Years B.C.   Michael Carreras, Aida Young/Hammer Films/Seven Arts, Great Britain, Filmed at Associated British, Elstree Studios and on Lanzarate, Canary Islands. Eastmancolor. Giant Panamation.

Director: Don Chaffey. *Stop-Motion—Visual Effects and Stop Motion Animation Created by* Ray Harryhausen. *Sculptor:* Arthur Hayward. *Process—Director of Photography:* Wilkie Cooper. *Camera Operator:* David Harcourt. *Miniatures—Miniatures and Explosions (Earthquake Sequence):* George Blackwell. *Special Service—Prologue:* Les Bowie (Bowie Films). *Prologue Crew:* Bob Cuff, Ray Caple, John Mackey, Ian Scoones.

Raquel Welch (as Loana) vs. the dinosaurs. After the short but disappointing introduction of a live iguana, Harryhausen offers a stop-motion pteranodon (and breed) and rhaphorhynchus, another airborne creature, a deadly fight between Triceratops and Ceratosaurus, Archelon, a Cretaceous marine turtle, Brontosaurus (which contrary to preproduction ideas only makes a brief appearance) and Allosaurus which is staked by Welch's lover Tumak (played by John Richardson). "[T]he lizard sequence was shot between 14 and 16 March, the Pteranodon between 17 March and 7 April, the Archelon between 12 and 30 April, the Allosaurus between 2 May and 3 June, the Triceratops and Ceratosaurus battle between 6

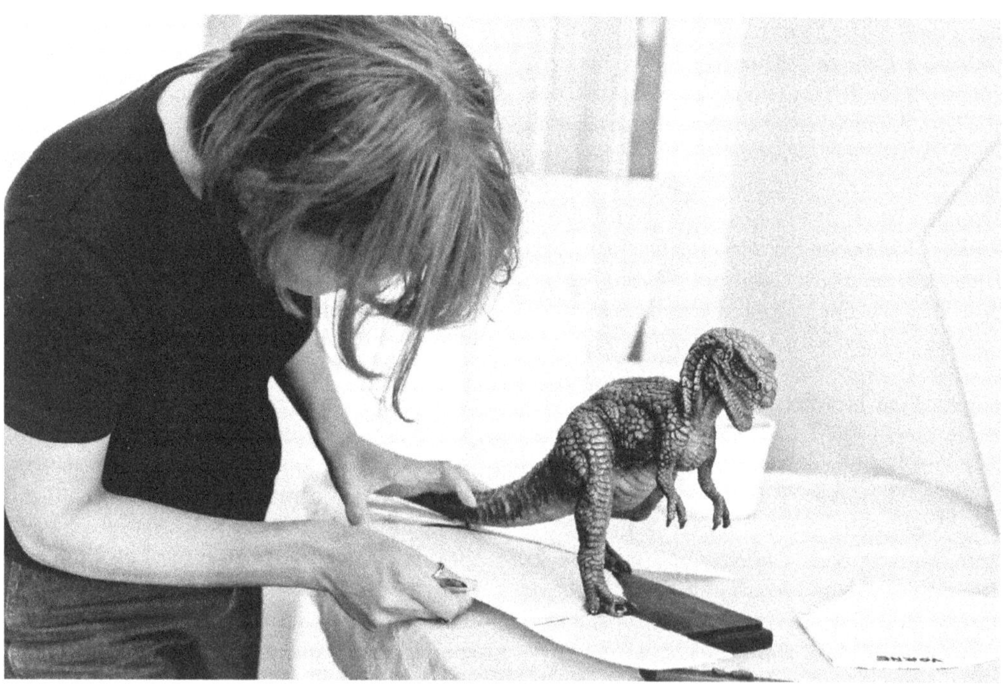

An artist prepares Ray Harryhausen's *One Million Years B.C.* Allosaurus for exhibition at Museum für Film und Fernsehen Berlin (courtesy Ray and Diana Harryhausen Collection as displayed by Deutsche Kinemathek Berlin).

June and 15 July, and the Brontosaurus and others between 18 and 29 July" (*Hammer Films: The Bray Studios Years*, p. 339). "The monster who grabs Miss Welch is realistically constructed; indeed so are all the others designed for the film by Ray Harryhausen—huge lizards, turtles, dinosaurs, et al. He has done a remarkable job in making these prehistoric animals not only to look genuine but to move about with surprising agility" (*Motion Picture Herald*, March 1967).

1967–68

Planet of the Apes Arthur P. Jacobs/Apjac–20th Century–Fox, U.S.A.

Director: J. Lee Thompson. *FX Makeup—Prosthetic Devices and Special Makeup:* John Chambers. *Special Makeup and Sculpts:* Daniel Striepeke, Werner Keppler, Wah Ming Chang. *Additional Makeup Artist:* Verne Langdon. *Consultant:* Fuminori Ohashi(?). *Photographic Effects—Photographic Effects Supervisor:* L.B. Abbott. *Visual Effects Cinematography:* Art Cruickshank. *Matte Paintings—Supervising Matte Artist:* Emil Kosa, Jr. *Matte Artist:* Matthew J. Yuricich. Academy Award (for Special Makeup): John Chambers.

John Chambers and his gang transformed actors Kim Hunter, Roddy McDowall, Maurice Evans and others into talking chimpanzees, orangutans and gorillas. At the end, astronaut Charlton Heston realizes that he is back on Earth when he sees the demolished Statue of Liberty (an impressive matte painting).

1968–69

Mackenna's Gold Carl Foreman/Columbia, Great Britain/U.S.A. Ultra Panavision 70, Technicolor.

Director: J. Lee Thompson. *Process—Plate Photography Consultant:* John Mackey. *Matte Paintings—Matte Artists:* Ray Caple, Lynette Lee, Bob Cuff, Joy Seddon. *Matte Process Cameraman:* Paul Cuff. *Special Effects—Mechanical Effects:* Willis R. Cook. *Effects Technicians:* Brian Loftus, John Johnson. *Special Service—Optical Cinematography:* Butler-Glouner, Inc.

This well-cast western involves the search for a lost *Canón del Oro*, a canyon of gold and features a spectacular special effects climax (physical effects, miniatures, process and mattes): An earthquake destroys all hope to get the gold.

1968–69

The Battle of Britain Harry Saltzman (for United Artists release), Great Britain

Director: Guy Hamilton. *Mattes—Matte Photography:* Wally Veevers. *Matte Artists:* Ray Caple, Bob Cuff, Peter Melrose. *Camera Assistant:* Martin Body. *Mechanical Effects—Explosives:* Cliff Richardson. *Process—Front Projection Equipment:* Jan W. Jacobsen. *Miniatures—Miniature Supervisor:* Glen Robinson. *Carpenter Model Aircraft and Cockpits:* William Creighton. *Mechanical Effects—Special Effects:* Wally Armitage, Alan Barnard, Jimmy Harris, Garth Inns, Robert Nugent, Roy Whybrow. *Additional Service—Aerial and Second Unit Director:* Derek Cracknell. *Aerial Cinematography:* Ronnie Wass. *Preproduction Effects Supervisor:* John P. Fulton. *Titles:* Maurice Binder.

R.A.F. and German *Luftwaffe* fight it out over London. Lots of model aircraft, explosions and front projection with makeshift cockpits. John P. Fulton died during preproduction in Spain. Plates were later reused in the British-Czech coproduction *Dark Blue World*.

1968–69

The Valley of Gwangi Charles H. Schneer/Morningside Productions (for Warner Bros.–Seven Arts release), Great Britain/Spain, Technicolor, *Process:* Dynamation.

Director: James O'Connolly. *Stop-Motion—Creator of Special Visual Effects/Stop-Motion Animation:* Ray Harryhausen. *Sculptor:* Arthur Hayward. *Photography—Director of Photography/Plates:* Erwin Hillier.

Although the late Willis O'Brien isn't mentioned in the credits, *Gwangi* was a pet project of his (he tried to get it off the ground in the 1940s while at RKO). Ray Harryhausen and producer Charles Schneer revived the idea in the late

1960s: Gwangi, a fierce allosaurus discovered in the Forbidden Valley, is lassoed by cowboys and brought to a circus. Freed from its cage, it runs amok in a Mexican town. Finally, it dies in a burning cathedral.

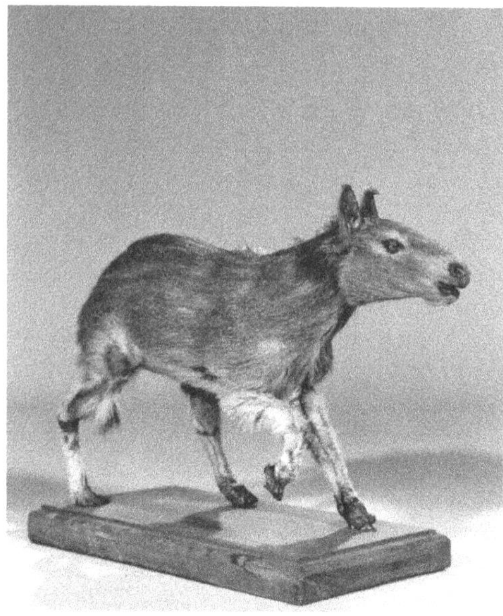

The Eohippus from *The Valley of Gwangi.*

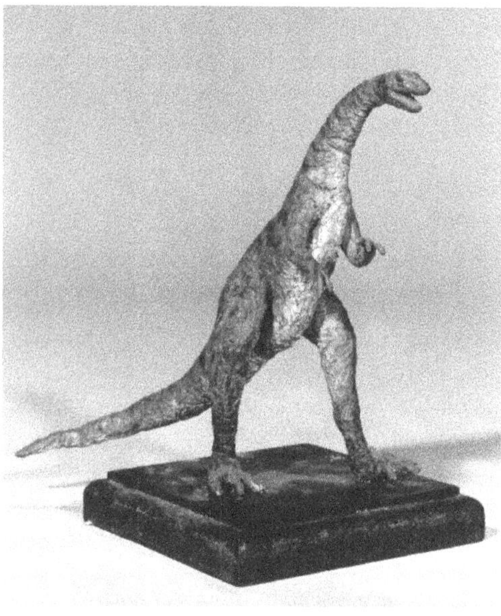

One of two Ornithomumus models from *The Valley of Gwangi* (all three courtesy Ray and Diana Harryhausen Collection as displayed by Deutsche Kinemathek Berlin).

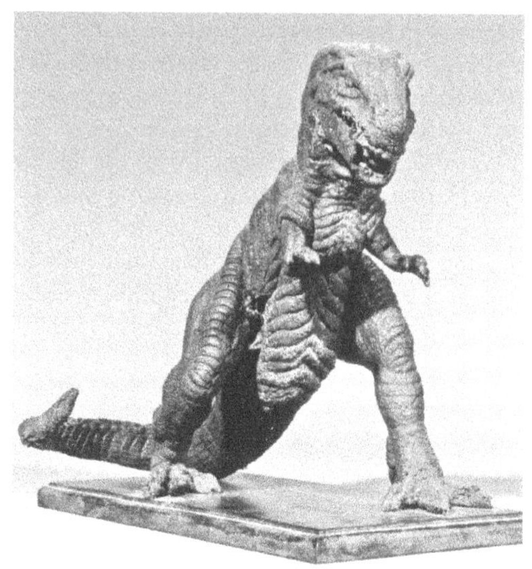

Gwangi from *The Valley of Gwangi.*

1968–71

When Dinosaurs Ruled the Earth   Hammer Film Productions Ltd./Seven Arts, Great Britain, Wide Screen, Technicolor.

Director: Val Guest. *Stop-Motion—Visual Effects, Matte Art and Stop-Motion Animation Created by* Jim Danforth (who also directed second unit on location and at Shepperton Studios). *Sculptor:* Roger Dicken. *Additional Stop-Motion Animation (Chasmosaurus Sequence/two shots of Baby Dinosaur):* David Allen. *Visual Effects—Effects Consultant:* Brian Johncock (Johnson*). Mechanical Effects—Special Effects Props:* Allan Bryce. *Effects Shop Supervisor at Shepperton Studios:* Ted Samuels. *Special Effects Technicians:* Martin Gutteridge, Brian Humphrey, Garth Inns. *Matte Paintings—Additional Matte Art:* Ray Caple, Les Bowie (Bowie Films Ltd.), Doug Ferris, Shepperton Matte Department.

Sort of a sequel to the successful *One Million Years B.C.* As Ray Harryhausen was not available, Jim Danforth was hired to create a chasmosaurus, plesioaurus, giant crabs, a rhamphorhynchus (flying reptile), a four-legged mother dinosaur and its kid. Danforth: "Lin Dunn had recommended me to Warner's post-production head, Rudi Fehr, who interviewed me. Hammer then contacted me. My employment was put on hold while Hammer was forced by the British unions to try to find a Britisher who could do the job. Roger Dicken was doing work for *Trog*. Hammer felt Roger's work would not be good enough, so that satisfied the union requirement and I was back on board" (E-mail from Jim Danforth). While studio footage was shot at Shepperton, stop-motion footage was executed at Bray Studios, additional matte art at Les Bowie Studios. "Its most engaging aspect is its special effects sequences, and we are shown a veritable prehistoric zoo of lumbering dinosaurs and salmon pink pterodactyls. There is an amusing takeoff of wildlife films in the sequences in which we watch the dinosaur's egg hatching of Victoria Vetri, like some primeval Michaela Denis, playing with a tame dinosaur" (*Films and Filming*, January 1971).

1968–[1998]

The Primevals Charles and Albert Band/ Darkzone/Empire/Full Moon, U.S.A. Color.

Director: David Allen. *Stop-Motion—Effects Company:* David Allen Productions. *Visual Effects Supervisor:* David Allen. *Stop-Motion and Effects Cinematography/Collaborators:* Dennis Muren, Ken Ralston, Phil Tippett, Randall William (Randy) Cook, Tom St. Amand/Dave Carson, Jon Berg/Chris Endicott.

Started as *Raiders of the Stone Ring*. It took decades to create this stop-motion tale of the Himalayas, a Yeti and alien reptile men, but it might never be finished. (Jim Danforth did not collaborate on the effects. His contribution was the story idea of the Lizard Men and their function as the adversaries of the story.) At one time it looked as if Hammer would get on the bandwagon, "then it turned out that what they wanted to do was simply to buy a part of the story; they wanted to make a picture called *Zeppelin vs. Pterodactyls*," Danforth revealed. "Well, there was a Zeppelin in the story which was Dave's idea. And there was a combat between the Zeppelin — the people in the Zeppelin — and the Pterodactyls, who protected the island.... Hammer wanted to just buy that, and said, 'You guys can still make the rest of the movie if you just sell the rights to this, and we'll make *Zeppelin vs. Pterodactyls*.'" (Danforth interviewed by Steve Archer in *Little Shoppe of Horrors*, February 1985, Number 10/11) Although Hammer had made up a poster and ran it in the trade magazines nothing came out of it. David Allen revived the original idea with producer Charles Band with whom he had a good working relationship and for some time it looked that the movie really would be finished. In fact, great parts were filmed and animated but Allen's sudden death complicated the process.

1969–70

Tora! Tora! Tora! Elmo Williams/20th Century–Fox, U.S.A./Japan. Panavision 70, Color by DeLuxe.

Director: Richard Fleischer. *Japanese Directors:* Toshio Masuda, Kinji Fukasaku. *Visual Effects— Visual Effects Supervisor:* L.B. Abbott. *Visual Effects Cinematography:* Art Cruickshank. *Pyrotechnical Effects—Explosives and Mechanical Effects:* A. D. Flowers. *Miniatures—Miniature Supervisors:* Gail Brown, Ivan Martin. *Miniature Preproduction:* Howard J. Lydecker. *Additional Service—Aerial Cinematography:* Vision Photography Inc. *Second Unit Director:* Ray Kellogg. Academy Award: L. B. Abbott, A. D. Flowers.

December 7, 1941: Pearl Harbor. Originally Akira Kurosawa was supposed to do the Japanese scenes but withdrew from the project. For a short moment there even was a chance for John Ford to direct American scenes. L.B. Abbott's unit had 40 days of shooting for the intricate miniatures: "The ship models were constructed by building plaster casts of the hulls. The hulls of both the American and Japanese ships turned out to be remarkably similar, which meant that only a relatively few casts had to be made. These casts were used to pour fireproof, fiberglass molds of the hulls. The superstructures were built separately in order to give each ship its distinctive appearance. In actual photography of the Battleship Row holocaust, the fireproof characteristic really paid off. We were able to blow up the ships, then reset the movable superstructure parts and replace the destroyed ones, repaint and reshoot with a minimal time loss" (L. B. Abbott, *Special Effects: Wire, Tape and Rubber Band Style,* p. 173).

1972–73

The Golden Voyage of Sinbad   Charles H. Schneer and Ray Harryhausen/Morningside Productions–Columbia, Great Britain/Spain

Director: Gordon Hessler. *Stop-Motion—Creator of Visual Effects/Stop-Motion Animation:* Ray Harryhausen. *Process—Director of Photography/Process Plates:* Ted Moore. *Traveling Matte Consultant:* Victor L.A. Margutti. *Mechanical Effects—Mechanical Effects Supervisor:* Manuel Baquero. *Miniatures—Miniature Supervisor/Art Director:* Fernando Gonzalez. *Glass Mattes—Glass Artist:* Emilio Ruiz del Rio. *Special Service—Special Masks:* Colin Arthur. *Stunt Coordinator:* Fernando Poggi.

Originally *Sinbad Goes to India* but then they had to change locales (no Indian rupees available) and be content with Spain. A golden amulet, which comes into the possession of Sinbad (John Philip Law), takes the sailor on a voyage to the legendary island of Lemuria, in search

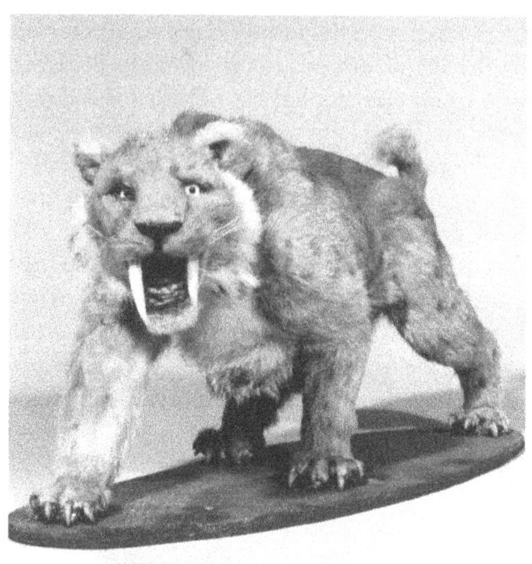

The saber-tooth tiger from *Sinbad and the Eye of the Tiger.*

of the fabled Fountain of Destiny. Also out to locate the spot is the evil sorcerer Koura (Tom Baker). Sinbad has to fight a six-armed bronze statue of goddess Kali, brought to life by Koura's black magic, and a cyclopean centaur that has killed a Griffin.

1971–74

Flesh Gordon   Graffiti, U.S.A. Prints by Metrocolor

Live-Action Directors: Michael Benveniste, Howard Ziehm. *Supervision/Production—Special Effects Design and Direction:* Howard Ziehm, Lynn Rogers, Walter R. Cichy. *Props and Miniatures—Special Effects Props:* Rick Baker, Tom Scherman. *Miniatures:* Gregory Jein. *Visual Effects—Photographic Effects:* Tom Scherman. *Stop-Motion—Stop-Motion Cinematography and Miniature Front Projection:* Dennis Muren. *Animation:* Mij Htrofnad (pseudonym of Jim Danforth), David Allen, Bill Hedge, Robert Maine, Jim Aupperle, Steven Czerkas. *Glass Shots:* Jim Danforth. *Effects and Stop-Motion Technicians:* Douglas Beswick, Russ Turner, Craig Nueswanger, Mike Hyatt, Mike Minor, Laine Liska, George Barr, Joe Clark, Joe Musso. *Opticals—Optical Effects:* Bob Costa. *Additional Optical Effects:* Ray Mercer & Company.

Unauthorized soft-porn spoof on the Flash

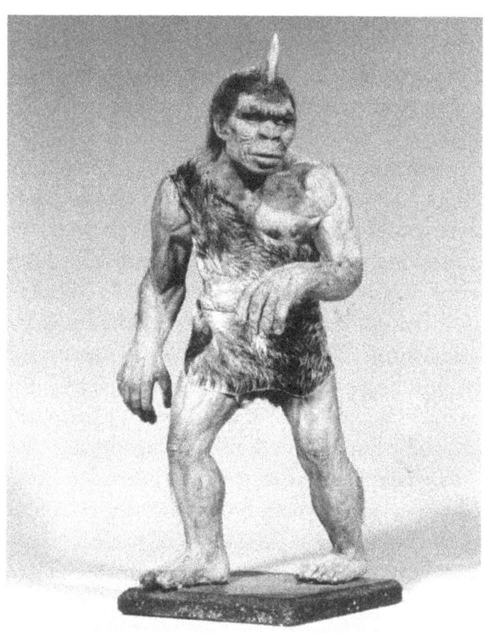

Trog from **Sinbad and the Eye of the Tiger** (both courtesy Ray and Diana Harryhausen Collection as displayed by Deutsche Kinemathek Berlin).

Gordon serials with surprisingly good, fanciful stop-motion sequences of Penisauri, Beetle Man and Great God Porno.

1973–74

Earthquake Jennings Lang/Filmmakers Group Inc.–Universal/MCA, U.S.A. Panavision 70, Technicolor.

Director: Mark Robson. *Matte Paintings—Matte Artist:* Albert Whitlock. *Matte Photography:* Roswell A. Hoffman. *Miniatures—Miniature Photography:* Clifford R. Stine. *Miniature Supervisors:* Glen E. Robinson, Charles A. Baker. *Mechanical Effects—Mechanical Effects Technicians:* Frank Brendel, Jack McMasters, Lou Ami. *Special Service—Titles and Opticals:* Universal Title. Academy Award: Frank Brendel, Glen Robinson and Albert Whitlock.

Whitlock had only a few weeks to finish 22 2x3-foot glass paintings for 40 cuts depicting the destruction of Los Angeles: "When I first heard about *Earthquake* it seemed like it would be overwhelming. Mark Robson, however, was very positive in his approach. He knew exactly what he wanted — which was a great help — and there was no vacillation in making decisions.... What makes many of the paintings in *Earthquake* work well is that we often put people in action right in front of the painting. For example, you see people running in front of a painting of the demolished Hollywood Boulevard. This gives the scene a sense of depth. Of course, it involves rotoscoping, the tedious cell-by-cell inking of individual frames to be filmed as a matte in order to superimpose the people on the painting" (*American Cinematographer*, November 1974, p. 1330–31). Then, also, the matte shots are very short, a glimpse of four seconds or so, which helps tremendously. *Earthquake* was presented in Sensurround.

1976

King Kong Dino De Laurentiis Corporation (for Paramount release), U.S.A. Panavision, Metrocolor.

Director: John Guillermin. *Photographic Effects—Optical Cinematography:* Van der Veer Photo Effects. *Optical Cinematography Supervisor:* Frank Van der Veer. *Optical Cinematography Assistant:* Barry Nolan. *Effects Cinematography:* Harold E. Wellman. *Matte Paintings—Matte Artist:* Louis Lichtenfield. *Mechanical Effects—Special Effects Kong Robot:* Carlo Rambaldi, Isidoro Raponi, Glen E. Robinson, Joe Day. *Kong Mechanical Effects Coordinator:* Eddie Surkin. *FX Makeup—Kong Gorilla Outfit Created and Worn by* Rick Baker. *Additional Action Scenes Played by* William (Bill) Shepard. *Assistant to Rick Baker:* Rob Bottin. *Kong Hair Design:* Michael Dino. *Kong Modeler:* Don Chandler. *Miniatures—Miniature Coordinator:* Aldo Puccini. *Special Service—Visual Effects Editors:* Margo Anderson, William Cruse. *Titles:* Pacific Title & Art Studio. Academy Award: Carlo Rambaldi, Glen Robinson and Frank Van der Veer.

Remake of the classic *Kong*. No stop-motion animation although both Harryhausen and Danforth had been contacted and were offered the job of animating some lizard. The much promoted giant robot Kong that finally appears for a minute of screen time or so does not work. ("The robot broke down frequently," says Bill Warren, an extra in the crowd fleeing from Kong.) Instead Kong is played by Rick Baker in a gorilla costume and killed on top of the landmark Twin Towers of the ill-fated, doomed World Trade Center. A Special Achievement Award for visual effects was granted to both the *Kong* remake and *Logan's Run*; Danforth protested by announcing his resignation from the Academy and returning his own Oscar nomination plaques: "[I]n my opinion, the effects are a joke, just absolutely terrible.... I wrote a letter to the Board to explain to them why I felt their actions were not justified. I went to great lengths to point out that Rick Baker was not in any way in my opinion to be considered a 'special visual effect.' No more than Bert Lahr could be considered a special effect when he played the Cowardly Lion in *The Wizard of Oz*. Or no more than a real gorilla would be considered a special effect if you put that in front of a blue screen and made it look 50 feet tall. You certainly wouldn't claim the gorilla was a special effect, only the optical part of it" (*Cinefantastique* Volume 5 Number 4, p. 24).

1976–77

Star Wars   George Lucas/Lucasfilm Ltd. in association with 20th Century–Fox, Great Britain/U.S.A. Panavision 70, Technicolor. Prints by De Luxe.

Director: George Lucas. *Visual Effects—Visual Effects Created by* Industrial Light & Magic Inc., a Division of Lucasfilm Ltd. *Visual Effects Supervisor:* John C. Dykstra. *Visual Effects Unit General Manager:* Jim Nelson. *Production Managers:* Bob Shepherd, Lon Tinney. *Production Staff:* Patricia Rose Duignan, Mark Kline, Rhonda Peck, Ron Nathan. *Visual Effects First Cinematographer:* Richard Edlund. *Visual Effects Second Cinematographer:* Dennis Muren. *Assistant Cameramen:* Douglas Smith, Kenneth Ralston, David Robman. *Second Unit Cinematographer:* Bruce Logan. *Traveling Matte Consultant London Unit:* Stanley W. Sayer. *Special Equipment—Electronic Design:* Alvah J. Miller, Miller Electronics, Jerry L. Jeffress. *Electronic Effects:* Ron Hayes. *Special Components:* James (Jamie) Shourt. *Special Components Assistants:* Masaaki Noriboro, Eleanor Porter. *Camera and Mechanical Equipment:* Jerry Greenwood, Douglas Barnett, Stuart Ziff, David Scott. *Art Department—Conceptual Art and C-3PO Design:* Ralph McQuarrie. *Production Illustrators:* Michael Minor, Alex Tavoularis. *Optical Cinematography—Optical Cinematography Supervisor:* Robert Blalack, Praxis Film Works Inc. *Optical Coordinator:* Paul Roth. *Optical Printers:* David Berry, David McCue, Richard Pecorella, Eldon Rickman, James Van Trees, Jr. *Blue Screen Adviser:* William Reinhold. *Optical Assistants:* Caleb Aschkynazo, John C. Moulds, Bruce Nicholson, Gary Smith, Bert Terreri, Donna Tracy, Jim Wells, Vicky Witt, Mark Vargo. *Production Supervisor:* George E. Mather. *Additional Optical Effects—* Dan Genis (Modern Film Effects), Ray Mercer, Sr. (Ray Mercer & Company), Frank Van der Veer (Van der Veer Photo Effects), Dick Bond (Master Film Effects), DePatie-Freleng Enterprises Inc. *Matte Paintings and Design—Supervising Matte Artist:* P.S. (Harrison) Ellenshaw. *Conceptual Art, Planet, Satellite and Matte Artist:* Ralph McQuarrie. *Production Designer and Illustrator:* Joseph (Joe) Johnston. *Additional Spacecraft Design:* Colin J. Cantwell. *Miniatures—Chief Miniaturist:* Grant McCune. *Model makers:* David Beasley, Jon Erland, Lorne Peterson, Steve Gawley, Paul Huston, David Jones. *Stop-Motion (Chess Sequence)—Stop-Motion Animation:* Jon Berg, Phil Tippett. *Stop-Motion Technician:* Laine Liska. *Effects Animation—Animation and Rotoscope Designer:* Adam Beckett. *Animators:* Michael Ross, Peter Kuran, Jonathan Seay, Chris Casady, Lyn Gerry, Diana Wilson, Nina Saxon. *Explosives—Pyrotechnical Effects:* Joseph Viskocil, Greg Auer. *Pyrotechnic Unit Production Manager:* David L. Lester. *Computer Animation—Graphic Displays:* Dan O'Bannon, Larry Cuba, John Wash, Jay Teitzell, Dominic Iaia, Image West. *FX Makeup and Creature Shop:—Makeup Supervisor:* Graham Freeborn. *Makeup Assistants:* Kay Freeborn, Christopher Tucker. *Hairdressing:* Pat McDermott. *Second Unit Makeup/Cantina Sequence Masks:* Rick Baker. *Consultant Cantina Sequence:* Charles E. Parker. *Cantina Sequence Assistants:* Douglas Beswick, Laine Liska, Jon Berg, Phil Tippett, Rob Bottin. *Additional Alien Design:* Ralph McQuarrie, Ron Cobb. *Mechanical Effects—Special Production and Mechanical Effects Supervisor:* John Stears. *Special Effects Technician:* Robert Nugent. *Effects Consultant in Britain:* Les Bowie. Academy Award: John Stears, John Dykstra, Richard Edlund, Grant McCune, Robert Blalack.

The second World War projected into outer space. George Lucas studied World War II dogfight footage and the British movie *The Dam Busters*. Richard Edlund: "At the start of the project, George Lucas had some very specific ideas about the starship shots. He had already edited the sequence using actual black-and-white battle footage and scenes from other airplane movies, and what he wanted us to do was to duplicate each of those shots using X-wings, or T.I.E. ships. Our shots would be cut right into his sequences and replace the black-and-white footage as they were shot. What he had done was pre-shoot and pre-edit the sequence in a sense — a storyboard on film. Using the black-and-white footage as a guide, we knew the shot length, ship motions, and direction of travel for *each shot*"

(*Cinefantastique* Double Issue, Vol. 6 No. 4/Vol. 7 No. 1, p. 22). This system is called today *pre-visualization*. Originally Lucas turned to Jim Danforth and Bill Taylor to help him start Industrial Light & Magic but Danforth turned him down because of lack of creative freedom. Douglas Trumbull, who also was not available, eventually referred Lucas to John Dykstra, who set up the shop and created Dykstraflex motion control that allowed operators to simulate and repeat extreme camera movements instead of moving the models. The movie was later retitled *Episode IV: A New Hope*.

1976–77

Close Encounters of the Third Kind Julia and Michael Phillips/Columbia, U.S.A. in association with EMI Films Inc. and Time Inc., Panavision 70, Metrocolor.

Director: Steven Spielberg. *Visual Effects—Visual Effects Company:* Future General Corporation. *Visual Effects Supervisor:* Douglas Trumbull. *Visual Effects Cinematographer:* Richard Yuricich. *Mothership Cinematographer:* Dennis Muren. *UFO Cinematography:* David Stewart. *Camera Operators:* Eugene Eyerly, Eldon Rickman, Dave Berry, Maxwell Morgan, Ron Peterson. *Assistant Cameramen:* David Hardberger, Alan Harding, Bill Millar, Bruce Nicholson, Richard Ripple, Scott Squires. *Still Photographer:* Marcia Reid. *Cinetechnician:* Robert Hollister. *Technical Assistants:* Glenn Erickson, Hoyt Yeatman. *Art Department—Storyboard Illustrator:* George Jensen. *Matte Paintings—Matte Artist:* Matthew J. Yuricich. *Assistant Matte Artist:* Rocco Gioffre. *Matte Cinematography:* Don Jarel. *Optical Cinematography—Optical Cinematography Supervisor:* Robert Hall. *Laboratory Technicians:* Don Dow, Tom Hollister. *Negative Cutter:* Barbara Morrison. *Project Supervision—Coordinator and Editor:* Larry Robinson. *Project Manager:* Robert Sheperd. *Project Coordinator:* Mona Thal Benefiel. *Production Secretary:* Joyce Goldberg. *Production Accountant:* Peggy Rosson. *Miniatures—Chief Model maker:* Gregory Jein. *Miniature Shop Coordinator:* J. Richard Dow. *Miniatures:* Paul Huston, David M. Jones, Jor van Kline, Michael McMillen, Kenneth Swenson, Robert Worthington, Peter Anderson, Larry Albright. *Effects Animation-Animation Supervisor:* Robert Swarthe. *Animator:* Harry Moreau. *Assistant Animators:* Carol Boardman, Eleanor Dahlan, Cy Didjurgis, Tom Koester, Connie Morgan. *Equipment—Front Projection Equipment:* Don Trumbull. *Camera and Mechanical Design:* B. G. Engineering, John Russell, Fries Engineering. *Electronics Design:* Jerry L. Jeffries, Alvah J. Miller, Peter Regla, Dan Slater. *Motion Control Technician:* Gregory L. McMurray. *Gaffer:* David Gold. *Key Grip:* Ray Rich. *Special Consultants:* Larry Albright, Richard Bennett, Ken Ebert, Kevin Kelly, Jim Lutes, George Randle, Jeff Shapiro, Rourke Engineering. *Special Puppets—Extraterrestrial Realization:* Carlo Rambaldi. *Assistant:* Isidoro Raponi. *Alien Makeup:* The Burman Studio, Ellis Burman, Tom Burman. *Extraterrestrial Choreography:* Susan Heldford. *Puppeteer:* Bob Baker. *Mechanical Effects—Mechanical Effects Supervisor:* Roy Arbogast. *Mechanical Effects Technicians:* George Polkinghorne, Michael Wood.

For the protagonists of Spielberg's movie, this so-called close encounter of the third kind (with a nod to UFO adviser J. Allen Hynek) means a frantic cross-country journey to a mountain in Wyoming, the Devil's Tower, and the unshakeable knowledge that extra-terrestrials are here already. For the effects work, Spielberg hired Trumbull (who initially had turned down a similar offer by George Lucas to work on *Star Wars*). Trumbull set up a shop in Marina del Rey for 65mm effects cinematography. Richard Yuricich was to become director of photography:

> We built a smoke room to photograph our UFOs, and that was done almost entirely by Bob Shepherd. We had one room that was set aside for the optical camera; another was set up as a line-up room; and yet another was set up for the matte camera. These three rooms were interconnected, but segregated from the rest of the building. They had their own air filtration system which we never did get to work quite right, but the rooms *did* stay clean and our dirt problems were kept to a minimum because the guys had good film handling procedures.... Then another building became available down the street. We took that over, too, and built an air conditioned animation room for our Oxberry, and a screening facility where we could see our dailies. Later, we shot the mothership footage there, also [*Cinefantastique* Double Issue Vol. 7 No. 3/Vol. 7 No. 4, p. 32/33].

In August 1980 a *Close Encounters of the Third Kind Special Edition* was presented with additional effects footage by Robert Swarthe, Robert Short and Dream Quest Inc.

1977–78

Superman Alexander Salkind, Ilya Salkind/International Film Production Inc./Warner Bros., Great Britain

Director: Richard Donner. *Art Department—Visual Effects Designer:* Dennis Rich. *Star Ship Designer:* Ed Gimmell. *Blue Screen and Composites—Optical Cinematography Supervisor:* Roy Field. *Optical Cinematography:* Roy Pace, Sheldon Elbourne. *Traveling Matte/Blue Screen Consultant:* Stanley W. Sayer. *Blue Screen Supervisor:* Dennis Bartlett. *Optical Liaison:* Martin Shortall, Harrow College of Technology and Art. Special *Optical Effects:* Camera Effects Ltd., Oxford Scientific Films Ltd.: Peter Parks, Sean Morris, National Screen Service Ltd., Gillie Potter Productions Ltd., Delecluse Realisations, Cinema Research Corporation, Peter Donen, Joe Wallikas, Rocky Mahoney, Charles Colwell, Rank Post Productions Ltd., Cinefex (London) Ltd., Vee Films Ltd., General Screen Enterprises Ltd. *Additional Optical Cinematography:* Van der Veer Photo Effects. *Additional Optical Cinematography Supervisors:* Greg Van der Veer, Frank Van der Veer, Barry Nolan. *Matte Paintings—Supervising Matte Artist:* Les Bowie. *Matte Artists:* Doug Ferris, Ray Caple. *Assistant Matte Artist:* Liz Lettman. *Matte Camera Operators:* Peter Harman, Peter Hammond. *Miniatures—Miniature Effects Supervisor:* Derek Meddings. *Miniature Photography:* Paul Wilson, Jack Atcheler. *Additional Miniature Effects Supervisors:* Brian Smithies, George Gibbs. *Additional Miniature Cinematography:* Harry Oakes, Robert Kindred, Leslie Dear. *Miniature Construction Manager:* Michael Redding. *Model makers:* Terry Reed, Cyril Forster, Andrew Kelly, Jeff Lund, Tony Dunsterville, Tadeusz Krzanowski. *Process and Front Projection—Process Cinematography:* Denys Coop. *Front Projection Supervisor:* Wally Veevers. *Front Projection Equipment:* Jan W. Jacobsen. *Process Systems:* Charles Staffell. *Process Unit Director:* Andre de Toth. *Zoptic Effects Supervisor:* Zoran Perisic. *Zoptic Operators:* David Speed, Mike Drew, James Aspinall. *Flying Unit Coordinator:* Dominic Fulford. *Mechanical Effects—Mechanical Effects Supervisor:* Colin Chilvers. *New York and Canadian Mechanical Effects Supervisor:* John Richardson. *New Mexico Mechanical Effects Supervisor:* Robert A. MacDonald. *Mechanical Effects Technicians:* Roy Spencer, Terry Schubert, Bob Nugent, Joe Fitt, Ron Burton, Brian Warner, Rodney Fuller, Michael Dunleavy, Jimmy Harris, Peter Biggs, Frank Richardson, Peter Pickering. *Wireworks:* Derek Botell, Bob Harman. *Additional Effects—Additional Effects Photography:* Howard A. Anderson Co. *Additional Effects Photography Supervisor U.S.A.:* Darrell A. Anderson. New York *Process Plate Cinematography:* Bob Bailin. *New York Process Stills:* Cervin Robinson. *FX Makeup—Special Makeup Supervisor:* Stuart Freeborn. *Effects Editors—Visual Effects Editor:* Peter Watson. *Assistant Visual Effects Editor:* Russell Woolnough. *Production Department—Visual Effects Coordinators:* Ernest Walter, Michael Campbell. *Titles—Main Titles:* Steve Frankfurt Communications, R/Greenberg Associates Inc. *End Titles:* Camera Effects Ltd. *End Title Cinematography:* Roy Pace, Sheldon Elbourne. Academy Award: Les Bowie, Colin Chilvers, Denys Coop, Roy Field, Zoran Perisic and Derek Meddings.

In 1938, an "abandoned" infant boy is found in the American Midwest and raised by a childless couple but the real parents are from Krypton, a planet which had exploded into its own sun. On Earth the boy, Clark Kent, grows to manhood (Christopher Reeve), gets a job as a reporter with *The Daily Planet* and moonlights as the costumed superhero Superman. The Man of Steel's exploits attract the attention of master criminal Lex Luthor (Gene Hackman) who is planning to reroute two U.S. rocket missiles and destroy the western half of California to increase the value of his own land holdings. Just in time, Superman is able to divert one of the missiles and reverse the effects of the earthquake caused by the other. Flying scenes were mostly created by front projection and the Zoptic Process.

1978–79

Alien Brandywine Productions Ltd.-Ronnie Shusett in Association with 20th Century–Fox,

Great Britain. Panavision 70, Eastman Color. Processed by Rank. Prints by De Luxe. *Director:* Ridley Scott. *Visual and Special Effects— Effects Director:* Brian Johnson. *Special Effects Supervisor:* Nick Allder. *Cinematographer:* Denys Ayling. *Camera Operator:* David Litchfield. *Assistant Cameraman:* Terry Pearce. *Key Grip:* Peter Woods. *Miniatures—Supervising Miniaturists:* Martin Bower, Bill Pearson. *Miniaturist:* Philip D. Rae. *Matte Paintings— Matte Artist:* Ray Caple. *Optical Cinematography—Special Opticals:* Filmfex Animation Services Ltd. *Mechanical Effects—Mechanical Supervisor:* Allan Bryce. *Mechanical Effects Technicians:* David Watkins, Phil Knowles, Roger Nicholls, Dennis Lowe, Neil Swann, Guy Hudson. *FX Makeup/Creature Shop—Alien Design:* H. R. Giger. *Alien Head Effects:* Carlo Rambaldi. *Alien Head Effects Co-Creator:* Isidoro Raponi. *Head Effects Assistant:* Ralph Cobis. *Small Alien Forms Co-Designer, Builder and Operator:* Roger Dicken. *Additional Alien Mechanics:* Carlo de Marchis, Dr. David Watling. *Alien Effects Coordinator:* Clinton Cavers. *Supervising Modeler:* Peter Boysey. *Modelers:* Eddie Butler, Shirley Denny, Patti Rodgers. Academy Award: Carlo Rambaldi, Brian Johnson, Nick Allder, Denys Ayling.

This was a reworking of some low-budgets efforts, *It! The Terror from Beyond Space* (1958) and *Terrore nello spazio* (1965, directed by Mario Bava), complete with an uncredited story idea (*The Voyage of the Space Beagle*) conceived by A. E. van Vogt. The result: a blockbuster starring a stunning alien designed by Swiss artist Hansruedi (Hans Rudolf) Giger (born 1940 in Chur).

1979

1941 A-Team Productions/Universal/Columbia, U.S.A. Panavision 70, Technicolor/Metrocolor.

Director: Steven Spielberg. *Visual Effects Creators—Visual Effects Supervisor:* Larry Robinson. *Visual Effects Cinematographer:* William A. Fraker. *Optical Consultant:* L.B. Abbott. *Traveling Matte/Blue Screen Consultant:* Frank Van der Veer, Van der Veer Photo Effects *Miniatures—*

Miniature Supervisor: Gregory Jein. *Miniature Lighting Designer:* Robin Leyden. *Assistant Miniature Supervisor:* Ken Swenson. *Miniature Coordinator:* Glenn Erickson. *Miniature Production Assistant:* Mitch Suskin. *Model Makers:* Tom Cengar, Michael Del Genio, Anthony Doublin, Ken Ebert, Frances W. Evans, David Heilman, Tim Huchthausen, Sharon Lee, Illyanna Lowry, Michael McMillen, Milius Romyn, Nicholas Seldon, Susan Turner, Gary Weeks, Robert Worthington, Ken Ralston, Will Guest, Jack Isaacs, Tom Sheldon, Steve Telsky. *Miniature Riggers:* Bill Aldridge, Michael Barrett, Don Hathaway, Robert Johnston, David Peterson, Doyle Smiley, Richard Stutsman, Matt Sweeney, Brad Turpin. *Special Miniature Consultants:* Larry Albright, Robert Short. *Matte Paintings— Matte Artist:* Matthew J. Yuricich. *Assistant Matte Artist:* Rocco Gioffre. *Mechanical Effects—Mechanical Effects Supervisor:* A.D. Flowers. *Mechanical Effects Technicians:* Logan Z. Frazee, Logan R. Frazee, Terry Frazee, Steve Galich, Steve Lombardi, Marlin "Buck" Jones, Gary Monak, Bill Myat, Don Myers, Joe Zomar, Eugene Crum, Kenneth Estes, Arthur Arp, Wilbur Arp, Thomas Arp.

How would the Lydecker brothers have rigged the miniatures? That was the question chief miniaturist Gregory Jein had in mind when he was asked to contribute to a hilariously funny story about war panic in L.A. following the Pearl Harbor attack. He solved the problem, especially model aircraft, with stunning results.

1979–80

The Empire Strikes Back George Lucas, Gary Kurtz/Lucasfilm Ltd., Great Britain/ U.S.A. Panavision 70, Color by Rank. Prints by DeLuxe.

Director: Irvin Kershner. *Visual Effects—Visual Effects Company:* Industrial Light & Magic Inc., a Division of Lucasfilm Ltd. *Visual Effects and Mechanical Effects Supervisor:* Brian Johnson (Great Britain). *Visual Effects Chief Cinematographer (San Rafael, California):* Richard Edlund (ILM). *Cinematographers:* Kenneth Ralston, Jim Veilleux. *Camera Operators:* Don Dow, Bill Neil. *Assistant Cameramen:* Selwyn Eddy, Jody Westheimer, Rick Fichter, Clint Palmer, Michael J. McAlister, Paul Huston, Richard Fish, Chris Anderson. *Key Grip:* Ted Moehnke. *Grips:* William Beck, Robert Finley, Leo Loverro, Edward Hirsh, Dick Dova, Ed Breed. *Blue Screen Consultant (Great Britain):* Stanley W. Sayer. *Still Photographer:* Terry Chostner. *Still Laboratory Assistant:* Roberto McGrath. *Equipment—Electronic Systems Designer:* Jerry L. Jeffress. *Systems Programmer:* Kris Brown. *Electronic Engineers:* Lhary Meyer, Mike MacKenzie, Gary Leo. *Special Project Coordinator:* Stuart Ziff. *Equipment Engineering Supervisor:* Gene Whiteman. *Design Engineer:* Mike Bolles. *Machinists:* Udo Pampel, Greg Beaumonte. *Camera and Movement Design:* Jim Beaumonte. *Special Optics Designer:* David Grafton. *Special Optics Fabrication:* J. L. Wood Optical Systems. *High Speed Camera Movements:* Mitchell Camera Corporation. *Ultra High Speed Camera:* Bruce Hill Productions. *Art Department—Art Director:* Joe Johnston. *Assistant Art Director:* Nilo Rodis-Jamero. *Matte Paintings— Supervising Matte Artist:* Harrison Ellenshaw. *Matte Artists:* Ralph McQuarrie, Michael Angelo Pangrazio. *Matte Cinematography:* Neil Krepela. *Assistant Matte Cameramen:* Craig Barron, Robert Elswit. *Additional Matte Cinematography:* Michael Lawler. *Stop-Motion—Stop-Motion Cinematography:* Dennis Muren. *Stop-Motion Animators:* Jon Berg, Phil Tippett. *Stop-Motion Technicians:* Tom St. Amand, Douglas Beswick. *Miniatures—Miniature Shop Foreman:* Steve Gawley. *Chief Miniaturist:* Lorne Peterson. *Miniaturists:* Paul Huston, Tom Rudduck, Michael Fulmer, Samuel Zolltheis, Charles Bailey, Ease Owyeung, Scott Marshall, Marc Thorpe, Wesley Seeds, Dave Carson, Rob Gemmel, Pat McClung. *Miniature Pyrotechnical Effects—Explosives:* Joe Viskocil, Dave Pier, Thaine Morris. *Effects Animation—Animation and Rotoscope Supervisor:* Peter Kuran. *Animators:* Samuel Comstock, Garry Waller, John Van Vliet, Rick Taylor, Kim Knowlton, Chris Casady, Nina Saxon, Diana Wilson. *Optical Cinematography—Optical Cinematography Supervisor:* Bruce Nicholson. *Optical Printer Operators:* David Berry, Kenneth F. Smith, Donald Clark. *Optical Line-up:* Warren Franklin, Mark Vargo, Peter Amundson, Loring Doyle, Thomas Rosseter, Tam Pillsbury, James Lim. *Optical Coordinator:* Laurie Vermont. *Laboratory Technicians:* Tim Geideman, Duncan Myers, Ed Jones. *Optical Printer Component Manufacturer:* George Randle Company. *Optical Printer Component Engineering:* Fries Engineering. *Additional Optical Effects:* Van der Veer Photo Effects (Frank Van der Veer, Barry Nolan), Modern Film Effects, Ray Mercer & Co. (Ray Mercer, Sr.), The Westheimer Company (Joseph Westheimer), Lookout Mountain Films. *Sfx Editing—Supervising Editor:* Conrad Buff. *Editor:* Michael Kelly. *Assistant Editors:* Arthur Repola, Howard Stein. *Apprentice Editor:* Jon Thaler. *Editorial Coordinator:* Roberta Friedman. *Production—General Manager, ILM:* Tom Smith. *Production Administrator:* Dick Gallegly. *Production Secretary:* Patricia Blau. *Production Associates:* Thomas Brown, Ray Scalice. *Assistant Accountants:* Glenn Phillips, Pam Traas, Laura Crockett. *Production Assistant:* Jenny Oznowicz. *Transportation:* Robert Martin. *Mechanical Effects (Great Britain Unit)—Mechanical Effects Supervisor:* Nick Allder. *Location Unit Supervisor:* Allan Bryce. *Technicians:* Neil Swann, David Watkins, Phil Knowles, Barry Whitrod, Martin Gant, Brian Eke, Gary Hudson, Dennis Lowe. *Engineers:* Roger Nicholls, Steve Lloyd. *Electrical Engineer:* John Hatt. *Electronics Consultant:* Rob Dickson. *Model Construction:* John Pakenham. *Assistant Technicians:* Alan Poole, Digby Milner, Robert McLaren. *Secretary:* Gill Case. *FX Puppets/Creature Shop—Special Creature and Makeup Design:* Stuart Freeborn. *Chief Makeup Artist:* Graham Freeborn. *Makeup Artists:* Kay Freeborn, Nick Maley. *Yoda Fabrication:* Wendy Midener. *Yoda played by* Frank Oz. Academy Award: Richard Edlund, Dennis Muren, Brian Johnson, Bruce Nicholson.

The show must go on. Stop-frame Imperial Snow Walkers, moving like enormous elephants, an animatronics puppet named Yoda and a rotoscoped lightsaber duel between Luke Skywalker and his (big surprise for audiences then) father, Darth Vader. Filmed in the new ILM location at San Rafael, Marin County. Dennis Muren, who photographed most of the stop-motion for the prologue (the plates were shot in Norway): "When we arrived, the ILM building was still under construction. Walls were being set, equipment was being shipped up from Los Angeles, storyboards were being redone, and the script was in its final stages. There was no electricity in the building. We moved up there in September [1978], we couldn't even turn on a stage light until February! We only had regular work lights. That was a long time. And we only had two cameras up until August of 1979 to shoot with — the Dykstraflex and the old Technirama. When we finally got the Empireflex working we started the stop-motion work. I think it took eight months to complete the facility" (*Cinefex* number 3, December 1980, p. 6).

1979–80

Star Trek: The Motion Picture Gene Roddenberry/A Century Associates Picture/Paramount, U.S.A. Panavision 70, Metrocolor.

Director: Robert Wise. *Visual Effects Future General Unit—Visual Effects Company:* Future General Corporation. *Visual Effects Director:* Douglas Trumbull. *Visual Effects Producer:* Richard Yuricich. *Effects Cinematography:* Richard Yuricich, David Stewart. *Camera Operators:* Don Baker, Phil Barberio, Don Cox, Douglas Eby, John Ellis, David Hardberger, Alan Harding, Lin Law, Clay Marsh, David McCune, Max Morgan, Scott Squires, Hoyt H. Yeatman Jr. *Cinematography:* Thane Berti, Glenn Campbell, Christopher George, Scott Farrar, Robert Friedstand, Robert Hollister, Ross McElhatton, Mike Peed, Lex Rawlins, Jonathan Seay, Steve Slocum, Bob Thomas. *Additional Cinematographers:* Jim Dickson, Bruce Logan, Charles F. Wheeler. *Visual Consultants:* Virgil Mirano, Guy Marsden. *Gaffer:* David Gold. *Key Grip:* Pat van Auken. *Equipment—Special Electronics and Mechanical Design:* Evans Wetmore, Richard Hollander. *Special Mechanical Designs:* George Randle Company, Precision Machine, Dieter Seifert, Rourke Engineering. *Art Department—Illustrators:* David Negron, Andy Probert, Tom Cranham, Robert McCall, Don Moore. *Matte Paintings—Matte Artist:* Matthew J. Yuricich. *Additional Matte Artist:* Rocco Gioffre. *Matte Cinematographer:* Don Jarel. *Miniatures—Miniature Supervisor:* Gregory Jein. *Miniaturists:* Bruce Bishop, Al Broussard, Mike Fink, Kris Gregg, Mike McMillen, Robert Short, Robert Spurlock, Rick Thompson, Don Wheeler. *Effects Animation and Graphics—Animators:* Deena

Burkett, Alison Yerxa, Lisze Bechtold, Merilyn Ching, Eirene Cowan, Cy Didjurgis, Leslie Ekker, Linda Harris, Nicola Kaftan, John Kimball, Thomas Koester, Deidre Le Blanc, Linda Moreau, Connie Morgan, Paul Olsen, Greg Wilzbach, Richard E. Hollander. *Special Electronics:* Kris Dean, Stephen Fog, John Gilman, Jim Goodnight, Fred Iguchi, Robin Leyden, Greg McMurray, Mike Myers, Josh Morton. *Optical Cinematography—Optical Consultants:* Alan Gundelfinger, Milt Laiken. *FX Editing:—Editors:* Jack Hinkle, Vicki Witt. *Special Editors:* Michael Backauskas, Kathy Campbell, Nora Jeanne Smith. *Production—Project Managers:* John James, Bill Millar. *Assistant to Douglas Trumbull:* Mona Thal Benefiel. *Assistant to Richard Yuricich:* Joyce Goldberg. *Special Assistants:* Leora Glass, Brett Webster. *Projectionist:* John Piner. *Transportation Coordinator:* Robert Mayne. *Visual Effects Apogee, Inc.—Visual Effects Company:* Apogee, Inc. *Visual Effects Supervisor:* John C. Dykstra. *Cinematography:* Cosmos Bolger, Dennis Dorney, Robert Elswit, Phil Gonzales, Greg Kimble, Ron Nathan, Michael Sweeney, Diane E. Wooten. *Camera Operators:* Chuck Barbee, Bruno George, Michael Lawler, Jerry Pooler, Doug Smith, John Sullivan. *Key Grips:* Mark Cane, Mark Kline. *Gaffer:* Chuck Embrey. *Visual Consultants:* Mike Middleton, Erik Nash, Phil Joanon. *Geometric Designs:* Ron Resch, Boston University. *Equipment—Special Electronics Design:* Alvah J. Miller, Mat Beck, Paul Johnston, Steve Sass. *Special Mechanical Design:* Dick Alexander, Bill Shourt, Donald Trumbull. *Special Optical and Mechanical Consultants:* B/G Engineering, Abbot Grafton, Gerald Nash. *Art Department—Illustrators:* Mark Kline, Syd Meade, Jack Johnson, John Shourt. *Miniatures—Miniature Supervisor:* Grant McCune. *Miniaturists:* David Beasley, Jon Erland, Joe Garlington, Pete Gerard, Rick Gilligan, Richie Helmer, Michael Joyce, Deborah Kendall, Don Kurtz, Pat McClung, Gary Rhodaback, John Ramsay, Dennis Schultz, David Scott, Dick Singleton, Richard Smiley, David Sosalla, Susan Turner, Don Webber, Gary Weeks. *Effects Animation—Special Animation:* Harry Moreau. *2D Animation and Graphics:* Angela Diamos, John Millerburg. *Optical Cinematography—Optical Cinematography Supervisor:* Roger Dorney. *FX Editing—Editors:* Denny Kelley, David Bartholomew,

Steve Klein, Steve Mark. *Production—Project Manager:* Robert Shepherd. *Assistant to Robert Shepherd:* Ann M. Johnston. *Assistant to John Dykstra:* Mimi McKinney. *Special Assistants:* Deborah Baxter, Janet Dykstra, Philip Golden, Proctor Jones, Tut Shurtleff. *Robert Abel & Associates Visual Effects Unit—Effects Company:* Robert Abel & Associates. *Supervisor:* Robert Abel. *Effects Designer:* Richard Taylor. *Project Manager:* Con Pederson. *Special Services—Process Cinematography:* Bill Hansard. *Special Animation:* Robert Swarthe. *Miniature Computer Motion Control System:* Bob Gehring. *Certain Miniatures:* Magicam Inc. *Magicam Supervisors:* James Dow, Ross Simpson. *Magicam Technicians:* Larry Albright, Peter Anderson, David Ascher, Brad Bluth, Bob Buckner, Chris Crump, Lee Ettleman, Nick Esposet, Rick Gutierrez, Dann Linck, Carey Melcher, Chris Miller, Paul Olsen, Tom Pahk, Richard Raymis, Chris Ross, Mark Stetson, Zuzana Swansea, Rick Thompson, Chris Tietz, George Trimmer, Paul Turner, Steve Wilson. *Additional Miniatures:* Brick Price Miniatures. *Mechanical Effects—Mechanical Effects Supervisor:* Alex C. Weldon. *Location Mechanical Effects Supervisor:* Joe Viskocil. *Mechanical Effects Technicians:* Darrell Pritchett, Ray Mattey, Marty Bresin.

Two then-important effects companies and a computer graphics studio offered their services to transfer for the first time TV's *Star Trek* to the big screen by enlarging a former TV episode to a multi-million dollar budget format which in that case didn't fulfill the spectators' expectations but couldn't harm the popularity of the *U.S.S. Enterprise.*

> The *U.S.S. Enterprise* is a cruiser-size star ship displacing 390,000 tons and manned by a crew of 400. Her spacious decks encompass a bridge, control rooms, crew quarters and many science labs and technical departments, along with commodious passenger accommodations and sufficient cargo and storage space for voyages of long duration. The *Enterprise's* mission includes scientific investigation and reconnaissance of previously unexplored worlds; providing aid and supplies for Earth colonies; diplomatic courtesy calls on alien civilizations; and the enforcement of laws regulating commerce with the Earth colonies [*Star Trek: Advance Information on 1966–67 Programming NBC Television Network*].

The original TV format created by Gene Rodenberry in contrast worked on a shoestring but nevertheless used the combined forces of several effects houses in Hollywood to photograph *Enterprise* models or beam animation: Howard A. Anderson Co. (Darrell Anderson), then located on the Desilu (former RKO) lot; Film Effects of Hollywood (Linwood G. Dunn) was supposed to take over from Anderson's which didn't work out; The Westheimer Company (Joseph Westheimer), Van der Veer Photo Effects (Frank Van der Veer), and Cinema Research. Among the individuals who worked on the shows at various times were Richard Edlund, William Reinhold, Albert J. Whitlock and MGM makeup artist Charlie Schram (who had done the Morlock masks for *The Time Machine* and now contributed the final version of the Spock ears), and on the list of prop makers we find such illustrious names as Wah Chang, Gene Warren and Jim Danforth (the latter as prop maker for the premiere episode "The Cage").

1979–81

Das Boot [U.S.: *The Boat*] Bavaria Atelier/ Radiant Film/WDR (Westdeutscher Rundfunk)/SDR (Süddeutscher Rundfunk), W. Germany, Fujicolor.

Director: Wolfgang Petersen. *Mechanical Effects—Explosives:* Karl Baumgartner. *Hydro Technician:* Ludwig Kurz. *Special Machines:* Heinrich Bader. *Special Effects Unit:* Max Gretmann, Willi Neuner, Michael Strohhofer, Nick Middleton, Fritz Kirschke. *Miniatures—Model Photography:* Ernst Wild. *Model makers:* Hans Nothof, Oliver Nothof. *Process—Front Projection:* Jan W. Jacobsen. *Front Projection Consultant:* Theodor Nischwitz. *Assistant Camera:* Thomas Gitt. *Optical Cinematography:* Jörg Michael Kunsdorff. *Assistants:* Rudolf Roemmelt, Sebastian Schwerte, Peter Maiwald, Hans Nachol, Gerhard Neumeier. *Special Service—Art Technician:* Frieder (Friedrich) Thaler. *Underwater Cinematography and Second Unit Director:* Egil S. Woxholt.

This film version of Lothar Günther Buchheim's book, originally intended as a tax write-off project (Donald Siegel was supposed to direct), became the greatest international box-

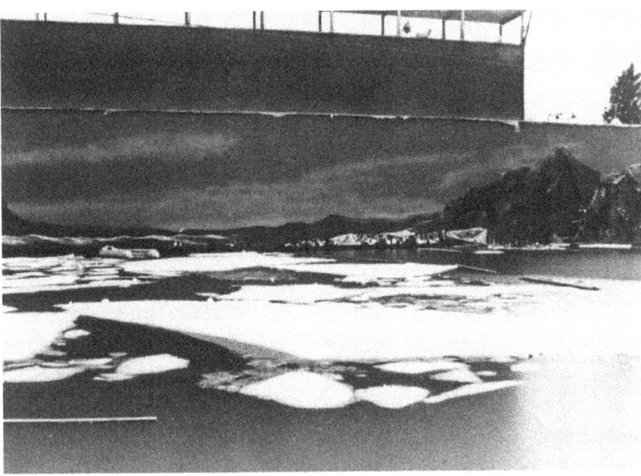

The tank at Bavaria Studios where Wolfgang Petersen and crew filmed the World War II submarine drama *The Boat* (courtesy Deutsche Kinemathek Berlin).

office success of German post-war cinema. They had three model World War II subs, the longest more than 30 feet, partly filmed on a real sea, and a replica of the tower for the protagonists (Jürgen Prochnow et al.) to act in front of a process screen.

1979–81

Clash of the Titans   Charles H. Schneer and Ray Harryhausen/Peerford Films–MGM, Great Britain

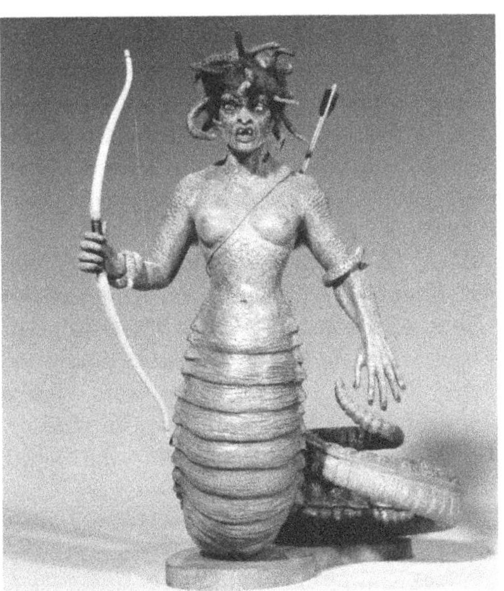

Director: Desmond Davis. *Stop-Motion—Creator of Special Visual Effects and Stop-Motion Animation:* Ray Harryhausen. *Assistants to Ray Harryhausen and Additional Stop-Motion Animation:* Jim Danforth, Steven Archer. *Sculptors:* Janet Stevens, Colin Chilvers, Lyle Conway. *Mechanical Effects—Floor Effects:* Brian Smithies. *Mechanical Effects Technician:* David Knowles. *Matte Paintings—Matte Artist:* Cliff Culley. *Blue Screen—Traveling Matte Supervisor/Blue Screen Consultant:* Dennis Bartlett. *Optical Cinematography:* Roy Field (Pinewood Studios). *Additional Optical Effects:* Frank Van der Veer, Barry Nolan (Van der Veer Photo Effects). *Special Service—Special Makeup:* Colin Arthur. *Stunt Coordinator:* Fernando Poggi.

Ray Harryhausen's swan song retells the ancient Greek myth of Perseus (Harry Hamlin) and his campaign to rescue and marry Princess Andromeda (Judi Bowker). It offers several exciting stop-motion creatures such as Andromeda's tormentor, Calibos, the disfigured Lord of the Marsh, and four-armed sea beast Kraken finally being petrified and turned to stone by the

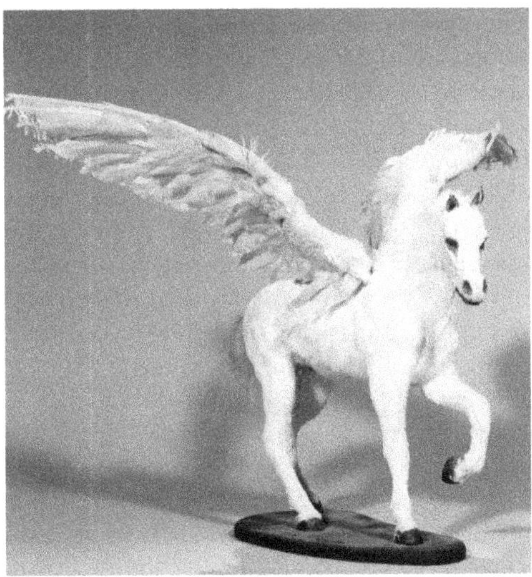

Medusa *(left)* and one of the three Pegasus models *(above)* from *Clash of the Titans* (both courtesy Ray and Diana Harryhausen Collection as displayed by Deutsche Kinemathek Berlin).

head of the decapitated snake lady Medusa, a Gorgon. Jim Danforth animated lively blue screen shots of the flying winged horse Pegasus.

1980–81

Caveman   Turman-Foster (for United Artists release), U.S.A. Technicolor.

Director: Carl Gottlieb. *Stop-Motion—Special Visual Effects/Stop-Motion Concepts:* Effects Associates Inc. *Visual Effects Supervisor and Sculptor:* Jim Danforth. *Visual Effects Supervisor and Stop-Motion Animation:* David Allen. *Stop Motion Crew:* Jim Aupperle, Randall William (Randy) Cook, Spencer Gill, Peter Kleinow, David Stipes, Laine Liska. *Model Construction:* Roger Dicken. *Additional Armatures:* Ernest D. Farino. *Matte Paintings—Matte Artists:* Dan Curry, Rocco Gioffre, Jena Holman. *Illustrator/Sketch Artist:* Michael Ploog. *Special Service—Abominable Snowman Created by* Chris Walas. *Mechanical Effects—Mechanical Effects Supervisor:* Roy Arbogast.

Ringo Starr Meets Slapstick Stop-Motion Dinosaurs in an homage to Willis O'Brien's early stone age comedies. "Everybody tells me, 'Dinosaur pictures are dead.' And I always say to them, 'The only thing that's dead is bad movies.' You can keep making dinosaur pictures as long as there are valid stories to be told that involve dinosaurs.... The challenge is finding new dimensions." Jim Danforth, who said that a decade before *Jurassic Park* (*Cinefex* No. 5, July 1981), didn't receive screen credit as co-director due to protests by the Directors Guild and quit the basically interesting but script-wise not very satisfying project about two-thirds of the way through (leaving it in the hands of certainly competent colleagues and co-workers).

1980–81

Dragonslayer   Paramount Pictures/Walt Disney Productions, Great Britain/U.S.A. Panavision 70, Color by Rank. Prints by Metrocolor.

Director: Matthew Robbins. *Visual Effects—*

Visual Effects Company: Industrial Light & Magic, a Division of Lucasfilm Ltd.. *Visual Effects Cinematography Supervisor:* Dennis Muren. *Cinematographers:* Rick Fichter, Michael J. McAlister. *Additional Cinematography:* Jim Veuillex. *Assistant Cameramen:* Selwyn Eddy III, Jody Westheimer. *Key Grip:* T. E. Moehnke. *Grips:* Patrick Fitzsimmons, Dick Dova, Bobby Finley III, Edward Hirsh, William Beck. *Aerial Cinematography:* Continental Camera Systems. *Camera Aircraft Pilot:* Clay Lacey. *Still Photographer:* Terry Chostner. *Assistant Still Photographers:* Roberto McGrath, Kerry Nordquist. *Go-Motion—Dragon Supervisors:* Phil Tippett, Kenneth Ralston. *Dragon Movers:* Tom St. Amand, Stuart Ziff, Gary Leo. *Closeup Dragon:* Chris Walas. *Dragon Set Design:* Dave Carson. *Dragon Consultant:* Jon Berg. *Dragon Set Builder:* Dave Carson. *Dragon Assistants:* Eric Jensen, Marc Thorpe, Wesley Seeds, Peter Stolz, Bess Wiley. *Pyrotechnical Effects:* Thaine Morris. *Equipment—Electronic Systems Designer:* Jerry Jeffress. *Equipment Engineering Supervisor:* Gene Whiteman. *Machinists:* Udo Pampel, Conrad Bonderson. *Computer Engineer:* Kris Brown. *Electronic Engineer:* Mike MacKenzie. *Electronic Technicians:* Marty Brenneis, Melissa Cargill, Cristi McCarthy. *Ultra High Speed Camera:* Bruce Hill Productions. *Art Department—Dragon Design, Graphics and Titles:* David Bunnett. *Matte Paintings—Supervising Matte Artist:* Alan Maley. *Matte Artists:* Chris Evans, Michael (Mike) Pangrazio. *Matte Cinematography:* Neil Krepela. *Assistant Matte Cinematography:* Craig Barron. *Miniatures—Miniature Shop Supervisor:* Lorne Peterson. *Miniaturists:* Ease Owyeung, Paul Huston, Charles Bailey, Michael Glenn Fulmer, Scott Marshall, Bruce Richardson. *Effects Animation—2D Animation Supervisor:* Samuel Cromstock. *Animators:* Dietrich Friesen, Garry Waller, Loring Doyle, John Van Vliet, Kim Knowlton, Judy Elkins, Sylvia Keulen, Scott Caple. *Additional Animation:* Visual Concept Engineering. *Additional Animation Supervisor:* Peter Kuran. *Additional Animators:* Susan Turner, Kathrine Kean, Pam Vick, Chris Casady, Len Morganti. *Animation Cameraman:* Robert Jacobs. *Optical Cinematography—Optical Cinematography Supervisor:* Bruce Nicholson. *Optical Coordinator:* Warren Franklin. *Optical Printers:* Kenneth Smith, John Ellis, David Berry. *Opti-*

cal Line-up: Tom Rosseter, Mark Vargo. *Optical Technician:* Duncan Myers. *Optical Cameraman:* James Hagedorn. *Optical Laboratory:* Alpha Cine Laboratories. *Additional Optical Effects: Rgb* Film Processing, Lookout Mountain Films, Modern Film Effects. *Optical Effects Consultant:* Roy Field. *FX Editing—Editors:* Arthur Repola, Howard Stein. *Assistant Editor:* Peter Amundsen. *Production—Production Supervisor, ILM:* Thomas Smith. *Production Coordinator:* Laurie Vermont. *Administration Coordinator:* Chrissie England. *Production Accountant:* Laura Kaysen. *Mechanical Effects and British Unit—Mechanical Effects Supervisor:* Brian Johnson. *Chief Technicians:* David Watkins, Philip Knowles, Neil Swann, John Gant, Peter W. Hutchinson, Andrew Kelly. *Technicians:* Barry Whitrod, Martin Gant, John Hatt, Norman Kerss, Ronald Hone, Nicholas J. Middleton, John Pakenham. *Assistant Technicians:* Clive Beard, Ian Corbould, Chris J. Gant, Guy Hudson, Digby Milner, Dennis Morgan, Donald Murphy, Sean Nagle, Alan Poole, Peter Skehan, Philip Smith, Anthony Speake, Mark Pickford. *Halo Crane:* Nick Allder, Dennis Lowe, Ray Evans. *Traveling Matte and Blue Screen Consultant at Pinewood Studios London:* Dennis C. Bartlett. *Walt Disney Studios—Additional Dragon Mechanic:* Danny Lee.

Go-Motion, the system that moved the dragon puppet, was a computer-controlled device with rods attached to the four limbs of the model programmed to recreate the moves during stop-frame exposure and thus creating a motion blur.

1980–81

Raiders of the Lost Ark George Lucas, Howard Kazanjian/Lucasfilm Ltd., U.S.A./ Great Britain. Panavision 70, Color by Rank and Metrocolor. Prints by Metrocolor.

Director: Steven Spielberg. *Visual Effects—Visual Effects Company:* Industrial Light & Magic Inc., a Division of Lucasfilm Ltd. *Visual Effects Supervisor:* Richard Edlund. *Cinematographer:* Jim Veilleux. *Camera Operator:* Bill Neil, Don Dow. *Assistant Cameraman:* Clint Palmer. *Still Photographer:* Terry Chostner. *Still Lab Technicians:* Roberto McGrath, Kerry Nordquist. *Art Department—Art Director:* Joe Johnston. *Assistant Art Director:* Nilo Rodis-Jamero. *Illustrator:* Ralph McQuarrie. *Matte Paintings—Supervising Matte Artist:* Alan Maley. *Matte Artist:* Michael Angelo Pangrazio. *Matte Cinematography:* Neil J. Krepela. *Assistant Matte Cameraman:* Craig Barron. *Miniatures—Miniature Shop Foreman:* Lorne Peterson. *Miniaturists:* Steve Gawley, Mike Fulmer, Wesley Seeds, Paul Huston, Charlie Bailey, Sam Zolltheis, Marc Thorpe, Bruce Richardson, Ease Owyeung. *Effects Animation—Supervising Animators:* Samuel Comstock, Dietrich Friesers. *Animators:* John Van Vliet, Kim Knowlton, Garry Waller, Loring Doyle, Scott Caple, Judy Elkins, Sylvia Keulen, Scott Marshall. *Additional Animation Supervisor:* Peter Kuran (Visual Concept Engineering). *Optical Cinematography—Optical Cinematography Supervisor:* Bruce Nicholson. *Optical Printer Operators:* David Berry, Kenneth F. Smith, John Ellis. *Optical Line-up:* Mark Vargo, Warren Franklin, Tom Rosseter. *FX Makeup—Special Makeup Effects:* Chris Walas. *SFX Editing—Editor:* Conrad Buff. *Assistant Editor:* Peter Amundson. *Production—Production Supervisor and General Manager, ILM:* Tom Smith. *Production Coordinators:* Patricia Blau, Laurie Vermont. *Production Associate:* Miki Herman. *Mechanical Effects—Mechanical Effects Supervisor:* Kit West. *Chief Technician:* Peter Dawson. *Technicians:* Terry Schubert, Rodney Fuller, Trevor Neighbour. *Engineer:* Terry Glass. *Equipment Supervisor:* William H. (Bill) Warrington. *Electrician:* Chris Condon. *Carpenter:* Roy Combes. *Assistant Technicians:* Ken Gittens, Ray Hanson. Academy Award: Richard Edlund, Kit West, Bruce Nicholson, Joe Johnston.

The old Saturday matinee serials blown up to epic proportions. The (rotoscoped) spirits of the Biblical Ark of the Covenant destroy a group of Nazi relic hunters striving for world domination

1981–82

Blade Runner The Blade Runner Partnership/The Ladd Company in Association with Sir Run Run Shaw, U.S.A. Panavision 70, Technicolor.

Director: Ridley Scott. *Visual Effects—Visual Effects Company:* Entertainment Effects Group. *Visual Effects Supervisor:* Douglas Trumbull. *Visual Effects Co-Supervisors:* Richard Yuricich, David Dryer. *Director of Miniature Photography:* David Stewart. *Additional Cinematography:* James R. Dickson. *Camera Operators:* Don Baker, Rupert Benson, Glen Campbell, Charles Cowles, David Hardberger, Ronald Longo, Timothy McHugh, Jon Seay. *Special Camera Technician:* Alan Harding. *Key Grip:* Pat van Auken. *Gaffer:* Gary Randall. *Equipment—Electronic and Mechanical Design:* Evans Wetmore. *Optical Cinematography—Optical Cinematography Supervisor:* Robert Hall. *Optical Line-up:* Philip Barberio, Richard Ripple. *Film Coordinator:* Jack Hinkle. *Cinetechnician:* George Polkinghorne. *Animation—Animation and Graphics:* John Wash. *Matte Paintings—Matte Artist:* Matthew Yuricich. *Additional Matte Artist:* Rocco Gioffre. *Assistant Matte Artist:* Michelle Moen. *Matte Cinematography:* Robert Bailey, Tama Takahashi, Don Jarel. *Miniatures—Special Projects and Miniature Coordinator:* Wayne Smith. *Miniature Technician:* Robert Spurlock. *Chief Miniaturist:* Mark Stetson. *Miniaturists:* Jerry Allen, Sean Casey, Paul Curley, Leslie Ekker, Thomas Field, Vance Frederick, William George, Kristopher Gregg, Robert Johnston, Michael McMillian, Thomas Phak, Christopher Ross, Robert Wilcox, George Trimmer, Rick Guttierrez, John Vidor. *Art Department—Illustrator:* Tom Cranham. *Special Service—Visual Displays:* Dream Quest, Inc. *Mechanical Effects—Mechanical Effects Supervisor:* Terry Frazee. *Mechanical Effects Technicians:* Steve Galich, Logan Frazee, William C. Curtis.

Like *Metropolis,* this *film noir* with Harrison Ford as a private eye and his pursuit of some androids in a City of the Future (Los Angeles) was mismanaged from the beginning but turned out a classic in the long run. Douglas Trumbull and cinematographer Richard Yuricich, joined by Yuricich's brother Matthew, an accomplished matte artist, created the awesome futuristic skyline and street canyons. Inspired by Philip K. Dick's sci-fi novel *Do Androids Dream of Electric Sheep?*

1981–82

E.T. the Extra-Terrestrial　Steven Spielberg, Kathleen Kennedy/Amblin Entertainment/Universal, U.S.A. 70mm, Spherical Panavision. Color by De Luxe. Prints by Technicolor.

Director: Steven Spielberg. *FX Puppet—E.T. Mechanical Creator:* Carlo Rambaldi. *E.T. Mechanical Co-Creator:* Isidoro Raponi. *Preliminary Design:* Rick Baker (uncredited). *E.T. Artistic Consultant:* Craig Reardon. *E.T. Technical Supervisor:* Steve Townsend. *Additional E.T. Effects:* Robert Short. *E.T. Eye Designer:* Beverly Hoffman. *E.T. Eye Makers:* Ocular Prosthetics. *Visual Effects—Visual Effects Company:* Industrial Light & Magic Inc., a Division of Lucasfilm Ltd. *Visual Effects Cinematography Supervisor:* Dennis Muren. *Effects Cinematographer:* Michael McAlister. *Camera Operators:* Robert Elswit, Don Dow. *Assistant Cameramen:* Pat Sweeney, Karl Herrmann, Selwyn Eddy III. *Key Grip:* T. E. Moehnke. *Grips:* Dave Childers, Harold Cole, Dick Dova, Bob Finley III, Patrick Fitzsimmons, Edward Hirsh, John McCleod, Thaine Morris, Peter Stolz. *Still Photographer:* Terry Chostner. *Still Laboratory Technicians:* Roberto McGrath, Kerry Nordquist. *Additional Visual Effects:* Dream Quest Inc. *Additional Visual Effects Supervisor:* Hoyt H. Yeatman, Jr. *Equipment—Equipment Maintenance:* Wade Childress, Michael Smith. *Electronic Systems Designer:* Jerry Jeffress. *Optical Cinematography—Optical Cinematography Supervisor:* Kenneth F. Smith. *Optical Coordinator:* Mitchell Suskin. *Optical Printer Operator:* David Berry. *Optical Lineup:* Ralph Gordon. *Optical Technicians:* Duncan Myers, Tim Geideman, Bob Chrisoulis. *Optical Printer Engineering:* Gene Whiteman, John Ellis. *Go-Motion—Go-Motion Models:* Tom St. Amand. *Miniatures—Miniature Shop Supervisor:* Lorne Peterson. *Chief Miniaturists:* Charlie Bailey, Mike Fulmer. *Miniaturists:* Scott Marshall, Ease Owyeung, Mike Cochrane, Suzanne Pastor, Michael Steffe, Jessie Boberg, Randy Ottenberg. *Miniature Electronics:* Gary Leo, Marty Brenneis. *Art Department—Spaceship Design:* Ralph McQuarrie. *Matte Paintings—Supervising Matte Artist:* Michael (Mike) Pangrazio. *Matte Artists:* Christopher Evans, Frank Ordaz. *Matte Cinematography:* Neil J. Krepela. *Assistant Matte*

Cameraman: Craig Barron. *Animation—Supervising Animator:* Samuel Comstock. *Animators:* Peggy Tonkonogy, Garry Waller, Terry Windell, Jack Mongovan. *FX Editing—Supervising Editor:* Conrad Buff. *Editor:* Howard Stein. *Production—General Manager, ILM:* Tom Smith. *Production Coordinators:* Warren Franklin, Laurie Vermont. *Production Accountant:* Laura Kaysen. Academy Award: Carlo Rambaldi, Dennis Muren, Kenneth F. Smith.

It may be hard to believe but *E.T.* came into being as the offspring of a horror movie titled *Night Skies*, kind of an extraterrestrial poltergeist. Rick Baker was hired to design the aliens whose look was pretty close to what was eventually seen on the screen in *E.T.* and then credited solely to Carlo Rambaldi. In the end, E.T. didn't turn out a monster but an extraterrestrial Christkind. Industrial Light & Magic contributed some matte paintings and miniatures (E.T.'s spaceship) as well as the go-motion system for a scene that shows a kid bicycling up to the sky.

1982–83

Return of the Jedi   George Lucas, Howard Kazanjian /Lucasfilm Ltd., Great Britain/ U.S.A. 70mm, JDC Scope, Color by Rank, Monaco and De Luxe. Prints by De Luxe.

Director: Richard Marquand. *Visual Effects—Visual Effects Company:* Industrial Light & Magic Inc., a Division of Lucasfilm Ltd. *Visual Effects Supervisors and Cinematographers:* Richard Edlund, Dennis Muren, Ken Ralston. *Camera Operators:* Don Dow, Michael J. McAlister, Bill Neil, Scott Farrar, Selwyn Eddy III, Michael Owens, Robert Elswit, Rick Fichter, Stewart Barbee, Mark Gredell, David Hardburger. *Assistant Camera Operators:* Pat Sweeney, Kim Marks, Robert Hill, Ray Gilberti, Randy Johnson, Patrick McArdle, Peter Daulton, Bessie Wiley, Maryan Evans, Toby Heindel, David Fincher, Peter Romano. *Key Grip:* Ted Moehnke. *Grip Foreman:* Patrick Fitzsimmons. *Grips:* Bob Finley III, Ed Hirsh, John McCleod, Peter Stolz, Dave Childers, Harold Cole, Merlin Ohm, Joe Fulmer, Lance Brackett. *Still Photography Supervisor:* Terry Chostner. *Still Photogra-*

phy: Roberto McGrath, Kerry Nordquist. *Steadicam Plate Cinematography:* Garrett Brown. *Ultra High Speed Cinematography:* Bruce Hill Productions. *Blue Screen Consultant (Great Britain):* Stanley W. Sayer. *Equipment—Electronic System Designers:* Jerry Jeffress, Kris Brown. *Electronic Engineers:* Mike MacKenzie, Marty Brenneis. *Equipment Engineering Supervisor:* Gene Whiteman. *Machinists:* Udo Pampel, Conrad Bonderson. *Apprentice Machinists:* David Hanks, Chris Rand. *Design Engineers:* Mike Bollers, Ed Tennler. *Equipment Maintenance:* Wade Childress, Michael J. White, Cristi McCarthy. *Art Department—Art Directors:* Joe Johnston, Nilo Rodis-Jamero. *Assistant Art Director:* Dave Carson. *Illustrator:* George Jenson. *Computer Graphics—Computer Graphics Supervisors:* William Reeves, Tom Duff. *Matte Paintings—Supervising Matte Artist:* Michael Pangrazio. *Matte Artists:* Christopher Evans, Frank Ordaz. *Matte Cinematography:* Neil J. Krepela, Craig Barron. *Miniatures—Miniature Shop Supervisors:* Lorne Peterson, Steve Gawley. *Chief Miniaturists:* Paul Huston, Charles Bailey, Michael Glenn Fulmer, Ease Owyeung. *Miniaturists:* William George, Marc Thorpe, Scott Marshall, Sean Casey, Larry Tan, Barbara Gallucci, Jeff Mann, Ira Keeler, Bill Beck, Mike Cochrane, Barbara Affonso, Bill Buttfield, Marghi McMahon, Randy Ottenberg, Chuck Wiley, Toby Heindel, Richard Davis. *Miniature Pyrotechnical Effects—Explosives:* Thaine Morris, Dave Pier, Peter Stolz. *Stop-Motion—Stop-Motion Animation:* Tom St. Amand. *Effects Animation—Animation Supervisor:* James Keefer. *Chief Animators:* Garry Waller, Kimberly Knowlton. *Animators:* Terry Windell, Renee Holt, Mike Lessa, Samuel Comstock, Rob La Duca, Annick Therrien, Suki Stern, Margot Pipkin. *Additional Animation Supervisor:* Peter Kuran (Visual Concepts Engineering). *Optical Cinematography—Optical Cinematography Supervisor:* Bruce Nicholson. *Optical Printers:* John Ellis, David Berry, Kenneth F. Smith, Donald Clark, Mark Vargo, James Lim. *Optical Line-up:* Tom Rosseter, Ed L. Jones, Ralph Gordon, Philip Barberio. *Laboratory Technicians:* Tim Geideman, Duncan Myers, Michael S. Moore. *Additional Optical Cinematography:* Van der Veer Photo Effects. *Additional Optical Supervisor:* Greg Van der Veer. *Additional Optical Effects:* Lookout

Mountain Films, Pacific Title & Art Studio, Monaco Film Labs, California Films, Movie Magic. *FX Editing—Editor:* Arthur Repola. *Editors:* Howard Stein, Peter Amundson, Bill Kimberlin. *Assistant Editors:* Robert Chrisoulis, Michael Gleason, Jay Ignaszewski, Joe Class. *Production—General Manager, ILM:* Tom Smith. *Production Supervisor:* Patricia Rose Duignan. *Production Coordinators:* Warren Franklin, Laurie Vermont. *Administration:* Chrissie England, Laura Kaysen, Paula Karsh, Karen Ayers, Sonja Paulsen, Karen Dube. *Production Assistants:* Susan Fritz-Monahan, Kathy Shine. *Mechanical Effects—Mechanical Effects Supervisors:* Kit West, Roy Arbogast. *Foreman:* William David Lee. *Floor Controller:* Ian Wingrove. *Chief Technician:* Peter Dawson. *Technicians:* John Baker, Joe Fitt, G. Clifford, David Beavis. *Location Technician:* Bob Harman. *Wire Flying Assistant:* S. Miles. *Creature Shop—Creature Designers:* Phil Tippett, Stuart Freeborn. *Articulation Engineer:* Stuart Ziff. *Assistant Articulation Engineer:* Eben Stromquist. *Armature Designer:* Peter Ronzani. *Plastic Designer:* Richard Davis. *Sculptural Designers:* Chuck Wiley, James Howard. *Chief Sculptors:* Dave Carson, Tony McVey, Dave Sosalla, Judy Elkins, Derek Howarth. *Chief Moldmakers:* Wesley Seeds, Ron Young. *Creature Consultants:* Jon Berg, Chris Walas. *Production Creature Coordinator:* Patty Blau. *Latex Foam Laboratory Supervisor:* Tom McLaughlin. *Animatronics Engineer:* John Coppinger. *Jabba the Hut Puppeteers:* Toby Philpott, Mike Edmonds, David Barclay. *Creature Puppeteers:* Michael McCormick, Deep Roy, Simon Williamson, Hugh Spirit, Swim Lee, Michael Quinn, Richard Robinson. Academy Award: Richard Edlund, Dennis Muren, Ken Ralston, Phil Tippett.

The film's highlight was a bike ride through a forest. Dennis Muren: "We knew from the start that the final bike chase would be a combination of live-action close-ups against bluescreen and then miniatures for the longer shots.... [W]e shot for about seven or eight days on our stage with the actors and full-size bikes against our new huge blue screen.... The bike chase is about two and a half or three minutes long, with something like a hundred shots — most of them no longer than about sixty frames" (*Cinefex* Number 13, July 1983, p. 52). For the high-speed

background plates, Lucasfilm hired Steadicam pioneer Garrett Brown.

1983–84

Indiana Jones and the Temple of Doom
George Lucas, Frank Marshall/Lucasfilm Ltd., U.S.A./Great Britain. Panavision 70, Color by Rank and Monaco. Prints by De Luxe.

Director: Steven Spielberg. *Visual Effects—Visual Effects Company:* Industrial Light & Magic Inc., a Division of Lucasfilm Ltd. *Visual Effects Supervisor:* Dennis Muren. *Chief Cinematographer:* Michael J. McAlister. *Cinematography:* Mike Owens. *Camera Operator:* Kim Marks. *Assistant Cameramen:* Pat Sweeney, Randy Johnson, Joe Fulmer. *Additional Cinematography:* Rick Fichter. *Key Grip:* Patrick Fitzsimmons. *Grip Coordinator:* Edward Hirsh. *Grips:* Bob Finley III, Dick Dova, John McCleod, Dave Childers, Harold Cole, Lance Brackett, Merlin Ohm, Mike Speakman, Don Watson. *Still Photographers:* Terry Chostner, Kerry Nordquist, Roberto McGrath. *Equipment—Electronic Engineering:* Michael MacKenzie, Wade Childress, Greg Beaumonte, Jerry Jeffress, Kris Brown. *Machinists:* Udo Pampel, Christopher Rand. *Optical Cinematography—Optical Cinematography Supervisor:* Bruce Nicholson. *Optical Printer Operators:* John Ellis, David Berry, Donald Clark. *Optical Line-up:* Tom Rosseter, Ed Jones, Peg Hunter. *Additional Optical Effects:* Modern Film Effects. *Additional Optical Line-up:* Jacques Protay. *Laboratory Technicians:* Tim Geideman, Jeff Doran, Louis Rivera. *Miniatures—Miniature Shop Supervisor:* Lorne Peterson. *Chief Miniaturists:* Paul Huston, Barbara Gallucci, Charlie Bailey, Ease Owyeung, Michael Fulmer. *Miniaturists:* Wesley Seeds, Barbara Affonso, Larry Tan, Marc Thorpe, Scott Marshall, Chuck Wiley, Pete Ronzani, Jeff Mann, Ira Keeler, Richard Davis, William George, Mike Cochrane. *Stop-Motion—Stop-Motion Animation:* Tom St. Amand. *Creative Consultant:* Phil Tippett. *Stop-Motion Technicians:* David Sosalla, Randy Ottenberg, Sean Casey. *Matte Paintings—Supervising Matte Artist:* Michael Pangrazio. *Matte Artists:* Christopher Evans, Frank Ordaz, Caroleen Green. *Matte*

Camera Supervisor: Craig Barron. *Matte Cinematography:* David Fincher, Deborah Morgan. *Animation—Animation Supervisor:* Charles Mullen. *Additional Animation Supervisor:* Peter Kuran. *Chief Animator:* Bruce Walters. *Animators:* Barbara Brennan, Jack Mongovan, Ellen Lichtwardt, Rebecca Petrulli, Sean Turner, Suki Stern. *Additional Animation:* Visual Concepts Engineering. *Pyrotechnical Effects—Explosives:* Ted Moehnke, Peter Stolz, Bob Finley, Jr. *FX Editing—Editor:* Michael Gleason. *Assistant Editor:* Michael Moore. *Production—General Manager, ILM:* Tom Smith. *Production Supervisor:* Warren Franklin. *Production Coordinator:* Arthur Repola. *Location Coordinator:* Patty Blau. *Administration:* Chrissie England, Cheryl Durham, Susan Monahan, Paula Karsh, Kathy Shine, Karen Ayres, Karen Dube, Ned Gorman, Geoffrey de Valois. *Mechanical Effects—U.K. and Asia Mechanical Effects Supervisor:* George Gibbs. *Chief Technician:* Richard Conway. *Floor Supervisor:* David Watkins. *London Second Unit Floor Supervisor:* David Harris. *Senior Technicians:* Trevor Neighbour, David Watson. *Technicians:* Bob Hollow, Brian Morrison, Rodger Shaw. *Assistant Technicians:* Peter Davey, Stephen Hamilton, Joss Williams. *Chief Wire Flying Technician:* Bob Wiesinger. *U.S. Mechanical Effects:* Kevin Pike. Academy Award: Dennis Muren, Michael McAlister, Lorne Peterson, George Gibbs.

An effects sequence to top *Raiders of the Lost Ark* and equal the bike ride of *Return of the Jedi*, the escape of Indy and his friends from the Temple of Doom in mine cars was a *tour de force* of well-blended live-action photography involving Harrison Ford, stunt people and mechanical effects and miniatures. For the brief cuts, FX supervisor Dennis Muren and his crew would need no more than thirty feet of film which would apply to a still camera and finally came up with a modified Nikon VistaVision format motion picture camera small enough to literally travel with ten-inch mine cars and stop-motion actors. This permitted the movie makers to reduce the size of the sets so that they would fit the ILM stage, that was only eighty feet long.

1983–84

Ghostbusters Black Rhino-Bernie Brillstein/Columbia, U.S.A. Panavision 70, Metrocolor.

Director: Ivan Reitman. *Visual Effects—Visual Effects Company:* Entertainment Effects Group. *Visual Effects Supervisor:* Richard Edlund. *Camera Operators:* James (Jim) Aupperle, John Lambert. *Assistant Cameramen:* Pete Romano, Jody Westheimer, Clint Palmer. *Still Photographer:* Virgil Mirano. *Equipment—Electronic Engineers:* Jerry Jeffress, Robin Leyden. *Software Programmer:* Kris Brown. *Special Optics Designers:* David Grafton, Harold Johnson. *Projector Manufacturer:* George Randle Co. *Art Department—Art Director:* John Bruno. *Matte Paintings—Supervising Matte Artist:* Matthew Yuricich. *Matte Artists:* Michelle Moen, Constantine Ganakas. *Matte Photography Supervisor:* Neil Krepela. *Matte Cinematographer:* Bill Neil. *Assistant Matte Cameraman:* Alan Harding. *Miniatures—Miniature Shop Supervisor:* Mark Stetson. *Miniaturists:* Gary Bierend, Leslie Ekker, Kent Gebo, Pete Gerard, Bob Hoffman, Pat McClung, Don Pennington, Milius Romyn, Nick Seldon, Paul Skylar. *Stop-Motion—Stop-Motion Animator:* Randall William (Randy) Cook. *Creature/Ghost Shop—Ghost Shop Head:* Stuart Ziff. *Ghost Shop Supervisor:* Jon Berg. *Sculptors:* Steve Neill, Mike Hosch. *Onion Head/Librarian Sculptor:* Steve Johnson. *Stay Puft Man Sculptors:* Linda Frobos, Bill Bryan. *Chief Mold Maker:* Gunnar Ferdinandsen. *Chief Mechanism Designer:* Steve Dunham. *Mechanism Designers:* Don Carner, John Alberti, Nicholas Alberti, Douglas Beswick, Lance Anderson. *Mechanism Builders:* John Franke, Kevin Dixon, Tom Culnan, Bill Sturgeon, Larz Anderson. *Creature Design Consultants:* Brent Boates, Terry Windell, Thom Enriquez, Berni Wrightson, Robert Kline, Kurt W. Conner. *Design Engineers:* Mike Bolles, Mark West. *Effects Animation—Animators:* Sean Newton, William Recinos, Bruce Woodside, Richard Coleman. *Technical Animators:* Annick Therrein, Peggy Regan, Sam Recinos, Pete Langton, Les Bernstein, Wendie Fischer. *Additional Animation:* Available Light Ltd. *Optical Cinematography—Optical Supervisor:* Mark Vargo. *Optical Printers Operators:* Chuck Cowles, Bruno

George, Bob Wilson. *Optical Line-up:* Phil Barberio, Mary E. Walter, Ronald B. Moore. *FX Editing—Editor:* Conrad Buff. *Production—Administrator:* Leona Phillips. *Special Projects Director:* Gary Platek. *Production Secretaries:* Laurel Walter, Leslie Falkinburg, Mary Mason. *Mechanical Effects—Mechanical Effects Supervisors:* Thaine Morris, Chuck Gaspar. *Foreman:* Joe Day. *Mechanical Effects Technician:* Robert Spurlock.

The spooky spoof with Onionhead ghosts, animated Terror Dogs and a 100-foot-tall version of the Stay Puft marshmallow man was the reason for Academy Award winner Richard Edlund to leave the safe harbor of Industrial Light & Magic in San Rafael and return to Los Angeles to take over the facilities of former Entertainment Effects Group from Douglas Trumbull and Richard Yuricich which became known thereafter as Boss Films. Edlund: "Basically, we had to totally change the place. Each existing department was reorganized, and several additional ones — including a stop-motion animation department and a 'creature shop' — were built from scratch. Plus I was able to assemble what I believe to be the best special effects film group ever. Every department head is very experienced and has all sorts of battle ribbons covering every successful special effects film made in the last eight years. Fortunately, *Ghostbusters* was a project which we, as a group, could easily move into, having covered some of the same terrain in *Poltergeist*" (*Cinefex* Number 17, p. 9).

1985

Cocoon 20th Century–Fox, U.S.A.

Director: Ron Howard. *Art Department— Conceptual Artist:* Ralph McQuarrie. *Visual Effects Art Director:* Phillip Norwood. *FX Makeup/Creature Shop—Alien Creatures:* Greg Cannom. *Special Creature Consultant:* Rick Baker. *Creature Effects Crew:* Stuart Artingstall, Robert Clark, Tony Gardner, Camilla Henneman, Tom Hester, Shawn McEnroe, Kevin Yagher, Adam Hill, Bill Sturgeon, Tim Turner. *Storyboard Artist:* James Cummins. *Visual Effects—Visual Effects Company:* Industrial Light & Magic Inc., a Division of Lucasfilm Ltd. *Visual Effects Supervisor:* Ken Ralston. *Visual Effects Creator:* Pamela Marcotte. *Visual Effects Photography:* Scott Farrar. *Visual Effects Assistant Cameramen:* Ray Gilberti, Randy Jonsson. *Visual Effects Stage Manager:* Edward Hirsh. *Visual Effects Supervising Stage Technician:* Pat Fitzsimmons. *Visual Effects Equipment Engineering Supervisor:* Mike MacKenzie. *Visual Effects Construction Coordinator:* Donald Pennington. *Cloud Tank Technician:* Robert Finley, Jr. *Still Photography:* Kerry Nordquist. *Matte Paintings—Matte Photography Supervisor:* Craig Barron. *Matte Photography:* Paul Huston. *Supervising Matte Artist:* Christopher Evans. *Matte Artist:* Caroleen Green. *Animation—Visual Effects Animation Supervisor:* Charlie Mullen. *Rotoscope Artists:* Barbara Brennan, Sandy Houston, Ellen E. Lichtwardt, Jack Mongovan. *Animation Camera:* Jay Riddle. *Stop-Motion—Stop-Motion Supervisor:* David Sosalla. *Stop-Motion Armatures:* Tom St. Amand. *Stop-Motion Technicians:* Margot Phillips, Anthony (Tony) Laudati, Sean M. Casey. *Miniatures—Modelshop Supervisor:* Steve Gawley. *Model Makers:* Marty Brenneis, William Beck, Michael Fulmer, Ira Keeler. *Optical Effects—Optical Supervisor:* David Berry. *Optical Camera Operators:* Donald Clark, James Lim, Kenneth Smith. *Optical Line-up:* Peg Hunter, Ed Jones, Tom Rosseter. *Mechanical Effects— Special Effects Coordinator:* Joseph A. Unsinn. *FX Editing—Editor:* Bill Kimberlin. *Assistant Effects Editors:* Michael Moore, Terrence Peck. *Production—General Manager ILM:* Warren Franklin. *Visual Effects Production Supervisor:* Mitch Suskin. *Visual Effects Production Coordinator:* Laurie Vermont. *Production Assistant:* Ned Gorman. Academy Award: Ken Ralston, Ralph McQuarrie, Scott Farrar, David Berry.

Heavenly aliens invite a group of silver (or "best agers") to the skies and "beam" their boat inside their spaceship. "At the climax, a boat floats up into the spaceship. Five long shots use a miniature boat with tiny animated puppets of the actors on board. This was a practical way to shoot the sequence (intercut with close shots of the actors) because it avoided the expense of hoisting a full-size boat up with a crane on a blue-screen stage, and also because the puppets are only required to make the slightest movements. They seem extremely realistic" (*The Stop-Motion Filmography*, p. 152).

1986–87

Innerspace Peter Guber, Jon Peters, Steven Spielberg, Kathleen Kennedy, Frank Marshall/Guber-Peters, U.S.A.

Director: Joe Dante. *Visual Effects—Visual Effects Company:* Industrial Light & Magic. *Visual Effects Supervisor:* Dennis Muren. *Visual Effects Photography:* Peter Kozachik, Kim Marks, Harry Walton, Don Dow. *First Unit Effects Cameramen:* John V. Fante, Peter Kozachik. *Visual Effects Cameraman and Go-Motion Animator:* Harry Walton. *Visual Effects Technician:* Christopher Daddy, Juniko Moody. *Stage Managers:* Pat Fitzsimmons, Edward Hirsh. *Stage Technicians:* Brad Jerrell, Buck O'Hare, Michael Olague, Craig Mohagen. *Still Photographer:* Kerry Nordquist. *Visual Effects Coordinator:* Caren Marinoff-Montante. *Process—Process Service:* Bill Hansard. *Art Department—Visual Effects Art Director:* Harley Jessup. *Conceptual Designer:* Richard Vander Wende. *Special Sculptor:* Henry Alvarez. *Optical Cinematography—Optical Supervisor:* Kenneth F. Smith. *Optical Camera Operators:* Jeff Doran, James Lim. *Miniatures—Modelshop Supervisor:* William (Bill) George. *Modelshop Project Chiefs:* Walter Conti, Cris Hammond, Ease Owyeung, Larry Tan. *Model makers:* Howie Weed, Rick Anderson, Eric Christensen, Ira Keeler, Scott McNamara, Rich Townsend, Mark Setrakian. *Puppeteer:* Blair Clark. *Sculptors:* Sean M. Casey, Jonathan Horton, Tony Hudson, Richard Miller, Wesley Seeds, Claudia Mullaly. *Animation—Effects Animation:* Gordon Baker, Gordon Clark, Chuck Eyler. *Animation Camera Operator:* John Knoll. *Mechanical Effects—Supervisor:* Michael Wood. *Special Effects Foreman:* Michael Edmonson. *Special Effects Technicians:* Al Broussard, Mike Paris, Joseph C. Sasgen, David Wood, Gary D. Bierend. *FX Editing—Editor:* Michael S. Moore. *Assistant Editor:* Timothy Eaton. *Production—General Manager, ILM:* Warren Franklin. *Visual Effects Manager, ILM:* Ned Gorman. *Production Supervisor:* Chrissie England. Academy Award: Dennis Muren, William George, Harley Jessup, Kenneth Smith.

Made along the lines of *Fantastic Voyage* with a miniaturized sub (*Kraken II*) traveling through the bloodstream of a human (Martin Short). Director Joe Dante: "Effects-wise our number one priority was to try to *not* make it look like *Fantastic Voyage*, because the idea of remaking a picture has never appealed to me and I knew we were already going to be in trouble because both films have the same premise. *Fantastic Voyage*, however, is much more stylized than would be permissible today where realism seems to be the name of the game. Knowing this, we tried to have it both ways. We tried to make *Innerspace* realistic enough to be convincing, but stylized enough to not be disgusting since there are a lot of people who find it difficult to look at things like gooey body parts" (*Cinefex* Number 32).

1987–88

RoboCop Jon Davison, Arne Schmidt, Stephen Lim, Edward Neumeier, Phil Tippett/Orion Pictures, U.S.A. Eastmancolor.

Director: Paul Verhoeven. *Second Unit Directors:* Mark Goldblatt, Monte Hellman. *Matte Paintings—Matte Artist:* Rocco Gioffre. *Matte Camera:* Don Baker, Michael Karp (Praxis Film Works). *Camera Operator:* Ute Leonhardt. *Optical Effects Supervisor:* Robert Blalack (Praxis Film Works). *Visual Effects—Special Photographic Effects:* Peter Kuran (VCE, Inc.). *Optical Effects (VCE):* Beverly Bernacki, Spencer Gill, Ed Harker. *Animation Effects:* Kevin Kutchaver, Jo Martin, Jammie Friday (VCE). *Administration:* Jacqueline Zietlow (VCE). *Plate Photography (ED-2000):* Rick Fichter. *Stop-Motion—ED-209 Sequences:* Phil Tippett. *ED-209 Designer-Creators:* Craig Davies, Peter Ronzani. *Visual Effect (ED-2000):* Harry Walton. *Stop-Motion Animation (ED-2000):* Randy Dutra. *Armature Design:* Tom St. Amand. *6000 SUX Commercial:* The Chiodo Bros. *Mechanical Effects—Special Effects Technicians:* Lawrence A. Aeschlimann, Dale L. Martin, William (Bill) Purcell, Keith Richins, Becky Ochoa, Don Waller. *FX Makeup—Makeup Effects (RoboCop Designer):* Rob Bottin. *Prosthetics:* Stephan Dupuis. *Sculptor:* Henry Alvarez.

A comic book film with Peter Weller as a cop, fatally injured in the line of duty, who is turned into a cyborg. The picture has a memorable stop-motion sequence with an ED 209 robot animated by Phil Tippett.

1987–89

Robot Jox   Charles and Albert Band/Empire Pictures, U.S.A Color.

Director: Stuart Gordon. *Visual Effects and Stop-Motion—Visual Effects Director:* David Allen. *Associate Effects Director:* Paul Gentry. *Stop-Motion Animation:* Paul Jessel, David Allen. *Stop-Motion Armatures:* Localmotion Machine Works. *Model makers:* Sandy Blaylock, Mark Setrakian, James Carson. *Animatronics:* Mark Rappaport. *Art Department—Conceptual Designers:* Ron Cobb, Stephen Burg. *Animation/Optical Cinematography—Special Photographic Effects:* Peter Kuran (VCE, Inc.). *Mechanical Effects—Special Effects:* Jurgen Heimann, Roy Goode

Similar in approach to *Japanese Giant Robot Wars* except that David Allen had to offer the plus of 45 stop-motion cuts: "There are three robot sequences, a brief one at the beginning and two lengthy battles, one ten minutes into the film, the other at the climax. In their own right, each is entertaining and technically impressive, but they are separated by tiresome live-action passages" (*The Stop-Motion Filmography*, p. 597).

1989

Honey, I Shrunk the Kids   Walt Disney Pictures/Silver Screen Partners III, U.S.A. Technicolor.

Director: Joe Johnston. *Mechanical Effects—Practical Effects and Creature Mechanicals:* Image Engineering, Inc. *Mechanical Effects Coordinator:* Peter Chesney. *Mechanical Effects Technicians:* Jurgen Heimann, David L. Hewitt, Jim Kundig. *Special Effects Foreman:* John McLeod. *Model Maker:* Steve Sanders. *Special Effects Assistant (Roark Productions):* Tim Turner. *Visual Effects—Visual Effects Director of Photography:* Rick Fichter. *Visual Effects Camera:* Michael Lawler. *Visual Effects Coordinator:* Michael Muscal. *Optical Cameraman (Illusion Arts, Inc.):* Mark Freund. *Stop-Motion—Creatures and Miniatures Supervisor:* David Sosalla. *Additional Photography:* Paul W. Gentry, Michael Paul Lawler. *Stop Motion Animator (Ant Sequence):* David W. Allen. *Scorpion Sequence:* Phil Tippett. *Scorpion Designer and Constructor:* Craig Hayes. *Additional*

Stop-Motion Animation: Tom St. Amand. *Animation—Visual Effects Animation:* Peter Kuran (VCE, Inc.), Jammie Friday, Kevin Kutchaver. *Animation Photography:* Joseph Thomas. *Additional Service—Digital Animator (Title Sequence):* Brian Jennings.

An experimental ray gun reduces some kids to microscopic size. Obviously inspired by *The Incredible Shrinking Man*. Director Stuart Gordon had the original idea but due to illness was not able to helm the production. So Joe Johnston, former storyboard artist at ILM, seized the opportunity.

1992–93

Jurassic Park   Steven Spielberg, Kathleen Kennedy, Gerald R. Molen/Amblin Entertainment–Universal, U.S.A. Technicolor.

Director: Steven Spielberg. *Visual Effects—Visual Effects Company and CGI:* Industrial Light & Magic. *Visual Effects Supervisor:* Dennis Muren. *Co-Supervisor:* Mark A.Z. Dippé. *Stage Technician:* Bill Barr. *Camera Operator:* Terry Chestner. *Camera Assistants:* Jeffrey Greeley, Robert Hill. *Camera Engineers:* Mike Bolles, Duncan Sutherland. *Additional Plate Photographer:* Scott Farrar. *Blue Screen Supervisor:* Stephanie Powell. *Visual Effects Coordinator:* Judith Weaver. *Art Department—Visual Effects Art Director:* TyRuben Ellingson. *Concept Artist:* Mark "Crash" McCreery. *3D Animation—ILM Lead Computer Graphics Supervisor:* Stefen M. Fangmeier. *Computer Graphics Animators:* Steve "Spaz" Williams, Eric Armstrong, Geoff Campbell, Steve Price, James Satoru Straus. *Computer Graphic Artists:* Jean M. Cunningham, Carl N. Frederick, Wade Howie, Thomas L. Hutchinson, Joe Letteri, Jeffrey B. Light, James D. Mitchell, Ellen Poon. *Computer Graphics Supervisors:* George Murphy, Alex Seiden. *Computer Graphics Technical Assistants:* Joel Aron, Michael Conte, Edwin Dunkley. *Computer Graphics Software Developer:* Paul Ashdown. *Digital Artists:* Kathleen Beeler, Barbara Brennan, David Carson, Lisa Dostrova, Bart Giovanetti, Sandy Houston, Greg Maloney, Carolyn Ensle Renda, Rita E. Zimmerman. *Computer Graphics Camera Matchmovers:* Charlie Clavadetscher, Patrick

T. Myers. *Computer Graphics Software Developers:* Eric Enderton, John Horn, Zoran Kacic-Alesic, Brian Knep, Michael J. Natkin. *Computer Graphics Systems Supporter:* Jay Lenci. *CG Department Production Manager:* Gail Currey. *Senior CG Department Manager:* Douglas Scott Kay. *CG Department Operations Manager:* John Andrew Berton, Jr. *Computer Graphics Coordinator:* Nancy Jill Luckoff. *Scanning Supervisor:* Joshua Pines. *Scanning Operators:* George Gambetta, Randall K. Bean. *Supervisor of Software and Digital Technology:* Thomas A. Williams. *Matte Paintings—ILM Matte Artists:* Christopher Evans, Yusei Uesugi. *Digital Matte Coordinator:* Diane Holland. *Modelshop—Chief Model Makers:* Steve Gawley, Lorne Peterson, Barbara Affonso, Ira Keeler, Christopher Reed. *Model Maker:* Scott Schneider. *Assistant Model Maker:* Jules Mann. *Compositing—Optical Supervisor:* John Ellis. *Optical Camera Operators:* Keith L. Johnson, James C. Lim. *Optical Line-up:* John O. Whisnant, Kristen D. Trattner. *Optical Coordinator:* Lisa Vaughn. *Mechanical Effects—Mechanical Effects Shop:* Stan Winston Studio. *Live-Action Dinosaurs:* Stan Winston. *Art Department:* Francesca Avila, Len Burge, David Beneke, Sebastien Caillabet, Michael J. Coughlin, Nathalie Fratti-Rapoport, Anthony Gaillard, Beth Hathaway, Adam Jones, Mark Jurinko, Eileen Kastner-Delago, Lindsay MacGowan, Kevin McTurk, Nick Marra, Eric Ostroff, Jeff Periera, Robert Ramsdell, Michiko Tagawa, Pierre–Olivier Thevenin, Scott "Gwidge" Urban, Kevin Willis. *Art Department Coordinator:* Shane Mahan. *Concept Artist:* Mark "Crash" McCreery. *Key Artists:* Bill Basso, Greg Figiel, Dave Grasso, Rob Hinderstein, Paul Mejias, Joey Orosco, Joe Reader, Andy Schoneberg, Shannon Shea, Ian Stevenson, Christopher Swift, Mike Trcic. *Mechanical Designers:* Evan Brainard, Jeff Edwards, Jon Dawe, Rick Galinson, Rich Haugen, Frank Charles Lutkus III, Tim Nordella, Alan Scott, Patrick Shearn, Alfred Sousa. *Hydraulic Engineer:* Lloyd Ball. *Technical Coordinator (T-Rex):* Craig Barr. *Dinosaur Skin Fabricator:* Marilyn Dozer-Chaney. *Master Mold Maker:* Tony McCray. *Mechanical Department Coordinators (Stan Winston Studio):* Craig Caton, Richard J. Landon. *Mechanical Department:* Matthew Durham, Greg Manion, Bruce Stark. *Master Welder:* Armando González. *Production Coordinators:* Mark Lohff, Tara Meaney-Crocitto. *Production Assistants:* Kimberly Verros, Chuck Zlotnick. *Special Dinosaur Effects—Special Dinosaur Effects:* Michael Lantieri. *Special Effects Engineer:* Joss Geiduschek. *Special Effects Foreman:* Donald Elliott. *Special Effects Shop Supervisor:* Tom Pahk. *Special Effects:* Cory Faucher, Kim Derry, Steve Bunyea, Erik Haraldsted, Terry W. King, Louie Lantieri, Matthew J. McDonnell, Bruce Minkus, Dan Ossello, Joe Porter, E. Wayne Rabouin, Brian Tipton, Thomas R. Homsher. *Custom Props:* Kevin Pike. *Stop-Motion/Direct Input (Tippett Studio)—Stop-Motion Animation:* Phil Tippett. *Production Supervisor:* Jules Tippett. *Stop-Motion Armatures:* Lionel Ivan Orozco. *Senior Animator:* Randal M. Dutra. *Animator:* Tom St. Amand. *D.I.D. Computer Interface Engineer:* Craig Hayes. *Engineers:* Nicholas Blake, Conrad Bonderson, Gary Platek, Bart Trickel, Stuart Ziff. *Computer Systems Technician:* Douglas Epps. *Animatics:* Kim Blanchette, Peter Konig, Eric Swenson. *Production Coordinator:* Sheila Duignan. *FX Editing—Visual Effects Editor:* Michael Gleason. *Assistant Editor:* Roberto McGrath. *Negative Cutter:* Louis Rivera. *Editorial Coordinator:* David Tanaka. *Production—General Manager, ILM:* Jim Morris. *Visual Effects Producer:* Janet Healy. *Plate Producer:* Mark. S. Miller. *Production Accountant (ILM):* Pamela Kaye. *Academy Award:* Dennis Muren, Stan Winston, Phil Tippett, Michael Lantieri.

While Phil Tippett and his company prepared for 50 Go-Motion dinosaur shots (things that mechanical effects supervisor Stan Winston was unable to do), Dennis Muren realized a breakthrough in computer technology which enabled them to add a motion blur to the animation and thereby eliminate stop-motion strobing. Eventually they did use some stop-motion to enhance digital techniques with the virtues of the mechanical age. Basics for a few minutes of CGI dinosaurs was a stop-motion system which allowed to transfer keyframe animation data onto a computer-generated creature, a Dinosaur or Direct Input Device (DID). Muren: "The DID was made because a third and final test showing the T-rex chasing the gallimimus herd had a serious jerky animation problem our animators couldn't fix" (Vaz/Duignan, *Industrial Light & Magic: Into the Digital Realm*, p. 218). "Initiating CG imagery with stop-motion DIDs, rather than conceiving the images in the computer, has the benefit of avoiding the unreal look of pure computer imagery. The hands-on-stop-motion element adds quirks, sudden changes of direction and touches of personality which prevent the finished image from looking too smooth and predictable. The DIDs only supply information about major movement — 'minor' animation of finger and toes was added by the computer animators and supervised by Tippett" (Neil Pettigrew, *The Stop-Motion Filmography,* p. 387). The DID Direct Input Device became the forerunner of today's motion capture, a biproduct of biomechanics, that already was used by the late Robert Abel for his legendary *Sexy Robot* spot.

Bibliography

Books

Abbott, L.B. *Special Effects: Wire, Tape, and Rubber Band Style*. Hollywood, CA: The ASC Press, 1984.

Ackerman, Forrest J. *Forrest J Ackerman's Fantastic Movie Memories*. Canoga Park, CA: New Media Books, 1985.

Agel, Jerome (ed.). *The Making of Kubrick's 2001*. New York: Signet, 1968.

Archer, Steven. *Willis O'Brien: Special Effects Genius*. Jefferson, NC: McFarland, 1998.

Barron, Craig, and Mark Cotta Vaz. *The Invisible Art: The Legends of Movie Matte Painting*. San Francisco: Chronicle Books, 2004.

Bessy, Maurice, and Lo Duca. *Georges Méliès, Mage*. Paris: J.J. Pauvert, 1961.

Brosnan, John. *Movie Magic*. New York: St. Martin's Press, 1974.

Bulleid, Henry A.V. *Special Effects in Cinematography*. London: Fountain Press, 1954.

_____. *Trick Effects with the Cine Camera*. London: Link House Publications, 1936.

Burns, Bob, with John Michlig. *It Came from Bob's Basement! Exploring the Science Fiction and Monster Movie Archive of Bob Burns*. San Francisco: Chronicle Books, 2000.

_____, as told to Tom Weaver. *Monster Kid Memories*. New York: Dinoship, 2003.

Clark, Frank P. *Special Effects in Motion Pictures: Some Methods for Producing Mechanical Special Effects*. Scarsdale, NY: Society of Motion Picture and Television Engineers, 1966.

Culhane, John. *Special Effects in the Movies: How They Do It*. New York: Ballantine, 1982.

A Directors Guild of America Oral History, Byron Haskin Interviewed by Joe Adamson. Metuchen, NJ: The Scarecrow Press, 1984.

Dohler, Don. *Film Magic: The Fantastic Guide to Special Effects Film-making*. Maryland: Cinema Enterprises, 1984.

Dunn, Linwood G., and George E. Turner (eds.). *The ASC Treasury of Visual Effects*. Hollywood, CA: The ASC Press, 1983.

Fielding, Raymond. *The Technique of Special Effects Cinematography*. London and Boston: Focal Press, 1985.

Finch, Christopher. *Special Effects. Creating Movie Magic*. New York: Abbeville Press, 1984.

Fleischer, Uwe, and Helge Trimpert (eds.). *Wie haben Sie's gemacht...? Babelsberger Kameramänner öffnen ihre Trickkiste*. Marburg: Schüren-Verlag, 2005.

Frazer, John. *Artificially Arranged Scenes. The Films of Georges Méliès*. Boston: G.K. Hall, 1979.

Fry, Ron, and Pamela Fourzon. *The Saga of Special Effects*. Englewood Cliffs, NJ: Prentice-Hall, 1977.

Galbraith, Stuart IV. *Japanese Science Fiction, Fantasy and Horror Films: A Critical Analysis of 103 Features Released in the United States, 1950–1992*. Jefferson, NC: McFarland, 1994.

_____. *Monsters Are Attacking Toyko! The Incredible World of Japanese Fantasy Films*. Venice, CA: Feral House, 1998.

Giesen, Rolf. *Alles über Kong*. Ismaning: TaurusVideo (KirchGroup), 1993.

_____. *Sagenhafte Welten: Der Trickspezialist Ray Harryhausen*. Frankfurt am Main: Deutsches Filmmuseum, 1988.

_____. *Special Effects: Die Tricks im Film*. Ebersberg: Edition 8½, 1985.

_____, and Claudia Meglin. *Künstliche Welten*. Hamburg/Zurich: Europa Verlag, 2000.

Godziszewski, Ed. *The Illustrated Encyclopedia of Godzilla*. Private publication.

Goldner, Orville, and George E. Turner. *The Making of King Kong*. New York: A. S. Barnes, 1975.

Harmetz, Aljean. *The Making of The Wizard of Oz*. New York: Knopf, 1997.

Harryhausen, Ray. *Film Fantasy Scrapbook*. New York: A. S. Barnes, 1972.

_____, and Tony Dalton. *Ray Harryhausen: An Animated Life*. London: Aurum Press, 2003. (American edition by Billboard Books, 2004.)

_____, and _____. *The Art of Ray Harryhausen*. London: Aurum Press, 2005.

Hayes, R.M. *3-D Movies: A History and Filmography of Stereoscopic Cinema*. Jefferson, NC: McFarland, 1989.

_____. *Trick Cinematography: The Oscar Special-Effects Movies.* Jefferson, NC: McFarland, 1986.

Hickman, Gail Morgan. *The Films of George Pal.* Cranbury, NJ: A. S. Barnes, 1977.

Hume, Alan, with Gareth Owen. *A Life Through the Lens: Memoirs of a Film Cameraman.* Jefferson, NC: McFarland, 2004.

Hutchison, David. *Film Magic: The Art and Science of Special Effects.* New York: Prentice-Hall, 1987.

Imes, Jack, Jr. *Special Visual Effects: A Guide to Special Effects Cinematography.* New York: Prentice-Hall Press/Van Nostand Reinhold, 1984.

Iwerks, Leslie, and John Kenworthy. *The Hand: Behind the Mouse.* New York: Disney Editions, 2001.

Kinsey, Wayne. *Hammer Films: The Bray Studios Years.* London: Reynolds & Hearn, 2002.

Lourie, Eugene. *My Work in Films.* San Diego/New York/London: Harcourt Brace Jovanovich, 1985.

McCarthy, Robert E. *Secrets of Hollywood Special Effects.* Boston/London: Focal Press, 1992.

McGilligan, Patrick. *Fritz Lang: The Nature of the Beast.* New York: St. Martin's Press, 1997.

Menningen, Jürgen. *Filmbuch Science Fiction.* Cologne: Studio Dumont, 1975.

Netzley, Patricia D. *Encyclopedia of Movie Special Effects.* Phoenix, Arizona: Oryx Press, 2000.

Opfermann, H.C., and Georg Kramer. *Die neue Trickfilm-Schule.* Seebruck am Chiemsee: Heering-Verlag, 1967.

Parish, James Robert, and Michael R. Pitts. *The Great Science Fiction Pictures.* Metuchen, NJ: The Scarecrow Press, 1977.

Perisic, Zoran. *Special Optical Effects in Film.* London and New York: Focal Press, 1980.

Pettigrew, Neil. *The Stop-Motion Filmography: A Critical Guide to 297 Features Using Puppet Animation.* Jefferson, NC: McFarland, 1999.

Rogers, Pauline B. *Art of Visual Effects: Interviews on the Tools of the Trade.* London: Focal Press, 1999.

Rickitt, Richard. *Special Effects: The History and Technique.* New York: Billboard Books, 2007.

Riley, Philip (ed.). *This Island Earth. Universal Filmscript Series — Classic Science Fiction Films Volume 1.* Absecon, NJ: Magicimage Filmbooks, 1990.

Ryfle, Steve. *Japan's Favorite Mon-Star: The Unauthorized Biography of "The Big G."* Toronto, Ontario: ECW Press, 1998.

Savini, Tom. *Grande Illusions.* Pittsburgh: Imagine, 1983.

Schechter, Harold, and David Everitt. *Film Tricks: Special Effects in the Movies.* New York: Harlin Quist, 1980.

Seeber, Guido. *Der Trickfilm in seinen grundsätzlichen Möglichkeiten.* Berlin: Verlag der "Lichtbildbühne," 1927 (reprinted by Deutsches Filmmuseum Frankfurt am Main in 1979).

Siegel, Don. *A Siegel Film: An Autobiography.* London and Boston: Faber and Faber, 1993.

Smith, Thomas C. *Industrial Light and Magic: The Art of Special Effects.* New York and London: Ballantine Books, 1986.

Solow, Herbert F., and Robert H. Justman. *Inside* Star Trek*: The Real Story.* New York: Pocket Books, 1996.

Strickland, A.W., and Forrest J Ackerman. *A Reference Guide to American Science Fiction Films Volume 1.* Bloomington, IN: T.I.S. Publications Division, 1981.

Tucker, Guy Mariner. *Age of the Gods: A History of Japanese Fantasy Films.* Brooklyn, NY: Daikaiju Publishing, 1996.

Vaz, Mark Cotta, and Patricia Rose Duignan. *Industrial Light & Magic: Into the Digital Realm.* New York: Del Rey/Ballantine Books, 1996.

Warren, Bill. *Keep Watching the Skies! American Science Fiction Movies of the Fifties. Volume I, 1950–1957,* and *Volume II, 1958–1962.* Jefferson, NC: McFarland, 1982 (Volume I) and 1986 (Volume II).

Wilkie, Bernard. *The Technique of Special Effects in Television.* London and Boston: Focal Press, 1971.

Wilson, S.S. *Puppets & People: Dimensional Animation Combined with Live Action in the Cinema.* San Diego/New York: A. S. Barnes; London: The Tantivy Press, 1980.

Periodicals

American Cinematographer, The BKSTS Journal, Cinefantastique, Cinefex, Cinemagic (1979–1987), *Cult Movies, Famous Monsters of Filmland, Fantascene* (Robert F. Skotak, ed.), *Fantasy Film Journal, Film & TV Kameramann, Filmfax: The Magazine of Unusual Film & Television, FKT Fernseh- und Kino-Technik, Forrest J Ackerman's Wonderama, FXRH* (1971–1976), *G-FAN* (Daikaiju Enterprises), *Just Imagine —The Journal of Film and Television Special Effects, Little Shoppe of Horrors, Markalite: The Magazine of Japanese Fantasy, Video Watchdog.*

Index